Future of Business and Finance

The Future of Business and Finance book series features professional works aimed at defining, analyzing, and charting the future trends in these fields. The focus is mainly on strategic directions, technological advances, challenges and solutions which may affect the way we do business tomorrow, including the future of sustainability and governance practices. Mainly written by practitioners, consultants and academic thinkers, the books are intended to spark and inform further discussions and developments.

Henrik Hvid Jensen

Circular Economy Opportunities and Pathways for Manufacturers

Manufacturing Renewed

Springer

Henrik Hvid Jensen
Copenhagen, Denmark

ISSN 2662-2467 ISSN 2662-2475 (electronic)
Future of Business and Finance
ISBN 978-3-031-75278-0 ISBN 978-3-031-75279-7 (eBook)
https://doi.org/10.1007/978-3-031-75279-7

This Springer imprint is published by the registered company Springer Nature Switzerland AG
The registered company address is: Gewerbestrasse 11, 6330 Cham, Switzerland

Foreword: A Contribution to the Transformation from a Linear Model Toward a Circular Economy

This book is written for manufacturers. The transition to the circular economy presents a unique opportunity to accelerate business growth and differentiate our value propositions in the increasingly competitive and complex global sourcing, manufacturing, and distribution markets. *Circular Economy Opportunities and Pathways for Manufacturers* highlights the business benefits of the circular economy and provides practical tools to navigate the necessary economic transformation. This book is a comprehensive guide for manufacturers seeking to unlock higher-order business value across the current and future capital creation landscape.

Strategic Frameworks and Models

In the book, Henrik Hvid Jensen presents the 1+5 Rs framework, a detailed and practical model for manufacturers. We think that this framework is essential for its comprehensive approach to circular practices, including:

- *Redesign*: Creating products for adaptability, repairability, and upgradability.
- *Redistribute*: Extending product lifecycles through recommerce and reuse.
- *Repair*: Developing efficient repair services to prolong product engagement.
- *Refurbish*: Offering high-quality refurbished products.
- *Remanufacture*: Designing for disassembly and reusing parts.
- *Recycle*: Ensuring materials are reintroduced into production cycles.

Each component is detailed with strategies and practical case studies, showcasing how businesses can implement each step to enhance their operations and financial performance.

Capability Maps for Strategic Execution

We find the detailed capability maps in this book to be invaluable. They serve as practical guides for aligning business operations with circular principles. These maps outline essential skills and processes, from advanced logistics for managing product returns to integrating lifecycle assessment techniques. They help businesses identify gaps, plan improvements, and ensure a smooth transition to circular practices.

The Nine Catalysts Reshaping Manufacturing

The book identifies nine key catalysts driving the transformation in manufacturing, which we believe are critical for understanding the broader context:

1. *Global climate impacts* prompting sustainable practices.
2. *Stakeholder advocacy* demands corporate responsibility.
3. *Renewable energy transformation* reduces fossil fuel dependency.
4. *Government initiatives* promoting circular practices through regulations and incentives.
5. *Long-term corporate commitments* to sustainability.
6. *Changing perceptions of waste* as a resource.
7. *Supply chain resilience* ensures robustness against disruptions.
8. *Enhanced value* through innovation in products and processes.
9. *Digital technologies* enable seamless integration and efficiency.

Each catalyst is thoroughly examined, offering manufacturers insights on leveraging these forces to stay innovative and competitive.

Compliance as a Competitive Advantage

This book discusses government initiatives and regulatory compliance. It explores the role of regulations such as right-to-repair laws, extended producer responsibility (EPR) policies, and digital product passports (DPP). These regulations, often seen as challenges, are reframed in the book as strategic opportunities. The strategic reflection checklists are helpful tools for businesses to navigate these regulations, develop comprehensive compliance strategies, and turn regulatory mandates into competitive advantages.

Digitization and the Sustainable Manufacturing Intelligence Framework (SMIF)

Digitization is essential for integrating circular principles into manufacturing. We are aligned with the author Henrik Hvid Jensen, who sees in the Sustainable Manufacturing Intelligence Framework (SMIF) a critical component of the transition management toward a circular economy, referring to:

- *Adaptating internal IT systems* to meet evolving requirements and regulations.
- *The value of digital business ecosystems* and the importance of collaborations beyond traditional supply chain partnerships.

- Establishing the *IoT and connected products* capability as a fundamental aspect
- *Ongoing customer interaction* to align their consumption behaviors with circular economy principles.
- *Data-driven circularity* enabling insights to understand customer behavior, improve operational efficiency, and identify innovation and waste reduction opportunities.

The digital capability maps and checklists provide a structured approach to implementing digital strategies, ensuring manufacturers can effectively drive the integration of digital technologies with circular goals.

Synthesizing Insights and Strategic Roadmaps

In the concluding chapters, Henrik Hvid Jensen synthesizes insights from the 1+5 Rs framework and the SMIF, offering a comprehensive approach to embracing circular and digital transformation. The two are closely related. The 10-Step Circular Advantage Guide in the final chapter provides a clear roadmap for manufacturers to integrate circular economy principles into their operations, ensuring long-term financial success through a holistic approach toward sustainability.

A Must-Read for Any Manufacturer

Circular Economy Opportunities and Pathways for Manufacturers is an essential resource for any manufacturer committed to embracing the circular economy idea. This book equips businesses with the knowledge and tools needed to turn the circular economy into a powerful growth and business success driver. We particularly appreciate the key messages at the beginning of each chapter and the checklists summarizing each chapter, which make the sections easily digestible. The journey toward a sustainable and profitable future can start today, and this book is your guide to navigating that journey with confidence and clarity.

Wolfgang Lehmacher and Attila Turos

This foreword has been penned by two seasoned circular economy professional leaders with rich international backgrounds who specialize in driving change toward clear visions.

Wolfgang Lehmacher and Attila Turos are globally recognized leaders in the circular economy space, with extensive international experience across Africa, the Americas, Europe, the Middle East, and Asia. Their expertise in driving transformative change through strategic relationships with top executives in both the private and public sectors has been instrumental in advancing circularity and sustainability initiatives worldwide, making them authoritative voices on the transition to a circular economy.

Wolfgang Lehmacher
Partner e.Circular ApS, Former Director,
Head of Supply Chain and Transport Industries.
World Economy Forum

Attila Turos
Senior Advisor, NextGen CDR,
Co-Founder and Business Development e.Circular ApS

Preface

The industrial landscape is undergoing a profound transformation. As we confront the mounting challenges of environmental sustainability and resource scarcity, the manufacturing sector stands at a pivotal crossroads. This book, *Circular Economy Opportunities and Pathways for Manufacturers*, is a comprehensive guide aimed at helping manufacturers navigate and thrive in this new era of economic activity.

For decades, the linear "take-make-dispose" model has dominated industrial practices, driving growth but also contributing to environmental degradation. However, the advent of the circular economy presents a revolutionary shift—a paradigm where products and materials are continuously reused, refurbished, and recycled, fostering an ecosystem that is not only sustainable but also economically advantageous.

This book emerges from the belief that the circular economy is more than a fleeting trend; it is the future of competitive manufacturing. With the support of digital technologies, businesses can innovate in ways previously unimaginable, reducing waste and optimizing resources while creating new revenue streams. I aim to equip you with the knowledge and strategies to embrace this transformative shift, ensuring your long-term success and resilience.

In *Circular Economy Opportunities and Pathways for Manufacturers,* we delve into the key drivers of change reshaping the manufacturing sector, including technological advancements, regulatory frameworks, and evolving consumer and customer expectations. We explore the "1+5 R model"—a strategic blueprint for integrating circular principles into your operations. This model emphasizes redesigning products and business models while focusing on five central circular business strategies: redistribute, repair, refurbish, remanufacture, and recycle.

To provide a robust foundation for your circular economy journey, this book, in addition to the 1+5R model, introduces several essential frameworks and guides:

- *Circular Economy Strategy Framework (CESF)*: A comprehensive approach to embedding circular principles into your business strategy.
- *Manufacturing Circular Maturity Framework (MCMF)*: A tool for assessing your current state and planning the transition towards circularity.
- *Capability Maps*: Detailed maps of the key business and digital capabilities required for successful circular economy practices.

- *Sustainable Manufacturing Intelligence Framework (SMIF)*: Insights into leveraging digital technologies to support sustainable manufacturing.
- *10-Step Circular Advantage Guide (CAG)*: A practical roadmap to help you implement circular economy principles and achieve competitive advantage.

Each chapter is designed to provide actionable insights, detailed frameworks, and real-world examples that illustrate how circular economy practices can be effectively implemented. Whether you are an established manufacturer seeking to transition from traditional methods or a new player aiming to build a circular business from the ground up, this book offers the guidance you need.

The journey to circularity is not without its challenges. It requires a fundamental shift in perspective, viewing waste as a resource and recognizing the extended value of products and materials. It demands collaboration across the value chain and the integration of advanced digital solutions to track, manage, and optimize the lifecycle of products. However, the rewards are significant: enhanced competitiveness, reduced environmental impact, and a more resilient business model capable of adapting to future market demands.

As we stand on the brink of this new economic transition, it is clear that those who adapt and innovate will lead the way. This book is an invitation to join this transformative movement, to embrace the principles of the circular economy, and to unlock the myriad opportunities it presents.

I hope *Circular Economy Opportunities and Pathways for Manufacturers* will serve as a valuable resource and a source of inspiration as you embark on this journey toward a sustainable and prosperous future. As the topic continues to evolve, the journey doesn't end with the book. Stay updated through my website https://circularpathwaysbook.com.

Copenhagen, Denmark — Henrik Hvid Jensen

Acknowledgments

I want to extend my heartfelt gratitude to several individuals and organizations whose support and encouragement have been instrumental in creating this book.

To my good friends Søren Hebsgaard, Gitte Werther, and Claus Berner, your great and inspiring feedback has been invaluable. Without your insights, this book would never have materialized. Thank you for your encouragement and always pushing me to strive for excellence.

To my employer, DXC Technology, thank you for trusting my ability to write a significant book to guide manufacturers toward becoming circular, clean, and digital. Your support and confidence have been crucial in providing the resources and environment needed to bring this vision to life.

Of course, to my wife, Anette Ljungstrøm Larsen, thank you for your patience and firm belief that I could finish this book. I know you may have thought I was a bit crazy when I first told you I wanted to write it, but your love, understanding, and unwavering support have been my anchor throughout this journey. I could not have completed this work without you by my side.

To my children, Victor Hvid and William Hvid, your dedication and focus on finding the right direction for your future have been truly inspiring. Your determination has motivated me to continue my journey of learning and growth. Thank you for being a constant source of inspiration.

In writing this book, I have utilized various tools and resources to enhance the quality and clarity of my work. I want to acknowledge the assistance provided by large language models (LLMs) such as ChatGPT, developed by OpenAI, Google Gemini, Grammarly, Microsoft CoPilot, and the AI Assistant from Adobe. These tools have served as invaluable sparring partners, sources of inspiration, and aids in improving the book's readability.

It is important to note that while these tools have contributed to the development of this book, I remain solely accountable for its content and authorship. The insights, interpretations, and conclusions presented here are my own and do not reflect the opinions or positions of the aforementioned tools or their developers.

Thank you for making this possible.

Sincerely,

Henrik Hvid Jensen

Contents

List of Figures

List of Tables

List of Examples

Part 1

Manufacturers' Future Competitiveness Hinges on Three Paradigms That Drive Growth Through Clean(er), Digital, and Circular Models

As history has shown, those who seize the economic transformative shifts pave the way for enduring success. The circular economy, bolstered by digital advancements, offers a path to sustainable and competitive manufacturing.

iStock Credit: Marut Khobtakhob

Circular Economy – The Next Transformative Shift in the Economy

1

Abstract

This chapter explores the transformative potential of the circular economy, drawing historical parallels to past technological revolutions such as the advent of electricity and railroads. It emphasizes that the circular economy is not just an environmental initiative but a robust business strategy that can enhance competitiveness by reducing resource dependency, cutting costs, and generating new revenue streams. The chapter highlights the role of technological innovations, including AI and robotics, in facilitating this shift and disrupting traditional economic models by creating continuous usage cycles.

The chapter outlines manufacturers' need to integrate clean, digital, and circular paradigms to remain competitive. It discusses the nine key catalysts reshaping manufacturing: global climate impacts, stakeholder advocacy, renewable energy transformation, government initiatives, long-term commitments, changing waste perceptions, supply chain resilience, enhanced value, and digital technologies. The chapter also introduces the concept of "born-circular" companies, which, like their digital counterparts, redefine markets through circular business models.

Additionally, it presents a strategic reflection checklist to help manufacturers assess their alignment with circular principles, identify immediate steps for integration, leverage technologies, form partnerships, and engage stakeholders. This sets the stage for the detailed exploration of transitioning to a circular economy that the book promises in subsequent chapters.

H. H. Jensen, *Circular Economy Opportunities and Pathways for Manufacturers*, Future of Business and Finance, https://doi.org/10.1007/978-3-031-75279-7_1

Key Messages

- *A Historical Parallel:* In the late nineteenth century, the introduction of electricity transformed manufacturing, making old steam-driven factories outdated. This change emphasized the importance of embracing new technologies to stay competitive. The same principle applies today with the rise of digital disruptors and the circular economy. Ignoring these changes means risking becoming obsolete in an increasingly competitive market.
- *A New Business Model: The circular economy goes beyond sustainability efforts; it's a strong business strategy that enhances competitiveness by reducing reliance on finite resources, cutting costs, and creating new revenue streams*. Companies that adopt circular principles can turn waste into assets, prolong the commercial life of products, and maximize resource efficiency.
- *Technological Innovation and Disruption:* Technological advancements, such as AI-driven material optimization and robotics in disassembly and recycling, play a role in this transformation. The circular economy disrupts established norms by shifting value creation from consumption to continuous usage cycles, creating new markets and eliminating old, unsustainable ones.
- *The Path Forward*: To stay competitive, manufacturers must incorporate clean, digital, and circular paradigms. This book will guide you through the complexities of transitioning to a circular economy, emphasizing strategic investments in technology and embracing these emerging paradigms for sustainable growth.
- *Embrace the Future: As history has demonstrated, those who fail to adapt to transformative changes are left behind. The circular economy, supported by digital innovation, offers a path to sustainable and competitive manufacturing.* By embracing these changes, manufacturers can ensure long-term success in an evolving economic landscape.
- *Nine Catalysts Reshaping the Future of Manufacturing:* The future of manufacturing is being transformed by nine key catalysts: global climate impacts, stakeholder advocacy, renewable energy transformation, government initiatives, long-term commitments, the shift in waste perception, supply chain resilience, enhanced value and innovation, and digital technologies. These catalysts drive changes beyond the factory floor, influencing customer behaviors, supply chains, and international trade dynamics. Manufacturers must re-evaluate their production practices and embrace these catalysts to remain competitive, sustainable, and innovative in a rapidly evolving industrial landscape.

Imagine you are a manufacturer at the end of the nineteenth century, just when revolutionary electric power burst onto the scene. Gone are the days of cumbersome belt drives and the constant thrum of steam engines. All that is required is a flick of the switch, and power surges into all the workstations, bringing with it a new way of

Fig. 1.1 Belt drives Kansas, in 1898. (Credit iStock photo/ilbusca)

doing things, more efficient and exact than what was previously imaginable (Fig. 1.1).

Electricity changed the rules of the game. Workshops and factories hummed not with the activity of human voices but with the electric hum of machinery that allows for operations well into the night, producing productivity levels that a decade ago would have seemed like witchcraft. The new multipurpose electric motor penetrated everything from sewing machines to printing presses, changing how fabrics manufactured products and whole industries.

But with this electric dawn comes a realization: to ignore this tide is to risk obsolescence. The electric train, so to say, is leaving the station, and those businesses not on board will consign themselves to the annals of history, their once-thriving workshops reduced to relics of a bygone era. The choices were obvious: either adapt and willingly accept the electricity, or see your competitors and new innovators move on with this invisible yet seemingly unstoppable force (Fig. 1.2).

Speaking of trains, consider railroads. Railroads didn't take over from steamships on rivers—they obliterated them. There wasn't only a change in transportation. It was a transformative shift that redefined the face of trading and industry. It afforded much more than hastened the movement of goods. The railroads managed to link markets that were thousands of miles apart at an efficiency and speed that was at that time unimaginable.

Fig. 1.2 Railway works. (Credit iStock photo/ilbusca)

This connectivity fostered a level of mass production and distribution that was previously unimaginable. Suddenly, big factories were churning out goods in ways never seen before, reshaping the local economies and the global trade networks. The ripple effect was profound, making it impossible for small artisans and local manufacturers to compete against the tidal wave of mass-produced goods. It was like watching a horde of giants trampling through a village, reshaping the very foundation of industry and commerce. If you weren't on board, you were more than just left behind; the march of progress swallowed you and rendered you obsolete.

Fast forward two centuries, after the railroads and electric power had reshaped the manufacturing landscape, a new breed of innovators came onto the horizon: born-digital disruptors such as Uber, Airbnb, and Amazon (Fig. 1.3). These are companies born and bred in the digital playground, which not only brought new services but also changed the very fabric of the economy. They defied traditional pearls of wisdom and business models set up centuries ago, using just a few keys and some creative coding. They are turning seemingly impregnable industries on their heads and forging new markets where none previously existed.

Uber has transformed personal transport, not by creating cars but by enabling the capability of connectivity and a shared economy to disrupt the dominion that century of the taxi industry had over the personal transportation market. Airbnb turned the hospitality industry upside down, with no hotel building; instead, it allowed a person to become a hotelier with a few clicks of a mouse. Amazon didn't revolutionize retail by opening even more stores; it revolutionized by creating an online marketplace where stores are brought right to your front door. They've not just redefined

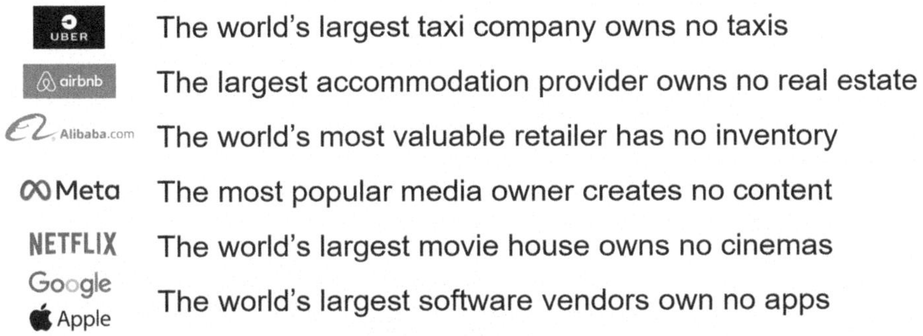

Fig. 1.3 Born-digital disruptors. (Inspired by Tom Goodwin)

what it takes to be a market leader but scared the living daylights of the established players by proving that agility, innovation, and a good grasp of digital platforms are crucial to success.

Example 1.1 The critical importance of timely adaptation in the face of economic and technological transformations

Here are examples illustrating the critical importance of timely adaptation in the face of economic and technological transformations. Once a giant in video rentals, Blockbuster failed to pivot to digital streaming and succumbed to bankruptcy as Netflix thrived. Kodak, despite being the inventor of the digital camera, clung too long to film and faced a similar fate. Nokia, a former leader in mobile phones, was outpaced by the smartphone revolution, leading to its decline and the eventual sale of its mobile division to Microsoft. BlackBerry, once dominant in business smartphones, could not compete with iOS and Android, resulting in a drastic market share loss. Lastly, Sears, a retail behemoth, did not effectively transition to e-commerce, leading to its bankruptcy and reduction to a minor player.

The digital age rewrites much more than just the rulebook; it sets the stage for the next transformative shift toward a circular economy (Sect. 1.2). Just as born-digital disruptors, electric manufacturing, and mass producing have upended traditional industries by reimagining what's possible, the circular economy is an alternative economic model that aims to transform our take on production and consumption. It's an economy that values reuse, repair, refurbishment, remanufacturing, and recycling, turning waste into a resource and challenging the linear "take-make-dispose" model that has dominated since the Industrial Revolution (Fig. 1.4).

This new and emerging paradigm sees a world where economic growth and competitiveness do not degrade the environment but ensure a flourishing economy on par with our planetary borders.

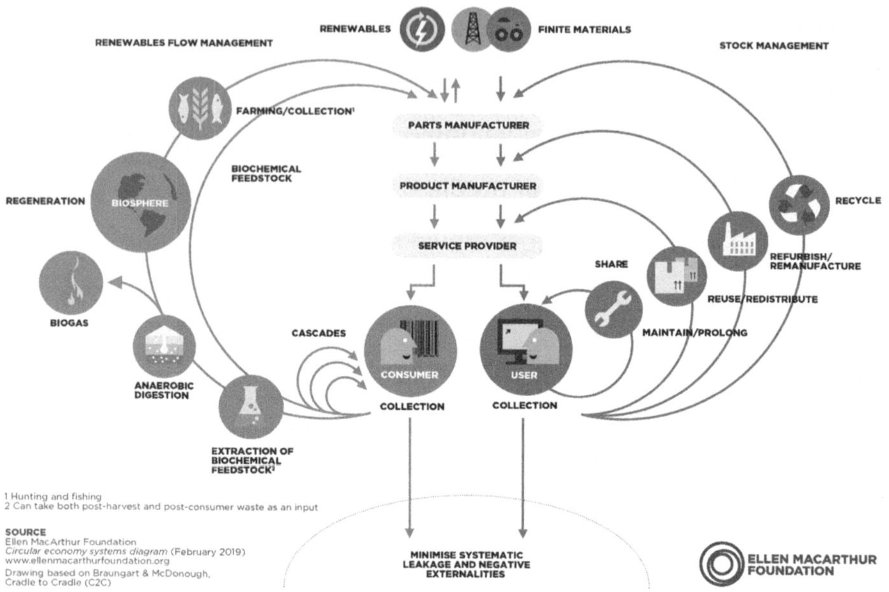

Fig. 1.4 Circular economy system butterfly diagram. (Copyright © Ellen MacArthur Foundation, 2019)
The circular economy system diagram, known as the butterfly diagram, illustrates the continuous flow of materials in a circular economy. There are two main cycles—the technical cycle and the biological cycle. In the technical cycle, products and materials are kept in circulation through processes such as reuse, repair, remanufacture, and recycling. In the biological cycle, the nutrients from biodegradable materials are returned to the Earth to regenerate nature (The Ellen MacArthur Foundation, 2019). Notice in this book, we will only focus on the technical cycle

The emergence of "born-circular" companies, founded with a circular business model at the core, promises to be as transformative as the impact of born-digital companies and disruptive firms leading the previous economic shifts. Like their digital predecessors, who redefined marketplaces by prioritizing digital capabilities and Internet-first strategies, born-circular companies focus on competitive resource efficiency as core to their business identity. They demonstrate that operating within ecological limits while achieving economic success is an attractive business model by embedding circular principles into every aspect of their operations, challenging existing paradigms.

However, it is important to recognize that born-circular companies face unique challenges compared to born-digital firms. Born-digital companies, which emerged without the need for significant investment in physical infrastructure, capitalized on the inherent advantages of digital platforms, enjoying both convenience and cost benefits. These companies were able to scale rapidly by leveraging existing digital infrastructure and focusing on innovation in technology and customer experience.

In contrast, born-circular companies must still invest heavily in manufacturing capabilities to realize their vision. This requirement creates a barrier to entry that can slow down their growth and impact compared to their digital counterparts. Consequently, with their established production capabilities and infrastructure, existing manufacturers are often better positioned to transition into the dominant "born-circulars" role within their industries. The ability to retrofit and innovate within their existing frameworks is critical to effectively leading the circular economy transition.

Given this landscape, catalysts such as customer pressure and regulatory frameworks become crucial in accelerating the transition to a circular economy (Sect. 1.4). Consumer demand for sustainable products and services compels companies to adopt circular practices to remain competitive. Meanwhile, regulations can provide the necessary impetus for companies to prioritize circular principles, ensuring that the market shifts in favor of sustainability.

1.1 What Is the Circular Economy?

The global economy mainly operates under a linear model known as "take-make-use-dispose." In this traditional economic system, raw materials are extracted and turned into parts, assembled into products, and then used and discarded as waste. This model heavily depends on large quantities of easily accessible resources and energy. It is characterized by a short-term consumption cycle that prioritizes economic growth, often at the expense of environmental health (Fig. 1.5).

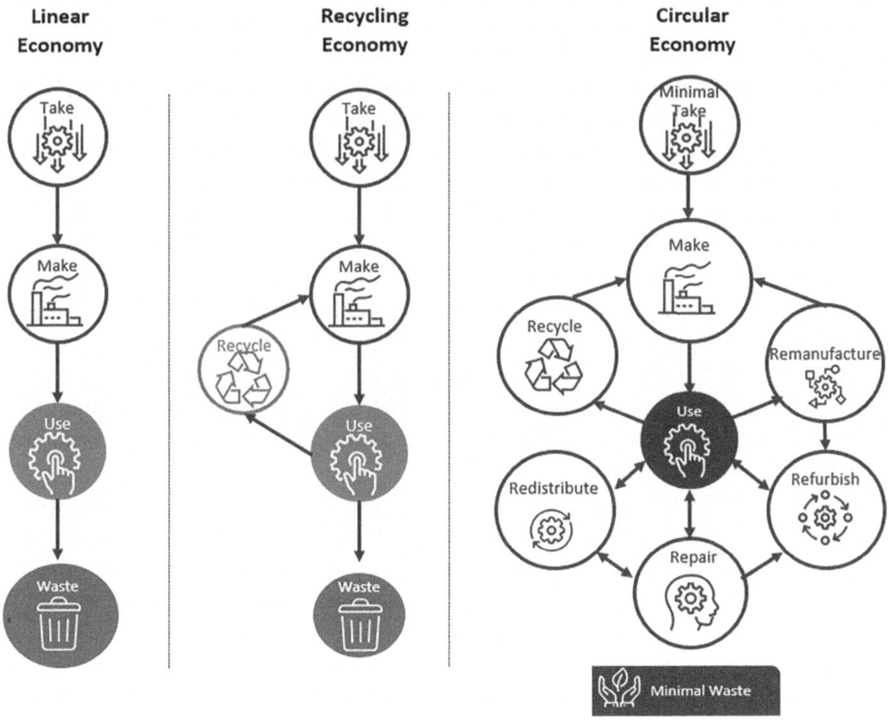

Fig. 1.5 The linear, recycling, and circular economy. (Credit DXC Technology)

Table 1.1 Circular principles

Circular principle	Description
Sustainable input	Renewable, recyclable, or biodegradable materials are prioritized to lessen ecological impacts It reduces costs over time, as these materials can often be cheaply sourced. It also enhances supply chain resilience by decreasing dependence on volatile raw material markets and maintaining control over material sources
Design for longevity	It involves creating products that are built to last, easy to repair, and capable of being upgraded This approach extends the product's life and reduces the demand for new items. It allows components to be refurbished to near-original conditions, which cuts down the time and resources needed for production from scratch, thereby increasing revenue potential
Use maximization	Encourages the sharing, leasing, and repurposing products to maximize their utility and reduce the need for new products This principle enables businesses to generate revenue throughout the product's lifecycle
Waste as a resource	Transforms waste management from a disposal challenge into an opportunity By viewing waste as a valuable resource, businesses can turn a disposal cost into an asset contributing to profitability

Recently, there has been a gradual shift toward what is sometimes called the recycling economy, an intermediate step toward more sustainable practices. This model includes increased efforts to recycle and manage waste more effectively than the outright disposal methods of the linear model. However, while beneficial, the recycling economy often still operates within the framework of the linear model—it aims to mitigate the environmental impacts of the "dispose" phase. Still, it does not fundamentally change how products are designed, used, and reused.

The circular economy is an approach that aims to transform how we view and utilize resources. It seeks to revolutionize the entire lifecycle of products by prioritizing sustainability, competitiveness, and efficiency, ensuring that repair, reuse, and recycling are not just add-ons to the process but central elements of production and consumption. This approach builds on core principles (Table 1.1) that strive to create a closed-loop system where waste is minimized, and every resource is used to its fullest potential. The circular economy introduces a more robust and competitive business model, positioning companies to reduce their environmental footprint and enhance their competitiveness.

Circularity aims to connect economic progress with ecological boundaries by promoting prosperity that replenishes rather than depletes our finite resources. The circular economy represents an adjustment and a complete redefinition of growth, visualizing a future where economic activities coexist with and nourish the natural environment. The European Union estimates that by adopting circular practices, GDP could increase by an additional 0.5%, and approximately 700,000 new jobs could be created by 2030 (European Commission, 2020).

Example 1.2 Stellantis' Dare Forward 2030

With 14 automotive brands worldwide, Stellantis is a significant industry player. Its "Dare Forward 2030" strategic plan embeds circular economy principles across its operations (Stellantis, 2022).

The strategy highlights several key initiatives and ambitions:

- Stellantis is planning to enhance its capabilities for reusing and remanufacturing parts. This will involve implementing a system for reconditioning vehicles, refurbishing parts, and recycling to ensure that all possible byproducts of the manufacturing and usage process are converted back into valuable industrial inputs (Stellantis, 2024).
- Stellantis aims to increase its recycling revenues tenfold by 2030, highlighting the company's strategy of turning waste into profitable assets (Stellantis, 2022).
- Vehicles and their parts are now being designed with the end-of-life stage in mind to maximize the ease and efficiency of recycling and reuse. The intention is to ensure that every component has the potential for a second life, either in its original form or as raw material for new products.
- Stellantis aims to generate over 2 billion Euros in revenues from circular economy activities by 2030 as part of its broader economic goals (Stellantis, 2022).

1.1.1 Flow in a Circular Economy

Figure 1.6 provides an overview of the flow within a circular economy, highlighting the various stages and processes involved in maintaining the lifecycle of products and materials. This is the circular economy flow we will be using throughout the book.

The circular economy starts with resource extraction, involving sourcing raw materials for manufacturing. The objective is to minimize the extraction of virgin materials by prioritizing using recycled and sustainable resources.

Energy and material suppliers provide the necessary inputs for manufacturing. In a circular economy, these suppliers focus on delivering renewable energy and sustainable materials to reduce the overall environmental footprint.

Tier suppliers manufacture components for final products and adopt circular practices by designing durable, easily repairable, and recyclable components.

Original Equipment Manufacturers (OEMs) assemble the final products using components provided by tier suppliers. These manufacturers use design principles that make it easy to disassemble, repair, and recycle the products. This ensures that the products can be effectively managed throughout their lifecycle and at the end of it.

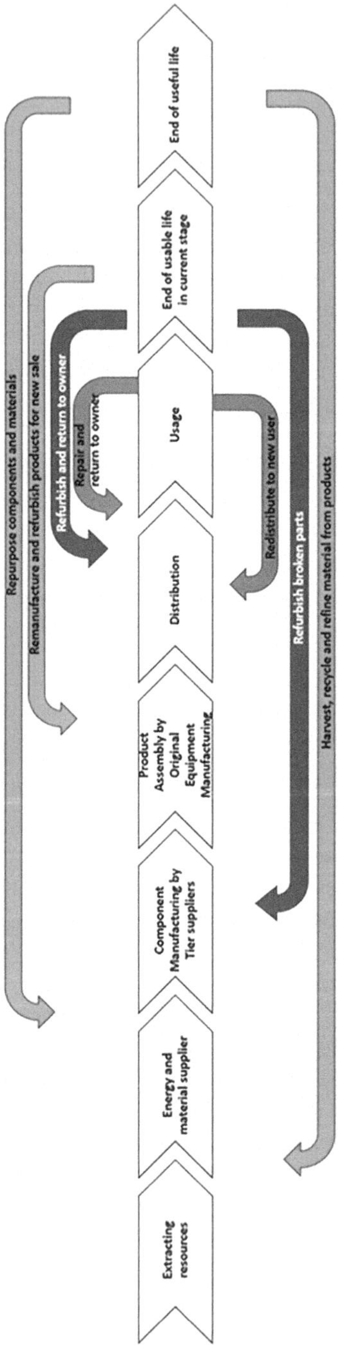

Fig. 1.6 The flow within a circular economy

Once products are assembled, they are distributed to customers through various channels. Efficient distribution strategies minimize transportation emissions and ensure products reach customers with minimal environmental impact.

Customers utilize the products for their intended purposes. During this phase, products are maintained to extend their usable life, reducing the need for premature disposal and replacement. When products need attention, they follow these paths:

- *Repairs are performed to restore the product to working condition and return it to the owner for continued use. Any exchanged parts are sent for refurbishment (not illustrated).*
- *Products can also be redistributed through recommerce and reuse models such as product as a service (PaaS) and the sharing economy, ensuring they continue to provide value and utility.*

When a product reaches the end of its usable life in its current stage, it undergoes further processes to reclaim its value:

- *Products can be refurbished or remanufactured. They are disassembled, cleaned, repaired, and reassembled to meet original specifications or better. These remanufactured products are then sold again.*
- *Individual broken parts are refurbished, used in other products, or sold separately.*

At the end of its useful life, a product undergoes additional processes to reclaim its value and reduce waste.

- *Components and materials that cannot be reused in their original form are repurposed for different applications, finding new life in other products.*

Finally, any remaining materials are harvested, recycled, and refined. These materials are then reintroduced into the supply chain, reducing the need for new raw material extraction.

1.1.2 New Business Opportunities in the Circular Economy

The circular economy presents numerous new business opportunities across various sectors (Table 1.2). Repair services are in high demand as customers and businesses aim to prolong the lifespan of their products. The shift to circularity creates a market potential for refurbishers and remanufacturers, who can take advantage of the growing market for refurbished and remanufactured products and provide high-quality alternatives to new products. It's important to note that repairers, refurbishers, and remanufacturers can be the manufacturers themselves or third-party service providers.

Table 1.2 New business opportunities in the circular economy

Sector	Business opportunities
Repair services	High demand for prolonging product lifespan through repairs
Refurbishers and remanufacturers	Market potential for refurbished and remanufactured products; can be manufacturers or third-party providers
Recycling companies	Increased supply of end-of-life products for material recovery and recycling
Tier suppliers	Demand for durable, repairable, and recyclable components; potential to resell refurbished parts, creating additional revenue streams
OEMs (Original Equipment Manufacturers)	New business models such as leasing, take-back schemes, and service-based offerings; generating multiple revenue streams from a single production cycle
Digital platforms	Facilitation of used and refurbished products; redistribution of products; matching service providers with customers
Logistic service providers	Increased demand for reverse logistics; optimization of logistics networks for circular supply chains

Recycling companies benefit from an increased supply of end-of-life products for material recovery and recycling, enhancing their capabilities for efficient material separation and recycling technologies.

Tier suppliers see opportunities in the demand for durable, repairable, and recyclable components, driving innovation in the design and production of sustainable components. They also have the potential to resell refurbished parts, creating additional revenue streams. *OEMs and tier suppliers can capitalize on the circular economy by generating multiple revenue streams from a single production cycle.*

Original Equipment Manufacturers (OEMs) can explore new business models focused on product lifecycle management, including leasing, take-back schemes, and service-based offerings. Digital platforms that facilitate the redistribution of used and refurbished products, such as recommerce platforms and models like product as a service (PaaS), can thrive by connecting sellers with buyers. Additionally, platforms that match service providers with customers needing repair, refurbishment, and recycling services gain opportunities by ensuring a vast network of reliable service providers and robust logistical support.

Logistic service providers are experiencing an increased demand for reverse logistics to handle product return, redistribution, and recycling. They are optimizing logistics networks to manage the complexities of circular supply chains, where all arrows in Fig. 1.6 require logistics.

By embracing these opportunities, businesses can contribute to environmental sustainability and achieve economic growth and resilience in the evolving market landscape driven by the circular economy principles. This book will explore these opportunities in detail, providing insights and strategies for leveraging the circular economy to create sustainable and profitable business models. Dive in to discover how you can transform your business for the future.

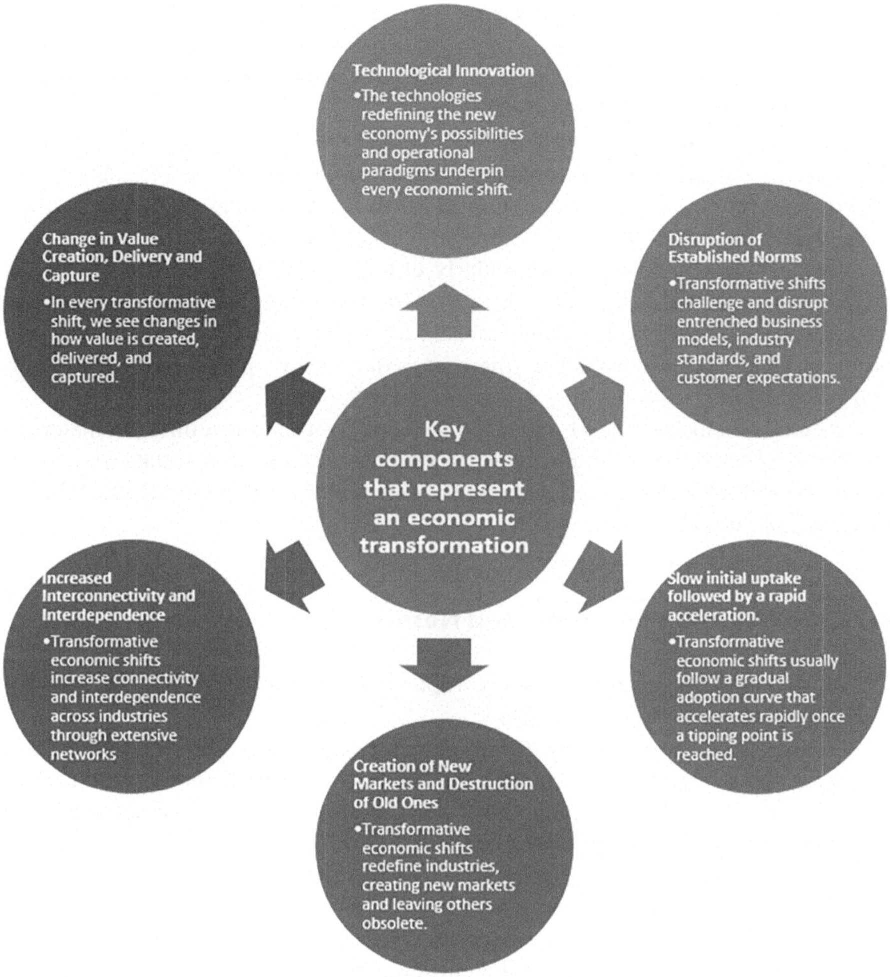

Fig. 1.7 Key components that represent an economic transformation

1.2 Why the Circular Economy Is an Economic Transformation

In the previous section, we explored the circular economy concept and its potential to transform the current economic model. This section will delineate the key components that represent such a transition and elucidate the reasons behind the characteristics of the circular economy as a transformative shift in the economy (Fig. 1.7).

1.2.1 Technological Innovation

The technologies redefining the new economy's possibilities and operational paradigms underpin every economic shift.

Augmented by digital technology, the circular economy introduces efficiencies in tracking, analyzing, and optimizing resources, components, and products across the business ecosystem. This technological infusion ensures that maximum lifetime value is extracted from products, components, and materials.

Advancements in robotics, particularly efficient parts harvesting and material extraction, are pivotal in this transformation. Modern robots equipped with cutting-edge sensors and powered by sophisticated algorithms can precisely disassemble products and extract valuable materials that were previously considered non-recoverable.

Artificial intelligence (AI) enhances the composition and utility of materials used in manufacturing. AI algorithms can analyze vast amounts of data to identify potential improvements in material compositions, making them more adaptable to recycling and reuse.

1.2.2 Disruption of Established Norms

Transformative shifts challenge and disrupt entrenched business models, industry standards, and customer expectations.

The disruption epitomized by the circular economy is the radical departure from the linear "take-make-dispose" model that has ruled industrial and economic practice for centuries. The restoration and regeneration of resources compel industries to reflect on their whole value chain, from raw material extraction to product design, manufacture, customer-use behavior, and management at the end of usage cycles, causing companies to innovate or lose out to obsolescence.

The circular economy shifts customer expectations toward a responsible and long-term value culture instead of the current culture of consumption and disposability. The increased adoption of circular economy principles by leading born-circular disruptors, customers, consumers, and governments will make it unsustainable to stay in a wasteful status quo. This will foster transformations in the economy's production, consumption, and value of goods.

1.2.3 Slow Initial Uptake Followed by a Rapid Acceleration

Transformative economic shifts usually follow a gradual adoption curve that accelerates rapidly once a tipping point is reached. This is often illustrated as a hockey stick graph depicting slow initial uptake followed by rapid acceleration.

Today, the circular economy is approaching such an inflection point, spurred by catalysts (Sect. 1.4) such as climate change, stakeholder advocacy, legislative changes, and digital innovation. The concept has been underway for a long time, as William McDonough and Michael Braungart published *Cradle to Cradle: Remaking the Way We Make Things* back in 2002, which many see as the manifesto for the circular economy.

The global analyst company Gartner predicts that circular supply chains will hit the "peak of inflated expectations" by 2024 and advance to the "plateau of productivity" within 5 to 10 years (Tohamy, 2023). *The trajectory indicates that by around 2030, circular economy practices will transition from niche to mainstream.* This shift will require manufacturers to prepare and strategically invest in circular capabilities. If they have not already done so, they must allocate resources to develop or expand these capabilities rapidly. This book will assist manufacturers in gaining an understanding of how to do so.

1.2.4 Creation of New Markets and Destruction of Old Ones

Transformative economic shifts redefine industries, creating new markets and leaving others obsolete.

In a circular economy, value will not come from focusing on consumption but from extending the life of products, renewing resources, and using resources efficiently. This shift creates many opportunities in remanufacturing, product as a service models, and materials recovery and recycling, enabling the development of new industries and business models. Companies that innovate to serve circular markets are entering growing markets with increasing demand, driven by rising customer awareness and regulatory pressures for sustainability.

1.2.5 Increased Interconnectivity and Interdependence

Transformative economic shifts increase connectivity and interdependence across industries through extensive networks, whether physical (e.g., railroads), utility-based (e.g., power grids), or virtual (e.g., digital platforms).

Circularity acknowledges the interconnectedness of industries and promotes collaborative networks. In this model, waste generated by one process becomes a resource for another, promoting cost efficiency and building resilience across the business ecosystem.

Fostering a closed-loop circular system requires and encourages extensive cooperation among traditionally siloed industries, such as waste management, material supply, product and service design, and customer involvement.

Digital technologies enable this interconnectivity by tracking, sharing, and managing resources across the entire value chain. Businesses become part of a larger, interconnected digital ecosystem that depends on and benefits from cooperation and resource sharing. This interconnectivity improves the resilience and sustainability of individual companies and contributes to a more robust and adaptable global economy.

1.2.6 Change in Value Creation, Delivery, and Capture

In every transformative shift, we see changes in how value is created, delivered, and captured.

The circular economy changes how value is created, shifting it from the point of production to the continuous usage cycles of the entire product. This change emphasizes the value of services, product longevity, and resource efficiency (Sect. 9.2 discusses the change in Value Creation, Delivery, and Capture).

Example 1.3 World Economic Forum's Circular Cars initiative

According to the World Economic Forum's Circular Cars initiative (Circular Cars Initiative, 2022), a shift to circularity could increase the revenue and profitability metrics across the automotive industry. Revenues per vehicle could increase approximately tenfold over its lifecycle, potentially reaching 15–20 times the initial sales price. Similarly, the overall profitability of the value chain could increase by about 1.5 times, with profits per vehicle throughout its lifespan potentially multiplying up to around 15 times.

Strategic Cost Reductions and Value Maximization

The industry can reduce production costs using modular designs and recycled materials, improving vehicle profitability.

Designing vehicles for easier maintenance and repair can extend their lifespan and lower the total cost of ownership.

Advanced recycling processes can decompose end-of-life vehicles and reintegrate them into the production cycle, reducing the need for raw materials and lowering material costs.

Innovative Revenue Streams and Customer Engagement

Circular strategies create new revenue streams by offering extended lifecycle services focusing on maintenance and repair, keeping customers engaged throughout the vehicle's enhanced lifespan.

Remanufacturing enables companies to provide sustainable and affordable products, meeting the growing demand for greener options.

The shift to service-based models like mobility as a service (MaaS) and product as a service (PaaS) changes the revenue model from one-off vehicle sales to recurring income, ensuring long-term financial stability and continuous customer engagement.

1.3 Why a Book on the Clean, Digital, and Circular Paradigms as the Cornerstones of Competitive Manufacturing

This book explores the concept of the transformative circular economy. As mentioned earlier, such transformation will lead to the emergence of new industry leaders and redefined economic norms. The book guides manufacturers, demonstrating how the circular economy can benefit the environment while being a superior business strategy.

A central theme is that manufacturers' competitiveness depends on how effectively they integrate three fundamental paradigms.

Cleaner production methods are crucial for minimizing environmental and climate impacts by reducing carbon footprints.

Digital technologies are essential to streamline operations, improve efficiency, and promote innovation.

Circular economy practices are necessary to establish regenerative resource loops that extend product lifecycles and reduce waste.

These paradigms are not individual strategies but foundational synergies for sustainable manufacturing growth, leading to advanced processes where competitiveness, efficiency, and sustainability intertwine (Fig. 1.8).

The transition to a circular economy may seem easy for startups with limited product lines, but it can be a complex challenge for established manufacturers. These manufacturers are accustomed to the traditional linear economy and must maintain their competitiveness in that model while transitioning to circularity. This book aims to assist these established manufacturers and inspire emerging circular businesses by emphasizing the importance of gradually re-engineering traditional practices to embrace this new economic model. It provides valuable insights into how integrating clean, digital, and circular paradigms can help maintain competitiveness and promote growth in an era where sustainability is an important economic consideration.

The following section will delve into the various catalysts transforming the manufacturing sector, accompanied by a chapter that explores governmental initiatives that support this shift. The second part will introduce the "1+5 R model," a framework designed to help manufacturers redesign and reinvent their products and business models for the circular economy. The 1+5 R model focuses on the core principles of redesign and the five essential circular business models: redistribute, repair, refurbish, remanufacture, and recycle. Each model is thoroughly examined to highlight the business benefits and challenges, offering readers clear and actionable insights into practical implementation. Moreover, Part II will provide key capability maps for each of the five Rs for successful adoption. Readers will also gain insights into the Circular Economy Strategy Framework (CESF) and the Manufacturing Circular Maturity Framework (MCMF), which offer strategic guidelines for assessing and enhancing their circular economy initiatives. By the end of Part II, readers will have a robust understanding of how to transition their operations

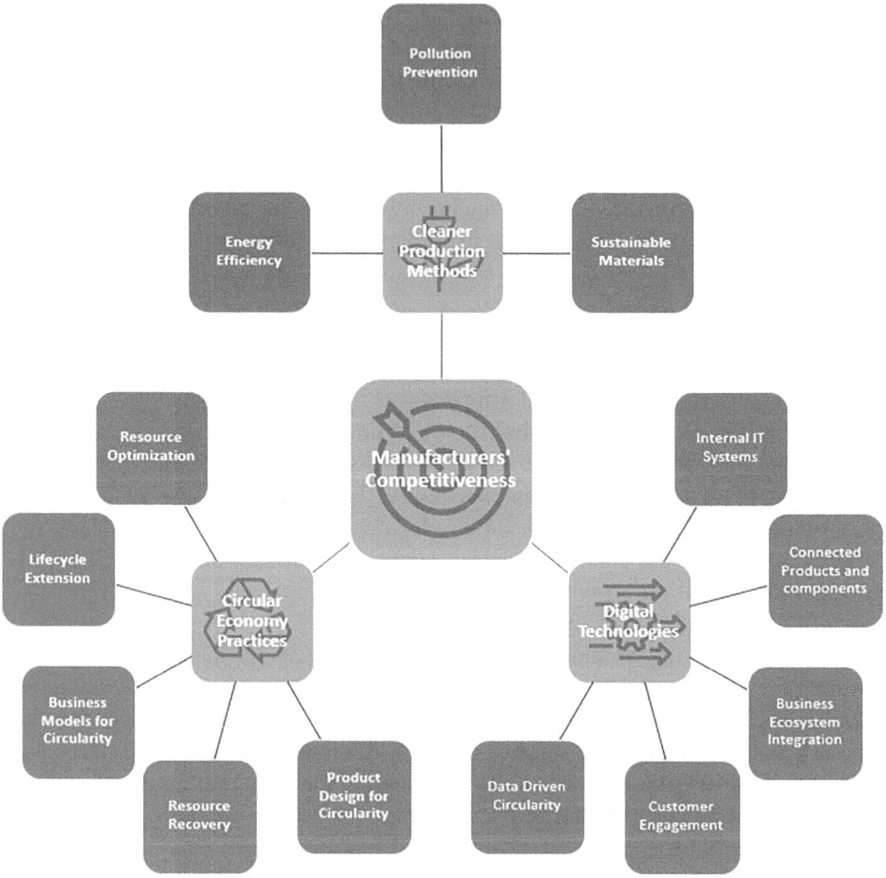

Fig. 1.8 Manufacturers' competitiveness

toward a circular economy, leveraging these models and frameworks to drive sustainability and profitability.

As we progress to Part III, the book shifts focus to the pivotal role of digitization in facilitating this transformation. This part is dedicated to unraveling how digital technologies intersect with and support the circular economy principles outlined in earlier chapters. This section illuminates the Sustainable Manufacturing Intelligence Framework (SMIF), which demonstrates how digitization supports the transition across various dimensions—customer experience, connected products, internal IT, business ecosystem, and data-driven circularity. Twelve key digital capabilities will be identified for each dimension.

Part IV combines all the insights and strategies discussed in the previous sections, culminating in a comprehensive and actionable conclusion. This part will outline the 10-Step Circular Advantage Guide (CAG), providing a detailed roadmap for manufacturers to navigate and thrive in the circular economy.

Through detailed discussions, case studies, and practical examples, we aim to show how leveraging digital tools can streamline processes, improve resource management, and foster innovations that align with circular economy objectives. This comprehensive coverage ensures that readers not only grasp the theoretical underpinnings of these changes but also understand the practical steps they can take to integrate these advanced technologies into their daily business practices.

Each chapter begins with an overview of its key messages, providing a roadmap of the main themes and critical points to be covered. The overview gives you a quick preview of what to expect.

At the end of each chapter, a checklist summarizes the key points covered. This practical checklist is designed to help you review and assess your understanding of the topic. It also provides actionable steps that you can implement to integrate the discussed strategies into your practices.

Given the extensive coverage of the clean paradigm/decarbonization in existing literature, this book will concentrate on the less-explored digital and circular dimensions and refer the readers to other resources dedicated to clean practices, like the International Energy Agency (IEA),[1] World Resources Institute (WRI),[2] United Nations Framework Convention on Climate Change (UNFCCC),[3] and the World Economic Forum (WEF).[4]

Upon reaching the last page of this book, readers will be equipped with theoretical knowledge, practical strategies, and insights that can change their manufacturing processes and usher in a new era of industrial efficiency, competitiveness, and environmental responsibility. This book bridges conventional manufacturing approaches and the sustainable industry's future, ensuring businesses can flourish in an economically viable and ecologically sound setting.

1.3.1 The Terms "Value Chain Customer" and "Customer"

The terms "value chain customers" and "customers" are used interchangeably to mean all entities and individuals involved as customers in the journey of a product. A value chain customer includes a host of stakeholders, such as resellers, distributors, retailers, and the end-users (either business or consumers)—the ultimate users of the product and who may not be engaging directly with manufacturers but whose preferences and consumption habits influence the product design, production processes, and sustainability practices.

[1] https://www.iea.org/

[2] https://www.wri.org/

[3] https://unfccc.int/

[4] https://www.weforum.org/

1.4 Nine Key Catalysts Reshaping the Future of Manufacturing

The cleaner, digital, and circular paradigms revolve around nine key catalysts that are reshaping the future of manufacturing. These changes go beyond just the factory floor and impact customer behaviors in the value chain, transform supply chains, and redefine international trade dynamics. As a result, there is a need to reevaluate production practices and take a fresh look at the relationships between manufacturers, customers, and the environment (Fig. 1.9).

1.4.1 Global Climate Impacts

The rate of global climate change is accelerating, and scientific research is providing a clear message to industries worldwide. The IPCC's Climate Change 2023 report (Lee & Romero, 2023) shows that human activities affect extreme weather and climate patterns worldwide. This is reflected in extremely high temperatures, heavy rainfall, prolonged droughts, and an increase in the frequency of tropical

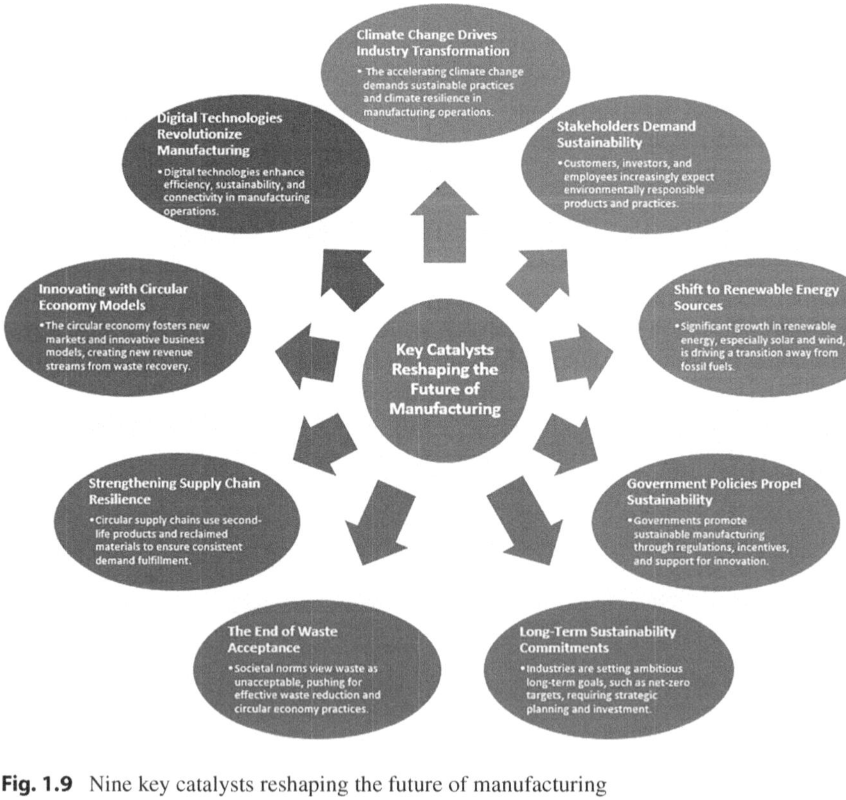

Fig. 1.9 Nine key catalysts reshaping the future of manufacturing

cyclones. These phenomena indicate that we need to fundamentally change our approach to the environment (Fig. 1.10).

In the World Economic Forum's Global Risks Report 2024 (World Economic Forum, 2024), extreme weather events stand out as significant short- and long-term concerns. Over the next 2 years, they are considered the second-most severe risk facing global stability. Looking further ahead, the 10-year outlook positions extreme weather as the most critical risk, underscoring the increasing challenges posed by climate change and environmental instability (Fig. 1.11).

1.4.2 Stakeholder Advocacy

Stakeholders, including customers, investors, the workforce, and regulatory bodies, continuously demand environmentally responsible products and practices.

Industry surveys highlight consumers at the forefront of this movement. Their growing environmental awareness strongly favors products that align with their values (Wood, 2022) (Fig. 1.12).

Sustainability has become an aspect of investment strategies, with implications for risk, return, and investor preference. It is no longer a niche market but a part of the global investment landscape. The shift reflects a growing awareness that sustainability issues are integral to financial success and stability today. The increasing trend toward ESG (environmental, social, and governance) investing is a response to environmental and social imperatives and a strategic financial approach to ensure resilience and profitability in an interconnected global economy (The Global Sustainable Investment Alliance, 2023). GSIA indicates a 20% increase in the percentage of sustainable investments, increasing from USD 18.2 to USD 21.9 trillion (Table 1.3).

The regulatory landscape is also changing, with initiatives like the European Green Deal aiming to transform the continent to climate neutrality by 2050. Such policy actions highlight the role of regulatory bodies in setting the standards for sustainable manufacturing practices (see Sect. 1.4.4).

The Global Millennial Survey (Deloitte, 2023) shows that today's workforce, particularly millennials and Gen Z, increasingly prioritizes sustainability and ethical practices when choosing employers. *"50% of Gen Zs and 46% of millennials say they and their colleagues are pressuring businesses to take action on climate change, which marks a slight increase from last year."* Many young professionals report seeking companies with strong environmental credentials and are likelier to stay long-term with an employer demonstrating commitment to social and environmental issues. This trend is driven by a broader desire among younger workers to contribute to positive social and environmental outcomes through employment. The survey highlights that companies that fail to adopt genuine sustainability practices may find themselves at a competitive disadvantage in attracting and retaining top talent.

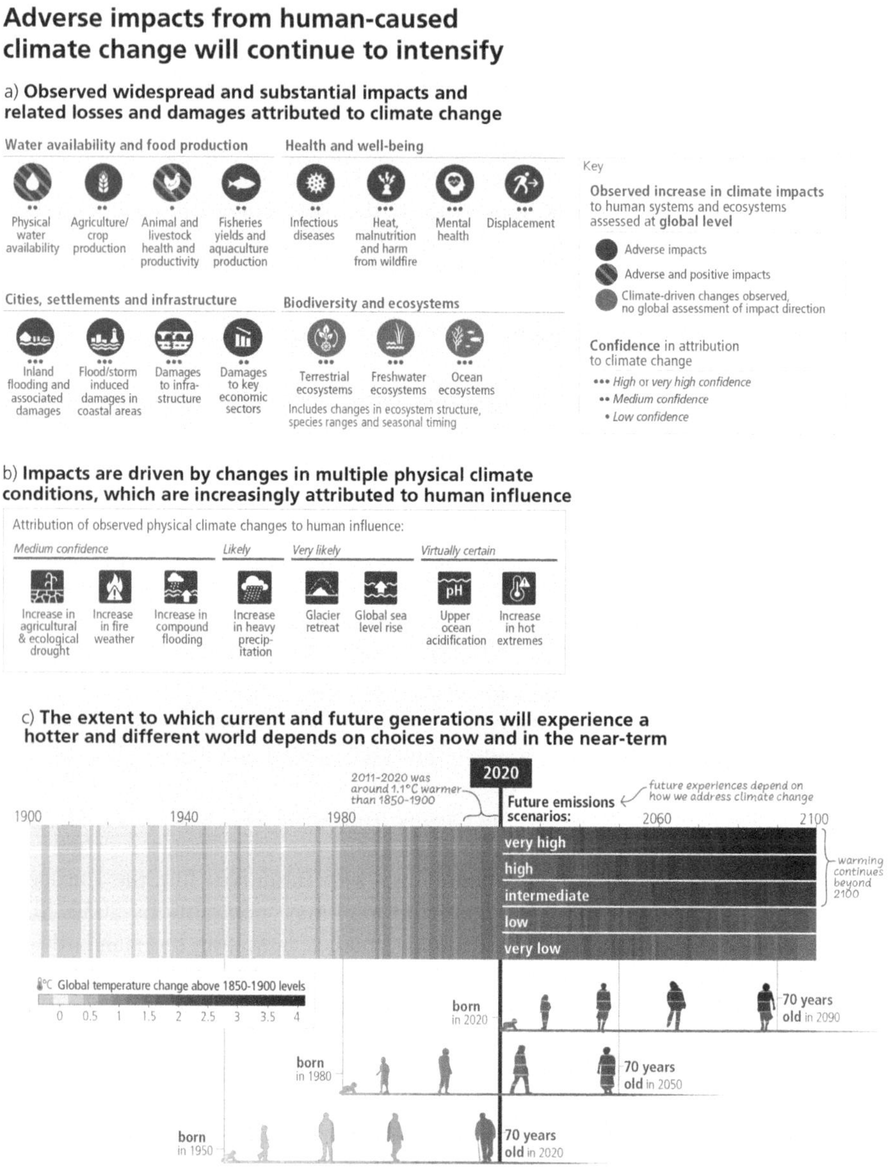

Fig. 1.10 Adverse impacts from human-caused climate change will continue to intensify (**a**) Climate change has already caused widespread impacts, related losses, and damages on human systems and altered terrestrial, freshwater, and ocean ecosystems worldwide. Physical water availability includes the balance of water available from various sources, including groundwater, water quality, and demand for water. Global mental health and displacement assessments reflect only assessed regions. Confidence levels reflect the assessment of attribution of the observed impact to climate change. (**b**) Observed impacts are connected to physical climate changes including many that have been attributed to human influence such as the selected climatic impact drivers shown. Confidence and likelihood levels reflect the assessment of attribution of the observed climatic

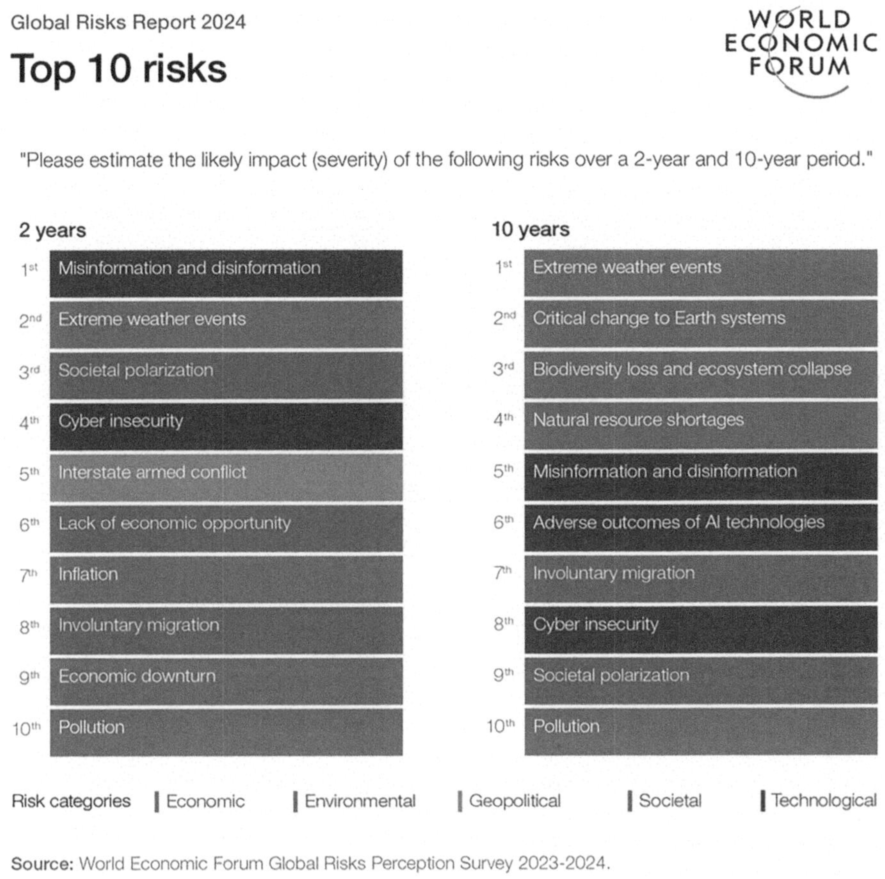

Fig. 1.11 Global risks ranked by severity over the short and long term. (The figure by the World Economic Forum is licensed under CC BY-NC-ND 4.0 (https://creativecommons.org/licenses/by-nc-nd/4.0/deed.en). Accessed from (World Economic Forum, 2024))

Fig. 1.10 (continued) impact driver to human influence. (**c**) Observed (1900–2020) and projected (2021–2100) changes in global surface temperature (relative to 1850–1900), which are linked to changes in climate conditions and impacts, illustrate how the climate has already changed and will change along the lifespan of three representative generations (born in 1950, 1980, and 2020). Future projections (2021–2100) of changes in global surface temperature are shown for very low (SSP1-1.9), low (SSP1-2.6), intermediate (SSP2-4.5), high (SSP3-7.0), and very high (SSP5-8.5) GHG emissions scenarios. Changes in annual global surface temperatures are presented as "climate stripes," with future projections showing the human-caused long-term trends and continuing modulation by natural variability (represented here using observed levels of past natural variability). Colors on the generational icons correspond to the global surface temperature stripes for each year, with segments on future icons differentiating possible future experiences. (Credit: IPCC, 2023: Summary for Policymakers. In: Climate Change 2023: Synthesis Report. Contribution of Working Groups I, II and III to the Sixth Assessment Report of the Intergovernmental Panel on Climate Change [Core Writing Team, H. Lee and J. Romero (eds.)]. IPCC, Geneva, Switzerland, pp. 1–34, https://doi.org/10.59327/IPCC/AR6-9789291691647.001)

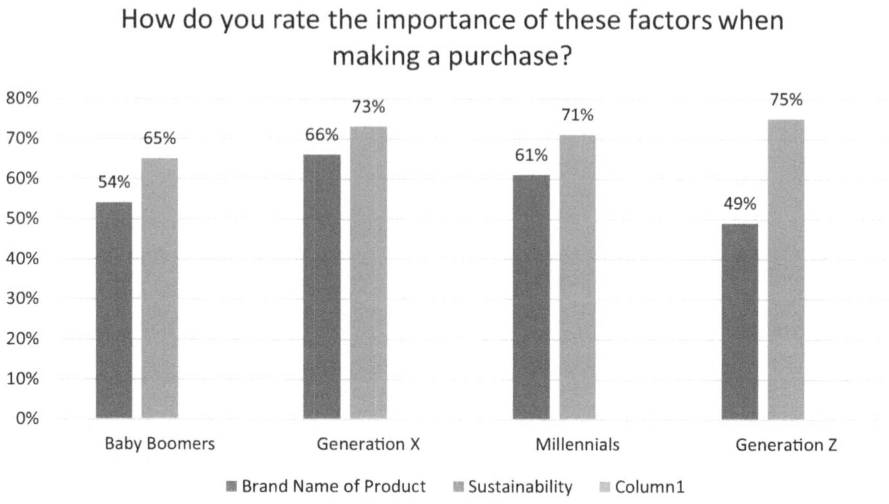

Fig. 1.12 75% of Gen Zs think sustainable purchases are more important than brand names

Table 1.3 Snapshot of global sustainable investing assets (The Global Sustainable Investment Alliance, 2023)

Region	2016	2018	2020	2022
EUROPE	12,040	14,075	12,017	14,054
Canada	1086	1699	2423	2358
Australia and New Zealand	516	734	906	1220
Japan	474	2180	2874	4289
Sub-total (USD billions)	14,115	18,688	18,220	21,921
% change		32%	−3%	20%
United States	8723	11,995	17,081	8400
Total (USD billions)	22,838	30,683	35,301	30,321
% change		34%	15%	n/a

GSIA changed the US methodology and the quantum of assets represented by this region; therefore, their trend analysis has been conducted, excluding the US data

1.4.3 The Renewable Energy Transformation

The energy landscape is transforming into an era in which renewable energy sources are viable and increasingly preferred over traditional fossil fuels.

According to the IEA's 2023 report (International Energy Agency (IEA), 2023), renewable energy has grown in recent years, primarily driven by solar photovoltaics (PV) and wind power. The IEA notes that solar PV installations have reached record highs, a trend that will continue as costs decline. Similarly, the EIA's 2023 Annual Energy Outlook highlights increased wind and solar capacities in the United States. Renewables are expected to account for most new power generation capacity (US Energy Information Administration, 2023).

REN21's 2023 report (REN21, 2023) complements these findings by pointing out that renewables are becoming increasingly competitive globally compared to fossil fuel sources. The report stresses that policy frameworks in over 50 countries have successfully supported the market's rapid expansion and integration into existing grids.

Looking ahead, the IEA projects that renewable energy will account for almost 95% of the increase in global power capacity through 2026, with solar and wind leading the charge. This is echoed by the EIA, which forecasts that renewable energy will provide nearly half of the global electricity output by 2050, driven by further technological advancements and decreasing costs.

REN21 offers a slightly more cautious outlook, emphasizing the need for sustained and enhanced governmental policy support to overcome systemic grid integration challenges and market dynamics. They advocate for a more aggressive policy shift to support the existing technologies and innovate new solutions that could integrate renewables more deeply into the energy mix.

1.4.4 Government Initiatives: Catalyzing a Global Shift Toward Sustainable Manufacturing

Governments worldwide are pivotal in steering the manufacturing sector toward a more clean and circular future. By offering support for research and development, implementing stringent regulations, introducing carbon taxes, and establishing trading systems, they're laying the groundwork for an industrial transformation. The commitment to sustainability has notably intensified among OECD nations from 2000 to 2020 (Kruse et al., 2022), evidenced by increased targeted policies, regulations, and financial incentives designed to foster eco-innovation.

For instance, the European Union's budget for 2021 to 2027, combined with the NextGenerationEU recovery instrument, totals €2.018 trillion (European Commission, 2021), with 30% dedicated to combating climate change. Similarly, the United States allocated about $80 billion in 2022 (U.S. Government Publishing Office, 2022) to tackle various challenges, including climate change, highlighting a concerted effort toward sustainable progress globally, including in regions such as the EU, China, the United States, the United Kingdom, and Japan (Jensen, 2023) (see Chap. 2).

1.4.5 Long-Term Commitments

The momentum for change has evolved beyond the typical short-term outlook of many executive agendas, signaling a long-haul dedication. For instance, setting an ambitious net zero target well before the global goal of 2050 underscores a paradigm shift in strategic foresight and planning (Fig. 1.13).

Industries must view this transformation not as a temporary change but as a fundamental shift that will shape the future of manufacturing. Successfully navigating

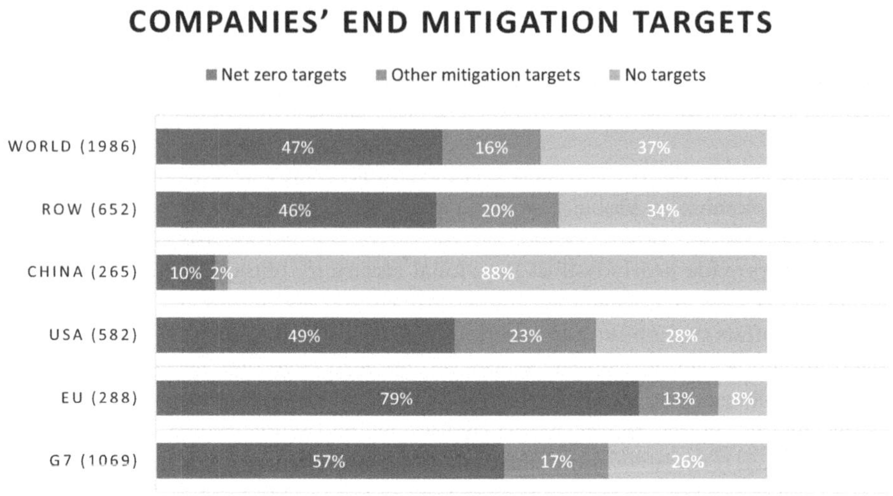

Fig. 1.13 Companies' end mitigation targets—covering the world's largest 2000 companies by revenue (Net Zero Tracker 2023)

this requires strategic foresight, technological investment, effective collaboration with government bodies, and a unified vision among all stakeholders.

1.4.6 Waste Becoming Unacceptable

As we approach 2030, the perception of waste undergoes a profound transformation, propelled by a collective awakening among consumers and reinforced by decisive governmental action (Gartner, 2019).

Nielsen's Global Sustainability Report (Nielsen, 2023) reveals that most consumers worldwide prioritize products with sustainable packaging and minimizing waste through their lifecycle. This change is driven by a growing awareness of environmental issues and a strong desire among consumers to contribute personally to sustainability efforts.

OECD Environmental Performance Reviews (EPR) (OECD, 2024) detail how governments respond to public pressure and recognize the economic benefits of enhanced waste management policies. These include reducing long-term costs associated with waste disposal and tapping into new job markets within the recycling and waste reduction sectors.

The shift toward considering waste as unacceptable creates opportunities for waste reduction. As societal norms evolve, waste becomes environmentally, socially, and economically untenable.

1.4.7 Supply Chain Resilience

In today's globalized economy, supply chain resilience has become crucial to business success. The COVID-19 pandemic highlighted the fragility of global supply chains, causing widespread disruptions and exposing vulnerabilities in the traditional linear supply chain models. Natural disasters, geopolitical tensions, and cyber-attacks further exacerbate these risks, making it essential for companies to build more robust and adaptable supply chains. According to (Elliott et al., 2023), the level of supply chain disruption reported by organizations is more than twice as high as pre-pandemic levels. Almost half of respondents (45.7%) experienced these issues with their closest suppliers at Tier 1, while 24.1% saw more disruptions at Tier 2.

The shift to a circular economy improves the resilience of supply chains. Circular supply chains, which prioritize the reuse, recycling, and remanufacturing of materials, decrease reliance on volatile raw material markets and help mitigate the risks related to supply interruptions. By incorporating circular principles, companies can establish closed-loop systems that are less vulnerable to external shocks. For instance, using recycled materials reduces the necessity for new resources, while remanufacturing and refurbishing products can prolong their lifespan, ensuring a consistent supply of goods even during disruptions.

1.4.8 Enhanced Value and Innovation

The circular economy enables enterprises to explore new markets and innovate with fresh business models and products.

Enterprises are adopting novel business models such as product as a service (PaaS), where products are offered on a usage basis rather than sold, encouraging better maintenance and recycling. Refurbishment and resale initiatives allow companies to extend product lifecycles by selling refurbished items at a discount, appealing to cost-conscious consumers and reducing waste. Sharing platforms in industries like automotive enable users to access products as needed. Firms are developing services to recover and repurpose waste materials, such as extracting precious metals from electronics or converting food waste into bioenergy, creating new revenue streams while mitigating environmental impact.

1.4.9 Transformation Through Digital Technologies

The manufacturing sector is transforming through digital technology, enhancing efficiency and sustainability.

AI and GenAI improve automation and optimize resource use. AI systems efficiently manage production and reduce waste by predicting maintenance needs and streamlining operations. GenAI further aids in designing and testing through algorithms, minimizing material use and speeding up development.

5G technology enhances factory connectivity, enabling real-time data exchange and supporting the widespread use of IoT devices, which optimize energy and operational efficiency. Collaborative robots (cobots) work alongside humans to ensure task precision and adaptability, promoting safer and more efficient practices.

Digital twins simulate production processes in virtual environments to optimize material and energy use, while advanced sensors monitor conditions to adjust operations dynamically, maintaining efficiency and sustainability.

Advancements in digital technologies like APIs, artificial intelligence, and digital platforms are integrating the value chain within the manufacturing sector. These technologies facilitate connectivity and communication across various manufacturing process components, from supply chain management to production and distribution.

Part III of this book will introduce the Sustainable Manufacturing Intelligence Framework, which guides manufacturers using digital tools to build a clean, circular manufacturing paradigm.

1.5 Strategic Reflection Checklist

As we start this book, it's important to consider how the principles and concepts we discuss apply to your business. Reflecting early on will help lay the groundwork for deeper insights and more detailed strategies as you read. This checklist is meant to encourage critical thinking and strategic planning from the start so you can refine and improve your approach as you go through the chapters (Table 1.4).

Table 1.4 Strategic reflection checklist

Strategic questions for reflection	Description
Business model alignment	
How does your current business model align with circular economy principles?	Evaluate the extent to which your business practices reflect circular economy principles
What changes are necessary to align your business model with these principles better?	Identify specific adjustments needed in your business strategy and operations
Immediate steps	
What immediate steps can you take to start integrating circular practices?	List actionable steps that can be implemented quickly
Who will be responsible for these initiatives, and what resources will they require?	Determine key personnel and resources needed for implementation
Technology benefits	
Which technologies could provide the most benefits for your operations?	Assess potential technologies that could enhance circular practices within your operations
How will you integrate these technologies into your existing systems?	Develop a plan for technology adoption and integration

(continued)

Table 1.4 (continued)

Strategic questions for reflection	Description
Partnership leverage	
How can you leverage partnerships to enhance your circular economy efforts?	Explore opportunities for collaboration with other organizations
What potential partners could offer the most value, and how will you engage them?	Identify and plan engagement with potential partners
Success metrics	
What metrics will you use to measure the success of your circular initiatives?	Define key performance indicators (KPIs) to track progress
How will you collect, analyze, and report these metrics?	Establish systems for data collection, analysis, and reporting
Long-term vision	
What is your long-term vision for integrating circular economy principles into your business?	Develop a strategic vision for the long-term implementation of circular practices
How will you ensure continuous improvement in your circular economy initiatives?	Plan for regular reviews and updates to your circular economy strategy
Stakeholder engagement	
How will you communicate your circular economy efforts to stakeholders?	Develop a communication strategy to inform stakeholders about your circular initiatives
How will you engage customers, employees, and investors in your circular economy journey?	Plan engagement activities to involve all relevant stakeholders

References

Circular Cars Initiative. (2022). Driving ambitions: The business case for circular economy in the car industry. *World Economic Forum*. From https://www.weforum.org/projects/the-circular-cars-initiative/

Deloitte. (2023). 2023 Gen Z and Millennial Survey. *Deloitte*. From https://www.deloitte.com/global/en/issues/work/content/genzmillennialsurvey.html

Elliott, R., Garcia, M. F., & Riglietti, G. (2023). *BCI Supply Chain Resilience Report 2023*. The Business Continuity Institute. From https://www.thebci.org/news/bci-launches-supply-chain-resilience-report-2023.html

European Commission. (2020). *A new Circular Economy Action Plan For a cleaner and more competitive Europe*. From https://environment.ec.europa.eu/strategy/circular-economy-action-plan_en

European Commission. (2021). *Supporting climate action through the EU budget*. Directorate-General for Climate Action. From https://climate.ec.europa.eu/eu-action/eu-funding-climate-action/supporting-climate-action-through-eu-budget_en

Gartner. (2019). *Gartner predicts circular economies will replace linear economies in 10 years*. Gartner. From https://www.gartner.com/en/newsroom/press-releases/2019-09-26-gartner-predicts-circular-economies-will-replace-line

International Energy Agency (IEA). (2023). *World Energy Outlook 2023*.

Jensen, H. H. (2023a). *Digitizing compliance: Unpacking Circular Economy legislations and their digital demands*. From Circular Bytes: https://www.linkedin.com/pulse/digitizing-compliance-unpacking-circular-economy-digital-jensen-3x7ae/

Kruse, T., Dechezleprêtre, A., Saffar, R., & Robert, L. (2022). *Measuring environmental policy stringency in OECD countries: An update of the OECD composite EPS indicator*. OECD Economics Department Working Papers. https://doi.org/10.1787/90ab82e8-en

Lee, H., & Romero, J. (2023). *Climate change 2023: Synthesis report.* Contribution of Working Groups I, II and III to the Sixth Assessment Report of the Intergovernmental Panel on Climate Change. Geneva: IPCC.

Net Zero Tracker. (2023). Net Zero Stocktake 2023. NewClimate Institute, Oxford Net Zero, Energy & Climate Intelligence Unit and Data-Driven EnviroLab. From https://ca1-nzt.edcdn.com/Reports/Net_Zero_Stocktake_2023.pdf

Nielsen. (2023). *Global sustainability report.* From https://www.nielsen.com/about-us/responsibility-and-sustainability/esg-report/

OECD. (2024). *Environmental country reviews.* OECD Environmental Performance Reviews (EPR) programme. From https://www.oecd.org/environment/country-reviews/

REN21. (2023). *Renewables 2023 global status report. Renewable energy policy network for the 21st Century (REN21).* From https://www.ren21.net/gsr-2023/

Stellantis. (2022, March). *Dare Forward 2030.* From Stellantis: https://www.stellantis.com/en/company/dare-forward-2030

Stellantis. (2024). *Stellantis Circular Economy reported strong growth in 2023 and is on track to increase this trend in 2024.* From https://www.media.stellantis.com/em-en/corporate-communications/press/stellantis-circular-economy-reported-strong-growth-in-2023-and-is-on-track-to-increase-this-trend-in-2024

Tohamy, N. (2023). *Hype cycle for supply chain strategy, 2023.* Gartner.

The Ellen MacArthur Foundation. (2019). The butterfly diagram: visualising the circular economy. From https://www.ellenmacarthurfoundation.org/circular-economy-diagram

The Global Sustainable Investment Alliance. (2023). *Global sustainability investment review 2022.* HSBC Global Research. From https://www.gsi-alliance.org/wp-content/uploads/2023/12/GSIA-Report-2022.pdf

The World Economic Forum. (2024). Global Risks Report 2024. *World Economic Forum.* From https://www3.weforum.org/docs/WEF_Global_Risks_Report_2024.pdf

US Energy Information Administration. (2023). *Annual Energy Outlook 2023.* From https://www.eia.gov/outlooks/aeo/narrative/

U.S. Government Publishing Office. (2022). *H.R.5376 - Inflation Reduction Act of 2022.* Congress.gov. From https://www.congress.gov/bill/117th-congress/house-bill/5376/text

Wood, J. (2022). Gen Z cares about sustainability more than anyone else – and is starting to make others feel the same. *The World Economic Forum.* From https://www.weforum.org/agenda/2022/03/generation-z-sustainability-lifestyle-buying-decisions/

2 Government Initiatives

Abstract

This chapter delves into the critical role of government initiatives in promoting the circular economy. It highlights how national and international regulations, such as right to repair, Extended Producer Responsibility (EPR), and Digital Product Passports (DPP), enforce circular practices and ensure compliance. The chapter underscores businesses' need to develop comprehensive compliance strategies to align with these regulatory mandates, integrating them into product design, manufacturing, and supply chain management.

Government incentives, grants, and subsidies are explored as vital support mechanisms for businesses transitioning to circular economy practices. The chapter presents a global perspective, showcasing diverse strategies employed by different countries. The European Union's Green Deal, the Netherlands' "Green Deals" program, China's Five-Year Circular Economy Plan, the United Kingdom's Green Industrial Revolution, and Japan's Sound Material-Cycle Society are discussed as leading examples of governmental efforts to drive sustainable development.

Key legislative trends supporting the circular economy, such as ecodesign directives, EPR schemes, right to repair laws, and Digital Product Passports, are examined. These regulations promote resource efficiency, sustainability, and transparency, reshaping how businesses produce, consume, and dispose of goods. The chapter also provides a strategic reflection checklist, guiding businesses in navigating the complex landscape of government regulations and leveraging available support to enhance their circular economy initiatives.

H. H. Jensen, *Circular Economy Opportunities and Pathways for Manufacturers*, Future of Business and Finance, https://doi.org/10.1007/978-3-031-75279-7_2

Key Messages

- *National and International Regulations:* Government regulations at national and international levels play a pivotal role in enforcing circular economy practices. Regulations such as right to repair, Extended Producer Responsibility (EPR), and Digital Product Passports (DPP) are key to this transformation.
- *Compliance Requirements:* Understanding and adhering to compliance requirements is crucial for businesses to operate sustainably and avoid legal repercussions. Aligning with these regulatory mandates requires developing a compliance strategy.
- *Compliance Strategy Development:* Businesses must develop comprehensive strategies to address regulatory requirements. This includes identifying relevant regulations, integrating these requirements into business operations, and ensuring ongoing compliance.
- *Operational Integration:* Integrating regulatory requirements into product design, manufacturing processes, and supply chain management supports achieving sustainability targets and maintaining competitive advantage.
- *Government Incentives and Support:* Various government incentives, grants, and subsidies are available to support businesses adopting circular economy practices. Identifying and leveraging these financial supports can aid the transition.

The shift toward a circular economy is evident in the diverse strategies employed by various countries. Each tailors its approach to its unique context while sharing a common goal of sustainable development (Fig. 2.1).

The European Union is taking the lead with its ambitious Green Deal to reshape its economy and achieve climate neutrality by 2050 (European Commission, 2020). This deal includes many policies, such as promoting circular economy practices and sustainable industries, focusing on biodiversity, and eliminating pollution. The main objective of this vision is to transition toward a modern, resource-efficient economy that balances economic growth with environmental responsibility.

Aiming for a fully circular economy by 2050, the Netherlands offers tax incentives and subsidies to encourage public-private participation in circular projects in the "Green Deals" program (Fraser, 2022).

China has committed to sustainable development through its Five-Year Circular Economy Plan. The plan emphasizes reducing waste, improving resource efficiency, and strengthening recycling industries. To achieve this, China has set targets for reducing pollutants, increasing the use of renewable resources, and integrating circular models into industries and urban planning (China Daily, 2012).

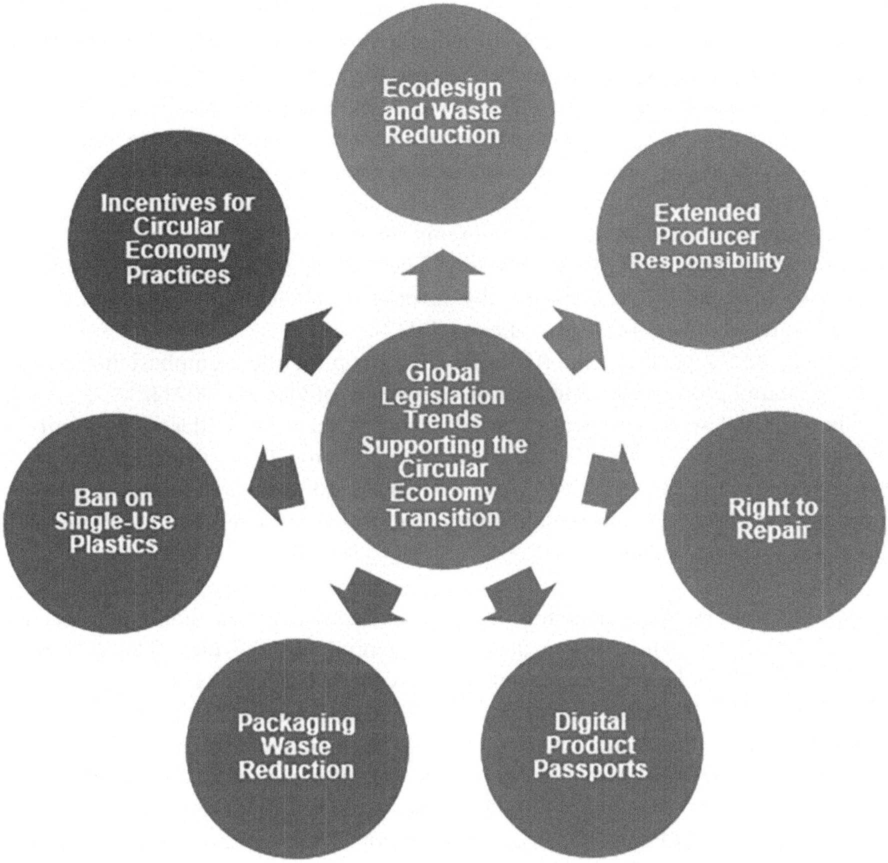

Fig. 2.1 Global legislation trends supporting the circular economy transition

The United Kingdom is pursuing a "Green Industrial Revolution"[1] to achieve net-zero carbon emissions by 2050. This approach involves investing in green technologies, sustainable transportation systems, energy-efficient housing, and green finance. The United Kingdom's Resources and Waste Strategy[2] incentivizes product design for longevity and recyclability, implements Extended Producer Responsibility schemes, implements plastic taxation, and supports the recycling sector through grants and investments (Department for Environment, Food & Rural Affairs, 2018).

In the United States, there are various initiatives at state and local levels aimed at promoting sustainable materials management and resource conservation despite the

[1] https://www.gov.uk/government/publications/the-ten-point-plan-for-a-green-industrial-revolution

[2] https://www.gov.uk/government/publications/circular-economy-package-policy-statement/circular-economy-package-policy-statement

lack of a cohesive national policy. Programs like the Recycling Partnership[3] and Closed Loop Fund[4] at the federal level indicate growing awareness and support for circular waste management and recycling approaches.

The California Circular Economy and Plastic Pollution Reduction Act[5] proposes measures to reduce waste from single-use products and packaging (Bruggers, 2022).

Japan is one of the early adopters of circular economy principles. They prioritize sustainable manufacturing and efficient waste management. The Japanese government has implemented policies encouraging businesses to adopt sustainable practices, reduce waste, and improve recycling. The country's primary goal is to achieve a "Sound Material-Cycle Society"[6] by leveraging technological innovation and strong public-private partnerships (Fraser, 2022).

Canada backs projects incorporating circular principles, emphasizing design innovation and product life extension (Government of Canada, 2021).

These global strategies, while varied in their execution, collectively signify a growing consensus on the need for a circular economy. These laws and directives aim to reshape how businesses produce, consume, and dispose of goods, emphasizing resource efficiency and sustainability. The following overview highlights key global legislative trends.

Ecodesign and Waste Reduction Many countries worldwide implement ecodesign directives to reduce waste and enhance product lifecycles. The European Union's Ecodesign Directive[7] sets out specific criteria for products to be considered environmentally friendly (European Commission, 2024). This directive has impacted product design, making it more energy-efficient and accessible to repair or recycle. In 2021, the current ecodesign measures covering 31 product groups resulted in EU consumers' energy expenditure savings of EUR 120 billion. They led to a 10% reduction in annual energy consumption by the products under the directive's scope (European Commission, 2022a, b).

Extended Producer Responsibility (EPR) End-of-life product management is increasingly becoming the responsibility of manufacturers through Extended Producer Responsibility (EPR) schemes. These schemes encourage companies to design products that can be disposed of sustainably or recycled easily. Countries like Japan (Johannes et al., 2021) and France (Dentons, 2023) have established EPR frameworks incentivizing companies to integrate environmental considerations into their product design and waste management practices.

[3] https://recyclingpartnership.org/

[4] https://www.closedlooppartners.com/

[5] https://calrecycle.ca.gov/circulareconomy/

[6] https://www.env.go.jp/en/recycle/smcs/index.html

[7] https://commission.europa.eu/energy-climate-change-environment/standards-tools-and-labels/products-labelling-rules-and-requirements/sustainable-products/ecodesign-sustainable-products-regulation_en

Right to Repair There is growing support for right to repair legislation, especially in the United States[8] and Europe.[9] These laws allow consumers to repair their devices or get third-party repairs, which goes against the culture of disposable technology. These regulations promote sustainable consumption by securing access to repair manuals, spare parts, and tools.

Digital Product Passports The Digital Product Passport (DPP)[10] initiative of the European Union is a prime example of employing digital solutions to promote circularity. These passports contain comprehensive information regarding a product's materials, source, repairability, and recyclability. This enhances transparency and facilitates circular business models. The Commission is currently developing the technical specifications for the DPP, and it is expected to become mandatory for specific product categories by 2026.

Packaging Waste Reduction Numerous nations are presently concentrating on decreasing packaging waste by enacting laws that require the decrease, reuse, or recycling of packaging materials. The Plastic Packaging Tax in the United Kingdom,[11] which obliges the payment of a tax on plastic packaging components containing less than 30% recycled plastic,[12] and Germany's Packaging Act (Der Grüne Punkt, 2024) are examples of such legislation. These laws are intended to reduce packaging waste and encourage using recycled materials.

Ban on Single-Use Plastics Many countries worldwide are implementing restrictions on single-use plastics to combat pollution (Giacovelli, 2018). These restrictions are part of a broader strategy to reduce plastic waste and promote using more environmentally friendly alternatives. For instance, the European Union has prohibited using single-use plastic straws, cutlery, and plates.[13] In California, cities such as San Francisco and Los Angeles have banned single-use plastic bags.[14]

---

[8] https://www.ncsl.org/technology-and-communication/right-to-repair-2023-legislation

[9] https://ec.europa.eu/commission/presscorner/detail/en/ip_23_1794

[10] https://commission.europa.eu/energy-climate-change-environment/standards-tools-and-labels/products-labelling-rules-and-requirements/sustainable-products/ecodesign-sustainable-products-regulation_en

[11] https://www.gov.uk/government/publications/introduction-of-plastic-packaging-tax/plastic-packaging-tax

[12] https://www.gov.uk/guidance/check-if-you-need-to-register-for-plastic-packaging-tax

[13] https://environment.ec.europa.eu/topics/plastics/single-use-plastics/eu-restrictions-certain-single-use-plastics_en

[14] https://www.cawrecycles.org/list-of-local-bag-bans

Incentives for Circular Economy Practices Governments incentivize businesses to adopt circular economy practices. These incentives may include tax benefits, grants,[15] loan programs,[16] or subsidies. For instance, the European Union offers tax breaks to businesses that use recycled materials in their products (DLA Piper, 2023).

The mentioned legislative trends promote a circular and sustainable economy, guiding manufacturers and consumers toward environmentally responsible practices (Jensen, 2023a, b). In the following section, we will focus on selected initiatives.

2.1 Right to Repair Legislations

Globally, right to repair legislations are emerging from EU to US state laws to ensure repairability, focusing on transparency, accessibility, and affordability. These laws compel manufacturers to provide necessary repair information, tools, and parts, easing and reducing the cost of repairs for consumers. They aim to dismantle manufacturers' repair monopolies, thereby prolonging product lifespans, reducing waste, and advocating for a more sustainable, repair-centric approach in contrast to traditional obsolescence models.

The critical points in right to repair legislation can be broken down into several distinct parts (Fig. 2.2).

Fig. 2.2 Key points in the right to repair legislations

[15] https://www.gov.uk/government/news/reducing-plastic-waste-in-the-environment-apply-for-funding

[16] https://www.eib.org/en/about/initiatives/circular-economy/index

Spare Parts Availability[17] Extends beyond just ensuring parts are available. It requires manufacturers to keep a stock of crucial components for a set period, often several years, post-production. This period aligns with the product's expected lifespan, ensuring consumers can repair their purchases long after the sale. This aspect is vital for products that need repairs or replacements of specific parts, such as electronics, appliances, and vehicles, guaranteeing a longer, more sustainable usage cycle.

Accessibility of Repair Manuals[18] It is about ensuring transparency in repair processes. It compels manufacturers to make detailed repair manuals and guides publicly available to authorized service centers, independent repair shops, and individual consumers. This access democratizes repair knowledge, enabling skilled individuals and third-party entities to perform repairs.

Design for Repairability[19] Emphasizes the need for products to be created with ease of repair. This includes using standardized components like screws instead of proprietary fasteners and designing products to avoid the use of permanent adhesives that make disassembly challenging. Such designs make repairs easier to conduct and extend the overall lifespan of products by making them more adaptable to part replacements and upgrades.

Preventing Software Restrictions[20] Targets the digital barriers to repair, particularly in modern electronics. These laws aim to restrict manufacturers from using software locks or firmware updates that would prevent third-party repairs. This ensures that digital products like smartphones, laptops, and smart appliances remain repairable even after software updates. The goal is to maintain consumers' ability to choose their repair service provider, fostering a competitive repair market and preventing manufacturers from monopolizing the repair process through software.

Transparency in Repair Pricing[21] Ensures consumers are fully informed about upfront repair costs. This requirement addresses inflated or hidden charges by obliging manufacturers and repair services to provide transparent, upfront pricing for repairs. This transparency helps consumers decide whether to repair or replace a product and fosters a fairer, more competitive repair market. It's a critical measure to protect consumers from unexpectedly high costs and to promote trust in the repair industry.

---

[17] https://www.edie.net/uks-right-to-repair-laws-come-into-force-in-bid-to-cut-electrical-waste/

[18] https://journals.sagepub.com/doi/10.1177/20438869231178037

[19] https://knowledge.insead.edu/operations/stakeholder-perspectives-right-repair-laws

[20] https://www.bbc.com/future/article/20231027-how-the-right-to-repair-might-change-technology

[21] https://ec.europa.eu/commission/presscorner/detail/en/ip_23_1794

The Consumer Right to Choose Repair Services[22] The law empowers consumers to select their repair providers, challenging the exclusivity of authorized service centers. This aspect of the law democratizes the repair market, giving consumers the freedom to seek more affordable or convenient repair options. It also fosters competition among repair providers, potentially leading to better service quality and pricing, and ensures that consumers are not limited to potentially expensive manufacturer-authorized repair services.

Warranty Protection[23] Safeguards consumers' warranties when they opt for third-party repairs. This provision ensures that consumers are not unfairly penalized for using independent repair services instead of manufacturer-authorized centers. By protecting warranties under these circumstances, the legislation aims to provide consumers more flexibility and choice in managing their products, fostering a fairer, more open repair market without fear of voiding their warranty.

2.1.1 Challenges in the Right to Repair Journey

Although implementing right to repair legislation can be advantageous, it poses challenges that must be addressed (Fig. 2.3).

One of the challenges of implementing the right to repair legislation is developing a diverse and competent repair market that can manage the required volume and variety of repairs. This involves increasing the number of skilled repair professionals and ensuring that they have access to the necessary equipment, parts, and information.

Manufacturers must maintain an inventory of spare parts for their products for several years after production, which can increase warehousing and inventory management costs. Balancing these costs while ensuring parts availability is a delicate task.

Another challenge is distributing spare parts to various repair centers or directly to consumers. Manufacturers must develop efficient supply chain management strategies to minimize delays and costs associated with part distribution.

There's a fine line between providing sufficient information for repairs and safeguarding proprietary technologies from potential misuse or infringement.

Effort is needed to create standardized repair manuals that are comprehensive yet accessible to a wide range of technicians, including third-party and DIY repairers.

As innovative technologies become more integrated into products, protecting customer data during the repair process is essential. Manufacturers and repair services must implement strict data protection measures to maintain consumer trust.

Besides repairing, it is important to develop markets for refurbished parts, which provide a sustainable and cost-effective repair option. To ensure the success of this aspect of the right to repair movement, establish a system that certifies the quality of refurbished parts and integrates them into the supply chain.

---

[22] https://biztechlawyers.com/the-right-to-repair-rebellion-consumers-take-control/

[23] https://www.ftc.gov/business-guidance/blog/2022/07/ftc-announces-three-right-repair-cases-do-your-warranties-comply-law

Fig. 2.3 Right to repair challenges

Example 2.1 Used Serviceable Material (USM) obtained from decommissioned aircraft

A steady supply of airplane spare parts in the aviation industry ensures operational efficiency.

One practice is to use Used Serviceable Material (USM) obtained from decommissioned aircraft, which companies like AerSale provide[24]. This approach allows airlines to maintain a consistent supply of necessary components, particularly during high demand or disruptions in the OEM supply chain.

The USM parts come with comprehensive documentation and certification to ensure that they comply with regulatory standards and are traceable. This helps maintain trust in their reliability and safety across the industry.

[24] https://www.aersale.com/

Each challenge requires concerted efforts from manufacturers, policymakers, repair professionals, and other ecosystem stakeholders to ensure an effective shift toward repairability.

2.2 Digital Product Passport

The European Union is implementing the Digital Product Passport (DPP) as part of its larger European Green Deal strategy to promote a sustainable and circular economy. The DPP is a tool that aims to create a detailed digital record of products throughout their entire lifecycle.

The European Commission has finalized the draft Digital Product Passports (DPPs) regulation.[25] The regulation outlines a framework to enhance sustainability across the EU market progressively. Key product groups targeted for early implementation of the DPP include batteries; iron and steel; aluminum; textiles; garments; footwear; furniture, including mattresses; tires; detergents; paints; lubricants; chemicals; information and communication technology (ICT) products; and other electronics.

These product groups have been selected for their environmental impact and potential to improve sustainability through ecodesign. The timeline for implementation will be defined in future delegated acts.

While many elements of the EU DPP, including its scope, technological aspects, and specific data requirements, are still being refined, the overarching goal is to create a comprehensive digital record for products throughout their lifecycle. The DPP will serve as a "digital twin" of physical products, containing detailed information from production to disposal, including raw materials, manufacturing processes, usage data, repair history, and recyclability. The DPP aims to ensure the accessibility, authenticity, and accuracy of detailed product information, thereby enhancing product traceability, facilitating sustainable practices, and enabling more informed decision-making among consumers, manufacturers, and regulators across various product lifecycle stages.

Implementing the DPP regulations will impact product lifecycle management. They will also apply to imported products and components, influencing the European market and global manufacturing and supply chains.

[25] https://eur-lex.europa.eu/procedure/EN/2022_95

Example 2.2 Battery Passport

The European Union is set to introduce the Battery Passport in February 2027 (European Commission, 2023). This digital document will compile around 90 different data attributes (see Fig. 2.4) from batteries with a capacity of over 2kWh used in electric vehicles, light transport, and industrial applications. These attributes are organized into seven clusters that include manufacturing details and environmental impact assessments, providing a comprehensive view of each battery's impact.

Fig. 2.4 Grouping the battery passport data attributes into seven content clusters (the Battery Pass consortium, 2023)

Content and Value of the Battery Passport

The Battery Passport is a central database storing battery information. This includes details about the manufacturer, the battery's composition, performance metrics such as energy capacity and durability, and environmental credentials like the carbon footprint. The comprehensive data collection has several strategic advantages that benefit the economy, environment, and society. From an economic standpoint, it promotes transparency and efficiency in the battery supply chain, potentially reducing costs associated with materials sourcing and environmental compliance. Environmentally, it encourages better recycling practices and waste management, ultimately helping to conserve resources and minimize ecological harm. Socially, the passport improves safety and reliability by providing clear information about battery handling and capabilities.

Practical Applications

The Battery Passport has numerous practical applications. For example, it enhances the recycling process by providing recyclers with precise information regarding the composition and health of batteries. This empowers them to customize their methods for optimal resource recovery and cost efficiency. Not only is this beneficial for the environment, but it is also economically advantageous as it reduces reliance on raw material extraction.

(continued)

Furthermore, the Battery Passport promotes market transparency by making detailed performance and environmental data available, enabling consumers and businesses to make informed choices. It fosters a competitive market where innovation thrives and is crucial for consumer trust and companies aiming to distinguish themselves based on sustainability.

Another application is the safe transport of used or waste batteries. The passport helps accurately assess transport risks by documenting a battery's history and current condition. This ensures that safety regulations are met during transit, preventing accidents and enhancing recycling channels' efficiency.

The Battery Passport also supports circular economy initiatives by detailing material compositions and potential for reuse. This information is invaluable for companies looking to repurpose or remanufacture batteries, allowing them to plan more effectively and reduce waste. It aligns with broader environmental goals of resource conservation and sustainability.

2.2.1 Key Points of the Digital Product Passport

In this section, we delve into the key points that define the Digital Product Passport and explore its impact on various aspects of product lifecycle management.

The DPP will standardize, store, and provide access to a wealth of data across a product's lifecycle. It aims to enhance transparency and accountability in manufacturing and usage by offering detailed insights into sourcing raw materials, production methods, energy consumption during manufacturing, and the environmental impact of each stage. By providing a holistic view of a product's journey, the DPP can help manufacturers make informed decisions and take action to minimize their products' environmental impact.

The DPP aims to promote circular economy practices such as sustainable product design, reuse, repair, and recycling by providing detailed product information. It encourages manufacturers to design products with longer lifespans and easier repairability, reducing waste and resource consumption. The availability of product information empowers consumers and recyclers to make informed decisions about product use, maintenance, and end-of-life management, fostering a circular culture. With comprehensive product components and materials data, repairers, recyclers, and waste managers can facilitate more efficient repair, recycling, and reuse processes (Fig. 2.5).

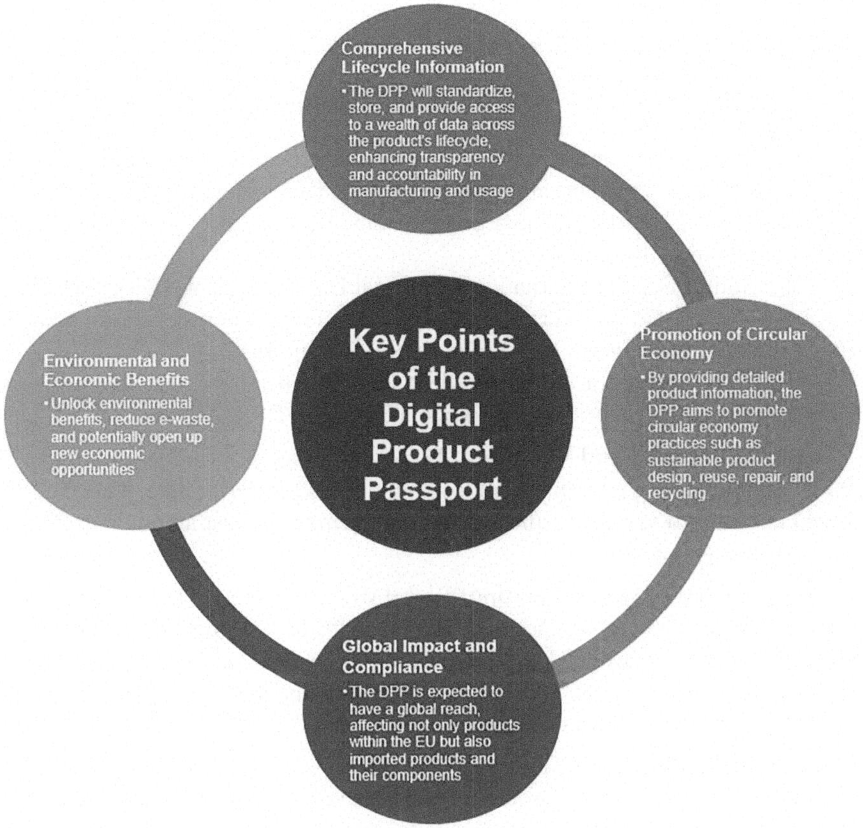

Fig. 2.5 Key points of a Digital Product Passport

The Digital Product Passport (DPP) is anticipated to have a widespread impact, affecting products within the European Union and imported products and their components. Manufacturers and suppliers worldwide must adhere to DPP regulations, which could influence international standards. This global impact could foster a more uniform approach to sustainability standards across borders, pushing industries worldwide toward more eco-friendly practices, thereby creating a level playing field regarding environmental responsibility.

Increased transparency and traceability of DPPs can unlock environmental benefits, reduce waste, and create new economic opportunities by making products' impacts more visible and traceable.

The Digital Product Passport (DPP) promotes transparent communication in the supply chain without compromising supplier confidentiality. It stores comprehensive product information but only allows relevant stakeholders to access it. Robust data security measures and access control protocols keep supply chain details private. The DPP ensures regulatory compliance without jeopardizing supplier relationships. Balancing transparency with confidentiality is crucial for the DPP's effectiveness.

Example 2.3 The International Material Data System (IMDS)

For over two decades, the automotive industry has navigated the complexities of material compliance within its extensive supply chain. The industry needed a robust system to manage, integrate, and share material compliance data, ensuring adherence to international environmental and safety regulations. The sheer volume of components and materials involved in automotive manufacturing heightened the complexity.

The solution was the International Material Data System (IMDS),[26] which has been operational for over 20 years and has become a cornerstone in managing material compliance data in the automotive industry.

While IMDS is not a Digital Product Passport, its successful realization offers lessons for industries preparing to adapt to DPP regulations.

Data Integration and Sharing: IMDS provides a platform for automotive OEM manufacturers and suppliers to input detailed material data. This web-based centralized system facilitates the management of vast amounts of data across the supply chain.

Supply Chain Communication: With IMDS, automotive companies can ensure that all vehicle components comply with environmental regulations like ELV (End of Life Vehicles Directive[27]) and REACH (Registration, Evaluation, Authorization, and Restriction of Chemicals[28]). It offers the ability to trace materials back through the supply chain.

Standardization and Efficiency: The system standardizes data collection and reporting, streamlining processes and reducing the likelihood of errors. It also enables efficient information exchange globally.

The implementation of the International Material Data System (IMDS) has had a significant impact on the automotive industry. With over 200,000 users from over 50,000 companies worldwide, IMDS plays a crucial role in ensuring that automotive products comply with global environmental standards, thereby reducing non-compliance risks. Additionally, IMDS supports the industry's sustainability objectives by aiding in identifying and reducing hazardous substances in vehicles. Moreover, the system has enhanced cost efficiency by streamlining data management processes, which reduces administrative burdens and associated costs.

(continued)

[26] https://www.mdsystem.com/imdsnt/startpage/index.jsp

[27] https://environment.ec.europa.eu/topics/waste-and-recycling/end-life-vehicles_en

[28] https://echa.europa.eu/regulations/reach/understanding-reach

The automotive industry's successful use of the International Material Data System (IMDS) for over two decades, involving thousands of businesses, serves as a valuable blueprint for managing complex material data and ensuring regulatory compliance across other sectors. This extensive experience is particularly relevant for industries preparing for the Digital Product Passport (DPP), which presents similar challenges on a larger scale. The DPP, like IMDS, aims to manage intricate product data across various industries, ensuring data transparency and security through robust systems for data integration, sharing, and protection. Furthermore, both the DPP and IMDS are designed to facilitate compliance with environmental and sustainability regulations, highlighting the critical role of advanced data management systems in achieving regulatory adherence.

2.3 Extended Producer Responsibility

EPR (Extended Producer Responsibility) policies and regulations differ across various legislations and industries. However, some overarching trends and principles broadly define the EPR landscape. EPR's primary objectives typically revolve around enhancing environmental responsibility among producers, promoting sustainable product design, and transferring the burden of waste management.

Extended Producer Responsibility (EPR) mandates that manufacturers take responsibility for the environmental impact of their products throughout the product's lifecycle rather than just at the point of sale. This includes product take-back, recycling, and final disposal. EPR incentivizes companies to innovate in product design, materials selection, and recycling technologies, providing them with a competitive advantage in the circular economy.

The traditional financial model for product lifecycle has favored producers and retailers, who profit from selling products. At the same time, environmental and social costs of responsibility and disposal are left to the environment, society, and public entities. This has led to unsustainable practices and provided little motivation for producers to consider their products' environmental impact and end-of-life management.

EPR addresses this issue by shifting the responsibility for waste management from public entities and consumers back to the producers. This aligns economic incentives with environmental outcomes by holding producers accountable for the entire lifecycle of their products, including their disposal. This approach encourages producers to consider the environmental costs of their products, leading to more sustainable product designs that are easier to recycle, repair, and reuse. Ultimately, this reduces waste and ensures that those who profit from the production are responsible for mitigating its environmental impact.

Example 2.4 The environmental impact of littered cigarette butts

Brown et al. (2023) address the environmental impact of littered cigarette butts, a pervasive issue worldwide. Cigarette filters, made primarily from cellulose acetate, a form of plastic, are one of the most discarded pieces of waste globally. Their small size and widespread presence pose a considerable challenge for waste management and environmental protection.

Cigarette butts are a major source of litter, contaminating urban streets, natural landscapes, and water bodies. They are not biodegradable and can persist in the environment for years. The filters contain harmful chemicals, including nicotine, heavy metals, and many other toxic substances that leach into soil and water, posing a threat to wildlife and aquatic ecosystems. Animals mistaking cigarette butts for food can ingest them, leading to internal blockages, poisoning, and often death.

As part of its broader efforts to tackle plastic pollution, the European Union has included cigarette filters in the Single-Use Plastics Directive, which requires member states to implement EPR schemes by 2025 to hold tobacco companies accountable for the environmental impact of their products.

Under the directive, tobacco product manufacturers will be required to contribute to the costs of waste collection for cigarette butts, including public litter cleanups and the establishment of waste management infrastructures specifically for tobacco products. By internalizing the cleanup costs, EPR schemes for tobacco product filters aim to incentivize manufacturers to innovate toward more environmentally friendly designs or alternatives to traditional filters.

Effective implementation of EPR for cigarette filters requires careful consideration of the logistics involved in collecting and processing this type of waste, given its ubiquity and small size. Widespread public engagement and education are also needed to ensure the success of such programs.

Given the sheer volume of cigarette butts littered annually, effective EPR schemes reduce environmental pollution and serve as a model for addressing other forms of micro-litter.

EPR also encourages eco-friendly design. Manufacturers are incentivized to develop products that are easy to disassemble, recycle, or repurpose, ensuring that environmental considerations are integrated right from the product's inception (Fig. 2.6).

Fig. 2.6 The key points of Extended Producer Responsibility

Example 2.5 British Columbia's Tire Stewardship BC (TSBC) program

Reduced rolling resistance and durability are aspects of Extended Producer Responsibility for tire manufacturers. By reducing tire rolling resistance, which accounts for 5–15% of a vehicle's fuel consumption, manufacturers can decrease fuel use and CO2 emissions, guiding them toward designing longer-lasting tires. Enhanced durability in tire design means fewer replacements over time, reducing the overall environmental impact.

An example of this can be seen in British Columbia's Tire Stewardship BC (TSBC) program.[29] This initiative includes an Advance Disposal Fee (ADF) for every new tire sold in the province. The revenue generated from these fees is dedicated exclusively to collecting, transporting, and recycling scrap tires and program-related activities.

EPR policies often encompass both carrots and sticks. They offer economic incentives such as tax breaks, subsidies, or reduced fees for sustainable practices while imposing penalties or higher fees for non-compliance. These financial mechanisms aim to motivate companies to adopt more environmentally friendly practices.

[29] https://tsbc.ca/

Example 2.6 EPR laws in Japan

EPR laws in Japan[30] place a portion of the cost of recycling and transportation on consumers to encourage product stewardship and reduce the overall environmental impact of waste.

EPR reshapes the production phase of a product's lifecycle by embedding environmental responsibility into the core of manufacturing processes.

EPR also has the potential to influence consumer behavior by raising awareness about products' environmental impact and encouraging more sustainable consumption choices. This includes participating in recycling programs and making more informed purchasing decisions.

EPR is a vital tool in promoting the principles of the circular economy. By incentivizing producers to develop products that are easier to recycle, repair, and reuse, EPR facilitates the shift from a linear to a circular model of production and consumption.

Example 2.7 Commercial Fishing Gear and Equipment

Brown et al. (2023) describe the use case of "Commercial Fishing Gear and Equipment" within the context of Extended Producer Responsibility (EPR). It addresses the environmental impacts of abandoned, lost, or discarded fishing gear, often called "ghost gear." This gear, including nets, lines, and other fishing equipment, can devastate marine ecosystems by entangling wildlife, damaging coral reefs, and contributing to the accumulation of marine debris. A substantial percentage of fishing gear is lost or discarded in the oceans each year.

Norway has established a voluntary EPR system named Nofir, which collects end-of-life (EoL) fishing gear for recycling. The program is partially self-funded by selling secondary materials derived from recycled gear. Nofir facilitates separate collection at port facilities and offers direct collection from gear owners upon request.

The Federation of Icelandic Fishing Vessel Owners and Fish Processing Plants has set up a voluntary EPR system to manage EoL fishing gear, partly to pre-empt national policies. Vessel owners clean, prepare the gear, and bear the transportation costs to collection centers. The cost is roughly equivalent to disposal fees for landfilling or incineration, making recycling a viable alternative.

(continued)

[30] https://pubs.acs.org/doi/pdf/10.1021/es072561x

The EU Single-Use Plastics Directive mandates that member states implement EPR fishing gear schemes by 2025. This directive aims to cover the costs of gear collection, recycling, and cleanup efforts and is expected to reduce the environmental impacts of ghost gear.

Shifting the financial responsibility of waste management from municipalities and fishing communities to gear manufacturers finances the collection, recycling, and proper disposal of EoL gear.

EPR fees incentivize manufacturers to design gear that is less likely to be lost, more durable, and easier to recycle or repair, promoting sustainability within the industry.

2.4 Packaging Waste Legislations

Numerous countries have enacted legislation to reduce packaging waste, increase recycling rates, and improve packaging material management.

European Union The European Union has established a framework to manage packaging waste[31]; it sets targets for recycling and recovery of packaging waste and requires member states to establish systems for collecting, returning, and recycling packaging. Furthermore, it includes specific measures to minimize the environmental impact of packaging.

United States Although no nationwide legislation fully addresses packaging waste, some states have implemented laws and regulations. For instance, California has set recycling requirements and content standards for packaging materials.[32] Other states have adopted different forms of Extended Producer Responsibility (EPR) laws, which hold producers responsible for managing their products and packaging at the end of their lifecycle.

Japan Japan's Container and Packaging Recycling Law[33] states that manufacturers and importers must recycle packaging materials such as glass, paper, plastic, and aluminum.

[31] https://environment.ec.europa.eu/topics/waste-and-recycling/packaging-waste_en

[32] https://calrecycle.ca.gov/packaging/

[33] https://www.jcpra.or.jp/english/tabid/613/index.php

South Korea South Korea has an Act on the Promotion of Saving and Recycling of Resources[34], which includes provisions for the proper disposal and recycling of packaging waste.

Canada Canada has various provincial regulations concerning packaging waste, with British Columbia being notable for its recycling program that covers all printed paper and packaging. The province operates under an EPR model, which has been explored or implemented in other provinces.

These examples reflect a global trend toward stricter packaging waste management and recycling requirements, driven by increasing environmental concerns and the need to promote sustainable packaging and waste management practices.

2.4.1 Key Points of the EU's Packaging and Packaging Waste Regulation (PPWR)

To illustrate the content of packaging waste regulations, we will examine the EU's framework.

The PPWR emphasizes the need for all packaging in the EU market to be recyclable and reusable wherever possible by 2030.[35] This represents a shift from focusing on disposable packaging to more sustainable solutions. The regulation also sets specific reusability targets for sectors such as catering and e-commerce. For instance, food packaging in these sectors must adhere to strict reusability guidelines. As a result, retailers and manufacturers must overhaul their packaging strategies to develop systems that support recycling and promote the reuse of packaging materials.

The PPWR has implemented a new rule to address the issue of overpackaging. According to the regulation, the space within packaging must not exceed 40% of the total packaging volume.[36] Excessive space often results in unnecessary material usage and waste. The rule is designed to promote packaging strategies that use resources more efficiently, minimize the environmental impact of excessive packaging materials, and encourage manufacturers to optimize their packaging designs.

The PPWR aims to address environmental concerns related to plastic waste by setting ambitious targets for using recycled content in plastic packaging.[37] Certain

[34] https://faolex.fao.org/docs/pdf/kor51892.pdf

[35] https://ec.europa.eu/commission/presscorner/detail/en/ip_22_7155

[36] https://protega-global.com/2023/05/25/will-eus-law-of-a-maximum-of-40-void-fill-be-adopted-by-the-uk/

[37] https://www.europarl.europa.eu/news/en/press-room/20231023IPR08128/packaging-new-eu-rules-to-reduce-reuse-and-recycle

types of plastic packaging will be required to contain a minimum percentage of recycled material by 2030, and these requirements will become more stringent by 2040. Specific targets include achieving a 77% separate collection target for plastic bottles by 2025, which will increase to 90% by 2029 (European Parliament, 2023). Additionally, there are goals to incorporate 25% recycled plastic in PET beverage bottles starting in 2025 and reaching 30% in all bottles by 2030.

The PPWR aims to standardize packaging across the EU by introducing comprehensive labeling requirements.[38] These labels will indicate the material composition of packaging and guide appropriate disposal and recycling methods. This standardization is expected to simplify the recycling process for consumers and waste management entities, making waste sorting and recycling operations more efficient. The labeling system will educate consumers about sustainable disposal practices and promote greater environmental awareness and responsibility.

2.5 Ecodesign Policy, Legislation, and International Frameworks

Ecodesign embeds environmental considerations into every aspect of the design process, from conception to disposal. It redefines the relationship between products and the environment, ensuring that each product lifecycle phase contributes positively to our planet's health. Figure 2.7 illustrates the three key principles of ecodesign.

Ecodesign is increasingly governed by a robust framework of policies, legislation, and international agreements that collectively set the global standard for sustainable product design. These regulatory mechanisms are pivotal in shaping industry practices and guiding manufacturers toward more environmentally responsible production methods.

Various national and regional laws, such as the European Union's Ecodesign Directive,[39] establish specific and enforceable energy efficiency and environmental performance standards, requiring companies to innovate and adhere to these standards. This directive has led to product designs that are more energy-efficient and easier to repair or recycle.[40] In 2021, the current ecodesign measures, which apply to 31 product groups, saved EUR 120 billion in energy costs for EU consumers, leading to a 10% reduction in annual energy consumption by the products covered by the directive (European Commission, 2024).

---

[38] https://ec.europa.eu/commission/presscorner/detail/en/ip_22_7155

[39] https://commission.europa.eu/energy-climate-change-environment/standards-tools-and-labels/products-labelling-rules-and-requirements/ecodesign-sustainable-products-regulation_en

[40] https://commission.europa.eu/energy-climate-change-environment/standards-tools-and-labels/products-labelling-rules-and-requirements/energy-label-and-ecodesign/about_en

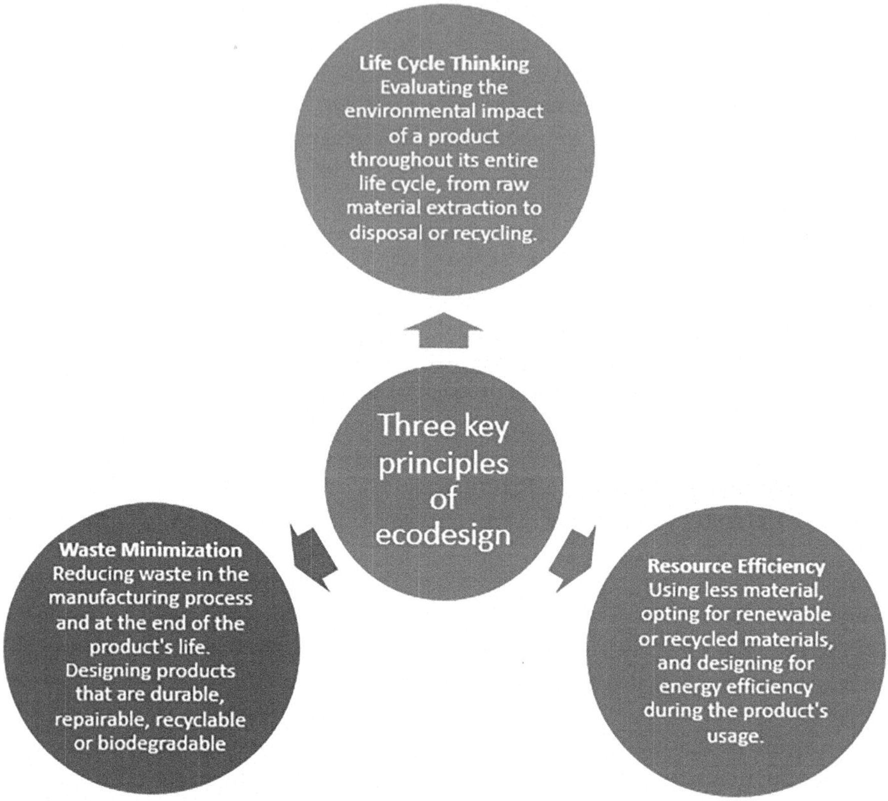

Fig. 2.7 The three key principles of ecodesign

The standards are not developed in isolation but are often in line with broader international environmental agreements, such as the Paris Agreement[41] and the United Nations Sustainable Development Goals.[42] These global frameworks emphasize the importance of sustainable design in achieving larger environmental goals and promoting international cooperation, enabling a unified approach to addressing environmental challenges.

[41] https://unfccc.int/process-and-meetings/the-paris-agreement

[42] https://sdgs.un.org/goals

2.5.1 Ecodesign Legislation Trends Around the Globe

Globally, ecodesign legislation continuously evolves, demonstrating an increasing commitment to sustainability across different regions. In the European Union, the Ecodesign Directive is a cornerstone, establishing strict criteria for environmentally friendly products, focusing on energy efficiency, resource use, and lifecycle impact. This directive has not only transformed product design within the EU but has also influenced global manufacturing practices.

Across the Atlantic, the United States has implemented initiatives such as the ENERGY STAR program,[43] which certifies products that meet high energy efficiency standards, guiding consumers toward more sustainable choices.

Countries like Japan and South Korea are at the forefront of integrating ecodesign principles into their policies in the Asia-Pacific region. They emphasize energy efficiency and waste reduction, particularly in their electronic and automotive industries, which are major contributors to their economies.

On the other hand, emerging economies such as Brazil and India are increasingly adopting ecodesign principles. These countries focus on sustainable development and environmental conservation, recognizing the dual benefits of environmental responsibility and economic growth. In these regions, ecodesign is often seen as a pathway to modernizing industry and enhancing competitiveness on the global stage.

These global trends in Ecodesign legislation collectively signify a shift toward a more sustainable and environmentally conscious approach to product design and manufacturing, transcending geographical and economic boundaries.

2.5.2 Common Threads in Global Ecodesign Legislation

Ecodesign legislations worldwide may vary in specifics, but they share several fundamental principles that define sustainable product design. Energy efficiency is a key focus, with regulations typically establishing strict standards for minimizing energy consumption throughout a product's lifecycle. This not only reduces environmental impact but also lowers operational costs for consumers. For example, the EU's Ecodesign Directive has implemented energy efficiency standards for heating and cooling equipment, such as boilers, air conditioners, and heat pumps.[44] These standards have contributed to improving the energy efficiency of these devices and reducing energy consumption in buildings.

Another aspect is the focus on resource efficiency and material selection, which encourages using sustainable, recyclable, or biodegradable materials, thereby reducing the ecological footprint from the extraction and disposal stages.

---

[43] https://www.energystar.gov/

[44] https://commission.europa.eu/energy-climate-change-environment/standards-tools-and-labels/products-labelling-rules-and-requirements/energy-label-and-ecodesign/energy-efficient-products/air-heating-and-cooling-products_en

Durability and repairability are also emphasized, advocating for products that are built to last and can be easily repaired or upgraded, thus extending their lifespan and reducing waste. For example, the EU's Ecodesign Directive sets the framework for product reparability, particularly regarding product design requirements and the availability of spare parts. It has so far led to the adoption of ecodesign requirements for 31 individual energy-related product groups, of which 8 are currently covered by reparability requirements (such as TVs and electronic displays, washing machines, dishwashers, and refrigerators).[45]

Additionally, reducibility and recyclability are key. Legislation often mandates that products be designed for easy disassembly and recycling at the end of their life.

Another common feature is the reduction of hazardous substances, with laws frequently restricting the use of certain harmful materials in products to safeguard the environment and human health.

Furthermore, consumer information and labeling are vital components. They require that products carry clear information about their environmental impact, energy consumption,[46] and recyclability, thus empowering consumers to make informed choices.

Lastly, compliance and monitoring mechanisms are integral to these legislations. They ensure that manufacturers adhere to the set standards and that products are regularly assessed for environmental performance. This ensures accountability and drives continuous improvement in product design.

2.6 Government Initiatives Checklist

Government initiatives drive the transition toward a circular economy. These initiatives include regulations, incentives, and support programs that guide and compel businesses to adopt sustainable practices. Understanding and leveraging these initiatives is essential for manufacturers aiming to align with the circular economy's principles and enhance their competitiveness.

This checklist is designed to help businesses navigate the complex landscape of government regulations and initiatives related to the circular economy. It provides a structured approach to identifying relevant regulations, developing compliance strategies, integrating regulatory requirements into operations, and leveraging available government support (Table 2.1).

[45] https://ec.europa.eu/commission/presscorner/detail/es/qanda_23_1795

[46] https://eur-lex.europa.eu/eli/reg/2017/1369/oj

Table 2.1 Government initiatives checklist

Category	Checklist Item
Understanding legislation and regulations	
Identify relevant regulations	Identify national and international regulations impacting your industry Determine specific laws on right to repair, EPR, or DPP that apply
Assess compliance requirements	Assess specific compliance requirements of these regulations Ensure systems are in place for ongoing compliance
Strategic planning and implementation	
Develop a compliance strategy	Develop a compliance strategy addressing all relevant regulations Assign responsibility for overseeing compliance
Integrate regulatory requirements into business operations	Integrate regulatory requirements into product design, manufacturing processes, and supply chain management Update operations to meet targets
Leveraging government support	
Identify available government support	Identify government incentives, grants, or subsidies for adopting circular economy practices Apply for financial support to aid the transition
Engage with government initiatives	Participate in government programs or initiatives promoting the circular economy Engage with policymakers to stay informed about new regulations
Enhancing product lifecycle management	
Adopt Digital Product Passports (DPP)	Implement DPPs for products to enhance traceability and sustainability Manage the required data and assign responsibility for maintaining it
Implement Extended Producer Responsibility (EPR)	Establish an EPR program for your products Design products for easy disassembly, recycling, and reuse
Collaboration and partnerships	
Foster industry collaboration	Collaborate with industry peers to address common regulatory challenges Form partnerships to enhance circular economy initiatives
Engage with supply chain partners	Work with supply chain partners to ensure compliance with circular economy regulations Ensure suppliers are aware of and compliant with regulations

2.7 Highlights from Part I

The circular economy represents the next transformative shift in the global economy, driven by several factors:

- The pressing need to address global climate change and environmental degradation has made the circular economy an imperative. By prioritizing resource efficiency, waste reduction, and sustainable value creation, businesses can contribute to global climate goals and ensure long-term ecological health.

- Governments worldwide are enacting regulations that necessitate adopting circular economy practices. From Extended Producer Responsibility to right-to-repair laws, regulatory landscapes are shifting to enforce sustainable manufacturing, making compliance a key driver of circular economy adoption.
- Modern consumers, particularly younger generations and employees, increasingly advocate for environmentally responsible products and practices. This stakeholder advocacy pushes businesses to integrate sustainability into their core operations to meet consumer expectations and attract and retain top talent.
- Digital technologies like AI, IoT, and platforms have matured to a point where they can support an ecosystem-centered business model like the circular economy. This model requires efficient resource management, transparency, and collaboration across value chains.
- The circular economy presents opportunities for economic growth. Businesses can enhance their competitiveness by reducing costs through optimized resource use and creating new revenue streams through innovative service and product offerings.
- The time to act is now. Inaction is not a viable strategy. As history has shown with previous economic shifts, businesses that fail to adapt will be left behind. For manufacturers to remain competitive and relevant in a rapidly evolving industrial landscape, they must embrace the circular economy.

In the next part of this book, we will explore how the circular economy provides a competitive advantage through decreased costs and increased revenue. We will delve into the business models manufacturers must master to thrive in a circular economy.

References

Bruggers, J. (2022). California Passed a Landmark Law About Plastic Pollution. Why Are Some Environmentalists Still Concerned? *Inside Climate News*. From https://insideclimatenews.org/news/12102022/california-plastics-pollution-bill/

Brown, A., Laubinger, F., & Börkey, P. (2023). *New Aspects of EPR: Extending producer responsibility to additional product groups and challenges throughout the product lifecycle*. OECD - Organisation for Economic Co-operation and Development. OECD Environment Working Papers. From https://www.oecd-ilibrary.org/deliver/cfdc1bdc-en.pdf

China Daily. (2012, 09). *Circular economy gets 5-year regulator boost*. From https://english.www.gov.cn/policies/policywatch/202107/08/content_WS60e639b0c6d0df57f98dc92b.html

Dentons. (2023, 07). *Extended producer responsibility: mandatory implementation of a prevention and eco-design plan for each of the sectors to which you belong*. From https://www.dentons.com/en/insights/articles/2023/july/4/extended-producer-responsibility

Der Grüne Punkt. (2024, 06). *The German Packaging Act – What's particularly important for online retailers?* From https://www.gruener-punkt.de/en/packaging-licensing/packaging-act

DLA Piper. (2023). *European Union reduced VAT rates for recycled products*. From https://www.dlapiper.com/en/insights/publications/vat-monthly-alert-series/2023/vat-monthly-alert-june-2023/european-union-reduced-vat-rates-for-recycled-products

Department for Environment, Food & Rural Affairs. (2018). *Resources and waste strategy for England*. From https://www.gov.uk/government/publications/resources-and-waste-strategy-for-england

European Commission. (2020). *A new Circular Economy Action Plan For a cleaner and more competitive Europe*. From https://environment.ec.europa.eu/strategy/circular-economy-action-plan_en

European Commission. (2022a). *Ecodesign for Sustainable Products Regulation*. From European Commission: https://commission.europa.eu/energy-climate-change-environment/standards-tools-and-labels/products-labelling-rules-and-requirements/sustainable-products/ecodesign-sustainable-products-regulation_en

European Commission. (2022b, March 30). *Green Deal: New proposals to make sustainable products the norm and boost Europe's resource independence*. From https://ec.europa.eu/commission/presscorner/detail/en/ip_22_2013

European Commission. (2024, 05). *Ecodesign for Sustainable Products Regulation*. From https://commission.europa.eu/energy-climate-change-environment/standards-tools-and-labels/products-labelling-rules-and-requirements/sustainable-products/ecodesign-sustainable-products-regulation_en

European Commission. (2023, 08). *Circular economy: New law on more sustainable, circular and safe batteries enters into force*. From https://environment.ec.europa.eu/news/new-law-more-sustainable-circular-and-safebatteries-enters-force-2023-08-17_en

European Parliament. (2023, 10). *Packaging: new EU rules to reduce, reuse and recycle*. From https://www.europarl.europa.eu/news/en/press-room/20231023IPR08128/packaging-new-eu-rules-to-reduce-reuse-and-recycle

Fraser, M. (2022). Pioneers of the future: The countries leading the way with circular economy policy. *Circle Economy*. From https://www.circle-economy.com/blogs/the-circular-economy-who-is-leading-the-way

Giacovelli, C. (2018). *Single-use plastics: A roadmap for sustainability*. UN Environment Progamme. From https://www.unep.org/resources/report/single-use-plastics-roadmap-sustainability

Government of Canada. (2021). *Get involved in the Circular Economy*. From https://www.canada.ca/en/services/environment/conservation/sustainability/circular-economy/get-involved.html

Jensen, H. H. (2023a). *Digitizing compliance: Unpacking Circular Economy legislations and their digital demands*. From Circular Bytes: https://www.linkedin.com/pulse/digitizing-compliance-unpacking-circular-economy-digital-jensen-3x7ae/

Jensen, H. H. (2023b). *Digitizing sustainability: Navigating the new era of EU's packaging and packaging waste regulation*. From Circular Bytes: https://www.linkedin.com/pulse/digitizing-sustainability-navigating-new-era-eus-packaging-jensen-dq2je/

Johannes, H. P., Kojima, M., Iwasaki, F., & Edita, E. P. (2021). Applying the extended producer responsibility towards plastic waste in Asian developing countries for reducing marine plastic debris. *Waste Management & Research 2021, 39*(5), 69–702. From https://journals.sagepub.com/doi/pdf/10.1177/0734242X211013412

The Battery Pass consortium. (2023). *Battery passport content guidance- executive summary*. The Battery Pass consortium. From https://thebatterypass.eu/assets/images/content-guidance/pdf/2023_Battery_Passport_Content_Guidance_Executive_Summary.pdf

Part II

The Path to Perpetual Value: Embracing Circularity in Manufacturing

The journey to circularity requires manufacturers to rethink not just products but entire value chains, ensuring every component serves a purpose beyond its initial use.

Stock Credit: Champpixs

1+5 Rs: The Blueprint for Circular Manufacturing

3

Abstract

This chapter introduces the transformative 1+5 Rs framework, guiding manufacturers in transitioning to circular manufacturing. It outlines a comprehensive approach to redesigning business models and operations to align with circular economy principles, ensuring long-term viability and success.

The framework comprises six key components:

- Redesign, Reinvent: This approach focuses on designing adaptable, repairable, and upgradable products and reinventing business models to support these attributes.
- Redistribute: Explores the redistribution of products through recommerce and reuse, leveraging extended product lifecycles and shared economy principles.
- Repair: This section highlights the importance of repairability in product design and the development of service models that make repair convenient and economical, fostering a maintenance culture.
- Refurbish: Emphasizes refurbishment as a core service offering, giving products a second life and promoting quality over quantity.
- Remanufacture: Discusses designing products for disassembly and reusing parts, supported by business models that enable take-back schemes and remanufacturing services.
- Recycle: Consider recycling a crucial element of the circular economy, discussing how business models can incorporate recycling materials and harvested parts as valuable resources.

The chapter also underscores the critical role of Logistics Service Providers (LSPs) in facilitating circular business models. LSPs are essential partners in the circular economy, enabling efficient collection, refurbishment, redistribution, and recycling of materials and products.

H. H. Jensen, *Circular Economy Opportunities and Pathways for Manufacturers*, Future of Business and Finance, https://doi.org/10.1007/978-3-031-75279-7_3

As we explore the next part of this book, we will delve into how embracing circularity can revolutionize manufacturing. This will offer businesses the tools and strategies to prosper economically and sustainably in this new economic landscape.

Shifting to circular manufacturing requires transforming product design, business models, and business operations. It's a journey from transient commodities to enduring assets, from products designed for obsolescence to ones created for a utility continuum. To navigate this terrain, manufacturers must look beyond the production line to the architecture of their business models, realigning them with the principles of circularity to ensure long-term viability and success.

This section delves into the 1+5 Rs (Fig. 3.1), a framework that serves as a guide and a strategic business blueprint for manufacturers aiming to thrive in the evolving circular economy. Each "R" outlines a distinct yet interconnected approach to innovating profitable circular business models. This integrated approach doesn't mean manufacturers must directly manage all aspects of the circular flow. Still, they should design their products and business models to seamlessly fit into and enhance the circular business ecosystem.

1st R: Redesign, Reinvent—Manufacturers ensure that products are redesigned to be adaptable, repairable, and upgradable. Simultaneously, we'll examine how to reinvent business models to enable and support these product attributes.

2nd R: Redistribute—This section delves into redistributing products and facilitating their recommerce and reuse, transforming business models to capitalize on extended product lifecycles and shared economy principles.

3rd R: Repair—We will explore the role of repairability in product design and create service models that make repair convenient, economical, and commonplace, fostering a culture of maintenance over replacement.

4th R: Refurbish—Here, the focus shifts to refurbishment as an integral service offering, providing a pathway for products to gain a second life and establishing a business case for quality over quantity.

5th R: Remanufacture—In remanufacturing, we focus on designing products for disassembly and reusing parts, supported by business models that enable take-back schemes and remanufacturing services.

6th R: Recycle—The final R considers the role of recycling in a circular economy. We discuss how business models can evolve to incorporate recycling materials and harvested parts as a resource stream, creating new value from old materials.

Manufacturers must grasp these principles. Adopting these practices means rethinking everything from product physical design to overarching business strategies. It's laying the groundwork for success in an era when sustainability and circularity aren't just nice to have; they're essential.

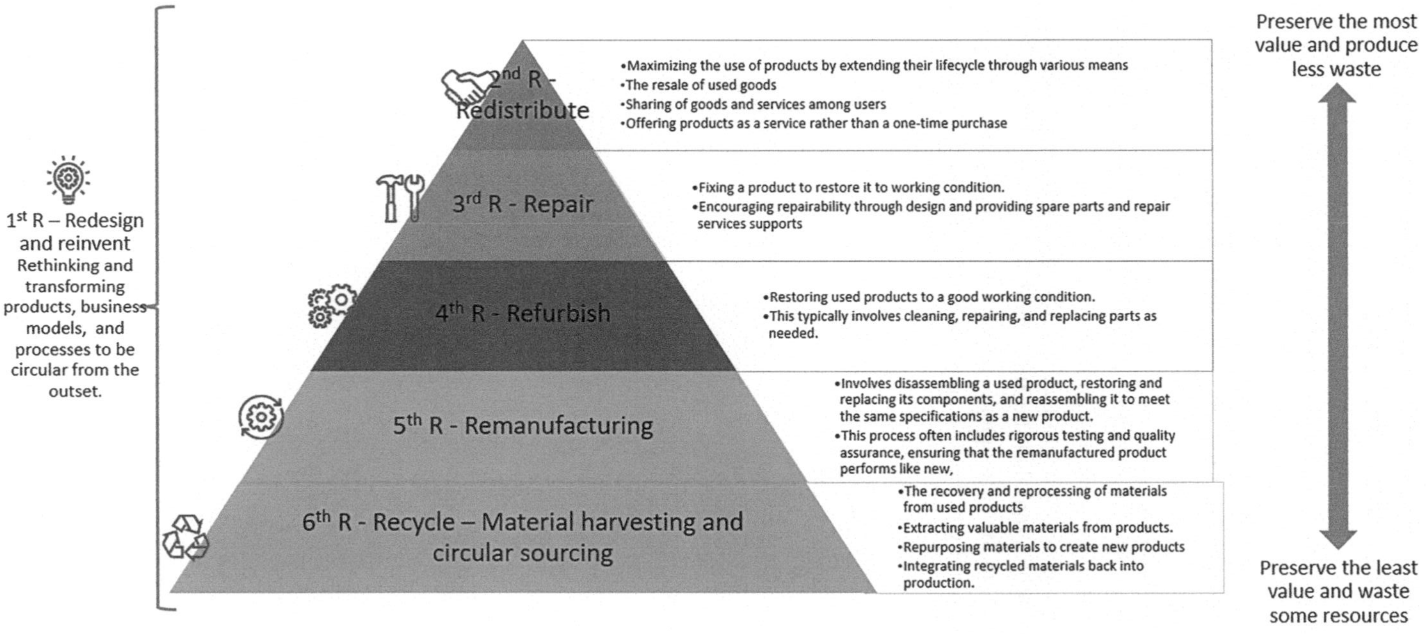

Fig. 3.1 The 1+5 Rs model: a guide and a strategic business blueprint for manufacturers aiming to thrive in the evolving circular economy

3.1 Logistics Service Providers Elevating Circular Economy Practices for Modern Manufacturers

The success of the circular economy hinges on the role of Logistics Service Providers (LSP), who emerge as indispensable partners for manufacturers navigating the shift toward circular manufacturing practices.

LSP will transition from traditional logistics roles to the backbone of circular business models, facilitating the seamless flow of resources through collection, refurbishment, redistribution, and recycling.

Manufacturers can expect LSP to roll out innovative circular service offerings. These services efficiently cycle materials and products back into the economy, minimizing waste and maximizing resource utilization. Manufacturers must consider integrating these LSP capabilities into their business models.

As we discuss the 1+5 Rs in the subsequent chapters, we will explore how LSP supports circularity and highlight how a manufacturer benefits from these partnerships.

1st R – Redesign and Reinvent: Laying the Foundation for Circular Success

4

Abstract

This chapter explores the critical role of redesigning and reinventing products and business models as the foundation for a successful transition to a circular economy. This transformation involves rethinking product design to ensure adaptability, repairability, and upgradability, essential for extending product lifecycles and promoting sustainability.

Key messages include the importance of implementing lifecycle assessment (LCA) techniques to minimize environmental impact and addressing internal challenges such as adapting production processes and retraining staff. The chapter also emphasizes the need for manufacturers to develop circular business models that focus on long-term customer relationships and ongoing services rather than one-time product sales.

Efficiently managing reverse logistics, integrating digital technologies like data analytics and IoT, and ensuring regulatory compliance are vital components of this transition. Training and upskilling the workforce and fostering a collaborative ecosystem with suppliers and partners are essential strategies for achieving circular success.

This section provides a comprehensive framework for manufacturers to redesign and reinvent their products and business models, setting the stage for a sustainable and economically viable future in the circular economy.

H. H. Jensen, *Circular Economy Opportunities and Pathways for Manufacturers*, Future of Business and Finance, https://doi.org/10.1007/978-3-031-75279-7_4

Key Messages

- *Redesign for Circularity:* The shift toward a circular economy begins with redesigning products to be adaptable, repairable, and upgradable, ensuring they can be efficiently reused and recycled.
- *Lifecycle Assessment:* Implementing lifecycle assessment (LCA) techniques helps manufacturers understand and minimize the environmental impact of products from creation to disposal, fostering more sustainable design practices.
- *Addressing Internal Challenges:* Transitioning to a circular economy requires overcoming internal challenges such as adapting production processes, retraining staff, and reorienting organizational KPIs and incentives to support circular goals.
- *Adapting Business Models:* Transitioning to circular business models requires manufacturers to rethink their sales strategies and KPIs, focusing on long-term customer relationships and ongoing services rather than one-time product sales.
- *Managing Reverse Logistics:* It is important to efficiently handle the return flow of products for reuse, refurbishment, or recycling. It requires skills in logistics planning, inventory management, and coordination of collection systems.
- *Integrating Digital Technologies:* Leveraging digital competencies, such as data analytics, IoT, and AI, is vital for tracking product lifecycles, predicting maintenance needs, and optimizing resource use in circular manufacturing processes.
- *Regulatory Compliance:* Stay informed about and compliant with environmental regulations. Employees must be skilled in interpreting and applying these regulations to ensure sustainable manufacturing practices.
- *Training and Upskilling:* Addressing the skill gap involves assessing current workforce capabilities and investing in targeted training programs focused on sustainable design, waste management, and circular business models. Attracting new talent with expertise in these areas is equally important.
- *Collaborative Ecosystem:* Achieving circularity requires collaboration across the entire value chain. Engaging with suppliers, partners, and customers to co-create a circular ecosystem ensures that materials, products, and data flow in closed loops, minimizing waste and maximizing value.

The first step—redesigning and reinventing—challenges every layer of an organization. It calls for reimagination from product design philosophy to operational value. This transition is as much about innovation in tangible product development as it is about a paradigm shift in intangible aspects of business strategy and market engagement.

The redesign imperative demands products crafted to fulfill an immediate need and endure multiple cycles of use and reuse. Redesign involves rethinking materials, construction, and every item's end-of-life potential. Reinvention goes beyond the product; it encompasses revamping the entire business model, including internal processes and KPIs, cultivating a workforce adept in circular principles, and fostering systems that champion longevity and renewability.

Navigating these internal challenges is just the beginning. On the ecosystem level, manufacturers must work with suppliers and distributors to catalyze change throughout their upstream and downstream value chains and ensure that the principles of circularity are upheld from the extraction of raw materials to the end-user's hands.

The challenges continue beyond the factory gate. External forces—regulatory frameworks, compliance mandates, cultural norms, and customer behaviors—pose hurdles. Manufacturers must maneuver these waters, championing advocacy for regulatory environments that encourage circular practices, shaping customer perceptions to value circularity and repairable products, and breaking through cultural barriers that resist the circular model.

This chapter will dissect these internal, ecosystem, and external challenges, offering insights and strategies for manufacturers to surmount them.

4.1 Internal Reinvention and Redesign: Navigating the Path to Circularity

The internal challenges include redesigning products and business models, transitioning sales strategies and KPIs, considering how to deliver circular service, the digital transformation required, and financing the shift.

4.1.1 Assessing Product Redesign for Circularity

The evaluation of the redesign of products for enhanced circularity involves analysis across three key dimensions; resource efficiency, materials stocks and flows, and product centric considerations (Shevchenko & Cluzel, 2023), each contributing to the circular potential of a product.

Resource efficiency emphasizes the judicious use of materials and energy throughout a product's lifecycle. This involves inspecting every stage, from manufacturing to end-user consumption, to ensure optimal resource utilization. The aim is to minimize waste generation and enhance the product's overall circularity, reducing the quantity of new materials and energy consumed and maximizing the value derived from each resource.

Evaluating resource efficiency requires a deep dive into the production processes and the product's performance during use. It also involves seeking opportunities to reduce resource intake and environmental footprint and identifying business models like product as a service, circular sourcing, and product use extension that benefit from resource efficiency.

Example 4.1 Smart thermostats

Smart thermostats combine energy efficiency with user-centric convenience.[1] Unlike traditional thermostats, which rely on manual adjustments, they utilize advanced algorithms and sensors to monitor daily routines.

The second dimension delves into the dynamics of materials stocks and flows, tracing the journey of materials from extraction through to their end of life. This analysis ensures that materials remain in the economic loop for as long as possible by assessing how materials are sourced (extraction, processing, and transportation), transformed, and eventually reused or recycled.

The goal is to establish a commercially attractive closed-loop system that minimizes environmental impact and continually repurposes materials. This would reduce reliance on virgin resources and diminish waste through business models like circular sourcing, recovery, and recycling.

Example 4.2 Apple incorporating recycled materials

Apple, a global technology leader, is incorporating recycled materials into its iPhone 13.

The iPhone 13 includes 100% recycled rare earth elements in all magnets. The Taptic Engine, which provides haptic feedback, contains 99% recycled tungsten. Apple uses recycled aluminum as well as aluminum smelted primarily with low-carbon sources of electricity for the iPhone 13 enclosures. The logic board and solder in the iPhone 13 are made with recycled tin.

The packaging for the iPhone 13 is designed to be smaller and lighter, reducing transportation emissions. It is made from 100% recycled wood fiber or responsibly managed forests.

The final assembly of the iPhone 13 takes place in facilities that run on 100% renewable energy and do not generate any waste sent to landfills (Apple, 2021).

Additionally, Apple has developed Daisy, a robot capable of disassembling iPhones to recover valuable materials (Sect. 13.4.1).

[1] https://www.nytimes.com/wirecutter/reviews/the-best-thermostat/

The third and most transformative dimension focuses on the product's design, functionality, and end-of-life handling. This dimension encourages a radical rethinking of product conception, emphasizing durability, repairability, upgradability, and recyclability.

The challenge is to transcend traditional design paradigms and business models and innovate to extend the product's lifespan and utility in a commercially attractive way. It can be via redistribution business models like the sharing economy or product use extension models like repair and refurbishment.

Example 4.3 Patagonia's Worn Wear program

Patagonia, a leading outdoor apparel company, has a Worn Wear program focused on repairing and reselling clothing to prolong its lifespan. The program offers free repairs on all Patagonia clothing items, regardless of age, covering common issues such as broken zippers and tears. In 2023, it repaired more than 23,000 pieces of clothing in Europe. By providing this service, Patagonia aims to help customers continue using their favorite clothing instead of disposing of it. Globally, more than 110 repair locations fix Patagonia clothing.

The Worn Wear program also includes a resale component in the United States, where gently used items are collected, inspected, refurbished and made available through the website and dedicated stores. This allows customers to buy high-quality Patagonia gear at reduced prices (Patagonia, 2024).

The results from these dimensions enable a manufacturer to place their product in a matrix, where the horizontal axis, product lifecycle extension, represents the extent to which a product's design and business model extend its useful life through durability, repairability, and upgradability and the vertical axis, material circularity, represents the degree to which materials used in products are biodegradable, recyclable, or made from renewable resources, aiming for minimal waste and maximum reusability or recyclability (Table 4.1).

4.1.2 Modularity

Modularity in product design is a strategy centered around creating products with interchangeable and easily separable components. This approach promotes more sustainable consumption and production by extending the lifecycle of products, enhancing their adaptability, and reducing waste. Modular designs offer several key advantages.

Table 4.1 Characteristics and strategies for product assessment

	Low product lifecycle extension	High product lifecycle extension
High material circularity	*Materially circular:* High use of recyclable, renewable, or biodegradable materials in products that may not have an extended lifespan *Strategy:* Focus on developing take-back schemes and recycling programs and exploring product as a service models to improve the product lifecycle Compostable coffee pods	*Fully circular models:* Designers create longer-lasting products using fully recyclable or biodegradable materials *Strategy:* Innovate in business models, such as offering products as services (PaaS) and establishing closed-loop systems to maintain product and material circulation Modular smartphones with parts that can be individually upgraded or recycled
Low material circularity	*Linear models:* Short-lived products, single-use materials, traditional "take-make-waste" approach *Strategy:* Identify opportunities for incremental product design and materials improvements to initiate the shift toward circularity Disposable plastic cutlery	*Longevity focused:* Products designed for long-term durability may not use circular materials *Strategy:* Enhance product design for repair and upgradeability while gradually introducing recyclable or renewable materials High-end appliances that are designed for long-term use with proprietary components that are not necessarily recyclable

Modular designs enhance a product's longevity and repairability by allowing individual components to be easily replaced or upgraded without discarding the entire product due to a single component's failure or obsolescence. By extending the usable life of the product, modular designs support a longer relationship between the product and its users.

Modular designs enable products to be updated with the latest technology or functionality by replacing or adding modules. This adaptability keeps products relevant and valuable over time, reducing the need for frequent complete product replacements. *From a business perspective, this means that the users have bought a platform that they can constantly update—they do not have to go out every few years to select a new product potentially from a competitor.* Instead, they can upgrade their existing platform for perhaps 15 years, creating a stronger customer relationship and reducing costs, as keeping a customer is generally five to seven times cheaper than acquiring a new one (Kumar, 2022).

Modular products can be disassembled at the end of their life, allowing materials and components to be efficiently sorted, recycled, or remanufactured. This process is more straightforward and cost-effective than monolithic designs, where disassembly and material separation can be challenging and resource-intensive. Efficient end-of-life processing reduces the overall environmental burden and cost of recycling supports, increasing the attractiveness of circular business models.

Modular designs offer customers the flexibility to customize or personalize their products according to their specific needs or preferences, enhancing user satisfaction and potentially leading to longer product retention. The ability to personalize products can also strengthen customer loyalty and enhance the product's perceived value, further embedding the customer within the brand's ecosystem.

Example 4.4 Dell's Concept Luna project

Dell's Concept Luna project is a prototype representing a shift in laptop design philosophy. Concept Luna designs components like the keyboard, display, battery, and motherboard for easy removal and replacement. This modular approach offers a range of benefits:

Extended lifespans*:* Instead of replacing the entire laptop when a component fails or becomes outdated, users could swap out the specific part, reducing electronic waste and promoting a more sustainable approach to technology consumption. Dell can benefit from an aftermarket for parts and services, driving continuous revenue after the initial laptop purchase.

Upgradability*:* Users can upgrade specific laptop parts, keeping the core functioning machine intact. This allows for greater personalization and extends the laptop's useful life. Upgradability enables Dell to offer customization options at the point of sale and beyond, allowing for upselling opportunities as users seek to enhance their laptops' performance or features over time. It is a platform from which Dell can continue to profit.

Simplified repairs*:* Concept Luna emphasizes a design that minimizes the use of adhesives and screws, making repairs quicker and easier. Easier repair processes enable Dell to expand its service network.

Concept Luna is a prototype that has given Dell insights into how to tweak how they make future products (Robson, 2021).

4.1.3 Product Lifecycle Management

Complementing the redesign effort is a robust product lifecycle management (PLM) strategy, which ensures that products are designed with circularity in mind and managed throughout their lifecycle to maximize their value and minimize waste. PLM encompasses a comprehensive framework for overseeing a product's journey from inception to its end-of-life and beyond, incorporating product return, refurbishment, and recycling mechanisms. Circularity involves a systemic integration of lifecycle thinking into the fabric of product development and operational processes, ensuring that every product's design considers its eventual recovery, reuse, or recycling.

Example 4.5 IKEA plans to transform into a completely circular business

By 2030, IKEA, a global leader in home furnishings, plans to transform into a completely circular business. This means all their products will be designed using renewable and recycled materials, following circular principles. In addition, IKEA will focus on helping customers obtain, maintain, and pass on products to minimize waste and maximize resource efficiency (IKEA, 2024).

IKEA aims to achieve its circular goals by 2030 through a comprehensive approach that includes circular product design, material innovation, and developing more circular services. By 2030, all products will be designed to be durable, repairable, reusable, resellable, and recyclable, using only renewable and recycled materials.

IKEA is currently experimenting with new business models to assist customers in prolonging the lifespan of their purchases. This includes implementing buy-back programs for secondhand items and offering assembly parts to facilitate repairs. Collaborations with suppliers, business partners, and other stakeholders are helping IKEA to transition to a circular economy more quickly. The company aims to drive systemic change by sharing knowledge and setting an industry-leading example.

IKEA's Circular Design Principles (IKEA, 2024)

Designing for Renewable or Recycled Materials: To develop sustainable products, choose renewable and recyclable materials from the beginning.

Designing for Standardization: Enabling care, repair, upgradability, refurbishment, and recycling through standardizing parts and materials.

Designing for Care: Extending product life through maintenance and prevention by designing durable products and providing care instructions.

Designing for Repair: Making products easy to repair with available spare parts and convenient solutions.

Designing for Adaptability: Creating products that adapt to evolving customer needs, allowing modifications instead of replacements.

Designing for Disassembly and Reassembly: Facilitating easy disassembly and reassembly to support reuse, refurbishment, and remanufacturing.

Designing for Remanufacturing: Using existing materials and parts in new products to conserve resources.

Designing for Recyclability: Ensuring products can be easily recycled using separable and recyclable materials.

Integrating the Digital Product Passport (DPP) (Sect. 2.2) into the PLM strategy improves the transparency and traceability of a product's lifecycle. The DPP includes comprehensive and standardized information about the product's materials, components, and lifecycle events, which can be accessed at different value chain stages.

4.1.4 Transitioning Sales Strategy

Adopting circularity means moving away from focusing on volume and sales of new products to valuing longevity, utility, and ongoing services. In this model, viewing products as platforms for continual services necessitates a change in sales strategies that impacts not only internal teams but also distributors, resellers, and retail partners.

For internal sales teams, the change requires understanding circular products and a shift in performance metrics and incentives (see Sect. 4.1.6). Sales goals emphasize long-term customer relationships and repeat engagements facilitated by circular products and services, moving away from traditional volume-based metrics. This approach focuses on building customer loyalty, promoting durable, repairable products and encouraging participation in take-back programs.

For distributors and resellers, the strategy evolves toward a collaborative model, ensuring they can effectively champion circular products, including incentives to actively adopt and promote circular principles. Incentive schemes might include rewards for long-term customer retention, bonuses for selling products with higher circular attributes, or shared revenue from the sale of refurbished items and repair services.

Retail partners educate and engage consumers with the principles of circularity, emphasizing the product and the broader ethos of circularity. While still selling the products, retail spaces should also serve as platforms for showcasing circular products' financial and environmental lifetime benefits to consumers, including the extended value and cost savings from reduced replacements and the availability of repair and take-back services. Incentive schemes for retail staff might include rewards for customer education on circular practices and bonuses for sales of products designed for longevity and reparability.

4.1.5 Decisions on Whom to Deliver Circular Services

Manufacturers face decisions about who should perform circular services related to their products. They can handle these services internally, collaborate with third-party providers, or let the market lead. Each option has distinct benefits, drawbacks, and impacts on potential earnings, brand reputation, and existing relationships with distributors, resellers, and retail partners.

4.1.5.1 Manufacturer-Managed Services

When manufacturers handle services internally, they control the quality and delivery, ensuring they meet their brand's standards. This direct management enhances brand loyalty and customer satisfaction through consistent, high-quality service experiences. It also provides direct feedback on product performance, aiding future improvements and innovations. However, this method requires investment in service infrastructure and skills, which can be costly and complex, particularly when scaling across different regions. While this increases operational expenses, it also creates opportunities for additional revenue through premium services and strengthens customer relationships.

4.1.5.2 Partnerships with Third-Party Service Providers

Partnering with third-party service providers allows manufacturers to utilize external expertise and infrastructure, enhance scalability, and manage the challenges of broad geographic service coverage without the associated costs. This strategy enables manufacturers to concentrate on their primary strengths, like product development, while outsourcing service operations. The downside involves reduced control over service quality, which could affect customer satisfaction and damage the brand's reputation. Dependence on external parties may also impact service reliability. Potential earnings are lower due to revenue sharing, but this approach minimizes operational risks and resource demands.

4.1.5.3 Market-Driven Services

Choosing a market-driven approach is the least costly investment, as it requires minimal development of internal service capabilities. This strategy fosters competitive innovation, potentially leading to more efficient and varied service options. However, it also poses service quality and consistency risks, adversely impacting the product lifecycle and customer experience. Additionally, manufacturers have minimal direct customer interaction, possibly weakening brand loyalty and engagement. The potential income is most limited with this model, with manufacturers benefiting indirectly through improved product longevity and brand reputation.

4.1.5.4 Strategic Considerations Involving Distributors, Resellers, and Retailers

In each approach, manufacturers must consider the economic effects on their existing partners, who may see a decrease in traditional income from product sales as services and durable products become more prevalent. By involving these partners in circular service models, perhaps through revised roles or revenue-sharing agreements, manufacturers can help maintain the profitability of traditional sales channels. Training and support ensure these partners deliver new services while maintaining quality and customer satisfaction. Integrating solutions that involve all stakeholders can distribute economic benefits more evenly and support a smooth transition to new business models.

This strategy reflects the transition of the early 2000s when businesses had to balance the advantages of direct online sales with the need to keep their traditional partners engaged and profitable. The success of this shift often relied on transparent communication, fair revenue sharing, and adequate support to all involved parties. Similarly, successfully moving to circular economy models will require carefully integrating new services with existing partner networks, maintaining their role and income while expanding into circular practices.

4.1.6 Reorienting Organizational KPIs and Incentives

As businesses transition toward circular economy models, there's a shift required in how internal goals, processes, and key performance indicators (KPIs) are defined and measured. This shift moves beyond traditional sales and production metrics that align with the linear "make-sell-dispose" model, redirecting focus toward the economic performance of circular activities.

These new KPIs reflect the profitability and cost generated from circular services, clearly showing their contribution to the business. It can also include sustainability KPIs like material reuse rates, waste reduction, and product lifecycle extensions, but this must be secondary. The KPIs must emphasize the economic viability and benefits for the business, for example, measuring the success of take-back programs regarding waste reduction and their ability to contribute to the bottom line through cost savings or new revenue streams.

Incentive structures must evolve to prioritize and reward the successful implementation and growth of circular services, ensuring that employees across all departments align with and actively contribute to the company's circular economy objectives.

By reorienting organizational KPIs and incentives toward the economic performance of circular activities, businesses can foster a culture that values sustainability and financial efficiency. This dual focus is key to achieving a successful and sustainable transition to circular models, ensuring that companies contribute positively to the environment and secure their competitive edge in the evolving marketplace.

Table 4.2 is a sample of key performance indicators (KPIs) tailored for different areas within organizations transitioning toward a circular economy. These KPIs illustrate both business-focused and sustainability-focused metrics, guiding sales, production, services, and product design teams. The business-focused KPIs emphasize economic performance, efficiency, and customer engagement specific to circular practices, while the sustainability-focused KPIs highlight environmental impact, resource utilization, and lifecycle considerations.

Table 4.2 Selection of key performance indicators (KPIs) tailored for different areas within organizations transitioning toward a circular economy

Area	KPI type	Key performance indicators (KPIs)
Sales	Business focused	Revenue from circular products and services
		Customer retention rate for circular services
		Percentage of sales from product as a service and sharing models
		Growth rate of recommerce and secondhand sales
		Number of take-back programs initiated and their conversion rates
Sales	Sustainability focused	Percentage reduction in virgin material usage through circular sales
		Carbon footprint reduction achieved through circular sales strategies
		Increase in sales attributed to products with recycled content
Production	Business focused	Cost savings from using recycled or remanufactured materials
		Efficiency improvements in remanufacturing processes
		Income generated from the sale of byproducts and waste materials
		Rate of innovation in product design for disassembly and reuse
		Inventory turnover rate of circular materials and components
Production	Sustainability focused	Percentage of products designed for easy disassembly
		Total amount of waste diverted from landfills due to circular production
		Energy consumption reduction in circular production processes
Product design	Business focused	Percentage of products meeting circular design criteria
		Time-to-market for circularly designed products
		Cost reduction achieved through circular design practices
		Number of circular design patents filed or obtained
		Customer feedback scores on circularly designed products
Product design	Sustainability focused	Percentage of recyclable materials used in new designs
		Reduction in product carbon footprint through circular design
		Increase in product lifespan due to circular design features

(continued)

Table 4.2 (continued)

Area	KPI type	Key performance indicators (KPIs)
Services	Business focused	Profit margins on circular services (repair, maintenance, refurbishment)
		Customer satisfaction and loyalty metrics for circular services
		Response and resolution times for repair and refurbishment services
		Recurring revenue generated from circular service contracts
		Cost efficiency of circular service operations
Services	Sustainability focused	Number of products successfully refurbished and re-entered the market
		Total lifetime extension achieved for products through circular services
		Reduction in resource use due to efficient circular service practices

4.1.7 Leveraging Digitization for Effective Product Redesign in the Circular Economy

Part III of this book will thoroughly explore how digitization integrates into circular business models. This section briefly overviews how digitization supports manufacturers in innovating, optimizing, and transforming their redesign processes to align with circular economy principles. This summary highlights key aspects of The Sustainable Manufacturing Intelligence Framework (SMIF) introduced in Part III, demonstrating how digital tools and strategies enhance customer experience, optimize product lifecycle management, foster business ecosystem collaboration, and drive data-driven circularity, ensuring long-term sustainability and economic viability.

Data from internal IT systems inform the redesign process. Advanced supply chain management (SCM) systems allow real-time tracking of product lifecycles, assisting designers in using reusable parts efficiently. Customer relationship management (CRM) systems analyze customer feedback to identify areas for improvement. Digital tools also aid in creating modular, repairable, and recyclable products from the beginning.

Connected products improve lifecycle management. IoT sensors monitor product condition and performance, providing data on usage patterns and potential failures. AI analyzes this data to recommend optimal redesign strategies for repair, refurbishment, and recycling, thus enhancing product durability and functionality.

Digitization improves collaboration and data sharing within business ecosystems. Platforms facilitate seamless interaction among suppliers, recyclers, and service providers. Digital Product Passports enhance transparency and traceability, aiding manufacturers in making informed design choices to support circularity.

Digitization integrates multichannel interactions and personalized engagement. Digital warranties encourage continuous customer interaction, providing valuable feedback for redesign. Personalization enables designers to create products tailored to individual customer needs and preferences.

Data-driven tools enable informed decision-making. Lifecycle assessment tools provide insights into products' environmental and economic impacts, guiding sustainable redesign. Predictive analytics optimize production based on recycled materials and market trends. Generative AI helps create innovative, efficient, and sustainable designs.

4.1.8 Financial Considerations in Transitioning to a Circular Economy

Moving toward a circular economy involves financial planning, starting with understanding the costs of this shift.

Businesses accustomed to linear models will incur upfront costs due to new technologies, infrastructures, and employee training needed for circular operations. These investments are necessary to set the foundation for a sustainable, circular business.

Companies must remain competitive in the existing linear market while adapting to circular practices. This balancing act is crucial—firms must innovate and invest within the circular model without losing their foothold in the traditional market. Managing this dual focus requires careful strategic planning and prioritization (see Sect. 4.6).

Circular business models fundamentally change revenue generation. Unlike traditional models, where profits are made at the point of sale, circular models often see profits accrue over a product's lifespan through services such as product as a service, maintenance, and refurbishment. This shift to deferred income means companies need initial capital to bridge the gap until these new revenue streams begin to pay off. However, the product's lifecycle profitability can be greater than that of linear models.

Businesses must understand the long-term value of investing in circular practices and plan their finances to support immediate needs and future growth.

Example Circular Business Models	Required Investment	Lost Traditional Income	Future Circular Income
Product as a Service	Developing leasing systems, IoT integration for tracking, and customer support infrastructure	Reduced upfront sales revenue due to shift from ownership to service-based models	Recurring subscription revenue, long-term customer relationships, and enhanced brand loyalty
Repair and Maintenance Services	Setting up service centers, training staff, and creating supply chains for spare parts	Decline in new product sales as repair services extend product lifespans	Income from service contracts, predictive maintenance, and customer satisfaction improvements

Example Circular Business Models	Required Investment	Lost Traditional Income	Future Circular Income
Refurbishment Programs	Building facilities for inspection, repair, and quality assurance of refurbished products	Decreased demand for new products as customers opt for refurbished options	Revenue from refurbished product sales, lower costs due to reuse, and access to new customer segments
Recommerce Platforms	Developing e-commerce platforms, logistics for reverse flows, and customer engagement tools	Loss of traditional retail channels as focus shifts to resale and recommerce	Profit from resale of used products, marketplace fees, and strengthened customer trust

4.2 The Ecosystem Approach to Circular Transformation

The circular economy requires transforming the upstream and downstream value chains. This is a necessary operation and a strategic imperative that reshapes the entire business ecosystem. This shift mirrors the transformative changes of the digital era, which redefined traditional roles, and new players emerged as pivotal forces. Achieving circularity requires a comprehensive reconfiguration of relationships and processes among manufacturers, suppliers, customers, and partners.

4.2.1 Upstream Challenges

Manufacturers must take a nuanced approach to redefine supply chain dynamics and address upstream challenges. The first step is expanding their supplier network to include new partners specializing in recycled materials and refurbished and remanufactured products to incorporate circularity into the production process from the beginning. At the same time, manufacturers must ensure that the transition to circular models remains economically attractive for their existing suppliers.

An aspect of transitioning toward a circular economy is establishing a network that efficiently manages the return of products. This network comprises various stakeholders involved in the value chain. Its primary goal is to enable the seamless flow of used products, parts, and materials into the manufacturing cycle for refurbishment, remanufacturing, or recycling. It is imperative to ensure that all the stakeholders are aligned toward the same objectives, creating a collaborative environment where every participant is motivated to act in the ecosystem's best interest. This involves creating shared value propositions, implementing reward systems for circular practices, or establishing agreements that benefit all parties involved in the circular flow of materials. The ecosystem reinforces the circular model by aligning these incentives, accentuating the value of materials and components throughout their lifecycle, and ensuring that every action taken by individual stakeholders contributes to the sustainability and efficiency of the entire system.

Navigating supply chain complexity introduced by circular practices is another aspect of upstream strategy. Circular supply chains, characterized by their focus on material recovery, product life extension, and resource efficiency, present an intricacy not typically encountered in traditional linear models. To effectively manage this complexity, manufacturers can harness advanced technologies such as artificial intelligence for system optimization (Chap. 15) and Digital Product Passports for enhancing transparency and traceability (Sect. 2.2). These technological solutions streamline circular supply chain operations, ensuring materials and information flow seamlessly.

4.2.2 Supply Chain Vulnerabilities

Geopolitical tensions, environmental challenges, and trade conflicts intensify supply chain vulnerabilities, underscoring the need for supply chain resilience. Beyond risk mitigation, resilience emerges as a strategic asset, offering a competitive edge.

By diversifying supply sources to include recycled materials, refurbished products, and remanufactured parts, manufacturers can diminish the risks of supply disruptions and secure a consistent flow of inputs. It empowers manufacturers to maintain control over the lifecycle of their resources; *this means ensuring parts and materials within their control never unintentionally exit their sphere of influence.* This control prevents resource loss and facilitates a smoother transition of materials back into the supply chain. Manufacturers ensure the continual utilization of resources by managing and recovering materials and components effectively. This proactive management aids in decoupling economic growth from resource consumption, cultivating an increasingly resilient supply chain in the face of external pressures (Fig. 4.1).

4.2.2.1 Local Production Capabilities

Circular economy principles align with growing political pressures to develop local production capabilities. The desire for economic resilience, job creation, and reduced

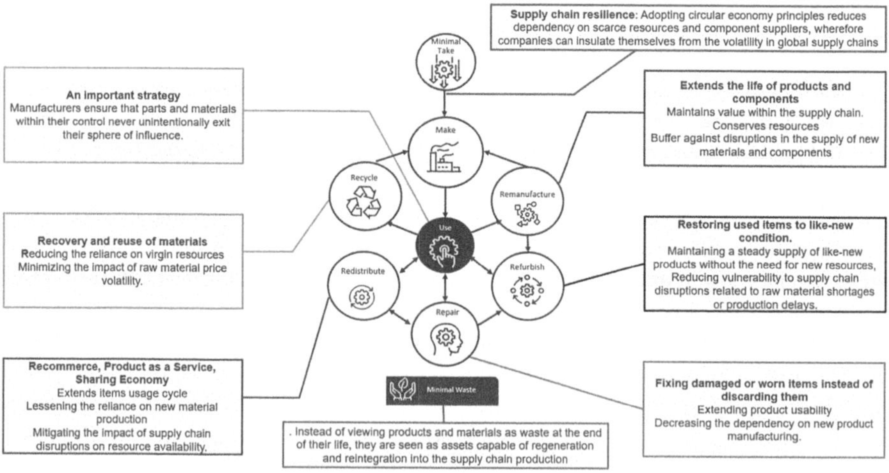

Fig. 4.1 How the circular economy enables supply chain resilience

global supply chain dependency drives this movement toward localization. An example is the US government's initiative, the CHIPS and Science Act that encourages local production by providing $52.7 billion for American semiconductor research, development, manufacturing, and workforce development, including incentives for manufacturing and R&D, aimed at bolstering domestic semiconductor production and reducing dependency on foreign supply chains (The White House, 2022).

The circular economy fosters the development of local circular service provider markets. This approach supports local businesses and encourages the growth of repair services, remanufacturing facilities, and recycling centers. By investing in local ecosystems that support the circular economy, regions can reduce their reliance on imported goods and materials, leading to more resilient regional economies. EU's Green Deal finds that setting criteria for circularity and an overall reduction of products' environmental and climate footprint will lead to more energy and resource independence and less pollution (European Commission, 2022).

Governments worldwide are beginning to implement measures to encourage businesses to adopt these practices, supporting the transition to more sustainable and self-sufficient local economies. These measures include incentives for sustainable product design, support for local recycling and remanufacturing industries, and regulations that favor using recycled materials in new products (Chap. 2).

4.2.3 The Circular Business Ecosystems

Manufacturers must adapt their operations to fit into circular business ecosystems. To participate in these ecosystems, manufacturers need to ensure their processes are optimized to enhance the efficiency of circular ecosystems. By improving the efficiency of product return, refurbishment, and recycling operations, they can reduce waste and increase resource recovery.

Manufacturers have a unique position that enables them to foster and even lead the evolution of a dynamic ecosystem of circular service providers. Promoting or establishing services that extend from repair to comprehensive product as a service platforms can enrich the ecosystem's diversity and vibrancy, making circular solutions more accessible and appealing to all stakeholders involved.

Manufacturers must assess their potential roles within circular business models and the broader service market, identifying areas where they can add value, from offering circular product lines to providing lifecycle services.

4.2.4 Roles in a Circular Economy Business Ecosystem

A company's role in a circular economy business ecosystem impacts its influence, opportunities, and overall success within the network. Understanding these roles is crucial for any company looking to engage effectively in a circular economy and maximize its value from such collaborations. The roles discussed below are inspired by Pidun et al. (2021) (Fig. 4.2).

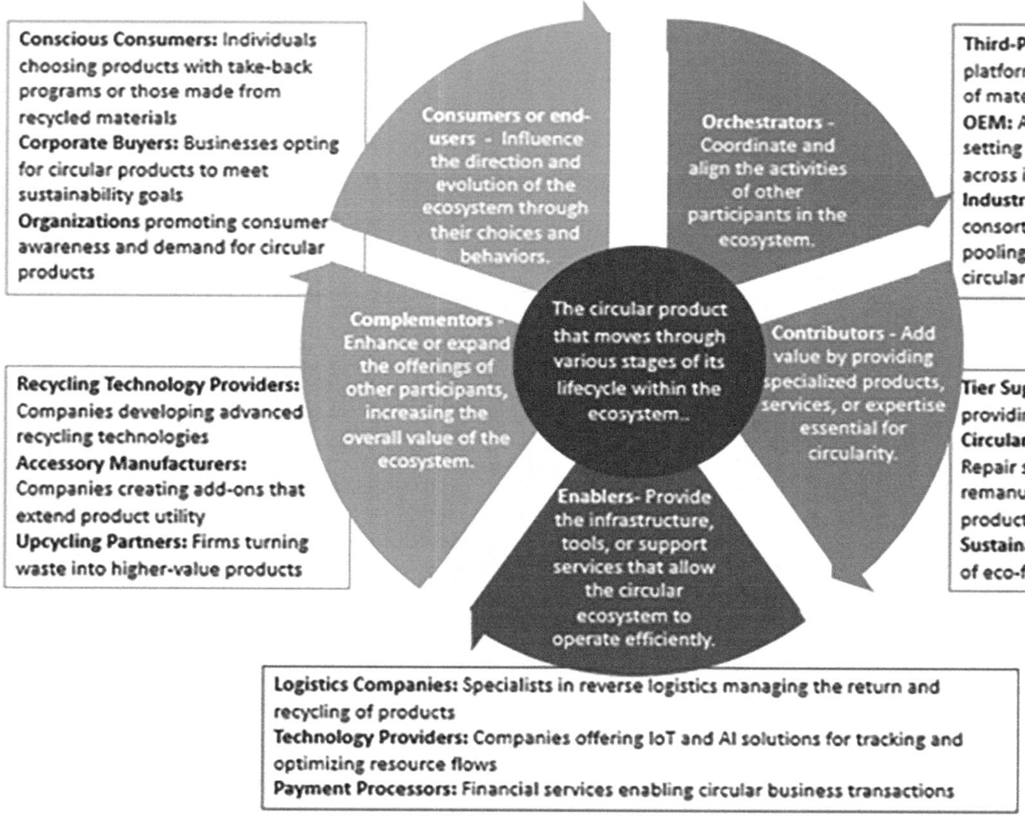

Fig. 4.2 The roles within a Circular Business Ecosystem and examples of entities

Orchestrator

The orchestrator plays a central role in a circular economy ecosystem by coordinating and aligning the activities of other participants. This orchestrator can be a third-party entity, an original equipment manufacturer (OEM), or an industry collaboration that takes on a leadership role within the ecosystem.

For example, a third-party orchestrator could manage a digital platform that enables the exchange of materials and information among all ecosystem participants, promoting seamless collaboration and efficiency. Alternatively, an OEM (original equipment manufacturer) could assume the role of orchestrator by establishing standards for circularity throughout its supply chain and coordinating efforts to ensure that products are designed, manufactured, and recycled in accordance with circular principles. Industry collaborations, such as consortia consisting of multiple companies within a sector, can also act as orchestrators by combining resources and expertise to drive sector-wide circular initiatives. Regardless of who assumes this role, the primary function of the orchestrator is to set the strategic direction, define common goals, and ensure that all participants collaborate effectively to achieve shared objectives.

Contributor

Contributors are businesses that enhance the circular economy ecosystem by offering specialized products, services, or expertise essential for achieving circularity. Although they may not be the leaders of the ecosystem, their role is crucial to its functioning. Contributors in a circular ecosystem can include tier suppliers, circular service providers such as repair shops, refurbishers, remanufacturers, and companies that develop sustainable materials or components.

For example, a tier supplier that provides recyclable electronic device components contributes to the ecosystem by ensuring that the end product can be easily disassembled and recycled. Similarly, repair shops and refurbishers play a critical role by extending the life of products, thus reducing the need for new resources and minimizing waste. Circular service providers like these are essential for maintaining the flow of materials within the ecosystem and supporting the overall goal of resource efficiency, competitiveness, and sustainability. While contributors may not control the ecosystem, their offerings are vital to achieving the network's sustainability and financial goals.

Enabler

Enablers provide the infrastructure, tools, or support services necessary for the circular ecosystem to operate efficiently. While they might not directly contribute to the final products, they are crucial in facilitating the interactions and processes that drive the ecosystem.

For instance, a logistics company specializing in reverse logistics—managing the return and recycling of products—acts as an enabler in a circular economy by ensuring that materials are efficiently collected and routed back into the production cycle. Enablers establish the conditions for other participants to collaborate, innovate, and deliver sustainable value.

Complementor

A complementor is a business that enhances or expands the offerings of other participants within the circular ecosystem. Complementors work closely with orchestrators and contributors, creating complementary products or services that increase the overall value of the ecosystem's offerings.

For example, a company that develops advanced recycling technologies that can handle mixed-material products complements the efforts of manufacturers and recyclers within the ecosystem. By making it easier to recycle complex products, the complementor enhances the sustainability and effectiveness of the entire ecosystem.

Consumers, customers, and end-users

In a circular economy, the consumer or end-user plays a critical role as a participant in the ecosystem. Through their choices, feedback, and behaviors, they influence the ecosystem's direction and evolution.

For example, consumers who prioritize purchasing products with take-back programs or those made from recycled materials drive demand for circular products and encourage companies to adopt more sustainable practices. Understanding consumer behavior is essential for all participants, as it helps shape the ecosystem's offerings and ensures its long-term sustainability.

Understanding Your Role

It's important for a company to figure out its place in a circular economy. This helps the company position itself strategically. Companies should evaluate their strengths, resources, and goals to decide whether they should lead, contribute to, support, complement, or engage with consumers in the ecosystem. Also, a company's role in the ecosystem can change over time. For example, a company that contributes to the ecosystem today might become a leader in the future as its influence and abilities grow.

Understanding how your company fits into an ecosystem and leveraging its role to create value is key. By recognizing and embracing your role, you can align your efforts with other participants to foster collaboration, innovation, and mutual success on the journey toward a profitable circular economy.

4.2.5 Embrace Innovative Digitization Strategies

Manufacturers need to adopt innovative digital strategies to remain competitive. To achieve digital integration, they must focus on their internal operations and broader business ecosystems. Internally, manufacturers must upgrade their systems to enable interoperability with external platforms and facilitate seamless data exchange throughout the value chain. This is particularly important for effectively managing circular processes, such as product returns, refurbishment, and recycling.

Manufacturers must promote the digitization of the entire business ecosystem. They can do this by advocating for and adopting standards and practices that encourage circularity. For instance, implementing digital product passports for improved traceability and using shared ecosystem artificial intelligence (AI) to support efficient collaboration can lead to establishing a digitally enabled circular economy. This digital transformation across the entire ecosystem facilitates more effective circular practices and opens up new avenues for innovation and collaboration among all stakeholders in the ecosystem.

Manufacturers must continuously assess the digital landscape, identifying emerging platforms and technologies that could present new opportunities or pose potential threats. This ongoing evaluation might include delving into platform-based business models that could redefine market dynamics or understanding how digital marketplaces might influence competitive landscapes.

The necessity for digital integration, internally and within the broader business ecosystem, underscores the complexity and interconnectedness of transitioning to circular models. Manufacturers must navigate this digital terrain thoughtfully, leveraging technology to enhance circular practices while remaining vigilant to the shifting digital landscape. Chapter 12 explores ecosystem digitization and its implications for circular manufacturing, providing deeper insights into harnessing digital innovation for circular success.

4.3 External Factor

Manufacturers must address the external factors that are beyond the immediate control of individual businesses. Successfully redesigning and reinventing in response to these outside challenges requires a proactive and strategic approach:

4.3.1 Supportive Policies and Incentives

The political landscape underscores the importance of supportive policies and incentives in facilitating this shift. Globally, various countries have launched initiatives to encourage circular practices. Chapter 2 provides detailed information about these initiatives, so they will not be repeated here. Opportunities like grants, tax incentives, and collaborative projects can support the transition to circular models. Manufacturers should actively explore these avenues, ensuring alignment with regulatory trends and consumer demands for sustainability. This can ease the path toward the successful integration of circular economy principles.

4.3.2 Overcoming Cultural Barriers and Engaging Customers

The transition from a linear "take-make-dispose" mindset to a circular economy framework represents a cultural shift. Overcoming these ingrained cultural barriers requires manufacturers to exemplify circular practices within their operations and champion these principles throughout their value chains and among their value chain customer base. By leading through example, manufacturers can illuminate the practicality and advantages of circular models, showcasing their efficacy in real-world applications.

Educational initiatives help demystify circular concepts and highlight their tangible benefits. Transparent communication allows manufacturers to articulate circularity's environmental and economic merits. This transparency and educational outreach can gradually reshape cultural norms, cultivating an ethos that embraces circular principles.

Simultaneously, engaging customers in this new paradigm is essential. Manufacturers can influence customer behavior by making circular products and services appealing and conveniently available. This involves developing marketing strategies emphasizing the positive impact of circular choices on the planet and the customer's wallet. By enhancing the accessibility and attractiveness of circular options, manufacturers can encourage customers to adopt more sustainable habits, further embedding circularity into societal norms.

Overcoming cultural barriers and engaging customers are intertwined challenges that manufacturers must address concurrently. Manufacturers can catalyze a cultural shift toward circularity through demonstration, education, and engagement, gradually transitioning away from linear consumption patterns and fostering a more sustainable, circular economy.

4.4 Skills and Knowledge for Circular Economy Transition

The shift toward a circular economy necessitates new skills and knowledge across various aspects of the manufacturing process. Manufacturers must assess their workforce capabilities and invest in training programs to upskill existing employees. Additionally, attracting new talent with expertise in circular economy principles, sustainable design, and green technologies will be needed to drive the transition (Fig. 4.3). This section outlines the required skills and knowledge and the strategies manufacturers can employ to address the skill gap.

In sustainable design, manufacturers require skills in ecodesign principles. This includes understanding and minimizing the environmental impacts of products from creation to disposal through lifecycle assessment (LCA). Additionally, modularity and disassembly design expertise is necessary to facilitate repair, reuse, and recycling. Knowledge of material efficiency, reducing hazardous substances, and enhancing product durability is also important. Integrating ecodesign terminologies from industry standards into product development processes ensures compliance and sustainability.

Waste management skills are needed to optimize resource use and minimize waste throughout the product lifecycle. Employees need to be proficient in techniques for reducing waste through recycling, reuse, and innovative waste-to-energy solutions. Understanding and implementing waste audit processes and strategies for effective waste segregation and processing are vital.

To effectively implement circular business models, manufacturers need to create and oversee business models that promote circular economy practices. This involves expertise in product as a service (PaaS), which entails transitioning from selling products to offering them as services through subscription models, leasing, and

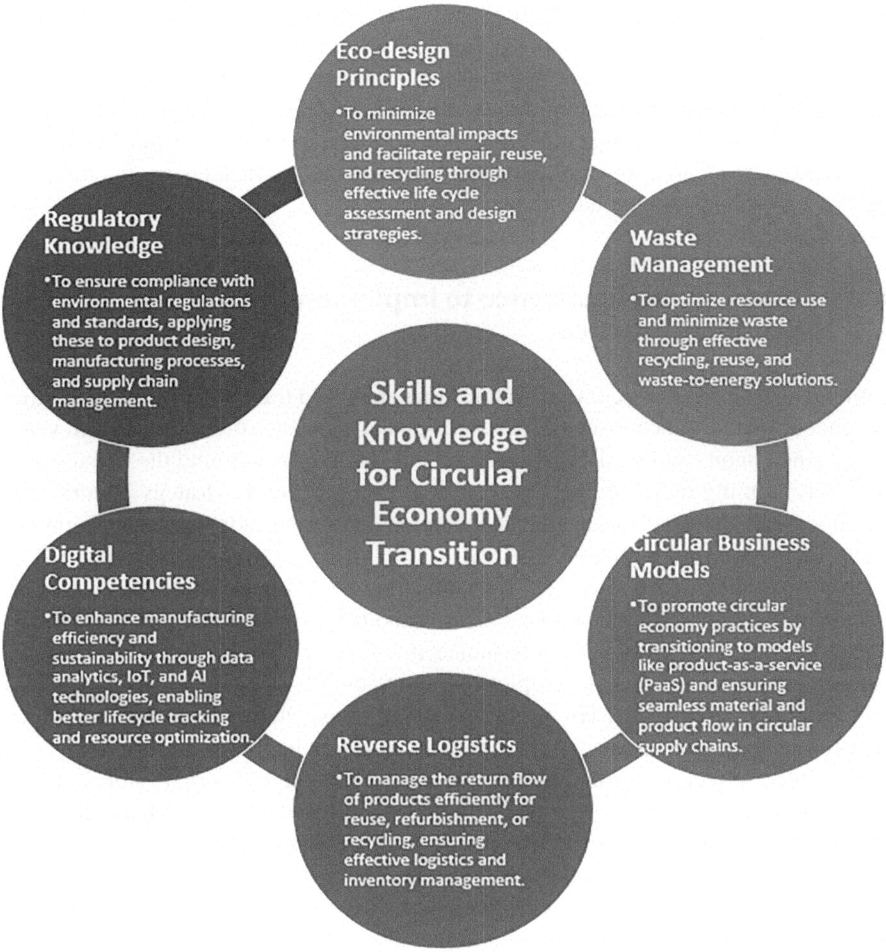

Fig. 4.3 Skills and knowledge for circular economy transition

pay-per-use. Additionally, having knowledge of circular supply chains, which enable the seamless flow of materials and products, is crucial.

Handling reverse logistics requires specialized skills in managing the return flow of products for reuse, refurbishment, or recycling. Employees must be adept at logistics planning, inventory management, and coordinating collection and processing systems. Skills in tracking and managing the lifecycle of products through digital platforms and databases are relevant for efficient reverse logistics operations.

Digital competencies are integral to this transition. Skills in data analytics are needed to track product lifecycle, predict maintenance needs, and optimize resource use. Implementing Digital Product Passports containing detailed information on product materials and lifecycle events will enhance transparency and traceability.

Additionally, skills in leveraging IoT and AI technologies can improve efficiency and sustainability in manufacturing processes (see Part III).

Regulatory knowledge is another key area. Staying informed about environmental regulations and ensuring compliance with relevant laws and standards is needed for effectively implementing circular economy practices. Employees must be skilled in interpreting and applying regulatory requirements to product design, manufacturing processes, and supply chain management.

4.5 Overcoming Resistance to Implementing Circular Economy Practices

Implementing a circular economy in the value chain is a transformative process that can encounter resistance from various actors. This resistance often stems from years of ingrained habits and well-established processes designed around the linear economy. Overcoming these challenges requires a comprehensive strategy encompassing education, communication, and engagement tailored to address each stakeholder group's concerns and motivations.

Internal stakeholders often resist circular practices due to a lack of awareness and understanding of their benefits, concerns about operational disruptions, and cost considerations. Addressing this resistance involves implementing comprehensive training programs to educate employees about circular practices' economic and environmental advantages. Highlighting industry case studies and success stories can provide tangible evidence of their benefits. Introducing incentives for teams that successfully integrate circular practices can motivate internal stakeholders. Additionally, starting with small-scale pilot projects can demonstrate feasibility and success, easing concerns about potential operational disruptions.

Suppliers may resist circular economy initiatives due to the complexity and potential disruption of existing supply chains, concerns about the quality and reliability of recycled or refurbished materials, and contractual or compliance issues. Engaging suppliers early in the transition process and fostering a collaborative approach can help develop circular solutions that benefit all parties. Implementing stringent quality control measures and providing certifications can address quality concerns. Working with legal teams to create flexible contract terms and ensuring compliance with relevant regulations can mitigate contractual and compliance issues.

Distributors might resist due to perceived logistics and inventory management complexities when dealing with refurbished or recycled products. There may also be concerns about their future role as the focus shifts from selling new products to circular services such as maintenance, repair, and refurbishment. To address these issues, manufacturers can collaborate closely with distributors to streamline logistics and create efficient systems for refurbished products. Training and support can help distributors understand the benefits and processes of managing circular products. Additionally, highlighting new business opportunities in circular services can help distributors see the potential for sustained profitability and growth.

Retailers may resist circular economy products due to concerns about consumer demand, shelf space, and inventory management challenges. They may also need clarification about their future role as the market shifts toward circular services instead of selling new products. To overcome this resistance, manufacturers can partner with retailers to educate them on the growing consumer demand for sustainable products and the long-term benefits of stocking circular products. Marketing support, point-of-sale materials, and clear product information can help retailers promote these items effectively. Developing flexible inventory management systems that accommodate circular products can ease the transition. Additionally, assisting retailers to explore new service-based revenue models, such as rental, leasing, and subscription services, can align their business strategies with the circular economy.

Customers may resist circular economy products due to perceptions of inferior quality, lack of awareness about the benefits of sustainable products, and cost concerns. Launching marketing campaigns to educate customers about the benefits of circular products, such as environmental impact and potential cost savings, shift perceptions. Providing transparent information about the lifecycle of products, including certifications and warranties, build trust in the quality of circular products. Offering incentives like discounts, loyalty programs, and trade-in options encourage customers to choose sustainable products.

Regulatory bodies and policymakers may present resistance due to existing regulations that do not support circular economy practices and slow adaptation to new policies. Manufacturers must engage with policymakers and regulatory bodies to advocate for supportive policies and regulations. Highlighting the economic and environmental benefits of the circular economy help in this advocacy. Developing and proposing new policies that support circular practices, such as tax incentives for sustainable businesses and stricter regulations on waste management, can facilitate the transition. Collaborating with industry associations and coalitions to present a unified voice strengthen efforts to achieve regulatory changes.

Overcoming resistance and transforming entrenched habits into circular practices demand a comprehensive and cohesive strategy that spans education, communication, and engagement. Combining education on circular practices' economic and environmental merits with support mechanisms can ease the transition for internal stakeholders and external partners. Effective communication strategies are central to dismantling years of linear habits, requiring broadcasting the benefits of circular initiatives and engaging in meaningful dialogue across all levels of the supply chain. By addressing the specific concerns of each actor in the value chain, manufacturers can foster a more collaborative and supportive environment for implementing circular economy practices.

4.6 Between Momentum and Caution: Navigating Fear of Missing Out and Fear of Being Early in the Circular Economy Shift

For established manufacturers, jumping headlong into circularity without a well-thought-out transition plan can be akin to betting the entire business on an untested model. The shift toward circular economy models requires a nuanced approach, balancing the innovation imperative against the need for stability and continuity in existing operations.

The Fear of Missing Out (FOMO) and the Fear of Being Early (FOBE) present a classic problem for businesses contemplating this transition. FOMO is the anxiety that competitors might leapfrog into market leadership positions by embracing sustainable practices more swiftly. Conversely, FOBE reflects the apprehension of investing too soon—before the market, technologies, or customer preferences have sufficiently matured to support a new model—potentially leading to wasted resources and strategic missteps.

Navigating this delicate balance is akin to walking a tightrope; veering too far in either direction could have consequences. Moving too hastily may disrupt well-established value chains without a ready alternative, while dragging one's feet might leave a company playing catch-up in an increasingly eco-conscious market landscape.

Businesses can turn to Geoffrey Moore's "Crossing the Chasm" framework to strategically time the adoption of circular economy practices. This framework offers insights into navigating the adoption lifecycle of groundbreaking technologies and practices. It aids in pinpointing the opportune moment for a pivot toward circular models, ensuring a business is neither prematurely jumping the gun nor lagging in the sustainable revolution (Moore, 2014).

4.6.1 Applying "Crossing the Chasm" to Circular Economy Adoption

Geoffrey Moore's "Crossing the Chasm" theory, initially devised for the diffusion of high-tech products, delineates a critical divide—the "chasm"—separating early adopters from the early majority. This chasm must be bridged for any innovation, including new business models like circular economy, to achieve widespread acceptance and success (Fig. 4.4).

Early Market At this stage, innovators and visionaries are leading the way as early adopters. They adopt new technologies or methodologies because they see the potential for gaining a competitive advantage. In the circular economy, these entities are the first to integrate sustainable practices, motivated by their ethical commitments or in anticipation of future regulatory mandates. They are willing to take risks and experiment to achieve long-term benefits.

The Chasm At this critical juncture, there is a challenging transition from a small group of visionaries to a larger, mainstream market. Many businesses face obstacles in scaling their innovative concepts into viable, profitable enterprises. It is the hurdle between small-scale, innovative pilot initiatives and robust, scalable models that resonate with a broader audience. The chasm is where practicality, scalability, and market readiness are tested, and only those models that can adapt from a visionary idea to a pragmatic solution can successfully navigate this gap.

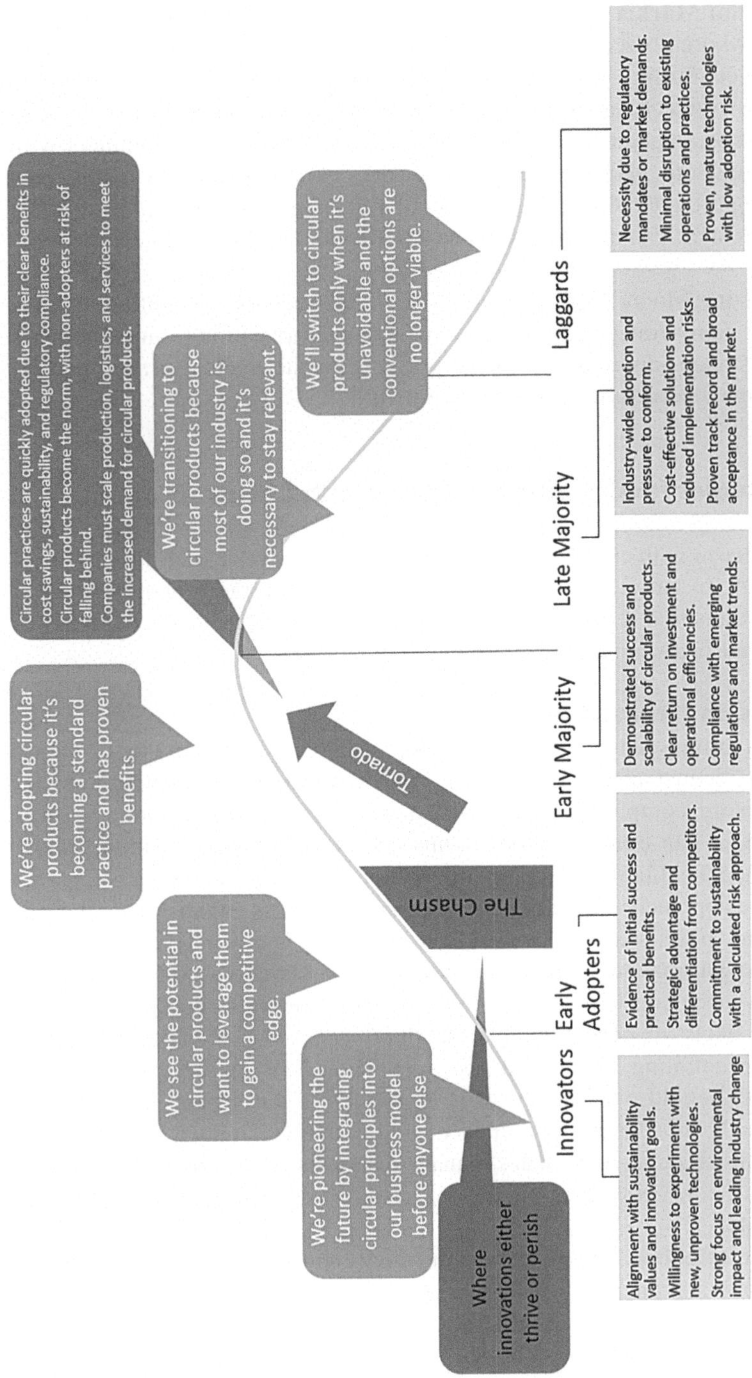

Fig. 4.4 The innovation distribution curve

The Mainstream Market This phase is dominated by pragmatists, the early and late majority, who embrace innovation when it presents tangible benefits, proven reliability, and conformity with established standards. For the circular economy to successfully cross the chasm and captivate this group, it must showcase its environmental credentials, economic viability, operational feasibility, and alignment with customer expectations and regulatory frameworks. The transition to mainstream acceptance hinges on demonstrating that circular economy models deliver superior performance, cost efficiency, and resilience compared to traditional linear models.

By contextualizing Moore's theory within the circular economy adoption journey, businesses can more strategically navigate the complex transition from niche innovation to mainstream adoption. Each stage presents unique challenges and opportunities, requiring tailored strategies to move forward.

4.6.2 Strategies for Crossing the Chasm with Circular Economy

Crossing the chasm with circular economy principles involves a multifaceted strategy that appeals to early adopters and resonates with the more pragmatic early majority. This transition is pivotal for gaining mainstream acceptance and requires a deliberate, well-orchestrated approach.

4.6.2.1 Focus on Target Niches

Begin by pinpointing specific sectors or market segments where circular economy principles offer distinct advantages, such as improved resource efficiency, cost savings, or regulatory compliance. By demonstrating clear value in these targeted niches, businesses can establish proof points and build credibility within a more focused audience, facilitating a smoother transition to broader markets.

This targeted approach is what Geoffrey Moore refers to as establishing a "beachhead." The term "beachhead," borrowed from military strategy, refers to the initial focus on securing a small, defendable position that can serve as a strong foundation for further advancement. Circular economy adoption implies choosing a market segment most likely to benefit from and adopting circular economy principles quickly. By concentrating efforts on this segment and achieving success, a business can create a stronghold or "beachhead" from which it can expand into adjacent markets, gradually broadening its influence and circular economy adoption across the industry. This strategic focus helps manage resources effectively and provides a tangible proof of concept that can be leveraged to overcome skepticism in broader market segments.

Drawing upon Geoffrey Moore's "bowling alley" concept (Fig. 4.5) is beneficial when focusing on target niches for circular economy adoption. This concept emphasizes the importance of achieving initial success within specific, well-defined market segments before scaling across broader markets. In the "bowling alley" phase, each niche market/beachhead is viewed as a "pin," and the objective is to knock down one pin at a time, leveraging the momentum from each success to tackle the next market segment.

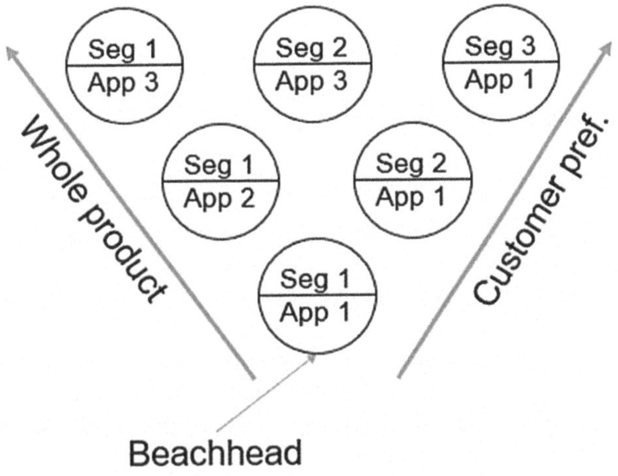

Fig. 4.5 "Bowling alley" for crossing the "chasm"

4.6.2.2 Identify High-Impact Niches

Select target niches where the circular economy can benefit significantly and immediately. These niches should have identifiable pain points that the circular economy can address, such as resource scarcity, regulatory pressures, or strong consumer demand for sustainable products. The idea is to choose segments where the circular economy's value proposition is most compelling and urgent.

4.6.2.3 Tailor Solutions to Specific Needs

As bowlers adjust their aim and throw for each pin, circular economy initiatives should be customized to meet each target niche's unique requirements and challenges. This involves a deep understanding of the niche's dynamics, stakeholder expectations, and existing gaps the circular economy can fill. By creating whole solutions that resonate with the specific needs of each segment, businesses can increase their chances of adoption and success.

4.6.2.4 Leverage Success to Expand

In Moore's analogy, knocking down the first pin creates a chain reaction that makes it easier to topple the subsequent pins. Similarly, achieving success in one niche can create a ripple effect, enhance credibility, and provide valuable case studies to showcase in adjacent markets. Success stories can serve as powerful testimonials, reducing the perceived risk for other segments and paving the way for broader circular economy adoption.

By integrating Moore's bowling alley strategy into targeting niches for circular economy adoption, businesses can approach the market with a more focused and effective strategy. This systematic approach facilitates initial entry and success within niche markets. It strategically positions enterprises to expand their circular economy practices across broader segments, leveraging the momentum gained from each targeted success.

Example 4.6 Patagonia expanded Worn Wear principles to a broader market

Patagonia launched its Worn Wear program in 2013 in the USA to encourage consumers to take better care of their outdoor gear by washing it and repairing it as needed (Hendriksz, 2016). It initially focused on creating a sustainable product cycle by encouraging customers to return used Patagonia gear in exchange for store credit[2]. These items were then repaired and resold through the Worn Wear online store and pop-up shops. This initiative targeted environmentally conscious consumers who valued sustainability and long-lasting products.

The Worn Wear program built a community of loyal customers who appreciated Patagonia's commitment to sustainability. This initiative resonated particularly well with younger consumers, who are more inclined to support brands with strong environmental values (Barkho, 2020).

Patagonia distinguished itself from competitors by promoting the idea of repairing and reusing garments rather than disposing of them. This approach aligned perfectly with their brand ethos of environmental responsibility.

After proving the concept with Worn Wear, Patagonia expanded these principles to a broader market through several key initiatives:

ReCrafted Collection: Patagonia introduced the ReCrafted Collection[3], which upcycles unsalvageable garments into new, unique items. This line was made available to a broader audience, further promoting the concept of circular fashion (Make Fashion Better, 2019).

Ironclad Guarantee and Repairs: Patagonia reinforced its commitment to durability with the Ironclad Guarantee[4], offering repairs and replacements for its products to extend their lifespan. This program supports sustainability and builds trust and loyalty among customers.

Mainstreaming Worn Wear: The success of Worn Wear led Patagonia to integrate this initiative more prominently into its business model. The Worn Wear program is now featured on Patagonia's main e-commerce site, encouraging customers to consider used items alongside new ones. This mainstream visibility has increased the reach and impact of their circular economy efforts.

---

[2] https://wornwear.patagonia.com/pages/trade-it-in

[3] https://wornwear.patagonia.com/collections/recrafted

[4] https://help.patagonia.com/s/article/Ironclad-Guarantee

4.6.3 Create Whole Product Solutions

Circular economy adoption is more compelling when presented as part of a holistic solution that addresses customers' broader needs. Creating whole-product solutions in a circular economy involves offering customers not just a product or service but a complete ecosystem that caters to all their needs around that solution. This ecosystem should include circular services, maintenance, education on circular practices, and integration assistance with existing systems and processes. By doing so, businesses can reduce the barriers to adoption, making the transition to circular economy practices more attractive and less risky for customers. The key to successfully crossing the chasm lies in recognizing the value of circular economy as a superior business model (see Sect. 9.3), not just an environmental imperative.

As businesses successfully navigate through the "chasm" and gain traction within the early majority, they may encounter what Moore calls the "tornado" phase. This phase is characterized by a period of mass market adoption, where the market recognizes the value of the new paradigm and rapidly moves to adopt it. This could manifest as a sudden surge in demand for circular products and services as more businesses and consumers become aware of and committed to circular practices' economic and environmental benefits.

To capitalize on the tornado, businesses must ensure their whole-product solutions (Fig. 4.6) are scalable and meet the increased demand, optimizing supply chains, enhancing production capabilities, and ensuring that circular support services are robust enough to handle the influx of inquiries and service requests.

In the wake of the tornado, market leaders will emerge—these are the "800-pound Gorillas" of the circular economy space. These dominant players have successfully scaled their operations, established strong brand recognition, and have a significant market share. Businesses aiming to become or compete with the 800-pound Gorilla must have a comprehensive product solution and continuously innovate and improve their offerings to maintain a competitive edge, involving investing in new technologies and digitization, exploring new business models within the circular economy framework, or expanding the range of services offered to ensure customers have a seamless, end-to-end experience.

Creating whole-product solutions in the circular economy is about providing a comprehensive, customer-centric experience that addresses all aspects of the product and service lifecycle. As businesses progress through the tornado phase, scalability and the ability to meet growing demand become paramount. Ultimately, the goal is to either become the 800-pound Gorilla in the circular economy space or develop robust competitive strategies to thrive alongside such dominant players, continually innovating and enhancing the whole-product solution to sustain long-term growth and success.

4.7 Capability Map for Redesign and Reinvent

Manufacturers must develop capabilities across various dimensions to successfully integrate redesign and reinvent principles in alignment with the circular economy. Based on the content in this chapter, a capability map to guide manufacturers through this transformation is presented in Fig. 4.7.

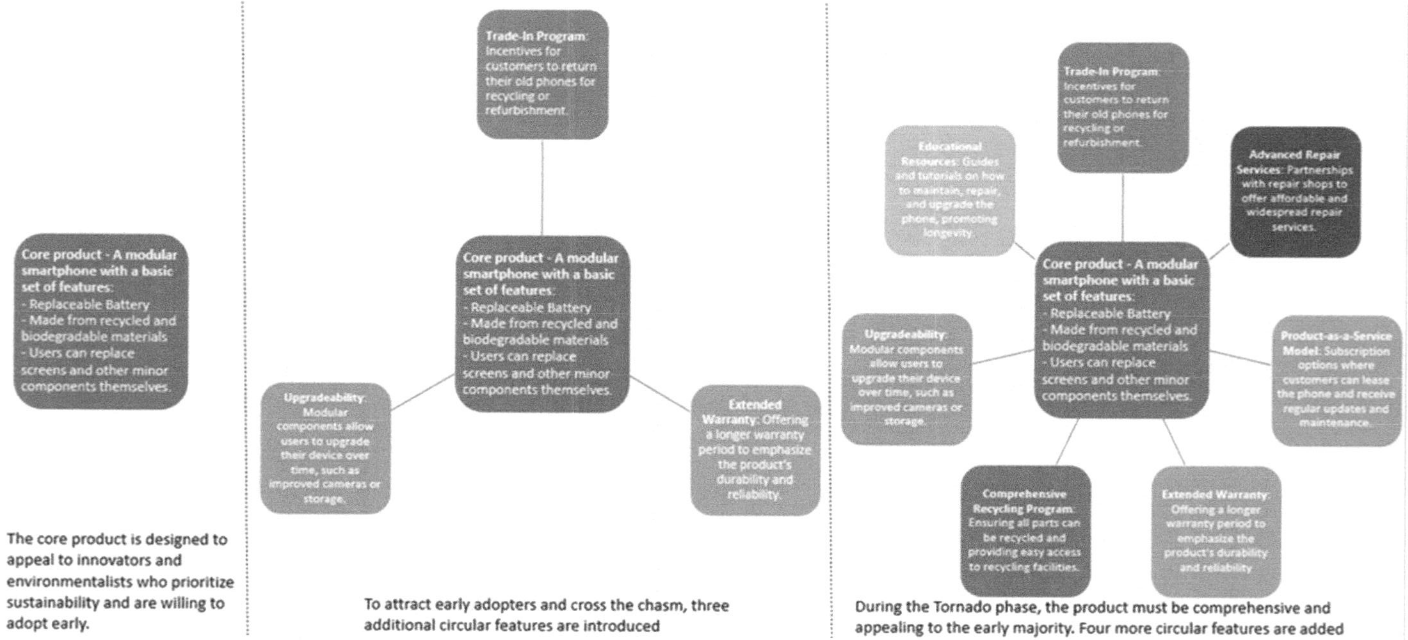

Fig. 4.6 The whole product

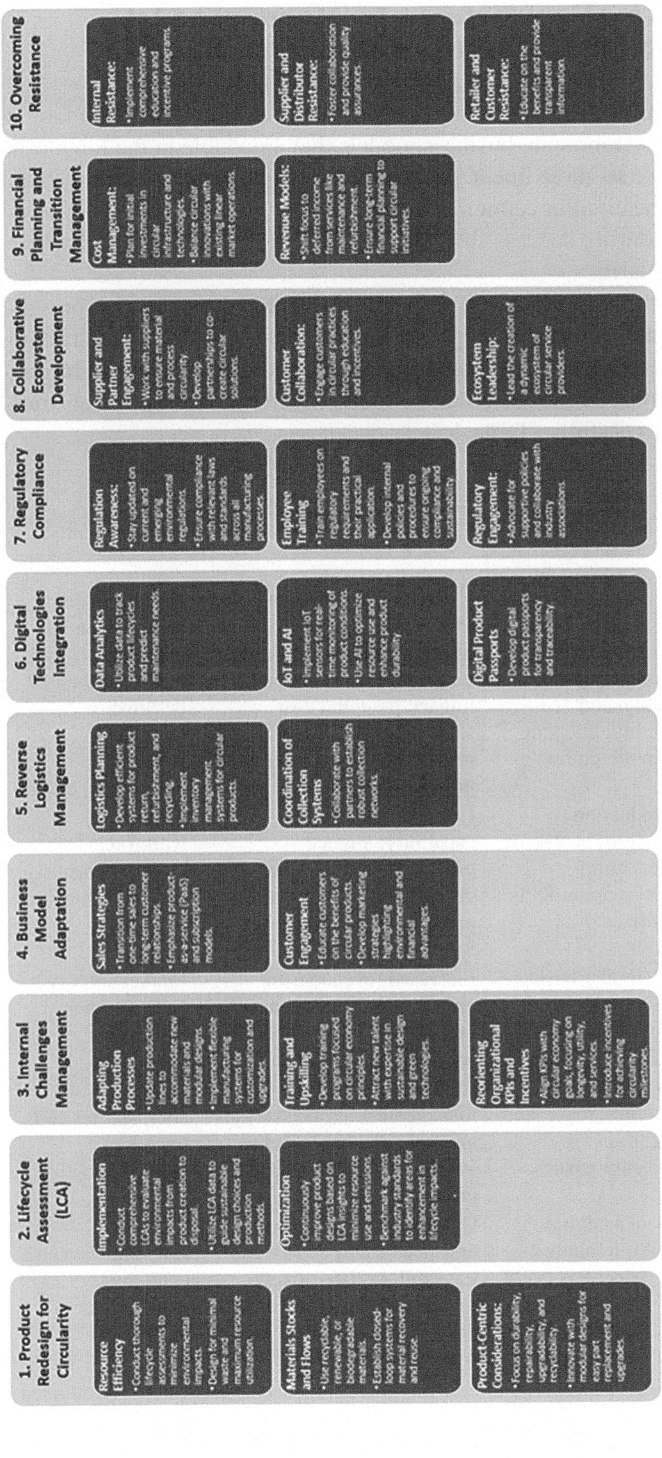

Fig. 4.7 Capability map for redesign and reinvent

4.8 A Checklist for Manufacturers to Integrate the 1st R—Redesign and Reinvent—into Their Strategies

The circular economy transition represents more than an environmental mandate; it is a strategic gateway to embracing business models that are viable in the long term and potentially superior to their linear predecessors. By judiciously timing their move and leveraging the circular economy's intrinsic benefits, businesses can position themselves for enduring success in a rapidly evolving landscape to prioritize sustainability and circularity.

The following chapters will delve into the tasks outlined in this checklist, providing detailed guidance and actionable steps. However, it would be best to start considering the tasks to prepare for the circular transformation. This overview highlights the key elements that must be integrated into a manufacturer's strategy to transition to circular practices successfully (Table 4.3).

Table 4.3 A checklist for manufacturers to integrate the 1st R—redesign and reinvent—into their strategies

Task	Methodology	Expected outcome	Risk mitigation
Redesign products for circularity	Implement lifecycle assessment (LCA); design for adaptability, repairability, and upgradability; integrate ecodesign principles	Products that are easier to repair, reuse, and recycle; minimized environmental impact; potential cost savings from reduced resource use; and extended product lifecycles	Avoid potential disruption Address potential design cost increases
Address internal challenges	Adapt production processes; retrain staff on circular economy principles; reorient KPIs and incentives	Enhanced workforce capability; aligned organizational goals with circular practices; improved operational efficiency and long-term cost savings	Prepare the workforce Reduce transition costs and internal resistance
Adopt circular business models	Develop circular business models and focus on long-term customer relationships and services	Increased revenue from circular services; stronger customer loyalty; stable and recurring income streams	Market entry risks and customer adoption challenges
Manage reverse logistics	Develop systems for product return, reuse, and recycling; train employees in logistics planning	Efficient product lifecycle management, reduced waste, and potential new revenue streams from refurbished products	Logistical complexities and tracking challenges
Leverage digital technologies	Utilize data analytics, IoT, and AI; implement Digital Product Passports	Optimized resource use; enhanced transparency and traceability; data-driven decision-making; increased operational efficiency and cost savings	Capturing real-time data and extracting meaning out of these data

(continued)

Table 4.3 (continued)

Task	Methodology	Expected outcome	Risk mitigation
Ensure regulatory compliance	Stay updated on environmental regulations; ensure compliance with design, manufacturing, and supply chain	Reduced legal risks; improved sustainability; avoidance of fines and penalties	Non-compliance with evolving regulations
Invest in training and upskilling	Assess current workforce capabilities; develop targeted training programs; attract new talent	A workforce with the necessary skills for circular economy transition, increased innovation and productivity, and long-term economic benefits	Skill gaps and talent retention challenges
Foster a collaborative ecosystem	Engage suppliers, partners, and customers; promote material, product, and data flow in closed loops	Minimization of waste; maximization of resource value; strengthened partnerships; economic benefits from improved resource efficiency and shared value creation	Collaboration complexities and alignment of goals among partner
Carefully Plan Financing	Develop a financial roadmap, assess initial investments, deferred income, and long-term profitability, and secure funding to bridge the gap.	Adequate resources to support circular transformation; minimized financial disruption; a balanced transition strategy.	Mitigate risks of cash flow disruptions by aligning investments with revenue timelines; prioritize scalable pilots

References

Apple. (2021). *Product Environmental Report - iPhone 13*. From https://www.apple.com/environment/pdf/products/iphone/iPhone_13_PER_Sept2021.pdf

European Commission. (2022). *Green Deal: New proposals to make sustainable products the norm and boost Europe's resource independence*. From https://ec.europa.eu/commission/presscorner/detail/en/ip_22_2013

IKEA. (2024). *Our circular agenda*. From https://www.ikea.com/global/en/our-business/people-planet/our-circular-agenda/

Kumar, V. (2022). *Customer relationship management: Concept, strategy, and tools*. Springer.

Moore, G. (2014). *Crossing the Chasm: Marketing and selling high-tech products to mainstream customers*. HarperCollins.

Patagonia. (2024, 06). *Worn Wear*. From https://eu.patagonia.com/gb/en/wornwear/

Pidun, U., Reeves, M., & Zoletnik, B. (2021, 10). BCG's series on Business Ecosystems. From BCG: https://www.bcg.com/publications/2021/how-to-succeed-as-a-business-ecosystem-contributor

Robson, G. (2021, 12). *Pushing the boundaries of sustainable PC design: Concept Luna*. From Dell: https://www.dell.com/en-us/blog/pushing-the-boundaries-of-sustainable-pc-design-concept-luna/

Shevchenko, T., & Cluzel, F. (2023). *A circular product design toolkit: Methodologial background, basic principles and building blocks*. in Proceedings of the International Conference on Engineering Design (ICED23), Bordeaux, France, 24–28 July 2023. DOI:10.1017/pds.2023.7

The White House. (2022). *The CHIPS and science act: Strengthening American semiconductor research, development, and manufacturing*. From https://www.whitehouse.gov/briefing-room/statements-releases/2022/07/29/fact-sheet-chips-and-science-act/

2nd R – Redistribute: Maximizing Product Utility

5

Abstract

This chapter explores the pivotal role of redistribution in the circular economy, emphasizing the extension of product lifecycles through recommerce and reuse. Manufacturers are urged to move beyond traditional "sell and forget" models, unlocking new revenue streams by maximizing the utility of existing products. This chapter delves into innovative business models, including product as a service (PaaS) and partnerships with P2P sharing platforms, facilitating effective redistribution.

Key messages include embracing digital transformation for managing reused products, fostering collaboration with partners and suppliers, and educating customers about the benefits of reuse. Redistribution challenges manufacturers to rethink product design, marketing, and support, ultimately transforming their role in the economy from mere sellers to stewards of continuous value creation. By adopting these practices, manufacturers gain a competitive advantage by aligning with the growing demand for eco-friendly products.

The chapter highlights the importance of digital platforms for product sharing and recommerce and the need for efficient logistics to handle returned goods. Furthermore, it underscores the necessity of customer engagement and education to foster participation in the circular economy. A detailed capability map guides manufacturers in adopting redistribution models. Through strategic redistribution, manufacturers can reduce waste, enhance resource efficiency, and contribute to a more sustainable economic model, ensuring long-term viability and success in an evolving market landscape.

H. H. Jensen, *Circular Economy Opportunities and Pathways for Manufacturers*, Future of Business and Finance, https://doi.org/10.1007/978-3-031-75279-7_5

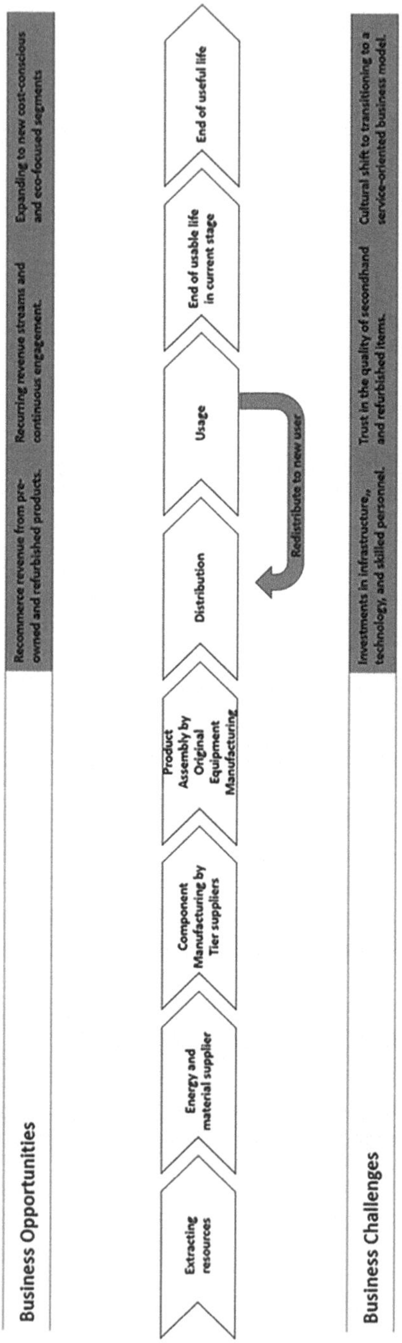

Fig. 5.1 Redistribution's placement in circular flow (Figure 1.6) and three significant business opportunities and challenges

Key Messages

- *Embracing the Circular Economy:* Redistribution emphasizes extending product lifecycles through recommerce and reuse.
- *Creating Value from Existing Products:* Focus on maximizing the utility of existing products to unlock new revenue streams and opportunities by ensuring efficient redistribution.
- *Challenging the "Sell and Forget" Paradigm:* Move away from traditional business models, and find ways to derive value from products throughout their lifecycle.
- *Innovative Business Models:* Explore and adopt models like product as a service (PaaS) and partnerships with P2P sharing platforms to facilitate redistribution effectively.
- *Digital Transformation:* Implement digital platforms for product sharing and recommerce and systems for efficiently managing reused and redistributed products.
- *Collaboration and Ecosystem Engagement:* Redistribution success requires active collaboration with partners, suppliers, and third-party service providers across the business ecosystem.
- *Customer Engagement and Education:* Educate customers about the benefits of reuse and recommerce to foster participation in the circular economy.
- *Sustainability and Competitive Advantage:* Adopting circular economy principles through redistribution contributes to sustainability and offers a competitive advantage by aligning with customer demand for eco-friendly products.

The 2nd R—Redistribute—covers areas like recommerce, reuse, product as a service, and the sharing economy. It represents a shift for manufacturers accustomed to the linear economy's "sell and forget" model, which centers profits at the initial point of sale, often marking the end of the manufacturer's involvement with the product's lifecycle. The circular economy's core principle is upending this traditional approach, urging manufacturers to tap into the revenue potential of redistribution (Fig. 5.1).

Redistribute necessitates reevaluating product design, marketing, and support. It moves from a model that emphasizes singular transactions to one that values ongoing engagement with products and value chain customers. This approach builds products for longevity, multiple usage cycles, and potential redistribution in various forms.

The move toward redistribution requires manufacturers to forge a deeper relationship with their products and customers. It's about recognizing that the product's journey doesn't end at the sale but transforms into a cycle of continuous value creation. This paradigm shift is both a challenge and an opportunity for manufacturers to redefine their role in the modern economy.

For manufacturers, adapting to this shift means exploring strategies to generate revenue beyond the initial sale. It involves developing partnerships within the circular ecosystem to facilitate product returns, resale, or repurposing, ensuring their products remain attractive and valuable in secondary markets.

Section 11.3 details the process steps for the various redistribution business models.

5.1 Recommerce

Recommerce, also known as reverse commerce, involves selling previously owned products. It is a strategy that includes returned, refurbished, or secondhand items. This section will discuss the decisions required for manufacturers considering entering the recommerce market. We will weigh the pros and cons of creating their recommerce site, using a third party, or letting the market operate independently. Additionally, we will explore opportunities for manufacturers to add value to recommerced items.

5.1.1 Strategic Decisions in Recommerce

Manufacturers must determine the best method for reselling returned, used, or refurbished products. This decision impacts operational processes, customer engagement, and brand image control. Manufacturers may evaluate three primary strategies: building their recommerce site, partnering with a third-party vendor, or adopting a market-driven approach where the resale market operates independently. Each strategy has advantages and disadvantages, and the choice depends on factors such as resource availability, brand management priorities, and market conditions.

5.1.1.1 Own Recommerce Site

Establishing a physical or virtual recommerce site gives manufacturers control over every aspect of the sales process. This approach allows them to create a tailored customer experience and maintain their branding consistently across all interactions. One of the benefits is the ability to directly engage with end-users, facilitating enhanced data collection and improved customer relationship management, helping manufacturers better understand and respond to customer needs and preferences.

However, this level of control and customization comes with its own challenges. Establishing and maintaining a recommerce site requires an initial investment. Manufacturers must set up and maintain a digital or physical infrastructure that effectively supports sales and customer interactions. The digital and physical infrastructure often must work together to create an optimal recommerce experience. Additionally, this strategy involves operational complexities that span various business functions, from logistics to customer service, efficiently managing returns and ensuring that the quality of resold items meets customer expectations from both a quality and a sustainability point of view. The platform must continuously be updated and improved to keep up with technology and customer expectations, requiring ongoing investments in technology and skilled personnel to manage operations efficiently.

While an own recommerce site offers control over the recommerce process and can improve customer engagement, it demands a financial and operational commitment. Manufacturers considering this option must prepare to invest the necessary resources to build and sustain a robust physical and/or online sales platform.

Example 5.1 IKEA's Buy Back & Resell program

IKEA has a Buy Back and Resell program.[1] The program starts with the online buyback estimator tool. This tool lets customers input details about their used furniture and get an estimated buyback value. This upfront financial incentive gives an additional touch point with the customer.

Once the buyback value is determined, customers prepare their items for return by ensuring the furniture is clean, fully assembled, and in good condition. This reduces IKEA's workload when processing the returned furniture.

Upon returning the furniture to the store, a co-worker will compare the furniture's condition to the estimate. If the condition differs, the quoted buyback price might be adjusted. Customers receive a voucher for the buyback amount, which can be used for future purchases at IKEA. The returned items are then inspected and resold in their As-Is section, creating a new source of revenue from products that might otherwise have been discarded (IKEA, 2023).

In 2023, IKEA gave more than 45.1 million products a second life, with 36.1 million products resold via the As-Is areas and more than 9 million repacked and sold in other areas (Ingka Group, 2023).

5.1.1.2 Using a Third Party

Manufacturers can use third-party platforms like eBay, Amazon, or specialized recommerce sites to reduce operational burdens. These platforms have the advantage of preexisting infrastructure, meaning that the platform handles much of the logistical work and customer interaction. By taking advantage of established networks, manufacturers can avoid the upfront costs associated with setting up their recommerce sites and sell returned, refurbished, or secondhand goods more quickly and cost-effectively.

[1] https://www.ikea.com/gb/en/customer-service/services/buy-back/

However, there are some downsides to using third-party platforms. One of the main disadvantages is the reduced control over the customer experience. Manufacturers are subject to the rules and interface designed by another company, which can limit how they present their products and engage with customers. This can lead to a customer experience that aligns differently with the manufacturer's brand image or service standards. Additionally, the financial returns from using third-party platforms may be lower due to platform fees and competitive pricing pressures.

Manufacturers depend on the third party's rules, fees, and data-sharing policies. The platform's terms of service may constrain manufacturers and limit their access to customer data, which is used to improve products and customer service. This dependence can make manufacturers vulnerable, as platform policy or fee structure changes could negatively impact their recommerce business.

While a third-party platform can provide easy access to an established customer base and reduce operational costs, it also comes with control, profitability, and independence trade-offs.

5.1.1.3 Letting the Market Decide

Manufacturers often let the market decide regarding recommerce, as it requires little investment and involvement. This approach allows end-users and independent resellers to drive the secondary market independently. However, it comes with risks and disadvantages. The most prominent concern is the lack of control over branding and the customer experience. When transactions are handled by third parties or through informal resale channels, manufacturers cannot ensure that the customer experience aligns with their brand values and quality standards.

Example 5.2 Habitat for Humanity's ReStores sell new and gently used products

Habitat for Humanity's ReStores[2] are nonprofit home improvement stores and donation centers that sell new and gently used furniture, appliances, home accessories, building materials, and more to the public at a fraction of the retail price. The proceeds from ReStore sales help Habitat for Humanity fund the construction of affordable homes for families in need (Habitat for Humanity, 2023).

By not participating directly in the recommerce market, manufacturers forgo potential revenue opportunities and lose a valuable touch point with customers that could help build long-term relationships, gather end-user insights, and drive repeat business. Moreover, manufacturers cannot monitor or rectify reputation issues from poor-quality resales.

[2] https://www.habitat.org/restores

While letting the market handle recommerce activities minimizes upfront investment and involvement, it also means forgoing control over important aspects of the customer experience and potentially exposing the brand to reputation risks. Therefore, manufacturers must consider whether the reduced costs and complexities justify the possible long-term impacts on brand integrity and customer loyalty.

5.1.2 Adding Value to Recommerced Products

Manufacturers can use the recommerce market to improve the appeal and value of recommerced products by focusing on additional services and assurances.

5.1.2.1 Transferable Warranty Rights

One approach is offering an extended warranty with transferable warranty rights. Customers can transfer the warranty to a new owner for a fee when selling a recommerced product. This feature reassures buyers that the manufacturer fully backs the quality and reliability of these items, just as they would with new products.

The ability to transfer warranty rights adds value to the recommerced item, alleviating buyers' concerns about the longevity and dependability of pre-owned products. This makes the investment more appealing and reduces the perceived risk of purchasing recommerced items.

To make things easier for customers and smooth out the process, it's best to digitally manage the transfer of warranty rights (Sect. 10.5). This way, the transition is automatic and efficient, requiring minimal effort from the customer. It also provides immediate reassurance that their newly purchased product is still under warranty.

Example 5.3 Apple's Certified Refurbished

Programs like Apple's Certified Refurbished[3] take previously owned products and have Apple's technicians meticulously test, clean, and repair the devices to ensure they meet the same functional standards as new products. Components that don't pass the tests are replaced with genuine Apple parts.

All certified refurbished products, like new Apple products, have a 1-year warranty. This warranty covers repairs and service, giving customers confidence in the quality and reliability of their purchase. Additionally, customers have the option to purchase AppleCare for extended coverage (Apple Inc. 2023).

5.1.2.2 Validation of Originality

Ensuring authenticity is an issue in the recommerce market, particularly for high-value items. To add value, manufacturers can provide a certificate or guarantee of authenticity with each sale, building trust and giving customers confidence that they are purchasing genuine products from either the maker or a certified seller.

[3] https://www.apple.com/shop/refurbished

To achieve this, manufacturers can employ various modern digital tools such as QR codes or NFC tags attached to the product or its packaging. When scanned, these digital verification tools can direct customers to a validation page confirming the product's details and authenticity.

A Certificate of Authenticity (CoA) can accompany each recommerced item, detailing its origin, specifications, and any refurbishment history. This certificate should include a unique identifier or serial number that customers can verify via the manufacturer's website.

Example 5.4 Cisco Refresh

Cisco, a global leader in networking solutions, offers a refurbishment program called Cisco Refresh. Each product is tested, updated with proprietary firmware and hardware, and has the same warranty and support as new products (Cisco, 2024).

To ensure the authenticity of its products and combat counterfeit and pirated goods, Cisco employs several authentication tools (Cisco Legal, 2024):

Carton Security Label: Found overlapping the edge of the carton's white label

Chassis Security Labels: Located on selective chassis products

PCBA Security Label: Holographic and other security features on most line cards and modules' printed circuit board assemblies

Module Security Label: Holographic security indicators on most optical transceivers and high-speed cable assemblies

5.1.2.3 Quality Assurance

Improving quality assurance practices can make recommerced products more appealing to potential buyers. Manufacturers can adopt strict quality checks and refurbishment processes. By promoting these high-quality assurance standards, manufacturers can assure potential buyers of the quality and performance of recommerce products. This positions these items as comparable to new ones regarding functionality and reliability.

Example 5.5 John Deere offers a Certified Pre-Owned (CPO) program

John Deere, a manufacturer of agricultural and construction equipment, offers a Certified Pre-Owned (CPO) program in the United States and Canada.[4] This program ensures that customers have access to high-quality, field-ready used machinery.

(continued)

[4] https://www.deere.com/en/agriculture/used-equipment/

Each piece of equipment undergoes a meticulous inspection process. Tractors have over 170 inspection points, while self-propelled sprayers and combines have more than 200. As part of the program, fluid is tested, reviewed, and approved.

Certified pre-owned equipment comes with a 1-year PowerGard Protection Plan, which covers major components and provides benefits similar to those of new machinery (John Deere, 2023).

5.1.2.4 Customer Support

Manufacturers can offer services designed for the recommerce segment. These services may include a dedicated help desk, troubleshooting assistance, and easy access to repair and maintenance services. Providing exceptional customer service improves the overall customer experience and helps build long-lasting relationships with customers, leading to repeat business and positive word-of-mouth referrals.

5.1.2.5 Exclusive Offers

Offering exclusive deals to customers who choose recommerce products can enhance their value proposition. Such deals may comprise discounts on future purchases, priority access to new products, or preferential pricing on bundled offers. These benefits help customers feel appreciated and can boost the perceived value of buying recommerce products.

Example 5.6 Patagonia's Worn Wear program offers store credit for trade-ins

The fashion sector is leveraging recommerce to address inventory challenges and tap into consumer demand for sustainable options. Patagonia's Worn Wear[5] program offers store credit for trade-ins. These items are then cleaned, repaired, and sold at a lower price, transforming used gear into a valuable asset, fostering customer loyalty, and opening up a secondary market (Patagonia, 2023).

5.1.2.6 Loyalty Programs

Integrating recommerce customers into existing loyalty programs, or creating new programs specifically for this group, can promote loyalty and encourage further purchases. In addition to earning points on purchases, customers could also accumulate rewards for participating in sustainability initiatives such as recycling old products.

---

[5] WornWear.com

5.1.3 Recommerce of Modules

Section 4.1.2 introduced the concept of modularity in manufacturing. This concept enabled manufacturers to see their products as platforms for continuous innovation and customization, and through interchangeable modules, they can support multiple configurations and upgrades.

Manufacturers can use the product as a platform to establish recommerce marketplaces specifically for modules, allowing the buying and selling of used and refurbished modules. These markets would also provide a platform for releasing new modules compatible with existing products. Such a design would keep customers engaged throughout the product's extended lifecycle. Customers are encouraged to upgrade modules instead of purchasing new products, fostering brand loyalty and repeated interactions. Notice that the product as a platform can also be supported by the sharing economy (Sect. 5.2) and the product as a service (Sect. 5.4).

Manufacturers can use customer data and purchase history to recommend modules that proactively enhance the user's experience. For instance, if a user frequently takes photos in low-light conditions, the manufacturer could recommend a camera module with better low-light performance.

To ensure compatibility, manufacturers can offer personalized advice and compatibility checks. They can also recommend modules that fit specific products so customers purchase modules that improve their setup without compatibility issues.

A recommerce market for modules creates a new revenue stream for manufacturers. It allows them to profit from the sale of primary products and the ongoing sale of new and recommerced modules and accessories.

5.1.4 Manufacturers' Opportunities

Recommerce is a practice that allows manufacturers to extend the life of their products, unlock new revenue streams, and support sustainability efforts. Recommerce involves selling pre-owned and refurbished goods at lower prices, which appeals to cost-conscious customers. By doing so, manufacturers can generate additional revenue and enhance customer loyalty through programs that offer credits for returning used items or selling certified pre-owned products.

Recommerce is also an environmentally friendly practice as it reduces waste by refurbishing and reselling used products, thereby decreasing the volume of waste directed to landfills and reducing the environmental impact of new goods production.

However, several challenges are associated with engaging in recommerce. Setting up and managing recommerce operations involves complex and expensive tasks such as collecting, inspecting, repairing, and certifying items before reselling them. Consistent quality standards are crucial; failing to do so can harm the brand's reputation if refurbished products do not meet the original specifications. Manufacturers must overcome customer skepticism about the quality and reliability of pre-owned or refurbished items to make recommerce a viable option.

Regulatory and compliance issues also pose challenges, as recommerce must adhere to various local and international regulations concerning warranties, customer rights, and product safety, which can vary between regions. Furthermore, pricing strategies for refurbished products need careful consideration to ensure they are attractive to buyers while still covering costs and generating profits without undercutting new product sales.

Manufacturers should focus on successfully integrating recommerce into their business models. They must develop robust processes to handle product returns and prepare them for resale. Educating customers about the benefits and quality of refurbished products can help shift perceptions and build trust.

Example 5.7 Toyota's Mechacomi

Toyota has launched a platform called Mechacomi[6] to change how auto repair shops manage their equipment needs. This initiative promotes a more sustainable and economically efficient approach by enabling workshops to trade and reuse specialized tools.

One common issue auto repair garages face is the accumulation of expensive, specialized equipment that is not required regularly. By encouraging a system where tools can be bought and sold, Toyota is helping to reduce the high capital costs typically associated with outfitting and updating repair shops. The platform helps to maintain a lean inventory, ensuring that tools are utilized to their fullest potential.

In addition, the complexity of servicing modern vehicles has increased with the introduction of computerized systems and electric drivetrains, necessitating a broader range of expensive equipment. Mechacomi facilitates easier access to necessary tools without significant upfront investment and promotes a shift in the industry from a "discard" to a "reuse" mindset (Toyota, 2023).

5.2 The Sharing Economy: Access Over Ownership

The sharing economy is a socio-economic system that uses technology to share goods, services, and resources among people and organizations. Unlike traditional models that focus on individual ownership, this approach emphasizes access over ownership, maximizing the use of each item and reducing the need for new products.

This model challenges traditional consumption habits and calls for durable, maintainable, and adaptable shared-use products. It also leads to new business models and closer customer interactions, requiring manufacturers to innovate and adapt to stay competitive.

[6] https://mechacomi.site/

Peer-to-peer (P2P) platforms like Airbnb and Uber are at the heart of the sharing economy. These digital marketplaces use the Internet and mobile technology to connect people with underused assets (such as homes, cars, or equipment) with those needing them. P2P platforms have transformed traditional ideas of ownership and access by making it easy for anyone to offer or obtain resources.

The rise of P2P platforms offers manufacturers opportunities and decisions. One strategy is creating branded P2P platforms tailored to their products and customers. This approach opens new revenue streams and allows manufacturers to control the customer experience, gain direct insights from users, and ensure their products are used correctly and maintained properly in the sharing economy.

On the other hand, manufacturers may become partners in existing P2P platforms, integrating their products into well-established sharing ecosystems. This route can provide immediate access to a broad user base and reduce the upfront investment of developing a new platform from scratch.

Example 5.8 Caterpillar's EquipmentShare[7]

Caterpillar partners with EquipmentShare, a platform that enables the sharing of construction equipment among contractors. This collaboration ensures that Caterpillar's machinery is utilized more efficiently across projects, reducing idle time and promoting a more sustainable use of resources.

Manufacturers can generate income by offering additional services like warranty and maintenance on top of the sharing, acknowledging that most income from sharing accrues to the platform owner. This model allows manufacturers to tap into new revenue streams while leveraging the platform's reach and capabilities.

To get data to refine their offerings and align more closely with market demands, manufacturers should secure agreements with P2P platforms to receive detailed information on their products, providing valuable insights into usage patterns, user preferences, and potential areas for product improvement.

5.2.1 Industrial Asset Sharing

The sharing economy, commonly known for its role in consumer goods and services, also plays a part in the industrial sector by enabling the sharing of industrial assets. This practice, known as Industrial Asset Sharing, helps manufacturers to cut costs, boost operational efficiency, and improve the use of costly equipment, machinery, and infrastructure.

[7] https://www.equipmentshare.com/

Example 5.9 John Deere MachineFinder

John Deere MachineFinder[8]: While primarily a marketplace for used equipment, John Deere facilitates a network where customers can list their machinery for resale or rent, indirectly promoting a peer-to-peer sharing system.

Our discussion includes both consumer-focused and industry-focused sharing models. However, it's important to note that industrial sharing can have unique features. For example, using a shared asset might require the user to relocate their production activities to the asset's location. This introduces logistical complexity, which affects how to share and utilize these assets in the industrial context.

Example 5.10 FLEXE's warehousing solution

FLEXE's warehousing solution[9] allows companies to share unused warehouse space and acts as a platform that connects companies with excess warehouse space to companies needing on-demand storage. Companies can avoid the high costs of fixed leases and only pay for the space they need when they need it, making it particularly valuable for seasonal businesses or those with fluctuating inventory levels (FLEXE, 2023).

5.2.2 Opportunities with the Sharing Economy

The sharing economy brings new opportunities for manufacturers by redefining traditional business models and opening up new avenues for growth and innovation. Manufacturers can leverage the sharing economy to enhance their product design, offer services rather than just products, improve sustainability and operational efficiency, expand their market presence, reduce inventory and production costs, and position themselves as industry innovators. Incorporating sharing economy models allows manufacturers to rethink how they design and sell products, engage with customers, manage resources, and position themselves.

To take advantage of the sharing economy, manufacturers must create modular, durable, and easily repairable products that can withstand repeated use by multiple users. They should also explore transforming the traditional transactional relationship with customers into a more engaged and ongoing one, enabling direct contact with their products' end-users and providing insights into product performance, usage patterns, and emerging market needs. This transition to offering services can open up continuous revenue streams and enable feedback, leading to product enhancements and new offerings that closely align with customer expectations.

[8] https://www.machinefinder.com/

[9] https://www.flexe.com/

By maximizing the utilization of each product and reducing periods of idleness, manufacturers can conserve resources and mitigate environmental impact. The sharing economy can also open new markets by making products more accessible to a broader audience. Products that may have been too expensive for specific customers to own outright can become accessible through sharing models, allowing manufacturers to tap into previously untapped segments. This increased accessibility can drive demand and expand the manufacturer's market presence.

By focusing on shared usage and service models, manufacturers can potentially reduce the costs of holding extensive inventories and continuous production. Lower inventory levels mean reduced storage costs and less capital in unsold goods. Furthermore, optimizing production based on actual usage data and demand from sharing platforms can lead to more efficient manufacturing processes and reduced waste.

Example 5.11 BMW's SHARE NOW

BMW's SHARE NOW[10] is a car-sharing service developed by BMW in collaboration with Daimler AG. It operates in numerous cities across Europe and North America, offering users the convenience of accessing a fleet of vehicles on-demand through a mobile app.

BMW has designed its SHARE NOW fleet with robust, easy-to-maintain vehicles, ensuring longevity and consistent performance.

BMW's ability to monitor vehicle usage and performance through digital platforms allows for predictive maintenance, further enhancing operational efficiency.

This approach has enabled BMW to tap into a market segment that values flexibility and cost-efficiency over ownership, expanding its market presence and customer base and offering a pathway to continuous revenue stream.

The program's mobile app collects user preferences, trip patterns, and vehicle performance data. This information is invaluable for ongoing product development and service optimization, ensuring that BMW can continuously enhance its offerings to meet evolving customer expectations.

5.2.3 Challenges

One of the most significant challenges is shifting from a product-centric approach to a service-oriented mindset. This transformation demands investments in new technologies and a complete reconfiguration of supply chain logistics. It also requires a cultural shift within organizations to prioritize long-term customer engagement and sustainable practices over the conventional focus on immediate product sales. This change touches every aspect of the business, from product design and marketing to sales and after-sales support.

The backbone of a sharing economy model is a robust digital infrastructure capable of managing shared assets, processing bookings, monitoring product usage, and

[10] https://www.share-now.com/

fostering customer relationships. Manufacturers must invest in or develop specialized digital platforms and applications that facilitate the seamless sharing of products.

Maintaining the quality and safety of products in a sharing model is imperative, as multiple users use products over extended periods. This challenge necessitates the establishment of quality control checks and efficient maintenance and repair processes. Manufacturers must ensure that shared products remain in optimal condition, which can involve frequent servicing and complex logistics for retrieving, repairing, and redeploying assets. Balancing these requirements with the need to keep operational costs manageable is a delicate task.

Manufacturers venturing into service-based offerings must navigate regulatory requirements and legal considerations, including compliance with safety standards, liability issues, and consumer protection laws, which can vary across different markets and jurisdictions. Staying abreast of these regulations and ensuring full compliance can be challenging.

Encouraging end-users to embrace shared products and services over traditional ownership models requires a shift in mindset. Manufacturers must invest in education and marketing to promote the benefits of the sharing economy, such as cost savings, flexibility, and environmental sustainability. Overcoming ingrained habits and perceptions about ownership versus access is a gradual process that demands consistent and effective communication.

In addressing these challenges, manufacturers must adopt a strategic and holistic approach, leveraging technology, rethinking internal processes, and engaging with consumers and other stakeholders.

5.2.4 Identifying Products Suitable for Sharing

By evaluating products based on their frequency of use and overall value, businesses can better understand which items are likely to succeed in a shared model (Table 5.1).

5.3 Industrial Symbiosis/Eco-industrial Parks

Industrial symbiosis or eco-industrial parks (EIPs) emphasize sharing valuable resources such as energy, water, materials, and by-products between industries. This approach aims to transform waste from one manufacturing process into valuable resources for another process (Fig. 5.2).

The mechanics of industrial symbiosis involve a network of diverse organizations that work together to optimize resource use. This system requires a coordinated approach in which one company's waste is another company's raw material. For example, heat generated from one process might power another process in a nearby facility.

Table 5.1 Characteristics and strategies for product sharing

	Low value	High value
High frequency of use	*Mass sharing:* Commonly used products that are lower in value. Perfect for widespread sharing models *Strategy:* Emphasize accessibility and convenience. These are typically low-cost items that can be scaled easily in large urban areas Bicycles in citywide bike-sharing programs	*Premium sharing:* Involves highly valuable and frequently used products. It is ideal for high-end shared services where quality and availability are critical *Strategy:* Focus on offering high-quality service with excellent maintenance. This quadrant often involves high investment in product care and customer service to maintain trust Luxury cars in a high-end car-sharing service
Low frequency of use	*Niche sharing:* Infrequently used and low-value items. These products are not typically profitable for widespread sharing models but can find a market in specialized niches *Strategy:* Identify specific groups or communities that need these items occasionally but might not afford or desire to own them Camping gear for city dwellers who rarely escape to nature	*Exclusive rental:* Rarely used products that are high in value. Suitable for rental models where the frequency of use does not justify the cost of ownership *Strategy:* Market to niche audiences looking for occasional access without the total purchase price. Provide high-quality options for temporary use Designer dresses or tuxedos for rent

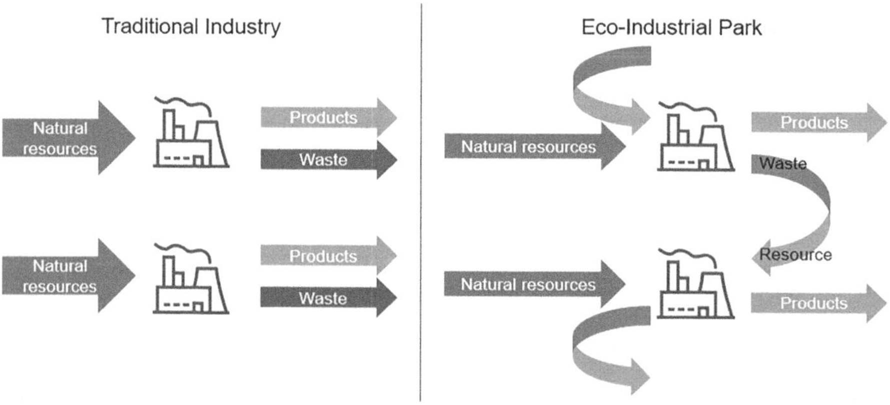

Fig. 5.2 Traditional industries vs. eco-industrial parks. (Based on Tao et al. (2015))

However, setting up industrial symbiosis networks can be challenging due to technical, regulatory, economic, and cultural barriers. Identifying and connecting complementary industrial processes is complex and requires innovative technological solutions. Different industries often face strict regulations, which can complicate the reuse of materials. Initial investments for the infrastructure needed to facilitate symbiosis can also be significant and risky. Additionally, companies often operate in isolation and are unaccustomed to sharing operational details with potential competitors, which can hinder symbiotic relationships.

Despite these challenges, industrial symbiosis presents numerous opportunities, such as reduced operational costs, environmental benefits, innovation, competitive advantage, and economic development. Successful implementation of symbiotic strategies can reduce companies' raw material and disposal costs. It can also reduce environmental impact by minimizing waste and conserving raw materials and energy. Regions can enhance economic resilience by fostering collaborative networks and creating new business opportunities.

Several examples of industrial symbiosis exist, such as the Kalundborg Symbiosis in Denmark.[11] The symbiosis annually reduces environmental impact by using 4 million cubic meters of surface water instead of groundwater, recycling 62,000 tons of residual materials, and cutting 586,000 tons of CO2 emissions. Since 2015, the symbiosis has reduced CO2 emissions by 80%, achieving CO2 neutrality in the local energy supply (Kalundborg Symbiosi, 2024).

Industrial symbiosis encourages shifting from traditional waste disposal and independent manufacturing processes toward integrated and cooperative approaches.

5.3.1 A Framework for Eco-industrial Parks

The United Nations Industrial Development Organization (UNIDO), the World Bank Group, and the Deutsche Gesellschaft für Internationale Zusammenarbeit (GIZ) GmbH have created a framework for the development and implementation of eco-industrial parks (EIP). This framework guides the establishment of EIP that are economically viable, socially responsible, and environmentally sustainable (Tas et al., 2021).

The framework highlights several core areas of focus:

Environmental Sustainability: EIP aims to minimize environmental impact and promote efficient use of resources, including water and energy management, reduction of greenhouse gas emissions, and responsible waste management.

Economic Performance: Businesses in EIP can improve their financial performance by becoming more competitive and innovative. This is achieved through better infrastructure and services and by promoting company collaboration.

Social Inclusivity: The framework emphasizes social factors to enhance workers' living conditions and ensure that development benefits are shared equitably within communities.

Governance and Management: The framework advocates for proper governance structures to ensure EIP operates under transparent and fair rules, providing a stable and supportive environment for businesses to thrive.

---

[11] https://www.symbiosis.dk/

This framework guides policymakers, industrial park operators, and other stakeholders in developing EIP. It integrates sustainable development principles to achieve global economic, social, and environmental goals.

5.4 Product as a Service

Another redistribution model is the "product as a service" (PaaS) model. This approach transforms traditional product ownership models into service-oriented frameworks, where value is derived from the product itself and the service it provides. Figure 5.3 categorizes this approach into distinct service delivery models, illustrating the continuum from pure product to pure service.

At one end of the spectrum, the value is predominantly embedded in the physical product. These models focus on tangible goods, where the primary interaction is with the product itself. Conversely, at the opposite end, the value is predominantly in intangible services. These models emphasize service provision over the physical product, often resulting in higher customer engagement through continuous service delivery.

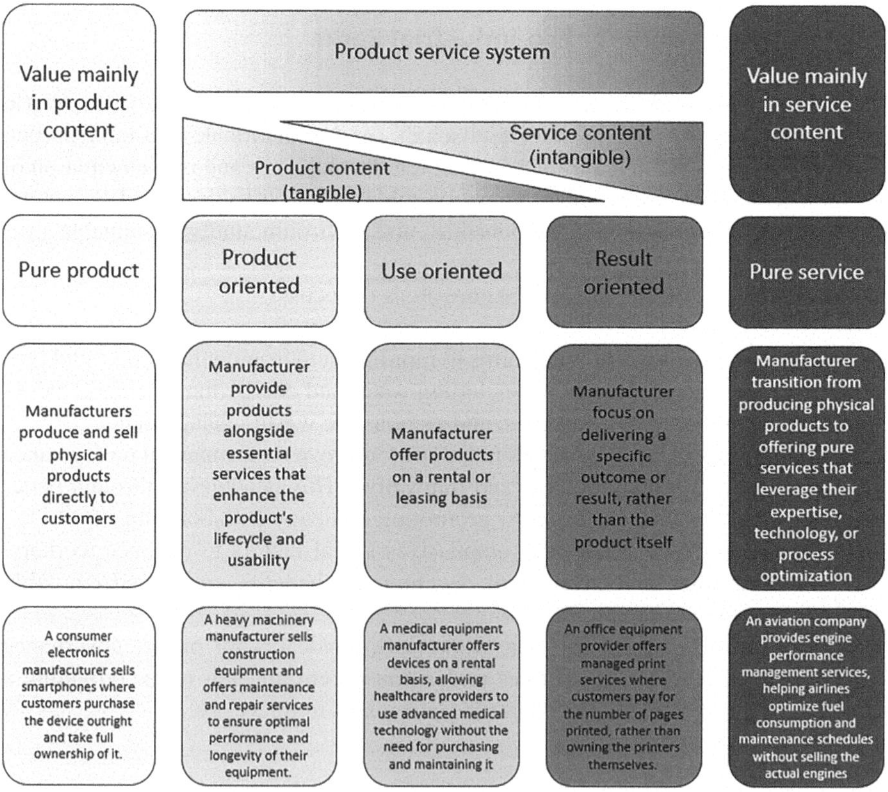

Fig. 5.3 Distinct service delivery models. (Based on Tukker and Tischner (2006))

In the pure product model, manufacturers produce and sell physical products directly to customers. The value proposition is centered entirely on the product's features, quality, and performance. Customers take ownership of the product and are responsible for its maintenance and end-of-life disposal.

In the product-oriented model, manufacturers provide products alongside essential services that enhance the product's lifecycle and usability. These services include maintenance contracts, extended warranties, and repair services.

In the use-oriented model, manufacturers offer products on a rental or leasing basis rather than selling them outright. Customers pay for the right to use the product for a specified period or frequency, reducing the burden of ownership. This model allows manufacturers to maintain product ownership, manage its lifecycle, and optimize resource utilization through multiple use cycles.

Example 5.12 Caterpillar's CAT Rental Store

Caterpillar's CAT Rental Store[12] allows businesses to rent rather than purchase equipment. It provides access to a wide array of Caterpillar equipment for any duration, which aids in managing project costs and addresses the underutilization of machinery (Caterpillar, 2023).

Example 5.13 Free2Move subscription model

Free2Move,[13] a subsidiary of Stellantis, offers a wide range of vehicles through a subscription model. Free2Move allows customers to access cars on demand without the long-term commitments or costs associated with traditional ownership. The service includes insurance, maintenance, and roadside assistance.

Customers book vehicles through the Free2Move app. Free2Move employs dynamic pricing models to offer competitive rates, adjusting prices based on demand, duration, and vehicle type to ensure affordability and accessibility. The app also constantly engages users, offering personalized recommendations, loyalty rewards, and customer support.

This model opens new revenue streams and market segments, including urban dwellers without private parking, environmentally conscious consumers, and those seeking temporary mobility solutions.

Maintaining a diverse and reliable vehicle fleet for Free2Move demands substantial investment and robust logistical coordination. Ensuring high service availability across varied geographic regions with different regulations presents operational challenges, requiring meticulous planning and execution (The Free2Move, 2023).

[12] https://www.cat.com/en_GB/products/rental/rental.html

[13] https://www.stellantis.com/en/brands/free2move

In the result-oriented model, manufacturers focus on delivering a specific outcome or result rather than the product itself. Customers pay for the performance or result achieved through product use. This model requires manufacturers to bundle their products with services that ensure the desired outcome, such as performance-based contracts, where payments are tied to achieving predefined performance metrics.

Example 5.14 Rolls-Royce's TotalCare

Rolls-Royce's TotalCare® program allows airlines to purchase engine power rather than physical engines.[14] Rolls-Royce maintains ownership of the engines and is responsible for maintenance and upgrades. Rolls-Royce is vested in producing long-lasting, easily maintainable engines, and airlines benefit from reduced upfront costs and predictable operating expenses (Rolls-Royce, 2023).

In the pure service model, manufacturers transition from producing physical products to offering pure services that leverage their expertise, technology, or process optimization capabilities. These services deliver value independently of any tangible product, focusing on outcomes such as increased efficiency, cost savings, or enhanced sustainability for their clients.

At the intersection of these models lies the Product Service System (PSS). This integrative approach combines both tangible product elements and intangible service elements to deliver comprehensive solutions that maximize customer value and minimize environmental impact. PSS encourages businesses to innovate in ways that decouple economic growth from resource consumption.

5.4.1 Distinction Between the Sharing Economy Model and the Product as a Service Model

From a manufacturer's perspective, the distinction between the sharing economy model and the product as a service (PaaS) model lies in the structure of ownership, customer engagement, and the flow of products and services. In sharing economy models, the emphasis is on maximizing the utility of a product by facilitating its access to multiple users, either through peer-to-peer platforms or by the manufacturer acting as a central hub for product sharing. This model promotes access over ownership, with products transitioning between users without a traditional sale. The sharing economy thrives on community-based platforms where users share, rent, or borrow products, extending the product lifecycle and reducing the demand for new products.

The PaaS model represents a more structured and direct approach where the manufacturer or a third-party provider retains ownership of the product and offers its utility

[14] https://www.rolls-royce.com/media/our-stories/discover/2017/totalcare.aspx

as a service to customers. This model can range from providing access to products (use-oriented service) to delivering specific outcomes without prescribing the product used (outcome-oriented service). PaaS is characterized by closer customer relationships, with manufacturers taking on a more active role in the product's maintenance, upgrade, and lifecycle management to ensure service quality and reliability.

For manufacturers, the key differences between these models are summarized in Table 5.2.

Table 5.2 Comparison of the key aspects of PaaS and sharing economy models from a manufacturer's perspective

Aspect	Product as a service (PaaS)	Sharing economy
Ownership and control	Manufacturers or third-party providers retain ownership and control, managing the product throughout its lifecycle	Ownership and control are more fluid. A platform or marketplace facilitates sharing, but ownership typically remains with the individual or entity that owns the asset
Revenue generation	Revenue is generated through service contracts or subscriptions, which provide continuous and predictable income over the product's service life	Revenue is generated through fees for access or usage, potentially involving multiple parties and offering less predictable income
Relationship dynamics	It involves direct, ongoing relationships between manufacturers or third-party providers and customers, focusing on service provision and customer satisfaction	It relies on platform-mediated relationships between users, with the manufacturer as a potential facilitator
Product design requirements	Requires products designed for durability, maintainability, and serviceability due to the manufacturer's responsibility for product performance	While durability is valued, the emphasis is on maximizing product usage among multiple users
Lifecycle management	Manufacturers manage the entire product lifecycle, including maintenance, repairs, and end-of-life disposal	Product lifecycle management may be less centralized, with users or platform operators sharing responsibilities
Customer engagement	High level of customer engagement and service orientation, ensuring satisfaction through consistent interaction and support	Customer engagement is often facilitated by the platform, with a focus on user-to-user interactions rather than direct manufacturer involvement
Market dynamics	Typically, it involves fewer parties, allowing for more controlled and stable market dynamics	It involves multiple parties and a dynamic marketplace, which can lead to more variable market conditions
Innovation focus	Drives innovation in service models, product design for longevity, and advanced maintenance solutions	Encourages innovation in platform technology, user experience, and ways to enhance sharing efficiency
Environmental impact	Strong alignment with circular economy principles, promoting sustainability through extended product lifespans and efficient resource use	Promotes sustainability by maximizing the use of existing products, though the focus is more on usage efficiency rather than lifecycle management

Different business models present unique opportunities and challenges for manufacturers. To plan their strategies accordingly, manufacturers must first understand the differences between these models. This involves considering their operational capabilities, market objectives, and sustainability goals.

5.4.2 Strategic Opportunities from a Product as a Service Model

Adopting product as a service (PaaS) models presents manufacturers with an opportunity to redefine their engagement with products and end-users, offering several advantages:

Manufacturers ensure their products' durability, performance, and continuous alignment with evolving market demands and sustainability standards by retaining ownership and oversight. This direct control facilitates the timely implementation of upgrades and innovations, extending the products' functional life and enhancing their overall value proposition.

Example 5.15 BlueMovement's service to lease appliances from brands like Bosch and Siemens

BlueMovement,[15] a service brand of BSH Household Appliances, offers a service that allows customers to lease appliances from brands like Bosch and Siemens. This service includes delivery, installation, maintenance, upgrade, and take-back of the replaced appliances.

At the end of a subscription, products are returned, cleaned, checked, and refurbished by Bosch professionals in BlueMovement's maintenance center, allowing more households to use the same product.

If a product cannot be refurbished, BlueMovement recycles it. The company partners with Wecycle[16] to ensure that all old appliances are recycled correctly. Customers can also give away other small electrical appliances, such as smartphones, toasters, or electric toothbrushes, for recycling (BlueMovement, 2023; Wecycle, 2023).

PaaS models allow manufacturers to mitigate resource scarcity risks and market volatility risks. By maintaining ownership, manufacturers can more effectively manage and forecast the demand for materials, buffer against price fluctuations, and implement more sustainable practices, contributing to a more resilient and stable operational environment.

The PaaS approach enables manufacturers to design end-of-life management into their products from the outset. As products return at the end of their service period, manufacturers can systematically disassemble them, salvaging components for refurbishment or repurposing, recycling materials, reducing waste, and conserving resources.

[15] https://www.bluemovement.com/

[16] https://wecycle.nl/

One of the benefits of PaaS models is the opportunity for manufacturers to engage with end-users continuously. This continuous interaction provides invaluable insights into product usage, satisfaction levels, and emerging needs. Such insights can inform product development, customization options, and the refinement of service offerings, leading to stronger customer loyalty and brand advocacy.

PaaS models introduce more predictable, recurring revenue streams than traditional one-off sales. By offering products as a service, manufacturers can establish long-term contracts with customers, provide steady income over time, and reduce the financial uncertainties associated with fluctuating sales cycles.

Example 5.16 Michelin tire management solutions

Michelin has ventured into tire management solutions by selling kilometers instead of tires, which aids the customers in budgeting and lowers upfront costs. Michelin is responsible for tire performance, maintenance, and entire lifecycle management, reducing fleet operators' operational burdens. This comprehensive service is enhanced by integrating sensors within the tires, enabling Michelin to monitor various metrics such as wear and tear, pressure, and temperature in real time. This technology facilitates predictive maintenance and streamlines fleet management by preemptively identifying maintenance needs and optimizing fleet operations and safety (Michelin, 2023).

Michelin maintenance services include inspections, rotations, and repairs, all aimed at prolonging tire life and minimizing the chances of roadside failures. Another cornerstone of their offering is tire lifecycle management services, encompassing tire selection, tracking, and recycling, ensuring a comprehensive approach from procurement to disposal (Michelin, 2024).

At the heart of Michelin's tire management solutions is a sophisticated technological framework:

Tire sensors are embedded in the tires to relay real-time data on performance metrics. This technology predicts service or replacement needs, minimizing downtime and enhancing fleet efficiency.

Telematics monitors fleet vehicles' location and performance, helping identify opportunities to improve fuel efficiency and lower emissions.

The collected data from tire sensors and telematics systems undergoes thorough analysis to uncover trends and patterns in fleet operations, empowering operators with actionable insights for informed decision-making.

Michelin's foray into tire management solutions exemplifies a strategic pivot toward value-added services, offering fleet operators a pathway to reduce costs, boost operational efficiency, and extend the durability of their tire assets.

Since the launch of the new service, Michelin has delivered fuel savings of 1.5 liters per 100 kilometers to trucking customers. Michelin will save more than 3 billion liters of fuel in 1 year, reducing 9 million tons of carbon dioxide emissions into the atmosphere and adding more than 3 billion US dollars to the trucking industry (or more than 1300 per vehicle per year) (Than, 2023).

5.4.3 Challenges for Manufacturers in Adopting PaaS Models

Transitioning to a product as a service (PaaS) model presents a shift for manufacturers, moving from traditional product sales to a service-oriented approach. While this model offers numerous benefits, it also brings forth several challenges that manufacturers must navigate:

Adopting a PaaS model necessitates reevaluating and redesigning the value chain. Manufacturers must reconsider everything from product design, focusing on durability and serviceability, to manufacturing processes that may need to become more flexible to accommodate customization. After-sales support requires robust maintenance, repair, and end-of-life management systems. This transformation demands investment, cross-functional collaboration, and a willingness to innovate at every level.

The transition to PaaS has implications for the network of manufacturer's distributors, dealers, and resellers. Traditionally geared toward selling physical products, these partners may alter their roles and revenue models. As manufacturers assume greater responsibility for the product throughout its lifecycle, partners must adapt to new roles in the service delivery process, potentially requiring new skills, resources, and operational strategies.

A successful PaaS model relies on advanced digital infrastructure to manage service contracts, monitor product usage, and ensure proactive maintenance. Manufacturers must invest in IoT technologies for product tracking, cloud-based platforms for customer engagement, and data analytics for operational insights. Building and maintaining this digital backbone require technological investment and expertise (details in Part III).

Moving to a PaaS model involves a cultural shift within manufacturing organizations. It challenges ingrained mindsets centered around product sales and requires a new focus on long-term customer relationships and service excellence. This shift can be particularly challenging to implement, requiring training, change management initiatives, and sometimes a reconfiguration of team structures and incentives.

As manufacturers assume ongoing responsibility for their products, they must also navigate an increasingly complex regulatory landscape. Compliance with safety standards, environmental regulations, and consumer protection laws becomes more complicated when products are not sold outright but offered as a service. Manufacturers must stay abreast of these regulations across all markets they serve, adding another layer of complexity to their operations.

Shifting end-user behavior from ownership to service usage requires market education and customer engagement efforts. Manufacturers must articulate the value proposition of PaaS, addressing any concerns about quality, reliability, and flexibility. Overcoming entrenched end-user preferences for ownership can take time and requires targeted marketing strategies.

The PaaS model alters manufacturers' financial dynamics, shifting from lump-sum product sales to recurring service-based revenue. This transition can impact cash flow and requires financial planning and management. Manufacturers must develop attractive pricing models for consumers while ensuring the sustainability and profitability of their service offerings.

Example 5.17 Volvo Car Mobility

In 2021, Volvo Car Mobility's shared vehicle initiative removed the equivalent of up to nine private vehicles from the roads for each shared car they introduced within the urban centers of Stockholm, Gothenburg, and Malmö. This shift brought tangible environmental benefits, particularly in the Stockholm area, where the initiative contributed to a 5% reduction in CO2 tailpipe emissions compared to the previous year, culminating in a decrease of up to 16,000 tons in CO2 emissions for 2021 (Cap Gemini Invent, 2021).

While this transformative approach fosters a greener, more sustainable urban environment, it does present a challenge for Volvo in the short term, notably a dip in new car sales. This decrease in immediate revenue requires Volvo to adopt a forward-thinking perspective, with the anticipation that the value generated over time from this sustainable model will not only compensate for the initial shortfall but will lead to greater financial returns in the long run.

5.4.4 Third-Party Product as a Service Models

Manufacturers must decide whether to offer their products as services directly to end-users or enable third parties to offer these services using their products. While the previous discussion has mainly focused on manufacturers directly providing PaaS, the alternative approach of third-party service provision presents a different set of dynamics, offering both opportunities and challenges.

Collaborating with third parties to provide PaaS introduces a partnership model wherein manufacturers supply the products. At the same time, external providers handle the service aspect, from customer interaction to maintenance and support. This partnership can expand the reach of manufacturers' products into new markets and customer segments, facilitated by the third party's expertise in service delivery and market penetration (Table 5.3).

Example 5.18 DXC's Evergreen is a monthly subcription for compute power

DXC's Evergreen, part of their Modern Workplace[17] suite, is a service that replaces the traditional purchasing, supplying, delivering, maintaining, and patching of Windows, replacing and upgrading devices with a simple monthly subscription for Compute Power. This service ensures that employees always have the proper computing performance. Evergreen reuses devices to maximize their lifespan. The equipment delivered through DXC's Evergreen service includes devices from, e.g., Dell, Apple, Lenovo, HP, and Microsoft.

The service reduces 51% of PC refreshes and 53% of carbon consumption from reduced manufacturing and logistics (DXC Technology, 2023).

---

[17] https://dxc.com/us/en/offerings/modern-workplace

Table 5.3 Key opportunities and challenges for manufacturers considering engagement with third-party PaaS models

Aspect	Opportunities	Challenges
Market expansion	Collaborating with third-party service providers can open up new market and manufacturer customer segments, leveraging the service providers' established networks and expertise	Ensuring third-party services meet the manufacturer's quality standards and brand image requires robust partnership agreements and ongoing oversight
Scalability and flexibility	Third-party PaaS providers can offer scalable and flexible service options that might be more difficult for manufacturers to achieve independently, especially if they lack the infrastructure or expertise in service management	Third-party providers' intermediary role means manufacturers might have limited direct interaction with customers, impacting their ability to collect firsthand product feedback and build customer loyalty
Focus on core competencies	Manufacturers can benefit from reduced direct involvement in service management, allowing them to focus on core competencies such as product innovation and manufacturing efficiency	Without direct control over the customer relationship, manufacturers might find their products more easily substituted by competitors' offerings within the service platform. This risk is particularly acute in markets where multiple products can meet the service requirements, and the differentiation is less about the product itself and more about the service quality or price point. Establishing strong brand loyalty and clear differentiators for the product, alongside strategic agreements with service providers to ensure product preference mitigates this risk (see the DXC Evergreen example below)
Reduced upfront investments	Engaging with third parties can lead to lower upfront investments in service infrastructure and digital technologies required for service delivery as these responsibilities shift to the service providers	Customer insights and data tend to be collected by third-party providers. Manufacturers must negotiate agreements to ensure the flow of this valuable information back to them to inform product development and enhancements
Risk sharing	By leveraging third-party providers, manufacturers can share some of the risks associated with the service provision, especially those related to fluctuating market demands and service operation logistics	The economic model with third-party providers typically involves revenue sharing, which might result in lower per-unit revenue for manufacturers than direct sales or in-house PaaS offerings
Brand visibility and reputation	Third-party PaaS offerings can serve as additional channels to increase brand visibility and reputation, especially if these providers are well-regarded in their service domains	Ensuring that third-party service providers' goals and values align with the manufacturer's can be challenging but is critical for long-term success. Misalignment could lead to conflicts or inconsistencies in customer service and brand representation

Navigating the third-party PaaS model requires selecting partners that align with their quality standards and brand values. Clear agreements outlining service expectations, quality control measures, and revenue-sharing models are essential to foster a mutually beneficial relationship.

Example 5.19 Manufacturing as a Service (MaaS)

Manufacturing as a Service (MaaS) enables companies to access advanced manufacturing capabilities and services on demand without requiring significant capital investment in equipment or infrastructure. This model provides broader access to high-end manufacturing technologies, optimizes resource utilization, reduces waste, and enhances overall efficiency.

MaaS works on a subscription or pay-per-use model, where manufacturers provide their production capabilities to other businesses. This can involve various services like machining, 3D printing, assembly, and more complex manufacturing processes. Using MaaS, companies can concentrate on their main strengths, such as design and marketing, and delegate manufacturing to specialized providers.

MAAS ensures that expensive manufacturing equipment is used to its maximum capacity, minimizing idle time. It avoids large upfront investments in manufacturing facilities and equipment, freeing up capital for other strategic initiatives, and providing the flexibility to scale production up or down based on demand. Small- and medium-sized enterprises (SMEs) can access cutting-edge manufacturing technologies that would otherwise be out of reach.

Xometry[18] is a platform connecting businesses with a network of manufacturing partners that provide on-demand manufacturing services, from CNC machining to 3D printing.

Fictiv[19] has built a custom manufacturing operating system to connect manufacturers to a group of globally networked and highly specialized manufacturing partners. Fictiv employs dedicated quality engineers, logistics specialists, and supply chain managers. Manufacturing as a Service (MaaS) encounters several challenges. These include maintaining consistent quality across different providers, requiring robust standardization and quality control measures, protecting sensitive data and intellectual property in a collaborative manufacturing environment, and integrating MaaS solutions with existing business processes and supply chains.

---

[18] https://www.xometry.com/

[19] https://www.fictiv.com/

Table 5.4 A Customer Integration and Service Intensity Matrix

	Low customer integration	High customer integration
High service intensity	*Full-service model:* The provider offers comprehensive services to maintain the product's functionality *Strategy:* Provide all-inclusive maintenance packages, focusing on service quality and reliability Industrial equipment leasing with complete maintenance	*Outcome-based model:* Customers pay for outcomes rather than access to the product *Strategy:* Develop and manage comprehensive service packages that guarantee specific results Performance-based contracts like Michelin's tire-as-a-service, where payment is based on mileage covered
Low service intensity	*Basic access model:* The focus is on providing access to the product with little to no customization *Strategy:* Maintain product quality and ensure availability Traditional car rental services, basic tool rentals	*Enhanced access model:* Customers can customize their experience but don't aim for specific outcomes *Strategy:* Engage with customers to tailor experiences and gather feedback for service improvements Car-sharing services like Zipcar and customizable tech gadget rentals

5.4.5 Identifying Products Suitable for PaaS

Table 5.4 helps manufacturers and service providers visualize and strategize different PaaS delivery models by categorizing them according to two key dimensions: customer integration and service intensity. The Horizontal Customer Integration Axis measures active engagement and customer customization with the service. Low customer integration implies product use with minimal customization, while high integration involves significant customer involvement in tailoring the product experience and providing feedback. The Vertical Service Intensity Axis assesses the extent and complexity of the services offered with the product. Low service intensity might include basic access and minimal maintenance, whereas high intensity encompasses comprehensive service offerings that may even guarantee specific performance outcomes.

5.5 Value Chain Considerations for OEMs and Tier Suppliers

Circular economy practices prioritize redistribution, recommerce, and reuse for Original Equipment Manufacturers (OEMs) and their tier suppliers. These principles apply to end products, and the components and materials suppliers contribute to manufacturing. In other words, the second "R" of redistribution serves as more than just a strategy for final products; it is a comprehensive approach that should integrate throughout the value chain, including the minor parts and materials that comprise the larger whole.

The challenge and opportunity for tier suppliers are to recognize that their products are still subject to the lifecycle extension practices of redistribution. The upcoming chapter on refurbishment and remanufacturing will provide more details on how components, once part of an end product, can begin new lifecycles within the same application or in entirely new contexts. This emphasizes tier suppliers' need to design and produce with circularity in mind, ensuring that their components are easy to disassemble, refurbish, and integrate into new products, thus avoiding the fate of becoming waste.

The strategic integration of the second "R" throughout the value chain requires a collaborative effort among manufacturers and their suppliers. *It involves a shift in perspective from seeing products and components as disposable to recognizing them as valuable assets with extended lifecycles.* This shift contributes to environmental sustainability by reducing waste and the demand for virgin materials while opening new revenue streams and business models for OEMs and their suppliers. By embracing practices that facilitate the redistribution of components, suppliers can position themselves as vital partners in the circular economy, contributing to and benefiting from the regenerative capabilities of their products.

5.6 Digitization Supporting Redistribution Models

The digitization of redistribution models is a strategic transformation. It requires a cohesive approach integrating digital customer touchpoints, robust internal IT systems, interconnected business ecosystems, IoT-enabled products, and advanced data analytics. Manufacturers can enhance transparency, efficiency, and collaboration among all stakeholders by adopting a comprehensive digital strategy.

This section highlights key insights from Part III, in which the Sustainable Manufacturing Intelligence Framework (SMIF) is introduced. SMIF provides a structured guide to navigating this digital transformation, ensuring that every digital initiative is part of a larger, cohesive mechanism to achieve circular economy goals.

5.6.1 Internal IT Systems

Internal IT systems support the redistribution process. These systems must be flexible to meet new standards, enable product traceability, and implement end-of-life strategies. Key internal IT functionalities include supply chain management for tracking returned items, CRM systems for maintaining sustainable customer communication, and quality control systems to ensure consistent refurbished product quality. Effective integration of internal systems with external circular service providers requires efficient API management and strong security measures.

5.6.2 Digital Business Ecosystems

Digital business ecosystems support redistribution models by enabling seamless interactions and data sharing among various stakeholders, including recyclers, repair services, and value chain customers. Digital platforms streamline processes across multiple participants, enhancing resource utilization and operational efficiencies. For instance, collaboration platforms support collective creativity, orchestration platforms ensure smooth process integration, and matching platforms optimize resource availability.

5.6.3 Connected Products

The Internet of Things (IoT) allows for real-time monitoring and data-driven decision-making, making it effective for redistribution models. IoT technologies enable continuous data transmission on product status and efficiency, facilitating predictive maintenance, extending product lifetimes, and reducing waste. This real-time data supports the transparency and adaptability necessary for redistribution models.

5.6.4 Digital Customer Touchpoints

The integration of digital customer touchpoints is essential for redistribution models. Digital engagement platforms enable manufacturers to interact with customers beyond the initial sale continuously. Advanced analytics and AI facilitate personalized product recommendations, proactive maintenance alerts, and incentives for circular behaviors, fostering deeper customer loyalty and sustainable usage patterns.

5.6.5 Data-Driven Circularity

Data-driven decision-making is at the heart of effective redistribution models. By leveraging data from customer interactions, business ecosystems, connected products, and internal IT systems, manufacturers can gain comprehensive insights into their circular business models. Advanced data analytics tools enable strategic decision-making and operational adjustments, including big data, business intelligence (BI), machine learning (ML), and predictive analytics. These tools enhance product lifecycle management, increase customer engagement, and improve operational agility, leading to more efficient resource use and reduced supply chain vulnerabilities.

5.7 The Role of Logistic Service Providers (LSP) in Redistribution

Manufacturers transitioning to circular business models require Logistic Service Providers (LSP) support. LSP facilitates redistribution, enhances recommerce, supports reuse, and provides operational excellence (Jensen, 2023).

To manage the redistribution of goods, LSP tailors their logistics networks efficiently. They should handle the return flows and secondary distribution to new users or markets with as much priority and efficiency as initial product deliveries. LSP also excels in complex transportation management, adapting to the unique challenges that redistributed goods present compared to traditional logistics.

To support recommerce, LSP organizes the logistics for quality checks and certification processes to ensure that products meet all necessary secondary-use standards. This includes efficiently managing the transportation of products to and from inspection facilities. Additionally, LSP must use advanced inventory and warehouse management systems to accurately track and store recommerced goods, maintaining detailed records of product conditions and specifications to meet market demand effectively.

In supporting reuse activities, LSP must handle product repair and refurbishment logistics. This includes organizing the collection, sorting, and transportation of items to designated refurbishment centers and managing the reverse logistics chain efficiently. They should also develop specialized packaging solutions to protect used and refurbished goods during transit and storage, ensuring their integrity until they reach new users.

LSP's solutions must be flexible and scalable to accommodate the volumes and types of goods processed in the circular system. Integrating advanced technologies such as artificial intelligence (AI) and the Internet of Things (IoT) enhances the tracking, routing, and handling of goods through the circular supply chain, ensuring efficiency and accuracy at all stages.

LSP contributes to sustainability by optimizing route planning and load management to reduce carbon emissions and increase environmental benefits. Additionally, they should provide manufacturers with valuable market insights to help them understand customer preferences, return patterns, and sales channel efficiencies. These insights, obtained through sophisticated data analytics, enable manufacturers to improve their product offerings and adjust strategies in response to real-time market conditions.

LSP must ensure regulatory compliance by navigating the complex regulatory landscape of handling, transporting, and selling used and refurbished goods across different markets. They manage all pertinent documentation and certifications required to operate legally and efficiently.

LSP act as connectors within the circular economy ecosystem, facilitating robust networks that link manufacturers with key partners for recommerce, reuse, and third-party service providers. Logistic Service Providers are more than just transporters; they are vital enablers that help manufacturers implement and thrive in the 2nd R paradigm. By fulfilling these comprehensive roles, LSP assists manufacturers in overcoming logistical challenges and leveraging new opportunities.

5.8 Capability Map for Redistribution Business Models in Manufacturing

The capability map presented in Fig. 5.4 is designed to guide manufacturers in adopting redistribution business models, leveraging the insights and strategies discussed in this chapter.

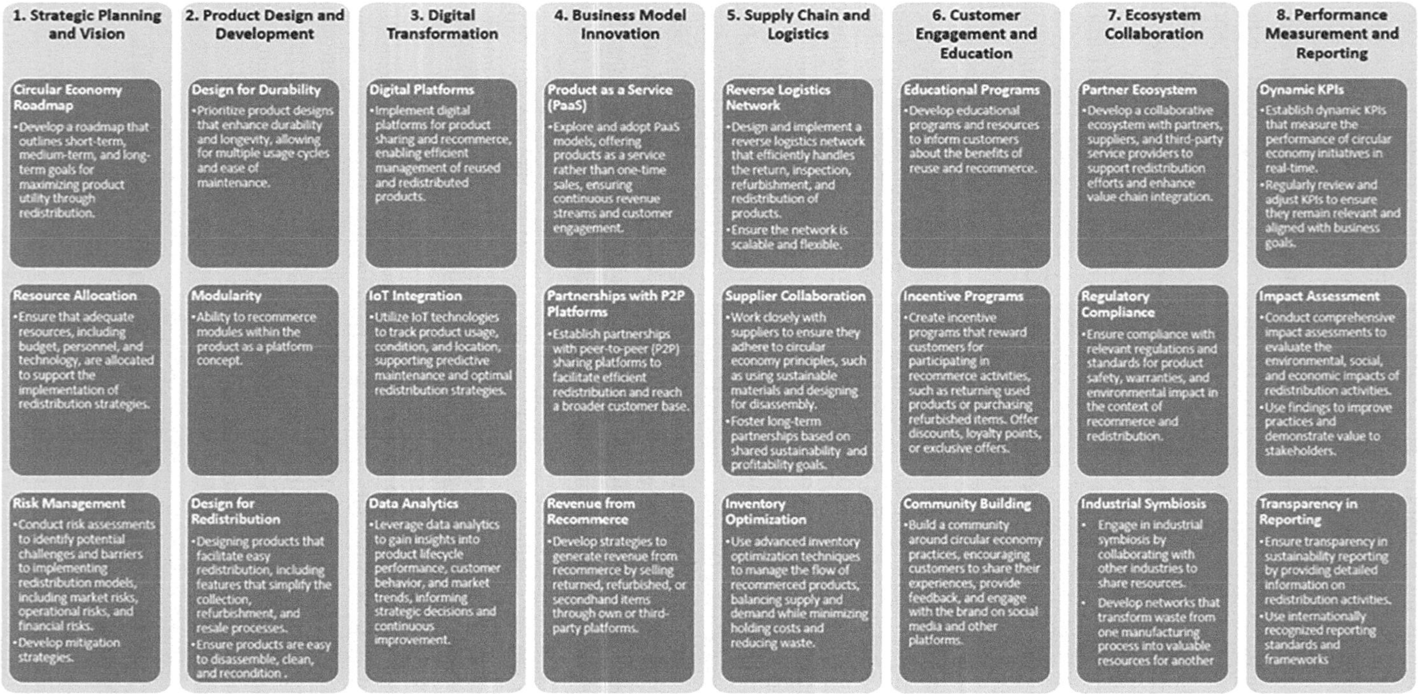

Fig. 5.4 Capability map for redistribution business models in manufacturing

Table 5.5 Checklist for embracing Redistribute, Recommerce, and Reuse

Task	Methodology	Expected outcome	Risk mitigation
Evaluate product portfolio for recommerce potential	Conduct lifecycle assessment to identify high-impact areas for circular interventions	Identification of products suitable for recommerce and reuse	Reduces risk of market misalignment
Design products for modularity and durability	Use design thinking workshops focused on modular and durable product design	Enable a redistribution market for modules	Missed opportunities for module recommerce
Establish partnerships with third-party providers	Create strategic alliance frameworks for collaborating with recommerce and reuse service providers	Expanded market reach and new revenue streams	Reduces dependency on internal resources
Implement extended warranties for reused products	Develop warranty and service contract models tailored to reused and recommerced products	Higher customer retention and brand loyalty	Lowers customer dissatisfaction risk
Educate customers on the benefits of recommerce	Launch customer awareness campaigns and incentive programs	Increased customer demand and engagement with circular offerings	Mitigates customer resistance to recommerce
Enhance digitization to support 2nd R	Analyze the current IT landscape and identify necessary digital capabilities to support 2nd R activities	Seamless integration of 2nd R practices into existing operations	Mitigates technology integration issues
Optimize logistics for recommerce and reuse	Implement advanced inventory and warehouse management systems	Efficient management of product returns and refurbishments	Reduces inefficiencies in the logistics chain
Collaborate with existing suppliers and partners	Develop programs and frameworks for engaging current suppliers and partners in circular practices	Enhanced alignment and support for circular economy goals	Reduces risk of supply chain disruptions and misalignment

5.9 Checklist for Embracing the 2nd R—Redistribute, Recommerce, and Reuse

To successfully navigate the transition towards the 2nd R of Redistribute, Recommerce, and Reuse, manufacturers must take strategic actions. This checklist is a roadmap for manufacturers to identify key focus areas, adopt effective methodologies, and achieve desired outcomes in embedding the 2nd R into their operations. By systematically addressing these areas, manufacturers can ensure they are well-positioned to capitalize on the opportunities presented by the circular economy while overcoming the inherent challenges (Table 5.5).

References

Apple Inc. (2023). *Apple certified refurbished products*. Retrieved from https://www.apple.com/shop/refurbished

BlueMovement. (2023). *BlueMovement Service*. Retrieved from https://www.bluemovement.com/

Cap Gemini Invent. (2021). *The impact of Volvo Car mobility on urban CO2 Emissions*. Retrieved from https://www.capgemini.com/invent/

Caterpillar. (2023). *CAT Rental Store*. Retrieved from https://www.catrentalstore.com/

DXC Technology. (2023). *DXC Evergreen*. Retrieved from https://www.dxc.technology/evergreen

FLEXE. (2023). *On-Demand Warehousing*. Retrieved from https://www.flexe.com/

Free2Move. (2023). *Vehicle Subscription Service*. Retrieved from https://www.free2move.com/us/en/

Habitat for Humanity. (2023). *ReStores*. Retrieved from https://www.habitat.org/restores

IKEA. (2023). *IKEA Buy Back & Resell Program*. Retrieved from https://www.ikea.com/global/en/newsroom/circular-economy

Ingka Group. (2023). *Annual & sustainability summary report FY22*. Retrieved from https://www.ingka.com/sustainability-report/

Jensen, H. H. (2023). *Logistics reimagined: Pioneering the circular transformation*. From Circular Bytes: https://www.linkedin.com/pulse/logistics-reimagined-pioneering-circular-henrik-hvid-jensen-fcsye/

John Deere. (2023). *Certified Pre-Owned Program*. Retrieved from https://www.deere.com/en/certified-pre-owned/

Kalundborg Symbiosis. (2024). *Environmental impact*. Retrieved from https://www.symbiosis.dk/en/

Michelin. (2023). *Tire Management Solutions*. Retrieved from https://www.michelin.com/eng/innovation/policy/

Michelin. (2024). *MICHELIN® Fleet Solutions*. From https://business.michelinman.com/freight-transportation/freight-transportation-services/michelin-fleet-solutions

Patagonia. (2023). *Worn Wear Program*. Retrieved from https://www.patagonia.com/worn-wear/

Rolls-Royce. (2023). *TotalCare® Program*. Retrieved from https://www.rolls-royce.com/products-and-services/civil-aerospace/totalcare.aspx

Tao, Y., Morgan, D., & Evans, S. (2015). How policies influence the implementation of industrial symbiosis: a comparison between UK and China. *Asian J. Management Science and Applications, 2*(1), 1–32.

Tas, A., Tyska, S., & Ludlow, T. (2021). *Framework for eco-industrial parks*. United Nations Industrial Development Organization (UNIDO). Retrieved from https://www.unido.org/resources-publications

Than, D. (2023). Michelin's strategy for sustainable mobility. *Journal of Automotive Innovation*.

Toyota. (2023). *Mechacomi Platform*. Retrieved from https://global.toyota/en/newsroom/

Tukker, A., & Tischner, U. (2006). *New business for old Europe: Product-service development, competitiveness and sustainability*. Greenleaf Publishing.

Wecycle. (2023). *Appliance recycling*. Retrieved from https://www.wecycle.nl/

3rd R – Revamping Business Through Repair

6

Abstract

This chapter examines how repair practices extend product lifecycles, shifting away from traditional linear economy models to create continuous revenue streams. This shift addresses planned obsolescence, a mid-twentieth-century strategy designed to shorten product lifespans for frequent replacements. Moving toward repairability reduces waste and increases revenue through prolonged product engagement.

Key messages include the right to repair movement, advocating for repair feasibility and affordability, and the importance of enhancing product design for repairability using durable materials and modular designs. Efficient repair services require reconfigured supply chains supported by digital systems for real-time inventory and logistics tracking. Manufacturers can embrace repair services through mobile repair units, partnerships with third-party networks, and innovative financial models, expanding service reach and enhancing customer satisfaction.

A shift in sales strategies is essential, emphasizing product longevity and service, integrating digital platforms for enhanced customer engagement, and offering extended warranties and subscription-based models. Educating customers about the benefits of circularity and offering loyalty programs, personalized maintenance schedules, and transparent repair tracking promotes a culture valuing product longevity and resource efficiency. Investment in training for employees and repair providers is required. Collaboration with Logistic Service Providers supports repairability by offering services like reverse logistics and repair hubs. The capability map guides manufacturers in adopting repair business models.

H. H. Jensen, *Circular Economy Opportunities and Pathways for Manufacturers*, Future of Business and Finance, https://doi.org/10.1007/978-3-031-75279-7_6

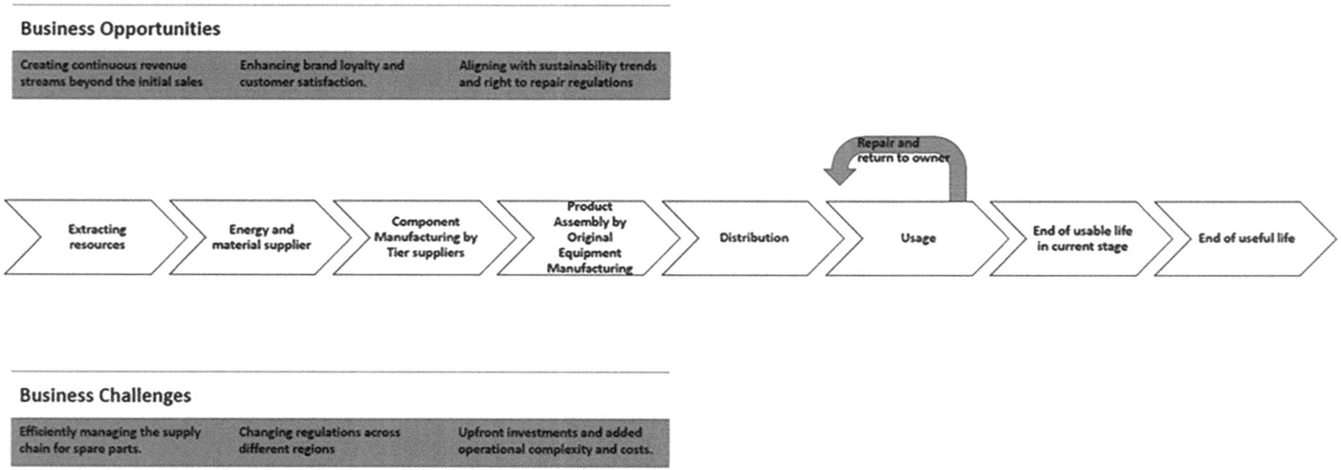

Fig. 6.1 Repair's placement in circular flow (Figure 1.6) and three significant business opportunities and challenges

Key Messages

- *Revamping Business Through Repair: Repair practices extend product life and create continuous revenue streams, shifting away from the traditional linear economy model.*
- *Addressing Planned Obsolescence*: Mid-twentieth-century strategies favored short product lifespans to drive frequent replacements. Moving away from planned obsolescence toward repairability can reduce waste and open opportunities for increased revenue through prolonged product engagement and additional services.
- *Right to Repair Movement*: The right to repair movement challenges the traditional buy-use-discard model, advocating for repair feasibility and affordability to foster sustainable consumption.
- *Enhancing Product Design for Repairability*: Manufacturers should design products for easy disassembly and repair, using durable materials and modular designs to extend product life and support recycling efforts.
- *Adapting Supply Chain Logistics*: Efficient repair services require reconfigured supply chains dedicated to spare parts, supported by digital systems for real-time inventory and logistics tracking.
- *Embracing Repair Services*: Manufacturers can embrace several opportunities in repair services, such as mobile repair units, partnerships with third-party repair networks, and innovative financial models to expand service reach and enhance customer satisfaction.
- *Shift in Sales Strategies*: Manufacturers must pivot their sales strategies to emphasize product longevity and service, integrate digital platforms for enhanced customer engagement, and offer extended warranties and subscription-based models.
- *Customer Mindset Shift:* Educating customers on the benefits of circularity and offering loyalty programs, personalized maintenance schedules, and transparent repair tracking can promote a culture that values product longevity and resource efficiency.
- *Training and Skill Development*: Investment in training for employees and repair providers ensures the ability to repair complex products, supported by detailed manuals and instructional resources.
- *Regulatory Compliance*: Keeping up with evolving repairability regulations and standards requires active engagement with policymakers and transparent communication with customers.
- *Collaboration with Logistic Service Providers*: Logistic Service Providers support repairability by offering services like reverse logistics and repair hubs within distribution centers.
- *Digital Support for Repairability*: Digital tools like Digital Product Passports enhance repair processes by providing detailed product information and ensuring compliance with regulations.

The following two chapters focus on Repair, Refurbishment, and Remanufacturing practices, which fall under the umbrella of Product Use Extension business models. These models contrast the traditional linear economy where products are sold and then "forgotten" by the manufacturer. Instead, they represent a shift towards sustainability and longevity. Manufacturers who adopt Product Use Extension models design their products to make them easily repairable, upgradable, and reusable. This approach extends the life of products and creates continuous revenue streams for businesses across multiple usage cycles. This chapter discusses the business opportunities and challenges that arise from improving product repairability (Fig. 6.1).

In the mid-twentieth century, the pursuit of continuous economic growth led to business strategies where products were intentionally designed for shorter lifespans or were uneconomical to repair. This approach is known as planned obsolescence (Iberdrola, 2024).

Planned obsolescence is designing and producing goods with a shorter lifespan to compel frequent replacements. Rapid technological advancements and evolving consumer behaviors drove this shift from durable to disposable goods. Manufacturers adopted this strategy to maximize profit by reducing the repairability and durability of products. This practice created a continuous demand for new products, creating a perpetual purchase and disposal cycle (FasterCapital, 2024).

While planned obsolescence supported economic growth by stimulating production, sales, and jobs in the manufacturing and retail sectors, it also increased resource consumption and waste. This strategy allowed companies to introduce new technologies and features by continuously updating products, keeping pace with competitors, enhancing consumer experience, and maintaining a steady revenue stream vital for research and development.

Proponents of planned obsolescence argue that it drives technological innovation and economic growth. However, it also results in increased environmental degradation and waste. Therefore, balancing economic incentives and sustainable practices is essential for long-term progress. Examples of planned obsolescence include technology companies designing smartphones with non-removable batteries or using proprietary screws, reducing repairability. In appliances, the integration of components often means that the failure of one part requires replacing the entire unit; for instance, I owned a toaster whose spring, meant to keep the handle down, broke. Since it was irreparable, I had to buy a new toaster because of a faulty spring. Fast fashion trends lead to clothing designed to be worn only a few times before losing shape or color. The Phoebus Cartel, an international consortium of light bulb manufacturers, was formed in 1924 to limit the lifespan of incandescent light bulbs to 1000 hours to inflate demand for new bulbs and increase profits artificially. Before the cartel's formation, light bulbs could last thousands of hours, but the Phoebus cartel deliberately introduced design flaws and manufacturing shortcuts to shorten their lifespan. For example, the Centennial Light demonstrates the potential durability of early bulbs. This bulb, housed at Fire Station 6 in Livermore, California, has glowed since 1901. Remarkably, it has been turned off only once, for 1 week during renovations in 1937 (Phoebus Cartel 1924).[1]

Externalizing environmental costs has historically enabled business models focused on the unrepairability of products to be financially viable for manufacturers. The broader environmental implications of producing, using, and disposing of goods—such as pollution and resource depletion—have often been overlooked in the pricing strategies of manufacturing firms. *Instead, these environmental burdens have fallen on society and natural ecosystems, creating a disconnect between the economic actions of manufacturers and their environmental and social impacts.* This practice has inadvertently supported models based on planned obsolescence, where the producers do not directly bear the consequences of waste and excessive resource consumption.

In response to these challenges, the right to repair movement emerges as a transformative force, advocating for a shift away from the "buy-use-discard" cycle. By mandating companies to ensure the feasibility and affordability of repairs, this initiative seeks to counteract the traditional business models and foster a culture of sustainable consumption.

The European Commission's introduction of the right to repair for consumers (European Commission, 2023) (Sect. 2.1) highlights that people often prematurely discard products that could still be repaired and are viable goods., resulting in 35 million tons of waste, 30 million tons of resources, and 261 million tons of greenhouse gas emissions in the EU annually. European Commission estimates that the financial toll on consumers who opt for replacement over repair is losses nearing EUR 12 billion annually. *Consumers could have used this expenditure to acquire new capabilities and enhancements, enrich individual consumers, and contribute to broader societal wealth instead of merely substituting defective products.* EU expects the initiative to bring about EUR 4.8 billion in growth and investment within the EU. This growth bolsters the economy and opens avenues for non-academic job opportunities, underscoring the multifaceted advantages of embracing repair and extending the lifecycle of products.

6.1 Embracing Repairability

Increased repairability challenges the global economic model, disrupting traditional production and consumption cycles. It calls into question the profitability of fast-turnover products and urges businesses to rethink their approach to product lifecycles and sustainability. These changes represent a holistic shift in how products are manufactured, marketed, and serviced and can create initial economic uncertainties for manufacturers who rely on frequent repeat sales.

Section 11.4.1 details the process steps for repair.

[1] https://www.lightbulbs.com/blog/worlds-oldest-light-bulb-that-still-works

6.1.1 Rethinking Product Design for Durability and Repairability

Designing products for durability and repairability requires a shift in design philosophy. This approach emphasizes the product's entire lifecycle—not just its initial performance and cost —including ease of repair, potential for upgrades, and end-of-life disassembly.

Designing products with disassembly in mind means that products can be easily taken apart and reassembled, simplifying the repair process and supporting end-of-life recycling efforts. This design consideration ensures that when a product can no longer be repaired or upgraded, its components can be efficiently recovered and reused. One key strategy in this shift is to move toward modular designs (see Sect. 4.1.2). This approach breaks down products into independently replaceable or upgradable modules, allowing specific components to be swapped out as needed without discarding the entire product.

Manufacturers must opt for durable materials resistant to wear and tear to ensure that products can withstand repeated use and repair and reduce the frequency of replacements.

Incorporating digital diagnostics and connectivity features into products represents another frontier in facilitating repairability. Digital tools can offer real-time insights into a product's performance and health, enabling predictive maintenance and streamlined troubleshooting. This digital layer adds intelligence to products, making them more adaptable to maintenance needs and reducing repair downtime (see Part III).

Achieving these design innovations requires a delicate balance between durability and other product attributes, such as performance and cost-effectiveness. Manufacturers must navigate this balance to ensure their products remain attractive. This balance is not static; it evolves with technological advancements and changing customer expectations, driving continuous innovation in product design and manufacturing practices.

6.1.2 Adapting Supply Chain Logistics for Repairability

Efficient repair services and the availability of spare parts require reconfiguring supply chain logistics and establishing dedicated supply lines exclusively for spare parts. New warehousing solutions must be developed to store these parts efficiently, and they should be readily accessible when needed.

Creating efficient distribution networks allows prompt delivery of spare parts to the required locations. This network must support forward logistics, from manufacturers to repair centers or customers, and reverse logistics, allowing for returning products needing repair and used spare parts from local repair and maintenance. The integration of digital systems plays a pivotal role in this process, providing real-time tracking of inventory, repair statuses, and logistics, thus enhancing overall transparency and responsiveness (see Sect. 6.5 for a more detailed discussion on LSP's role).

6.1.3 Decentralize Repair Service

Manufacturers can make repair services more accessible to end-users by decentralizing them. They can do this by forging partnerships with local repair shops or service centers. This strategy makes repair services more convenient for customers, supports local economies, and reduces the environmental impact of transporting products over long distances for repair. In addition, focusing on sustainable packaging solutions for shipping spare parts and repair products aligns with environmental sustainability goals.

6.1.4 Pivoting Sales Strategies Toward Longevity and Service

Manufacturers prioritizing increasing unit sales must change their strategies to promote longevity and service. Sales teams should be trained to effectively communicate the benefits of product longevity and repairability to customers. They need to emphasize not only the immediate features of the products but also their long-term value, sustainability benefits, and positive impact on the total cost of ownership for the customer.

New pricing strategies that adhere to the principles of longevity and repairability can increase product appeal. Manufacturers can ensure that products are covered for repairs beyond the standard warranty period by offering a warranty extension for an additional fee. Another approach is to introduce subscription models where customers pay a recurring fee for access to a product, along with comprehensive maintenance and repair services. Some high-end appliance brands offer subscription services, including maintenance, repairs, and upgrades.

Example 6.1 HP All-In Plan

Transitioning toward service-based models requires manufacturers to look beyond the initial sale. HP All-In Plan exemplifies this shift with its printer as a service model. Consumers pay a monthly fee for a new printer, automatic ink replenishment, 24×7 support, printer replacement, and upgrades. This model establishes a continuous revenue stream for HP, providing consumers with reduced printer management hassle. HP can monitor performance, implement upgrades, and extend product life by maintaining ownership (HP, 2024).

Integrating digital platforms into sales strategies can streamline the customer journey from purchase to service, fostering a deeper connection with the brand. Sales teams can leverage these platforms to offer personalized services, direct access to repair options, and transparent pricing structures, thereby enriching the customer experience.

6.1.5 Facilitating a Customer Mindset Shift

Manufacturers must put concerted efforts toward shifting the end-user mindset toward longevity. They can achieve this through customer education campaigns highlighting the economic and environmental benefits of opting for repairable and durable products. Additionally, manufacturers can offer tangible incentives to make repair more attractive. For instance, manufacturers can extend warranties to include comprehensive repair coverage, offer discounts on repair services or parts, or even implement loyalty programs that reward sustainable behaviors. These strategies can foster a culture of sustainability and promote a shift in customer attitudes toward valuing product longevity. Ultimately, this can strengthen the relationship between brands and their customers.

Example 6.2 Bosch's online repair service for its power tool customers.

Bosch has implemented an online repair service for its power tool customers (Bosch, 2023).

The service simplifies repair by offering free collection and delivery of defective tools. This feature removes logistical barriers for customers, making it easier to opt for repairs rather than replacing their tools. By handling the transportation logistics, Bosch ensures that the products are transported safely to and from the repair centers, minimizing the risk of damage and the carbon footprint associated with multiple transport phases.

Each successful chargeable repair is backed by a 1-year warranty, providing customers with assurance of the quality and reliability of the repair work. This warranty acts as a trust-building measure that supports Bosch's commitment to high service standards and customer satisfaction.

Bosch enhances transparency and customer engagement through regular email updates about the status of the repair. Bosch keeps customers informed from the moment Bosch collects their tool to the completion of the repair process. This continuous communication helps manage customer expectations and reduces the anxiety associated with waiting for the return of tools.

The service gives transparent costs. Before sending a tool for repair, customers can view an estimate of the repair costs on Bosch's website, allowing them to make informed decisions based on potential repair expenses versus the price of a new purchase. This transparency builds trust and loyalty with customers, who can avoid unexpected charges and assess the economic benefits of repairing over replacing.

The data collected through the service can help Bosch identify common faults or areas for product improvement, driving innovation and efficiency in product design and support services (Bosch, 2024).

6.1.6 Training and Skill Development

Manufacturers must invest in properly training their employees and authorized repair providers to ensure they possess the skills to repair increasingly complex and durable products. This training should include comprehensive technical knowledge of new product designs and customer service training to handle repair inquiries effectively. In addition, manufacturers should consider making detailed repair manuals and instructional videos available to independent repair services and Do-It-Yourself (DIY) enthusiasts to support the growing consumer demand for the right to repair and foster a culture of transparency and empowerment in product maintenance and repair. These resources can facilitate a broader range of repair options for consumers, contributing to the longevity and sustainability of products in the market.

6.1.7 Regulatory Compliance and Standards

Manufacturers face the challenge of keeping up with the evolving regulations related to product repairability, such as the right to repair laws and standards for product durability. To comply with these regulations, they must actively engage with policymakers and industry groups to influence beneficial rules. The regulatory landscape can vary across different countries or regions, making it necessary to adopt a tailored approach to ensure that products meet local legal requirements. To avoid confusion, manufacturers must transparently communicate with customers, informing them about their right to repair and the availability of repair services.

Additionally, it is vital to ensure that all supply chain partners, particularly component suppliers, align with these repairability standards. This will help create a cohesive strategy for managing the product lifecycle. Certifications and eco-labels signify high repairability and sustainability standards, which can also serve as a marketing advantage, guiding customer choices toward more sustainable options.

6.2 Understanding the Right to Repair Legislation

Section 2.1 provides an in-depth discussion of the Right to Repair legislation. In summary, the Right to Repair movement advocates for multiple measures to empower consumers to repair their purchased products. These measures include the availability of spare parts, accessibility of repair manuals, designing products for easy repairability, preventing software restrictions, transparency in repair pricing, consumer right to choose repair services, and warranty protection. These measures aim to promote a fair and competitive repair market, extend the lifespan of products, and safeguard consumers' right to repair their purchases (Figs. 6.2 and 6.3).

Fig. 6.2 Key points in right to repair legislations (from Sect. 2.1)

Fig. 6.3 Repairability Business Models

6.3 Tier Suppliers

This focus on repairability extends beyond just Original Equipment Manufacturers (OEMs) and includes all suppliers in the supply chain. All suppliers must prioritize repairability when designing and providing components for final products. This collaborative approach designs the entire product for longevity and ease of maintenance, not just at the surface level.

Prioritizing component repairability is not just a nod to sustainability but a strategic move for enhancing competitiveness in the manufacturing sector. As the industry moves toward a more repair-centric approach, tier suppliers who design efficiently repairable components will have a competitive advantage. OEMs, driven by customer demand for durable products and compliance with right to repair laws, will prefer suppliers whose components contribute to the repairability and longevity of their products.

This shift represents an opportunity for tier suppliers to strengthen partnerships with OEMs and secure their place in the supply chain. By aligning their offerings with emerging repairability standards, suppliers can ensure their relevance in a market where the ability to repair and maintain products is becoming increasingly important. This strategic alignment can open new revenue streams by providing spare parts and repair services, further solidifying their competitive stance.

6.4 Unveiling Repairability Business Models

This section explores various business models that manufacturers can adopt to harness the benefits of repairability. From mobile repair services and partnerships with repair networks to innovative financial models and digital support tools, we will delve into how each model works, its advantages for manufacturers in terms of competitiveness and profitability, and the challenges that may arise while implementing these strategies (Fig. 6.3).

6.4.1 In-House Repair Centers

Manufacturers that establish their own repair centers have direct control over the repair process. This ensures that services meet the standards associated with their brand. Being involved in repairs allows manufacturers to offer exceptional service quality, which reinforces brand reliability and customer trust. In-house repair centers provide a seamless customer experience from the initial purchase through the repair process, creating a stronger connection between customers and the brand.

In-house repair centers provide numerous benefits for manufacturers. These include new revenue streams from repair services and cost savings from handling these processes internally. This approach also meets customer demand for sustainable and long-lasting products, giving a competitive advantage. Additionally, offering direct repair services helps build stronger customer relationships, offers valuable insights, and boosts brand loyalty.

Manufacturers face numerous challenges when establishing in-house repair centers. These include the initial investment required to set up and staff the repair centers, ensuring that technicians are well-trained to maintain the brand's standards, and managing the logistics of parts supply and repair appointments. Additionally, manufacturers must stay updated on evolving right to repair legislation to ensure their services comply with legal requirements and customer expectations.

For in-house repair centers to be successful, they need to generate profit. This can be achieved by offering premium services such as expedited repairs and extended warranties, which can be priced higher. Refurbishing and reselling products at the centers can also bring in extra revenue while reducing waste. Taking advantage of repair interactions to cross-sell and upsell compatible accessories or new models can help increase sales. Implementing subscription-based maintenance plans can provide a consistent revenue stream and improve customer loyalty.

Before establishing in-house repair centers, manufacturers should thoroughly analyze market demand to assess the need for repair services within their target market. They should also examine the competitive landscape to understand how competitors handle repairs and whether in-house centers could provide a competitive advantage. It's important to consider the complexity and specialization of the products, as more advanced products may benefit from dedicated in-house repairs to maintain their quality. This decision must align with the brand strategy and value proposition, especially if the brand emphasizes quality and customer satisfaction. Finally, assessing resource availability and operational capacity ensures that the organization can support and sustain the repair centers without compromising other areas of operation.

6.4.2 Mobile Repair Services

Deploying mobile repair units enables manufacturers to offer customers on-the-spot repairs, which enhances their convenience and minimizes product downtime. This proactive approach can lead to increased revenue streams from repair services and potentially higher profit margins due to the premium nature of immediate, on-location service. Mobile repair services facilitate direct customer interaction, deepening their brand engagement. This heightened level of service can boost brand loyalty, encouraging repeat business and positive word-of-mouth referrals. Through these mobile units, manufacturers can maintain a continual presence in their customers' lives, reinforcing the value and reliability of their products and services.

However, implementing mobile repair services brings several challenges for manufacturers. These challenges include the logistical complexity and costs of managing a fleet of mobile units equipped for diverse repairs. Training and retaining skilled technicians add to operational costs. Coordinating efficient scheduling and routing to meet customer needs across vast areas requires sophisticated software and real-time communication tools, increasing the investment needed. Ensuring consistent quality of service across all units to maintain brand integrity involves setting up strict quality control measures. Additionally, navigating regulatory and insurance requirements in different regions can introduce further complexity and costs.

6.4.3 Partnerships with Repair Networks

Collaborating with third-party repair networks is a cost-effective way for manufacturers to offer repair services to customers. It allows them to expand their service reach without investing heavily in new facilities or staff. This model can increase revenue opportunities and offer higher profit margins as it leverages existing repair infrastructure, reducing the costs associated with setting up and operating dedicated repair centers. It also ensures that repairs meet the manufacturer's standards, which enhances brand reputation and customer loyalty. By partnering with repair networks, manufacturers can provide convenient repair options and reduce the risk of repair quality and warranty issues. Additionally, frequent interactions through the repair process can increase customer engagement, providing valuable feedback for product improvement and fostering long-term customer relationships.

However, there are challenges that manufacturers need to overcome when forming partnerships with repair networks. It requires standardization and continuous monitoring to ensure consistent quality across a diverse network of repair shops, which can be resource-intensive. Manufacturers must also navigate the complexities of integrating their processes and systems with those of independent repair services, which can vary widely in terms of technology, capabilities, and customer service standards. Protecting brand reputation becomes challenging, and any lapse in a partner's service quality or customer experience can reflect poorly on the manufacturer. Additionally, aligning warranty and service policies between the manufacturer and the repair network can be complex, requiring clear agreements to prevent conflicts and misunderstandings.

6.4.4 Innovative Financial Models for Repair Services

Adopting innovative financial models for repair services can bring numerous benefits to manufacturers. Fixed repair fees offer transparency, which can help build customer trust and loyalty, leading to repeat business and referrals. Subscription-based repair services create a continuous revenue stream, smoothing income fluctuations and enhancing financial stability. Extended warranties serve as an additional revenue source and reassure customers about product quality, improving brand perception and competitive advantage.

Example 6.3 Fnac Darty's repair subscription service

Fnac Darty, a European retailer specializing in electronics, cultural goods, and household appliances, has launched a repair subscription service. Three different offers are available, depending on the number of appliance types the customer wants covered. As of 2023, Fnac Darty has 1.1 million subscribers (Fnac Darty, 2023).

This service offers customers a convenient and cost-effective way to maintain and prolong the lifespan of their electronic and household products. It provides unlimited repairs for a fixed annual fee, ensuring that customers have continuous access to professional repair services without the financial burden of individual repair costs.

The subscription includes major household appliances such as washing machines, laptops, and televisions. The service eliminates the uncertainty of repair costs and ensures that products can be fixed when needed, giving customers a sense of security and trust in their purchases.

Additionally, subscribers get access to expert advice and maintenance tips, which help them understand how to care for their products and avoid potential problems.

The repair subscription also benefits Fnac Darty economically by generating consistent revenue and reducing the expenses related to product returns and replacements.

These financial models save costs by optimizing repair operations and leveraging economies of scale in service provision.

One of the primary concerns when adopting these financial models is the upfront investment in developing digital platforms for managing subscriptions, fixed fees, and extended warranties. Another challenge lies in balancing the pricing structure to ensure it's attractive to customers while still covering the costs and generating a profit for the manufacturer. Setting prices too high may deter customers from opting for repair services, while too low prices might not cover the costs, affecting profitability.

Implementing subscription-based models introduces the risk of end-user underutilization or overutilization. Underutilization can lead to missed revenue opportunities, whereas overutilization can strain resources and erode profit margins. These financial models require a cultural shift within the organization, moving from a transactional sales mindset to a service-oriented approach, involving changes in sales strategies, customer service operations, and organizational structure.

There's also the challenge of market acceptance. Customers accustomed to traditional ownership models may hesitate to embrace subscription or service-based models, requiring manufacturers to invest in customer education and marketing to highlight the benefits.

6.4.5 Remote Diagnostics and Repair Support

Manufacturers increase profit by incorporating remote diagnostics and repair support into their service offerings. This cost-efficient approach resolves issues without costly physical interventions, reducing costs associated with traditional repair services.

Remote diagnostics offer a competitive advantage in the market, positioning the manufacturer as a customer-centric brand willing to leverage technology to improve service efficiency and convenience. However, building a robust digital infrastructure for remote diagnostics requires technology investment and staff training to ensure customer satisfaction.

It's important to note that not all customers are comfortable following remote repair instructions. Additionally, some repairs may require physical service interventions, and remote diagnostics carry a higher risk of misdiagnosis, leading to incorrect repairs, additional costs, and diminished customer trust.

To overcome these challenges, manufacturers must plan meticulously, communicate transparently with customers, and continuously invest in technology and staff training to ensure reliable and secure remote diagnostics and repair services. Furthermore, data privacy and security must be paramount, demanding stringent cybersecurity measures to protect customer information and comply with regulations.

6.4.6 Do It Yourself (DIY) Repair Kits and Tutorials

Manufacturers can increase their profits by selling DIY repair kits and tutorials to customers as an alternative to costly professional repair services. Offering this option can decrease operational costs associated with after-sales services and enhance customer engagement and loyalty, as customers often feel a greater sense of satisfaction and attachment to products they have personally maintained or repaired. This hands-on experience can lead to increased brand advocacy and repeat business, as customers appreciate the empowerment and support to extend the life of their purchases.

However, some challenges come with introducing DIY repair kits and tutorials. Manufacturers must ensure the accuracy and comprehensibility of the instructions to prevent misuse or further damage to the product, which could lead to customer dissatisfaction or safety concerns. Companies must also determine which repairs are suitable for DIY and which should be left to professionals to maintain product integrity and safety. Encouraging DIY repairs might inadvertently reduce the demand for professional repair services, potentially impacting relationships with service partners and affecting the manufacturer's service-based revenue streams. Manufacturers must ensure that DIY efforts do not void warranties or lead to legal liabilities when promoting self-repair options.

Example 6.4 Apple's Self-Service Repair program

Apple's Self-Service Repair program is for customers with the technical skills to fix their devices. It provides access to genuine Apple parts, tools, and repair manuals, allowing individuals to carry out out-of-warranty repairs on their iPhones and Macs. By ensuring that only genuine parts and professional-grade tools are used, Apple upholds high repair standards and protects product integrity (Apple, 2024).

Customers should start by consulting the relevant repair manual for their device to understand the necessary steps, parts, tools, and materials. They can purchase genuine Apple parts and tools from an authorized online store. After completing the repair, Apple provides a post-repair software tool called System Configuration to finalize the process and ensure the repair's success. Additionally, Apple encourages customers to return the parts they have replaced for recycling.

This program fulfills the need for high-quality repairs and generates revenue from selling parts and tools. It also enhances customer trust by enabling them to use original components to maintain their devices' performance and safety.

6.4.7 Spare Part Profitability and OEM-Supplier Dynamics

Spare parts sales often present a higher profit margin than new products for manufacturers. Manufacturers can enjoy substantial profit margins on these parts by ensuring that the price of individual spare parts is lower than the cost of purchasing a new product. This strategy hinges on a delicate balance: making spare parts affordable enough to encourage repair over replacement while capturing revenue.

The move toward increased repairability and the direct sale of spare parts introduces a nuanced challenge between Original Equipment Manufacturers (OEMs) and their tier suppliers. In a traditional setup, tier suppliers manufacture components that the OEMs assemble into the final product. However, as the focus shifts toward repairability, there's an emerging opportunity for tier suppliers to sell their spare parts directly to end-users or repair services, bypassing the OEMs. This direct sales model can benefit tier suppliers by opening up new revenue streams but may create competitive tensions with OEMs who traditionally manage the aftermarket parts supply.

To navigate this potential conflict, OEMs and their tier suppliers must establish clear agreements and collaborative strategies supporting the circular economy principles while respecting each party's business interests. This might involve joint ventures in the aftermarket sector, revenue-sharing models, or exclusive supplier agreements that benefit both sides. The key is to foster a transparent and cooperative relationship that leverages the strengths of each party to promote a repair-oriented approach within the industry.

6.4.8 Product Lifecycle Management Services

Manufacturers can offer lifecycle management services where they take responsibility for their products' maintenance, repair, and eventual recycling or disposal. This approach is appealing to corporate clients looking to outsource the management of their equipment to extend product lifespans, reduce unexpected breakdowns, and ensure compliance with regulations.

For manufacturers, product lifecycle management (PLM) services create steady revenue streams, enhance customer loyalty, and provide valuable insights for product innovation. By taking a proactive role in the lifecycle of their products, manufacturers can leverage data from maintenance and usage to improve product designs, offer value-added services, and expand their market reach.

6.5 Collaboration with Logistic Service Providers

In a landscape where repairability is becoming an aspect of product design and consumer expectations, manufacturers seeking to capitalize on the business opportunities presented by increased repairability must look toward Logistic Service Providers (LSP) for support. LSP, positioned uniquely within the supply chain, can offer a range of services that facilitate the repair process and enhance its efficiency and reach. Here's what manufacturers should expect from LSP to support the shift toward more repairable products:

Manufacturers should leverage LSP's distribution centers' evolving role, transforming them into multifunctional hubs. These centers go beyond storage and sorting, incorporating circular services like minor repairs and refurbishing activities directly within. This integration reduces the need for additional transportation, reducing carbon emissions and boosting operational efficiency.

Expect LSP to create collaborative spaces within their distribution centers. These innovative zones allow circular service providers (CSP) to conduct specialized circular services, combining LSP's logistical expertise with CSP's repair and refurbishment skills. This symbiotic relationship benefits manufacturers by providing repair facilities in any geographic location, minimizing waste, and maximizing resource utilization by effectively reviving returned products.

Manufacturers should anticipate that LSP will elevate reverse logistics from a secondary to a primary operational strategy. LSP must adeptly manage the collection, processing, and reintroduction of products into the supply chain, turning end-of-life products into valuable resources—this strategic shift bolsters circular business models.

LSP is refining its reverse logistics strategies to optimize logistics labor and transport assets, especially in collections and returns. By improving these processes, LSP aims to minimize unnecessary costs and move returned goods in the most resource-efficient manner possible.

With the anticipated rise in demand for readily accessible spare parts, manufacturers must work closely with LSPs to develop specialized supply chains dedicated to these components. This collaboration ensures the availability of spare parts and their efficient distribution. However, manufacturers must navigate potential conflicts of interest, particularly between OEMs and their suppliers, to provide a collaborative and mutually beneficial approach.

Manufacturers should leverage LSP's capabilities in digital integration to streamline operations. This includes advanced inventory management systems for spare parts, sophisticated route planning for reverse logistics, and digital platforms for collaborative repair services. These digital solutions manage the complexities of repair services.

By aligning with LSPs offering these advanced services, manufacturers can successfully transition to business models prioritizing repairability. This shift responds to consumer and regulatory demands for more sustainable products, opens new revenue streams, enhances customer engagement, and strengthens competitive advantage in an increasingly circular economy.

6.6 Digitization: A Catalyst for Sustainable Repair Business Models

Digitization is integral to supporting repair models within the circular economy. By enhancing internal IT systems, fostering collaborative ecosystems, connecting products, improving customer experiences, and leveraging data-driven insights, manufacturers can effectively transition to profitable repair models. The Sustainable Manufacturer Intelligence Framework (SMIF) (presented in Chapter 10) provides a cohesive approach to navigating this transformation, ensuring that every digital initiative contributes to a unified, efficient, and resilient circular economy.

This section highlights how digitization supports repair models based on insights from Part III, which focuses on the digitization of the circular economy.

6.6.1 Internal IT System

Digitization enhances internal IT systems, making them the backbone of repair models. These systems enable manufacturers to monitor, manage, and optimize repair processes effectively. Advanced supply chain management systems track products throughout their lifecycle, ensuring seamless integration of reverse logistics for returned items. Real-time data exchange improves the efficiency of routing and processing returned products, facilitating repair, refurbishment, and recycling.

Modern CRM systems facilitate continuous engagement with customers, offering educational content on product use, maintenance, and disposal. Automated follow-ups at lifecycle milestones encourage customers to participate in repair activities. Integrated waste management systems (WMS) with AI capabilities optimize waste sorting and processing, ensuring sustainable waste management within the repair process. These systems provide insights into the lifecycle of materials, aiding in the effective reuse and recycling of components.

Quality control systems (QCS) ensure that repaired and refurbished products meet consistent quality standards, incorporating feedback loops for continuous improvement. These systems help maintain the reliability and performance of products over extended lifecycles. Inventory management systems (IMS) manage the flow of spare parts and monitor the availability of recycled inputs, optimizing inventory levels to support repair activities. This ensures timely access to necessary components, reducing downtime in repair processes.

6.6.2 Business Ecosystem

Digitization enhances the business ecosystem by fostering collaboration and efficient resource utilization, which supports effective repair models. Digital platforms, such as collaboration platforms, enable partners to share ideas and resources, promoting collective creativity and innovation in repair processes. Orchestration platforms streamline processes across multiple participants, ensuring smooth interaction and coordination within the supply chain.

Interconnectivity and real-time communication are facilitated by IoT sensors and advanced analytics, allowing for real-time data sharing among stakeholders and dynamic adjustments for optimal efficiency. Predictive analytics forecast material availability and optimize resource planning, supporting a resilient and responsive repair ecosystem. Digital ecosystems simplify adherence to regulations by automating compliance tracking and reporting, ensuring that all participants meet regulatory standards, and enhancing transparency and trust within the ecosystem.

6.6.3 Connected Products

Connected products support repair models through continuous monitoring and data-driven decision-making. IoT technologies enable real-time monitoring of product performance, identifying potential issues before they escalate. Predictive maintenance driven by IoT data extends product lifecycles and reduces waste. Digital Product Passports (DPPs) (discussed further in Sect. 6.6.6) provide detailed product information, facilitating easier and more accurate repairs. Technicians and repair services can access comprehensive product specifications, enhancing the quality and efficiency of repairs.

6.6.4 Customer Experience

Digitization improves customer experience, promoting repair models and fostering customer loyalty. Advanced analytics and AI enable personalized product recommendations and proactive maintenance alerts, encouraging responsible consumption. Customers receive tailored incentives for circular behaviors, fostering deeper loyalty and engagement. Digital platforms provide transparent repair tracking and cost estimates, empowering customers to make informed decisions. Regular updates and communication enhance customer trust and satisfaction throughout the repair process.

6.6.5 Data-Driven Circularity

Data-driven approaches optimize repair models and improve resource efficiency. Integrating data from various touchpoints provides a comprehensive view of product lifecycles, supporting strategic decision-making in repair processes. Advanced business intelligence (BI) and machine learning (ML) tools analyze data to identify patterns and opportunities for improvement in repair and recycling processes. AI-driven decision support tools recommend optimal repair activities based on product conditions, market demand, and service provider capabilities. These tools enhance operational agility, reduce supply chain vulnerabilities, and improve profitability.

6.6.6 Utilizing Digital Product Passports to Enhance Repairability

The Digital Product Passport (DPP) (Sect. 2.2) will play a pivotal role in supporting the repair business model for manufacturers by streamlining access to product information and fostering transparency.

Consider a scenario where a consumer electronics manufacturer integrates DPPs into their smartphone line. Repair centers can scan a QR code on the device to access a digital passport detailing each component's specifications, the right tools for opening the device, and guidelines for replacing specific parts like the screen or battery.

The DPP provides technicians and repair services access to detailed product specifications and schematics, enabling them to better understand product compositions and the relationships between different parts. DPP can reduce the time and effort needed to diagnose issues and perform repairs. For instance, the digital product passport can reveal the exact type of screws used in a device, the arrangement of internal components, and guidelines for safe disassembly.

The DPP ensures that repair processes are consistent regardless of the location or service provider by centralizing and standardizing access to manuals, repair guides, and specifications. This standardization helps maintain the quality and reliability of repairs and reduces the risk of damage during the repair process.

DPP helps repair businesses comply with regional and international standards regarding product handling, waste disposal, and recycling. For example, knowing the exact materials in a product can ensure that hazardous substances are properly handled or disposed of, adhering to environmental regulations and avoiding potential fines.

DPP's transparency allows value chain customers to verify parts' authenticity and the repair methods' eco-friendliness.

With DPPs, manufacturers can track which parts are most often repaired or replaced, gathering data that can inform future design improvements to reduce

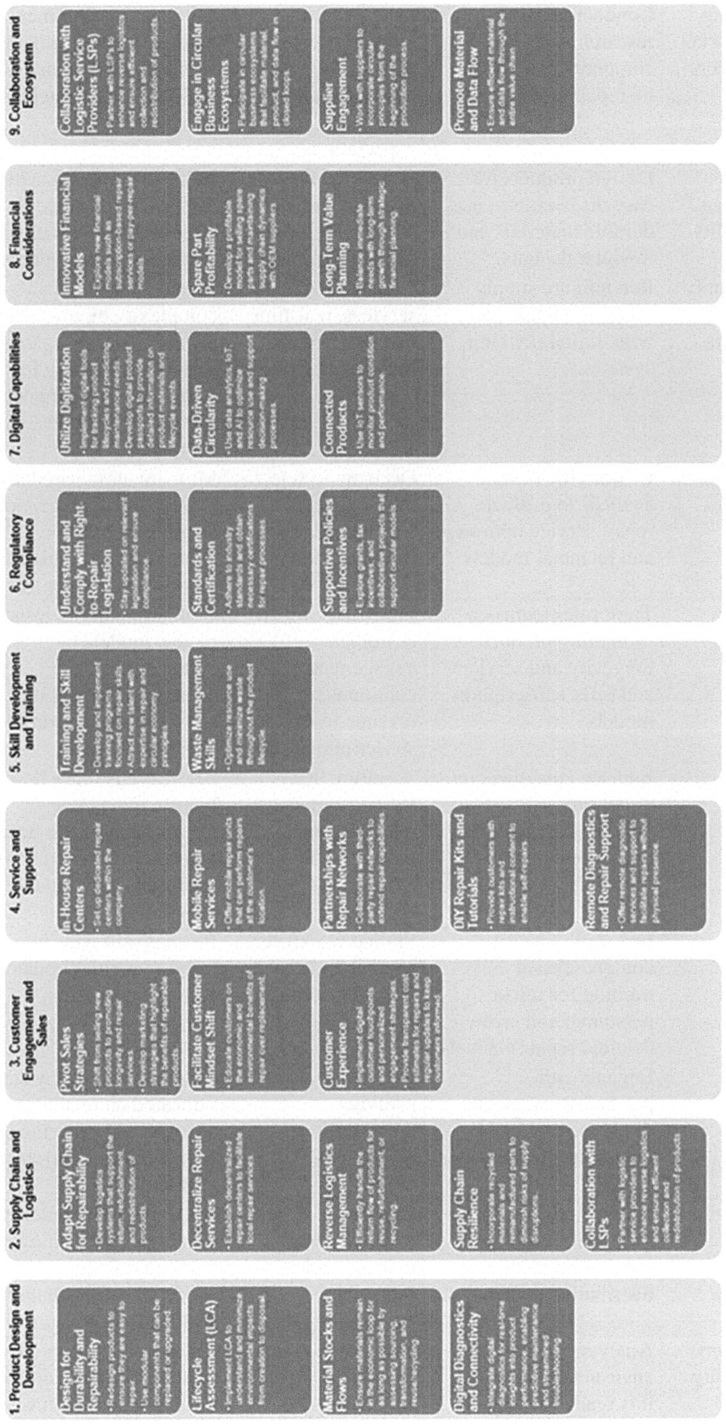

Fig. 6.4 Capability map for repair business models in manufacturing

Table 6.1 The checklist for enhancing repairability within manufacturing

Task	Methodology	Expected outcome	Risk mitigated
Understanding the repair market and competitors' position	Conduct market research and competitive analysis on repair services	Insights into market demand, competitor strategies, and customer expectations	Mitigate misalignment with market trends by regularly updating market analysis and adjusting strategies accordingly
Enhancing product design for repairability	Design products for easy disassembly; use durable materials and modular designs	Simplified repair process, reduced waste, and support for recycling	Balance durability with performance and cost-effectiveness to maintain market competitiveness
Adapting supply chain logistics for spare parts	Reconfigure supply chains for spare parts with digital tracking systems	Efficient repair services, real-time inventory, and logistics tracking	Manage logistical complexity by investing in advanced digital systems and robust training for supply chain personnel to prevent delays and shortages
Embracing repair services	Utilize cost-benefit analysis to evaluate repair service options and financial models	Decision to select the best repair service and financial models	Mitigate unpreparedness for market shifts by developing adaptable business strategies and continuously monitoring market trends
Shift in sales strategies	Train sales teams on promoting product longevity and service and offer subscription models	Increased customer engagement, continuous revenue from subscriptions	Counter potential resistance to new models by demonstrating the economic benefits of subscription and long-term savings
Customer mindset shift	Educate customers on circularity Offer loyalty programs and personalized maintenance schedules	A culture that values product longevity and resource efficiency	Address customer hesitancy by providing clear information on the benefits and ease of participating in repair and maintenance programs
Training and skill development	Invest in comprehensive training for repair personnel and create detailed repair manuals	Skilled workforce capable of handling complex repairs	Prevent skill gaps by offering regular updates and ongoing education programs
Regulatory compliance	Engage with policymakers, ensure transparency, and communicate customer rights	Compliance with evolving repairability regulations	Avoid legal risks by staying informed on regulatory changes and ensuring all practices meet current standards
Collaboration with logistic service providers	Utilize LSPs for reverse logistics and repair hubs within distribution centers	Enhanced efficiency and reduced carbon footprint	Mitigate coordination issues by establishing clear agreements and regular communication channels with LSPs
Digital support for repairability	Analyze the IT environment to ensure it is ready to support repair business models	Streamlined repair processes, enhanced product transparency	Mitigate the risk of IT systems being incompatible or insufficient by investing in necessary upgrades and staff training

failure rates and enhance durability. This feedback loop improves product design and optimizes inventory management for spare parts, ensuring that resources are used more efficiently.

6.7 Capability Map for Repair Business Models in Manufacturing

The capability map for repair (Fig. 6.4) outlines key capabilities for manufacturers to enable profitable repair business models.

6.8 Embracing Repairability

This chapter explored the various dimensions of increasing product repairability, from legislative drivers like right to repair laws to innovative business models that manufacturers can adopt to harness the benefits of an enhanced focus on repair.

Manufacturers must place repairability at the core of their operations as they reimagine their approach to product design, supply chain logistics, and customer engagement. This shift requires a balance of technological innovation, such as integrating IoT for predictive maintenance and using digital platforms for customer interaction, alongside a rethinking of traditional business models to include services like mobile repair units and partnerships with repair networks.

The challenges range from logistical complexities to the need for quality control in repairs and spare parts management. However, the opportunities for manufacturers to differentiate themselves, build deeper customer relationships, and tap into new revenue streams are equally compelling. Embracing repairability allows manufacturers to align with evolving customer expectations and regulatory landscapes.

The checklist for enhancing repairability within manufacturing (Table 6.1) outlines strategic actions, methodologies, and expected outcomes.

References

Apple Inc. (2024). *Self-Service Repair Program*. Retrieved from https://www.apple.com/self-service-repair

Bosch. (2023). *Online Repair Service for Power Tools*. Retrieved from https://www.boschtools.com/repair-service

Bosch. (2024, 06). *Online Repair Service*. From https://www.bosch-professional.com/gb/en/service/after-sales-service/online-repair-service/

European Commission. (2023). *Introduction of the right to repair for consumers*. Retrieved from https://ec.europa.eu/right-to-repair

FasterCapital. (2024). *The impact of planned obsolescence on the economy*. Retrieved from https://www.fastercapital.com/planned-obsolescence

Fnac Darty. (2023). *Repair Subscription Service*. Retrieved from https://www.fnacdarty.com/repair-subscription

HP. (2024, 06). *HP All-In Plan*. From https://www.hp.com/us-en/all-in-plan/printers.html

Iberdrola. (2024). *The concept of planned obsolescence*. Retrieved from https://www.iberdrola.com/planned-obsolescence

Phoebus Cartel. (1924). *History of the Phoebus Cartel and Light Bulb Lifespan Limitation*. Retrieved from https://www.phoebuscartel.com/history

4th and 5th R – Maximizing Product Lifecycles: Integrating Refurbishment and Remanufacturing Strategies

7

Abstract

This chapter delves into the strategic integration of refurbishment and remanufacturing, highlighting their environmental and economic benefits. These processes extend product lifecycles, offering a sustainable alternative to disposal and reducing the need for new raw materials, thus supporting cost savings and increased profitability. By tapping into the market of price-sensitive customers, manufacturers can diversify their revenue streams, enhancing financial stability and profitability. Remanufacturing also incurs lower material and labor costs than new manufacturing, leading to higher profit margins.

The chapter emphasizes brand differentiation through high-quality, certified remanufactured products, appealing to eco-conscious consumers and enhancing brand reputation. Operational agility is achieved by reusing existing resources, allowing companies to adapt quickly to market demand and supply chain dynamics. Remanufacturing is also positioned as a future-proof strategy, addressing sustainability trends and regulatory demands, thereby establishing manufacturers as leaders in the circular economy.

Additionally, the chapter covers the similarities between refurbishment and remanufacturing, including the business decisions and challenges involved. Both processes aim to prolong product life, minimize waste, and maximize resource value, making them essential to a circular business strategy. By integrating these strategies, manufacturers can achieve comprehensive benefits, including financial gains, improved market positioning, enhanced supply chain resilience, and increased customer satisfaction, preparing them for a sustainable future.

H. H. Jensen, *Circular Economy Opportunities and Pathways for Manufacturers*, Future of Business and Finance, https://doi.org/10.1007/978-3-031-75279-7_7

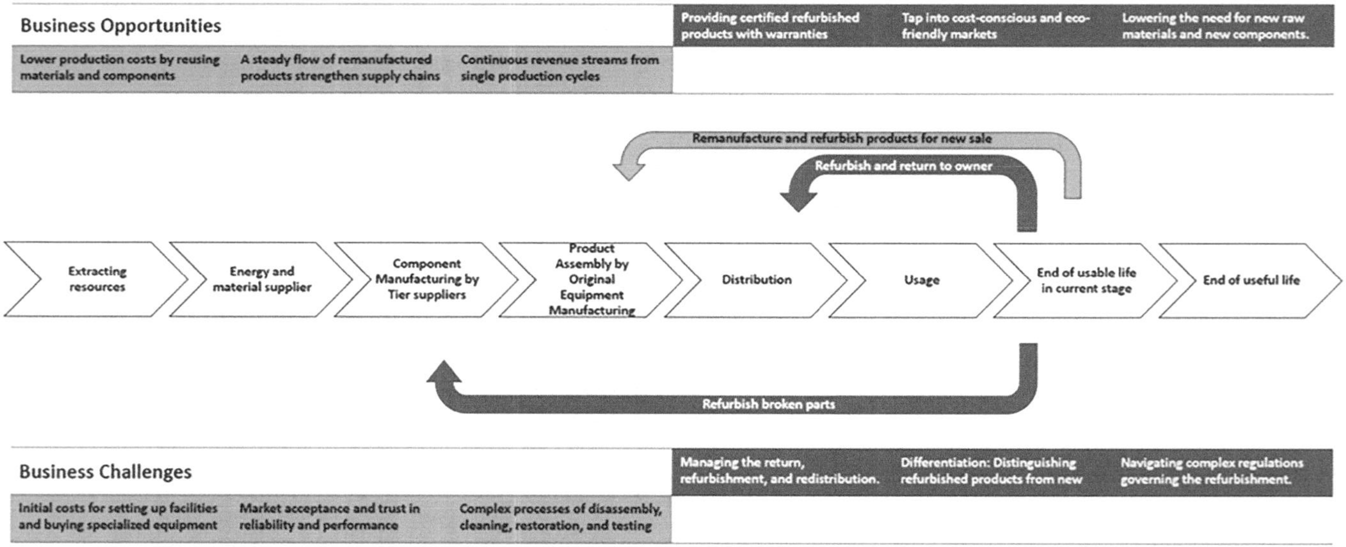

Fig. 7.1 Refurbishment and remanufacturing's placement in circular flow (Figure 1.6) and three significant business opportunities and challenges

Key Message

- *Environmental and Economic Benefits*: Remanufacturing transforms used products into valuable assets, offering an environmentally friendly alternative to disposal and reducing the demand for new raw materials. This process supports sustainability goals while contributing to cost savings and increased profitability.
- *New Revenue Streams*: By remanufacturing products, manufacturers can tap into a growing market of price-sensitive customers seeking high-quality items at reduced prices. This diversification enhances financial portfolios and boosts overall profitability.
- *Cost Advantages*: Remanufacturing used products often incurs lower material and labor costs than manufacturing new ones. This leads to higher profit margins and more stable production costs, as manufacturers are less affected by raw material price fluctuations.
- *Brand Differentiation*: Implementing remanufacturing strategies allows manufacturers to distinguish themselves by promoting high-quality, certified products. This appeals to eco-conscious customers and enhances brand reputation and customer loyalty.
- *Operational Agility*: Remanufacturing enables manufacturers to maintain operational agility. By reusing existing resources, companies can quickly adapt to changes in market demand and supply chain dynamics.
- *Future-Proofing*: As the manufacturing landscape shifts toward sustainability and efficiency, remanufacturing becomes a strategic element of business planning. It addresses customer trends and regulatory demands, positioning manufacturers as leaders in the circular economy.
- *Comprehensive Benefits*: Remanufacturing offers diverse benefits, including financial advantages, improved market positioning, enhanced supply chain resilience, and increased customer satisfaction. By investing in remanufacturing capabilities, manufacturers meet current market demands and prepare to lead in a sustainable future.

Refurbishment and remanufacturing are often seen as separate processes in a circular economy. However, the business decisions and challenges involved in these activities are similar, and the distinction between them can be unclear. Both processes aim to prolong the life of products, minimize waste, and maximize the value derived from resources, making them essential components of a circular business strategy (Fig. 7.1).

Refurbishment involves restoring used products to good working condition by repairing or replacing components as needed. On the other hand, remanufacturing takes this further by restoring products to a performance level equal to or better than new products. Although there are technical differences, businesses often face similar considerations, including quality control, cost management, market acceptance, and regulatory compliance.

Given these similarities, this chapter combines the discussions of refurbishment and remanufacturing into a single comprehensive guide to provide a holistic understanding of the opportunities and challenges associated with product revitalization.

If we consider the three categories of product use extension

Repair addresses specific faults or malfunctions within a product, aiming to restore its functionality without necessarily enhancing its overall condition. Repair is a targeted intervention that resolves immediate issues and enables the product to resume its intended function.

Example 7.1 Repairing a compressor

For instance, repairing a compressor requires identifying and fixing specific faults or damaged components to restore the compressor to working condition. This process may involve replacing faulty parts, such as seals or valves, and addressing immediate mechanical issues. The objective is promptly returning the compressor to operational status with minimal intervention, ensuring it can continue functioning as intended without requiring extensive overhauls.

Refurbishment is repairing and revitalizing products to a functional state, often without replacing all components. While refurbishment does not necessarily restore products to their original condition, it ensures that they are fully operational and can continue to serve their intended purpose.

Here's a breakdown of the refurbishment process (Vela, 2024):

- *Evaluation:* Used products are assessed to determine the repair needed. This evaluation identifies faulty or damaged components that require attention.
- *Repair and Replacement:* Damaged or worn components are repaired or replaced to restore the product's functionality. This might involve fixing minor defects, replacing worn-out parts, or upgrading specific components.
- *Testing:* Refurbished products undergo testing to ensure the repaired components function correctly and meet quality standards.
- *Cosmetic Improvement:* In addition to functionality, cosmetic aspects such as cleaning, repainting, or replacing worn surfaces might be addressed to improve the product's appearance.

Example 7.2 Compressor Refurbishment

Refurbishment involves disassembling the compressor, cleaning all components, replacing worn parts, and making necessary cosmetic improvements. Refurbishment may also include performance enhancements to ensure the compressor operates more efficiently and reliably. The goal is to extend the compressor's lifespan and improve its overall functionality and appearance, making it more appealing and valuable.

Remanufacturing involves disassembling the device, evaluating, cleaning, restoring or replacing, and testing each part to ensure it meets or exceeds original performance standards.

Here's a breakdown of the remanufacturing process (Vela, 2024):

- *Disassembly:* Used products are separated into components to evaluate each part for reuse or replacement.
- *Cleaning and Inspection:* Components undergo cleaning, inspection, and testing to identify defects, wear, or damage. Parts not meeting required standards are replaced.
- *Reassembly:* Once components are cleaned and inspected, they are reassembled into a remanufactured product according to original specifications or improved designs.
- *Testing:* Remanufactured products undergo extensive testing to meet or exceed new products' quality and performance standards.

Example 7.3 Compressor remanufacturing

When a compressor undergoes remanufacturing, it is completely disassembled to its core elements. Each component is thoroughly inspected for wear and functionality, and all parts are replaced or restored to meet or exceed original specifications. The remanufacturing process ensures the compressor is rebuilt to a "like new" condition, often incorporating the latest technology and improvements. This method extends the compressor's lifespan, offering performance and reliability comparable to a new unit.

While remanufacturing is more labor-intensive and potentially more expensive than refurbishment, it offers value by providing customers with a device that is "like new" in quality and reliability. Both allow manufacturers to obtain value continuously from a single production cycle investment.

In summary, refurbishment focuses on quickly and cost-effectively restoring and enhancing a product's functionality and aesthetics. At the same time, remanufacturing involves a detailed and thorough rebuilding process that delivers a product of like-new quality and reliability.

Section 11.4.2 details the process steps for remanufacturing.

Refurbishment and remanufacturing extend products' usability and reduce the need for new materials and energy consumption associated with manufacturing, thus lessening environmental impact. Additionally, refurbishment and remanufacturing present attractive business models for manufacturers, offering opportunities to enter secondary markets and increase the revenue potential of their products.

For example, the global refurbished electronics market is estimated to reach $48.29 billion in 2023 and $94.10 billion by 2030, showing a compound annual growth rate (CAGR) of 10% (Coherent Market Insights, 2024).

In the rest of this chapter, "remanufacturing" will be used as an umbrella term covering refurbishment and remanufacturing processes for clarity and to avoid confusion. In the examples, the use of the term "refurbishment" or "remanufacturing" reflects the language used by the company in the example.

Example 7.4 Caterpillar's Cat Reman

Caterpillar's Cat Reman restores used parts and components to their original performance specifications, providing cost-effective solutions for Caterpillar's customers.

First, the used components, or "cores," are thoroughly inspected upon receipt. The eligible cores then undergo a comprehensive disassembly, and each piece is cleaned and examined. Advanced techniques such as laser cladding and machining restore the parts' original characteristics.

One key distinction of Cat Reman products is that they are not merely rebuilt or refurbished but completely remanufactured. This ensures that each part meets strict OEM performance specifications before re-entering the supply chain. Caterpillar's 12-month warranty underscores this commitment to quality.

The remanufacturing process reduces greenhouse gas emissions, with Cat Reman operations producing 65–87% fewer emissions than traditional manufacturing. Additionally, this process uses 80–90% less raw material and energy.

Cat Reman parts provide cost benefits, priced between 45 and 85% of the cost of equivalent new parts, contingent on the return of the core component. This pricing strategy makes Cat Reman parts an attractive option for reducing the total cost of ownership for equipment operators. Additionally, the availability of remanufactured parts helps maintain machine uptime and reduce operations delays (Caterpillar, 2024).

7.1 Strategic Product Selection

Manufacturers carefully evaluate several key factors when selecting products for remanufacturing (Fig. 7.2). The primary consideration is market demand for remanufactured items. Understanding customer preferences, emerging trends, and the competitive landscape helps identify products that will sell well once remanufactured.

Apart from market demand, the value of the materials used in the original products also plays a role in the selection process. High-value materials, such as aluminum and copper, retain their worth over time and contribute to the cost-effectiveness of remanufacturing. Utilizing high-value materials aligns with environmental objectives by reducing waste and minimizing the demand for virgin materials.

When selecting a product for remanufacturing, its design must be considered, particularly its suitability for disassembly and reassembly. Products that are

Fig. 7.2 Strategic product selection for remanufacturing

modular by design (Sect. 4.1.2) or have features that allow for easy dismantling without damaging the components and without requiring specialized tools are the ideal candidates for remanufacturing. Modularity enables manufacturers to update individual components instead of replacing the entire product. The design-for-disassembly approach simplifies the remanufacturing process and reduces the risk of damaging valuable components, thereby preserving their functional and economic value.

A product designed for remanufacturing should use standardized parts wherever possible, making it easier to interchange components and reducing the complexity and cost of storing spare parts. Standardization is complemented by durable materials and construction techniques that can withstand multiple use cycles and remanufacturing. This will help ensure that the product can be used for an extended period, reducing the environmental impact and saving resources. Additionally, the selection process should also consider the product's technological lifecycle. In fast-evolving industries like electronics, where technological obsolescence can quickly render a product irrelevant, manufacturers must carefully assess the potential lifespan of remanufactured items. Products with longer expected lifecycles or those that can be easily updated or upgraded to meet current standards are better suited to remanufacturing. This ensures their continued usefulness and desirability in the market.

Example 7.5 Cummins Inc has designed its new engines with remanufacturing in mind

Cummins Inc., a global leader in power solutions, has designed its new engines with remanufacturing in mind. Up to 85 percent of an engine can be remanufactured, and Cummins engines are constructed to be remanufactured multiple times. Cummins' remanufactured parts are designed for seamless integration, ensuring minimal downtime for fleets. The plug-and-play nature of these parts simplifies maintenance and streamlines fleet management. Their remanufacturing facilities utilize advanced diagnostic and cleaning equipment, precision machining tools, and automated assembly lines to ensure that each remanufactured engine meets quality standards (Cummins, 2024).

7.2 Remanufacturing Business Opportunities

Remanufacturing strategies offer manufacturers a broad spectrum of business opportunities, enhancing their sustainability credentials and bottom line through new revenue streams, reduced costs, and expanding customer choice.

7.2.1 New Revenue Streams

Remanufacturing products allow manufacturers to diversify their revenue streams beyond selling new items. By upgrading used products to meet specific quality standards, manufacturers can create a "like-new" product category that appeals to a different market segment. This approach not only prolongs the economic lifespan of their products but also introduces multiple income streams from the same asset, thereby enhancing overall profitability. The resale of remanufactured products, especially when supported by a warranty, can attract price-sensitive customers who still demand high quality, opening up new market opportunities. Additionally, this strategy can strengthen customer loyalty and brand reputation, demonstrating a commitment to sustainability and value. By tapping into the growing demand for sustainable and cost-effective alternatives, manufacturers can position themselves as leaders in the circular economy, capturing a share of the expanding market for remanufactured goods.

Example 7.6 Danfoss' refurbished high-pressure pump

Refurbishment is essential in industries like desalination, where longevity and efficiency are paramount. Danfoss, a global leader in engineering solutions, designed the APP high-pressure pump to supply seawater at high pressure to reverse osmosis membranes, a critical function in desalination (Danfoss, 2022).

Danfoss's refurbished high-pressure pump setups are made of high-quality stainless steel. They are very heavy to move and expensive to produce. However, Danfoss is giving its parts a second life. When Danfoss receives a pump for renovation, it refurbishes the parts, replaces worn-out ones, tests for full functionality, and grants the customer a new warranty period.

The service provides several advantages. The affordability makes the technology accessible to a wider range of operators, potentially expanding the market. Danfoss ensures material efficiency and reduces environmental impact as components and materials are kept in use for as long as possible. Additionally, offering an energy-efficient, cost-effective, and reliable refurbished option sets Danfoss apart in a competitive market.

7.2.2 Opportunities Within Parts Supply

Remanufacturing products create opportunities in parts supply. As products undergo remanufacturing, components are often replaced, leading to a steady demand for high-quality parts. This demand can establish a profitable market for parts manufacturers.

The growing market for remanufactured goods has increased the demand for specific components, including electronic parts and mechanical replacements. This ongoing demand creates a steady revenue stream for manufacturers capable of supplying reliable parts. By ensuring the availability of components, manufacturers support remanufacturers in maintaining the quality and functionality of remanufactured goods, thereby contributing to overall market stability and growth.

However, manufacturers must deal with several challenges. It can be difficult to ensure the availability of parts for older or less common models and to establish an efficient logistics network to distribute parts promptly and cost-effectively.

7.2.3 Strategic Approaches to Capitalize on the Remanufacturing Market

This section examines different remanufacturing strategies, outlining the benefits and challenges of each approach (Fig. 7.3).

Fig. 7.3 Strategic Approaches to Capitalize on the Remanufacturing Market

7.2.3.1 In-House Remanufacturing

In-house remanufacturing involves the manufacturer establishing dedicated remanufacturing centers within their facilities. These centers have the necessary tools, technology, and trained personnel for remanufacturing.

> **Example 7.7** Cummins ReCon facilities use collaborative robots
>
> Cummins ReCon facilities use advanced technologies such as collaborative robots, delivery robots, and laser cleaning to improve workplace safety and efficiency. Metal additive manufacturing, also known as 3D printing, enables Cummins to create replacement parts when suppliers stop production, extending the lifespan of their products. Metal 3D printing reduces material waste and processing steps, supports local production, allows for engineering and performance updates, and streamlines the supply chain (Cummins Inc, 2024).

This approach enables manufacturers to uphold rigorous quality control throughout the remanufacturing process, guaranteeing that the remanufactured products adhere to the same standards as new ones. Furthermore, direct oversight helps to maintain brand integrity and ensures uniform customer satisfaction. Manufacturers also retain control over proprietary technologies and processes and can directly access the revenue and profit opportunities of the remanufacturing market.

In-house remanufacturing enables a direct and continuous connection with customers. This connection offers valuable insights into customer needs and product performance, fostering loyalty and trust. The feedback loop generated through this interaction is utilized for continuous improvement and innovation, empowering manufacturers to adjust and refine their products to better align with expectations.

Setting up in-house remanufacturing centers requires capital investment in equipment, facilities, training, and digitization. Managing a remanufacturing operation adds complexity to the existing business operations, and scaling in-house operations quickly in response to varying demands can be challenging.

Diverting resources to remanufacturing can shift focus from primary manufacturing activities, hindering new product development and innovation-driven initiatives for staying competitive in dynamic markets.

Example 7.8 Vestas' program for remanufacturing wind turbines

Vestas, one of the top manufacturers of wind turbines, has developed a program for remanufacturing wind turbines.[1] This process starts with a detailed disassembly of each turbine down to its core components, which are carefully cleaned, inspected, and restored to meet or exceed their original functionality. The refurbishment covers everything from minor mechanical repairs to major overhauls of blades and electrical systems.

By remanufacturing used turbines, Vestas can reuse up to 95% of the component material, reducing the carbon footprint by avoiding the emissions of producing new materials. Additionally, the refurbished turbines usually generate around 60% less CO2 emissions compared to new parts, taking into account the logistics of reverse transportation (Vestas, 2024).

Vestas ensures that each turbine is aesthetically restored and subjected to rigorous performance tests to ensure that they function as well as new units. This level of attention guarantees that the turbines meet the technical and aesthetic standards expected of new products and offer an extended service life, with many assessed to have over 15 years of operational viability left.

This strategic refurbishment approach helps Vestas and its customers to benefit from lower upfront costs and reduced maintenance expenses.

[1] https://www.vestas.com/en/energy-solutions/refurbished-turbines

7.2.3.2 Third-Party Remanufacturing

Third-party remanufacturing involves collaborating with specialized external companies to remanufacture products on behalf of the manufacturer.

This approach can be more cost-effective than maintaining in-house operations, especially for smaller batches or occasional remanufacturing needs. Third-party firms often have specialized expertise and experience, ensuring high-quality remanufacturing. It also allows manufacturers to quickly scale up or down based on demand without significant capital investment. Additionally, partnering with third-party remanufacturers can open new revenue streams and profitability for manufacturers through the remanufactured products market.

This cost-effective approach allows manufacturers to focus their financial and operational resources on core manufacturing and innovation activities while reaping the benefits of remanufacturing.

However, maintaining the desired quality standards when working with third-party remanufacturers can be difficult. Depending on external firms introduces potential risks related to partner reliability and performance. Any issues with the third-party remanufacturing process can affect the manufacturer's brand reputation. Additionally, the costs incurred by third-party remanufacturers can sometimes be significant, impacting the overall cost-efficiency of this approach.

7.2.3.3 Market-Driven Remanufacturing

In a market-driven approach, manufacturers permit independent remanufacturers and secondary markets to renovate and resell their products, relying on a robust secondary market ecosystem.

Manufacturers do not need to invest in remanufacturing facilities or processes, and the secondary market can efficiently match supply and demand for remanufactured products, reaching different market segments and geographical areas.

The quality of remanufactured products can vary widely, potentially affecting brand perception. Manufacturers have little control over the remanufacturing process and standards, which can lead to inconsistent product quality and customer experiences, thereby diluting the manufacturer's brand. Additionally, manufacturers do not generate significant revenue from this remanufacturing approach. However, manufacturers can still benefit by validating the quality of independently remanufactured products and offering warranties. They can also choose to resell these verified products themselves. Nonetheless, this approach risks building a competitive market where independent remanufacturers may start to compete with the manufacturers' offerings.

Example 7.9 Amazon Renewed

Amazon Renewed allows third-party sellers to offer refurbished products meeting Amazon's quality standards, enabling independent refurbishers to access a broad customer base while ensuring high product quality and customer satisfaction.

(continued)

The refurbisher thoroughly tests and inspects the refurbished products to ensure they function like new ones and meet Amazon's standards.

Amazon Renewed products come with the Amazon Renewed Guarantee, which offers customers a warranty period. Typically, standard products have a 90-day warranty, while premium products have a warranty of up to 1 year. This guarantee boosts customer confidence and ensures that the refurbished products meet their expectations in terms of quality and reliability (Amazon, 2024).

7.2.3.4 Recycling Non-suitable Products and Parts

Some parts and products are not suitable for remanufacturing. Recycling is the best option for these items to ensure materials are recovered and reused, minimizing environmental impact.

7.2.3.5 End as Waste

When products are not remanufactured or recycled, they are discarded as waste.

It is the most straightforward approach, requiring no additional processes or infrastructure. This allows manufacturers to focus exclusively on producing and selling new products without the added complexity of remanufacturing.

Disposing of products as waste contributes to environmental pollution and resource depletion while also missing out on potential revenue streams from remanufactured products. Increasing regulations around waste may pose compliance risks. Furthermore, this approach does not meet the growing customer expectations for sustainability and no-waste practices, potentially harming the manufacturer's reputation.

7.2.4 Cost-Effectiveness

Adopting a remanufacturing strategy offers cost advantages for manufacturers compared to producing new goods.

When manufacturers remanufacture existing products, they use fewer raw materials than when they manufacture new ones. Manufacturers can reduce material costs by reusing components and materials from returned or used products. This helps to lower expenses and lessen the impact of fluctuating raw material prices, leading to more stable and predictable production costs.

Remanufacturing allows manufacturers to consistently extract value from a single production cycle investment and generate revenue from assets that would otherwise be considered at the end of their lifecycle, maximizing return on investment and contributing to a more efficient business model.

Example 7.10 Schaeffler's refurbishment service for axle box bearings

Schaeffler is a global manufacturer of rolling bearings, components, and systems for engine, transmission, and chassis applications.

The railway industry is under pressure to ensure reliability, decrease downtime, and manage costs. To address these challenges, Schaeffler provides a refurbishment service for axle box bearings. This program examines and assesses used rail bearings to determine their suitability for refurbishment. Bearings that meet the criteria undergo a thorough cleaning process, and all worn-out components are replaced. The bearings are then reassembled, regreased, and sealed, ensuring they meet the quality standards.

By offering this service, Schaeffler ensures that railway operators can make the most of their bearings. Instead of replacing entire bearing sets, which can be expensive and resource-intensive, operators can refurbish their existing bearings, thus extending their service life and reducing overall lifecycle costs (Schaeffler, 2022).

The labor required to remanufacture products is often less intensive than that needed for full-scale production. Skilled technicians can upgrade and restore products more quickly than assembling new ones from scratch.

Remanufactured products often result in higher profit margins. Due to lower materials and labor costs, manufacturers can price remanufactured items competitively while maintaining healthy margins. The increasing customer demand for sustainable and cost-effective products can also lead to higher sales volumes, further boosting profitability.

Remanufacturing enables manufacturers to manage their inventory more flexibly. By remanufacturing returned or unsold products, manufacturers can quickly adjust to market demand changes without increasing new production. This flexibility helps reduce excess inventory and associated holding costs, resulting in a more cost-effective supply chain.

Numerous regions provide financial incentives and regulatory advantages for businesses that embrace sustainable practices, such as remanufacturing. By taking advantage of these incentives, manufacturers can lower costs and enhance their market position. Furthermore, adherence to environmental regulations can help avoid fines.

Example 7.11 Tetra Pak's refurbishment operations

Tetra Pak, a leader in processing and packaging solutions, has embraced refurbishment as a component of its business model. The company's refurbishment approach underscores the need for highly skilled personnel with the technical understanding required to refurbish complex machinery and a mindset attuned to sustainability and precision. This dual requirement ensures

(continued)

that Tetra Pak's refurbished machines meet high standards in terms of performance and reliability.

The refurbishment process at Tetra Pak involves a thorough inspection to identify components needing repair or replacement, cleaning, and, often, software updates to enhance efficiency.

Quality assurance plays a pivotal role in Tetra Pak's refurbishment operations. The company adheres to stringent quality standards, ensuring that each refurbished machine not only looks new but operates with a level of efficiency and reliability comparable to new equipment. Rigorous testing is a part of the process, ensuring that every machine meets Tetra Pak's standards before it is ready for resale.

In marketing these refurbished machines, Tetra Pak positions them as a sustainable and cost-effective alternative to new equipment. This strategy appeals to customers with budget constraints and those keen on making environmentally responsible purchasing decisions. By differentiating refurbished machines from new ones, Tetra Pak sets clear expectations about the product, including its warranty, performance, and price, effectively preventing any potential cannibalization of sales of new machines.

Tetra Pak provides comprehensive services, including installation, maintenance, and troubleshooting, ensuring that customers enjoy the same level of support as they would with new equipment. This level of service, coupled with a limited warranty, offers customers peace of mind and reinforces the value proposition of Tetra Pak's refurbished machines.

Through its refurbishment program, Tetra Pak addresses the needs of a diverse customer base, offering high-quality, reliable, and environmentally friendly alternatives to new equipment (Tetra Pak, 2024).

7.2.5 Remanufacturing as a Pillar of Supply Chain Resilience

Integrating remanufacturing into manufacturing operations is important in today's globalized economy. With supply chains extending across borders and continents, there is always a risk of disruptions due to geopolitical tensions, logistical challenges, or environmental factors. Remanufacturing provides autonomy and control over the supply chain, enhancing resilience and stability in these global uncertainties.

Remanufacturing improves supply chain resilience. Manufacturers can overcome the challenges of resource scarcity and supply chain disruptions by managing their products' lifecycles, improving remanufacturing processes, and carefully balancing inventory with new products and components. This strategy ensures a consistent and dependable production flow, protecting against market fluctuations and supply chain disruptions.

Efficient return systems are needed to allow manufacturers to recapture valuable components at the end of their current life. This sets the stage for reintroducing these components into the production cycle. Effective inventory management also plays a role in remanufacturing. It involves maintaining a balanced inventory of reclaimed components awaiting refurbishment and finished remanufactured products ready for market. This ensures manufacturers respond quickly to market demands, providing a buffer against supply chain fluctuations and disruptions.

7.3 Challenges

While remanufacturing offers numerous environmental and business opportunities, it also comes with challenges that must be addressed to establish a successful remanufacturing program. Key issues include maintaining consistent product quality, managing reverse logistics complexities, ensuring core parts' availability, and addressing potential brand perception concerns. Additionally, navigating regulatory requirements and gaining market acceptance require strategic planning and execution.

7.3.1 Skill Set Requirement

Remanufacturing complex machinery requires a skilled workforce to diagnose, repair, and update older models to meet modern standards. This task can be challenging, especially when products manufactured in one region require remanufacturing elsewhere, introducing logistical and knowledge-transfer hurdles. Therefore, local teams must have the expertise and understanding of the original manufacturing context. This scenario necessitates strategic investments in training and development alongside robust systems for knowledge sharing and technical support across different locations.

Remanufacturing technicians must understand the intricate workings of the machinery they are revitalizing. This includes specialized training in mechanical and electrical components and any software that controls the equipment. This ensures technicians can accurately identify and rectify various issues, from wear and tear to outdated technology.

Diagnosing the condition of returned products requires a knowledge base to distinguish between cosmetic blemishes and critical functional defects. It is important to understand how each component contributes to the overall operation of the machinery. Developing this diagnostic insight is necessary to determine the feasibility of remanufacturing and the extent of work required.

Remanufacturing may involve troubleshooting complex problems that do not have standard solutions. Technicians must possess strong problem-solving skills, enabling them to devise innovative solutions for repairing and upgrading equipment. This might involve repurposing parts, custom fabricating components, or creatively overcoming obsolescence issues to extend the equipment's life.

A commitment to sustainability is integral to the remanufacturing process. Employees must understand the environmental impact of their work and be motivated to recover and repurpose as much of the original product as possible.

7.3.2 Navigating the Financial Frontiers of Remanufacturing

Embracing a remanufacturing business model entails navigating a complex landscape of initial investments and process optimization. This transformative journey requires manufacturers to equip themselves with the specialized machinery necessary for the efficient disassembly, inspection, and rejuvenation of used components.

7.3.2.1 Investment in Specialized Equipment

The success of a remanufacturing process relies on the acquisition of specialized equipment. This includes advanced machinery tailored to the precise tasks of disassembling products to salvage valuable components. It also involves advanced diagnostic tools that can accurately assess the condition of used parts, providing insights into components' wear, integrity, and functionality. These diagnostic tools range from high-resolution imaging systems to sophisticated scanning and sensor technologies, enabling the detailed analysis of parts at a granular level. By accurately identifying areas of wear or damage, these diagnostic tools help target remanufacturing efforts, ensuring optimal utilization of resources.

Sophisticated remanufacturing machinery is designed to cater to various remanufacturing needs, such as cleaning, decontamination, repairing, and reconditioning parts. These technologies ensure the thorough and efficient remanufacturing of parts, contributing to the consistency and quality of the remanufacturing process.

Testing and quality assurance equipment ensure that remanufactured components meet quality standards, maintaining customers' trust and confidence. This includes dynamic testing rigs that simulate operational conditions, environmental testing chambers that assess durability under various conditions, and quality control systems that employ manual and automated inspection techniques.

7.3.2.2 Workforce Training and Development

As mentioned in Sect. 7.3.1, a skilled workforce is indispensable in remanufacturing. Therefore, remanufacturers must invest in employee training and development to ensure the team possesses the required technical skills.

7.3.2.3 Implementation of IT Systems

The remanufacturing process requires IT infrastructure to track each component's life cycle carefully. This digital backbone allows for precise management of components from intake through remanufacturing and back into the production cycle, ensuring quality control and traceability at every stage. Developing and integrating such IT systems into remanufacturing require an initial investment. (Part III discusses digitization in detail.)

7.3.2.4 Overcoming Financial Barriers

Investing in remanufacturing can present unique financial challenges, particularly for smaller manufacturers or those with limited budgets. These challenges can be further compounded by the need to continue investments in existing business operations to maintain market competitiveness and drive growth during the transition.

To effectively navigate these financial challenges, businesses should explore innovative financing solutions, leverage governmental fiscal incentives for sustainable practices, and consider strategic partnerships to share the investment burden and gain operational advantages.

7.3.3 Mastering Quality Assurance

Achieving consistent quality in remanufactured parts is challenging due to the varied conditions and histories of used components. Unlike new parts produced under controlled manufacturing environments, remanufactured components have a history of use that can impact their condition. Various factors, such as varying levels of wear and tear, differing exposure to environmental conditions, and diverse maintenance practices, contribute to the uniqueness of each part, adding layers of complexity to the remanufacturing process.

Due to the inherent variability of used components, the remanufacturing process requires a flexible yet rigorous approach. Unlike in traditional manufacturing, where standardized processes are employed, remanufacturing must account for the individual nuances of each part. This means that two seemingly identical components may require different remanufacturing approaches based on their condition and history. Manufacturers are challenged to devise a remanufacturing process that can adapt to the unique needs of each component while remaining efficient and cost-effective.

To address the challenge, manufacturers must create comprehensive testing and quality assurance protocols. These protocols accurately evaluate each component's condition and determine necessary remanufacturing steps to restore it to the desired quality standard.

Advanced diagnostic technologies and skilled labor are important to achieving consistent quality in remanufactured parts. Diagnostic tools identify defects and wear patterns, helping to target remanufacturing efforts. Additionally, skilled technicians apply their expertise to the remanufacturing process, using specialized knowledge and techniques to restore each component effectively. Custom remanufacturing approaches may sometimes be necessary, especially for complex or heavily worn components.

Navigating the landscape of quality assurance in remanufacturing requires investment in advanced diagnostics, skilled technicians, and potentially custom remanufacturing techniques. However, this investment must be balanced against the costs and resources needed to achieve these high standards. Ultimately, it is a delicate balancing act that manufacturers must perform to ensure the best possible outcome.

7.3.4 Tackling Logistical Complexities

Managing the logistical complexities of remanufacturing requires strategic planning and innovative solutions. Manufacturers must delve deeply into the intricacies of supply chain management, specifically tailored to the unique demands of remanufacturing. These strategies must consider the inherent variability in the returned items' condition, type, and volume. Unlike traditional manufacturing supply chains, which deal with consistent and predictable inputs, remanufacturing supply chains must be able to adapt to various variables. Manufacturers must create systems that can handle fluctuations in the availability and quality of used components, ensuring that these variances do not disrupt the remanufacturing process.

7.3.4.1 Efficient Collection, Sorting, and Evaluation Mechanisms

One aspect of addressing the challenges in remanufacturing is establishing efficient systems for collecting, sorting, and evaluating used products, which requires a deep understanding of the product lifecycle.

Manufacturers face the challenge of motivating customers to return products for remanufacturing. They can implement incentive programs like trade-in discounts or loyalty rewards to address this. Transparent and convenient return policies and processes encourage customers to participate in remanufacturing programs.

Manufacturers can leverage their existing value chains to ease the return process for product owners. By utilizing established distribution and retail networks, manufacturers can create convenient and accessible customer return points.

Example 7.12 Grundfos' Take Back program

Grundfos, a multinational pump manufacturer with over 80 years in the industry, embeds circularity principles across the lifecycle of their products. Since 2014, Grundfos has been recovering used pumps through its Take Back program in collaboration with installers, wholesalers, and HVAC OEM manufacturers. The program is deployed in several markets, including the Netherlands, the United Kingdom, Italy, Germany, France, Denmark, and Sweden.

Grundfos provides its Take Back partners with a collection box, where installers can dispose of the end-of-life circulators collected at homeowners. Once a box is full, it is shipped to their disassembly facilities. Through manual disassembly carried out by workers with disabilities, the returned pumps are sorted into clean fractions. Some fractions are sent for recycling through internal recycling facilities or in collaboration with waste managers, while others are remanufactured to be reused in future products.

In 2023, Grundfos and one of its global customers, NIBE AB, launched a strategic partnership to expand its already existing Take Back collaboration and purchased 10,000 circulators made with remanufactured components. This was a significant step for Grundfos in providing a solution to extend the

(continued)

life of its pumps, reduce waste, and offer remanufactured products that maintain the quality standards of new pumps.

The benefits of this program are as follows:

- Reduction in landfill waste, conservation of resources, and decreased energy consumption in the production process
- Cost savings, enhanced customer satisfaction, bolstering Grundfos' reputation as a responsible, sustainable organization

In 2023, Grundfos received 134,098 kg of pumps through its take-back scheme, a 109% increase over the 2022 figures. To reach its 2025 target of 500,000 kg, Grundfos will intensify its focus on building partnerships across the value chain to increase the volume of products customers return for remanufacturing (Grundfos, 2023).

Upon arrival at the remanufacturing center, returned products undergo thorough inspection and sorting. This stage identifies which products are suitable for remanufacturing, which can be harvested for parts, and which should be recycled. The complexity here lies in the need for specialized knowledge, techniques, and tools to assess each product's condition accurately. Moreover, this process must be efficient to prevent bottlenecks in the remanufacturing pipeline and ensure that viable products are quickly identified and moved forward. This meticulous evaluation ensures that only suitable materials enter the remanufacturing cycle and helps maintain the quality and reliability of the remanufactured products.

7.3.4.2 Collaboration with Logistics Partners

Due to its complexities, collaborating with logistics partners is often necessary to streamline the remanufacturing supply chain. These partners possess logistics and material handling expertise that can make the process more efficient and scalable. They offer advanced reverse logistics capabilities and extensive distribution networks, which enhance the efficiency and reach of collection and redistribution efforts. This, in turn, reduces lead times, minimizes costs, allows access to a broader range of used products, and uncovers valuable materials that might otherwise be overlooked.

7.3.4.3 Leveraging Advanced Technologies

Manufacturers must document each product's journey from initial collection to final resale to maintain quality control, manage inventory, and provide transparency to customers and regulatory bodies.

Manufacturers can adopt advanced tracking and inventory management technologies to manage remanufacturing logistics efficiently. These technologies help them keep track of their products throughout their lifecycle, from collection to remanufacturing to redistribution. With sophisticated tracking systems, manufacturers can access real-time data on returned items' location, condition, and status. This information enables them to make informed decisions and allocate resources efficiently. Advanced inventory management systems, on the other hand, can optimize the storage and handling of components, ensuring that they are readily available whenever needed for remanufacturing.

Effective reverse logistics also requires sophisticated data management systems to track returned products through remanufacturing. The variety and condition of returned products compound this data management challenge, requiring adaptable systems that can handle complex information.

7.3.4.4 Sustainability

Ensuring the sustainability of return flows is paramount. This involves minimizing the carbon footprint of transportation, ensuring that remanufacturing processes are energy-efficient, and responsibly managing waste materials. Manufacturers must continually seek ways to optimize these processes, such as by localizing remanufacturing centers to reduce transportation distances or employing renewable energy sources.

7.3.4.5 Regulatory Landscape

Navigating the regulatory landscape related to product returns and remanufacturing adds another complexity to reverse logistics. Compliance with local and international laws regarding waste, transportation, and remanufactured products avoids legal pitfalls and maintains the legitimacy of the remanufacturing program. This requires manufacturers to stay informed about relevant regulations and implement processes ensuring compliance at every reverse logistics chain stage.

7.3.5 Market Positioning of Refurbished Products

The market positioning of remanufactured products is a complex strategy that requires manufacturers to carefully navigate the fine line between leveraging the value of remanufactured items and maintaining the premium perception of their new products. This balance ensures that both product lines thrive without encroaching on each other's market space.

7.3.5.1 Branding and Product Differentiation

One strategy for market positioning involves creating unique branding for remanufactured products. Manufacturers can establish a distinct visual identity for their remanufactured product line by using specific sub-brands or labels with unique logos, color schemes, and packaging designs that identify a product as remanufactured. This helps to set customer expectations immediately. The branding strategy can create a separate but related brand identity. When combined with clear product features, aesthetics, and packaging differentiation, remanufactured products can stand out as a value proposition without directly competing with new offerings.

Example 7.13 Remanufactured products as separate brand

For example, does Caterpillar offer a line of remanufactured engines and parts under the "Cat Reman" brand,[2] Bosch operates a remanufacturing division under the brand Bosch eXchange,[3] and Volvo Group, which produces trucks, buses, and construction equipment, has a remanufacturing brand called Volvo Reman.[4]

To make this strategy more effective, manufacturers should emphasize the rigorous testing and quality assurance processes that remanufactured products undergo. Providing certifications or seals of approval can help build trust and signal reliability to customers. Transparency about the steps taken to restore the product can alleviate concerns about quality and performance. Therefore, packaging and marketing materials should include detailed information about the remanufacturing process.

It's essential to emphasize the unique benefits of remanufactured products, such as cost savings, positive environmental impact, and warranty coverage. Highlighting these advantages can make remanufactured items more appealing to price-sensitive and eco-conscious customers.

Example 7.14 John Deere's remanufacturing program

John Deere, a global agricultural and construction equipment leader, has a remanufacturing program. It details the remanufacturing program on its remanufactured parts page (John Deere Reman, 2024). This includes an overview of:

Benefits of Using John Deere Reman Parts:

- Increased uptime with a fast, low-cost repair option
- Faster than rebuilding parts
- 20–30% average lower cost than brand-new OEM parts
- The same or better quality as brand-new OEM parts
- Fully inspected, rigorously tested, and built to the latest specifications
- A John Deere Reman warranty that offers the same or better coverage as new OEM parts

John Deere explains the difference between Remanufacturing vs Repairing, Rebuilding, and Reconditioning.

(continued)

---

[2] https://www.cat.com/en_US/products/new/parts/reman.html

[3] https://www.boschoffhighway.com/xc/en/product-portfolio/remanufactured

[4] https://www.volvotrucks.us/parts-and-services/parts/remanufactured/

In the section "How John Deere Reman Works," they describe the remanufacturing process, starting with the removal of failed parts and components and ending with their return to like-new or better quality with a John Deere Reman factory warranty.

To further increase confidence, John Deere has the section "*See What John Deere Dealers Are Saying*" where dealers highlight increased confidence, value, and choice.

Manufacturers should define their target segment for remanufactured products and educate customers about their benefits and value. Addressing common misconceptions and highlighting remanufactured items' sustainability and economic advantages can further enhance their appeal. Collaborating with environmental organizations or influencers who advocate for remanufactured products' benefits can strengthen brand credibility and reach new audiences.

Sell remanufactured and new products through different sales channels. Online platforms may focus on remanufactured products, while traditional retail stores could prioritize new products. This reduces direct competition and leverages the strengths of each channel.

Manufacturers must educate customers about the remanufacturing process to build trust and credibility. Transparent communication regarding remanufactured products' origin, specifications, and cosmetic differences compared to new products is essential. This helps set the right expectations and reduces customer dissatisfaction.

Introducing different tiers of remanufactured products, such as "certified refurbished" and "like-new" categories, can meet customers' varying preferences and budgets, making the products more distinct. Offering solid after-sales support and warranties for remanufactured items can assure buyers and alleviate concerns about purchasing these products.

Example 7.15 Dell Outlet three tiers of certification for refurbished computers

Dell Outlet offers three tiers of certification for refurbished computers.

The top tier is "New & Unused." These products are either factory-sealed or open-box items that have never been used by a customer and have the software seal intact. They are typically overstocked or returned orders. "New & Unused" products do not have any cosmetic damage, ensuring that customers receive an essentially brand-new product.

The middle tier consists of "Like New (Refurbished)." Dell's highest-grade certified refurbished systems have undergone a rigorous refurbishing process to meet Dell's quality and performance standards.

(continued)

The last tier includes "Scratch & Dent" products, certified refurbished with cosmetic blemishes that do not affect performance or the device's functionality. This tier offers a cost-effective option for budget-conscious customers prioritizing performance over aesthetics.

While prices vary based on each level, products under all three tiers come with the same warranty and support included with new Dell computers (Dell, 2024).

Strategically time the release of remanufactured products to avoid direct competition with new products, for instance, introducing remanufactured versions into the market at a different point in the product lifecycle, perhaps when the new model has already saturated its primary market segment.

Example 7.16 Apple's Certified Refurbished program

Apple's Certified Refurbished program exemplifies branding and product differentiation for refurbished products.

Apple uses the "Certified Refurbished" label to differentiate refurbished products from new ones. This branding sets customer expectations regarding the product's status while maintaining the Apple brand's high standards.

Apple provides a certification that guarantees the refurbished product meets the same functional standards as new products.

Apple offers detailed information about refurbishment on its website, ensuring transparency and building customer trust. Customers know what they are getting, including the benefits of buying refurbished.

The Certified Refurbished products are marketed with an emphasis on cost savings, environmental benefits, and the inclusion of a one-year warranty. This highlights the value proposition and appeals to budget-conscious and eco-friendly customers.

Refurbished products are packaged in new boxes with all accessories, maintaining the premium unboxing experience that Apple customers expect.

Apple educates customers through its website and marketing materials about the benefits of buying refurbished, addressing common misconceptions and highlighting the program's sustainability benefits.

Apple offers the same customer support and service for refurbished products as it does for new ones, including access to AppleCare, which further reduces perceived risks and enhances customer satisfaction.

Through these practices, Apple positions its refurbished products as high-quality, reliable alternatives to new products, strengthening customer trust and loyalty while promoting sustainability (Apple, 2024).

7.3.5.2 Warranty and Support Services

The warranty terms are important when positioning remanufactured products. Providing a warranty that guarantees reliability while being different from new products can be attractive. For instance, manufacturers can offer a shorter warranty period or a different type of coverage for remanufactured products. Additionally, tailored support services, like dedicated helplines or maintenance packages, can enhance the value proposition of remanufactured products.

7.3.5.3 Pricing Strategy

Manufacturers must develop a strategic pricing model for remanufactured products. They need to set prices that reflect the value added through the remanufacturing process, remanufacturing costs, customer price sensitivity, and the residual value of the items. At the same time, the prices should be lower than those of new products to attract price-sensitive customers. Employing dynamic pricing strategies that consider product age, demand, and remanufacturing costs can help maintain this balance.

Manufacturers must analyze customer behavior and willingness to pay for remanufactured items to set appealing and profitable prices. Utilizing customer data and market insights to adjust pricing models can help maintain competitiveness and profitability. By consistently reviewing and fine-tuning pricing strategies based on market trends and customer feedback, manufacturers optimize their pricing approach to align with business goals and customer expectations.

7.3.5.4 Strategic Sales Channels

Another aspect of market positioning involves selecting the appropriate sales channels for remanufactured products. These channels should address the unique challenges and opportunities of selling remanufactured items, such as establishing customer trust and managing product perceptions.

Online platforms offer two distinct approaches: manufacturer-controlled platforms and third-party platforms. A manufacturer-controlled platform allows complete control over branding, customer experience, and product presentation. This direct approach enables manufacturers to access valuable customer data and feedback, fostering improvements and more effective marketing strategies. Additionally, a dedicated platform can reassure customers about the quality and reliability of remanufactured products through detailed product information, warranty offers, and customer reviews. However, developing and maintaining such a platform require investment in technology and marketing, and attracting traffic can be challenging and costly.

Example 7.17 HP Business Outlet

On HP Business Outlet[5], HP sells certified refurbished notebooks, desktops, and workstations.

[5] https://www.hp.com/us-en/sbso/buspurchase_refurbished.html

On the other hand, third-party platforms such as Amazon See example or eBay provide access to a vast customer base, which can increase potential sales volume. These established platforms are often trusted by customers, which can reduce skepticism about purchasing remanufactured items. Additionally, using an existing platform can be less expensive than developing a new one. However, the intense competition on these platforms can pressure pricing and margins, and manufacturers have less control over branding and customer experience. Furthermore, third-party platforms charge fees, which can impact profitability.

Example 7.18 eBay Refurbished program

eBay offers a refurbished product program that ensures consistency and reliability across its inventory, providing buyers with confidence and simplicity when purchasing refurbished items.

To sell products under the eBay Refurbished program, sellers must meet stringent criteria to maintain high standards and customer trust:

- Must be an eBay Top Rated Seller
- Sellers must maintain at least a 98% positive feedback rating
- Item Not as Described Rate must be less than 4%
- Items Not Received Rate must be less than 1%
- Sellers must be in good standing with eBay

For products to be listed as Certified Refurbished, sellers must also provide a purchase order or a letter of authorization from their manufacturer partners.

Items listed under the eBay Refurbished program must be fully functional, thoroughly tested, and refurbished to a high standard. Once accepted into the program, products are graded based on predefined criteria set by eBay:

Certified Refurbished: These items are refurbished by the manufacturer or a manufacturer-approved vendor, come with a manufacturer-backed warranty and are restored to like-new condition.

Excellent: Items in excellent condition are fully functional, with minimal signs of use and high cosmetic standards.

Very Good: These items are fully operational with some signs of use but remain in great condition.

Good: Functional items that may show more noticeable signs of use but still offer reliable performance.

Retail outlets with dedicated sections for remanufactured products can help build customer trust and credibility. This approach allows customers to physically inspect and test the products, addressing concerns about quality. It also helps distinguish remanufactured products from new ones, emphasizing their unique identity and targeting consumer-focused products. However, this retail space strategy involves costs such as rent, staffing, and utilities, and sales are limited to the locations of the retail outlets. Managing stock levels across multiple locations can also be complex and costly.

Specialized reseller networks offer a channel for reaching business customers looking for affordable, reliable products for their operations. These resellers understand the remanufactured market and can effectively communicate the value proposition. This approach allows for targeted marketing to specific niches and customer segments and can reduce the manufacturer's costs related to sales and distribution. However, manufacturers must share profits with resellers, impacting margins, and there is reduced control over branding and customer interactions. Relying on resellers can limit direct engagement with end customers and restrict data collection.

Selling remanufactured products in bulk to wholesalers through wholesale sales channels allows for quick movement of large inventory quantities and improved cash flow. This approach is ideal for targeting business customers seeking cost-effective operational alternatives. Dealing with fewer, larger orders simplifies logistics and distribution. However, wholesale pricing generally offers lower margins than direct sales, and maintaining brand integrity can be challenging when products are resold through various channels. Additionally, reduced direct interaction with end-users limits the ability to gather feedback and improve products.

Table 7.1 summarizes the strategic sales channels for remanufactured products, outlining their descriptions, advantages, and challenges. Manufacturers must carefully select and balance these channels to address the unique challenges and opportunities in selling remanufactured items, building customer trust, and managing product perceptions effectively.

7.3.6 Cost Management

Successful remanufacturing programs depend on effective cost management. This involves optimizing logistics, improving processes, strategic sourcing, labor management, and making technological investments (Fig. 7.4).

Optimizing the logistics of collecting and transporting used products for remanufacturing reduces costs. This can be achieved by implementing regional collection hubs, partnering with logistics companies for cost-effective transportation solutions, and incentivizing customers to return products directly. Additionally, bulk transportation and strategically locating remanufacturing centers closer to major collection points can improve cost efficiency (Sect. 7.3.4).

The diagnostics phase assesses each returned product to determine if it can be remanufactured. Investing in automated diagnostic tools and training technicians to help them identify issues quickly and accurately will reduce the time and labor costs

Table 7.1 Strategic sales channels for remanufactured products

Sales Channel	Description	Advantages	Challenges
Manufacturer-Controlled Online Platform	Direct sales channel managed by the manufacturer, providing complete control over branding, customer experience, and product presentation	Full control over branding. Direct customer feedback. Detailed product information. Warranty offers and customer reviews	High investment in technology and marketing. Attracting traffic can be challenging and costly
Third-Party Online Platforms	Utilizes established platforms like Amazon or eBay to sell remanufactured products, leveraging their vast customer base and established trust	Access to a large customer base. Reduced customer skepticism. Lower initial cost compared to developing a new platform	Intense competition. Pressure on pricing and margins. Fees charged by platforms
Retail Outlets	Physical stores with dedicated sections for remanufactured products, allowing customers to inspect and test items, building trust and credibility	Builds customer trust through physical inspection. Distinguishes remanufactured products from new ones	High costs for rent, staffing, and utilities. Limited to store locations. Complex stock management
Specialized Reseller Networks	Partnerships with resellers who understand the remanufactured market, allowing targeted marketing to specific niches and reducing manufacturer sales and distribution costs	Effective communication of value proposition. Targeted marketing. Reduced sales and distribution costs	Shared profits with resellers. Reduced control over branding and customer interactions
Wholesale Sales Channels	Selling remanufactured products in bulk to wholesalers, facilitating quick inventory turnover and improved cash flow	Quick movement of large inventory. Improved cash flow. Simplified logistics and distribution	Lower margins than direct sales. Maintaining brand integrity is challenging. Limited feedback from end-users

associated with this stage. Additionally, a modular product design will simplify the repair and upgrade process, leading to quicker turnaround times and reduced labor costs.

Achieving economies of scale in remanufacturing leads to cost reductions. Standardizing the remanufacturing process across similar product lines allows for the streamlining of operations, better inventory management of spare parts, and more predictable labor costs. Bulk purchasing commonly replaced parts and materials also saves costs.

Cost management includes sourcing the necessary parts and components for remanufacturing, building relationships with suppliers to obtain favorable terms,

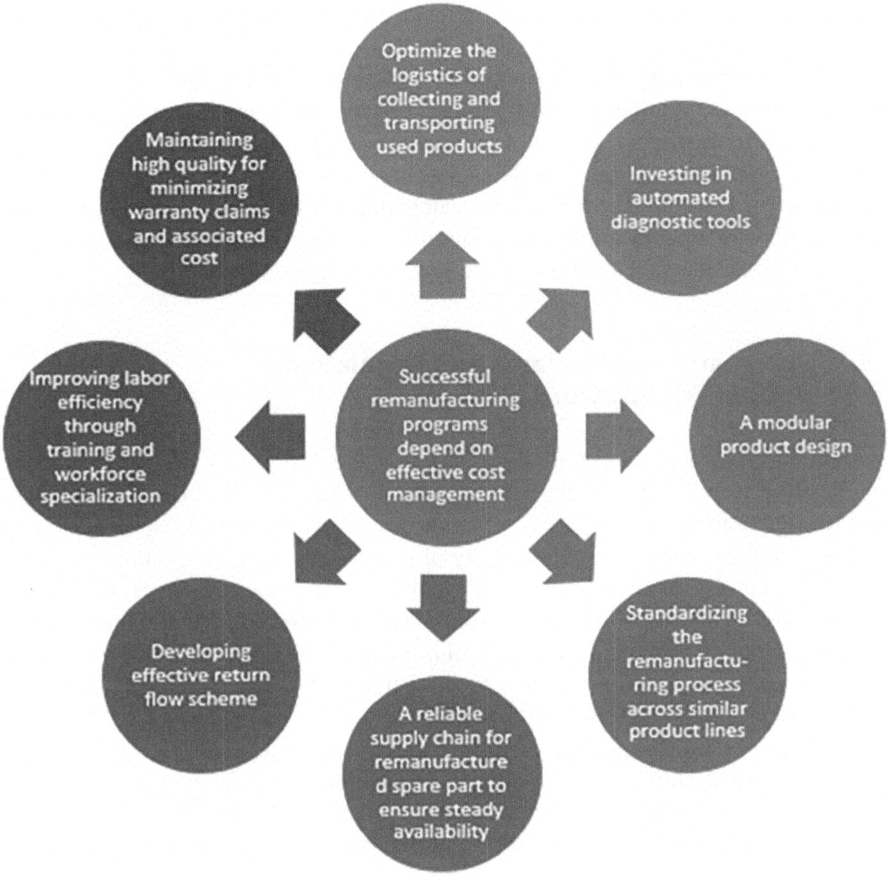

Fig. 7.4 Successful remanufacturing programs depend on effective cost management

considering aftermarket or generic parts as alternatives, and implementing efficient inventory management, all of which help to lower material costs. Furthermore, implementing a just-in-time inventory system reduces holding costs and minimizes waste. Manufacturers must prioritize integrating refurbished and remanufactured spare parts into their remanufacturing process. This requires establishing a reliable supply chain for such parts to ensure their steady availability to meet remanufacturing demands. Also, notice the example in Sect. 7.2.3 where Cummins creates replacement parts when suppliers stop production.

To maintain efficient operations, manufacturers must ensure a constant flow of products for remanufacturing. Developing effective return flow processes, such as buy-back or trade-in programs, is necessary. These initiatives help secure a continuous supply of items suitable for remanufacturing. Furthermore, offering customer incentives, like loyalty programs or discounts for returning old products, can further boost the collection of items, ensuring manufacturers have a consistent stream of products to remanufacture.

Labor costs are a significant part of remanufacturing expenses. Improving labor efficiency through ongoing training and workforce specialization can boost productivity. Implementing incentive programs that reward efficiency and quality work motivates staff and align their goals with the remanufacturing program.

To minimize warranty claims and associated costs, manufacturers must maintain high quality in remanufactured products. Implementing strict quality control checks throughout the remanufacturing process can help prevent issues that result in costly returns. Offering a balanced warranty that protects the customer and the manufacturer can help manage cost exposure due to product failures.

7.3.7 International Standards and Regulations: A Dual-Edged Sword

International standards and regulations ensure product safety, quality, and environmental protection. They set the benchmarks that remanufactured products must meet to suit the market.

However, the diversity and complexity of these standards and regulations across different countries and regions can pose challenges for remanufacturers. Each market may have its unique set of requirements, making it difficult for remanufacturers to ensure compliance and gain access to multiple markets. This complexity can lead to increased costs and a longer time to market, which can discourage businesses from pursuing remanufacturing initiatives.

The definition of a remanufactured product may vary between regions, including the processes used, the expected quality, and the required certification. For example, a product considered remanufactured in one country may be referred to as repaired or refurbished in another, and each classification may be subject to different regulations.

Due to the rigorous certification processes and documentation requirements, small- and medium-sized enterprises (SMEs) may struggle to comply with international standards.

Remanufacturers face added complexity due to varying environmental regulations related to hazardous substances, waste management, and emissions.

Navigating IP rights and compliance standards can be challenging when remanufacturing involves patented products or processes.

Although regulatory barriers challenge the remanufacturing industry, they are not insurmountable. Remanufacturers can overcome these challenges through strategic measures such as harmonizing standards, collaboration, investing in compliance infrastructure, leveraging technology, and engaging with policymakers.

7.3.7.1 Extended Producer Responsibility and Product Use Extension Models

Extended Producer Responsibility (EPR) (Sect. 2.3) supports product use extension strategies. EPR emphasizes the manufacturer's obligation throughout a product's entire lifecycle, focusing on end-of-life management responsibilities, including waste collection, recycling efforts, and environmentally friendly disposal.

The EPR regulatory framework mandates manufacturers to manage their product's aftermath, leading to the development of business models centered on product use extension. It also compels manufacturers to design products that are easier to remanufacture, repair, and recycle. The obligation to accept product returns under EPR legislation can motivate companies to adopt product use extension models, which often present more profitable avenues than material recycling or disposal as waste.

7.3.8 Upstream and Downstream Value Partners

Remanufacturing poses a challenge because existing upstream and downstream value partners may resist it. Downstream partners like retailers and distributors may prefer to sell new items and show reluctance toward remanufactured products. This is often due to the perception that remanufactured products are less profitable than new ones and that they diminish the value of new products, overshadowing the potential business benefits of participating in the remanufacturing process. On the other hand, upstream partners may feel that their roles are being diminished as remanufacturing focuses on extending the life of existing products rather than creating demand for new ones.

Overall, the success of a remanufacturing program hinges on the seamless integration and cooperation of both upstream and downstream partners. By working together, OEMs, tier suppliers, and downstream partners can create a robust remanufacturing ecosystem.

In some cases, tier suppliers may be best suited for remanufacturing their parts; this requires the OEM and tier suppliers to establish remanufacturing facilities. This integrated approach leverages the specialized knowledge and capabilities of tier suppliers, who are often more familiar with the intricacies of their components. By setting up dedicated remanufacturing facilities, tier suppliers can increase their attractiveness as suppliers.

Moreover, this collaborative effort between OEMs and tier suppliers enhances the overall efficiency and effectiveness of the remanufacturing process. OEMs benefit from reduced costs and increased availability of remanufactured parts, while tier suppliers can expand their business models and revenue streams through remanufacturing. This partnership necessitates strong communication and alignment on quality standards, processes, and logistics to ensure seamless operations and consistent product quality.

Downstream partners, including distributors, retailers, and service providers, also play a pivotal role in the remanufacturing ecosystem. They are responsible for marketing and selling remanufactured products to end customers, providing the necessary support and service to ensure a positive customer experience. Effective collaboration with downstream partners ensures that remanufactured products reach the right markets and are supported with appropriate warranties, customer service, and after-sales support.

To address these challenges, manufacturers must develop well-thought-out incentive schemes that align all partners' interests with the remanufacturing program's goals. Education also plays a role in changing perceptions about remanufactured products. By informing partners about the rigorous processes involved in remanufacturing and the quality of the finished products, manufacturers can alleviate fears that remanufactured goods are inferior to new ones.

Fostering a collaborative environment that encourages transparency and shared goals will be vital to integrating remanufactured products into the business models of both upstream and downstream partners.

7.4 Part Harvesting and Repurposing

Part harvesting involves extracting usable components from products that are not suitable for remanufacturing. These harvested parts are then repurposed into different products unrelated to the original, maximizing the value extracted from otherwise unusable items.

Repurposing through part harvesting helps to save costs by reducing the need for new raw materials and lowering production expenses. This approach also helps to minimize waste, which is great for the environment. Additionally, parts from products that can't be remanufactured can be sold or used to create new products, creating additional revenue opportunities.

However, part harvesting poses several challenges. It involves identifying and extracting usable parts from products that cannot be remanufactured, which can be labor-intensive and require specialized skills and equipment. Another challenge is to ensure that repurposed parts meet the necessary quality and safety standards for their new applications. Integrating these parts into new products often requires redesign and testing to ensure compatibility and performance. Market acceptance can also be a hurdle, as customers may have concerns about the reliability and quality of products made with repurposed parts.

Example 7.19 Parts harvested and used in entirely different products

In the automotive industry, parts from vehicles that cannot be remanufactured might be harvested and used in entirely different products, such as machinery or industrial equipment. For example, a transmission from an old vehicle could be repurposed in a factory conveyor system. This extends the part's life, provides cost savings, and reduces environmental impact.

7.5 Digitization Supporting Remanufacturing Models

The Sustainable Manufacturing Intelligence Framework (SMIF) offers a structured approach to integrating digital technologies into remanufacturing processes, ensuring efficiency and sustainability. This section presents key findings from Part III on the role of digitization in supporting remanufacturing across key areas: internal IT systems, business ecosystems, connected products, customer experience, and data-driven circularity.

7.5.1 Internal IT Systems

Internal IT systems are the backbone of remanufacturing models, providing the necessary infrastructure to support various remanufacturing processes. These systems facilitate real-time monitoring, efficient resource management, and integration with circular practices.

Effective Supply Chain Management (SCM) systems track products throughout their lifecycle, including returned items for remanufacturing. They transform reverse logistics into a strategic asset, ensuring that products can be efficiently returned, inspected, and remanufactured.

Evolved Customer Relationship Management (CRM) systems foster sustainable dialogues with customers, encouraging them to return products for remanufacturing. These systems manage customer interactions throughout the product lifecycle, promoting responsible consumption and facilitating the collection of end-of-life products.

Advanced Waste Management Systems (WMS) integrate AI to optimize waste sorting and processing within remanufacturing facilities, ensuring sustainable and efficient waste management.

Quality Control Systems (QCS) ensure that remanufactured products meet consistent quality standards. They incorporate feedback loops for continuous improvement, ensuring that remanufactured products are as reliable as new ones.

Inventory Management Systems (IMS) manage the flow of refurbished parts and monitor recycled inputs, optimizing inventory levels to support remanufacturing and reduce waste.

7.5.2 Business Ecosystem

A robust digital business ecosystem enables seamless interactions and data sharing among various stakeholders. This ecosystem extends beyond traditional supply chains to include remanufacturers, repair services, and value chain customers, fostering a culture of shared responsibility.

Collaboration platforms enable internal and external partners to collaborate on remanufacturing projects, harnessing collective creativity and innovation. Orchestration platforms streamline remanufacturing processes across multiple participants, ensuring smooth interaction between different stages of the product lifecycle. Creation platforms empower partners to develop new remanufacturing methods, products, and business models, driving innovation in remanufacturing practices. Matching platforms connect the supply of used products with the demand for remanufactured goods, optimizing resource utilization and operational efficiencies in remanufacturing.

7.5.3 Connected Products

IoT-enabled connected products allow for real-time monitoring and data-driven decision-making. These technologies ensure efficient tracking and management of products throughout their lifecycle. They provide continuous product condition and performance data, enabling predictive maintenance and timely remanufacturing interventions. Connected products generate valuable data that inform remanufacturing processes, ensuring optimal resource utilization and waste reduction.

7.5.4 Customer Experience

Enhancing customer experience through digital touchpoints enables customers to become active participants throughout the product lifecycle, contributing to the circular economy by returning products for remanufacturing.

Digital tools ensure a consistent and engaging customer journey, encouraging customers to return products for remanufacturing. Advanced analytics and AI enable personalized communication, offering incentives for returning products and participating in remanufacturing programs. Easily transferable and verifiable digital warranties encourage customers to invest in remanufactured products, enhancing trust and participation in circular practices.

7.5.5 Data-Driven Circularity

Data-driven circularity emphasizes using data as the central intelligence in a manufacturer's remanufacturing efforts. Integrating data from customer interactions, business ecosystems, connected products, and internal IT systems provides a comprehensive view of remanufacturing processes.

Big Data and Business Intelligence (BI) tools convert large volumes of data into actionable insights, improving decision-making and operational efficiency in remanufacturing. Predictive analytics forecast return volumes and optimize remanufacturing operations. AI supports enhanced decision-making, improving product lifecycle management and reducing supply chain vulnerabilities. By leveraging data across various dimensions, manufacturers can make strategic decisions that enhance the efficiency and profitability of remanufacturing processes.

7.5.6 Leveraging Digital Product Passports for Enhanced Remanufacturing Business Models

Digital Product Passport (DPP) (Sect. 2.2) provides transparent and accessible information for efficient product lifecycle management.

The instant availability of detailed historical data, including repair records, parts replacements, and maintenance checks, enables accurate and cost-effective remanufacturing planning. This efficiency reduces the time and resources spent evaluating returned or used products.

Remanufacturing companies can optimize resource allocation using specific components and material information to minimize waste and improve turn-around times.

DPPs can help guarantee that remanufactured products adhere to safety, quality, and environmental regulations by providing traceability and proof of compliance with required standards. This can simplify obtaining necessary certifications and permits, reduce administrative obstacles, and build trust with customers and regulators.

Offering a Digital Product Passport with remanufactured products can boost customer trust. Customers can access a verifiable product history, including details of all remanufacturing and the quality of parts used. This helps assure them of the product's reliability and value. Transparency builds customer confidence and potentially increases the market value of remanufactured goods. Buyers are more likely to invest in products when their lifecycle is fully documented and trustworthy.

7.6 Capability Map for Remanufacturing Business Models in Manufacturing

This capability map (Fig. 7.5) outlines the essential capabilities manufacturers must develop and maintain to successfully implement refurbishment and remanufacturing business models.

7.7 Capitalizing on Remanufacturing

Remanufacturing is an environmentally responsible choice and a compelling business strategy. In this chapter, we have discussed how embracing remanufacturing can improve a manufacturer's competitive edge, create new revenue streams, and establish strong market differentiation while optimizing operational efficiencies.

Remanufacturing offers new opportunities to generate income by transforming used products into valuable assets. Manufacturers can tap into a growing market of price-conscious and environmentally conscious customers by offering products with "like-new" quality at discounted prices. This enables them to diversify their financial portfolio and enhance overall profitability. Remanufacturing used products often involves lower material and labor costs than manufacturing new ones, potentially leading to higher profit margins.

Remanufacturing enables manufacturers to maintain agility in their business operations. By reutilizing existing resources, companies can quickly adapt to market demands and changes in supply chain dynamics, demonstrating resilience.

The checklist (Table 7.2) highlights essential tasks for building remanufacturing business models.

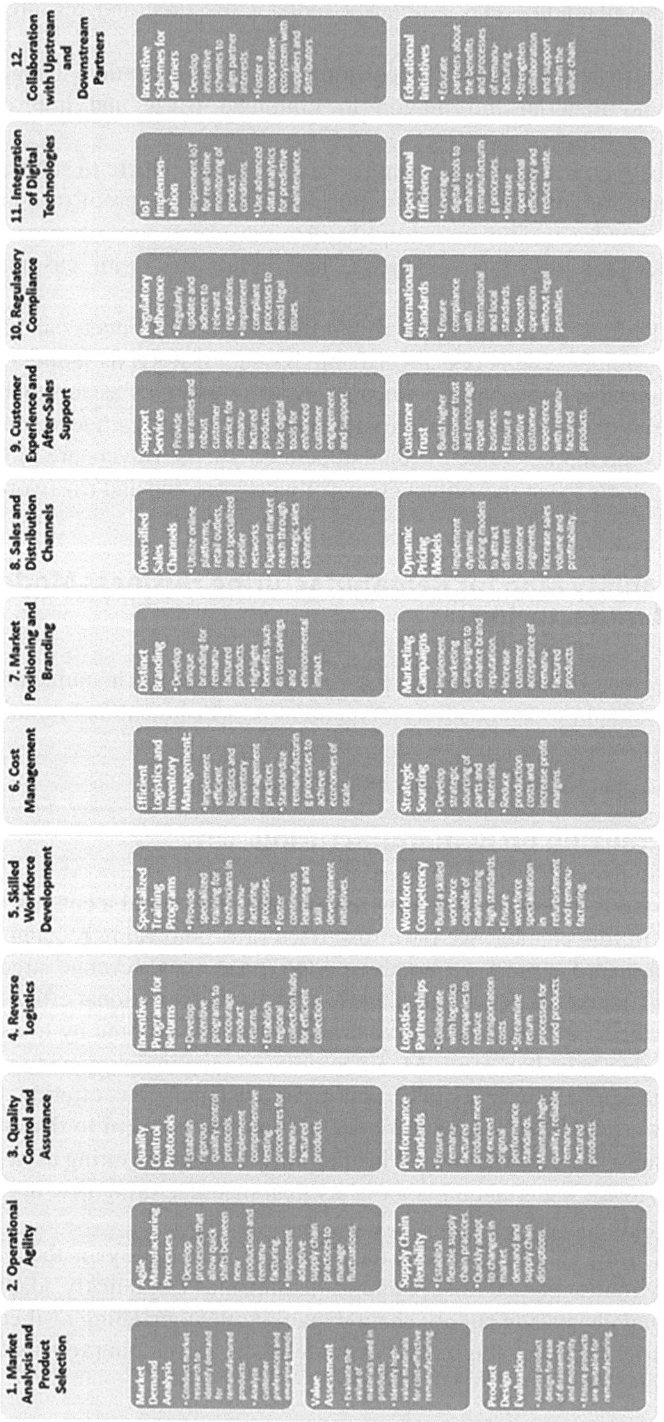

Fig. 7.5 Capability map for remanufacturing business models in manufacturing

Example 7.20 HP's refurbishment initiatives

HP Inc. has incorporated refurbishment into its business model as an element of its circular economy strategy. This initiative aligns with its broader aim to achieve 75% circularity for products and packaging by 2030 (HP, 2024).

HP Workforce Solutions is a standalone global business unit that reports directly to the CEO. This unit oversees the entire lifecycle of products, including refurbishment of PCs and printers, which HP has found can be profitable. By managing the refurbishment processes with both internal contract manufacturing partners and approved third-party licensed refurbishers, HP has been able to deliver high-quality multi-life devices (Bland & Shull, 2024).

HP is also working on a digital passport system to accompany refurbished PCs. The device's passport would provide detailed information about the unit's product history, including previous repairs and refurbishments. This is all to build a positive experience when using a refurbished device (Bland & Shull, 2024).

HP promotes its refurbished products as high-quality, cost-effective alternatives to new products. These products are aimed at environmentally conscious customers and budget-sensitive markets. HP provides warranty and support services for refurbished products to ensure customers receive the same assurance and reliability as new products.

HP's refurbishment initiatives demonstrate how a well-executed circular economy strategy can drive sustainability and profitability. By integrating refurbishment into its core operations, HP extends the lifecycle of its products and meets the growing demand for sustainable and cost-effective solutions. For example, France requires that 20 percent of the items going into government tender be recycled or reused (Bland & Shull, 2024).

Table 7.2 Checklist for building remanufacturing business models

Task	Methodology	Expected outcome	Risk mitigated
Assess market potential	Conduct market research and analysis	Identify demand and target segments	Misjudging market demand
Develop remanufacturing strategy	Define processes, standards, and goals	A clear roadmap for operations	Lack of direction
Design for remanufacturing	Implement design principles for easy disassembly and reassembly	Cost-effective and efficient remanufacturing	High remanufacturing costs
Establish quality standards	Develop and adhere to strict quality assurance protocols	High-quality remanufactured products	Customer dissatisfaction

(continued)

Table 7.2 (continued)

Task	Methodology	Expected outcome	Risk mitigated
Set up remanufacturing centers	Establish in-house facilities or partner with third parties	Efficient remanufacturing operations	Operational inefficiencies
Train skilled workforce	Provide specialized training for technicians	Competent staff for high-quality remanufacturing	Inadequate remanufacturing skills
Implement reverse logistics	Develop a system for collecting and transporting used products	Efficient collection and transportation	Logistical delays and high costs
Develop marketing campaigns	Highlight the benefits of remanufactured products	Increased customer awareness and demand	Low customer interest
Price refurbished products strategically	Employ dynamic pricing models	Competitive yet profitable pricing	Pricing too high or too low
Create dedicated sales channels	Use online platforms, retail outlets, and reseller networks	Wider reach and customer access	Limited market reach
Establish after-sales support	Offer warranties and robust customer service	Enhanced customer trust and satisfaction	Low post-purchase satisfaction
Monitor regulatory compliance	Stay updated with relevant regulations and ensure compliance	Avoid legal issues and fines	Regulatory non-compliance
Evaluate and optimize operations	Regularly review and refine processes based on feedback	Continuous improvement and operational efficiency	Stagnation and inefficiency
Plan Investments Strategically	Analyze required capital for facilities, technology, and marketing, ensuring alignment with projected returns	Optimized resource allocation and sustainable growth	Over- or under-investing in critical capabilities

References

Amazon. (2024). *Grow your business by selling on Amazon Renewed*. Retrieved from https://sell.amazon.com/programs/renewed

Apple. (2024, 06). *Certified Refurbished*. From https://www.apple.com/shop/refurbished

Bland, R., & Shull, D. (2024, March). *How HP is finding success in circularity*. From McKinsey Sustainability. Retrieved from https://www.mckinsey.com/capabilities/sustainability/our-insights/how-hp-is-finding-success-in-circularity

Caterpillar. (2024). *Cat® Reman*. Retrieved from https://www.cat.com/en_US/products/new/parts/reman.html

Coherent Market Insights. (2024). *Refurbished electronics market analysis*. Retrieved from https://www.coherentmarketinsights.com/market-insight/refurbished-electronics-market-6166

Cummins Inc. (2024). *How Cummins Recon® products can help your sustainability goals*. Retrieved from https://www.cummins.com/news/2024/02/01/how-cummins-reconr-products-can-help-your-sustainability-goals

Danfoss. (2022). *Annual Report 2021 - The greenest energy is the energy we don't use.*

Dell. (2024). *Everything you need to know about refurbished computers.* Retrieved from https://www.dell.com/en-us/dfh/lp/outlet-why-refurbished

Grundfos. (2023). *Sustainability Report.* Retrieved from https://www.grundfos.com/sustainability/sustainability-report-2023

HP. (2024, 05). *HP Business Outlet.* From https://www.hp.com/us-en/sbso/buspurchase_refurbished.html

Schaeffler. (2022, Sept). *From more efficient product design to data-based reconditioning service: Sustainability as a driver of innovation in rail transport.* Retrieved from https://www.schaeffler.com/en/media/press-releases/press-releases-detail.jsp?id=87860997

Tetra Pak. (2024). *Tetra Pak® Upgrades.* Retrieved from https://www.tetrapak.com/solutions/services/service-offerings/upgrades

Vela, R. A. (2024, Jan 14). *Exploring remanufacturing and refurbishment processes.* From Planet SCM. Retrieved from https://www.linkedin.com/pulse/exploring-remanufacturing-refurbishment-processes-rafael-a-vela-yjzfe/

Vestas. (2024). *Vestas refurbished turbines.* Retrieved from https://www.vestas.com/en/energy-solutions/refurbished-turbines

6th R – Recycle: Circular Closure

8

Abstract

This chapter explores the role of recycling in the circular economy, emphasizing its importance in extending material lifecycles and reintroducing them into production. This final stage of the product lifecycle determines whether materials are discarded as waste or given a new life. The chapter discusses resource harvesting, focusing on collecting and processing materials, and circular sourcing, which integrates recycled materials into manufacturing to reduce reliance on virgin resources.

Legislative frameworks worldwide are increasingly mandating the use of recycled materials. Extended Producer Responsibility (EPR) policies encourage manufacturers to design products with recycling in mind, ensuring end-of-life management is accounted for from the outset. Challenges in recycling complex materials, such as advanced plastics and composites, necessitate innovations in recycling technologies and strategic product redesign.

The chapter also addresses customer and market dynamics, highlighting the importance of building trust in recycled materials and effectively communicating their benefits. Technological integration and efficient reverse logistics are crucial for optimizing recycling processes. Manufacturers can systematically enhance their recycling initiatives by leveraging the capabilities outlined in the capability map, ensuring sustainability, reducing environmental impact, and unlocking new economic opportunities within the circular economy.

H. H. Jensen, *Circular Economy Opportunities and Pathways for Manufacturers*,
Future of Business and Finance, https://doi.org/10.1007/978-3-031-75279-7_8

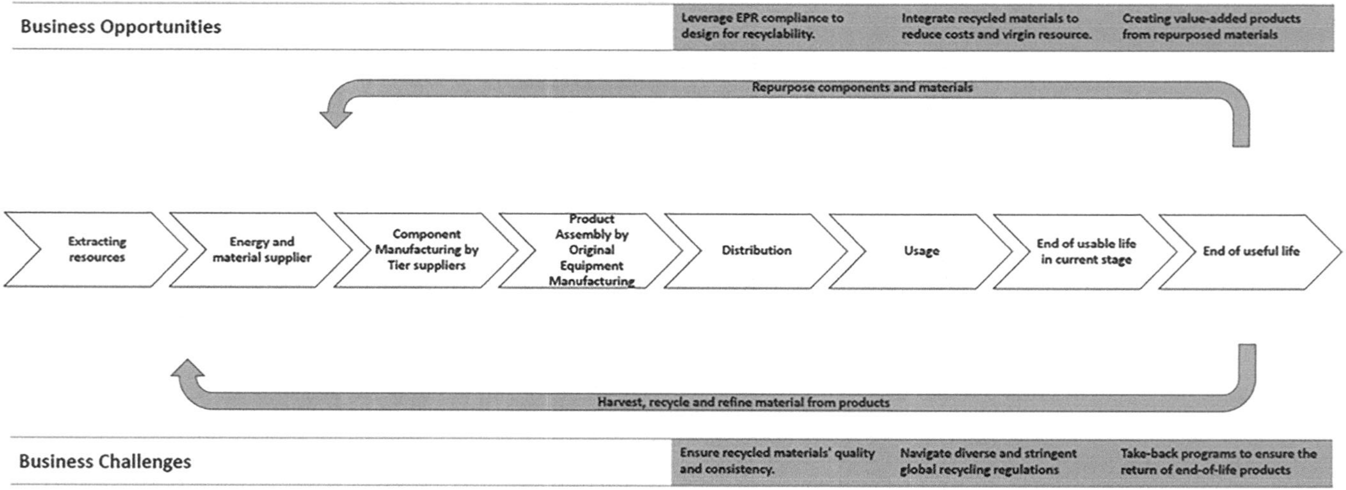

Fig. 8.1 Recycling's placement in circular flow (Figure 1.6) and three significant business opportunities and challenges

Key Messages

- *Critical Role of Recycling in the Circular Economy*: *Recycling is the final stage in a product's lifecycle. It is pivotal for extending the life of materials by reintroducing them into the production cycle.* This stage determines whether products will be discarded as waste or given another life.
- *Economic and Environmental Challenges*: Recycling faces financial challenges due to the low residual value of products and the high costs associated with recycling processes. The financial feasibility of recycling is often questioned, particularly for less valuable materials or those available in small quantities. Despite these challenges, the environmental benefits of recycling are substantial, providing a compelling reason for its adoption.
- *Resource Harvesting*: Focuses on collecting products for recycling and extracting materials through recycling processes.
- *Circular Sourcing*: Emphasizes integrating recycled materials strategically into manufacturing processes to reduce reliance on virgin raw materials.
- *Legislative Frameworks and Global Trends*: Governments worldwide are implementing stricter laws to enhance the use of recycled materials and improve product recyclability. These regulations are designed to reduce environmental impact and promote sustainable practices. Compliance with these regulations can also offer strategic advantages, such as access to international markets and improved competitive positioning.
- *Domestic Resilience and Strategic Shifts*: *Countries increasingly focus on recycling and circular economy principles to enhance domestic resilience.* By retaining critical materials within their borders, nations aim to reduce dependency on international supply chains and bolster environmental sustainability.
- *Extended Producer Responsibility (EPR)*: EPR policies make producers responsible for the end-of-life management of their products, incentivizing innovation in product design for enhanced recyclability and reduced environmental impact. This approach ensures recycling considerations are integrated from the product design stage.
- *Challenges in Recycling Complex Materials*: Recycling advanced plastics and composites is challenging and costly due to their intricate structures and material properties. Innovations in recycling technologies, such as chemical recycling and advanced sorting systems, are essential to address these challenges.
- *Circular Sourcing and Market Integration*: Circular sourcing involves balancing economic viability with environmental sustainability. This approach faces challenges with material quality, consistency, and market acceptance but offers benefits in reducing environmental impact and dependency on virgin materials.
- *Customer and Market Dynamics*: Manufacturers must address customer skepticism regarding the quality of recycled materials and align their brand

(continued)

positioning with circular practices. Effective communication and marketing strategies promote the environmental benefits of recycled products without compromising perceived value.

- *Technological Integration and Reverse Logistics*: Integrating tracking technologies and optimizing reverse logistics are critical for efficient recycling processes. Manufacturers can enhance transparency, improve decision-making, and reduce costs by leveraging advanced logistics solutions and digital tools.

After exploring redesign, reinvention, redistribution, recommerce, repair, refurbishment, and remanufacturing, we now arrive at the final stage: recycling, which extends the lifecycle of materials by reintroducing them into the production cycle (Fig. 8.1).

This final stage of a product's lifecycle determines whether it will be discarded as waste or given another life. However, this stage also poses challenges. The residual value of the product is typically at its lowest point, making it a critical moment in the circular economy. This is because the financial incentive to recycle is minimal compared to earlier stages (Fig. 3.1). Additionally, recycling facilities require investment to achieve economies of scale while handling many types of specialized waste.

The economic feasibility of recycling is frequently questioned, as the costs associated with these processes can exceed the value of the recovered materials, especially for less valuable materials or those in small quantities. This dilemma often leads to a situation where the environmental benefits are clear, but the economic incentives are not sufficiently compelling to motivate all stakeholders.

Example 8.1 Dell's Closed-Loop Supply Chain

Dell's closed-loop supply chain exemplifies how an OEM manages the recycling phase. Many people think that recycling immediately transforms materials back into their original forms. However, many materials are "downcycled" into new materials of lower quality or reduced functionality. In contrast, closed-loop systems recycle and reuse materials repeatedly, which reduces the need for virgin resources and minimizes waste creation.

A key element of closed-loop systems is recycling materials within the same product category or industry. At Dell, this translates to reusing old computers to make new ones. Dell has used recycled plastics from sources like water bottles in its monitors and OptiPlex desktops for some time. Their closed-loop system involves incorporating plastics from old computers into new computer parts.

(continued)

The recycling process involves separating plastics by type and shipping them to manufacturing partners in China. Other materials from the recycled computers are similarly processed and sold on the commodities market for reuse. At the manufacturing facilities, the plastics are shredded, melted, and blended (with 35% recycled content) before being molded into new parts. The cycle from the old computer to the new part takes approximately 6 months (Dell, 2024).

Customers frequently seek environmentally friendly products that do not come with extra costs or performance sacrifices. Dell's closed-loop plastic supply chain addresses this demand by offering energy-efficient products made from recycled materials at a reduced cost. According to a study by TruCost, Dell's closed-loop process delivers a net natural capital benefit of 44%, valued at $1.3 million annually, as opposed to using virgin plastics (Bolton & Kao, 2015).

In this chapter, we delve into the multifaceted role of recycling within the manufacturing landscape. We cover both recycling concepts:

Resource Harvesting This approach emphasizes collecting products for recycling and extracting materials through recycling processes.

Circular Sourcing This approach emphasizes strategically integrating recycled materials into manufacturing processes.

8.1 Political and Legislative Frameworks Governing Recycling

Governments worldwide are enacting stricter laws on the use of recycled materials and improving the overall recyclability of products. This is aimed at reducing the environmental impact of waste and promoting more sustainable practices.

The various regulatory requirements in different regions create challenges for global manufacturers. Adapting to new policies, regulations, and guidelines while ensuring compliance across all operational territories requires a strong strategy. Manufacturers must navigate different requirements related to product recycling, waste disposal, and using recycled materials, which can impact their operational efficiency, supply chain decisions, and broader business strategies.

Nevertheless, complying with global recycling standards and demonstrating a dedication to sustainability can also provide a strategic advantage, enabling access to international markets and improving competitive positioning.

In the following sections, we will explore several legislative trends across different regions that promote recyclability.

8.1.1 Promoting Domestic Resilience Through Recycling and Circular Economy

Various countries and regions have implemented legislation to strengthen domestic resilience by retaining critical materials within their borders through enhanced recycling practices and circular economy principles. These initiatives reflect a strategic shift toward reducing dependency on international supply chains and improving environmental sustainability.

The European Union's Critical Raw Materials Act (European Commission, 2023) is designed to utilize circular economy principles to secure a sustainable supply chain for essential materials crucial for the EU's green and digital transitions. The Act emphasizes the importance of recycling by improving the collection and processing of critical material-rich waste and transforming it into secondary raw materials.

Example 8.2 The European defense industry relies on suppliers outside the EU for critical raw materials

The European defense industry relies heavily on suppliers outside the EU for critical raw materials, which poses strategic and operational risks. Around half of the essential raw materials needed for defense production come from outside the EU. This heavy dependence exposes vulnerabilities that could impact the EU's defense capabilities and autonomy. In response to these challenges, the European Union established the Incubation Forum for Circular Economy in European Defense (IF CEED), focusing on critical raw materials, additive manufacturing, sustainable ecodesign, green procurement, and circular data management. IF CEED aims to reduce the risks associated with the EU's reliance on non-EU suppliers and promote a more self-sufficient and sustainable defense industry (Girardi et al., 2023).

Australia has introduced the Critical Minerals Strategy 2023–2030 (Bogdanich et al., 2023), focusing on developing and processing domestically sourced critical minerals. A component of this strategy is enhancing the capability to recycle critical minerals from extractive waste, thus supporting sustainable practices and reducing reliance on imported materials.

South Korea has implemented a comprehensive Resource Circulation Plan to increase resource use efficiency and promote recycling. Additionally, South Korea's Critical Materials Strategy for Economic Security targets stabilizing supply chains for essential industrial materials, emphasizing the importance of domestic sourcing and recycling to mitigate risks associated with foreign supply disruptions. These policies underscore South Korea's efforts to bolster national security and economic stability by fostering a robust internal market for critical materials and recycled goods (Lee & Cha, 2020).

These legislative frameworks demonstrate a global trend toward reinforcing domestic economies through the strategic use of recycling and circular economy practices. These countries aim to enhance their technological independence, economic resilience, and environmental stewardship by focusing on keeping critical materials within their regions. Australia's strategy aligns with this trend by supporting critical minerals projects to ensure processing remains within the country. This involves enhancing local capabilities in refining and processing minerals, building resilient and sustainable supply chains to maintain critical materials within the region, attracting investment in domestic mineral processing and related infrastructure, and engaging local communities to share in the benefits of the mineral sector (The Australian Government, 2023).

8.1.2 Maximizing Recycling Impact Through Extended Producer Responsibility (EPR)

Extended Producer Responsibility (EPR) (Sect. 2.3) is an important concept in product use extension models (Chaps. 6 and 7) and the recycling phase. EPR works by making producers responsible for the end-of-life management of their products. This policy approach shifts the burden of waste management from public entities, citizens, and the environment to manufacturers.

EPR incentivizes companies to innovate in product design for enhanced recyclability and reduced environmental impact. It also underscores the manufacturer's responsibility throughout the product lifecycle, unlocking fresh business prospects from end-of-life products. This approach ensures that recycling considerations are integrated from the beginning of a product's creation.

Example 8.3 Extended Producer Responsibility (EPR) to address textile waste management

The textile sector's rapid production cycles and the disposability of fashion items contribute to a substantial volume of textile waste (Brown et al., 2023). Despite the potential for recycling, many textiles still end up in landfills or incinerators, leading to environmental pollution and resource wastage.

The fast fashion industry, which produces cheap and trendy clothing with a high turnover rate, encourages consumers to dispose of their clothes frequently. This model perpetuates the generation of textile waste, leading to environmental problems. Furthermore, recycling mixed-fiber garments poses technical challenges, and the inadequate infrastructure for textile collection and processing contributes to the prevailing low rates of textile recycling worldwide.

(continued)

The way we dispose of textile waste has an impact on the environment. When textiles are dumped in landfills, they release methane, a harmful greenhouse gas. On the other hand, the incineration of textiles releases CO2 and other toxic substances, which only exacerbates the environmental problems caused by the textile industry. In 2020, the textile purchases made in the EU generated approximately 270 kg of CO2 emissions per person, meaning that the textile products consumed in the EU generated greenhouse gas emissions equal to 121 million tonnes (European Parliament, 2024).

Various Extended Producer Responsibility (EPR) schemes have been implemented to address textile waste management in response to these challenges. Refashion, for example, operates as part of France's Extended Producer Responsibility (EPR) legislation, overseeing waste management and resource preservation in the textile industry. Textiles are sorted according to a five-level waste hierarchy. Refashion is primarily financed by 95% of French brands and importers through a fee system under the EPR scheme. This legislative framework mandates producers to take responsibility for the end-of-life management of their products, thus promoting sustainable practices and ensuring the proper disposal and recycling of textiles. In addition to its regulatory role, refashion provides valuable resources through its ecodesign platform, offering a step-by-step guide for transitioning to sustainable materials. Furthermore, its recycle platform is a centralized hub connecting stakeholders involved in textile recycling efforts (Refashion, 2021).

Similarly, several states have introduced EPR programs targeting specific items like carpets and mattresses in the United States. These initiatives aim to improve recycling rates for bulky items that contribute to landfill volumes. For instance, California's Carpet Stewardship Program involves a stewardship fee at the point of sale, which finances carpet recycling efforts. Likewise, mattress recycling programs in states like California, Connecticut, and Rhode Island facilitate the collection and recycling of mattresses, diverting them from landfills (The California State Assembly, 2010).

8.1.3 Product Standards and Certification

Meeting the strict standards and certifications required for recycled products is essential to ensure that the products meet specific safety, quality, and performance criteria. However, recycled materials have inherent variability in quality and properties, making it more challenging to meet these standards than virgin materials. As a result, manufacturers may need to invest in additional processing, quality control measures, and certification processes to ensure that their products containing recycled content meet industry standards and certifications. This additional investment leads to extra costs and requires a thorough understanding of the standards and close collaboration with certification bodies.

8.2 Redesigning Products for Recycling

When devising strategies to redesign products for recycling, manufacturers encounter the challenge of creating economically feasible systems for themselves that are attractive to end-users and recycling companies. The objective is to develop products that are appealing enough at the end of their life to be returned and processed by recycling firms, even though they may not directly generate income through recycling for the manufacturers.

Balancing these factors requires careful consideration. Manufacturers must ensure that any redesign aligns with customer expectations for functionality and aesthetics to maintain or improve the product's market appeal. At the same time, the redesigned products should be designed to make recycling easy, increasing the chances that recycling companies will buy discarded items for their valuable materials rather than having the manufacturers or end-users pay for recycling.

Manufacturers must select materials conducive to recycling by assessing their recyclability, availability, and environmental impact. This strategic decision influences products' environmental sustainability, economic viability, and market competitiveness (Table 8.1).

Design for disassembly, modular design, and component standardization are strategies manufacturers can adopt to enhance product recyclability and streamline end-of-life management (Table 8.2).

Example 8.4 Timberland's circularity platform

Timberloop™ is Timberland's circularity platform for design and take-back. Their "Designed for Circularity" products use a sole construction in which the outsoles can be removed by cutting one seam, and each part can be put into its recycling stream. This new modular construction method lessens the chemical-based cements used in manufacturing.[1]

Recycling helps manufacturers minimize the volume of waste sent to landfills, reducing waste disposal fees. Disposal costs can be significant, especially in regions with strict waste management regulations and high landfill taxes. Manufacturers can achieve cost reductions by diverting materials from the waste stream and into recycling.

[1] https://www.timberland.com/en-us/responsibility#timberlooptakeback

Table 8.1 Strategic material selection for recycling

Strategic decision	Description
Recyclability	The choice of materials should prioritize those that can be easily and efficiently recycled. Certain metals, glass, and some plastics retain their properties after recycling, making them particularly valuable. Manufacturers need to consider the degradation of material properties through recycling processes and opt for materials that can withstand multiple reuse cycles
Reduce material variability	This approach uses mono-materials wherever feasible and engineering products for straightforward disassembly and material separation
Environmental impact	The environmental impact of extracting, processing, and recycling materials must be evaluated. Materials that require less energy and fewer resources to produce and recycle are preferable
The availability of recyclable materials	Manufacturers must assess the supply chains of these materials to ensure stable sourcing. Using locally sourced recyclable materials can reduce transportation costs and carbon footprints, aligning with economic and environmental goals
Financial considerations	The financial aspects of material selection are pivotal. The cost-effectiveness of recycling processes and the overall impact on product pricing must be considered. Materials that are costlier upfront but offer savings in disposal and recycling stages may prove more economically viable in the long run
Customer preferences	Understanding market trends and customer preferences toward sustainable products can guide material selection. There is a growing consumer demand for products made from recycled and sustainable materials. Manufacturers can leverage this trend by choosing materials that meet recycling criteria and appeal to environmentally conscious consumers. 86% of those aged 45 and under are willing to pay more for sustainable packaging, and 68% of consumers have chosen a product in the last 6 months based on its sustainability credentials, showing a shift from awareness to action (Trivium Communications, 2022)

8.3 The Challenge of Recycling Complex Materials

Recycling advanced plastics and complex composites can be challenging and costly, mainly because of their intricate structures and unique material properties. Composites are used in industries like automotive and aerospace due to their exceptional strength and lightweight properties. Composites comprise two or more materials with different physical or chemical properties, such as carbon fiber or fiberglass that are bound together to create strong bonds between the fibers and the matrix material. Recycling these composites requires separating them into their components, such as fibers and resin, which is technically demanding and often beyond the capabilities of traditional mechanical recycling methods. Additionally, the chemical recycling processes capable of breaking down these complex bonds tend to be costly and energy-intensive, adding further barriers to the recycling of complex composite materials.

Table 8.2 Streamline end-of-life management

Design for end-of-life management	Description
Design for disassembly	This approach focuses on crafting products that can be easily taken apart at the end of their lifecycle. The key is to design connections that can be easily undone, such as using screws instead of glues, which enables the separation of components without damaging them. This ease of disassembly enables efficient recycling processes as it allows for the precise separation of different materials and facilitates the recovery and reuse of components
Modular design	A modular design (Sect. 4.1.2) strategy allows products to be constructed from independently replaceable parts or modules. This design approach makes repair and upgrades easier and aids in the recycling process. Manufacturers ensure that individual modules can be easily removed and recycled without discarding the entire product by designing products in a modular fashion. This extends the product's life, minimizes waste, and supports material recovery at the end of the module's useful life
Standardization of components	Standardization of components enhances the recyclability of products by creating uniformity across various product lines. This uniformity benefits the recycling process in several ways: *Increased efficiency in material recovery*: When components are standardized, recyclers can process larger batches of the same material or component type at once rather than handling a diverse mix *Economies of scale*: Standardization facilitates economies of scale in recycling operations. With a more predictable and consistent stream of similar components entering the recycling stream, recyclers can invest in more specialized technologies that specifically target these components, ultimately reducing processing costs and increasing the volume of materials that can be processed effectively *Reduction in contamination*: Standardized components reduce the likelihood of contamination during the recycling process. When diverse materials are mixed, the risk of contamination is higher, which can degrade the quality of recycled materials. Standardization minimizes this risk by simplifying the sorting process and ensuring that similar materials are processed together *Simplified sorting and disassembly*: When components are standardized, sorting and disassembling products are simplified. Recyclers and dismantling facilities can quickly identify and categorize components if they are familiar and consistent across multiple products

Advanced plastics, which are high-performance polymers used in various industries like electronics, automotive, and medical devices, pose a challenge for recycling due to their intricate chemical structures. These structures are tailored for specific functions, such as heat resistance or enhanced strength, making it difficult to break down and process them using conventional recycling techniques. Moreover, these plastics often contain additives, fillers, and reinforcement fibers, adding another layer of complexity to the recycling process. To produce pure recycled material, it is necessary to use advanced and often costly separation technologies to remove these contaminants, which compounds the challenge of recycling advanced plastics.

Example 8.5 INEOS Infinia recycles polyethylene terephthalate

INEOS Infinia is an innovative solution to one of the biggest challenges the recycling industry faces—the efficient recycling of polyethylene terephthalate (PET). Unlike traditional mechanical recycling processes, Infinia uses advanced chemical recycling technology to break down PET waste that is unsuitable for mechanical recycling due to contamination or degradation. This includes colored, opaque, complex multilayer PET materials commonly found in food trays, colored bottles, and laminated packaging. The Infinia process breaks these materials down into their basic monomers, which are then utilized to produce new PET materials of virgin-like quality suitable for use in clear, food-grade packaging (INEOS, 2024).

Recycling complex composites and advanced plastics is challenging due to the high costs and lack of scalable technologies. Although specialized recycling techniques like pyrolysis, solvolysis, and chemical depolymerization show promise in handling these materials, they must be more scalable and economically viable for broad industrial applications. The financial burden of recycling these complex materials is higher than that of simpler materials like PET or HDPE plastics. This is due to the investment in advanced technology, increased energy consumption, and the need for specialized handling and processing facilities.

A comprehensive approach is necessary to tackle the issues related to recycling complex materials. One fundamental strategy is to design materials and products with recycling in mind at the end of their life. This can be achieved by simplifying the materials used in composites, choosing more suitable materials for recycling processes, or creating products that can be easily dismantled and separated.

Collaborative efforts across the industry, with manufacturers, researchers, and recycling facilities working together, can lead to the development of standardized processes and innovative technologies. This can help manage the complexities of these materials more effectively and cost-efficiently.

Example 8.6 CETEC (Circular Economy for Thermosets Epoxy Composites)

Wind turbine blades are crucial in generating renewable energy. However, disposing of them presents environmental challenges. Traditionally, these blades, mainly composed of complex materials joined together with epoxy resins, have ended up in landfills after they have served their purpose. The durability and resilience of epoxy make these blades particularly resistant to decomposition, which potentially wastes valuable materials. In the next few years, thousands of turbines will be decommissioned or repowered, presenting a sustainability challenge and an opportunity to use the materials they are made of.

(continued)

By 2030, it is estimated that over 52,000 tons of wind turbine blades will need to be recycled annually in Europe alone, underscoring the importance of this initiative (Stena Recycling, 2023).

Vestas,[2] one of the leading manufacturers of wind turbines, has collaborated with Aarhus University, Danish Technological Institute, and Olin in the CETEC project[3] to develop an innovative solution that addresses the problem of waste generated by wind turbine blades. Vestas' new technology is a two-step process. In the first process, the composite is disassembled, and the epoxy is released from the materials. After separating the materials, the second step focuses on converting the epoxy resin used in wind turbine blades into virgin-grade materials. This process can help repurpose the materials from the blades, including the epoxy resin from decommissioned blades, and transform the materials into valuable resources for producing new blades or other industrial components.

CETEC (Circular Economy for Thermosets Epoxy Composites) has developed a technology that potentially recycles epoxy-based turbine blades currently in landfills and those from ongoing operations. This technology helps mitigate the use of landfills and reduces the need for new raw materials. Notably, the technology does not require any redesigning of existing blades, which makes it possible to implement it without any changes to the current turbine designs or interfering with the production of new turbines. This practical and immediately applicable solution will be scaled up to handle the thousands of blades decommissioned in the coming years (Project CETEC, n.d.).

Stena Recycling,[4] experts in managing waste and recycled materials, have partnered with Vestas to tackle one of the most challenging aspects of blade recycling: the efficient large-scale processing and recycling of these complex composites to create a closed-loop system where end-of-life turbine blades are not seen as waste but as valuable resources for producing new products.

8.4 End-of-Life Product Control

Manufacturers must decide on the control level they want over their products' lifecycle, which is often a legal requirement under EPR legislation. Their decisions can affect material harvesting and circular sourcing. Effective product lifecycle management is necessary to ensure that valuable materials stay in the manufacturer's control and are not lost unintentionally. Below are strategic options that manufacturers can consider when deciding the amount of control they want over their products' lifecycle.

[2] https://www.vestas.com/en/media/company-news/2023/vestas-unveils-circularity-solution-to-end-landfill-for-c3710818

[3] https://www.project-cetec.dk/uk/

[4] https://www.stenarecycling.com/da/nyheder-indsigt/nyheder/2023/wind-turbine-blade-recycling-boosts-circularity-in-fossil-free-wind-energy/

8.4.1 Sell and Forget

This approach involves the least control, where the product is sold, and no further efforts are made to manage its end-of-life.

Example 8.7 Pandora uses 100% recycled silver and gold in all of its jewelry

Pandora, the largest jewelry brand in the world by volume, uses 100% recycled silver and gold in all of its jewelry. These precious metals can be recycled indefinitely without losing quality, making them perfect for circular strategies. Mining for silver and gold is an energy-intensive process that contributes to greenhouse gas emissions. Recycled silver reduces Pandora's carbon footprint by two-thirds, while recycled gold emits less than 1% of the carbon compared to newly mined gold (Pandora, 2024).

Instead of having take-back programs to control the return, Pandora has ensured that all its suppliers meet strict sustainability standards, specifically the Responsible Jewellery Council Chain of Custody.[5] This standard ensures that recycled materials are carefully tracked and managed, preventing any mixing with newly mined metals and maintaining the integrity of the supply chain.

8.4.2 Redistribution Business Models

Redistribution business models allow manufacturers to maintain relationships with their products and customers throughout the product's lifecycle. These models are beneficial in identifying when products are ready for recycling and extending offerings to the owner.

The product as a service (PaaS) model, as detailed in Sect. 5.4, exemplifies this approach. This model fosters continuous engagement with the product, enabling the PaaS supplier to continuously gather insights into the product's condition and usage patterns. These insights help determine the best time for recycling. The PaaS model can vary in terms of control.

Manufacturer-Controlled In this scenario, the manufacturer maintains complete control over the product, from distribution to eventual recycling. This direct control enables efficient material recovery, as the manufacturer can decide when to reclaim products for recycling.

Third-Party Controlled Alternatively, control can be exercised through partnerships with third parties who manage the product's deployment and maintenance. While this reduces direct oversight, it can be strategically managed through agreements that include provisions for material harvesting. These agreements can specify

[5] https://www.responsiblejewellery.com/wp-content/uploads/RJC-CoC-2017-V2-Standard-2-1.pdf

processes and terms under which the third party will return products for recycling, ensuring that the manufacturer still benefits from the reclaimed materials.

8.4.3 Product Use Extension Business Models

These models aim to increase product lifespan through maintenance, repair, refurbishment, and remanufacturing. Manufacturers can opportunistically harvest materials throughout the product's use cycle by maintaining continuous contact with customers and products. This dialogue also enables manufacturers to offer targeted deals to customers at the end of a product's life to reclaim it for material recovery. This model enhances the manufacturer's control over the recycling process and strengthens customer relationships and loyalty by providing extra value through extended product life.

8.4.4 Take-Back Programs

Manufacturers can benefit from take-back programs as a solution to the limitations of the "sell and forget" approach and to complement product use extension and redistribute business models. By allowing manufacturers to regain control of their products at the end of their lifecycle, take-back programs make recycling materials more efficient.

There are several ways in which manufacturers can encourage customers to return used products. For example, discounts on future purchases can help maintain customer engagement and mitigate the "sell and forget" model. Direct buy-back schemes can provide immediate financial benefits to customers for returning their products and integrate well with redistribution models. Setting up controlled return points in convenient locations can also help ensure that products are returned in a manageable and predictable manner, complementing product use extension strategies.

Example 8.8 The Timberloop™ platform

Timberland, a global outdoor footwear and apparel leader, has launched the Timberloop™ platform. This platform allows customers to return their old Timberland® products when they can no longer use them. Customers can bring their old gear to any US retail or outlet store. Timberland will then assess and recycle the returned items through our partners. As a thank you, customers will receive a 20% discount code to use immediately for an in-store purchase[6].

[6] https://www.timberland.com/en-us/responsibility#timberlooptakeback

Additionally, manufacturers can offer pickup services to make it easier for customers to participate in recycling initiatives, especially for larger or more cumbersome products. Finally, incorporating take-back initiatives into loyalty programs can motivate returns and keep customers engaged with the brand throughout the product lifecycle, enhancing both redistribution and product use extension models.

Example 8.9 Dell's prepaid shipping labels

Dell's recycling initiative[7] offers prepaid shipping labels for customers to return their old electronics for recycling. This service is offered at no cost to the customer, making it accessible and straightforward.

Participating in industry-wide take-back initiatives can benefit manufacturers from collective expertise, shared resources, and established logistics networks. This approach reduces operational costs and simplifies the process for consumers and businesses, making it easier for them to return products. Harmonized schemes allow for consistent communication and marketing efforts, reinforcing the importance of recycling and the ease of participation.

Example 8.10 PaintCare oversee recycling leftover paint

PaintCare is a non-profit organization created by paint manufacturers to oversee recycling leftover paint. It operates in several US states with paint stewardship laws. PaintCare provides convenient drop-off locations for consumers and businesses to return unused paint. The collected paint is then recycled into new products or used in other applications. To date, PaintCare has collected 69.7 million gallons of paint.[8]

8.4.5 End-of-Life Control of Third-Party Managed Components

Managing product lifecycles within a circular economy can be challenging when third parties, such as repair technicians or automotive service centers, control end-of-life components instead of the product's owner. When a component like a washing machine motor or a car part is replaced during repair, the old part, which may still have residual value, is usually left with the third party.

These third-party entities often possess components that could be refurbished, remanufactured, or recycled. The challenge here is the ambiguous ownership status: technically, the replaced parts still belong to the product's owner, who, however, may have no interest in their recovery or further use.

[7] https://www.dell.com/en-us/dt/corporate/social-impact/advancing-sustainability/how-to-recycle.htm

[8] https://www.paintcare.org/

This disinterest transfers the proper disposal or recycling responsibility to the third party. However, without formal ownership or direct incentive, these parties lack the motivation or means to ensure that these components enter a recycling stream or are otherwise disposed of in an environmentally responsible manner. This scenario leads to suboptimal recycling outcomes, where valuable materials are not reclaimed efficiently.

Manufacturers and policymakers should consider expanding take-back programs to cover components under third-party control. Such programs would need guidelines and incentives for third parties to return components at the end of their life. This could include logistical support, financial incentives, or partnerships with certified recycling centers responsible for the proper pickup and processing of the product.

Example 8.11 Nestle's Nespresso recycling program for its aluminum capsules

Nestle's Nespresso, a global producer of coffee and coffee machines, has implemented a dedicated recycling program for its aluminum capsules. Aluminum is chosen for Nespresso capsules due to its properties for preserving the quality and freshness of coffee and its recyclability.

Nespresso provides multiple options for customers to return used capsules, including dedicated collection points, postal return schemes where customers can send back used capsules free of charge, and, in some regions, home collection services. This ensures customers' ease of access and convenience, encouraging higher participation rates in the recycling program.

Once collected, the capsules are transported to specialized third-party facilities where they undergo treatment to separate the coffee grounds from the aluminum. The coffee grounds are often repurposed as compost or bioenergy, contributing further to environmental sustainability efforts.

The aluminum recovered from the capsules is then melted and purified to create new aluminum, which can be used to produce new coffee capsules or other aluminum products. Recycling aluminum uses less energy than producing new aluminum from ore, reducing energy consumption and greenhouse gas emissions (Nespresso, 2024).

8.4.6 Transparency and Involvement

Transparency in the recycling process helps establish trust with customers. Manufacturers can inform customers about the journey of their products through recycling, highlighting the usage of recycled materials and the environmental impact of their participation.

Manufacturers can strengthen their customer relationships by involving them in recycling programs. When customers feel they are making a meaningful contribution toward a greater environmental cause, they are more likely to develop an emotional connection with the brand.

8.4.7 Integration of Tracking Technologies

Incorporating tracking technologies into products, such as RFID tags, sensors, or QR codes, can optimize recycling processes. However, the decision to use these technologies depends heavily on the chosen business model, the take-back strategy, and the nature of the products.

For some products, real-time tracking via sensors can provide continuous data on the condition and location of the product, enabling timely recycling decisions. Alternatively, technologies like RFID and QR codes are suitable for less frequent updates and can help determine the optimal timing for product recycling. However, in some business models, tracking may be optional. In cases where products are disposable, or the cost and complexity of implementing tracking systems do not justify the recycling value, opting out of tracking technology might be the more practical approach.

Example 8.12 Volvo utilizes digital tracking and monitoring systems to oversee the lifecycle of batteries

Volvo Cars partners with battery recycling companies to ensure that the batteries from its electric vehicles can be sustainably recycled·. (CATL, 2024) describes that Volvo Cars will collect retired batteries and hand them to downstream suppliers certified by Volvo Cars for recycling and extracting metals, including nickel, cobalt, and lithium. CATL, a global leader in innovative new energy technologies, will use these recycled materials to produce new batteries to power electric vehicles manufactured by Volvo Cars.

Volvo utilizes digital tracking and monitoring systems to oversee the lifecycle of batteries. Analytics tools assist in predicting when batteries will reach the end of their life, ensuring that they are efficiently sent to recycling facilities. After a battery has completed its primary task in a vehicle or bus, Volvo uses detailed battery data to determine whether it needs a few cells replaced or a total overhaul. This enables Volvo to decide the battery's next purpose. The batteries are prepared for their next mission following inspection and any necessary repairs. They may return to the roads to power vehicles or take on a new role, such as serving as part of a battery energy storage system. As each battery nears the end of its lifecycle, the goal is to extract and reuse essential materials like lithium, cobalt, and nickel (Volvo, 2024).

The digitization of components will be discussed in Chap. 13.

8.4.8 What Do Manufacturers Do with Their Control of Recycle-Ready Products?

Manufacturers do not usually handle the recycling process directly for products containing materials suitable for harvesting. They delegate this task to specialized recycling companies that can achieve economies of scale, making the process more cost-effective and efficient. Manufacturers sell end-of-life products and scrap materials containing valuable components for recycling to add economic value and reduce waste. This allows them to recuperate some value from products that have completed their lifecycle, turning what would otherwise be waste into a financial asset. After recycling, companies process these materials and return them to the market as clean, usable resources. Manufacturers purchase these recycled materials.

In practical terms, manufacturers begin the recycling process by determining the optimal times to sell scrap and choosing recycling partners. However, they typically only control the materials indirectly once they exit their facilities. Their control is manifested economically through selling scrap and purchasing recycled materials rather than through direct stewardship of specific materials.

Example 8.13 The Royal Mint recycle gold from electronic waste

The Royal Mint is one of the world's oldest institutions that mints coins. They have launched a program to recycle gold from electronic waste (e-waste). The program is expected to process up to 90 tonnes of UK-sourced e-waste every week, which will help repurpose hundreds of kilograms of gold annually.

In collaboration with Excir,[9] The Royal Mint uses a novel chemical process that selectively recovers over 99% of gold from electronic components found in discarded laptops and mobile phones. It is worth noting that electronic waste contains a significant amount of gold, estimated at up to 100 times more gold per tonne than gold ore. E-waste is the world's fastest-growing waste stream and is estimated to hold about seven percent of the world's gold (The Royal Mint, 2023).

The gold recovered from the e-waste will be processed and utilized within its products, starting with its jewelry collection, 886 by The Royal Mint.

8.5 Recycling Packaging and Managing Packaging Waste

Many countries have implemented stringent regulations to improve the recycling of packaging materials (Chap. 2).

Example 8.14 Washington's plastics law

Washington's plastics law[10] mandates that manufacturers include a minimum percentage of post-consumer recycled content in specific types of plastic packaging, such as beverage containers, trash bags, and household cleaning product containers. The law requires manufacturers to report the amount and

(continued)

[9] https://www.excir.com/

[10] https://ecology.wa.gov/waste-toxics/reducing-recycling-waste/plastics/2021-plastic-pollution-laws/recycled-content-minimums

source of recycled content in their products to the Washington Department of Ecology. Compliance is enforced by the Department of Ecology, which may impose penalties for non-compliance. The recycled content requirements are subject to periodic review and potential increases to reflect changes in market conditions and technological advancements. The primary goal of this law is to reduce plastic waste and promote the use of recycled materials in packaging. Each product category is phased in with increasing post-consumer recycled content (PCRC) requirements over the next 15 years. By 2036, all packaging for covered product categories must include at least 50 percent post-consumer recycled content, except for trash bags, which only contain 20 percent after 2027 (Washington State Department of Ecology, 2021) (Fig. 8.2).

	2023	2024	2025	2026	2027	2028	2029	2030	2031	2032	2033	2034	2035	2036
Plastic trash bags	10%		15%		20%									
Beverage containers	15%			25%					50%					
Household cleaners and personal care products			15%			25%			50%					
Plastic wine container (187 milliliters)						15%			25%					50%
Dairy milk container						15%			25%					50%

Fig. 8.2 Minimum recycled content phases. (Credit: Washington State Department of Ecology (2021))

The percentage indicates the amount of a product that must be made from post-consumer resin starting in that year.

Efficient packaging design plays a pivotal role in the recyclability of materials. Designing for recyclability involves using fewer materials, selecting materials that are easier to recycle, and designing products that can be easily disassembled. This makes the recycling process more straightforward and enhances the economic feasibility of recycling by improving the quality of recovered materials.

Example 8.15 Electrolux's new packaging is free from Expanded PolyStyrene (EPS)

Electrolux,[11] a worldwide leader in home appliances, has introduced new packaging for its Electrolux and AEG small appliances. The new packaging is free from expanded polystyrene (EPS), which is difficult to recycle and often

[11] https://www.betterlivingelectrolux.com/actions/introduce-recycled-and-more-resource-efficient-product-packaging

ends up in landfills. Instead, the company has opted for packaging made from paper-based materials that are certified by the Forest Stewardship Council (FSC).[12]

The printing process for this new packaging utilizes four-color print technology, which reduces ink usage by 70%. Electrolux minimizes the release of volatile organic compounds (VOCs) during printing by reducing ink use. VOCs are known for their negative environmental impact.Electrolux's adoption of more resource-efficient packaging solutions lowers its material costs and helps reduce the costs associated with waste disposal and management.

However, recycling packaging waste presents several challenges. One issue is contamination, as packaging waste often contains various materials that are difficult to separate, such as plastic films on paper or multi-layered materials. This contamination can make recycling less efficient and more costly. Additionally, effective recycling depends heavily on consumer participation in waste separation and disposal. Educating the public and encouraging proper recycling habits increase recycling rates. Another challenge is the cost associated with collecting, sorting, and recycling packaging materials, which can be particularly high for materials that do not have a well-established market for recycled products. Subsidies, incentives, and technological innovations are often necessary to make recycling economically viable.

Various strategies can be used to improve packaging waste management. Extended Producer Responsibility (EPR) schemes involve producers being responsible for collecting, recycling, or properly disposing of packaging waste. These schemes can motivate producers to create more recyclable packaging and share the cost of recycling. Advances in recycling technology can help tackle contamination and enhance the efficiency of recycling processes. For example, improved sorting technologies can automate and improve the accuracy of separating different materials.

Additionally, developing and adopting global standards for packaging recyclability are essential (Table 8.3). These standards harmonize the recycling process, increase recycling rates worldwide, and create a more consistent market for recycled materials.

The global standards set consistent guidelines and practices to ensure that packaging is designed with recyclability. This makes recycling more accessible and more efficient across different regions. By accessing and adhering to these standards, manufacturers can align with best practices in packaging sustainability.

[12] Home | Forest Stewardship Council (fsc.org)

Table 8.3 Key standards for packaging recyclability

Standard	Description
ISO 18601 to ISO 18606 Series[a]	These ISO standards encompass general requirements, optimization, reuse, material recycling, energy recovery, and organic recycling for packaging. They are designed to offer comprehensive guidelines to ensure that packaging is environmentally sustainable and efficiently recyclable
EN 13430:2004[b]	This European standard specifies requirements for packaging recoverable by material recycling. It ensures that packaging materials can be effectively collected, sorted, and recycled within the existing waste management infrastructure
ASTM D7611/D7611M – 20[c]	This standard practice for coding plastic manufactured articles for resin identification helps in the sorting and recycling of plastic materials by providing a clear and consistent coding system
Global Protocol on Packaging Sustainability (GPPS)[d]	Developed by the Consumer Goods Forum, this protocol provides a common language and framework for packaging sustainability, helping businesses to communicate and implement sustainable packaging practices effectively

[a]https://www.iso.org/standard/55869.html
[b]https://standards.iteh.ai/catalog/standards/cen/4f92e1b9-0e0c-4b85-987d-045c83ccd6ce/en-13430-2004
[c]https://www.astm.org/d7611_d7611m-20.html
[d]https://www.theconsumergoodsforum.com/wp-content/uploads/2017/11/Global-Protocol-on-Packaging.pdf

8.6 Handling Waste from Production

This section will delve into the strategies and best practices for handling waste generated during production, emphasizing the importance of waste reduction, reuse, and recycling within manufacturing operations.

8.6.1 Minimizing Production Waste

Minimizing waste at the source is the first and most critical step in handling production waste. Manufacturers can implement lean manufacturing principles, which focus on identifying and eliminating waste throughout production. This includes optimizing material usage, improving process efficiency, and reducing defects.

Key strategies for minimizing production waste include:

- *Process Optimization*: Streamlining manufacturing processes to reduce waste generation. This can involve improving production planning, enhancing equipment efficiency, and adopting just-in-time (JIT) inventory practices to minimize excess material usage.

- *Material Efficiency*: Selecting materials that generate less waste during processing and exploring alternative materials that are easier to recycle or have a lower environmental impact.
- *Quality Control*: Implementing stringent quality control measures to reduce the incidence of defective products that need to be discarded or reworked.

8.6.2 Reusing Production Waste

Reusing production waste involves finding ways to reintegrate waste materials back into the production cycle or other applications within the manufacturing facility. This approach reduces waste disposal costs and conserves raw materials and energy.

Examples of reuse strategies include:

- *Internal Recycling Loops*: Creating internal recycling loops where waste materials, such as metal shavings, plastic scraps, or water, are collected, processed, and reused within the same production facility.
- *By-product Utilization*: Identifying valuable by-products that can be used in other processes or sold to other industries. For instance, waste heat from manufacturing processes can be used for heating purposes or energy generation.

Example 8.16 Volkswagen Group recycle production waste

Volkswagen Group Components demonstrates the recycling of production waste within its closed-loop processes. At the foundry in Kassel, all aluminum chips generated on-site are reintegrated into the casting process. The plant produces around 20 metric tons of aluminum chips daily, which are then melted down. This recycling initiative is expected to reduce energy requirements by approximately 3250 MWh annually and cut CO2 emissions by over 1400 metric tons annually (Volkswagen Group, 2021).

At Volkswagen's Wolfsburg plant, plastic waste produced during the manufacture of gasoline tanks through co-extrusion is recycled to make diesel tanks using mono-extrusion. This process enables the reuse of approximately 1600 metric tons of plastic waste each year, which would otherwise be disposed of as waste. This recycling initiative helps the plant save 2500 metric tons of CO2 emissions and €2 million in material costs annually (Volkswagen Group, 2021).

8.6.3 Recycling Production Waste

When reuse is not feasible, recycling production waste is the next best option. Effective recycling programs require a well-structured system for collecting, sorting, and processing waste materials to ensure they can be reintroduced into the production cycle or sold as secondary raw materials.

Key elements of successful recycling programs include:

- *Segregation at Source*: Implementing systems for segregating waste materials at the point of generation to enhance the purity and quality of recyclable materials. This involves providing clearly labeled bins and training employees on proper waste segregation practices.
- *Advanced Recycling Technologies*: Investing in advanced recycling technologies, such as chemical recycling for complex plastics and composites, to improve the efficiency and effectiveness of recycling processes.
- *Partnerships with Recycling Facilities*: Collaborating with specialized recycling facilities that can handle specific types of waste materials and ensure they are processed in an environmentally responsible manner.

Example 8.17 Audi's Aluminum Closed Loop Project

Audi's Aluminum Closed Loop Project, launched at the Neckarsulm plant in 2017, exemplifies the implementation of recycling production waste. In this initiative, aluminum waste generated from sheet-metal parts in the press shop is collected and delivered back to suppliers. These suppliers then recycle the scrap aluminum to produce new material, which Audi reuses in the press shop (Volkswagen Group, 2021).

8.6.4 Waste-to-Energy Conversion

For waste materials that cannot be reused or recycled, waste-to-energy (WTE) conversion offers a viable solution. WTE technologies, such as incineration and gasification, convert waste materials into energy, reducing the volume of waste sent to landfills and generating renewable energy.

Considerations for implementing WTE solutions include:

- *Environmental Impact*: Evaluating the environmental impact of WTE technologies, including emissions and by-products, to ensure they align with sustainability goals.
- *Energy Recovery*: Assessing the potential for energy recovery from waste materials and integrating WTE systems with existing energy infrastructure to maximize efficiency.

8.6.5 Regulatory Compliance and Reporting

Compliance with regulatory requirements is essential for managing production waste responsibly. Manufacturers must stay abreast of local, national, and international regulations governing waste management, including those related to hazardous waste, recycling, and emissions.

Key compliance strategies include:

- *Regular Audits*: Conducting regular audits of waste management practices to ensure compliance with regulations and identify areas for improvement.
- *Transparent Reporting*: Maintaining transparent records of waste generation, management practices, and recycling rates to demonstrate compliance and support continuous improvement efforts.

8.7 Repurpose

Repurposing offers manufacturers an opportunity to innovate and create value from end-of-life products. Unlike traditional recycling, which focuses on breaking down materials to develop new raw materials, repurposing is taking products or components that have reached the end of their original life and finding new uses without significant reprocessing. This method can reduce the environmental impact of waste, decrease the demand for virgin raw materials, and offer additional income. For example, old tires can create playground surfaces, and shipping containers can be transformed into modular housing units.

For repurposing to be truly effective, it should not be treated as a mere patch on a linear business model. Instead, it must be integrated into a manufacturer's broader circular economy strategies. This means embedding repurposing principles into product design, production processes, and business models.

One opportunity lies in innovative product development. Manufacturers can design products with future repurposing in mind. For instance, creating modular furniture that can be easily disassembled and reconfigured for different uses can extend product life. Additionally, offering customizable products that can be repurposed enables manufacturers to meet diverse customer needs. This can include products designed for multiple uses or components that can be repurposed into entirely new products.

Exploring new market segments offers valuable opportunities. Creating products tailored for secondary markets, where there's a demand for repurposed goods, can generate new revenue streams—for instance, selling repurposed industrial components to smaller manufacturers or hobbyists. Embracing upcycling and transforming waste materials into higher-value products can appeal to niche markets like eco-friendly fashion or home décor. For instance, used denim can be transformed into bags, cushions, or even new garments. Utilizing fabric scraps to create patchwork designs can reduce textile waste and create unique, handcrafted products.

Repurposing end-of-life products can reduce waste disposal costs and generate revenue from selling repurposed items.

Example 8.18 ReCORK's cork recycling initiative

Used wine corks can be repurposed into flooring tiles, insulation materials, and craft supplies. ReCORK,[13] a leading cork recycling initiative, has collected over 70 million natural wine corks for repurposing. ReCORK's process starts with collecting used wine corks from partner locations, including wineries, bars, restaurants, and individuals. Once collected, the corks undergo a granulation process to be transformed into various products, ranging from footwear soles to yoga blocks.

Collaboration and partnerships with organizations and businesses specializing in repurposing can enhance capabilities and reach new markets. Engaging with local communities to support grassroots repurposing initiatives can also be beneficial.

Marketing campaigns and product information can educate customers about the benefits and possibilities of repurposing and foster a culture of sustainability. Offering take-back programs and incentivizing end-users to return products for repurposing can further encourage participation.

8.8 Integrating Reverse Logistics in Recycling Business Models

Reverse logistics, which involves handling end-of-life products and ensuring their efficient return to recycling facilities, presents manufacturers with a new challenge. For instance, collecting end-of-life products from widely dispersed locations can be challenging and expensive. Manufacturers must develop efficient collection networks that cover large geographic areas without prohibitive costs. Additionally, coordination among various stakeholders, including recyclers, logistics providers, and product owners, is necessary to establish a reliable supply chain for recyclable products.

Logistics service providers specializing in handling returns play a role in this process by picking up and transporting products from owners or collection points to recycling facilities. By working with these providers, manufacturers can optimize transportation routes, streamline the collection process, and reduce transit times.

Manufacturers can implement various solutions, whether through third parties or themselves. For example, they can utilize sophisticated logistics and supply chain management software to forecast demand for recycling services, optimize routes, and manage inventory more effectively. They can also set up decentralized collection points or partner with local businesses to reduce the distances products need to travel back to recycling centers, lowering transportation costs and environmental impact. Implementing technology solutions such as RFID tracking, IoT devices, or QR codes can enhance the transparency and efficiency of reverse logistics. These technologies provide real-time product location and status data, facilitating better decision-making and process optimization.

[13] https://recork.com/

Reverse logistics is a component of recycling business models that requires detailed attention to the design and execution of collection and transportation systems. Manufacturers can overcome the inherent complexities and establish effective reverse logistics systems by partnering with experienced logistics providers and employing strategic planning and technology solutions.

8.9 Circular Sourcing

Circular sourcing involves incorporating recycled or renewable materials into the production cycle, which reduces or replaces the need for virgin raw materials. This section will delve into the different aspects of circular sourcing, such as balancing recycled materials with traditional inputs, ensuring material quality, and tackling economic and market-related challenges.

Example 8.19 Ford reuse spent 3D-printed powders

Ford, a global automotive manufacturer, has partnered with HP to reuse spent 3D-printed powders and parts by converting them into injection-molded vehicle parts. These parts have better chemical and moisture resistance than conventional versions, are 7% lighter, and cost 10% less (Ford, 2021).

HP is collecting and recycling 3D-printed parts, such as those from oral care companies, to increase Ford's volume.

Lavergne, a resin producer, transforms molds and discarded powder from Ford's 3D printers into high-quality recycled plastic pellets suitable for injection molding. Ford's supplier, ARaymond, then molds these pellets into fuel-line clips.

8.9.1 Balancing Recycled Materials with Traditional Raw Materials

To remain competitive in the linear supply chain during the transition to circular business models, manufacturers must determine the most practical combination of recycled and traditional materials. Manufacturers must keep a close eye on the market demand for recycled materials and the availability and pricing of traditional raw materials. Manufacturers can adjust their procurement strategies by analyzing market trends and supply chain dynamics to optimize cost-effectiveness and resource efficiency while ensuring a steady supply.

Integrating recycled materials as an extra source complicates a manufacturer's sourcing strategy. Quality, cost, availability, and sustainability considerations must be carefully balanced across multiple sourcing channels to manage this complexity and optimize overall supply chain performance.

8.9.2 Material Quality and Consistency

Manufacturers face challenges when incorporating recycled materials into their production processes due to their varying quality and consistency. Recycling involves recovering materials from a wide range of end-of-life products, contributing to this variability. Manufacturers must thoroughly assess their quality and performance to ensure recycled materials suit their specific applications and product requirements. Through extensive testing and evaluation, manufacturers can identify opportunities to substitute traditional raw materials with recycled alternatives without compromising product quality or performance.

8.9.2.1 Sources of Variability

The variability in recycled materials comes from various factors that make the recycling process challenging. Recycled materials come from different sources, each with its unique history, composition, and level of contamination. This diversity means that plastics from consumer packaging could be mixed with those from industrial applications, and each type reacts differently during recycling.

These materials are prone to contamination and degradation throughout their use and by the time they reach the end of their lifespan. Contamination may range from food residues to adhesives, and for polymers, degradation may result from exposure to elements like sunlight, chemicals, or mechanical stress, which can alter the material's inherent properties.

The effectiveness of the collection and sorting systems determines the purity and consistency of the recycled output. Inadequate sorting mechanisms can lead to material cross-contamination, amplifying the hurdles faced during recycling efforts and highlighting the complex interplay of factors contributing to the variability of recycled materials.

8.9.2.2 Impact on Manufacturing

Due to their inherent variability, using recycled materials in manufacturing poses several challenges for manufacturers. Quality and consistency issues with recycled materials can result in compromised properties such as strength, flexibility, and thermal stability fluctuations. This can make it challenging to maintain the performance standards of final products.

To overcome these inconsistencies, manufacturers may need to adapt their production processes. This could involve making modifications such as adjusting processing temperatures and pressures or incorporating compatibilizers and stabilizers to achieve the desired product quality. However, these adaptations can complicate the production landscape and potentially increase costs.

Ensuring that recycled materials align with product specifications requires more stringent quality control and testing protocols. This can prolong the production timeline and allocate additional resources, impacting manufacturing efficiency and cost-effectiveness.

These challenges highlight the need for innovative solutions to integrate recycled materials into production cycles, emphasizing the complex interplay between recycled material variability and manufacturing processes.

Manufacturers can overcome the challenges posed by recycled materials' variability and complexity. Advanced sorting and processing technologies such as near-infrared (NIR) spectroscopy and AI-driven systems can enhance the purity and consistency of recycled materials, making them more suitable for high-quality production. Establishing stronger collaborations with recycled material suppliers to develop precise specifications and standards leads to a more reliable and consistent supply of high-quality recycled materials.

8.9.3 Navigating Economic Challenges

Manufacturers who wish to adopt circular sourcing business models may face economic challenges such as cost implications and market volatility. The prices of recycled materials can be volatile and change frequently due to changes in the supply and demand dynamics within the global recycling market. Changes in waste management policies, fluctuations in the availability of recyclable materials, and shifts in the consumer behavior can all impact the supply side. On the demand side, variations in manufacturing output, technological advancements, and shifts toward more sustainable materials can influence the demand for recycled materials. This volatility makes financial planning and budgeting challenging for manufacturers as the cost of inputs can fluctuate over time, affecting profit margins and the overall cost-effectiveness of recycling initiatives.

To overcome these economic challenges, manufacturers must plan strategically and may take advantage of government incentives, subsidies, or partnerships to reduce the initial financial burden. Developing flexible procurement strategies that adapt to market volatility ensures a steady supply of recycled materials at competitive prices.

8.9.4 Tackling Customer and Market Challenges

Manufacturers face challenges in adopting circular sourcing due to customer acceptance, brand positioning, and market coexistence during the transition to circular practices.

One of the biggest challenges in promoting recycled materials in products is addressing customer skepticism or hesitancy about their quality, performance, and aesthetic appeal. Despite advancements in recycling technologies that often preserve or enhance the quality of recycled content, customer perceptions may still be influenced by outdated beliefs that equate recycled materials with inferior quality. This skepticism can discourage people from using recycled products, as concerns about durability, functionality, or aesthetics persist. Therefore, building customer trust is crucial, and manufacturers must ensure that their products made from recycled materials match or exceed the quality of those made from virgin resources while effectively communicating these quality assurances to customers.

Manufacturers face a challenge aligning their brand with a recycling business model while still using virgin materials in some products. To overcome this challenge, they must develop effective communication and marketing strategies highlighting recycled materials' environmental benefits. At the same time, they must ensure that their product's perceived value and quality are not compromised. This is critical as customers seek eco-friendly products but are unwilling to compromise on quality or functionality, even though many are willing to pay a premium for sustainability (PDI Technologies, 2024). Therefore, manufacturers need to position their brands so that incorporating recycled materials is an added value that improves the product's appeal without detracting from its quality.

As manufacturers transition toward more circular practices, they must ensure their new, sustainable offerings coexist with products from virgin raw materials without cannibalizing their existing market. This delicate positioning requires careful market segmentation and product differentiation strategies to cater to diverse customer preferences. Manufacturers must communicate the value of products made from recycled materials in a way that complements their existing product lines, ensuring that sustainability adds to the brand's value proposition rather than diluting it.

8.10 Digitization Supporting Recycling Models

Digitization facilitates seamless integration and efficient management of recycling processes. The Sustainable Manufacturing Intelligence Framework (SMIF) outlines how digital capabilities can support recycling business models, providing a comprehensive approach to integrating digitization within recycling operations. This section will highlight the role of digitization in recycling based on the insights from Part 3 of the book. SMIF comprises five key areas: Internal IT systems, Business Ecosystems, Connected Products, Customer Experience, and Data-Driven Circularity.

8.10.1 Internal IT Systems

Internal IT systems manage and optimize recycling processes. Effective Supply Chain Management (SCM) systems track products throughout their lifecycle, including end-of-life stages where products are collected for recycling. These systems facilitate reverse logistics management, ensuring returned products are efficiently processed and directed to appropriate recycling channels. By integrating real-time data exchange and predictive analytics, SCM systems can optimize the logistics and handling of recyclable materials, enhancing operational efficiency and resource recovery.

Customer Relationship Management (CRM) systems extend their functions beyond traditional sales to foster ongoing customer engagement. These systems can encourage customers to return products for recycling through incentive programs and provide educational content on proper disposal methods. By maintaining continuous customer communication, CRM systems help drive participation in recycling initiatives and ensure compliance with regulatory requirements.

Waste Management Systems (WMS) integrate advanced technologies such as AI and machine learning to optimize waste sorting and processing. These systems can predict waste generation patterns, improving the efficiency of waste treatment processes and ensuring sustainable waste management. Quality Control Systems (QCS) ensure that recycled materials meet required standards, incorporating feedback loops for continuous improvement and regulatory compliance.

8.10.2 Business Ecosystem

A robust digital business ecosystem enables seamless interactions and data sharing among stakeholders, including recyclers, manufacturers, and third-party service providers. Digital ecosystems facilitate the coordination of recycling activities across the supply chain, ensuring efficient material recovery and processing.

Collaboration platforms within the ecosystem enable stakeholders to collaborate on recycling initiatives, sharing knowledge and resources to optimize recycling processes. Orchestration platforms streamline operations, ensuring smooth interactions between different stages of the recycling value chain. These platforms manage material collection, processing, and redistribution logistics, enhancing transparency and operational efficiency.

Matching platforms connect supply with demand, aligning the availability of recyclable materials with manufacturers' needs. This coordination helps ensure that materials are efficiently recycled and reintroduced into production cycles, supporting circular economy goals. By leveraging the capabilities of digital ecosystems, manufacturers can enhance their recycling efforts, reduce waste, and promote sustainable resource use.

8.10.3 Connected Products

Connected products allow for real-time monitoring and data-driven decision-making. IoT sensors embedded in products can track usage and condition throughout their lifecycle, providing valuable data for recycling processes.

Real-time monitoring enables the timely identification of products that are ready for recycling, facilitating efficient collection and processing. IoT technologies also support predictive maintenance, ensuring that products remain in good condition for as long as possible before being recycled.

Connected products produce data that helps in developing recycling strategies. This includes identifying the best methods for separating and processing materials. Manufacturers can improve the transparency and efficiency of their recycling operations by integrating IoT technologies. This ensures that materials are recovered and reused in the most sustainable and profitable manner.

8.10.4 Customer Experience

Enhancing customer experience through digital engagement promotes recycling behaviors. Digital tools and platforms provide customers with easy access to information and services related to recycling, encouraging responsible disposal practices.

A seamless multichannel customer journey ensures customers can easily participate in recycling programs through various touchpoints, such as mobile apps, web platforms, and in-store kiosks. Personalized communication and incentive programs, facilitated by advanced analytics and AI, can motivate customers to return products for recycling, increasing participation rates and promoting sustainable behaviors.

Digital contracts support recycling by providing customers with clear product returns and recycling terms. These digital tools simplify the process of returning products, making it more convenient for customers to engage in recycling activities. By enhancing customer experience, manufacturers can foster a recycling culture and drive greater participation in circular economy initiatives.

8.10.5 Data-Driven Circularity

Data-driven circularity emphasizes using data as the central intelligence in managing recycling processes. By integrating data from customer interactions, business ecosystems, connected products, and internal IT systems, manufacturers can gain a comprehensive view of their recycling operations and make informed decisions.

Big Data and Business Intelligence (BI) tools convert large volumes of data into actionable insights, improving operational efficiency and resource recovery. Predictive analytics forecast return volumes and optimize recycling operations, ensuring materials are collected and processed on time. AI supports decision-making by analyzing product conditions and market demand and recommending the most effective recycling activities.

Integrated data analysis enables manufacturers to track their recycling initiatives' performance, identify improvement areas, and ensure compliance with regulatory requirements. By leveraging data-driven insights, manufacturers can enhance the efficiency and profitability of their recycling operations, supporting their transition to a circular economy.

8.10.6 The Role of Digital Product Passports and Extended Producer Responsibility

Digital Product Passports (DPPs) (Sect. 2.3) advance recycling business models. DPPs contain product information, including their composition, origin, and lifecycle, facilitating more efficient and effective recycling processes.

Digital Product Passports provide detailed data about the materials and components used in a product. This transparency allows recyclers to identify the exact nature of materials, including hazardous substances, material types, chemical compositions, and recycling instructions. This information can improve sorting and processing efficiency. Advanced sorting technologies, such as AI and robotics, can leverage DPP data to automate and optimize the sorting process, ensuring that materials are correctly categorized and processed. This precision reduces contamination and enhances the quality of recycled materials.

Governments and regulatory bodies are increasingly enforcing stricter recycling and waste management practices. DPPs assist manufacturers and recyclers in meeting these regulations by offering a transparent and easily accessible record of a product's lifecycle, including its adherence to environmental standards and recycling requirements.

Extended Producer Responsibility (EPR) (Sect. 2.3) policies hold producers accountable for their products' entire lifecycle, including end-of-life management. DPPs are essential for EPR as they enable producers to monitor their products throughout their lifecycle, even after they have been sold. This monitoring capability empowers producers to better plan and execute take-back schemes, recycling programs, and other EPR initiatives, ensuring that products are recycled responsibly and efficiently.

DPPs can make information about product materials and proper recycling accessible to consumers, promoting responsible consumer behavior and increased participation in recycling programs.

8.11 Capability Map for Recycling Business Models in Manufacturing

This capability map is based on findings from the chapter on the recycling business model, highlighting key capabilities that manufacturers can leverage to benefit from recycling business models (Fig. 8.3).

8.12 Checklist for Manufacturers Embarking on Recycling Initiatives

Implementing effective recycling strategies reduces environmental impact and provides economic and strategic advantages. However, initiating a recycling program involves addressing various complexities, from assessing material recyclability to ensuring regulatory compliance.

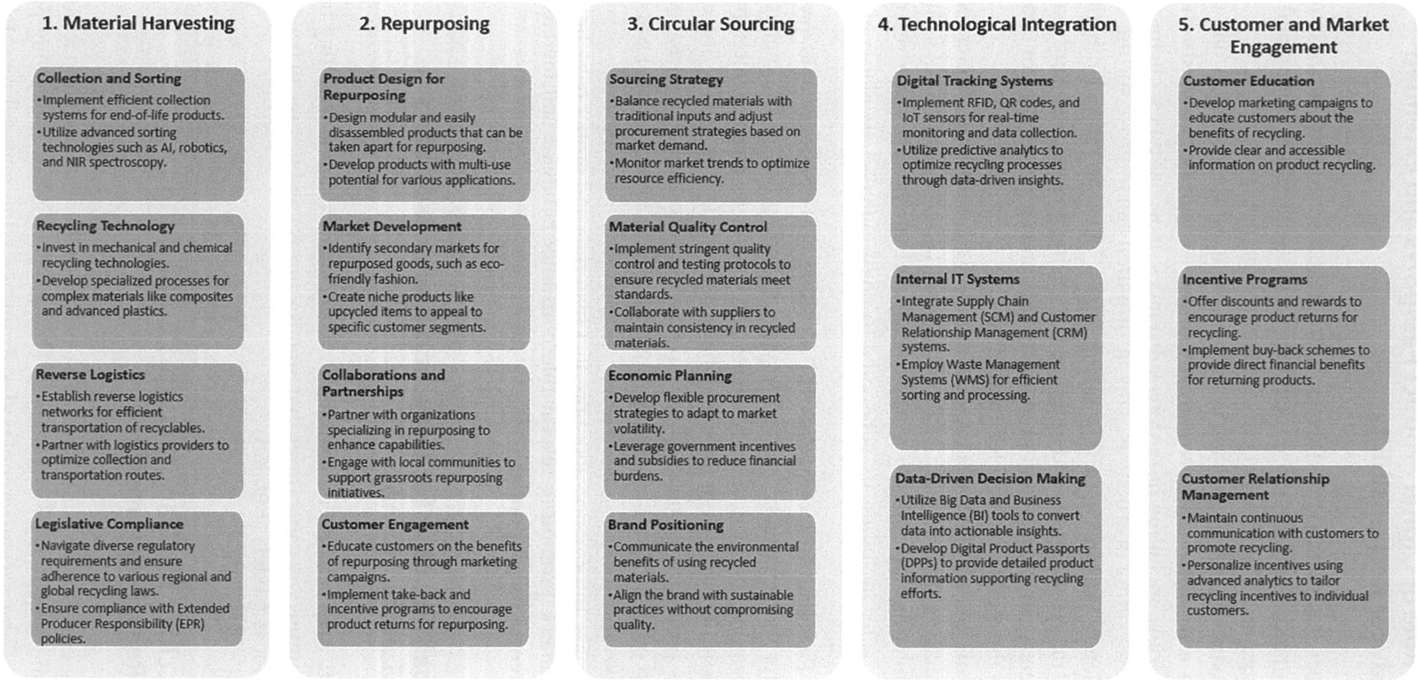

Fig. 8.3 Capability map for recycling business models in manufacturing

The checklist (Table 8.4) is intended to assist manufacturers in completing the necessary tasks for successful recycling integration. Each task is accompanied by a specific methodology, expected outcome, and risk it mitigates. Using this checklist, manufacturers can systematically tackle recycling challenges, improve their sustainability efforts, and reduce potential risks.

The checklist is designed to help integrate recycling into manufacturing processes in a structured way, ensuring that efforts are efficient and impactful. Use this checklist to guide your recycling plans into practical steps that align with your business goals and sustainability commitments.

Table 8.4 Checklist for manufacturers embarking on recycling initiatives

Task	Methodology	Expected outcome	Risk mitigated
Assess the feasibility of recycling	Conduct a cost-benefit analysis of recycling operations	Determine the financial viability and potential benefits	Financial loss due to high recycling costs compared to material value
Evaluate material recyclability	Test and analyze the recyclability of different materials	Identification of materials that can be effectively recycled	Inability to recycle due to unsuitable material properties
Establish a supply chain for recycled materials	Develop partnerships with suppliers and recycling facilities	Secure a reliable source of recycled materials	Supply chain disruptions and material shortages
Implement Extended Producer Responsibility (EPR)	Design and implement EPR programs	Increased recovery and recycling rates of products	Environmental impact and regulatory non-compliance
Optimize product design for recycling	Integrate Design for Disassembly (DfD) and modular design	Easier and more efficient recycling processes	High recycling costs and low recovery rates
Develop customer take-back programs	Establish take-back schemes with incentives for customers	Higher return rates of end-of-life products	Low participation and high disposal rates
Ensure compliance with regulations	Regularly review and update recycling practices per regulations	Compliance with local and international recycling standards	Legal penalties and market access issues
Train and educate employees	Provide training programs on recycling best practices	Increased employee awareness and involvement	Ineffective recycling operations due to a lack of knowledge
Monitor and report recycling efforts	Implement tracking and reporting systems	Transparent and accountable recycling processes	Lack of transparency and stakeholder trust
Engage with stakeholders	Collaborate with industry, government, and community groups	Stronger support and collaboration in recycling initiatives	Isolation and lack of industry support
Evaluate environmental impact	Conduct lifecycle assessments (LCAs)	Understanding and mitigating the environmental impact	Negative environmental impact and poor public perception

(continued)

Table 8.4 (continued)

Task	Methodology	Expected outcome	Risk mitigated
Explore circular economy opportunities	Investigate reuse, repurposing, and remanufacturing options	Diversified revenue streams and reduced waste	Over-reliance on recycling and missed opportunities for other circular practices
Balance recycled and traditional raw materials	Analyze market trends, material quality, and supply chain dynamics	Optimized sourcing strategy combining recycled and raw materials	Supply chain inefficiencies, inconsistent material quality, and cost fluctuation

References

Bogdanich, I., Hardcastle, B., Donnelly, D., Axup, K., & Manderson, K. (2023). *Australia's critical minerals strategy 2023–2030*. Allens. Retrieved from https://www.allens.com.au/insights-news/insights/2023/06/Australias-Critical-Minerals-Strategy-2023-2030/

Bolton, S., & Kao, G. (2015). *Valuing the net benefit of Dell's more sustainable plastic use at an industry scale*. Trucost. Retrieved from https://i.dell.com/sites/doccontent/corporate/corp-comm/en/documents/circular-economy-net-benefits.pdf

Brown, A., Laubinger, F., & Börkey, P. (2023). *New Aspects of EPR: Extending producer responsibility to additional product groups and challenges throughout the product lifecycle*. OECD – Organisation for Economic Co-operation and Development. Retrieved from https://www.oecd-ilibrary.org/deliver/cfdc1bdc-en.pdf

CATL. (2024, April). *CATL and Volvo Cars join hands for sustainable development*. Retrieved from https://www.catl.com/en/news/6234.html

Dell. (2024). *Closed-loop recycled content. From design for environment*. Retrieved from https://www.dell.com/learn/vg/en/vgcorp1/corp-comm/closed-loop-recycled-content

European Commission. (2023). *Critical Raw Materials Act*. Retrieved from https://single-market-economy.ec.europa.eu/sectors/raw-materials/areas-specific-interest/critical-raw-materials/critical-raw-materials-act_en

European Parliament. (2024). *The impact of textile production and waste on the environment*. Retrieved from https://www.europarl.europa.eu/topics/en/article/20201208STO93327/the-impact-of-textile-production-and-waste-on-the-environment-infographics

Ford. (2021). *Leading a sustainable revolution: Ford and HP to collaborate to transform 3D waste into auto parts*. Retrieved from https://media.ford.com/content/fordmedia/fna/us/en/news/2021/03/25/leading-a-sustainable-revolution.html

Girardi, B., Patrahau, I., Cisco, G., & Rademaker, M. (2023). *Strategic raw materials for defence: Mapping European industry needs*. The Hague Centre for Strategic Studies. Retrieved from https://hcss.nl/wp-content/uploads/2023/01/Strategic-Raw-Materials-for-Defence-HCSS-2023-2.pdf

INEOS. (2024). *INEOS Infinia*. Retrieved from https://www.ineos.com/businesses/ineos-aromatics/ineos-infinia/

Lee, K., & Cha, J. (2020). Towards improved circular economy and resource security in South Korea. *Sustainability, 13*(1), 17. https://doi.org/10.3390/su13010017

Nespresso. (2024, June). *How to recycle your coffee pods*. Retrieved from https://www.nespresso.com/uk/en/sustainability/recycling

Pandora. (2024). *Recycled silver and gold*. Retrieved from https://pandoragroup.com/sustainability/circular-innovation/recycled-silver-and-gold

PDI Technologies. (2024, April). *U.S. Consumers willing to pay more for sustainable products*. NACS. Retrieved from https://www.convenience.org/Media/Daily/2024/April/24/4-US-Consumers-Pay-Sustainable_Products_Research

Project CETEC. (n.d.). *New coalition of industry and academia to commercialise solution for full recyclability of wind turbine blades*. Retrieved from https://www.project-cetec.dk/uk/about/

Refashion. (2021). *The platform that connects textile and footwear recycling professionals*. From https://recycle.refashion.fr/en/

Stena Recycling. (2023, December). *Collaborative project for recycling wind turbine blades boosts circularity in fossil-free wind power*. Retrieved from https://www.stenarecycling.com/news-insights/newsroom/2023/wind-turbine-blade-recycling-boosts-circularity-in-fossil-free-wind-energy/

The Australian Government. (2023). *Critical minerals strategy 2023–2030*. Retrieved from https://www.industry.gov.au/sites/default/files/2023-06/critical-minerals-strategy-2023-2030.pdf

The California State Assembly. (2010). *California Assembly Bill 2398, Chapter 681, Statutes of 2010*. From Legiscan: https://legiscan.com/CA/text/AB2398/id/60892

The Royal Mint. (2023, January). *Recycled gold at The Royal Mint*. Retrieved from https://www.royalmint.com/invest/discover/invest-in-gold/recycled-gold-at-the-royal-mint/

Trivium Communications. (2022). *Buying green report 2022*. Retrieved from https://www.trivium-packaging.com/news-media/reports/buying-green-report-2022/

Volkswagen Group. (2021). *Circular Economy*. From https://www.volkswagen-group.com/en/publications/more/circular-economy-2342/

Volvo. (2024, June). *It all revolves around the batteries*. Retrieved from https://www.volvoenergy.com/en/how-we-do-it.html

Washington State Department of Ecology. (2021). *Recycled content minimums*. From https://ecology.wa.gov/waste-toxics/reducing-recycling-waste/plastics/2021-plastic-pollution-laws/recycled-content-minimums

Circular Economy Business Models Reinvent Value

9

Abstract

The circular economy represents a transformative shift in value creation, capture, and delivery, akin to the digital revolution. This paradigm shift demands companies transition from one-time transactions to ongoing value provision, focusing on durability, modularity, and ease of repair. Value capture involves retaining or extracting value from products through recommerce, reuse, part harvesting, resource recovery, refurbishing, and remanufacturing. Service-oriented models redefine value delivery, generating recurring revenue through subscriptions or service contracts.

Circular business models outperform linear ones by reducing material and component costs, shortening production times, and generating multiple income cycles from repair and redistribution. They enhance resilience, mitigate supply chain disruptions, and reduce environmental impact. Key challenges include redesigning products for circularity, reconfiguring supply chains, shifting consumer attitudes, managing financial investments, integrating digital technologies, developing employee skills, complying with regulations, and fostering ecosystem collaboration.

By leveraging the Circular Economy Strategy Framework and following the Circular Economy Transition Checklist, companies can systematically address these challenges, leading to sustainable growth and competitive advantage.

The Manufacturing Circular Maturity Framework provides a structured pathway for assessing and advancing circularity.

H. H. Jensen, *Circular Economy Opportunities and Pathways for Manufacturers*, Future of Business and Finance, https://doi.org/10.1007/978-3-031-75279-7_9

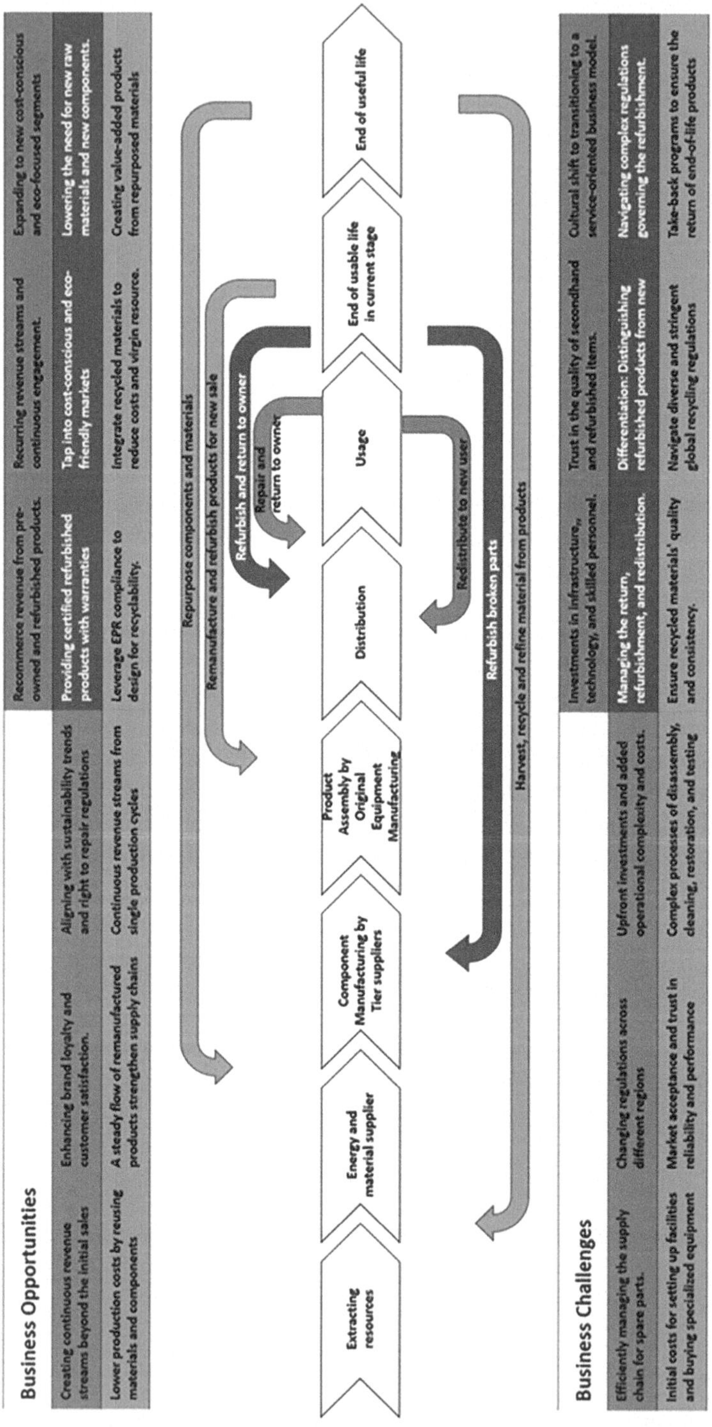

Fig. 9.1 The circular flow (Figure 1.6) and significant business opportunities and challenges

Key Messages

- *A Paradigm Shift in Value Creation:* The circular economy represents a transformative shift in how businesses create, capture, and deliver value, similar to the digital revolution of the late 1990s. Companies that recognize and adapt to this shift will lead in innovation and market share, much like early adopters of digital technologies outpaced their peers.
- *Reinventing Value Creation:* In the circular economy, value creation is not a one-time transaction but an ongoing process. Companies must shift from selling products to providing continuous value through long-term customer relationships. This involves designing products for durability, modularity, and ease of repair, integrating digital technologies for lifecycle tracking, and embracing sustainable materials and manufacturing processes. Regulatory and compliance factors also play a role, with stricter regulations driving the need for resource efficiency and waste reduction.
- *Capturing Value Through New Revenue Models:* Value capture in the circular economy involves retaining or extracting value from products and materials for as long as possible. This is achieved through business models such as recommerce, reuse initiatives, part harvesting, resource recovery, refurbishing, and remanufacturing. By moving away from single transaction revenue models, companies can unlock new growth opportunities, enhance resilience, and gain a competitive edge in a resource-constrained world.
- *Delivering Value as a Service:* Value delivery in the circular economy is redefined through service-oriented models that maintain or enhance product value over time. Manufacturers can transition from selling products to selling the utility these products provide, generating recurring revenue through subscriptions or service contracts. This approach fosters continuous customer engagement and opens new revenue streams from aftermarket services, including repair, refurbishment, and recycling.
- *The Circular Economy Outperforms Linear Models:* The circular economy offers advantages over traditional linear business models. It reduces material and component costs through refurbishing and remanufacturing, leading to shorter production times and multiple income cycles from repair and redistribution. Greater customer intimacy is achieved through continuous engagement and improving product offerings and relationships. Circular products are designed for reuse and repair, reducing overall costs and creating new revenue streams from remanufactured products and recovered materials. This model enhances resilience by providing a buffer against supply chain disruptions and material price volatility. Environmental benefits include lower energy use, reduced greenhouse gas emissions, resource conservation, waste minimization, and biodiversity protection. The circular economy provides a more sustainable and profitable business model by continuously capturing value and benefiting the environment.

(continued)

- *Overcoming Challenges and Seizing Opportunities:* Transitioning to a circular economy presents several challenges, including redesigning products for circularity, reconfiguring supply chains, shifting consumer attitudes, managing financial investments, integrating digital technologies, developing employee skills, complying with regulations, and fostering ecosystem collaboration. However, manufacturers that actively address these challenges will gain competitive advantages and pave the way for a sustainable future.
- *The Manufacturing Circular Maturity Framework:* To aid manufacturers in navigating the complexities of circular practices, the Manufacturing Circular Maturity Framework provides a structured pathway to assess their current position and strategically advance their circularity. The framework divides the journey into five stages: awareness, engagement, implementation, integration, and leadership, each with specific traits, objectives, and opportunities.

We have now gone through the 1+5R model, which illustrates the business opportunities and challenges of the circular economy (Fig. 9.1). To understand its potential impact on our business landscape, we can look back to the late 1990s, when visionary thinkers predicted a major shift in business models with the upcoming digital transformation. Harvard Business School Professor Clayton Christensen was at the forefront with his 1997 book *The Innovator's Dilemma* (Christensen, 1997), where he introduced the concept of disruptive innovation (Christensen et al., 2015).

His key insight was that technological shifts often blindsided established companies. *Their focus remained on refining products for existing customers, leaving them vulnerable to new, groundbreaking business models.*

Nicholas Negroponte, founder of the MIT Media Lab, also played a pivotal role in shaping this vision. In his 1995 book *Being Digital* (Negroponte, 1995), he predicted the extensive impact of digital technologies on life and work, envisioning a future where information technology was intricately woven into everyday life, reshaping how value was created and delivered.

These thought leaders highlighted the Internet's transformative potential and digital technologies. They emphasized the need for businesses to overhaul their approach to creating, capturing, and delivering value.

Their insights were often met with skepticism from established businesses, which were slow to adapt and underestimated the full extent of the digital revolution's impact on traditional business value models.

9.1 The Circular Economy Reshapes Value Innovation

Today, many companies focus on refining their existing products and services for their current customer base rather than exploring the transformative potential of the circular economy. However, this approach overlooks that the circular economy, like the Internet in the late 1990s, redefines how businesses create, capture, and deliver value (Sect. 9.2).

The circular economy's transformative impact is similar to the Internet's because it challenges and changes the traditional linear model. In the late 1990s, the Internet was a nascent technology often underestimated by established businesses. Today, the circular economy is in a similar position. However, the pace of change is much faster due to technological advancements, new legislation, environmental pressure, and shifting consumer preferences.

As we approach 2030, companies that embrace this shift will lead in innovation and market share, much like early adopters of digital technologies outpaced their peers. The rest of this decade will be crucial for businesses to adapt to this new paradigm, where being clean, digital, and circular is no longer a choice but an essential component of success.

In the upcoming sections, we will explore the transformative impact of the circular economy based on our 1 + 5R model. Specifically, we will discuss how the circular economy affects value creation, capture, and delivery. Following that, we will explain why circular business models are superior to linear ones. In the third section of this chapter, we will discuss the primary business challenges that have been identified. Lastly, we will present the Manufacturing Circular Maturity Framework as a conclusion to the 1 + 5R model.

9.2 The Circular Economy Reinvents Value

In a circular economy, value creation, capture, and delivery require a business strategy and operational shift. This transformation goes beyond tweaking existing processes; it involves rethinking and redesigning the entire value chain. The business strategy and the creation, capturing, and delivery of values are placed in the middle of the Circular Economy Strategy Framework (Fig. 9.2).

Table 9.1 shows some approaches to value analysis that manufacturers can employ to identify how they benefit from the shift. In the Circular Economy Strategy Framework (Fig. 9.2), these approaches are illustrated in the boxes with blue outlines.

9.2.1 The What —Value creation by Delivering Ongoing Value

Creating value in a circular economy involves providing continuous value to customers rather than just selling a product. Companies must shift from one-time transactions to long-term partnerships by understanding their customers' changing needs. This entails offering customizable solutions and services that encourage the extended use of products. A strong feedback and engagement framework is necessary to ensure that products and services align with customer needs as they evolve.

Value-in-use requires high quality and durability in product design. It promotes using sustainable materials and manufacturing processes that prolong product lifespan. It also encourages customers to participate in circular practices, such as returning products for refurbishment or recycling.

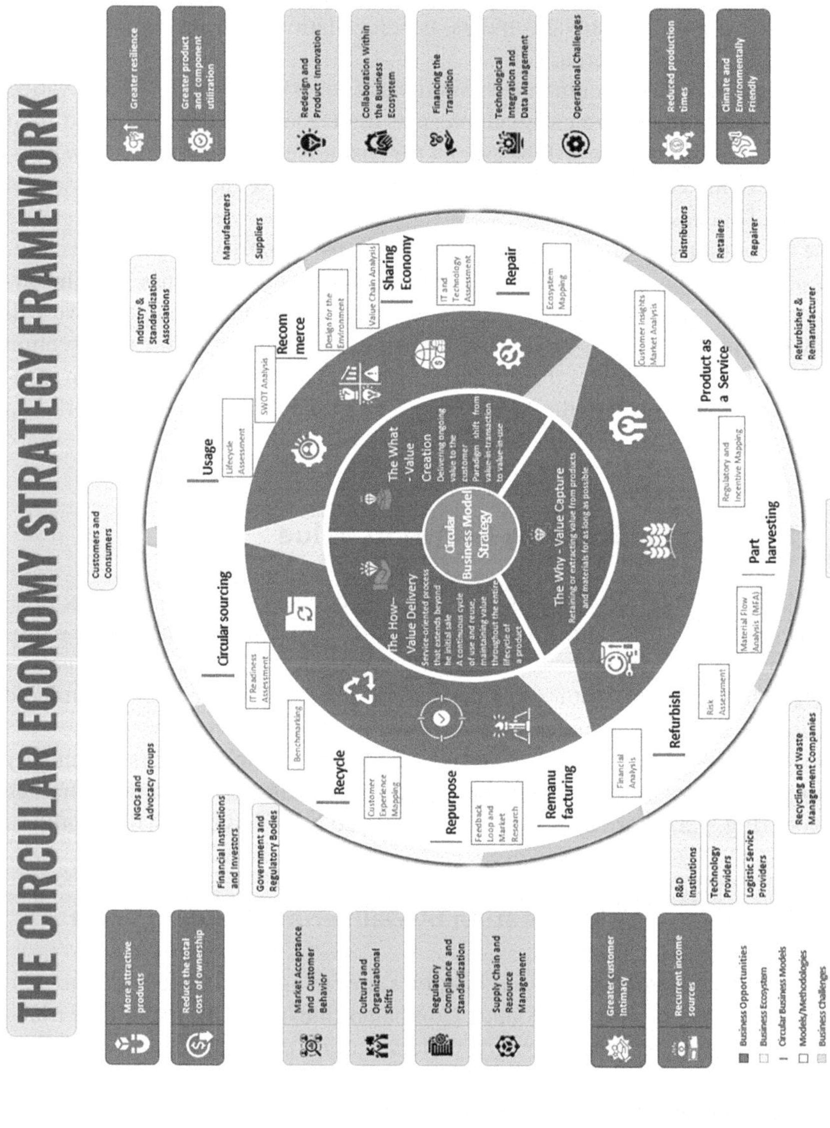

Fig. 9.2 The Circular Economy Strategy Framework

Table 9.1 Overview of various methods for value analysis

Method/tool	Description	Benefits	Key focus	Example
Lifecycle assessment (LCA)	Evaluates the environmental effects of each stage of a product's life, from raw material extraction to disposal or recycling	Identifies waste reduction opportunities, optimizes resource utilization, and improves sustainability	Environmental impact	A company uses LCA to assess the carbon footprint of a new smartphone from raw material extraction to disposal
Material flow analysis (MFA)	Systematic evaluation of the movement and storage of materials within a system to assess resource utilization efficiency	Highlights opportunities for recycling, reuse, and reduction of materials	Resource efficiency	A beverage manufacturer analyzes the flow of aluminum cans to find ways to increase recycling rates
Design for the Environment (DfE)[a]	Integrates environmental considerations into product design to minimize impact throughout its lifecycle	Encourages eco-friendly materials and designs for repairability, upgradeability, and recyclability	Product design	A furniture company designs modular desks that can be easily repaired and upgraded, reducing waste
Customer insights and market analysis	Study of market dynamics, trends, customer preferences, and competition to understand sustainability impacts on business strategy	Identifies opportunities for circular products and competitive advantages in the circular economy	Market trends and strategy	A retailer studies the growing demand for eco-friendly clothing to adjust its product lines accordingly
SWOT analysis	Tool for strategic planning that identifies internal strengths, weaknesses, and external opportunities and threats	It helps businesses recognize technological capabilities, market opportunities, and regulatory threats	Strategic planning	A recycling company uses SWOT analysis to identify the opportunity to expand into the e-waste recycling market
Value chain analysis	Examines business activities to enhance customer value, focusing on efficient resource use and waste reduction	Identifies areas for efficiency improvement and material recovery in the value chain	Process efficiency	A manufacturer identifies that recycling scrap metal can reduce costs and increase resource efficiency

(continued)

Table 9.1 (continued)

Method/tool	Description	Benefits	Key focus	Example
Feedback loop and market research	Collects and analyzes customer data to understand satisfaction, preferences, and requirements	Helps redesign products and services to meet customer expectations and align with circular economy goals	Customer insight	A tech company surveys customers and finds demand for devices with longer lifespans and more repair options
Financial analysis	Evaluates the viability, stability, and profitability of business or projects, including potential revenue from circular business models	Assesses profitability of circular practices, such as refurbishing products and offering services	Financial performance	A retailer analyzes the cost-benefit of refurbishing returned products for resale versus manufacturing new items
Technology assessment	Evaluates technologies for efficiency, capabilities, and cost-effectiveness in supporting circular economy practices	Identifies tools to improve resource efficiency and support recycling and reuse processes	Technological efficiency	An electronics company assesses a new disassembly technology for its potential to increase recycling rates
Benchmarking	Compares company processes and performance to industry best practices to identify areas for improvement	Pinpoints gaps and opportunities for enhancing circularity and efficiency	Performance improvement	A packaging company benchmarks its recycling practices against industry leaders to improve its own processes
Risk assessment	Identifies and evaluates risks impacting operations, including supply chain disruptions and compliance issues	It helps in mitigating risks related to circular economy practices and technology adoption	Risk management	A company evaluates risks associated with potential supply chain disruptions in sourcing recycled materials
IT readiness assessment	Evaluates current IT infrastructure to determine if it supports circular business models and initiatives	Ensures IT systems can support lifecycle tracking, resource management, and new business models	Technological readiness	A logistics company assesses whether its current IT systems can support real-time tracking of recycled materials

(continued)

Table 9.1 (continued)

Method/tool	Description	Benefits	Key focus	Example
Regulatory and incentive mapping	To stay updated with regulations and incentives that support circular practices and align them with business strategies	It helps ensure compliance and identify incentive opportunities that support circular economy practices	Regulatory compliance and strategy	A manufacturer aligns its business strategies with new government recycling and waste reduction incentives
Customer experience mapping	Maps the customer journey to identify touchpoints for ongoing services such as maintenance, upgrades, and end-of-life management	Enhances customer satisfaction and retention by providing continuous value through ongoing services	Customer journey	A home appliance company maps the customer journey to provide maintenance services and end-of-life recycling options
Ecosystem mapping	Identifies key partners and stakeholders within the value network to foster strong relationships and collaboration	Facilitates collaboration, innovation, and optimized resource use across the value network	Network collaboration	A tech company maps its ecosystem to identify potential partners for developing new recycling technologies

[a]https://www.gdrc.org/uem/lca/text.html

Value creation begins at the design stage, where products are conceived with durability, modularity, and ease of repair. This approach allows for individual components to be replaced or upgraded, extending the life of products and enhancing their utility and value over time.

Integrating digital technologies for product lifecycle tracking enhances transparency and accountability for products and materials. This digital traceability supports the circular economy by enabling more efficient resource management, facilitating the reuse and recycling of materials, and ensuring that products and components can find their way back into the production cycle.

Regulatory and compliance factors affect value creation in the circular economy as governments impose stricter regulations on resource efficiency, waste reduction, and recycling. Adapting to legal requirements proactively mitigates risks and opens new markets and customer segments.

Creating value in the circular economy is linked to environmental sustainability. By designing products for longevity, facilitating reuse and recycling, and minimizing waste, manufacturers contribute to resource efficiency and environmental preservation. The economic benefits of this approach include extended customer retention, diversified revenue streams from service offerings, and enhanced brand loyalty.

9.2.2 The Why—Revenue Models Evolve Through Circular Value Capture

Value capture is a concept that highlights the reasons behind why value is delivered, focusing on the benefits and rationale. In the circular economy context, value capture involves retaining or extracting value from products and materials for as long as possible. This is achieved through business models that leverage the lifecycle of products and materials to generate sustained and sustainable revenue streams. By moving away from traditional revenue models based on single transactions, companies can unlock new growth opportunities, enhance resilience, and gain a competitive edge in a resource-constrained world.

Circular Business Models for Value Capture

Recommerce and reuse (Chap. 5) initiatives extend the life of products by reselling or repurposing them. This adds value beyond the initial sale and generates additional revenue by offering cost-effective and sustainable alternatives to new products. These initiatives appeal to budget-conscious customers and environmentally conscious buyers, providing companies with new market segments to explore. Moreover, recommerce platforms facilitate easy buying and selling of pre-owned items, fostering a culture of reuse and sustainability.

Part harvesting and resource recovery (Chap. 8) involve reclaiming parts from end-of-life products and transforming waste materials into raw inputs. These initiatives help reduce the demand for new materials, decrease production costs, and capture value from materials that would otherwise be considered waste. By establishing efficient part harvesting systems, companies can maintain a steady supply of valuable components, reducing reliance on raw material extraction and minimizing environmental impact. Resource recovery also supports closed-loop manufacturing processes, where waste materials are continuously reintegrated into production cycles.

Refurbishing and remanufacturing (Chap. 7) are key strategies for value capture. These initiatives involve restoring old or used products to like-new conditions or original specifications, extending their life and saving resources that would have been used to produce new items. Refurbished and remanufactured products often come with warranties and guarantees, providing customers with confidence in their quality and reliability. This not only enhances customer trust but also promotes brand loyalty and repeat business.

Product-as-a-Service (PaaS) models (Sect. 5.4) offer another avenue for value capture by shifting the focus from selling products to providing access to them. Customers pay for the utility or functionality of a product rather than owning it outright. This model generates recurring revenue through subscription fees or service contracts and fosters continuous customer engagement. Companies benefit from longer-term customer relationships and can offer maintenance, upgrades, and end-of-life management as part of the service, ensuring ongoing value capture throughout the product lifecycle.

Repurposing involves transforming waste materials or obsolete products into new, higher-value items (Sect. 8.7). This innovative approach not only captures value from what would otherwise be discarded but also opens up unique marketing opportunities. Upcycled products often carry a story of sustainability and creativity, appealing to niche markets and environmentally conscious consumers. Companies can leverage upcycling to differentiate their brand and create a distinct market presence.

Collaborative consumption models, part of the sharing economy (Sect. 5.2), facilitate the shared use of products and resources among multiple users. This reduces the need for individual ownership and maximizes the utilization of assets. Examples include car-sharing, tool libraries, and co-working spaces. These models capture value by optimizing resource use and reducing idle time, while also fostering community engagement and sustainable consumption patterns.

Adhering to regulatory requirements and leveraging government incentives can also enhance value capture (Chap. 2). Regulations that promote recycling, waste reduction, and resource efficiency create opportunities for companies to capitalize on compliant practices. Government incentives, such as tax breaks and grants for sustainable initiatives, can offset initial investment costs and improve the financial viability of circular business models.

Example 9.1 GE Aerospace's TrueChoice services

GE Aerospace offers a range of services called TrueChoice that focuses on value capture in the aviation industry. This is particularly important as engine component lifecycle management is critical for economic and environmental sustainability.

TrueChoice aims to extend the operational life of aviation engines. It consists of different categories, each focusing on engine maintenance and optimization. The categories include overhaul, material, and repair solutions, among others. These services enable airlines and other operators to maintain engine performance, efficiency, and reliability without purchasing new parts or engines, thus capturing value from existing assets.

Part harvesting and resource recovery are important aspects of GE Aerospace's value capture strategy. The company refurbishes and repairs parts from engines approaching the end of their service life. These parts are reintroduced into the service cycle once restored to their original specifications or better. This provides a cost-effective alternative to manufacturing new components (GE Aerospace, 2024).

Strategies for Value Capture

Digital platforms and the Internet of Things (IoT) (Chap. 13) enhance the efficiency and transparency of circular processes. They enable improved product tracking, customer engagement, and data-driven insights, ultimately helping businesses optimize their operations. By utilizing IoT, companies can monitor product usage, predict maintenance needs, and extend product lifecycles through proactive service interventions. Digital platforms facilitate real-time data collection and analysis, providing valuable insights into product performance and customer behavior, which can inform future design and service improvements.

Collaborative ecosystems (Chap. 12) formed through partnerships within and across industries can enhance value capture. By pooling resources, sharing expertise, and co-creating value-added services, these partnerships accelerate the transition to profitable circular business models. Companies can collaborate with suppliers, technology providers, recyclers, and even competitors to develop innovative solutions that address shared challenges. These partnerships can lead to the creation of closed-loop systems where materials and products are continuously cycled back into the production process, reducing waste and optimizing resource use.

Businesses should ensure regulatory compliance and take advantage of incentives to promote sustainability and circular economy practices. Governments worldwide are increasingly implementing regulations aimed at resource efficiency, waste reduction, and recycling. Staying ahead of these regulatory changes can mitigate risks and unlock opportunities for funding and support. Companies can benefit from tax breaks, grants, and other incentives designed to encourage sustainable practices. Proactively adapting to regulatory requirements not only avoids potential penalties but also enhances the company's reputation as a responsible and forward-thinking industry leader.

Harnessing data analytics (Chap. 15) is essential for effective value capture. Advanced analytics can help companies understand customer preferences, predict market trends, and optimize inventory and supply chain management. By analyzing data from IoT devices, customer interactions, and operational processes, businesses can identify inefficiencies, forecast demand, and tailor their offerings to meet specific customer needs. This data-driven approach enhances decision-making and enables companies to deliver more personalized and sustainable products and services.

Enhancing customer engagement through digital tools and platforms is another strategy for value capture (Chap. 14). Providing customers with interactive platforms for feedback, product customization, and support fosters a sense of loyalty and trust. Engaged customers are more likely to participate in circular practices such as returning products for refurbishment or recycling. Additionally, offering educational resources and incentives for sustainable behaviors can further strengthen the customer-company relationship and promote the adoption of circular economy principles.

Building resilient supply chains is critical for value capture in the circular economy. Companies need to develop robust systems that can withstand disruptions and adapt to changing market conditions. This involves diversifying suppliers, investing in local sourcing, and incorporating recycled and renewable materials. Resilient supply chains not only ensure business continuity but also support sustainability goals by reducing dependency on finite resources and minimizing environmental impact.

Investing in innovation is key to staying competitive in the circular economy. Companies should continuously explore new technologies, materials, and business models that support circular principles. This includes research and development efforts focused on creating products that are easier to repair, refurbish, and recycle. Innovations in material science, such as biodegradable plastics and advanced recycling techniques, can provide advantages. Companies that prioritize innovation will be better positioned to capture value and drive industry transformation.

9.2.3 The How —Value Delivery as a Service-Oriented Process

This describes how value is delivered or reclaimed through the value chain. In a circular economy, value delivery is redefined through service-oriented models that maintain or enhance product value over time.

Circular Business Models for Value Delivery

Manufacturers can transition from selling products to selling the utility that these products provide by adopting models such as Product as a Service (PaaS) (See Sect. 5.4). This approach enables businesses to generate recurring revenue through subscriptions or service contracts and foster continuous customer engagement. Manufacturers can build more resilient and sustainable revenue streams by shifting focus from one-time sales to ongoing service.

Transitioning to a service-based model allows manufacturers to diversify their revenue sources beyond initial sales. Offering comprehensive maintenance, upgrades, and end-of-life management services creates additional revenue channels and strengthens customer relationships. These services ensure that customers receive continuous value from their products, increasing their satisfaction and loyalty.

The provision of aftermarket services, such as repair, remanufacturing, and recycling, generates consistent revenue and fosters opportunities for repeat business. These services foster customer loyalty by maintaining products in optimal condition throughout their lifespan. Moreover, manufacturers can use these services to minimize the risks associated with product obsolescence and market fluctuations.

By using data analytics, manufacturers can tailor products and services to better meet individual customer needs. This customization improves customer satisfaction and retention, as products are adjusted to specific preferences and requirements. Furthermore, data-driven insights enable manufacturers to set premium pricing and distinguish themselves in competitive markets. Understanding customer usage patterns and preferences allows manufacturers to provide targeted upgrades and services, ensuring continuous delivery of value.

Continuous engagement with customers using service models offers valuable insights into customer needs and behaviors. These insights assist manufacturers in improving their products and identifying new business opportunities as market demands change. By maintaining strong customer relationships, manufacturers can swiftly adjust to market changes and create innovative solutions to meet emerging needs.

Strategies for Value Delivery

Investing in digital platforms increases efficiency and scalability when delivering value. This approach enables manufacturers to reach broader markets and streamline their operations. By using these platforms, manufacturers can collaborate more effectively, create innovative products and services, and sell directly to end-customers, bypassing traditional distribution channels. Digital platforms also facilitate better customer interactions and support, enhancing overall satisfaction and loyalty.

The Internet of Things (IoT) technologies have the potential to convert conventional products into "smart" solutions that provide enhanced functionalities, remote services, and improved user experiences. Products equipped with IoT capabilities can offer real-time data and insights, enabling manufacturers to provide proactive maintenance and personalized services. These innovative solutions can extend the lifespan of products, improve performance, and generate new revenue streams through subscription-based models offering advanced features and services.

Manufacturers can position themselves as providers of high-quality, long-lasting solutions by focusing on product durability and repairability. Designing products with longevity in mind reduces waste and builds customer trust and loyalty. Offering easy-to-repair products encourages customers to maintain and upgrade their items, fostering repeat business and reducing the environmental impact of product disposal.

By adopting circular principles, manufacturers can capture early market share and establish themselves as industry leaders. Circular business models, such as Product as a Service (PaaS) and take-back schemes, help manufacturers create closed-loop systems that minimize waste and maximize resource efficiency. Early adoption of these principles positions manufacturers as pioneers in sustainability, appealing to environmentally conscious consumers and differentiating them from competitors.

Engaging in strategic partnerships and integrating circular principles into supply chains can help manufacturers deliver comprehensive solutions that address complex customer needs. Collaborations with suppliers, recyclers, and other stakeholders enable manufacturers to develop innovative solutions that leverage shared expertise and resources. These partnerships can expand market reach and capabilities, making manufacturers not only suppliers of products but also providers of recovered materials and components, tapping into new business-to-business markets.

Digital tools such as customer portals, mobile apps, and online communities can enhance customer engagement and provide valuable insights into customer preferences and behaviors. These tools enable manufacturers to offer personalized experiences, gather feedback, and rapidly respond to customer needs. Enhanced customer engagement helps manufacturers refine their offerings and develop new products and services that align with evolving market demands.

Advanced technologies such as artificial intelligence (AI), machine learning, and robotics can optimize manufacturing operations, reducing costs and improving efficiency. These technologies enable predictive maintenance, quality control, and supply chain optimization, leading to more reliable and cost-effective production processes. By adopting these technologies, manufacturers can enhance their competitiveness and deliver greater customer value.

9.2.4 Overview of Strategies for Value Creation, Capture, and Delivery

Table 9.2 provides an overview of strategies for value creation, capture, and delivery within the circular economy.

9.2.5 The Business Ecosystem as the Value Network

The business ecosystem functions as a value network in a circular economy, emphasizing interconnected relationships and collaborations essential for driving innovation, efficiency, and sustainability. The business ecosystem leverages circular economy principles to maximize resource utility, reduce waste, and create new business opportunities. In the Circular Economy Strategy Framework (Fig. 9.1), the business ecosystem is illustrated with the green boxes.

Identifying opportunities within the business ecosystem involves mapping key partners and stakeholders, fostering strong relationships, and utilizing digital technologies for transparency and data sharing. Collaborative efforts to develop new solutions and business models can lead to more sustainable and efficient processes. Ensuring aligned incentives among ecosystem participants fosters commitment and cooperation, driving collective success.

The business ecosystem creates value by incorporating input from all participants to ensure that products are designed for durability, repairability, and recyclability. Collaborative innovation within the ecosystem involves conducting joint research and development with suppliers, partners, and customers to create high-quality, sustainable products. By integrating insights from various stakeholders, manufacturers can continuously enhance product design and functionality, in line with principles of the circular economy. Moreover, the ecosystem facilitates the efficient use of shared resources and expertise, resulting in products that minimize environmental impact and maximize efficiency.

Value capture is strengthened within the business ecosystem by collectively extending product lifecycles and reclaiming value from materials. The ecosystem enables redistribution and recommerce by facilitating secondary markets and the reselling of used products through ecosystem partners, thus extending product lifespans. It also supports refurbishing and remanufacturing by collaborating with specialized partners to restore used products to like-new conditions, reducing the need for new resources. Additionally, the ecosystem coordinates part harvesting and resource recovery by working with recycling and recovery partners to reclaim valuable components and materials from end-of-life products, reducing waste and lowering production costs.

Table 9.2 Circular economy strategies: value creation, capture, and delivery

Strategy	Value Creation	Value Capture	Value Delivery
Customer Engagement and Feedback	Building long-term partnerships, offering customizable solutions and services, adapting to evolving customer needs	Enhancing customer loyalty and trust through continuous engagement	Using digital tools for customer feedback, customization, and support to improve satisfaction and retention
High Quality and Durability in Design	Using sustainable materials, designing for longevity, modularity, and ease of repair	Capturing value by extending product lifespans, reducing resource use, and encouraging refurbishment and recycling	Positioning products as high-quality, long-lasting solutions, enhancing brand reputation
Digital Technologies and IoT	Integrating lifecycle tracking, enhancing transparency, and resource management	Utilizing IoT for product monitoring, predictive maintenance, and optimized performance	Offering smart products with enhanced functionalities, real-time data, and remote services
Circular Business Models	Implementing Product-as-a-Service (PaaS), recommerce, refurbishing, remanufacturing, part harvesting, and take-back schemes to create closed-loop systems	Generating recurring revenue through redistribution, refurbishing, remanufacturing, recommerce, and part harvesting	Transitioning from product sales to service-based models, providing comprehensive maintenance, upgrades, and end-of-life services
Collaborative Ecosystems and Partnerships	Forming partnerships to share resources, expertise, and co-create value-added services	Expanding market reach and capabilities, optimizing resource use through shared systems	Delivering comprehensive solutions addressing complex customer needs through collaboration
Regulatory Compliance and Incentives	Adapting to stricter regulations on resource efficiency, waste reduction, and recycling	Capitalizing on government incentives, avoiding penalties, enhancing reputation	Ensuring compliance and leveraging incentives for sustainable practices
Advanced Data Analytics	Gathering and analyzing data to refine products and services, understanding market demands	Identifying inefficiencies, predicting trends, and tailoring offerings to specific needs	Enhancing decision-making, delivering personalized and sustainable products and services
Resilient Supply Chains	Developing robust systems, diversifying suppliers, and incorporating recycled and renewable materials	Ensuring business continuity, reducing dependency on finite resources	Supporting sustainability goals, optimizing supply chain operations
Innovation and R&D	Investing in new technologies, materials, and business models to support circular principles	Creating products that are easier to repair, refurbish, and recycle	Staying competitive, driving industry transformation through innovative solutions

The business ecosystem improves value delivery through integrated, service-oriented models that maintain or enhance product value over time. This includes offering leasing, subscription-based models, and comprehensive maintenance services through a network of partners, ensuring continuous value to customers. The ecosystem also plays a crucial role in customer engagement by using digital platforms and tools to facilitate ongoing interactions with customers, collect feedback, and offer personalized services that meet customer needs. In addition, seamless coordination among various stakeholders within the ecosystem ensures that products remain in use longer, thereby enhancing customer satisfaction and loyalty.

By optimizing business ecosystems as value networks, companies can enhance their ability to create, capture, and deliver value in a circular economy, driving sustainable growth and competitive advantage.

9.2.6 How to Read and Use the Circular Economy Strategy Framework

The Circular Economy Strategy Framework (Fig. 9.2) is a visual guide designed to help businesses transition from traditional linear economic models to more sustainable circular practices. At the heart of this framework lies the goal: the Circular Business Model Strategy, which defines how you create, capture, and deliver value. This central core emphasizes value creation by delivering ongoing customer engagement, value delivery through a service-oriented process, and value capture by retaining and extracting value from products and materials for as long as possible.

The framework illustrates several methodologies for defining the right circular business models. These methodologies are represented by the primary components of the framework, depicted in blue segments around the core. They include Circular Sourcing, Usage, Recommerce, Sharing Economy, Repair, Refurbishment, Remanufacturing, Repurposing, Recycling, Part Harvesting, and Product as a Service. Each component represents a key strategy that businesses can adopt to integrate circular economy principles into their operations.

Various actions, tools, and assessments, illustrated in blue outline boxes, support these primary components. These include IT Readiness Assessment, Lifecycle Assessment (LCA), Customer Experience Mapping, Financial Analysis, and Risk Assessment. These elements reinforce the primary strategies and ensure their successful implementation.

The framework also highlights the business ecosystem partners, illustrated in green boxes surrounding the primary components. These partners include Customers and Consumers, Manufacturers, Suppliers, Financial Institutions and Investors, NGOs and Advocacy Groups, Industry & Standardization Associations, and Government and Regulatory Bodies. Engaging with these stakeholders is essential for successfully transitioning to a circular economy.

The dark blue boxes represent eight business opportunities you should consider benefiting from in your value journey (Sect. 9.3). These opportunities include creating more attractive products, reducing the total cost of ownership, enhancing resilience, and increasing product and component utilization. These opportunities can provide significant advantages and drive economic growth within a circular economy model.

However, the transition to a circular economy also comes with challenges (Sect. 9.4), represented by the light blue boxes. These challenges include redesigning products, fostering collaboration within the business ecosystem, financing the transition, and managing technological integration and data. Awareness of these challenges and developing strategies to address them is critical for a smooth transition.

To use the framework effectively, map your current business practices against the framework's components to understand where your organization stands. Evaluate the highlighted business opportunities to identify potential benefits specific to your business and assess stakeholder involvement to leverage the support of key partners. Implement the supporting actions to reinforce your strategies and be prepared to address the operational challenges listed in the light blue boxes.

You can adapt and improve your strategies by continuously monitoring the performance of your circular economy initiatives and using tools like benchmarking and customer insights analysis. Begin with components that align closely with your current operations, engage stakeholders early, leverage technology, and iterate and improve based on feedback and performance data.

This framework is a comprehensive guide for businesses aiming to innovate and thrive in a sustainable economy, ensuring long-term economic resilience and competitive advantage.

Strategy Area	Purpose
Strategies for Identity and Access Management	Implementing secure identity and access management is crucial for API security
Strategies for Service Discovery Mechanism	Ensuring the secure discovery of services is vital for maintaining a resilient API infrastructure
Strategies for Secure Communication Protocols	Secure communication between clients and services, as well as between services, is essential
Strategies for Security Monitoring	Continuous monitoring of API interactions is crucial for detecting and responding to security threats
Availability/Resiliency Improvement Strategies	Maintaining the availability and resiliency of APIs is critical to ensure uninterrupted service
Integrity Assurance Strategies	Ensuring the integrity of API data and interactions is fundamental for maintaining trust and reliability
Countering Internet-based Attacks	Protecting APIs from internet-based attacks is essential for securing the API ecosystem

9.3 The Circular Economy Transforms Business in Eight Ways

During the discussion of the 1 + 5R model, we have identified eight areas where circular business models outperform traditional linear models. This section summarizes these areas.

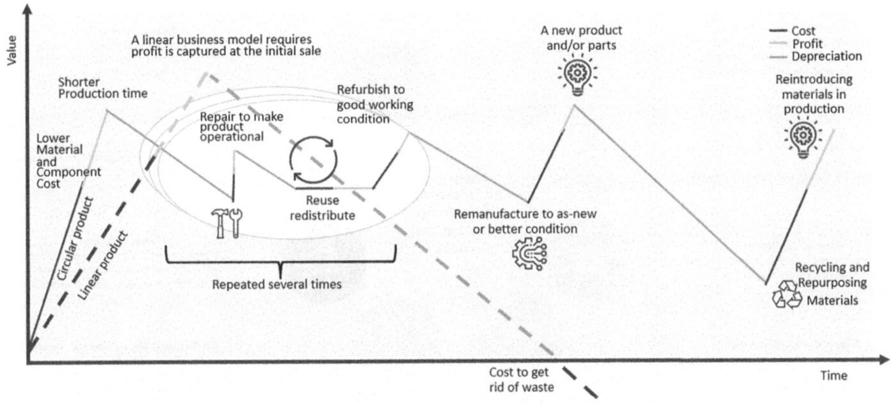

Fig. 9.3 A circular product accumulate more profits during its life cycles

Figure 9.3 visualizes the contrasting economic trajectories of linear and circular products over time. With "Value" plotted on the vertical axis and "Time" on the horizontal axis, the graph looks at how different business models fare across the product lifecycle.

The graph illustrates that a linear product (with a dotted line) has revenue concentrated at the initial sales stage. Following this, the product's value depreciates, eventually incurring a cost when it becomes waste that must be disposed of. The curve representing the linear product shows a steady decline in value over time, reaching a point where the disposal cost becomes a financial burden.

The behavior of a circular product's curve is markedly different in contrast:

Lower Material and Component Cost: The graph illustrates how a circular product benefits from reduced materials and component costs through circular sourcing, refurbishing, and remanufacturing.

Shorter Product Time: The graph illustrates that circular products spend less time in production due to reduced reliance on the extraction and refining of new materials, decreased manufacturing of new parts, and increased remanufacturing.

Smaller Upfront Price: The circular product can be sold at a lower initial cost thanks to the lower production cost and the circular business model, which allows value to be captured throughout the product's lifecycle.

Multiple Income Cycles: Unlike its linear counterpart, the circular product enjoys several spikes in value through cycles of repair, redistribution, and refurbishment.

Remanufacturing: Another increase in value is observed during remanufacturing, where a new product is created and returned to the initial sales stage.

Recycling and Repurposing Income: The curve also considers the revenue generated from recycling or repurposing the product at the end of its lifecycle. However, this may also incur a cost due to Extended Producer Responsibility legislation. The materials are then ready to be reintegrated into production at a lower cost than mining and refining raw materials from the earth.

Fig. 9.4 Eight ways the circular economy outperforms linear business models

The graph shows that the value of a circular product does not diminish over time. Instead, it undergoes a series of recoveries via various circular services, which enable it to regain some or all of its original value. This approach to value capture makes the circular product a more profitable and sustainable business model compared to its linear counterpart in eight ways, which will be discussed in the following sections (Fig. 9.4).

9.3.1 More Attractive Products

According to a study by McKinsey and NielsenIQ, there is a strong connection between ESG-related claims and consumer behavior (Frey et al., 2023). The study revealed that products with these claims experienced higher growth and increased customer loyalty and positively impacted sales. Products making ESG-related claims averaged a 28% cumulative growth over 5 years, compared to 20% for products without such claims. This indicates an 8% growth advantage for sustainable products.

Moreover, the study emphasizes that brands with a larger share of sales from products with ESG-related claims experience higher consumer loyalty. Specifically, brands that derive over half of their sales from ESG-related products have repeat purchase rates of 32–34%, compared to under 30% for brands with less than 50% of sales from ESG-related products. This indicates that a more significant commitment to ESG practices can improve brand loyalty and consumer retention.

Additionally, the study found that products with multiple ESG-related claims tend to grow approximately twice as fast as those with only one claim. This emphasizes the value of a comprehensive and multifaceted approach to sustainability in product offerings.

The Wharton School of the University of Pennsylvania found that consumers' reason to purchase sustainable products and brands was their intention to improve the environment (30%), reduce production waste (23%), reduce their carbon footprint (22%), and address concerns about animal welfare (17%) (First Insight, 2021).

With circular business models, waste becomes an asset rather than a liability to discard. Renewable and recyclable inputs become essential parts of production, lowering or eliminating waste, pollution, and biodiversity loss, strengthening the main reasons for purchasing sustainable products.

Example 9.2 Adidas' partnership with Parley for the Oceans

In partnership with Parley for the Oceans, has addressed environmental concerns and consumer demand for sustainable products by making its sneakers from recycled ocean plastics. That will lead to more than 15 million pairs of shoes being produced with Parley Ocean Plastic.

The sneakers are crafted using yarns from intercepted and upcycled marine plastic waste, transforming pollution into high-performance footwear. Adidas's use of recycled ocean plastics has created a more attractive product by tapping into th narrative of environmental stewardship, which resonates with eco-conscious consumers (Adidas, 2020).

9.3.2 Greater Customer Intimacy

In the linear economy, manufacturers sell new products to the next in line, leaving the continued customer dialogues to their downstream partners. However, circular business models require more than just one-way communication. Redistributing, extending product use, and recycling all demand continuous dialogue throughout the entire business ecosystem over the product's lifetime. This increased intimacy allows for consistent communication, helping manufacturers better understand customer usage patterns and perceptions.

Many manufacturers will experience continuous end-user dialogues for the first time, and they need to learn how to make them relevant, timely, and engaging.

Example 9.3 Signify offers "Light as a Service"

Signify offers "Light as a Service" (LaaS). This approach enables customers to enjoy energy-efficient, cutting-edge lighting without the upfront cost of purchasing the lighting hardware. Instead, Signify takes ownership of the fixtures and installations, while customers pay for the lighting service over time (Signify, 2024).

This service model assures reduced energy consumption and lower maintenance costs, which is attractive to a wide range of sectors, from municipalities to large corporations. Signify handles all aspects of the lighting lifecycle,

(continued)

including design, installation, maintenance, upgrades, reverse logistics, and part harvesting. This ensures that lighting systems are always at the forefront of technology and efficiency without incurring extra expenses or effort for the client or impact on the environment.

The transition from selling light bulbs to providing lighting as a service is a shift in business strategy. Previously, lighting firms would manufacture and sell light bulbs, leaving the user's responsibility for maintenance and energy consumption. The transaction would conclude at the point of sale, with limited ongoing interaction between the supplier and the customer unless new purchases were made. In contrast, Signify's LaaS model promotes continuous engagement with the end-user.

9.3.3 Reduce the Total Cost of Ownership

Circular products are designed to be reused, repaired, remanufactured, and disassembled, extending their lifespan and reducing the need for frequent replacements. This design philosophy ensures customers get more value from each product they purchase over time. Furthermore, the repair design reduces overall maintenance costs. The availability of refurbished parts and components at a lower cost than new ones also contributes to more affordable repairs.

Programs that provide incentives for returning used products for refurbishment or recycling can decrease the total cost of ownership. While they may no longer be relevant to the current owner, circular products may still hold value through reselling, repurposing, or recycling. This potential for continued use by others provides an opportunity to recoup some of the initial investment and reduces waste disposal fees, further lowering the total cost of ownership.

Example 9.4 SKF offers oil-as-a-service with its RecondOil offering

Sweden-based bearings supplier SKF offers oil-as-a-service with its RecondOil offering. It uses a double separation technology (DST) approach to remove even the smallest contaminants from oil to be cleaned and reused. Unlike an industrial 7-year production cycle requiring 30 oil changes, oil-as-a-service can complete the same 7 years with no additional oil or logistical costs and no lost production time (SKF, 2024).

9.3.4 Recurrent Income Sources

Circular business models offer sustained revenue streams through continuous selling and reusing of products. Unlike traditional models, circular models emphasize several key aspects. Redistribution and repair allow refurbished and repaired products to be resold, extending their lifecycle and creating frequent sales opportunities.

Remanufactured products, restored to like-new condition, meet consumer demand for high-quality, affordable goods.

Recovering components and materials from disassembled products results in valuable parts and raw materials, which can be sold in secondary markets to maximize their value. Instead of treating waste and by-products as liabilities, they are regarded as assets that can be sold to other businesses, transforming potential disposal problems into profitable resources.

Service-based models, such as subscriptions, leasing, and pay-per-use arrangements, provide a steady income and predictable revenue. Innovative recycling programs recover and repurpose materials, reducing costs and creating new revenue streams. Additionally, extended producer responsibility (EPR) schemes involve companies taking back products for recycling or remanufacturing, reducing environmental impact and generating income from recovered materials.

Example 9.5 Nike Grind initiative

Nike, a global leader in athletic footwear and apparel, has incorporated circularity into its business model to promote environmental consciousness while increasing revenue. One way is through its Nike Grind initiative, which involves collecting and processing discarded shoes, manufacturing scraps, and repurposing them into secondary raw materials. These materials are used to make new products, such as footwear, apparel, and sports surfaces. By doing this, Nike not only diverts waste from landfills but also creates a closed-loop system that contributes to ongoing revenue while reducing the need for virgin materials (Nike Grind, 2024).

In addition to the Nike Grind program, Nike has launched the Nike Refurbished initiative, further supporting its circular economy goals while generating additional income. This program revitalizes returned and slightly used footwear, which is then sold at reduced prices. Each pair undergoes a thorough inspection, cleaning, and refurbishing process to ensure they meet Nike's quality standards before being offered for sale again. Nike Refurbished extends the lifespan for three types of footwear: like-new (maybe worn for a day or 2 before being returned), gently worn (a little longer), and cosmetically flawed (something like a small snag that happened in manufacturing).

This initiative appeals to cost-conscious consumers and opens up a new market segment for Nike, providing a continuous revenue stream from products that would otherwise contribute to waste (Nike, 2024).

9.3.5 Greater Resilience

In today's world, with global markets and supply chains becoming more uncertain, manufacturers need to prioritize resilience (Henrich et al., 2022). This can be achieved by adopting circular economy models focusing on reclaiming and reusing components and materials. When products are designed for circularity, the ability to recover valuable components and materials helps create a buffer against the uncertainties of external supply chains. This internal process of recovery and reuse offers multiple layers of resilience.

Firstly, it reduces dependency on external suppliers who may be affected by geopolitical tensions, natural disasters, or other disruptions. By reclaiming components from returned products, a manufacturer becomes less vulnerable to supply chain bottlenecks and delays, thereby improving the overall robustness of its operations.

Example 9.6 H&M's clothing collection initiative

The global fashion retailer H&M launched a clothing collection initiative in its stores, encouraging customers to drop off unwanted garments from any brand in any condition (H&M, 2024). These collected clothes are then either:

- Reused/re-weared: Wearable clothes are marketed as second-hand clothing.
- Reused: If the clothes or textiles are unsuitable for re-wear, they're turned into other products, such as remake collections or cleaning cloths.
- Recycled: All other clothes and textiles are shredded into textile fibers and used to make insulation materials, for example.

H&M expects to reduce its dependence on raw materials by integrating recycled fibers into its production,[1] enhancing its resilience against disruptions in the supply of virgin textiles (H&M Group, 2024).

Another benefit of recycling is that it safeguards against material price volatility. Manufacturers can avoid the risks associated with sudden price hikes in raw materials by consistently recycling and reusing materials. This financial stability can give businesses a competitive advantage by maintaining consistent customer pricing while improving their profit margins.

Circular models offer greater adaptability and flexibility in changing market demands and regulations. This is because they operate within a closed-loop system where the necessary resources are already available. This is particularly important in sectors with rapid technological advancements, where materials and components can quickly become obsolete.

Circularity can aid in the planning of business continuity. If a disruption occurs, having an internal supply of materials can be the difference between halting production and continuing operations. This enables taking advantage of market opportunities when competitors may be struggling.

Furthermore, BCG (2023) identifies three key components essential for the future success of supply chains: resilience, digitization, and sustainability. While

[1] https://hmgroup.com/sustainability/circularity-and-climate/materials/

resilience is covered by the circular economy, as discussed, digitization involves leveraging advanced technologies to enhance supply chain visibility and agility. This includes implementing AI-driven analytics (Chap. 15), IoT devices (Chap. 13), and ecosystem integration (Chap. 12) to track and manage inventory more effectively. The last key component, sustainability, is inherently supported by circular economy practices, which minimize waste and reduce environmental impact by keeping materials in use for as long as possible.

By integrating these components—resilience through internal recycling loops, digitization for real-time decision-making, and sustainability through circular practices—manufacturers build robust, future-proof supply chains adaptable to current and emerging challenges.

Example 9.7 Stellantis utilize 'local loops' to maintain products and materials within countries

Stellantis' Circular Economy Business Unit aims to utilize "local loops" to maintain products and materials within countries, thereby expediting customer deliveries. In Brazil, crucial components such as starter motors and alternators from Stellantis brand vehicles are remanufactured, distributed, and sold through 1000 local dealerships (Stellantis, 2022).

9.3.6 Greater Product and Component Utilization

Linear economy business models are based on the user owning a product, often resulting in poor utilization. For instance, cars remain parked around 95% of the time (Morris, 2016).

On the other hand, Product-as-a-Service and sharing economy models aim to increase product utilization, leading to higher income per unit.

Circular products and business models are designed to be reused, repaired, reconditioned, and upgraded, resulting in increased utilization. Similarly, components will be harvested, remanufactured, and used again, and ultimately the materials will be recycled. Each step in this process not only extends the life and utility of the product but also provides opportunities to generate additional income from the same production cycle.

9.3.7 Reduced Production Times

Circular business models reduce production times by focusing on refurbishing and remanufacturing products and components. When products or components stop working, they can be restored to like-new conditions. This approach eliminates the need to manufacture many new components from scratch, streamlining the production process and conserving valuable resources.

The refurbishment and remanufacturing processes are typically faster than the full production cycle required for new products. Existing materials and parts are reused, reducing the time spent on sourcing, processing, and assembling raw materials. Additionally, the inspection and quality assurance phases are expedited, as the foundational elements of the products are already in place.

Example 9.8 Refurbishing existing wind turbines

Murywed (n.d.) finds that the demand for renewable energy surges worldwide and the traditional model of manufacturing new wind turbines struggles to keep up. Some manufacturers face lead times of up to 2 years. Refurbishing existing wind turbines reduces this waiting period, completing the process in 4 months.

These refurbished turbines, updated to meet modern mechanical and electrical standards, are primarily destined for developing regions. Once considered obsolete in markets like Germany and Denmark, these turbines find new life in countries across Africa and South America and specific parts of Europe such as the northern United Kingdom and southern Italy. These areas often include small-scale operators like farmers or small industrial businesses who greatly benefit from the availability, cost efficiency, and quick deployment of refurbished turbines.

The process makes these turbines more affordable and customizes them to comply with evolving local regulations and grid code requirements.

9.3.8 Climate and Environmentally Friendly

Recycling, repairing, remanufacturing, and reusing circular products and materials require less energy and have less impact on the environment than conventional methods. This includes biodiversity loss, foresting and mining, component and product manufacturing, and transporting raw materials. Also, organizations that adopt safe disposal methods can lower their environmental impact.

Reduction in Greenhouse Gas Emissions According to a report by the Ellen MacArthur Foundation, in partnership with the McKinsey Center for Business and Environment, adopting a circular economy could reduce CO2 emissions. The report suggests that Europe alone could cut emissions by 48% by 2030 and by 83% by 2050 if it embraces strategies such as recycling, remanufacturing, and extending the lifecycle of products (John et al., 2023).

Resource Efficiency The World Economic Forum has reported that by 2025, the circular economy could generate $1 trillion in economic savings annually and prevent 100 million tons of waste globally (Mohindra, 2014).

Example 9.9 n2s' sustainable IT asset management solutions

One example is n2s, an industry leader in sustainable IT asset management solutions that advocate reuse in line with the European Hierarchy of Waste Management.[2] n2s aims to reuse or redeploy devices first, with recycling as a secondary outcome for items beyond economic repair. In 2021, n2s recycled 149,489 tons of PCBs and 189,914 tons of electric cable. That means they recovered 129 tons of copper last year alone. It would take between 12,900 and 20,640 tons of copper ore to yield the same pure copper through traditional mining (n2s, 2024).

Water Usage According to the United Nations Environment Programme, circular water management practices could reduce water consumption. For example, recycling water within industrial processes can decrease freshwater withdrawal, which is significant given that industry accounts for around 20% of global water use (Lindner, 2023).

Biodiversity Loss The European Environment Agency (EEA) has highlighted the circular economy's potential in mitigating biodiversity loss. The report presents how the circular economy can directly and indirectly benefit biodiversity conservation (European Environment Agency, 2024). With the circular economy, the need for raw material extraction decreases, which is important since mining and logging cause habitat destruction and species displacement. Reduced waste generation is also beneficial as it lessens the environmental pressures on ecosystems. Furthermore, reduced industrial pollution helps protect water bodies and land areas that support a wide array of biodiversity.

Energy Savings Fragkos (2022) has analyzed the practices of circular economy and their impact on energy dynamics. The report found that industries can reduce their energy consumption by decreasing the need for energy-intensive production of new materials and reducing their reliance on freshly extracted raw materials. Traditionally, raw material extraction, processing, and transportation involve high energy costs. Furthermore, they can also achieve indirect savings through optimized logistics and distribution networks.

Example 9.10 Renault Group's subsidiary, the Re-Factory in Flins

Renault Group is a global player in the automotive industry. Through its subsidiary, the Re-Factory in Flins, the company is implementing a circular economy factory approach encompassing the entire automotive industry value chain.

(continued)

[2] https://environment.ec.europa.eu/topics/waste-and-recycling/waste-framework-directive_en

Renault's remanufacturing processes, especially for engines and gearboxes, consume up to 80% less energy than traditional manufacturing processes that rely on new materials. Additionally, retrofitting older vehicles is another energy-saving measure adopted by Renault to extend their lifespan or update their technology to comply with current environmental standards. This approach reduces the energy required to produce an entirely new vehicle instead of manufacturing new ones (Renault Group, 2023).

9.4 Main Challenges Manufacturers Will Encounter During Their Journey Toward Circularity

The 1 + 5R model highlights the challenges manufacturers must overcome as they transition to a circular economy. This analysis emphasizes that the journey to circularity is complex. Manufacturers who actively tackle these challenges will gain a competitive advantage.

9.4.1 Market Acceptance and Customer Behavior

Gaining market acceptance for circular products and business models takes time and effort, especially in markets accustomed to disposable, short-lived goods. Manufacturers must educate customers on the benefits of circular products and build trust in their quality and longevity. Marketing strategies should emphasize circular products' environmental and economic advantages, promoting them as superior alternatives to traditional options. Additionally, changing customer behavior to embrace responsible consumption and participation in redistribution and product use extension models, product return, and recycling programs is crucial. Incentives and awareness campaigns play a role in driving this behavioral shift.

9.4.2 Cultural and Organizational Shifts

The transition to a circular economy demands a cultural shift within organizations. Companies must move from a linear mindset of producing, selling, using, and disposing of products to a more holistic view that sees products and materials as valuable assets with extended lifecycles. This requires educating and training employees at all levels to understand and embrace circular economy principles. Leadership must champion this cultural shift, fostering an environment that encourages innovation, collaboration, and sustainable practices. Overcoming resistance to change and aligning all departments with the new circular vision can be challenging but is essential for a successful transition.

9.4.3 Regulatory Compliance and Standardization

As governments worldwide increasingly focus on sustainability, manufacturers must navigate a complex and evolving regulatory landscape. Complying with new laws and standards related to waste reduction, recycling, and using sustainable materials can take time and effort. Companies must stay abreast of regulatory changes and ensure their practices meet or exceed these requirements. Standardization is also crucial for seamless integration within the circular economy. Developing and adhering to common standards across the industry can facilitate collaboration and efficiency but requires concerted effort and coordination among various stakeholders.

9.4.4 Supply Chain and Resource Management

Reconfiguring supply chains to support the availability of spare parts for repair services requires investment in new warehousing solutions and digital systems for real-time inventory tracking. Efficient spare part logistics ensure that necessary components are readily available for repairs and refurbishments.

Establishing reverse logistics systems to handle end-of-life products is equally important. This involves developing collection networks and partnering with logistics service providers to facilitate the efficient return of products. These reverse logistics systems must be capable of handling the complexities of collecting, sorting, and transporting used products back to manufacturers, circular service providers, or recyclers.

Companies must develop advanced capabilities to track, assess, and process returned items, transforming reverse logistics from a cost-centric function into a strategic asset.

Ensuring the continuous flow of materials and products back into the economy requires robust logistics systems and close collaboration with suppliers, partners, and recycling facilities.

Geopolitical tensions, environmental challenges, and trade conflicts further complicate supply chain resilience. Diversifying supply sources to include recycled materials, refurbished products, and remanufactured parts is necessary but requires strategic planning and investment.

9.4.5 Redesign and Product Innovation

Transitioning from traditional design philosophies to emphasizing easy disassembly, durability, and repairability poses a challenge. Manufacturers must ensure that products can be easily taken apart and made with durable materials, complicating the design process. Additionally, products must be designed for optimal usage to compete with linear products and ready for circular practices such as repair, remanufacturing, and recycling. This dual focus requires a careful balance between maintaining performance and functionality while enabling circularity. Developing modular designs and standardizing components to streamline repair and recycling processes requires product design and engineering practice changes. Ensuring compatibility and interchangeability of components across different product lines adds another layer of complexity. Engaging tier suppliers to produce components that support circularity adds another layer of complexity to the supply chain.

9.4.6 Collaboration Within the Business Ecosystem

Ensuring that the entire business ecosystem works cohesively is a challenge in the circular economy. Manufacturers, suppliers, recyclers, and service providers must align their goals and practices to create closed-loop systems where materials are continuously reused. This requires transparent communication, data sharing, and collaborative platforms facilitating cooperation and coordination. Building trust and establishing common standards across different entities can be difficult but is essential for maximizing resource efficiency and achieving sustainability goals. Overcoming competitive barriers and fostering a culture of collaboration within the business ecosystem are critical steps toward a thriving circular economy.

Example 9.11 The Circular Electronics Partnership (CEP)

The Circular Electronics Partnership (CEP)[3] is a joint initiative to promote a circular economy within the electronics industry. This partnership unites major companies, governments, NGOs, and other stakeholders to advocate for circular design principles, which involve creating long-lasting, repairable, and recyclable electronics using sustainable and recycled materials. The goal is to extend the lifespan of products through better design, maintenance, and repair and to support business models that encourage longer use of devices.

9.4.7 Financing the Transition

Financing the transition to a circular economy while maintaining competitiveness in the linear economy is a delicate balancing act. Manufacturers must continue to invest in their existing linear operations to remain viable and generate the revenue needed to fund their circular initiatives. This challenge is compounded by the need to allocate substantial resources for research and development, technology integration, and process redesign associated with circular practices. Strategic financial planning and securing investment for current operations and future circular endeavors are crucial for effectively navigating this transition.

[3] https://cep2030.org/

9.4.8 Technological Integration and Data Management

The integration of advanced technologies and effective data management is also challenging. Manufacturers must invest in IT systems and digital tools to track, manage, and optimize resources throughout the product lifecycle. This includes implementing IoT technologies for real-time monitoring, AI for predictive maintenance, and advanced analytics for informed decision-making. However, the high costs associated with these technologies and the need for skilled personnel to manage and interpret data can take time and effort. Additionally, ensuring data privacy and security is paramount as companies handle vast amounts of sensitive information.

9.4.9 Operational Challenges

Shifting to circular practices demands capital expenditure to develop and implement new recycling, remanufacturing, and material recovery processes. These investments can be particularly burdensome for small- and medium-sized enterprises, which may struggle to secure the necessary funding. During the transition period, manufacturers may face operational inefficiencies as they integrate new processes into their existing systems. This can lead to disruptions in production and increased operational costs. Streamlining these processes to maintain efficiency while achieving circular economy goals requires careful planning and execution. The circular economy is an emerging discipline where rapid technological advancements pose a risk of obsolescence for newly implemented processes and systems. Manufacturers must be prepared to continually update and upgrade their operations to stay competitive and leverage the latest technological innovations.

9.4.10 Summarizing the Challenges

Table 9.3 outlines the main challenges manufacturers will encounter during their journey towards circularity and strategies for mitigating them. Each challenge is described in brief, followed by specific actions that can be taken to address it effectively.

9.5 Manufacturing Circular Maturity Framework

The shift from a linear to a circular economy in manufacturing is a complex and multifaceted process involving numerous stakeholders, including designers, suppliers, regulators, and end-users. As manufacturing organizations strive to adopt the principles of the circular economy, they must understand their current level of maturity in this transition to facilitate targeted growth and strategy development. The "Manufacturers Circularity Maturity Framework" is a roadmap to help manufacturers evaluate their position in the circular economy journey. This framework identifies the challenges they will likely face and outlines the opportunities that arise as companies mature.

Table 9.3 Main Challenges Manufacturers Will Encounter During Their Journey Towards Circularity

Main Challenge	Description	Mitigation
Market Acceptance and Customer Behavior	Gaining market acceptance for circular products and business models	Educate customers on benefits; build trust in quality and longevity; use marketing strategies emphasizing environmental and economic advantages; drive behavioral shifts through incentives and awareness campaigns
Cultural and Organizational Shifts	Transitioning to a holistic view of products and materials as valuable assets	Educate and train employees on circular economy principles; leadership to champion cultural shifts and foster innovation and collaboration; overcome resistance and align all departments with the circular vision
Regulatory Compliance and Standardization	Navigating a complex and evolving regulatory landscape	Stay updated on regulatory changes; ensure practices meet or exceed requirements; develop and adhere to industry-wide standards
Supply Chain and Resource Management	Reconfiguring supply chains for spare parts and reverse logistics	Invest in warehousing solutions and digital systems for real-time inventory tracking; develop collection networks and partnerships for efficient product returns; diversify supply sources to include recycled and remanufactured materials
Redesign and Product Innovation	Shifting to designs emphasizing disassembly, durability, and repairability	Balance performance with circularity; develop modular designs and standardize components; engage suppliers to produce components supporting circularity
Collaboration Within the Business Ecosystem	Ensuring cohesive operations within the business ecosystem	Promote transparent communication, data sharing, and collaborative platforms; build trust and establish common standards; foster a culture of collaboration among stakeholders
Financing the Transition	Balancing investment in linear operations and circular initiatives	Strategic financial planning; secure investments for both current operations and future circular endeavors; allocate resources for R&D and process redesign
Technological Integration and Data Management	Integrating advanced technologies and managing data	Invest in IT systems and digital tools; implement IoT for monitoring, AI for maintenance, and analytics for decision-making; ensure data privacy and security
Operational Challenges	Developing and implementing new recycling and recovery processes	Plan and execute process integration carefully; streamline operations to maintain efficiency; continually update and upgrade to stay competitive with technological advancements

The Manufacturers Circularity Maturity Framework divides the journey toward circularity into five progressive stages: awareness, engagement, implementation, integration, and leadership. Each stage is characterized by specific traits and objectives that align with increasing levels of circular integration within manufacturing processes. This structured approach helps manufacturers recognize the opportunities for innovation and competitive advantage at each level, guiding strategic planning and execution.

To effectively utilize this framework, manufacturers should initially determine their current position within the maturity model by evaluating their existing business practices against the criteria outlined for each stage. This assessment enables them to pinpoint the most relevant objectives and opportunities currently within reach and plan strategic actions necessary for advancement to subsequent stages. Regular reassessment is advised to ensure ongoing progress and adapt to emerging technology trends, market demands, and regulatory standards (Table 9.4).

9.6 Checklist for Manufacturers Transitioning to a Circular Economy

Transitioning to a circular economy represents a paradigm shift for manufacturers. This transformation necessitates rethinking traditional business models, product designs, supply chains, and customer engagement strategies. By moving away from the linear "take-make-dispose" model to a circular approach, manufacturers can unlock new revenue streams, enhance resource efficiency, and build more resilient and sustainable businesses.

This checklist (Table 9.5) is a practical tool for manufacturers to systematically address the multifaceted challenges and opportunities of the circular economy. By following these steps, manufacturers can lead innovation, sustainability, and market leadership.

Table 9.4 The manufacturers circularity maturity framework

Stage	Characteristics	Objectives	Opportunities	Challenges
1. Awareness	Limited understanding of circular economy concepts Minimal integration of circular principles Initial recognition of benefits	Educate leadership and employees Conduct an initial review of current practices and products Lay the groundwork for a strategic advantage through initial exploration	Identify quick wins to demonstrate potential benefits Build momentum for broader initiatives	Overcoming initial resistance to change Establishing a baseline understanding across the organization
2. Engagement	Growing commitment among management and staff Development of basic circularity policies Initial partnerships are exploring circular opportunities	Formalize sustainability goals, including circular targets Begin integrating circular principles into design Establish a foundation for future growth and competitive edge	Engage stakeholders in developing new practices Test new circular processes in controlled settings	Aligning various departments and processes with circular objectives Finding partners for collaboration

(continued)

Table 9.4 (continued)

Stage	Characteristics	Objectives	Opportunities	Challenges
3. Implementation	Active redesign of products/processes for resource efficiency Implementation of recycling, remanufacturing, or refurbishing Measurement of circular metrics	Improve product life extension and waste reduction Innovate through circular solutions like PaaS Drive cost reductions and product innovation for market leadership	Enhance product value and lifecycle Reduce costs through improved processes	Integrating circular practices at scale Managing costs and logistical complexities of new processes
4. Integration	Comprehensive integration of circular practices across operations Robust systems for product take-back and material recovery Strong collaborations	Optimize the supply chain for circularity Enhance customer engagement and education on circular benefits Secure a competitive market position through comprehensive circular integration	Achieve operational efficiencies Strengthen brand reputation and customer loyalty	Ensuring consistency and reliability in circular supply chains Adapting to evolving regulatory and market conditions
5. Leadership	Industry-leading adoption and promotion of circular practices Influence on policy and industry standards Continuous improvement in circular practices	Drive sector-wide changes Circularity central to competitiveness Develop new technologies and concepts for circularity Establish industry leadership and drive systemic change through circular innovation	Set industry benchmarks Open new markets and business models Lead in circularity and innovation	Staying ahead of technological advancements Leading amidst increasing competition and higher stakeholder expectations

Table 9.5 Circular economy transition checklist

Task	Methodology	Expected outcome	Risk mitigated
Evaluate environmental and resource efficiency	Conduct lifecycle assessment (LCA) Perform material flow analysis (MFA)	Identify waste reduction opportunities Optimize resource utilization	Minimize environmental impact Ensure regulatory compliance
Design and redesign products for circularity	Integrate Design for the Environment (DfE) Analyze value chain	Create durable, repairable, and modular products Enhance product value and lifecycle	High costs and waste from non-repairable products Inefficient processes
Understand and respond to market and customer needs	Gather customer insights Market analysis Establish feedback loop and market research	Identify opportunities for circular products Redesign products/services to meet evolving customer needs	Missing market trends Misalignment with customer expectations
Develop and implement circular business models	Conduct financial analysis Map customer experience	Assess the profitability of refurbishing products and offering services Enhance customer satisfaction and retention	Unsustainable business practices Poor customer engagement
Integrate and leverage technology for circularity	Conduct technology assessment Assess IT readiness	Identify tools to improve resource efficiency and support recycling Ensure IT systems support lifecycle tracking	Technology inefficiencies Inadequate IT support for circular practices
Benchmark and improve operational practices	Benchmark against industry best practices Perform risk assessment	Pinpoint gaps and opportunities for circularity Mitigate risks related to circular economy practices	Lagging behind industry standards Supply chain disruptions
Navigate and comply with regulatory requirements	Map regulatory and incentive landscape	Ensure compliance with regulations Identify supportive incentives	Non-compliance with regulations
Foster collaboration and ecosystem integration	Map ecosystem	Facilitate collaboration and innovation in resource use	Lack of collaboration and innovation opportunities
Assess and advance circular maturity	Utilize the Manufacturing Circular Maturity Framework	Evaluate the current circularity level Plan strategic actions for advancement	Stagnation in circular economy transition Inability to identify growth opportunities
Create continuous value for customers	Shift from one-time transactions to long-term partnerships	Provide ongoing value through customizable solutions and services	Loss of customer engagement Short product lifespan

References

Adidas. (2020). *Adidas aims to end plastic waste with innovation + partnerships as the solution.* Retrieved from https://news.adidas.com/running/adidas-aims-to-end-plastic-waste-with-innovation%2D%2D-partnerships-as-the-solutions/s/be70ac18-1fc9-45c1-9413-d8abaac2e849

BCG. (2023, August). *Building the supply chain of the future. From BCG's build for the future series.* Retrieved from https://www.bcg.com/publications/2023/building-the-supply-chain-of-the-future

Christensen, C. M. (1997). *The Innovator's dilemma: When new technologies cause great firms to fail.* Harvard Business School Press.

Christensen, C. M., Raynor, M. E., & McDonald, R. (2015). What is disruptive innovation? *Harvard Business Review.* Retrieved from https://hbr.org/2015/12/what-is-disruptive-innovation

European Environment Agency. (2024). *The benefits to biodiversity of a strong circular economy.* Retrieved from https://www.eea.europa.eu/publications/the-benefits-to-biodiversity

First Insight. (2021). *The state of consumer spending. Gen Z influencing all generations to make sustainability-first purchase decisions.* Retrieved from https://www.firstinsight.com/white-papers-posts/gen-z-influencing-all-generations-to-make-sustainability-first-purchasing-decisions

Fragkos, P. (2022). Analysing the systemic implications of energy efficiency and circular economy strategies in the decarbonisation context. *AIMS Energy.* Retrieved from http://www.aimspress.com/journal/energy

Frey, S., Am, J. B., Doshi, V., Malik, A., & Noble, S. (2023). *Consumers care about sustainability—and back it up with their wallets.* McKinsey and NielsenIQ. Retrieved from https://nielseniq.com/global/en/insights/report/2023/consumers-care-about-sustainability-and-back-it-up-with-their-wallets/

GE Aerospace. (2024). *TrueChoice Commercial Services.* From https://www.geaerospace.com/commercial/services/true-choice

H&M. (2024, June). *Let's close the loop.* Retrieved from https://www2.hm.com/en_gb/sustainability-at-hm/our-work/close-the-loop.html

H&M Group. (2024, June). *How we work with materials.* Retrieved from https://hmgroup.com/sustainability/circularity-and-climate/materials/

Henrich, J., Li, J., Mazuera, C., & Perez, F. (2022). *Future-proofing the supply chain.* McKinsey & Company.

John, I. B., Adekunle, S. A., & Aigbavboa, C. O. (2023). *Adoption of circular economy by construction industry SMEs: Organisational growth transition study.* MDPI. Retrieved from https://www.mdpi.com/2071-1050/15/7/5929

Lindner, J. (2023). *Global water consumption statistics.* Gitnux Marketdata Report 2024. From https://gitnux.org/global-water-consumption-statistics/

Mohindra, D. (2014). Circular economy can generate US$ 1 trillion annually by 2025. World Economic Forum. From https://www.weforum.org/press/2014/01/circular-economy-can-generate-us-1-trillion-annually-by-2025/

Morris, D. Z. (2016). *Today's Cars Are Parked 95% of the Time.* Retrieved from Fortune: https://fortune.com/2016/03/13/cars-parked-95-percent-of-time/

Murywed, M. (n.d.). *Turbine transformation—A new lease of life for ageing wind turbines.* PES Wind. Retrieved from ABB: https://new.abb.com/docs/librariesprovider135/wind-power-solutions/turbine-transformation%2D%2D-a-new-lease-of-life-for-ageing-wind-turbines.pdf

n2s. (2024, June). *Redefining the technology lifecycle.* Retrieved from https://www.n2s.co.uk/

Negroponte, N. (1995). *Being Digital.* Knopf Doubleday Publishing Group.

Nike. (2024, June). *Watch How Nike Refurbished Works.* Retrieved from https://about.nike.com/en/newsroom/releases/nike-refurbished-circularity-model

Nike Grind. (2024, June). Nike Grind. Retrieved from https://www.nikegrind.com/

Renault Group. (2023, December). *The future is NEUTRAL strengthens its coverage of the circular economy value chain.* Retrieved from https://media.renaultgroup.com/the-future-is-neutral-strengthens-its-coverage-of-the-circular-economy-value-chain/

Signify. (2024, June). *Our purpose is to unlock the extraordinary potential of light for brighter lives and a better world.* Retrieved from https://www.signify.com/global

SKF. (2024). SKF RecondOil. From https://www.skf.com/dk/services/recondoil

Stellantis. (2022). *Stellantis fosters circular economy ambitions with dedicated business unit to power new era of sustainable manufacturing and consumption.* Retrieved from https://www.stellantis.com/en/news/press-releases/2022/october/stellantis-fosters-circular-economy-ambitions-with-dedicated-business-unit-to-power-new-era-of-sustainable-manufacturing-and-consumption

Part III

The Role of Digitization in Circular Economy Transformation

Digitization offers manufacturers a blueprint for achieving circularity, driving economic success, and environmental stewardship.

iStock Credit: Siripak Pason

Digitization as the Enabler of Circularity 10

Abstract

Digitization is critical for integrating circular principles into manufacturing, supported by the Sustainable Manufacturing Intelligence Framework (SMIF). APIs serve as the backbone of digital integration, enabling seamless communication and data exchange across various platforms. Event-driven architectures enhance operational efficiency through real-time processing and response, improving decision-making and resource management. Digital warranties foster trust and encourage participation in circular practices by making warranties easily transferable, extendable, and verifiable. Smart contracts streamline circular economy agreements, ensuring efficiency and transparency without intermediaries.

In Part III, we connect circular business models with digital strategies, providing manufacturers with tools and knowledge for excelling in a digitally enabled circular economy. The SMIF outlines essential digital capabilities for embedding circular principles, emphasizing customer engagement, IT system adaptation, IoT integration, and data-driven decision-making. This framework aligns digital transformations with circular goals, reducing operational inefficiencies. Additionally, the Digitization Checklist offers specific steps to implement these strategies, ensuring manufacturers can effectively navigate the digital landscape and achieve sustainable growth and competitive advantage.

H. H. Jensen, *Circular Economy Opportunities and Pathways for Manufacturers*, Future of Business and Finance, https://doi.org/10.1007/978-3-031-75279-7_10

Key Messages

- *Digitization is essential for embedding circular principles into manufacturing operations.* The Sustainable Manufacturing Intelligence Framework (SMIF) guides manufacturers through digital transformation, which is crucial for supporting circular economy strategies.
- *APIs are the backbone of digital integration:* They enable seamless communication and data exchange across various platforms, supporting customer interaction, product lifecycle management, and integration with circular service providers.
- *Event-driven architectures enhance operational efficiency and adaptability.* Real-time processing and response to events improve decision-making, resource management, and customer satisfaction, which is essential for a digitized circular economy.
- *Digital warranties promote trust and participation in circular practices:* Easily transferable, extendable, and verifiable warranties encourage customers to invest in repair, refurbishment, and reselling, enhancing product longevity.
- *Smart contracts streamline circular economy agreements:* These self-executing contracts ensure efficiency, transparency, and seamless integration across the circular ecosystem, reducing the need for intermediaries.

In Part II, we discussed the "1 + 5 R" model, which emphasizes the shift toward circular business practices. In Part III, we focus on the importance of digitization in enabling and enhancing these circularity strategies.

To help manufacturers navigate this complex digital landscape, we introduce the Sustainable Manufacturing Intelligence Framework (SMIF) (Fig. 10.1). This framework is designed to guide manufacturers through the intricacies of digital transformation, which is crucial for embedding circular principles into their operations.

The SMIF is divided into five categories, each necessary for implementing a comprehensive digital overhaul that supports successful circular economy initiatives. Figure 10.2 illustrates these categories, which are explained in detail in the subsequent chapters.

Throughout this part, we will connect the dots between the circular business models discussed in Part II and the digital strategies that enable them. The aim is to equip manufacturers with the tools and knowledge necessary to excel in a digitally enabled circular economy.

10.1 Introducing the Sustainable Manufacturing Intelligence Framework

The SMIF outlines how digital capabilities maintain customer engagement beyond the initial sale. These capabilities also help facilitate responsible consumption and effective resource stewardship. As discussed in the 1 + 5 R model, customers need

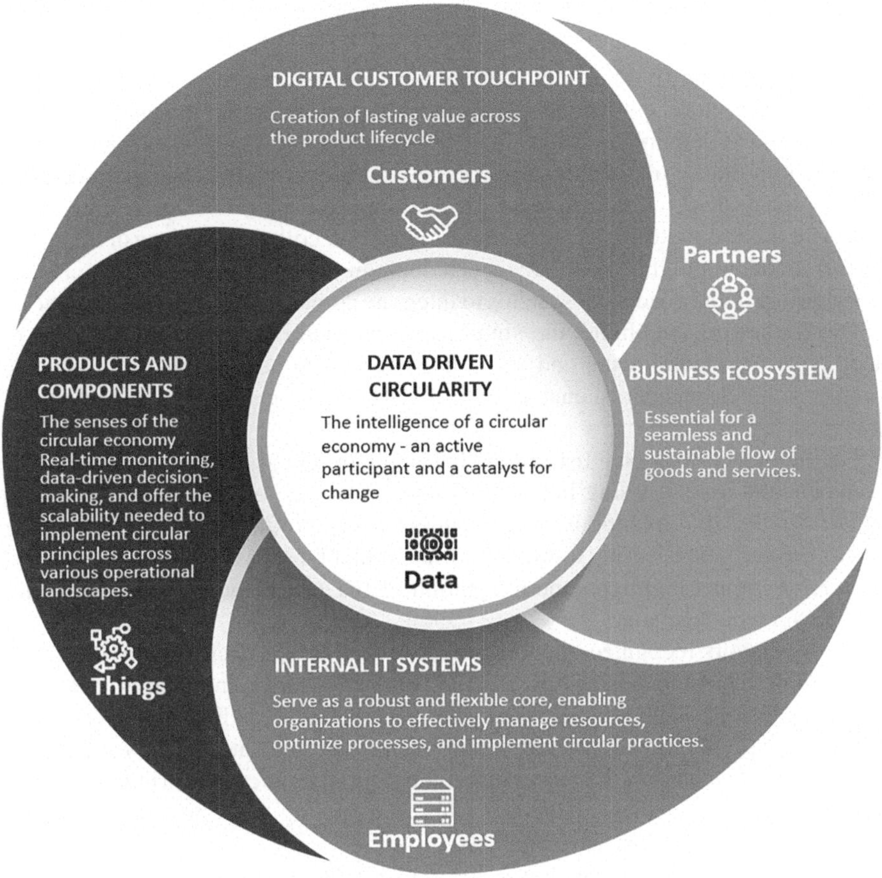

Fig. 10.1 Digitizing circular business models encompass five key components of a Sustainable Manufacturing Intelligence Framework

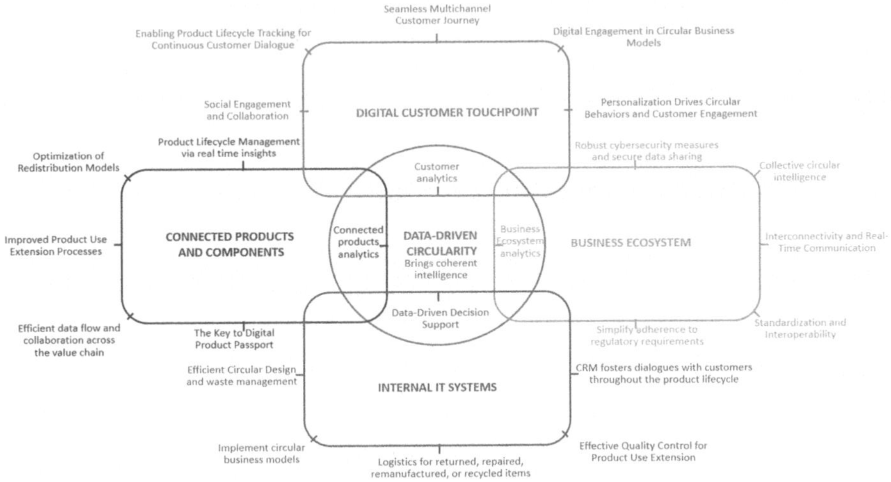

Fig. 10.2 Key benefits to expect from each capability

ongoing interaction to align their consumption behaviors with circular economy principles. Therefore, continuous engagement is vital for sustaining circularity.

The framework emphasizes the value of digital business ecosystems and recognizes the importance of collaborations beyond traditional supply chain partnerships. This approach involves stakeholders such as recyclers, repair services, third-party refurbishers, and distributors, creating a culture of collective responsibility. The 1 + 5 R model highlights the interconnectedness in circular manufacturing, emphasizing the need for broader ecosystems to integrate comprehensive circular practices.

The framework highlights the significance of adapting internal IT systems to meet evolving requirements and regulations. These systems must be flexible to comply with new standards, enable product traceability, and implement end-of-life strategies.

The framework has established the "IoT and Connected Products" capability as a fundamental aspect. Using IoT technologies to enable real-time monitoring and data-driven decision-making is essential in extending product lifetimes, optimizing resource usage, and ensuring transparency in circular business models. For instance, the 1 + 5 R model highlights the integration of IoT to enhance product durability and lifecycle management.

The framework recognizes the importance of data-driven decision-making. Data-driven tools can help businesses efficiently convert large amounts of data into actionable insights. These insights are essential for understanding customer behavior, improving operational efficiency, and identifying innovation and waste reduction opportunities. The 1 + 5 R model highlights how BI tools can assist manufacturers in responding to immediate challenges while anticipating future trends in customer preferences and regulatory environments.

SMIF simplifies the journey toward a circular economy by aligning manufacturers' digital transformations with their circular goals, mitigating the risk of disjointed efforts that could lead to operational inefficiencies.

Figure 10.2 illustrates the key benefits a manufacturer should expect from each capability. At the end of each chapter, it will expand with the 12 key capabilities a manufacturer should master to enable competitive circular business models.

Before exploring each capability in the following chapters, let's examine concepts relevant to all capabilities.

10.2 API-Driven Access Opportunities

Application Programming Interfaces, or APIs (Fig. 10.3), are the digital glue connecting disparate software applications, enabling them to communicate and exchange data seamlessly. They are, therefore, essential for all parts of the Sustainable Manufacturing Intelligence Framework (SMIF). APIs are the backbone of digital integration and are critical to the effective functioning of every component within the framework. For this reason, APIs are covered separately here and will be referenced throughout the chapter on each capability.

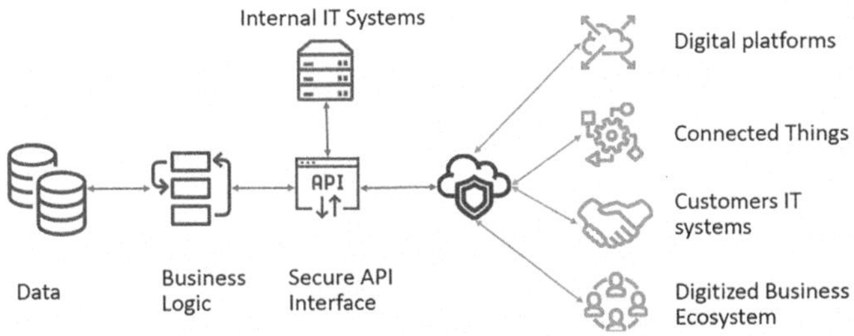

Fig. 10.3 APIs are the digital glue connecting disparate software applications, enabling them to communicate and exchange data seamlessly

APIs provide a consistent platform for manufacturers to offer services, making them easily consumable by internal and external digital systems. This unified approach ensures that manufacturers' digital offerings can seamlessly integrate into various platforms and services, enhancing their reach and accessibility.

Strategically deploying APIs allows for a multichannel approach to customer interaction and commerce. Customers can engage with manufacturers' offerings across multiple touchpoints, from mobile apps to web interfaces. APIs enable manufacturers to broaden their reach across various digital platforms, providing customers with convenient access to a wealth of information and services related to product lifecycle management, including repair, recycling, and upgrade options.

Integrating APIs extends to interfacing with any value chain customer's systems, enhancing product integration and interoperability. This advanced connectivity allows manufacturers to ensure that their products seamlessly fit into broader digital ecosystems. Such integration facilitates features like remote monitoring, predictive maintenance, and comprehensive data analytics, thereby enhancing the utility and desirability of the products.

APIs offer manufacturers the ability to engage in external workflows that are coordinated by third-party systems. This feature is essential in a circular economy, where collaboration among various stakeholders is crucial. By connecting to external systems, manufacturers can more effectively participate in and contribute to the shared objective of competitive circularity. For instance, manufacturers can use APIs to seamlessly integrate their systems with those of recycling centers, remanufacturers, third-party recommerce, or repair shop facilities, resulting in smoother, more efficient, and transparent material recovery and repair processes.

APIs are technical tools and strategic assets in manufacturers' digital transformation journeys in the circular economy. They mitigate the risk of disjointed efforts that could lead to operational inefficiencies. APIs provide a cohesive framework for integrating various digital components, ensuring a streamlined and effective approach to achieving circular economy objectives.

To effectively enable APIs, manufacturers should follow a systematic approach. First, they must define clear objectives by identifying specific goals and use cases for API implementation. These could include enhancing customer interaction

Table 10.1 API Security Measures

Strategy Area	Purpose
Strategies for Identity and Access Management	Implementing secure identity and access management is crucial for API security
Strategies for Service Discovery Mechanism	Ensuring the secure discovery of services is vital for maintaining a resilient API infrastructure
Strategies for Secure Communication Protocols	Secure communication between clients and services, as well as between services, is essential
Strategies for Security Monitoring	Continuous monitoring of API interactions is crucial for detecting and responding to security threats
Availability/Resiliency Improvement Strategies	Maintaining the availability and resiliency of APIs is critical to ensure uninterrupted service
Integrity Assurance Strategies	Ensuring the integrity of API data and interactions is fundamental for maintaining trust and reliability.
Countering Internet-based Attacks	Protecting APIs from internet-based attacks is essential for securing the API ecosystem

throughout the product lifecycle, improving interoperability with partners involved in recycling and refurbishment, or enabling IoT functionalities for better resource management and product traceability.

Next, they must create a strong, expandable, secure API structure. This includes outlining the API endpoints, data formats, and communication protocols to ensure smooth integration and exchange internally and across the circular ecosystem.

Manufacturers utilize API management tools to monitor and secure APIs. They must implement robust security measures, including authentication, authorization, and encryption. Additionally, APIs should adhere to relevant standards and regulations to safeguard data integrity and privacy. For more information on protecting API, please see Chandramouli (2019).

Table 10.1 highlights the key strategies from the NIST document that are essential for API security.

Manufacturers promote collaboration among internal teams and external partners, offering comprehensive documentation and support to assist in integrating APIs into various systems and workflows.

Embracing industry API standards and best practices ensures that APIs are consistent and interoperable, simplifies integration, and improves compatibility with external systems.

By following this systematic approach, manufacturers effectively enable APIs, leading to seamless integration, enhanced operational efficiency, and support for their journey toward a circular economy.

10.3 Event Thinking

An "event" refers to a significant business occurrence or change in state within a system or environment. This information is captured and communicated to subscribers to trigger subsequent actions or responses. Manufacturers are encouraged

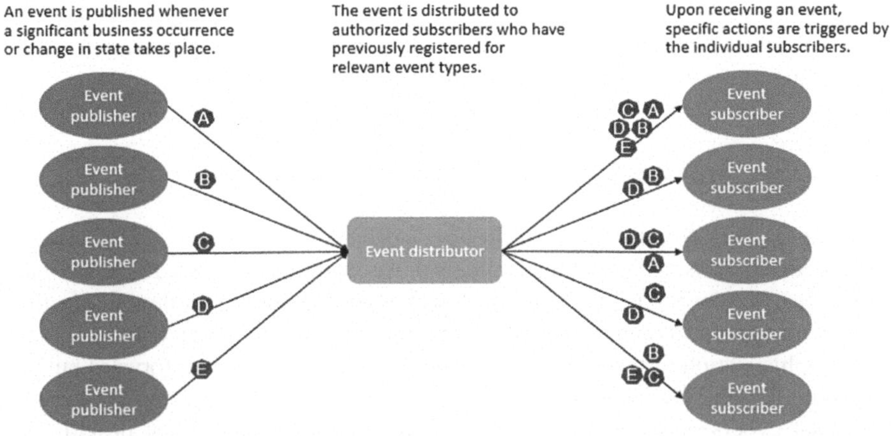

Fig. 10.4 Event thinking

to adopt event thinking to enhance operational efficiency and adaptability in a digitized circular economy. Event thinking focuses on real-time processing and response to events, which can improve decision-making, resource management, and customer satisfaction.

A key mechanism within event thinking is the publish-subscribe (pub-sub) model. In this model, events are published by event producers (such as sensors, applications, or systems) and consumed by subscribers who have expressed interest in those events. Events are distributed to subscribers as soon as they occur. This real-time dissemination ensures that relevant stakeholders and systems are immediately informed, enabling swift and appropriate responses (Fig. 10.4).

For instance, if a sensor detects a malfunction in machinery, it submits an event that maintenance teams subscribe to, allowing for quick intervention and minimizing downtime; when a repair center receives a product for repair, it submits an event that the owner of the product and the logistic partner subscribes to; when a shared product reaches the end of its use cycle, an event is triggered to notify the service provider, who can then schedule the collection and preparation of the product for the next user; when a refurbished product is ready for sale, the refurbishing center submits an event that retailers and potential buyers subscribe to, enabling the product to reenter the market quickly. As partnerships for resource sharing are established, events can be submitted to inform all involved parties, facilitating coordination and efficient resource utilization.

The pub-sub model separates event producers and subscribers, allowing producers to operate without knowledge of subscriber identity or quantity. This promotes scalability and flexibility, as subscribers can independently handle events, enabling efficient system scaling. Additional subscribers can be incorporated without affecting the event producer, making the architecture resilient and adaptable to business growth. Real-time event processing and distribution enable immediate action, which is particularly beneficial in manufacturing for proactive maintenance, inventory management, and customer service. The pub-sub model permits adding new event types and subscribers without significant system modifications, increasing flexibility in a circular economy that often requires dynamic adjustments.

10.4 The "Braking System" of Trust in Circular Economy

In the high-stakes world of race car driving, a driver's confidence in approaching a curve at top speed is less about the engine's power and more about trust in the braking system. Similarly, trust is the invisible yet crucial factor in seamless interaction and collaboration in complex digital ecosystems. It's not the sheer volume of data or the sophistication of technology that propels a digital ecosystem forward but the underlying layers of security and trust.

Robust cybersecurity measures are akin to reliable brakes. They provide the peace of mind for stakeholders to fully engage in data sharing, collective decision-making, and open collaboration. Digital identities and digital signatures serve as the verified "credentials" that parties present when entering these digital interactions. These tools ensure that the company you share data with is who it claims to be, lending an additional layer of credibility and security to the complex web of transactions.

As manufacturers transition to digital operations to enable their circular business models, they must adapt to new security skills. This is not just a one-time effort but a continuous process. Protecting customer data, securing IoT-enabled products, and participating in trustworthy digital ecosystems require comprehensive and adaptive cybersecurity measures. Moreover, the growing reliance on internal IT systems necessitates stringent protective measures to safeguard sensitive information from cyber threats.

Manufacturers can use various trusted sources for cybersecurity advice to address these challenges. One such source, the NIST Cybersecurity Framework, offers a reliable and proven basis for creating and improving security measures. Although this book doesn't cover all the intricate details of cybersecurity, it's important to emphasize certain essential NIST framework aspects relevant to manufacturers. By following this framework, manufacturers can feel confident in their cybersecurity practices (NIST, 2024):

Identify: This function helps manufacturers understand their environment to manage cybersecurity risk to systems, assets, data, and capabilities. It includes asset management, business environment, governance, risk assessment, and risk management strategy.

Protect: This function outlines appropriate safeguards to ensure the delivery of critical infrastructure services. It includes access control, awareness and training, data security, information protection processes and procedures, maintenance, and protective technology.

Detect: This function defines activities to identify the occurrence of a cybersecurity event. It includes anomalies and events, continuous security monitoring, and detection processes.

Respond: This function includes appropriate activities to take action regarding a detected cybersecurity event. It comprises response planning, communications, analysis, mitigation, and improvements.

Recover: This function identifies appropriate activities to maintain resilience plans and restore any capabilities or services impaired due to a cybersecurity incident. It includes recovery planning, improvements, and communications.

Manufacturers can build a resilient and trustworthy digital ecosystem by integrating these elements into their cybersecurity strategies. This will enable them to fully leverage the benefits of the circular economy while ensuring robust protection against cyber threats.

10.5 Digital Warranties in the Circular Economy

During our discussion of the 1 + 5R model in Part II, we repeatedly identified extendable warranties as enablers of a circular economy. By leveraging digital capabilities, manufacturers can create easily transferable, extendable, and verifiable warranties (Fig. 10.5).

Digital warranties should be easily transferable to new owners or users. This ensures the warranty's value is retained throughout the product's lifecycle, even as it changes hands. A seamless digital transfer process enhances trust and incentivizes customers to participate in circular practices, such as reselling or sharing products.

Warranties should be extendable after a product undergoes repair or refurbishment. To do that efficiently, digital verification processes confirm that repairs or refurbishments meet the required standards, qualifying the product for an extended warranty.

Products remanufactured to meet original specifications should receive a new warranty. This reassures customers of the product's quality and durability and promotes confidence in remanufactured goods.

Manufacturers digitally verify and issue warranties for products sold by third parties, including recommerce platforms and certified refurbishers. This ensures that customers buying refurbished or pre-owned products receive the same level of warranty protection.

To avoid customer confusion, manufacturers should consider standardizing digital warranties. A standardized approach simplifies warranty management for customers, repairers, and refurbishers who might otherwise struggle with multiple, varying digital warranty concepts.

Digital warranties integrate seamlessly with IoT devices and circular service providers' IT systems. This integration allows for automatic tracking and verification of repairs, making it easier for repairers and product owners to understand what is covered under warranty and for manufacturers to issue warranties after repair.

Manufacturers must ensure that repairs, refurbishments, and remanufacturing processes meet the required standards. Digital verification tools can authenticate that all procedures have been correctly followed, thus qualifying the product for warranty extension or reissuance.

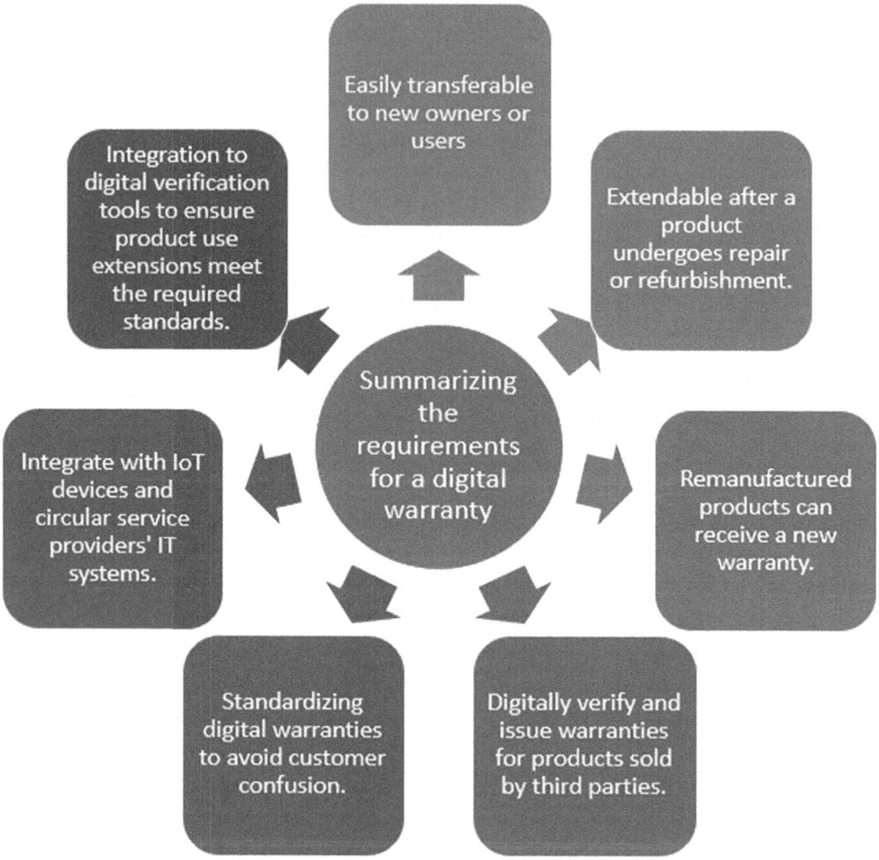

Fig. 10.5 Summarizing the requirements for a digital warranty

10.6 Digital Contracts in the Circular Economy

In a circular economy, there will be an increase in agreements and contracts across various phases, including redistribution, extending the use of products through repair and remanufacturing, and recycling. These contracts often involve multiple providers within the circular ecosystem. Incorporating digital contracts into the circular economy framework supports managing the increased agreement volume. Contracts created by things authorized by their owners, such as IoT-enabled devices that can request repairs, add another layer of complexity. Digitizing and standardizing contracts ensures efficiency, transparency, and seamless integration across the ecosystem.

Smart contracts are an emerging technology designed to standardize and automate agreements. These contracts are self-executing, with the terms written directly into the code. They are often stored on a blockchain, making them immutable, transparent, and secure. Smart contracts automatically execute actions when specific conditions are met. This automation reduces the need for intermediaries, speeds up processes, and minimizes the risk of human error. For example, a smart contract could initiate a repair request when a product's sensor detects a malfunction, streamlining the maintenance process. Another smart contract could automatically release payment to a recycling vendor as soon as the delivery of recycled materials is confirmed and validated through connected IoT devices. Additionally, a procurement order for refurbished parts could be triggered when inventory levels at a manufacturing facility drop below a specified threshold.

10.7 Digitization Checklist

This chapter has examined the fundamental digitization aspects essential for integrating circular principles into manufacturing operations. The checklist below outlines specific steps manufacturers should follow to execute the strategies discussed (Table 10.2).

Table 10.2 Digitization Checklist

Task	Methodology	Expected outcome	Risk mitigated
Understand how the SMIF enables a digital circular economy	Read this book	Comprehensive understanding of digital circular economy strategies	Misalignment with circular economy goals
Implement APIs	Define API endpoints and develop management tools	Seamless data exchange and improved system integration	Incompatibility issues between different systems
Ensure API security	Implement authentication and encryption protocols	Secure data transmission and enhanced trust	Data breaches and unauthorized access
Develop event-driven architecture	Create a real-time event processing system and pub-sub model	Improved decision-making and operational efficiency	Delayed responses to critical events
Develop digital warranties	Create a digital warranty platform and ensure easy transferability	Increased customer trust and participation in circular practices	Lack of customer confidence in warranty processes
Implement smart contracts	Develop and test self-executing contracts	Streamlined agreements and reduced human error	Delays and errors in contract execution

References

Chandramouli, R. (2019, August). *NIST SP 800–204 – Security strategies for microservices-based application systems*. Retrieved from NIST – Computer Security Resource Center: https://csrc.nist.gov/pubs/sp/800/204/final

NIST. (2024). *The CSF 1.1 Five Functions*. Retrieved from https://www.nist.gov/cyberframework/getting-started/online-learning/five-functions

Internal IT: The Backbone System of Circular Business Models

11

Abstract

Internal IT systems enable manufacturers to transition to a circular economy. These systems support real-time monitoring, product ecodesign, waste management, and green procurement. Effective supply chain management tracks, assesses, and processes returned items, transforming reverse logistics into a strategic asset. Evolved CRM systems foster sustainable dialogues with customers throughout the product lifecycle, promoting responsible consumption and facilitating recycling and returns.

Internal IT must support redistribution business models like recommerce, Product-as-a-Service, and sharing economy models, optimizing resource utilization and customer engagement. Modules for repair, refurbishment, and remanufacturing extend product lifecycles, ensuring products remain functional longer. Systems facilitate efficient logistics for product returns and recycling, ensure regulatory compliance, and optimize the use of recycled materials.

Waste Management Systems (WMS) should integrate AI to optimize waste sorting and processing. Quality Control Systems (QCS) ensure consistent quality standards for repaired, refurbished, and remanufactured products. Inventory Management Systems (IMS) manage refurbished parts and recycled inputs, supporting circularity and reducing waste. Circular design tools enable the creation of sustainable products with extended lifespans. Lifecycle Assessment (LCA) tools provide comprehensive metrics, emphasizing resource efficiency and regulatory compliance.

A strategic overhaul of internal IT systems, leveraging AI, IoT, and predictive analytics, is essential for a thriving circular economy.

H. H. Jensen, *Circular Economy Opportunities and Pathways for Manufacturers*, Future of Business and Finance, https://doi.org/10.1007/978-3-031-75279-7_11

Key Messages

- *Internal IT Systems Capabilities to Support Circularity:* Internal IT systems facilitate manufacturers' transition to a circular economy by providing real-time monitoring, product ecodesign, waste management, and green procurement.
- *Supply Chain Management:* Effective circular supply chains require capabilities to track, assess, and process returned items, transforming reverse logistics into a strategic asset.
- *CRM Systems Evolution:* CRM systems must extend beyond sales to foster sustainable dialogues with customers throughout the product lifecycle, promoting responsible consumption and facilitating recycling and returns.
- *Redistribution Business Models:* Internal IT systems must support various roles in redistribution, including managing recommerce, Product-as-a-Service, and sharing economy models to optimize resource utilization and customer engagement.
- *Product Use Extension:* Modules for repair, refurbishment, and remanufacturing processes are essential for maximizing product lifecycles, ensuring products remain functional and valuable for longer periods.
- *Recycling Support:* Systems must facilitate efficient logistics for product returns and recycling, ensure compliance with regulations, and optimize the use of recycled materials in production.
- *Waste Management Systems (WMS):* WMS must integrate advanced technologies like AI to optimize waste sorting and processing, ensuring waste is managed sustainably and efficiently.
- *Quality Control Systems (QCS):* QCS ensure that repaired, refurbished, and remanufactured products meet consistent quality standards, incorporating feedback loops for continuous improvement.
- *Inventory Management System (IMS):* IMS manages the flow of refurbished parts and monitors recycled inputs, optimizing inventory levels to support circularity and reduce waste.
- *Circular Design Tools:* These enable designers to create modular, sustainable products with extended lifespans, incorporating real-time feedback and AI for material selection.
- *Lifecycle Assessment Tools:* LCA systems provide comprehensive lifecycle metrics, emphasizing resource efficiency and compliance with circular economy regulations and standards.
- *AI-Driven Decision Support:* AI tools analyze product conditions, market demand, and service provider capabilities to recommend optimal circular activities, integrating with supply chain management systems for streamlined operations.
- *Procurement Systems:* Procurement systems must evaluate the lifecycle cost of products, facilitate the purchase of recycled materials, and manage contracts with suppliers involved in circular practices.
- *Technical Debt Management:* Addressing technical debt is crucial for modernization and a successful transition to a circular economy, as existing debts can hinder agility and innovation.

Internal IT systems facilitate manufacturers' transition to a circular economy. They are not just operational backbones but multifunctional hubs that empower real-time monitoring, product ecodesign, waste management, and green procurement. These systems derive value from connected products, customer interactions, business intelligence, and business ecosystem initiatives. They streamline traditional and circular business processes, providing the necessary capability, data, and insights for a confident and successful transition to a circular business model.

The specific capabilities of an internal IT system depend on the chosen circular business models and the manufacturer's role within the circular economy. Whether focusing on product lifecycle extension, resource recovery, or service-based models, IT systems must be adaptable and robust to meet these varying needs. This chapter will delve into the capabilities that internal IT systems must support depending on the chosen business model, inspiring manufacturers to understand and adopt the necessary technological enhancements. Some of these capabilities may be new to many manufacturers, or their coverage may need to be expanded beyond their present scope.

By understanding the intersection of IT systems and circular business models, manufacturers can identify and implement digital tools and processes that align with their strategic objectives, ensuring they are well equipped to thrive in a circular economy.

To demonstrate the combined role of the internal IT system, a fictive example has been created in Example 1. We will follow the role of the internal IT throughout a product's lifecycle. The details will be covered in the rest of the chapter.

Example 11.1 A fictive example of internal IT Systems involved in a product's lifecycle

SmartFlow Pumps Inc. is a fictive manufacturer of high-efficiency pumps. The company's internal IT supports the entire lifecycle of its products, from design and production to usage, maintenance, and end-of-life management.

SmartFlow Pumps Inc. designs pumps that are modular and easy to disassemble. The design phase leverages Circular Design Tools integrated with the company's internal IT systems. The procurement system ensures products are made from recyclable materials and designed for longevity and repairability. AI-driven decision support tools analyze materials and predict their lifecycle impacts, optimizing the design for sustainability.

Initially, the pumps are offered to industrial clients and residential customers through a PaaS model. Each pump is equipped with IoT sensors and a digital product passport.

Under the PaaS model, the pumps continuously send performance data back to SmartFlow's central IT system. This real-time data is analyzed using predictive analytics to monitor the pumps' health and efficiency. For industrial clients, predictive maintenance alerts mean optimal performance and

(continued)

reduced downtime. Residential users benefit from automated maintenance reminders and tips accessible through a mobile app connected to SmartFlow's CRM system.

The PaaS model's billing is based on the volume of liquids pumped. The IoT sensors measure the liters of liquids pumped, and this data is sent back to SmartFlow's central system. The usage data is then used to generate accurate billing for customers, ensuring they are charged only for the actual volume pumped.

SmartFlow's internal IT infrastructure supports an event-driven architecture that responds to anomalies detected by the IoT sensors. The system triggers a maintenance request when a pump's performance deviates from its expected parameters. This request can automatically schedule a technician visit, order necessary parts from inventory, and update the digital warranty records. The warranty management system ensures all repairs are documented and covered under the product's digital warranty, which can be extended based on the product's usage data.

At the end of each PaaS contract, pumps are returned to SmartFlow for inspection and refurbishment. The Quality Control System (QCS) thoroughly checks each pump, ensuring it meets high-quality standards before sending it to the following user. This process involves cleaning, repairing, and upgrading the pumps as necessary. The digital product passport is updated to reflect the pump's maintenance history and readiness for the next deployment.

Once refurbished, the pumps are reassigned to new customers. The Inventory Management System tracks the availability and condition of each pump, and the Supply Chain Management (SCM) system coordinates the logistics for their delivery to the following user.

At the end of their overall lifecycle, pumps are returned to SmartFlow for final recycling. The SCM manages the return logistics. Functional parts are harvested from the pumps for reuse in new products or refurbished pumps. The Inventory Management System tracks the returned products, the harvested parts, and the recycled material.

11.1 Supply Chain Management for the Circular Economy

Traditional linear supply chains move products from production to consumption, while a circular approach also manages the product's lifecycle through redistribution, product use extensions, and recycling.

A supply chain management (SCM) system must encompass several capabilities that address the challenges and opportunities of circular operations. It should enable manufacturers to track their products from the raw materials via the production cycle to the end of use. This includes maintaining a record of returned, repaired, refurbished, or recycled products and their reintroduction into the supply chain. By providing better visibility, manufacturers can monitor their products' status, location, and condition at any stage in the production cycle. This makes it easier for them to make informed decisions about resource allocation, product design, and reverse logistics.

11.1.1 Reverse Logistics

Digitization transforms reverse logistics from a traditionally cost-centric function into a strategic asset. Reverse logistics involves managing the return of products from end-users to the manufacturer or the appropriate point in the supply chain for refurbishment, remanufacturing, or recycling. This requires a sophisticated integration of forward and reverse logistics powered by real-time data exchange among all supply chain participants.

Manufacturers require the ability to track, evaluate, and handle returned items to reclaim value from products at the end of their lifecycle. This involves managing return orders, inspecting and grading returned products, and implementing an efficient routing system to determine the best action for each item, whether reselling, refurbishing, or recycling.

Seamless data exchange among all participants in the supply chain is necessary for quick and accurate decision-making, improving the overall efficiency and effectiveness of reverse logistics operations. It is also important to integrate with external circular service providers. The systems should enable easy connections with these providers, allowing convenient access to repair, refurbishment, and recycling services.

Digitization must also support incentive programs that smooth reverse logistics. For example, a clothing retailer could implement a digital platform that tracks and rewards customers for returning worn garments. By offering store credit, discounts on future purchases, or even a deposit return, the retailer can encourage customers to bring back their used items. Similarly, an electronics manufacturer could use a digital system to offer trade-in credits or loyalty points for returning old devices, which can be refurbished or recycled. This digital approach streamlines the process, making it easier for customers to participate and for the company to manage returns efficiently.

11.1.2 Analytics

Circular supply chains are complex and require advanced data analytics to operate efficiently and drive innovation (Chap. 15 details the aspects of data-driven circularity). Predictive analytics can be used to forecast return volumes, optimize reverse logistics operations, and identify opportunities for improvements in products or processes. Meanwhile, prescriptive analytics can offer actionable recommendations to enhance circularity, such as adjusting manufacturing schedules based on the availability of recycled materials or identifying products suitable for refurbishment based on market demand.

Corporate sustainability reporting is becoming increasingly important. SCM can automate the collection and reporting of sustainability metrics throughout the supply chain. This can simplify the reporting process on circular economy efforts and their outcomes, which is valuable for stakeholders and regulatory bodies.

11.1.3 Regulations

As circular economy practices become more regulated, SCM must track and manage compliance with local and international waste, recycling, and product lifecycle management regulations. This includes supporting Extended Producer Responsibility (EPR) (Sect. 2.3), which requires manufacturers to manage their products' entire lifecycle, including take-back, recycling, and disposal. Tracking capabilities, information on product end-of-life handling, and take-back programs will benefit EPR compliance.

Compliance management tools offer real-time insights into regulatory changes and help manufacturers adapt their processes accordingly, ensuring continuous compliance and keeping them ahead of regulatory developments.

11.2 CRM Systems: Beyond Sales to Sustainable Dialogues

Customer relationship management (CRM) systems are designed to manage customer relationships across the product lifecycle, supporting circularity through continuous engagement and efficient management of circular activities. Traditionally, in the linear economy, a manufacturer's CRM system focused on interactions with immediate sales partners like distributors or resellers. In a circular economy, CRM must evolve beyond conventional functions to involve value chain customers throughout the product lifecycle. This shift means prioritizing continuous communication with end-users beyond the initial sales process.

An advanced CRM system should integrate various features and capabilities to promote a circular economy. This includes encouraging responsible consumption; these systems deliver educational content on correct product use, maintenance, and disposal to customers. Automated follow-up communications can engage customers at lifecycle milestones, prompting actions such as recycling or product returns. Efficient warranty management within the CRM system ensures seamless tracking and processing of repairs and replacements, enhancing compliance and customer satisfaction.

Transparency about products' materials and components, including their origins and recyclability, fosters trust and informed decision-making. Incentive programs can be developed to reward customers who participate in circular practices, such as take-back programs for recycling or opting for repairs.

CRM systems should also offer visibility into the circular supply chain, from sourcing recycled materials to end-of-life processes. They should streamline resource recovery and recycling services, facilitating product collection, processing, and recycling at the end of their lifecycle.

Integrating external circular service providers into the CRM platform includes tracking customer engagements with repair, refurbishment, and recycling services and facilitating easy access to these services directly through the CRM platform.

11.3 Redistribution Business Models

Manufacturers can take on various roles in redistribution business models (Chap. 5) that their internal IT systems must support.

11.3.1 Recommerce

A recommerce module facilitates the management of the entire recommerce lifecycle, from product intake, refurbishment, quality assurance, and inventory management to resale. This ensures a smooth process from the product's return to its resale, maintaining high product quality standards and customer satisfaction. The module enables tracking products through various stages of the reverse supply chain, from the collection and sorting to refurbishment and resale, minimizing disruptions and enhancing operational efficiency.

Advanced analytics and reporting capabilities track key performance metrics such as sales trends, refurbishment costs, and customer behavior, providing insights for making data-driven decisions, optimizing processes, and enhancing both profitability and sustainability of the recommerce operations.

Enhancing the customer experience supports personalized customer journeys, making it easy for customers to sell or exchange used products. Features such as detailed product information, including refurbishment history and quality assurance, build trust and loyalty. Additionally, offering incentives like store credits for returned items and streamlined checkout processes can improve customer satisfaction.

Real-time visibility into inventory and automated workflows automate routine tasks and provide real-time updates on inventory levels, refurbishment status, and customer orders. This reduces manual effort, minimizes errors, and ensures timely processing of recommerce activities.

The module must include robust security features to protect data integrity and confidentiality and support compliance with regulatory requirements related to data protection and environmental standards.

The process steps and their digitization are covered next (Fig. 11.1).

11.3.1.1 Product Usage

Customers use the product for its intended lifespan, which requires continuous monitoring of its performance and condition to understand wear and tear over time.

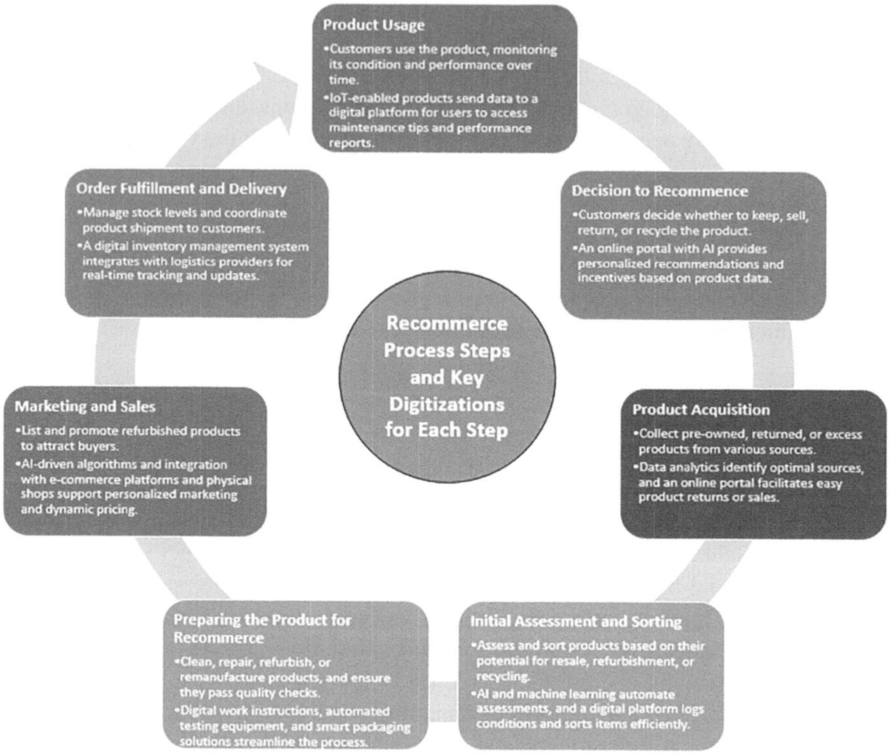

Fig. 11.1 Recommerce process steps and key digitizations for each step

Manufacturers provide a digital platform where users can access product usage data, maintenance tips, and performance reports. IoT-enabled products send usage and performance data back to the manufacturer, helping predict when the product will reach the end of its useful life.

11.3.1.2 Decision to Recommence

Customers decide whether to keep, sell, return, or recycle the product. Manufacturers offer incentives such as buyback programs, discounts on new purchases, or loyalty points for returning products.

An online portal or mobile app allows customers to evaluate the product's value, receive recommendations for the next steps based on product data, and initiate the return or sale process. AI offers personalized incentives and recommendations, supporting personalized customer journeys and improving customer satisfaction. Machine learning models can predict the best time for a customer to recommence based on usage patterns and historical data.

11.3.1.3 Product Acquisition

Collect pre-owned, returned, or excess products from consumers, businesses, and retailers. This step involves organizing the logistics for product return.

Data analytics identify optimal sources for product acquisition. An online portal enables customers to return or sell their products easily. The module enables tracking products through various stages of the reverse supply chain, minimizing disruptions and enhancing operational efficiency.

11.3.1.4 Initial Assessment and Sorting

Assess the condition of the acquired products to determine their potential for resale, refurbishment, or recycling. Products are sorted based on predefined criteria.

AI and machine learning automate initial assessments. A digital platform logs product conditions and sorts items efficiently. Real-time visibility into inventory and automated workflows provide updates on inventory levels, refurbishment status, and customer orders. Image recognition technology can quickly assess the physical condition of products.

11.3.1.5 Preparing the Product for Recommerce

This is where products are cleaned, repaired, refurbished or remanufactured, tested, and quality checked. Section 11.4.2 provides more details.

11.3.1.6 Marketing and Sales

List refurbished products on e-commerce platforms, the manufacturer's recommerce site, and physical shops. Implement marketing strategies to attract buyers, including digital advertising and social media campaigns.

AI-driven algorithms support personalized marketing and dynamic pricing. Integration with e-commerce platforms, own recommerce site, and physical shop systems ensures seamless listing and sales management. Advanced pricing and valuation algorithms optimize sales while supporting sustainability objectives.

11.3.1.7 Order Fulfillment and Delivery

Manage stock levels and prepare products for shipment. Coordinate logistics for timely and efficient delivery to customers.

A digital inventory management system integrates with logistics providers for real-time tracking and updates. Customers receive real-time tracking information, ensuring timely processing of recommerce activities.

11.3.1.8 Customer Support and Returns

Offer customer support to address inquiries and resolve issues. Manage returns efficiently, ensuring products are assessed for potential refurbishment or resale.

A CRM system manages customer interactions. A customer service management system supports ticketing and streamlines the return process. Chatbots and AI-driven support systems provide customers with instant assistance and troubleshooting.

11.3.1.9 Data Analysis and Continuous Improvement

Gather customer feedback on products and services. Analyze sales data, customer feedback, and operational metrics to identify areas for improvement.

Advanced analytics and machine learning identify trends and opportunities for process optimization. A dashboard monitors key performance indicators (KPIs). Advanced analytics and reporting capabilities track key performance metrics, providing insights for data-driven decisions and enhancing profitability and sustainability. Customer sentiment analysis tools gauge feedback from various channels, guiding strategic improvements.

11.3.2 Product-as-a-Service (PaaS)

A Product-as-a-Service (PaaS) module for manufacturers transitioning from traditional product-based models to service-oriented approaches includes various functionalities to ensure efficient management of subscriptions, usage-based billing, service delivery, and customer engagement.

The following section outlines the steps of a Product-as-a-Service process and the necessary digitization to support these steps (Fig. 11.2).

11.3.2.1 Product Design and Development

The journey begins with the meticulous design and development of products, focusing on durability, ease of maintenance, and upgradeability to extend their lifecycle.

Digital design tools and simulations optimize products for longevity and minimal environmental impact. Digital twins are implemented to monitor and improve product performance over time.

11.3.2.2 Subscription or Leasing Agreement

Following the design phase, products are offered to customers through subscription or leasing models rather than outright purchase.

An online platform manages these subscriptions, handles order management capabilities, and handles recurring billing and service contracts. Automated billing cycles manage various pricing models, ensuring accurate invoicing based on customer usage patterns.

11.3.2.3 Delivery and Installation

Once a subscription or leasing agreement is in place, the next step is to deliver and install products at the customer's location, ensuring proper setup and integration.

Logistics management software optimizes delivery routes and schedules, while IoT-enabled devices provide remote installation support and setup verification.

11.3.2.4 Usage Monitoring and Maintenance

After installation, the product's performance and condition are continuously monitored to ensure optimal functionality and preemptive maintenance.

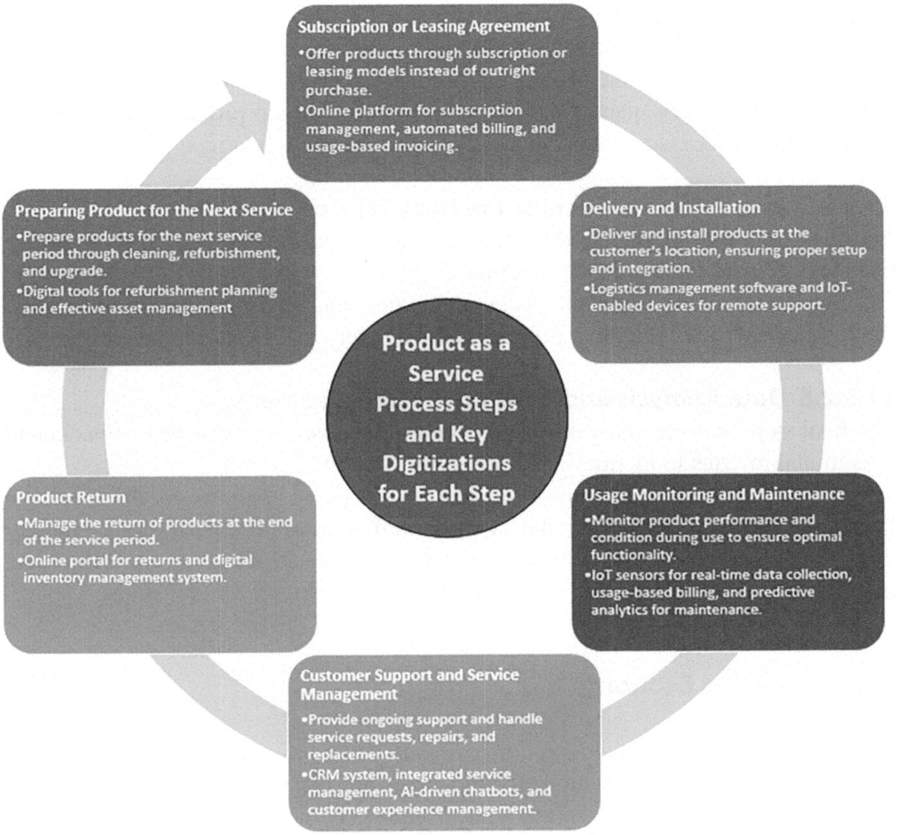

Fig. 11.2 Product-as-a-Service process steps and key digitizations for each step

IoT sensors collect real-time data on usage and performance, enabling usage-based billing and real-time consumption-based invoices. Predictive analytics facilitate predictive maintenance, reducing downtime and enhancing service reliability.

11.3.2.5 Customer Support and Service Management

Customer support is provided throughout the product's use, handling service requests, repairs, and replacements as needed.

A customer relationship management (CRM) system tracks and manages customer interactions, while integrated service management handles service orders, field service operations, and maintenance schedules. AI-driven chatbots offer instant support and troubleshooting, and customer experience management uses insights from customer behavior and preferences to deliver personalized services and proactive support.

11.3.2.6 Product Return

At the end of the service period, the product return process is managed efficiently through an online portal facilitating easy returns.

A digital inventory management system tracks returned products and manages refurbishment processes, ensuring a seamless transition to the next phase.

11.3.2.7 Preparing Product for the Next Service

Returned products are prepared for the next service period through cleaning, refurbishment, remanufacturing, and upgrades.

Effective asset management tracks, maintains, and optimizes the use of assets throughout their lifecycle, maximizing value delivery and extending asset life.

11.3.2.8 Data Analysis and Continuous Improvement

The final step involves analyzing data from product usage, customer feedback, and operational metrics to identify areas for improvement.

Advanced analytics and machine learning provide insights to optimize the Product-as-a-Service (PaaS) model. A dashboard monitors key performance indicators (KPIs), and continuous integration of customer feedback and interaction data helps enhance service offerings and build stronger customer relationships.

11.3.3 Sharing Economy

The sharing economy aims to maximize resource utilization through shared access, collaborative consumption, and efficient asset and service management. Digital support should include various functions to support resource sharing, improve operational efficiency, and promote stakeholder collaboration.

Real-time tracking of shared assets using an asset management module ensures the availability and condition of the shared resource. This includes monitoring usage patterns, scheduling maintenance, and predicting when assets will be returned or available.

Integrating booking systems enables customers to reserve shared assets easily. These systems should include calendar synchronization, availability checks, and automated notifications to streamline the reservation process.

Advanced analytics optimizes asset allocation, improves customer satisfaction, and identifies new sharing opportunities by gathering data on asset utilization, customer preferences, and the sharing model's overall performance.

Enhanced CRM capabilities are tailored to the sharing economy, focusing on managing customer interactions, feedback, and service requests. This includes features like personalized offers, loyalty programs, and detailed usage history to improve customer retention and satisfaction.

Flexible billing solutions handle pricing models typical in the sharing economy, such as pay-per-use, subscription-based, or hybrid. Secure and efficient payment processing systems ensure smooth transactions.

Facilitate communication and collaboration among users, enabling them to share experiences, provide reviews, and coordinate the use of shared assets. This fosters a sense of community and enhances the overall user experience.

11.4 Product Use Extension Modules

Product use extension modules are for manufacturers aiming to maximize the lifecycle and value of their products through repair (Chap. 6), refurbishment, and remanufacturing processes (Chap. 6.9). These modules help ensure that products remain functional and valuable for longer periods. By integrating these modules into their IT systems, manufacturers can efficiently manage and execute these processes.

11.4.1 Digitization Requirements for the Repair Process in a Circular Economy

The repair process restores defective or malfunctioning products to a functional state. This section details the steps involved in the repair process and outlines the digitization requirements essential for each step to enhance efficiency, quality, and customer satisfaction (Fig. 11.3).

11.4.1.1 Initial Assessment and Triage

The repair process begins when a customer contacts the service channel—be it an online portal, hotline, or in-store visit—or when an IoT-enabled product automatically reports an issue. Detailed information about the problem, including the symptoms and usage conditions, is collected. A preliminary diagnosis determines whether the issue can be resolved remotely or if the product requires physical inspection. This initial assessment helps streamline subsequent steps by ensuring only products needing detailed inspection are forwarded to repair centers.

The digitization of this step involves a repair module that facilitates the creation and management of maintenance orders. This system captures comprehensive information about the repair work required, including logging customer complaints and preliminary diagnoses. Integration with diagnostic tools and IoT devices is needed for real-time monitoring of product performance, enabling automated fault detection and reporting. Additionally, predictive maintenance capabilities should be incorporated to analyze historical and real-time data for potential failures, allowing for preemptive repairs and reducing downtime. AI-driven repair recommendations can further enhance the accuracy and efficiency of preliminary diagnoses.

11.4.1.2 Collection and Transportation

Once it is determined that the product needs physical inspection, logistics arrangements are made for collection or drop-off at a designated repair center. Proper packaging and secure transportation are essential to prevent further damage. This step

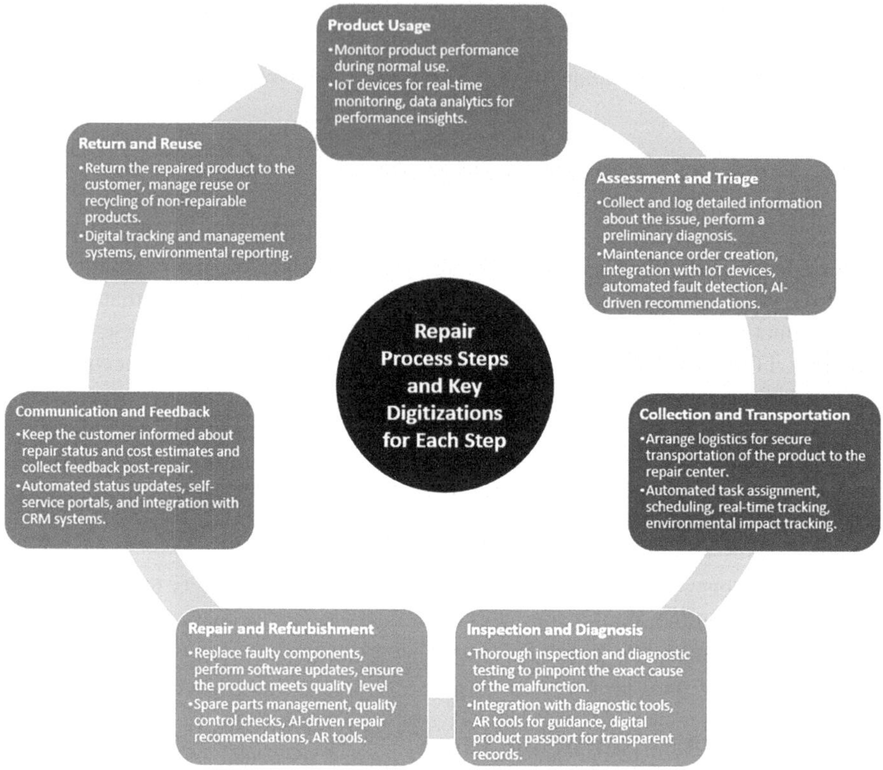

Fig. 11.3 Repair process steps and key digitizations for each step

ensures the product reaches the repair facility in good condition, ready for detailed inspection and repair.

The repair module automates the workflow from the initial repair request to the collection and transportation by assigning tasks, scheduling activities, and tracking each product's progress through the collection and transportation phases. This automation enhances operational efficiency, reduces delays, and ensures that all logistical aspects are handled smoothly and promptly. Mobile accessibility for logistics personnel to update and track transportation status in real time is also essential. Additionally, integrating environmental impact tracking to monitor the carbon footprint of logistics activities aligns with sustainability goals.

11.4.1.3 Detailed Inspection and Diagnosis

Upon arrival at the repair center, the product undergoes a thorough inspection to assess its condition. Diagnostic testing using advanced tools helps pinpoint the exact cause of the malfunction. Based on these findings, a detailed repair plan specifies the required parts and labor. This step is fundamental to ensure the repair addresses all underlying issues, restoring the product to optimal functionality.

The repair module must integrate seamlessly with diagnostic tools to facilitate accurate issue identification. Capturing and specifying the required parts and labor within the system is vital for creating detailed maintenance orders. Augmented reality (AR) tools can assist technicians with real-time guidance and interactive troubleshooting during inspections, improving accuracy and efficiency. Utilizing digital product passport or blockchain technology for the transparent and traceable recording of diagnostic results and repair histories can further enhance reliability and accountability.

11.4.1.4 Repair and Refurbishment

The repair involves replacing faulty or worn-out components with refurbished or new parts and prioritizing reused or recycled materials where possible. Necessary software updates or reinstallations are performed to restore functionality. Rigorous testing ensures that the repair meets the required quality and safety standards. This step is crucial for guaranteeing the product is fully functional and reliable post-repair.

Effective spare parts management is essential for timely repairs. The repair module should track the availability of spare parts, manage inventory levels, and automate reordering processes to ensure necessary components are always on hand. Additionally, incorporating quality control checks at various stages of the repair process within the system ensures compliance with industry standards and regulations, maintaining high repair quality. AI can provide technicians with repair recommendations based on past data and patterns, speeding up the repair process and enhancing decision-making. AR tools for detailed guidance and secure access to repair manuals and procedures further support the repair work.

11.4.1.5 Customer Communication and Feedback

Throughout the repair process, keeping the customer informed about the status of their repair is essential. Regular updates, cost estimates, and notifications upon repair completion help maintain transparency and trust. After the repair, collecting customer feedback improves service quality. This step ensures the customer remains engaged and satisfied, reinforcing loyalty.

The repair module should include features for seamless communication with customers. Automated status updates, repair cost estimates, and post-repair feedback collection enhance the customer experience. Developing self-service portals where customers can track their repair status, view diagnostic reports, approve cost estimates, and provide feedback increases engagement and satisfaction. Integrating CRM systems to provide a holistic view of the customer journey enhances personalized communication and service.

11.4.1.6 Return and Reuse

Once the repair is completed, the product is returned to the customer, ensuring it is well-packaged and includes any necessary documentation, such as warranty details and a repair report. For products beyond repair, parts are assessed for reuse or recycling, and nonreusable components are disposed of properly. This step closes the repair loop, promoting sustainability by extending product life or recycling materials.

Automating the return and reintegration processes within the repair module helps streamline operations. Ensuring efficient handling of repaired or non-repairable products through digital tracking and management systems supports the overall circular economy goals by promoting reuse and proper recycling practices. Tracking and reporting the environmental impact of the return and reintegration processes, including carbon footprint and waste generated, further supports sustainability objectives.

11.4.1.7 Continuous Improvement

Analyzing repair data to identify common issues and trends is essential for continuous improvement. This analysis contributes to product design enhancements and reduces future failures. Ongoing training for repair technicians ensures that skills are up-to-date with new technologies and repair techniques. Strengthening partnerships with suppliers of sustainable repair parts also plays a key role in this step.

Advanced analytics capabilities within the repair module provide insights into repair performance, common issues, and technician efficiency. Reporting tools help track key performance indicators (KPIs) and identify areas for improvement. Predictive maintenance insights and recommendations drive product innovation and enhance the overall efficiency of the repair process. Integration with CRM systems for a comprehensive view of customer interactions and feedback further supports improvement.

11.4.1.8 Customer Education and Engagement

Educating customers on proper product usage and maintenance is vital to prolonging their lifespan. Promoting repair services as a sustainable alternative to product replacement encourages responsible consumption. This step engages customers, fostering a deeper connection to the brand and its sustainability initiatives.

Implementing digital platforms to share product care tips and promote repair options enhances customer engagement and awareness. Mobile accessibility ensures a wider reach. Remote assistance tools, where experts guide customers through minor repairs using video calls and real-time annotations, increase engagement and satisfaction.

11.4.2 Remanufacturing Process Steps and Key Digitizations

In this section, we combine remanufacturing and refurbishment processes under the umbrella term "remanufacturing" (Chap. 7). Both processes involve restoring used products to a functional or like-new condition but differ in scope and depth. Remanufacturing typically involves a comprehensive disassembly and rebuilding of the product, while refurbishment may focus on minor repairs and cosmetic improvements. This section outlines the steps in remanufacturing and the digitizations required to support each step, ensuring efficiency, quality, and sustainability (Fig. 11.4).

Fig. 11.4 The remanufacturing process steps and key digitizations to support these steps

11.4.2.1 Product Return and Collection

The remanufacturing process begins when manufacturers collect end-of-life or used products. These products are returned to designated collection points or retrieved through a coordinated logistics system. This step ensures a steady supply of remanufactured products.

Integration with supplier systems includes logistics, handling returns, and coordinating with suppliers for parts. Predictive analytics is used to forecast the amount and condition of returned products.

11.4.2.2 Initial Inspection and Sorting

After collection, the products undergo an initial inspection to assess their condition. This inspection involves a preliminary check to identify defects and determine their potential for remanufacturing. The products are then sorted based on their condition, separating those suitable for remanufacturing from those that need recycling or disposal.

The module oversees all aspects of remanufacturing orders, from the initial assessment to the final quality checks. This involves logging the condition of returned products, planning necessary refurbishment tasks, and tracking the progress of each order through the remanufacturing process. An accurate assessment of the product's condition supports detailed inspections, grading products based on wear and tear, and determining the necessary refurbishment.

11.4.2.3 Disassembly

Products suitable for remanufacturing are carefully disassembled into individual components. This step requires meticulous attention to ensure proper handling of each part to avoid damage. Disassembly is crucial for a thorough cleaning, inspection, and eventual reassembly.

Digital support for structured disassembly and reassembly provides step-by-step guidance for technicians, ensuring that each component is handled correctly and reassembled. This includes maintaining a parts list and managing the workflow to ensure efficiency and accuracy.

11.4.2.4 Cleaning

After disassembly, each component is cleaned to remove dirt, debris, and residues that may have accumulated during use. Proper cleaning is essential to prepare the parts for inspection and testing and remove all contaminants.

The availability of remanufacturing instructions ensures that cleaning protocols are consistently followed, providing detailed guidelines for the appropriate cleaning methods and solutions for each type of component.

11.4.2.5 Inspection and Testing

Cleaned components are then inspected and tested to assess their functionality and quality. This step involves rigorous testing procedures to identify any defects or wear that may affect the performance of the remanufactured product. Components that fail to meet quality standards are either repaired or replaced.

Digitization ensures that remanufactured products meet stringent quality standards and integrates comprehensive quality control checks throughout the process, from initial inspection to final testing. This includes automated testing procedures and compliance with industry standards.

11.4.2.6 Repair and Replacement

Defective components identified during inspection are repaired or replaced with new or refurbished parts. This step ensures that all components used in the remanufacturing process meet the required performance and reliability standards.

Components that may be repurposed have their Digital Product Passport updated to reflect their new status and history. Efficient parts inventory management tracks the availability of components needed for rebuilding products, manages stock levels, and automates reordering processes. This ensures that necessary parts are always available when needed. It accurately tracks all remanufacturing costs, including labor, parts, and overheads. The module supports detailed cost analysis, enabling businesses to determine the profitability of their remanufacturing activities. This includes generating cost reports and processing billing.

11.4.2.7 Reassembly

Once all components are cleaned, inspected, repaired, or replaced, the product is reassembled. This step involves compiling the parts according to the original specifications, ensuring the product functions as intended.

Digital support for structured disassembly and reassembly provides step-by-step guidance for technicians, ensuring that each component is handled correctly and reassembled. Additionally, the Digital Product Passport is updated to reflect the remanufactured product, capturing all relevant details about the refurbishment process, parts replaced, and quality checks performed to ensure transparency and traceability.

11.4.2.8 Final Testing and Quality Control

The reassembled product undergoes final testing to meet the original specifications and quality standards. Comprehensive quality control checks are integrated throughout this process, from initial inspection to final testing, to ensure the remanufactured product is reliable and performs like new.

Ensuring that remanufactured products meet quality standards integrates quality control checks throughout the process, from initial inspection to final testing. This includes automated testing procedures and compliance with industry standards.

11.4.2.9 Painting and Finishing

After passing the final quality control checks, the product may require painting or finishing to restore its appearance. This step ensures that the remanufactured product looks as good as new and is ready for sale or use.

Advanced analytics tools offer robust reporting capabilities, tracking key performance indicators (KPIs) such as turnaround time, cost efficiency, and quality standards.

11.4.2.10 Packaging

The remanufactured product is then packaged for delivery or storage. Proper packaging protects the product during transportation and ensures it reaches the customer in excellent condition.

Integrating packaging modules ensures compliance with packaging waste legislation. This includes tracking packaging materials and processes to meet environmental standards.

11.4.2.11 Distribution and Sale

Packaged remanufactured products are distributed to customers or sales channels. This step involves coordinating logistics and ensuring timely delivery to meet demand.

Integration with partners' IT systems, including customer and supplier systems, facilitates distribution handling, streamlines operations, improves transparency, and enhances customer satisfaction by providing real-time updates and efficient supply chain management.

11.4.2.12 Continuous Improvement

Data from the remanufacturing process is analyzed to identify trends and areas for improvement. This step refines processes, enhances product design, and improves efficiency and quality.

Ensuring compliance with environmental regulations and sustainability goals supports tracking and reporting on sustainability metrics, such as waste reduction and the use of recycled materials.

11.5 Supporting Recycling and Circular Sourcing

While manufacturers typically do not conduct recycling themselves, they are often responsible for ensuring their products are efficiently returned to recyclers. This responsibility is driven by Extended Producer Responsibility (EPR) legislation or a business case for recycling. Managing internal production waste will be discussed in Sect. 11.6. Here, we outline the requirements for systems that support recycling and circular sourcing.

11.5.1 Facilitating Products for Recycling

Systems must enable logistical planning for the collection of end-of-life products. This includes long-term and short-term route planning to optimize the collection of materials from customers or designated drop-off points. Efficient route management ensures the timely and cost-effective transportation of materials back to recycling facilities. Third parties often handle return logistics.

Systems should support the integration of subcontractors and recycling partners to facilitate seamless operations. This includes managing order and contract data, handling incoming documents, and automating the creation of relevant order documents.

Real-time tracking of collected materials provides transparency over the material flow, from collection to recycling. This involves integrating mobile order management to document and track each step, ensuring accurate invoicing and efficient fleet utilization.

Systems must support comprehensive reporting functions to analyze recycling costs and ensure adherence to Extended Producer Responsibility (EPR) mandates, including calculating and projecting recycling fees. This ensures manufacturers meet legal obligations and sustain responsible product lifecycle management.

11.5.2 Sourcing Recycled Materials

Effective circular sourcing requires matching collected materials with production needs. Systems must support the detailed planning and management of material flows to ensure the right amount of recycled material is available for production. Optimization tools help in resource management and maintaining supply chain sustainability.

For circular sourcing, systems must facilitate the integration of recycled materials into new production. This requires accurate tracking of recycled content in materials, ensuring compliance with regulatory standards, and enabling manufacturers to meet sustainability goals.

11.6 Waste Management System (WMS)

Traditionally, waste management has been a linear process where waste is created and sent to landfills. However, in a circular economy, waste is considered a new input for another process, not the end product. Companies must integrate waste management systems beyond basic waste sorting to achieve this. These systems should ensure that waste from production processes is managed sustainably and efficiently (Sect. 8.6).

Enhanced waste management systems have features to help comply with waste management regulations. These include tracking hazardous materials, managing reporting requirements, and meeting international standards. This ensures that waste management activities follow the law and environmental guidelines.

Integrating AI and machine learning in waste management improves waste sorting and processing. These technologies can predict waste generation patterns, enabling the optimization of waste treatment processes. By leveraging predictive analytics, companies can better manage waste streams and anticipate future needs. Additionally, economic analysis tools are essential for assessing the cost-effectiveness of waste management initiatives and facilitating financially informed decisions that align with business goals. Advanced algorithms optimize resource use within waste management, ensuring sustainable and economically viable practices. These technologies help minimize waste generation, maximize recycling and reuse, and enhance overall resource efficiency.

Waste management systems (WMS) should integrate with external collaboration platforms to enable efficient information sharing and cooperation among stakeholders, including waste processors, regulatory bodies, and other businesses. This integration helps manage the complexities of waste management logistics by ensuring that all parties are informed and coordinated, leading to more effective waste handling and disposal.

Furthermore, integrating with by-product trading platforms allows enterprises to connect seamlessly with external platforms where waste materials can be sold, exchanged, reused, or repurposed in different industrial processes. This creates new revenue streams and reduces the environmental impact of waste by finding new uses for materials that would otherwise be discarded.

Example 11.2 Volkswagen Group's procurement division system for recovering waste materials

Volkswagen Group's procurement division has established a group-wide system for recovering waste materials that can generate income, such as paper, plastics, wood, electronic components, and metal (Volkswagen Group, 2021).

Modern waste management systems must be robust, incorporating advanced technologies and integration capabilities to support a circular economy. By doing so, companies can transform waste into valuable resources, comply with regulations, and achieve both environmental and economic benefits.

11.7 Quality Control Systems (QCS) for Product Use Extension

Quality Control Systems are implemented to ensure that repaired, refurbished, and remanufactured products meet the required quality standards. These systems should be designed to manage internal processes and oversee the quality of work done by third-party service providers involved in extending the use of products.

Manufacturers must establish standardized quality metrics for new and extended-use products. These quality standards help ensure that all items, whether new, repaired, refurbished, or remanufactured, meet consistent quality criteria. Implementing such standards provides a uniform basis for quality assurance across all product life stages.

The Quality Control Systems should adapt to different product types and extension processes, allowing customization and adjusting quality parameters for each item's specific needs.

Quality Control Systems should allow easy data exchange and quick communication with third-party providers specializing in repair, refurbishment, and remanufacturing. Shared digital platforms, standardized data formats, and APIs help efficiently flow information to ensure all parties have access to the necessary data to maintain quality standards.

A monitoring and verification system for the quality of work done by third parties is necessary. This can be achieved by conducting regular audits, tracking refurbishment processes in real time, and providing access to quality control results within the Quality Control System.

Feedback loops facilitate continuous improvement of quality control processes. They incorporate input from third-party service providers and customer feedback on product quality to inform ongoing adjustments to quality metrics and processes.

11.8 Inventory Management System (IMS)

Traditional inventory management systems aim to maintain optimal inventory levels for efficient operations. However, to support circularity, these systems need enhancements. Enhanced IMS will ensure minimal holding costs, reduce waste, and procure or produce resources based on actual demand, contributing to more sustainable and efficient operations.

Manufacturers must manage the flow of harvested and refurbished parts they receive. This includes monitoring the quantity, condition, and availability of components and products that have undergone refurbishing processes and are being reintroduced into the supply chain. An effective IMS should track these components meticulously to maintain a seamless flow of materials and parts.

IMS monitors recycled inputs' quality, type, and availability and incorporates this data into the production planning process. This ensures the efficient use of recycled materials that comply with quality standards, supports sustainable manufacturing practices, and reduces dependency on virgin materials.

Optimizing finished goods inventory involves monitoring products undergoing use extension processes and accurately forecasting demand. Manufacturers analyze market trends and customer behaviors by understanding and predicting the demand for items designated for redistribution. This enables better forecasting of the need for additional products, facilitating informed decision-making on increasing or decreasing production.

Differentiating between virgin and extended-use products, components, and materials is crucial. Proper classification and management help maintain transparency and integrity in product marketing and sales, aiding in reporting compliance and sustainability metrics. This distinction ensures customers are well informed about the nature of the products they purchase and supports regulatory compliance.

Predictive analytics enhance demand forecasting and inventory optimization. This capability allows manufacturers to accurately predict future inventory requirements by analyzing historical data and current market trends. Manufacturers can better align production with actual market needs by accounting for fluctuating demands for refurbished or remanufactured products.

Developing seamless integration capabilities with suppliers and circular service providers is essential. Real-time updates on supply chain activities help synchronize supply with demand and reduce inventory discrepancies. Such integration enables a more agile response to changes in the supply chain, enhancing overall efficiency.

The improved IMS should have advanced features such as real-time tracking systems for all inventory items, including raw materials, refurbished parts, and finished goods. This will enable immediate adjustments based on current inventory levels and demand. It should also integrate quality assurance processes to ensure that all refurbished and recycled materials meet the required standards before being reintroduced into the production cycle. Additionally, the IMS should encompass comprehensive product lifecycle management, tracking each item's journey from initial production through multiple use phases and eventual recycling or disposal. By incorporating sustainability metrics into the IMS, detailed reporting on the environmental impact of inventory practices, including carbon footprint, waste reduction, and resource efficiency, can be facilitated. Lastly, the use of automated reordering systems that trigger procurement processes based on real-time inventory levels and predictive demand analytics will ensure that materials are available when needed without overstocking.

Manufacturers can achieve more sustainable and efficient operations by enhancing traditional inventory management systems to support circular economy principles. These systems will optimize inventory levels, reduce waste, and ensure that resources are used effectively.

11.9 Circular Design Tool

Circular design tools allow designers to create products intended for use, redistribution, product use extension, and recycling. These tools incorporate advanced technologies and real-time feedback mechanisms to improve every stage of the design process.

Incorporate functionalities that enable the bill of materials (BOM) to be updated based on continuous feedback from the product lifecycle. This feedback includes data from customer use, returns, recycling procedures, and supplier innovations. By continually refining the BOM, designers can ensure that the materials and components are suited for circularity.

Equip designers with tools to create modular products that are easier to upgrade, repair, and recycle. This capability supports the extension of product lifespans by making it simple to replace individual components instead of entire products.

Design tools should incorporate feedback on environmental impact and product usability to enhance circularity. This feedback can improve disassembly ease and material durability.

Designers can select sustainable and recyclable materials by connecting design tools with current supplier databases. This ensures access to the latest materials that align with circular principles.

11.9.1 Analysis

AI analyzes extensive material properties and sustainability metrics databases to help select materials that meet functional needs and align with circular economy goals. It then suggests optimal options for specific product applications.

Simulation tools help designers incorporate circularity considerations early on, ensuring optimal performance throughout the product lifecycle, including product use extension and recycling. These tools also enable the exploration of different end-of-life options. By simulating disassembly, designers can assess how easy it is to take a product apart for repair, refurbishment, or recycling and identify opportunities for remanufacturing.

By incorporating life cycle cost analysis tools into the design process, designers can evaluate their circular design choices' economic and environmental impacts. These tools can analyze the cost-effectiveness and environmental benefits of using recycled materials, easy disassembly, and other circular practices.

11.9.2 Supporting Packaging Waste Management

A circular design tool offers tracking and reporting features to monitor packaging materials. This includes detailed household and non-household packaging records and branded and unbranded items. Accurate data tracking enables companies to maintain comprehensive documentation for internal sustainability goals and external regulatory reporting.

To manage packaging waste obligations (Sect. 2.4), the module must integrate with existing systems to extract and analyze relevant data on packaging compositions and material flows. This will help companies fulfill their responsibilities in managing the lifecycle of packaging materials, reducing waste, and increasing recycling rates. It should also stay updated with the latest regulatory changes and ensure that all packaging materials and designs comply with current laws. Additionally, the module should generate accurate and timely reports for regulatory authorities, simplifying compliance processes and reducing the administrative burden on companies.

The tool simulates and evaluates the economic and environmental impact of different packaging materials and designs. It provides insights into the lifecycle impacts of various packaging options, helping companies make informed decisions. This includes recommendations for using recyclable or biodegradable materials and strategies for minimizing excess packaging, thus enhancing overall performance.

Modules for tracking compliance with regulations and standards related to materials and product design ensure that all designs adhere to the latest regulatory requirements, thereby reducing non-compliance risk.

Example 11.3 Henkel opted for SAP Responsible Design and Production

Henkel AG,[1] a company with a legacy spanning over 145 years, is known for its brands in hair care, laundry and home care, adhesives, sealants, and functional coatings.

To successfully distribute its products in Spain and the United Kingdom, Henkel faced challenges due to strict plastics tax laws. Additionally, the company had to furnish its customers with comprehensive sustainability data to adhere to local regulations and enable them to evaluate the environmental impact of their product selections.

To tackle these challenges, Henkel opted for SAP Responsible Design and Production. This helped create compliant and efficient tax reports for business users, reduce manual and time-consuming data validation and reporting, and improve the accuracy of sustainability data through intelligent processing.

Moreover, Henkel gained valuable insights into product and packaging design, leading to increased efficiency and value. The company improved collaboration, analytics, forecasting, and simulations for sustainable packaging (SAP, 2024).

11.10 Lifecycle Assessment Tools

Lifecycle assessment (LCA) systems provide tools to analyze and enhance products' environmental and economic performance throughout their lifecycle. These systems should include comprehensive lifecycle metrics to evaluate impacts across redistribution, repair, refurbishment, remanufacturing, and recycling. Real-time

[1] https://www.henkel.com/

feedback mechanisms should integrate with product design tools to provide immediate insights into design choices' environmental and economic impacts.

LCA systems should emphasize resource efficiency by evaluating material recovery rates, durability, and potential for future reuse or remanufacturing. They must also simulate various end-of-life strategies to balance economic feasibility and environmental impact. Compliance monitoring and detailed reporting ensure adherence to circular economy regulations and standards.

Moreover, LCA tools should facilitate sharing of detailed lifecycle data with all stakeholders in the circular economy ecosystem, from material suppliers to end-users and third-party refurbishers. Predictive analytics within these systems can anticipate the effects of different lifecycle options and prepare for changes in product usage patterns, such as increased demand for refurbishment services. Monitoring materials across multiple usage cycles gives insight into the circular supply chain, ensures transparency, and builds trust among customers and stakeholders regarding the circularity of materials and products.

11.11 AI-Driven Decision Support Tools for Circular Activities

Manufacturers must identify their products' most effective circular activities throughout their lifecycle. Leveraging artificial intelligence (AI) can enhance this process. AI-driven decision support tools analyze various factors, such as the product's condition, market demand, and the capabilities of circular service providers, to suggest optimal next steps for each product.

The AI tool begins by assessing the product's physical condition using data from sensors, inspections, or user inputs. It evaluates wear and tear, functionality issues, and other factors that impact the viability of reuse, repair, refurbishment, or recycling. It then analyzes current market trends to understand the demand for different circular outputs. For instance, high demand for refurbished items in a specific category would lead the tool to prioritize refurbishment activities.

Additionally, the tool assesses the availability and capabilities of circular service providers, determining which providers can handle specific activities like repair or refurbishment and their capacity to manage the products. Following a comprehensive analysis, the AI tool recommends specific circular activities for each product based on environmental impact, cost-effectiveness, potential recovery value, and alignment with sustainability goals.

The decision support tool integrates with broader supply chain management systems to ensure seamless operations, coordinating logistics, scheduling, and inventory management with the recommended circular activities. This integration streamlines operations and enhances efficiency across the supply chain.

Furthermore, the AI tool features a continuous feedback loop, learning from outcomes and feedback. As products undergo recommended circular processes and market conditions evolve, the AI system adapts its algorithms to refine future recommendations, improving accuracy and relevance over time.

11.12 Procurement Systems for Circular Economy

Procurement systems should consider the entire lifecycle cost of products and accurately value those designed for circularity. These systems must facilitate the purchase of virgin materials and recycled content and engage in industrial symbiosis, ensuring diverse material sources.

Procurement systems equipped with lifecycle cost analysis tools enable the evaluation of the total cost of ownership throughout the product lifecycle. This aids in prioritizing products with longer lifespans and ease of maintenance, repair, refurbishment, or recycling. These systems also support sourcing refurbished and remanufactured products and components.

Comparative analysis capabilities allow procurement systems to evaluate the cost-effectiveness and practicality of owning products versus procuring services. This helps companies decide between leasing or subscribing to services and owning physical assets, determining the most beneficial approach.

Procurement systems facilitate the procurement of repair, maintenance, refurbishment, and recycling services to simplify buying circular services. Efficient contract management ensures that terms are met and logistics for returning products are smoothly executed, effectively managing contracts with suppliers involved in take-back programs for product return or end-of-life management.

Transparency and traceability features ensure verification of recycled content claims and responsible material sourcing, thus maintaining supply chain integrity.

11.13 Technical Debt: A Mounting Challenge in the Circular Transition

Technical debt is the cost of delaying necessary work during software system development. It is the price you pay to choose a quicker and easier solution instead of using a better approach that might take longer. Like financial debt, technical debt accumulates "interest" over time through increased costs and complexity. Organizations end up spending more resources on maintenance and remedial work instead of innovation.

In the traditional linear economy, businesses already face challenges posed by technical debt. Whether it's legacy systems that cannot be easily replaced or shortcuts taken to reach the market quickly, these debts must be managed carefully to maintain growth and responsiveness.

The circular economy is introducing new levels of complexity for companies. As they adopt new circular business models, they must incorporate new circular capabilities into their existing systems. This integration process requires reconfiguring and upgrading internal systems, ranging from customer relationship management to supply chain management. Such changes may aggravate existing technical debts.

The move to a circular economy amplifies the need for modernization. If not addressed, existing technical debts can slow down this transformation. However, the focus should be on more than just managing this debt. Instead, the emphasis should be on modernizing the entire operational framework to make it compatible with circular principles.

Modernization in the context of a circular economy involves more than just fixing old systems. It requires creating a robust, adaptable, intelligent core supporting circular business models. This core equips organizations with the ability to be more innovative and agile, enabling them to navigate the complexities of a circular economy effectively.

Therefore, modernization should be considered an immediate priority. Delaying this process will make it more challenging and more resource-intensive to transition to a circular model later on. Addressing technical debt is not a future concern but a pressing priority today. As organizations incorporate circularity into their core business models, the "interest" on existing technical debt will accelerate. Neglecting this could hinder a company's agility and innovation in evolving its circular business models.

11.14 Key Digital Capabilities Required for Internal IT Systems in Circular Business Model

The capability map in Fig. 11.5 outlines the essential digital capabilities that manufacturers must integrate into their internal IT infrastructure to support and thrive in circular business models.

11.15 Checklist to Adopt Internal IT Systems to Support Circular Business Models

This transition to circularity necessitates a strategic overhaul of internal IT systems to support new business models. Internal IT systems are the backbone of circular business models, coordinating and optimizing various functions such as supply chain management, customer relationship management, waste management, and quality control. By leveraging advanced technologies like AI, IoT, and predictive analytics, these systems provide real-time insights and capabilities crucial for a thriving circular economy.

This checklist guides manufacturers through the tasks, methodologies, expected outcomes, and risk mitigations required to align their internal IT systems with circular business principles. By following this roadmap, manufacturers can ensure they are well equipped to thrive in a sustainable and economically viable future (Table 11.1).

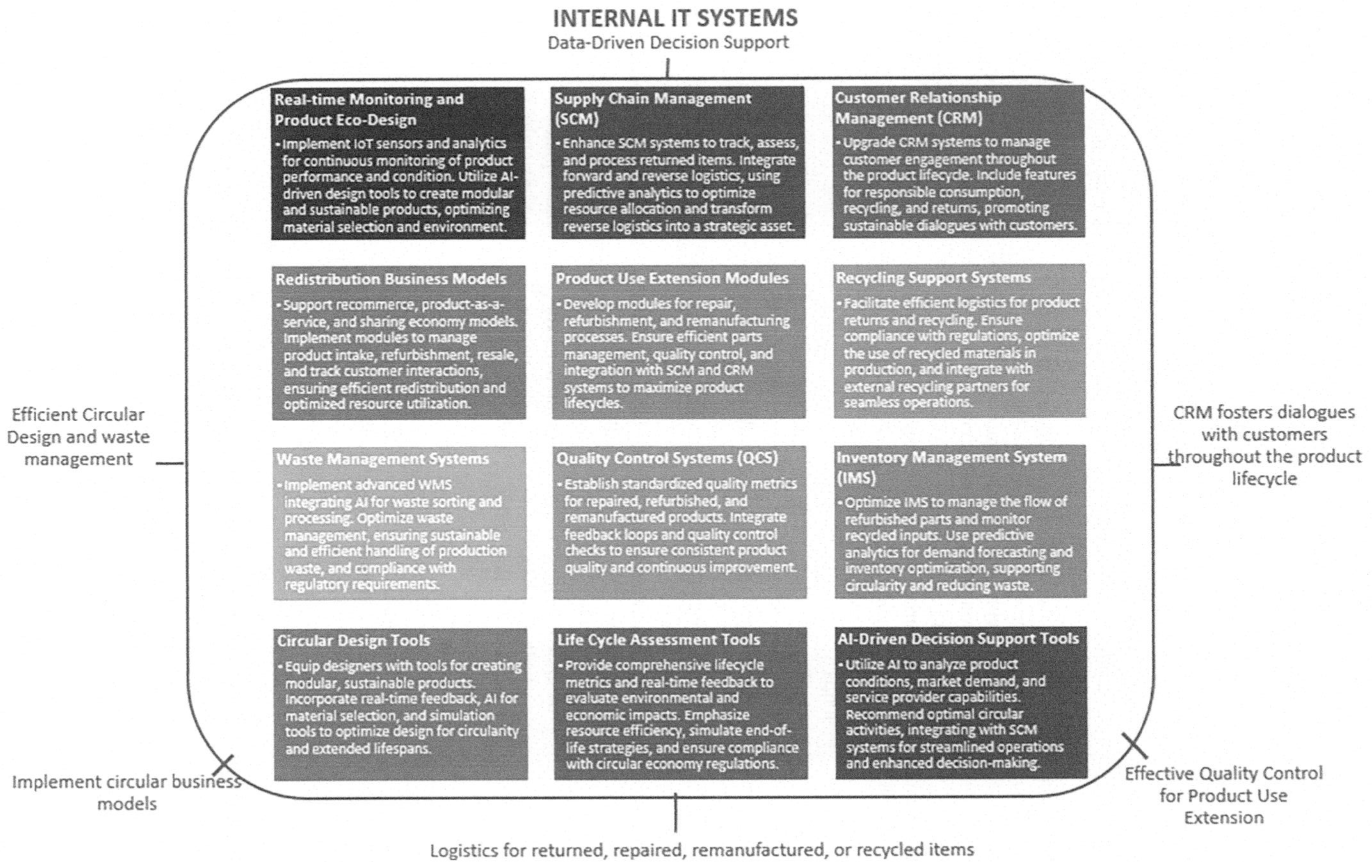

Fig. 11.5 Key digital capabilities required for internal IT systems in circular business model

Table 11.1 Checklist to adopt internal IT systems to support circular business models

Task	Methodology	Expected outcome	Risk mitigated
Implement advanced SCM systems	Integrate forward and reverse logistics, utilizing real-time data exchange and predictive analytics	Improved tracking and processing of returned items, optimized resource allocation	Inefficiency in reverse logistics and inability to recapture value from end-of-life products
Upgrade CRM systems	Extend CRM capabilities to include customer engagement for product lifecycle and integrate sustainability features	Enhanced customer dialogues, increased participation in recycling and returns	Lack of customer engagement and low participation in circular practices
Integrate Waste Management Systems (WMS)	Utilize AI and machine learning for waste sorting Integrate with external collaboration platforms	Optimized waste management, improved regulatory compliance	Inefficient waste processing and failure to meet regulatory requirements
Enhance Quality Control Systems (QCS)	Implement standardized quality metrics, integrate with third-party providers, and establish feedback loops	Consistent quality of repaired, refurbished, and remanufactured products	Variability in product quality and customer dissatisfaction
Optimize inventory management system (IMS)	Monitor recycled inputs, integrate predictive analytics, and differentiate between virgin and extended-use products	Efficient use of recycled materials and reduced inventory costs	Overstocking and underutilization of recycled components
Deploy circular design tools	Use AI for material selection and incorporate feedback on environmental impact	Creation of modular, sustainable products with extended lifespans	Designing products that are not aligned with circular economy principles
Implement lifecycle assessment (LCA) tools	Integrate real-time feedback, emphasize resource efficiency, and simulate end-of-life strategies	Comprehensive lifecycle metrics, improved compliance with circular economy regulations	Incomplete understanding of product lifecycle impacts and non-compliance with regulations
Utilize AI-driven decision support	Analyze product conditions and market demand, recommend circular activities, and integrate with SCM systems	Optimized decision-making for circular activities, streamlined operations	Suboptimal product lifecycle management and missed opportunities for value recovery
Upgrade procurement systems	Evaluate lifecycle costs, facilitate the purchase of recycled materials, and manage contracts with circular suppliers	Cost-effective sourcing, increased use of recycled materials	High procurement costs and lack of transparency in material sourcing

(continued)

Table 11.1 (continued)

Task	Methodology	Expected outcome	Risk mitigated
Manage technical debt	Assess current technical debt, prioritize modernization, and create an adaptable and intelligent IT core	Modernized IT infrastructure, reduced technical debt	Increased maintenance costs and slowed innovation due to legacy systems
Support redistribution models	Implement modules for recommerce, Product-as-a-Service, and sharing economy, and track customer interactions and feedback	Efficient management of redistribution activities and increased customer engagement	Inability to efficiently manage recommerce and sharing economy models
Develop product use extension modules	Integrate repair, refurbishment, and remanufacturing processes, ensuring efficient parts management and quality control	Maximized product lifecycles, maintained product value	Inability to extend product lifecycles and high disposal costs
Facilitate recycling support	Plan logistics for product returns, integrate with recycling partners, and ensure compliance with EPR regulations	Efficient product return and recycling processes, improved regulatory compliance	Ineffective recycling processes and failure to meet EPR requirements

References

SAP. (2024). *Henkel Gains Sustainability Insights with SAP Responsible Design and Production.* Retrieved from https://www.sap.com/products/responsible-design-and-production.html

Volkswagen Group. (2021). *Circular Economy.* From https://www.volkswagen-group.com/en/publications/more/circular-economy-2342/

Digital Business Ecosystem's Role in a Circular Economy

12

Abstract

Digital ecosystems are pivotal for circular economies, enabling seamless interactions and data sharing among stakeholders. They foster interconnectivity and real-time communication, allowing dynamic adjustments for optimal efficiency and sustainability. Data-driven decision-making leverages powerful analytics for transparency and informed choices, while automation and AI synchronize activities to minimize waste and optimize resources. These ecosystems ensure supply chain transparency, compliance, and efficiency, supported by strong cybersecurity measures to establish trust. Standardization and interoperability facilitate smooth integration among diverse platforms, and automated regulatory compliance systems keep up with regulatory changes. Manufacturers can enhance collaboration, make informed decisions, and efficiently manage complex stakeholder interactions by participating in such ecosystems, ultimately supporting sustainable and innovative business models.

The capability map highlights essential digital capabilities manufacturers need to thrive in such ecosystems, such as API management, event thinking, and enhanced supply chain transparency. Additionally, a checklist guides manufacturers through the tasks and methodologies required to participate effectively in digital circular ecosystems, ensuring seamless integration, robust security, and efficient resource utilization.

H. H. Jensen, *Circular Economy Opportunities and Pathways for Manufacturers*, Future of Business and Finance, https://doi.org/10.1007/978-3-031-75279-7_12

Key Message

- *The importance of digital ecosystems*: Digital ecosystems are essential for the circular economy as they enable seamless interactions and data sharing among various stakeholders.
- *Interconnectivity and real-time communication*: Interconnectivity and real-time communication act as the nerve system of the digital circular ecosystem, allowing stakeholders to adjust processes dynamically for optimal efficiency and sustainability.
- *Data-driven decision-making*: Digital ecosystems utilize powerful analytics to benefit all ecosystem stakeholders, driving transparency and informed decisions through collective circular intelligence.
- *Automation and AI*: Digital ecosystems enhance efficiency across the digital ecosystem by coordinating and automating activities among multiple stakeholders.
- *Supply chain transparency*: Digital ecosystems ensure visibility into the lifecycle of materials, parts, and products for compliance, traceability, and efficiency.
- *Trust and security*: Digital ecosystems establish trust through solid cybersecurity measures and secure data sharing to enable open collaboration in digital ecosystems.
- *Standardization and interoperability*: Digital ecosystems facilitate seamless communication and integration among diverse platforms and stakeholders through standardized protocols.
- *Regulatory compliance*: Digital ecosystems simplify adherence to regulatory requirements with automated systems that keep up with the latest regulatory changes.

A business ecosystem is a dynamic network of interconnected organizations, such as suppliers, producers, competitors, and customers, who collaborate and compete to create and deliver products and services. Unlike traditional supply chains, a business ecosystem is characterized by a more complex and mutually beneficial set of relationships that drive innovation, scalability, and efficiency. The ecosystem is enriched by the unique contributions of each participant, such as their capabilities, resources, or access to markets.

Technology and shared platforms, the backbone of digital business ecosystems, enable seamless interactions within the ecosystem, empowering participants to respond efficiently to new opportunities and challenges. These digital platforms provide the necessary infrastructure for smooth communication, transaction processing, and data sharing among entities. They help ecosystems to scale quickly by connecting more participants, managing complex data flows, and supporting new business models such as sharing economy, platform-based recommerce, coordination of product use extension, and data-driven decision-making.

Businesses that operate within a circular economy rely on a network of partners, including suppliers, manufacturers, value chain customers, consumers, and circular service providers. Each partner has a specific role to play in extending the lifespan of products. By participating in such ecosystems, companies can capitalize on each other's strengths, pool resources, and reduce waste, leading to cost savings and improved efficiency.

Example 12.1 Catena-X creates a standardized data exchange across the entire automotive value chain

Catena-X is a collaborative, open, and secure data ecosystem designed for the automotive industry. It was founded by industry leaders, including BMW, Mercedes-Benz, Volkswagen, Siemens, SAP, Robert Bosch, ZF Friedrichshafen, and Deutsche Telekom.

Catena-X is built to create a seamless and standardized data exchange across the entire automotive value chain. The initiative aims to enhance transparency, efficiency, circularity, and sustainability by enabling real-time data sharing among all participants.

Catena-X offers several key components to build a robust digital circular economy ecosystem.

Interoperable data platforms form the backbone of Catena-X. The ecosystem emphasizes the importance of standardized data formats and protocols to ensure interoperability among manufacturers, suppliers, and recyclers.

Collaborative networks are another cornerstone of Catena-X. It is essential to align the objectives of all stakeholders and make the incentives for participating in the ecosystem clear, whether they are cost savings, regulatory compliance, or market competitiveness.

Catena-X ensures that the digital ecosystem complies with existing regulations and anticipates future policies. Catena-X addresses this by aligning its operations with international standards and regulations related to data protection, environmental impact, and automotive industry requirements (Catena-X, 2024).

To illustrate the digitization of the entire circular business ecosystem, Example presents a fictive example featuring SmartFlow Pumps Inc. This fictive company manufactures industrial pumps and demonstrates how a digital business ecosystem enables circular economy practices throughout the product lifecycle. The digital concepts enabling such collaboration are covered in the rest of the chapter.

Example 12.2 A fictive example of the business ecosystem interactions

During the design phase, SmartFlow uses a collaboration platform to co-create with partners, including material suppliers and design experts. The platform enables sharing design blueprints and receiving real-time feedback from humans and GenAI, ensuring that the selected materials are sustainable and that designs are optimized for longevity and recyclability.

SmartFlow connects its purchasing system to an orchestration platform to manage the manufacturing process. This platform connects with suppliers, ensuring timely delivery of materials and parts.

SmartFlow implements IoT sensors on each pump, monitoring real-time performance and usage data. These sensors are connected to a centralized platform that tracks the pump's location and operational status, providing transparency to authorized users throughout the supply chain.

The IoT sensors send data to SmartFlow's analytics platform. The platform uses AI to predict maintenance needs. When a pump needs maintenance, the system automatically posts the task on a platform. Autonomous intelligent agents, authorized by the relevant party, negotiate the best maintenance deal based on preprogrammed instructions. The agreement is digitally signed in a smart contract. The autonomous agent schedules a technician visit and orders necessary parts.

Automated systems streamline the maintenance process. AI algorithms analyze usage data to predict failures and schedule proactive maintenance. Technicians receive detailed repair instructions via augmented reality (AR) tools, ensuring efficient and accurate repairs.

Maintenance activities are logged in a Digital Product Passport (DPP), which records all interventions, part replacements, and repair and recycling instructions. This transparency helps maintain compliance with environmental regulations and supports future recycling efforts.

When a pump reaches the end of its useful life, SmartFlow's digital platform facilitates its return. Customers can use the platform to find recycling or refurbishing partners, ensuring the pump is not discarded.

The platform uses collective data from various parties, like logistics service providers and recycling facilities, to optimize recycling processes. Shared dashboards provide insights into material availability and recycling opportunities, enabling SmartFlow and its partners to maximize resource recovery.

SmartFlow's digital ecosystem ensures compliance with environmental regulations through automated tracking and reporting systems. These systems keep abreast of regulatory changes and adjust processes accordingly, minimizing non-compliance risk and associated penalties.

To ensure trust and security, participants in the business ecosystem implement strong cybersecurity measures, such as encrypted data transmission and regular security audits. Digital identities and signatures verify stakeholder interactions, ensuring data integrity and secure collaboration.

Everyone in the ecosystem adheres to standardized API protocols to ensure seamless system-to-system communication. This standardization facilitates smooth data exchange, reducing operational inefficiencies and enhancing overall ecosystem performance.

12.1 Four Types of Digital Platforms Support Business Ecosystems

To participate in business ecosystems, manufacturers must consider four types of digital platforms: collaboration, orchestration, creation, and matching platforms. These platforms provide opportunities to optimize resources, enhance operational efficiencies, and drive profitability.

Collaboration platforms enable internal and external business ecosystem partners to collaborate and harness collective creativity. Manufacturers can, for example, share their invention ideas with a community and receive feedback.

Example 12.3 OpenIDEO's Circular Design Challenge

OpenIDEO organized the Circular Design Challenge to promote innovative designs that could contribute to a more circular economy. Participants from various industries were invited to share their ideas on how to redesign the way we produce and consume everyday products, with a particular emphasis on keeping materials in use and regenerating natural systems. Manufacturers, designers, and inventors submitted their concepts and received feedback from a global community. They collaborated to refine solutions that promote reuse, recycling, and sustainable manufacturing practices (Openideo, 2024).

Orchestration platforms streamline processes across multiple participants in the circular economy. They ensure smooth interaction between different stages of product lifecycles and supply chains.

Example 12.4 The International Material Data System (IMDS)

The International Material Data System (IMDS) is a platform that automotive manufacturers (OEM) and their suppliers use to manage and share comprehensive material data required for production and compliance. IMDS supports all parties' compliance with environmental regulations, such as the European Union's End-of-Life Vehicles (ELV) Directive.

IMDS is used by 95% of the world's automotive OEMs and thousands of tier suppliers, which amount to over 130,000 individual companies, to submit and manage their material data.

In IMDS, each company retains control over its data submissions; however, the data cannot be withdrawn once submitted. Data owners decide how much information they want to share and with whom, ensuring that sensitive information remains protected while supporting the industry's need for material transparency and traceability. This feature is critical for maintaining proprietary rights and data security (IMDS, 2024).

Creation platforms empower partners in business ecosystems to develop new applications, products, services, and business models. For instance, YouTube enables content creators to share their content with audiences, and audiences can also generate content.

Example 12.5 Thingiverse enables users to share and collaborate on 3D printable designs

Thingiverse[1] is a platform where users can share and collaborate on 3D printable designs. It has a variety of open-source designs that individuals and businesses can upload and access (Thingiverse, 2024).

Matching platforms connect supply with demand. They are aligning the availability of resources or services with those who need them.

Example 12.6 Rheaply facilitates resource exchange among businesses and institutions

Rheaply[2] is a platform that facilitates resource exchange among businesses and institutions. It allows them to list their surplus assets and materials on the platform for other entities to discover and acquire. In addition, Rheaply integrates environmental impact tracking, which provides participating organizations with data on their sustainability efforts and the positive environmental benefits derived from their participation in the reuse economy (Rheaply, 2024).

12.2 Who Controls the Digital Business Ecosystems

Manufacturers who want to incorporate digital platforms into their business processes must understand the control mechanisms governing them. How a platform is controlled can affect operational efficiencies, data governance, innovation potential, and competitive dynamics within the industry. The control over the platform can dictate the nature of interactions within the ecosystem, influence the interfaces between ecosystem participants, and determine the management and flow of data. This control enables the platform owner to analyze transactional data, continuously learn from interactions, and potentially become more intelligent with every transaction.

Manufacturers must consider whether a platform's control structure aligns with their strategic objectives and operational models. The choice of control mechanism—whether centralized, distributed, decentralized, or hybrid—has implications for how businesses interact with the platform, manage their data, and adapt to changes within the marketplace (Table 12.1). We will explore these control

[1] https://www.thingiverse.com/

[2] https://rheaply.com/

Table 12.1 Comparing controls in a digital business ecosystem

Aspect	Centralized control (orchestration)	Distributed control (choreography)	Decentralized control	Hybrid control (centralized orchestration with distributed data ownership)
Description	A trusted third party oversees all activities and decisions, ensuring harmony and coherence	Each participant performs their role independently, guided by predefined standards and protocols	Uses technologies like blockchain and smart contracts for autonomous coordination without central oversight	Combines centralized orchestration with distributed data ownership, maintaining centralized process control
Advantages	Efficiency and simplicity in decision-making and execution	Greater resilience and flexibility, allowing for innovation and quick responses	No single entity owns the platform	Streamlined decision-making with centralized oversight while ensuring data privacy and security
Challenges	Risk of monopolistic conditions and disproportionate power over the ecosystem	Difficulties in integration and coordination, slow adaptation to changes	Complicated dispute resolution and unanimous decision-making; potential inefficiencies if misaligned with business strategy	Balancing centralized and distributed elements creates potential conflicts between the central orchestrator and data owners
Decision-making	Quick and streamlined by one company	No central approval is needed; decisions are made independently by participants	Decisions are made through consensus mechanisms, ensuring no undue control	Centralized decision-making for processes, distributed control, and management of data
Integration and coordination	Central conductor ensures integration and coherence	Ensuring seamless interaction between autonomous operations is challenging	Autonomous coordination across a network without central oversight	Centralized process orchestration ensures harmony; distributed data ownership requires careful governance
Innovation and adaptability	Potentially stifled by central control	High flexibility allows for rapid innovation and adaptation	Innovation is driven by consensus but can be slowed by a lack of centralized direction	Balances centralized innovation direction with the flexibility of distributed data control
Risk of monopolization	High, as the central entity can dominate the market	Low, as no single entity has control	None, as platform ownership is decentralized	Medium requires governance to prevent central orchestrators from overpowering data owners

(continued)

Table 12.1 (continued)

Aspect	Centralized control (orchestration)	Distributed control (choreography)	Decentralized control	Hybrid control (centralized orchestration with distributed data ownership)
Data ownership	Centralized, controlled by the overseeing entity	Distributed among participants, guided by standards	Fully decentralized, managed autonomously across the network	Data ownership remains distributed, while process control is centralized
Use case suitability	Suitable for scenarios needing efficient and quick decision-making	Ideal for environments requiring high flexibility and rapid response to changes	Best for industry collaborations where central control is undesirable	Suitable for industry-wide platforms where centralized process control and distributed data privacy/security are needed
Example	Private companies or industry associations overseeing activities	Manufacturers, suppliers, and service providers work independently but collaboratively to create, maintain, and repurpose products	Blockchain-based platforms with smart contracts	International material data system (IMDS) platform

mechanisms below, discussing their advantages, challenges, and impact on the business ecosystem's functionality and the manufacturer's role.

12.2.1 Centralized Control (Orchestration)

Centralized control in ecosystem platforms is akin to an orchestra led by a conductor. A trusted third party, such as a private company or an industry association, oversees all activities and decisions. The central conductor ensures that each section plays at the right time, maintaining harmony and coherence across the platform.

The primary advantage of this setup is its efficiency and simplicity. As decisions are made by one company, decision-making and execution can be quick, streamlining operations and reducing time to market.

However, this model also introduces challenges. The centralized platform business landscape often exhibits a "winner-takes-all" scenario, where the controlling entity can emerge as the new industry leader, dominating the market, as we have seen with major tech companies in various sectors (Chap. 1). This poses the risk of creating monopolistic conditions where the platform controller has disproportionate power over the ecosystem.

12.2.2 Distributed Control (Choreography)

Distributed control in ecosystem platforms can be compared to a dance ensemble without a central coordinator. Each participant performs their role independently, guided by predefined standards and protocols. This approach offers greater resilience and flexibility, allowing for innovation and quick response to changes without centralized approval.

However, the lack of a central overseer can cause difficulties in integration and coordination, as ensuring seamless interaction between autonomous operations is challenging. Establishing and adopting robust standardization and mutual agreements can be challenging, and adapting them to changing conditions can be slow. This can impede the platform's agility, potentially delaying responses to new opportunities or threats.

In summary, while distributed control offers advantages in terms of flexibility and innovation, it requires standardization and collaboration frameworks to ensure integration and coordination across the platform.

12.2.3 Decentralized Control

Decentralized control leverages technologies like blockchain to store transactional data and smart contracts to autonomously coordinate ecosystem-wide processes to manage transactions and interactions autonomously across a network without central oversight. Within such platforms, decisions are made through consensus mechanisms, ensuring no single entity has undue control or influence.

A key advantage of decentralized control is that no single entity owns the platform. This makes it a candidate for industry collaborations where central control is undesirable, as it eliminates the possibility of one participant manipulating the platform for their advantage.

However, this model comes with its challenges. The lack of centralized decision-making can complicate the resolution of disputes or the making of unanimous decisions quickly. Additionally, the effectiveness of decentralized control can diminish if implemented alongside centralized technologies contradicting its fundamental principles. For instance, using decentralized technologies to uphold a fundamentally centralized business model could create inefficiencies and contradictions, potentially leading to failure. Therefore, evaluating whether decentralized technologies align with the intended business strategy and model ensures they are implemented only in environments where their benefits can be fully realized.

12.2.4 Hybrid Control (Centralized Orchestration with Distributed Data Ownership)

Hybrid control models combine aspects of centralized orchestration with distributed data ownership. The International Material Data System (IMDS) platform described previously in Sect. 12.1 is one example. In this model, the orchestration of processes and decision-making is centralized, while the control and management of data remain distributed among individual participants. This structure provides the efficiency and coherent governance of a centralized system, which ensures that all ecosystem or industry-wide interactions are harmonized and streamlined.

One advantage of the hybrid model is its ability to facilitate a streamlined decision-making process with centralized oversight while maintaining data privacy and security through distributed ownership. This model is often suitable for ecosystems or industry-wide platforms where competitive data should not be revealed to third parties and the benefits of centrally orchestrated processes are still desired.

Hybrid models also have challenges, particularly in balancing the centralized and distributed elements. Ensuring that the central orchestrator does not overpower the distributed nature of data ownership requires careful governance structures and transparent policies to prevent conflicts. Additionally, potential conflicts may arise between the central orchestrator and data owners regarding data access and utilization, necessitating robust conflict resolution mechanisms to maintain the platform's integrity and functionality.

Example 12.7 The EU's Vision for a Hybrid Control Model in Digital Product Passports

The European Union (EU) envisions the Digital Product Passport (DPP) as a key element in achieving a sustainable and circular economy. The DPP is designed to provide comprehensive information about a product's entire lifecycle, enhancing transparency, traceability, and sustainability. The EU's hybrid control model for DPPs merges centralized orchestration with distributed data ownership, balancing efficiency, transparency, and data sovereignty.

Centralized Orchestration

In the hybrid model, centralized orchestration involves the European Commission (EC) and other regulatory bodies setting standards, guidelines, and the overall framework for the DPP system. This centralized approach ensures that the system is cohesive and compliant with EU regulations, such as the Ecodesign for Sustainable Products Regulation (ESPR) and the Circular Economy Action Plan (CEAP).

- *Standardization and Compliance:* The EC will develop and enforce standards to ensure that DPPs contain essential information about the product's origin, composition, environmental impact, and end-of-life handling. This standardized framework ensures uniformity across all member states and industries, making it easier for stakeholders to comply with regulations and for consumers to understand product information (European Commission, 2024).
- *Central Registry and QR Codes:* The DPP will utilize a centralized registry for essential data storage, managed by the EC or a designated authority. Each product will have a unique identifier, such as a QR code, physically

present on the product. This QR code will link to the centralized registry, allowing stakeholders to access detailed product information easily. This centralized approach ensures that critical data is available and consistent across the entire EU (University of Cambridge Institute for Sustainability Leadership (CISL) and the Wuppertal Institute, 2022).

Distributed Data Ownership

Distributed data ownership allows individual stakeholders—manufacturers, suppliers, and recyclers—to manage their specific data contributions to the DPP. This approach maintains data privacy and security while fostering innovation and flexibility.

- *Data Privacy and Security:* By managing their data, stakeholders can ensure that sensitive information is protected. This approach aligns with the General Data Protection Regulation (GDPR) and other data protection laws, ensuring secure personal and proprietary information.
- *Innovation and Flexibility:* Distributed control enables stakeholders to innovate independently within the standardized framework. This flexibility allows for quicker adaptation to market changes and technological advancements, supporting the development of new business models and practices.

12.3 What Should Manufacturers Expect from the Digital Business Ecosystem?

This section will outline the key attributes that manufacturers can expect from digitized circular ecosystems. While it is improbable that a single platform will encompass all the desired features, these characteristics build a cohesive circular business ecosystem. By understanding these attributes, manufacturers will be empowered to make informed choices about the tools and strategies they implement.

12.3.1 Interconnectivity and Real-Time Communication as the Nerve System of the Digital Circular Ecosystem

The interconnectivity and real-time communication within a digital ecosystem serve as the central nervous system, synchronizing and defining the interaction among various stakeholders. This ensures that data flows seamlessly and stakeholders can instantly share and act upon data.

IoT sensors can, for example, send signals to the manufacturer, recycling facility, and raw material supplier when a product ends its useful life. This real-time communication allows for timely product retrieval for refurbishment, remanufacturing, or recycling. This interconnectivity enables the entire network of stakeholders to adjust their processes in real time.

Advanced analytics and AI can leverage real-time data to optimize an ecosystem's operations dynamically. Predictive analytics can also forecast when certain materials will be available for recycling, enabling other stakeholders to adjust their resource planning accordingly. A digital ecosystem's real-time, interconnected capabilities create a "living" circular economy that can continuously sense, respond, adapt, and optimize. This allows for a more resilient, efficient, and sustainable system than any organization could achieve alone.

12.3.2 Collective Circular Intelligence

In a digital business ecosystem, data-driven decision-making is no longer limited to the boundaries of a single organization. The ecosystem uses powerful analytics tools that benefit all stakeholders, including manufacturers, suppliers, retailers, and customers. By collecting data from various touchpoints, the ecosystem provides a comprehensive view of product lifecycles, resource utilization, waste generation, and other metrics.

For example, shared dashboards offer real-time insights into the availability of recyclable materials within a region, helping multiple manufacturers plan their production cycles collaboratively. Data drives transparency in the supply chain, helping businesses and their partners make informed decisions on sourcing materials that are not only high-quality but also ethically and environmentally sound.

This collective approach to data-driven decision-making enables all stakeholders to create decisions that benefit the ecosystem. When data flows freely and securely among ecosystem stakeholders, it forms the basis for collective intelligence that can tackle complex challenges beyond the capabilities of any individual company. Therefore, in a digitally interconnected ecosystem, data doesn't just inform—it transforms.

12.3.3 Automation and AI Are Synchronizing Efficiency Across the Digital Ecosystem

Automation and AI technologies are more than just tools for optimizing tasks within a single organization. They orchestrate ecosystem-wide efficiencies, dynamically coordinating activities among multiple stakeholders to streamline resource utilization and minimize waste.

For example:

- AI algorithms can analyze data from multiple producers and recyclers to optimize the routing and scheduling of material collection and recycling operations. Such coordination can reduce transportation costs and emissions.
- AI-driven demand forecasting can help manufacturers, suppliers, and retailers synchronize their operations, ensuring that materials and products are produced,

transported, and delivered just in time. This reduces inventory costs and prevents overproduction.
- AI can aggregate and analyze data from multiple companies to provide comprehensive reports on the collective environmental impact.
- AI-driven platforms can connect manufacturers with excess materials to those in need, promoting resource sharing and reducing waste. For instance, AI can match manufacturers with surplus inventory to other companies that can use those materials and coordinate the logistics to transport materials where they are needed most.

12.3.4 Supply Chain Transparency

In the circular economy, every material has a story to tell, and a transparent supply chain is the story's narrator. Unlike traditional supply chains, where the focus is predominantly linear and confined within organizational boundaries, the supply chain in a circular digital ecosystem is an interconnected web of multiple stakeholders, each playing a unique role in a product's or material's lifecycle.

Digital tools such as Digital Product Passports and Internet of Things (IoT) sensors amplify this transparency by capturing, storing, and sharing data about every phase of a product's life—from material extraction to design, manufacturing, usage, and end-of-life management. However, the impact of these technologies is not just additive; it's multiplicative when integrated into a larger digital ecosystem that involves suppliers, manufacturers, recyclers, regulators, and even consumers.

Data shared on unified platforms with authorized stakeholders provides a single "source of truth" and facilitates the coordination of circular practices such as reverse logistics or closed-loop recycling.

In a connected digital ecosystem, compliance with circular and sustainability standards can be automated and shared, enhancing stakeholder trust and cooperation.

Enhanced supply chain transparency also allows end-users to scan a QR code on a product, for instance, and immediately gain access to information about the product's origin, materials, and carbon footprint via the Digital Product Passport.

In a transparent digital ecosystem, compliance with environmental regulations and standards becomes a collective responsibility. Automated systems can simplify the reporting process, creating auditable records that can be accessed and verified by regulators and other stakeholders.

With complete visibility into the supply chain, stakeholders can more readily identify bottlenecks, inefficiencies, or unsustainable practices and take collective action.

Supply chain transparency becomes integral to an automated, adaptive, resilient circular economic model. It allows for coordination, trust, and efficiency, enabling the circular economy to function effectively on a large scale.

Example 12.8 The Excess Materials Exchange (EME) manages excess materials through digital platforms

The Excess Materials Exchange (EME)[3] manages excess materials through digital platforms. EME serves as a high-value marketplace for companies to exchange materials, transforming waste into valuable resources.

The Resources Passport is created to give materials an identity. This passport is a detailed database that records comprehensive information about a product, component, or material throughout its lifecycle. It includes origin, composition, toxicity, embedded energy, and carbon emissions. This structured format enables the efficient exchange of materials by making their characteristics and availability transparent and predictable.

EME's system integrates various identification technologies, such as barcodes, QR codes, NFC chips, and RFID chips, to ensure that materials can be followed throughout their lifecycle. This capability allows EME to predict when, where, and how many materials will become available, facilitating efficient and timely exchanges.

The Valuation module in EME's platform quantifies excess materials' financial, environmental, and societal value. This module evaluates a material's economic worth and environmental impacts, such as CO_2 emissions, water use, and transportation distances. The nonfinancial values are expressed through the "Eco-cost" indicator, which, combined with the financial value, is presented as the "Total Value" indicator. This holistic valuation approach enables decision-makers to make informed, data-driven choices about the best uses for their excess materials.

Matchmaking is at the core of EME's functionality. The platform uses data from the Resources Passport, Tracking and Tracing, and Valuation modules to identify high-value, circular uses for materials across different industries and sectors. EME facilitates matchmaking by actively assisting companies in finding optimal matches that maximize the materials' lifecycle and value. The matchmaking process is supported by AI tools and EME's extensive knowledge and experience in the circular economy.

Europe, especially the Netherlands and Belgium, meets 47% of the EU's carpet tile demand. Unfortunately, only 3% of the 1.6 million tons of carpet tile waste is recycled, with the remaining amount being either incinerated or landfilled. The EME model aims to improve the recyclability and reusability of carpet tiles.

The Resources Passport contains detailed product information to help recyclers distinguish between recyclable and contaminated carpet tiles.

[3] https://www.excessmaterialsexchange.com/

The Tracking and Tracing system uses technologies like barcodes and RFID chips to monitor carpet tiles throughout their lifecycle. This system provides real-time data on the quality and location of materials, optimizing logistics and ensuring timely collection and processing.The Valuation module evaluates carpet tiles' financial, ecological, and social value. It provides a comprehensive value assessment, including eco-costs and total value indicators, to assist stakeholders in making informed decisions.EME's matchmaking platform connects carpet tile manufacturers with users of recycled materials, facilitating the high-value reuse of materials by matching supply and demand across sectors, such as using nylon from recycled carpets in new products (Excess Materials Exchange, 2019).

12.3.5 Standardization and Interoperability

Imagine a well-coordinated orchestra where each musician plays a different instrument but follows the same sheet of music to create a harmonious melody. In this context, standardized protocols are akin to sheet music. The ease with which different instruments blend their unique sounds to form a cohesive musical experience reflects interoperability, like how violins, flutes, and drums can combine to produce a symphony; various platforms and technologies within a digital ecosystem must function in sync to ensure an efficient ecosystem.

Standardization enables stakeholders with different backgrounds and technical capabilities to communicate seamlessly using a common language.

Consider a scenario involving three key players: the owner of a fleet of industrial machinery, the manufacturer of these machines, and a network of specialized repair shops. In this collaboration, the equipment has IoT sensors that monitor machine performance and detect when maintenance or repair is needed. The owner's systems use standardized API-based dialogues (Sect. 10.2) to automatically communicate with the manufacturer's proprietary software to verify the type and scope of the needed repairs. The manufacturer's system then uses another set of APIs to contact the repair service provider and schedule maintenance work. This standardized interaction ensures that the necessary information about the machinery's model, the nature of the problem, and the required parts are accurately communicated to the repair shop, which can prepare in advance for the specific service needed.

Standardization and interoperability are frameworks that form the basis for scalable, adaptable, and efficient circular systems. Like how a symphony cannot achieve its full potential if each musician follows their own set of rules, a digital ecosystem will not optimize the circular model if each stakeholder adheres to a unique set of protocols.

Example 12.9 The ISO 59000 series

The ISO 59000 series[4] provides a common business language, enabling companies to effectively align their operations and communicate circular strategies.

Consider a scenario in the construction industry, where a company is sourcing sustainable materials for a large-scale project. The company outlines its circular economy objectives using the ISO 59000 framework, ensuring clear and consistent communication with potential suppliers. One supplier responds with an Environmental Product Declaration (EPD).

An EPD is a standardized document that transparently reports the environmental impact of a product throughout its lifecycle, including data on raw material extraction, manufacturing, distribution, use, and end-of-life stages. It provides key metrics such as carbon footprint, energy use, and recyclability, following international standards like ISO 14025[5] and EN 15804[6]. EPDs enable businesses to compare the environmental performance of similar products objectively, supporting more sustainable procurement decisions.

In this scenario, the construction company can compare EPDs from multiple suppliers, confident that the standardized format ensures consistency and accuracy. Moreover, through standardized digital interfaces (APIs), the EPD data is seamlessly integrated into the company's resource management system, enabling real-time tracking of the project's environmental performance.

This combination of a shared business language (ISO 59000) and a technical standard (EPDs) not only simplifies decision-making but also enhances transparency and operational efficiency. By adopting such standards, businesses can build scalable, adaptable, and efficient systems that support their circular economy goals.

12.3.6 Regulatory Compliance and Reporting

Digitized circular ecosystems can simplify regulatory compliance and reporting by automating the collection, processing, and submission of necessary regulatory data. This, in turn, reduces the burden of compliance and minimizes the possibility of human error.

For example, a digital platform can automatically track material reuse and recycling throughout the supply chain, providing auditable records that can be accessed during regulatory reviews or audits.

[4] https://www.iso.org/sectors/environment/circular-economy

[5] https://www.iso.org/standard/38131.html

[6] https://circularecology.com/en-15804-a2-epd-update.html

These systems should always be up-to-date with the latest regulatory changes, automatically adjusting processes to maintain compliance. Nevertheless, configuring these systems to reflect the complex and frequently changing regulatory landscape is the primary challenge.

12.4 Four Benefits and Four Challenges

To conclude, digital business ecosystems are critical in the circular economy, so let's examine their most important benefits and challenges.

12.4.1 Benefits

Collaborative Digital business ecosystems create a collaborative environment where various parties can share and utilize each other's capabilities. This networked approach enables organizations to pool resources, share knowledge, and synergize efforts, resulting in higher levels of business value. The interconnectedness allows participants to engage in co-creation and collective problem-solving, leading to innovative solutions and services that may not be possible within a single organization.

Informed A well-integrated digital business ecosystem ensures all participants can access the information to make informed decisions. This transparency benefits the entire ecosystem and enhances decision-making at every level, from strategic planning to operational execution. By offering a comprehensive view of the ecosystem's operations, each participant can act to support their interests and the ecosystem's collective objectives.

Adjustable Digital business ecosystems' constantly changing nature allows for real-time adjustments without compromising the quality or timeliness of the information. Adaptability empowers businesses to respond quickly to new challenges and opportunities in a rapidly changing market environment. Digital ecosystems make it possible to scale operations up or down, modify supply chain logistics, or integrate new technologies, enabling a nimble and responsive approach.

Mitigate Complexity As the number of participants in ecosystems grows, managing their relationships becomes more complex. This is where digital business ecosystems come into play. They are designed to manage this complexity through advanced data analytics and streamlined processes. These ecosystems have tools that help manage multiple interactions, ensuring the system remains manageable and efficient as the network grows.

12.4.2 Challenges

Creating an effective digital business ecosystem to support circular business models presents challenges that manufacturers and other stakeholders must overcome. Here are the four most significant challenges to consider:

Data Integration and Interoperability One of the primary challenges is achieving seamless data integration and interoperability among diverse actors. Each stakeholder often operates on different platforms and uses varied data formats and protocols. Ensuring these systems can communicate and exchange information efficiently is essential for the real-time collaboration required in a circular economy. Overcoming these technical disparities to achieve seamless integration requires solutions that can translate and synchronize data across the ecosystem.

Complexity of Stakeholder Collaboration A circular business ecosystem involves various participants, each with its objectives, capabilities, and constraints. Aligning these diverse interests toward a common goal is challenging. Managing such a varied group demands advanced coordination mechanisms and robust governance models to ensure that all parties are committed and contributing effectively.

Regulatory Compliance and Standardization Navigating the regulatory landscape is another hurdle. Sustainability, data protection, and specific business practices are regulated differently across regions and sectors. A digital circular business ecosystem must be agile enough to adapt to these varying regulations to prevent them from impeding the flow of information and materials. Furthermore, while standardization across processes and data can aid in addressing these challenges, reaching a consensus on these standards is often lengthy and complex.

Intellectual Property Concerns Sharing information about materials, processes, and designs is necessary to maximize resource utilization and enable recycling and refurbishing efforts. However, this need for openness often clashes with the desire to protect intellectual property (IP). Companies naturally aim to safeguard their competitive advantage by protecting their IP, which can hinder the collaborative spirit needed in a circular economy.

12.5 Digital Capabilities for Manufacturers in Digital Circular Business Ecosystems

Manufacturers must adopt a range of digital capabilities to effectively participate in digital circular business ecosystems. Figure 12.1 outlines the key digital capabilities required for manufacturers to thrive in such ecosystems.

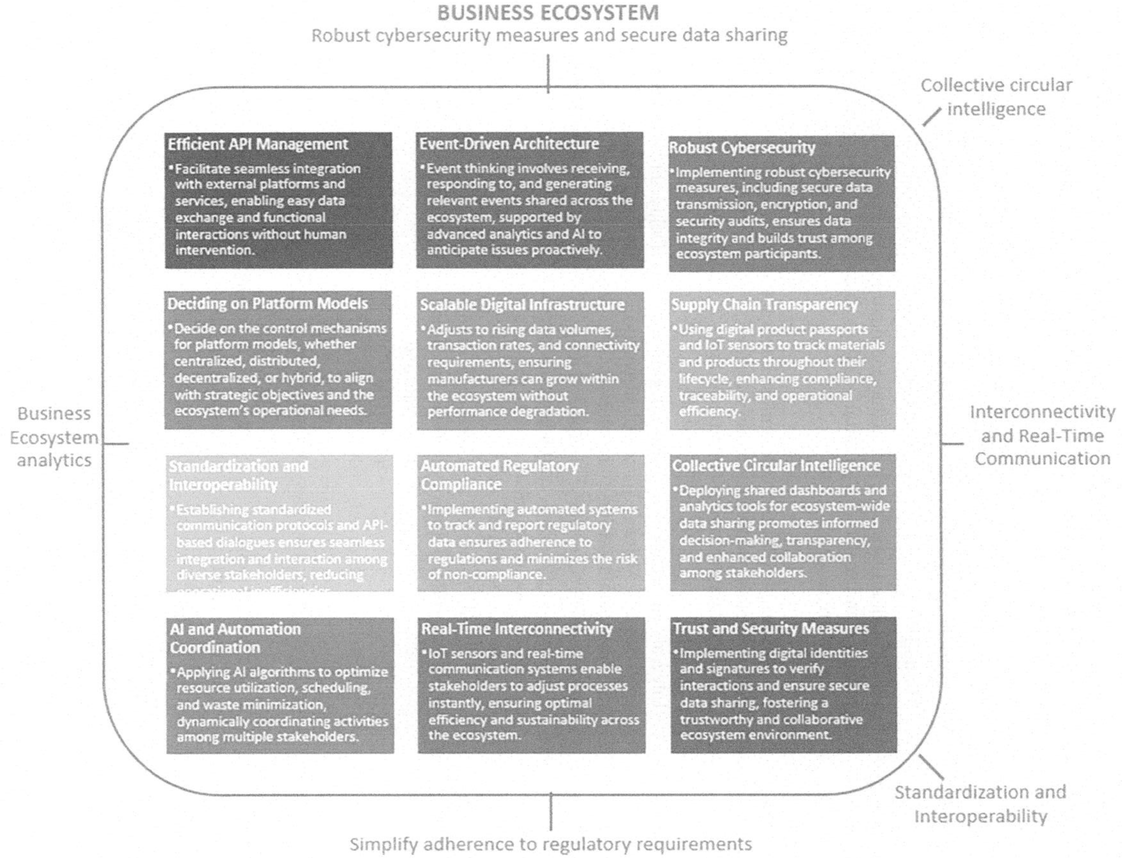

Fig. 12.1 Digital capabilities for manufacturers in digital circular business ecosystems

12.6 Checklist for Manufacturers to Participate in Digital Circular Ecosystems

Participating in a digital circular ecosystem requires manufacturers to implement specific tasks and methodologies to ensure seamless integration, data sharing, and collaboration with other stakeholders. This checklist provides a structured approach to guide manufacturers in this process, highlighting the expected outcomes and the risks mitigated (Table 12.2).

Table 12.2 Checklist for manufacturers to participate in digital circular ecosystems

Task	Methodology	Expected outcome	Risk mitigated
Develop digital infrastructure	Invest in cloud-based solutions and scalable architecture designs	Scalable and flexible digital infrastructure	Inability to handle increased data volumes and connectivity requirements
Implement efficient API management	Use advanced API management systems to facilitate data exchange	Seamless integration with external platforms and services	Data silos and integration inefficiencies
Adopt event thinking	Integrate advanced analytics and AI for real-time data handling	Proactive issue anticipation and resolution	Delayed responses to critical issues
Ensure robust security measures	Implement secure data transmission protocols, encryption standards, and regular security audits	Enhanced data integrity and privacy	Cybersecurity threats and data breaches
Enhance supply chain transparency	Use Digital Product Passports and IoT sensors for lifecycle tracking	Increased visibility into the lifecycle of materials and products	Lack of traceability and compliance issues
Standardize protocols and interoperability	Establish standardized communication protocols and API-based dialogues	Seamless communication among diverse stakeholders	Miscommunication and operational inefficiencies
Automate regulatory compliance	Implement systems to track and report regulatory data automatically	Simplified regulatory adherence and reporting	Non-compliance and regulatory penalties
Leverage collective circular intelligence	Deploy shared dashboards and analytics tools for ecosystem-wide data sharing	Informed decision-making and enhanced transparency	Data isolation and uninformed decisions
Integrate automation and AI	Apply AI algorithms to optimize resource utilization and scheduling	Efficient coordination and minimized waste	Operational inefficiencies and resource wastage
Foster trust and security	Use digital identities and digital signatures to verify stakeholders	Secure and trustworthy data-sharing environment	Lack of trust and data integrity issues

References

Catena-X. (2024). *Catena-X: Collaborative and secure data ecosystem for the automotive industry*. Retrieved from https://www.catena-x.net

Excess Materials Exchange. (2019). *Carpet recycling with EME*. Retrieved from https://excessmaterialsexchange.com/case-study/carpet-recycling/

IMDS. (2024). *International material data system: Comprehensive material data management*. Retrieved from https://www.mdsystem.com

OpenIDEO. (2024). *Circular design challenge*. Retrieved from https://www.openideo.com/circular-design-challenge

Rheaply. (2024). *Rheaply: Resource exchange platform*. Retrieved from https://www.rheaply.com

Thingiverse. (2024). *Thingiverse: Collaborative 3D design platform*. Retrieved from https://www.thingiverse.com

Connected Products and Components – The Senses of the Circular Economy

13

Abstract

Connected products and components powered by IoT technology are crucial for the circular economy. They enable real-time data collection and analysis, optimizing product design, enhancing customer satisfaction, and extending product lifespans. These products facilitate efficient redistribution models by providing real-time insights into product status and usage, supporting Product-as-a-Service models through predictive maintenance and real-time monitoring, and improving asset tracking and transparency in the sharing economy. Connected technologies enhance recommerce by ensuring the quality and reliability of used products and optimizing redistribution logistics through precise tracking. They also extend product use by enabling timely interventions and support recycling operations through improved sorting and material recovery.

A robust IT infrastructure for connected products is essential, incorporating coherent architecture, IoT platform connectivity, advanced analytics, and multi-layered security to support scalable and secure operations. This chapter explores how connected products drive sustainability, efficiency, and profitability in the circular economy, focusing on SmartFlow Pumps Inc. as a fictive example. It also discusses the importance of data privacy, edge computing, and the role of sensors in recycling. The capability map and checklist provide manufacturers with a structured approach to implementing connected products, ensuring optimized processes, enhanced product lifecycle management, and a more sustainable and profitable circular economy.

H. H. Jensen, *Circular Economy Opportunities and Pathways for Manufacturers*, Future of Business and Finance, https://doi.org/10.1007/978-3-031-75279-7_13

Key Message

- *Redesign for Circularity*: Real-time data from connected products enables manufacturers to optimize product design based on actual usage patterns, enhancing customer satisfaction and extending product lifespan.
- *Leveraging Connected Products in Redistribution Models*: Connected products facilitate efficient redistribution models by providing real-time insights into product status and usage, enhancing the value and lifecycle of products in the circular economy.
- *Enhancing Product-as-a-Service Models*: Connected products transform Product-as-a-Service models through predictive maintenance and real-time monitoring, ensuring optimal product performance and customer satisfaction.
- *Connected Products in the Sharing Economy*: Integrating connected products into the sharing economy improves asset tracking, security, and transparency, driving efficiency and user trust in shared services.
- *Recommerce and Secondary Markets*: Detailed data from connected products enhances the transparency and reliability of used products, boosting customer confidence and facilitating robust secondary markets.
- *Optimizing Redistribution Logistics*: Connected technologies streamline logistics by providing precise tracking and condition monitoring of products, ensuring efficient and timely redistribution.
- *Enhancing Product Use Extension*: Continuous product health monitoring through connected products allows for timely interventions, extending product life and optimizing resource use in repair, refurbishment, and remanufacturing processes.
- *The Role of Sensors in the Recycling Phase*: Sensors and IoT technologies improve the efficiency and accuracy of recycling operations, enabling precise sorting and material recovery.
- *Manufacturer's IT Infrastructure*: A robust IT infrastructure for connected products is essential. It must incorporate coherent architecture, IoT platform connectivity, advanced analytics, and multilayered security to support scalable and secure operations.

At the forefront of the circular economy are connected products and components propelled by the transformative power of IoT technology. These products equip manufacturers with real-time data on product performance in diverse environments. QR codes, barcodes, and NFC tags enable product tracking throughout its lifecycle, enhancing connectivity for accessing product information. The real-time data collected, analyzed, and transmitted is a game-changer for manufacturers and product owners. It empowers them to monitor, control, and optimize product performance and resource utilization.

This chapter explores how connected technologies establish insights into product usage, streamline maintenance processes, predict potential failures before they occur, and ensure efficient product usage for each phase of the 1 + 5R model.

Example is a fictive example that features SmartFlow Pumps Inc. It illustrates the coherent flow and practical application of connected products and components within a circular economy. This company manufactures industrial pumps and utilizes IoT technology to enhance its product lifecycle management. This chapter will delve into the digital opportunities presented in this example, emphasizing how real-time data and connected technologies drive sustainability, efficiency, and profitability in the circular economy.

Example 13.1 A fictive example of connected products and components in a circular economy

SmartFlow Pumps installs sensors in their pumps to collect real-time data on performance, usage patterns, and environmental conditions. This data provides valuable insights into how their pumps are utilized in various industries. For example, they discover that certain components deteriorate more quickly in specific environments, leading to redesigns that improve durability and performance.

SmartFlow's R&D team has analyzed operational data to identify design improvements that can extend the lifespan of its pumps. For instance, they found that a specific seal type degrades quickly in acidic conditions, prompting the development of a new design using more resistant materials.

SmartFlow provides a Product-as-a-Service (PaaS) model in which customers lease pumps instead of buying them outright. These pumps are fitted with IoT technology, allowing SmartFlow to monitor their performance remotely. Real-time data collection enables predictive maintenance, ensuring optimal operation and minimizing unexpected failures.

One of SmartFlow's clients is a large water treatment facility. The facility benefits from continuous monitoring and timely maintenance of its pumps. SmartFlow uses data analytics to predict when a pump is likely to fail and schedules maintenance before issues arise. This predictive maintenance reduces downtime, lowers operational costs, and enhances the overall reliability of the service.

SmartFlow collaborates with different industries to establish a sharing economy model for their pumps. By incorporating advanced tracking and access control technologies, SmartFlow guarantees secure and efficient asset management. This allows companies to share pumps across multiple facilities, optimizing utilization and reducing the necessity for new units.

For instance, a group of small manufacturers shares a pool of SmartFlow pumps. Each pump is monitored in real-time, and its availability is visible to all members. This sharing model maximizes the utilization of each pump, reducing overall equipment costs and minimizing environmental impact by reducing the need for new pumps.

SmartFlow uses detailed data from connected pumps to improve the recommerce market. When a pump is returned, SmartFlow assesses its condition using the collected data to determine any necessary repairs or refurbishments. This process ensures that only high-quality, reliable pumps reenter the market.

SmartFlow provides customers looking to purchase used pumps with transparent access to detailed usage history. This allows them to retrieve information about the pump's performance, maintenance history, and remaining lifespan. Consequently, customers can feel more confident when purchasing refurbished units. SmartFlow's data-driven approach also enables the company to extend warranties on used pumps based on their actual condition.

SmartFlow's connected technology optimizes pump logistics with real-time tracking and condition monitoring, ensuring efficient routing and resource optimization.

SmartFlow enhances recycling through sensors and IoT (Internet of Things) technologies. When a pump reaches the end of its useful life, sensors collect data on its condition and material composition, facilitating efficient recycling. This accurate sorting and recovery process guarantees that valuable materials are recovered and reused.

For example, SmartFlow utilizes advanced robotics with sensors to dismantle pumps and recover metals, plastics, and other materials.

13.1 Redesign for Circularity

The constant feedback loop of operational data from connected products and components provides manufacturers with valuable insights and building blocks for a more intelligent and responsive approach to product design. These technologies collect and analyze usage data, enabling manufacturers to make well-informed design decisions that closely align with customer behavior and market demands.

Embedded sensors provide real-time data on how products are used, revealing patterns that can be used to design products that align with customer needs.

Real-time customer feedback allows for dynamic product adaptation and customization. Tailoring products to meet evolving preferences fosters a more robust customer connection and optimizes manufacturing processes and inventory management.

Data from connected products enables benchmarking across product lines, identifying performance standards, pinpointing areas for improvement, and informing decisions about product lifespan and maintenance strategies. Analyzing real-world usage data helps manufacturers understand how long products last in customers' hands. This can reveal whether products are failing prematurely or exceeding expectations.

Performance data can also identify components that wear out quickly or require frequent repairs. This insight can be used to design more accessible and cost-effective products, extending their lifespan.

Insights into user behavior and preferences drive a user-centric design philosophy. This philosophy ensures that products are crafted to meet genuine needs, reducing the likelihood of unused features and wasted materials.

Incorporating real-time usage data into lifecycle analysis assists manufacturers in comprehending the environmental and economic effects of their products throughout their lifecycle. This can help design decisions that minimize environmental impact while maximizing financial returns, especially in resource allocation and end-of-usage management. For instance, this approach results in designs that streamline the disassembly process, which supports efficient repair, refurbishment, and recycling.

A digital twin is a virtual replica of a physical product that can simulate and test various design scenarios without creating physical prototypes. Employing digital twins allows manufacturers to experiment with different designs in a virtual environment, speeding up the innovation process, reducing R&D costs, and ensuring that the product that goes to market is optimized for performance and price.

The actionable insights provided by these technologies enable a shift from reactive to proactive design strategies, reducing costs, enhancing customer appeal, and driving higher profitability and lower environmental impact.

13.2 Leveraging Connected Products in Redistribution Models

The advancement of connected products and components transforms how products are reused, recommenced, and shared. This section explores the role of connected products in enabling efficient and profitable redistribution models.

13.2.1 Enhancing Product-as-a-Service Models Through Connected Products

Connected products increase the efficiency of Product-as-a-Service (PaaS) models by enabling real-time monitoring, predictive maintenance, and improved customer engagement. These technologies transform how services are delivered, creating more value for the provider and the customer. (See Sect. 11.3.2 for a process flow) (Fig. 13.1).

Connected products with IoT technology can transmit continuous data about their operational status and environment to service providers. This real-time monitoring allows for dynamic adjustments to product settings to optimize performance and energy efficiency, which can be particularly beneficial in PaaS models that maximize product utility and lifespan.

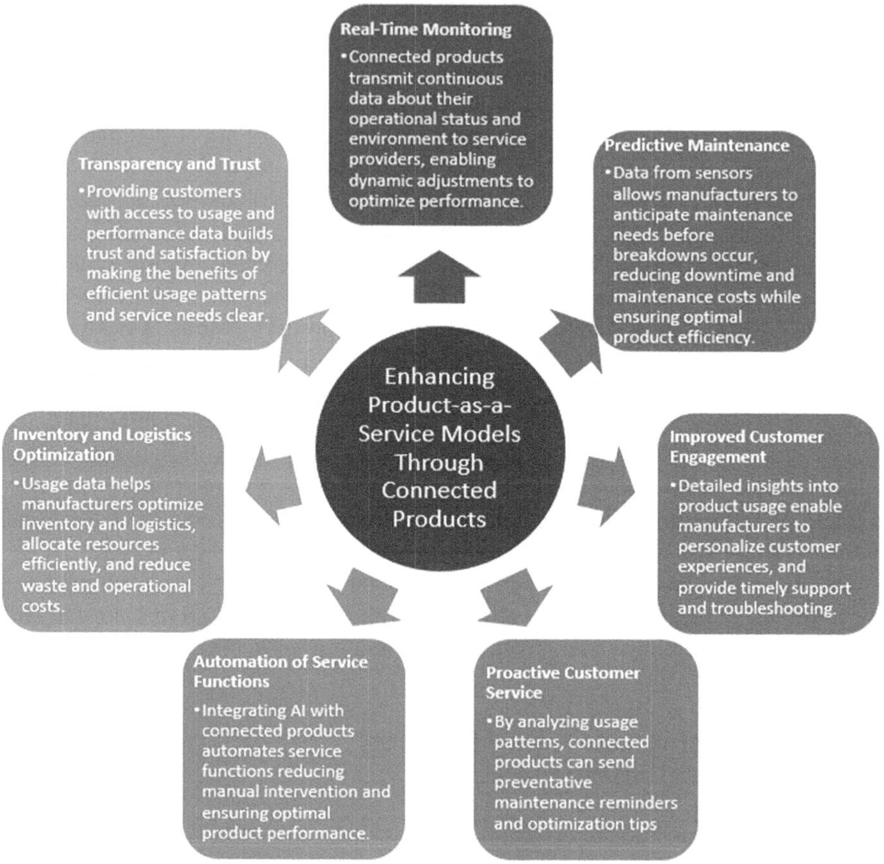

Fig. 13.1 Enhancing Product-as-a-Service Models Through Connected Products

Utilizing data gathered from sensors integrated into products, manufacturers can anticipate when a product will require maintenance or part replacement before a breakdown happens. This proactive strategy reduces downtime and maintenance expenses while guaranteeing that products operate at optimal efficiency, ultimately enhancing the overall reliability of the service.

Connected products give manufacturers and service providers detailed insights into how customers use products. This rich data can be leveraged to personalize the customer experience, tailor services to individual user needs, and provide timely support and troubleshooting.

By analyzing usage patterns, connected products can proactively contribute to customer service by sending preventative maintenance reminders to users and offering usage optimization tips like adjusting settings or changing how and when the product is used. This helps maintain the product in optimal condition and reduces the likelihood of unexpected failures.

Example 13.2 Michelin's Smart Predictive Tire

Michelin's Smart Predictive Tire[1] helps fleet managers and service providers monitor tire pressure, temperature, and wear and tear in real time. The solution notifies them of an abnormality so they can take appropriate action to avoid potential safety hazards for drivers and road users.

In addition, the solution generates a weekly predictive maintenance report that allows for the anticipation and prioritization of vehicle downtime, helping to avoid multiple mechanical and tire interventions. This is made possible by Michelin's automatic wear and tear diagnosis system and a pressure sensor that checks tire pressure in real time. Predictive algorithms convert data into personalized recommendations adapted to each fleet, increasing tire life by 9%, reducing fuel and CO2 emissions by 3%, and reducing incidents by 80% (Michelin, 2024).

Integrating advanced technologies such as AI and machine learning with connected products can automate many service functions. For example, software updates can be pushed automatically to products based on the data received about their performance and usage patterns. This automation reduces the need for manual intervention and ensures that all products in the service remain up-to-date and perform optimally.

Connected product data helps manufacturers understand usage patterns across customer segments and geographic areas. This information is vital for optimizing inventory and logistic decisions, allocating resources efficiently, and reducing waste and operational costs.

Giving customers access to data about the usage and performance of their rented or leased products can build trust and transparency in the PaaS model. Customers who can see the benefits of efficient usage patterns or understand their service needs through tangible data are likelier to feel in control and satisfied with the service.

Example 13.3 Rolls-Royce TotalCare® shows the integration of connected products within a PaaS model

Rolls-Royce, a major player in aerospace engineering, offers a service called TotalCare® that shows the integration of connected products within a PaaS model. This service allows airlines to pay for the engines and maintenance based on operation hours rather than purchasing them outright.

[1] https://connectedfleet.michelin.com/solution/predictive-tyre-maintenance/

Rolls-Royce equips its engines with sensors that continuously collect data on various operational parameters. These sensors monitor everything from engine efficiency to wear and tear and even environmental conditions affecting the engine during flights.

The data collected is analyzed using advanced predictive analytics to anticipate maintenance needs before any issues become critical. This proactive maintenance approach minimizes aircraft downtime and ensures optimal engine performance.

By analyzing the data, Rolls-Royce can provide insights into operational efficiency and suggest adjustments to improve fuel consumption and reduce emissions.

The TotalCare® program shifts the airline's engine maintenance and performance responsibility to Rolls-Royce, aligning the company's interests with those of its customers. Rolls-Royce is incentivized to keep engines running efficiently and reliably (Rolls Royce, 2024).

13.2.2 Connected Products in the Sharing Economy

This section explores the advantages connected products bring to sharing economy business models. We will not repeat the general benefits discussed in the PaaS section, such as predictive maintenance and operational efficiency. Consequently, this section is shorter, and we recommend reading both sections to understand better the benefits connected products offer to the sharing economy.

Connected products enable businesses to track shared assets' precise location and usage status, such as bicycles or cars, ensuring they are efficiently distributed and available when and where needed.

Security and trust are paramount in the sharing economy. Connected products incorporate sophisticated access control technologies, such as digital keys and biometric verification, to ensure that only authorized users can access the services.

Integrating connected products provides stakeholders greater transparency into asset utilization and environmental impact. Transparency is vital for maintaining user trust and complying with regulations.

13.2.3 Recommerce and Secondary Markets Through Connected Products

Connected products impact the recommerce and secondary markets by enhancing the transparency and reliability of information available on used products. This allows for the certification of the quality and reliability of used products through detailed data. Connected technologies foster a healthier ecosystem for recommerce goods, benefiting sellers and buyers (Fig. 13.2) (see Sect. 11.3.1 for a process flow).

Fig. 13.2 Recommerce and secondary markets through connected products

Usage and condition data is used to assess the quality and functionality of items intended for recommerce. Manufacturers and sellers can use this information to certify the quality and estimate the remaining lifespan of these items. This certification process enhances customer trust in the quality of used products, making them more likely to invest in recommerce goods.

The data collected can identify any necessary repairs or refurbishments before reselling the product. This proactive approach ensures that all recommerced items meet high-quality and functionality standards, further bolstering customer confidence. By addressing repair needs before resale, manufacturers extend the product's life and enhance its value in the secondary market, creating a stronger proposition for potential buyers.

Transparency allows potential buyers to access comprehensive information about the product's history and condition. This openness increases customer confidence as buyers understand what they are purchasing, reducing the perceived risk associated with used goods.

Product usage and wear data allow manufacturers to confidently extend warranties on recommerce goods based on actual usage data rather than standard time frames. This capability increases the attractiveness of refurbished or second-hand products and gives customers greater assurance about the reliability and longevity of their purchases.

Automating the process of valuing used items based on real-time product data and market demand data enables dynamic and accurate pricing. This helps sellers maximize returns, and buyers get fair prices.

Connected products can help ensure compliance with safety and quality standards for certain products. Providing data proving that the used items still meet regulatory requirements allows these products to be sold in secondary markets with confidence in their safety and functionality.

13.3 Enhancing Product Use Extension Through Connected Products

Real-time data on product usage and condition enables manufacturers and service providers to make informed decisions about when and how to intervene, extending the product's life and optimizing resource use. This section explores how connected products advance repair, refurbishment, and remanufacturing processes, making them more adaptive, customer-focused, and environmentally sustainable (Fig. 13.3).

Before exploring the specific applications within each product use extension model, we will understand the overarching role of connected products in enhancing these models.

Connected products continuously monitor product health and performance. These devices collect and analyze data in real time, allowing manufacturers and service providers to see how products are used and detect early signs of wear or failure. This ongoing monitoring helps identify maintenance needs before they become critical, ensuring timely interventions that prolong product lifespans and optimize performance. Connected products leverage artificial intelligence and machine learning to predict future product failures and optimize maintenance schedules based on usage patterns and environmental conditions. These predictive capabilities allow for more targeted interventions, reducing unnecessary maintenance, enhancing product performance, and extending the product's useful life.

With access to extensive lifecycle data, manufacturers can better manage products from cradle to grave. This information aids in identifying the optimal times for refurbishment or remanufacturing, ensuring that products are not discarded prematurely. Effective lifecycle management helps extend the usability of products, reducing the need for new resources and maintaining high-quality standards throughout the product's extended life.

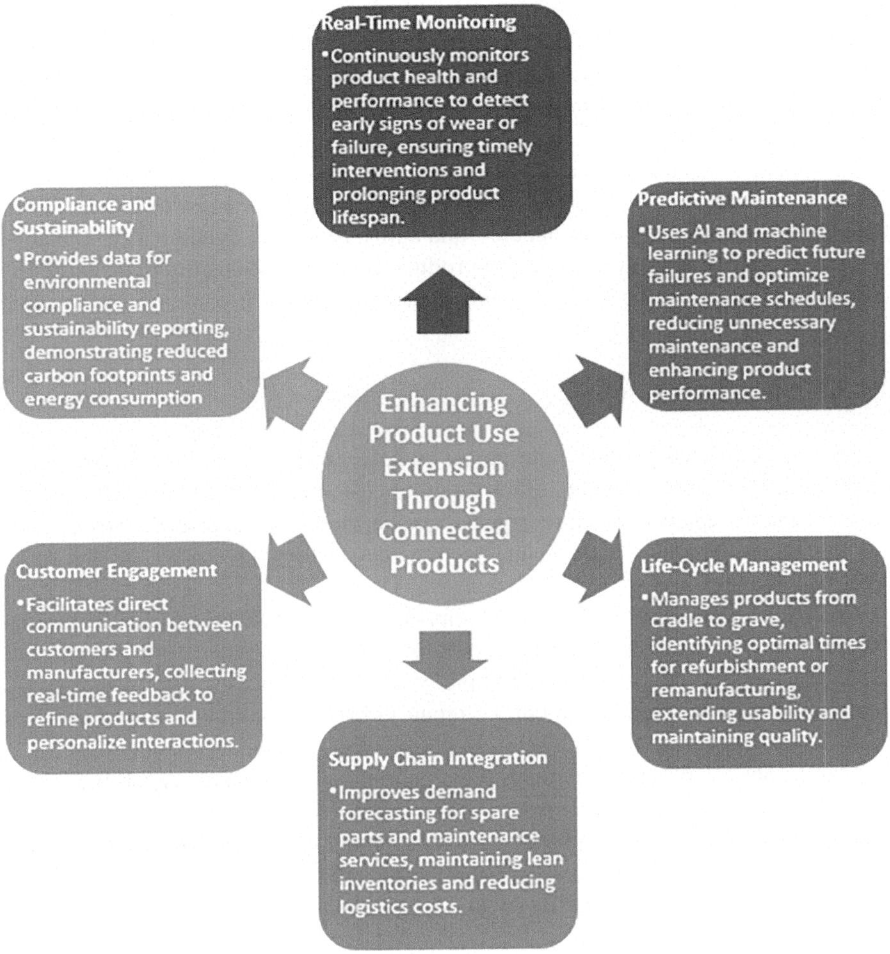

Fig. 13.3 Enhancing product use extension through connected products

Integrating connected product data with supply chain management systems improves demand forecasting accuracy for spare parts and maintenance services. This seamless integration helps manufacturers maintain lean inventories, reduce logistics costs, and ensure that parts and services are available when and where needed.

Connected products facilitate direct communication between customers and manufacturers. By continuously collecting data on user experiences and product performance, manufacturers can receive real-time feedback that can be used to refine products and personalize customer interactions. This ongoing engagement helps build stronger customer relationships, fostering loyalty and encouraging repeat business.

Usage and performance data are invaluable for compliance with ever-tightening environmental regulations. Manufacturers can use this data to prove compliance, report on sustainability initiatives, and demonstrate the environmental benefits of their product use extension strategies, such as reduced carbon footprints and lower energy consumption.

Connected technologies offer visibility into the repair, refurbishment, and remanufacturing operations. This transparency enables businesses to monitor real-time workflows, identify inefficiencies, and adjust processes dynamically. The ability to track and measure every aspect of product use extension ensures that operations are efficient and meet the high standards expected.

13.3.1 Specific for Repair

Integrating connected products into repair models transforms traditional approaches by introducing higher precision, efficiency, and customer service levels. These technologies enable repairs to be more targeted, quicker, and less intrusive, thereby extending the life of products and enhancing user satisfaction. (See Sect. 11.4.1 for a process flow.)

Connected products provide detailed information about the components or systems that are failing or likely to fail. This allows localized repairs where only the affected parts are addressed rather than undertaking broader, more invasive repair actions. By pinpointing the areas needing attention, repair efforts can be more focused and less resource-intensive, resulting in faster turnaround times and reduced labor costs.

Many connected products incorporate automated diagnostic capabilities that instantly analyze and interpret error codes or performance anomalies. This automation speeds up the diagnosis process, reduces human error, and ensures the correct repair procedures are followed. For manufacturers and service providers, this means quicker response times and higher accuracy in addressing product issues.

Example 13.4 Tenaris IoT sensors detect failures

Tenaris is a global manufacturer of steel pipes and related services for the energy industry. The company implemented IoT sensors at its Dalmine, Italy factory to detect failures in bearings, voltage, power, and other areas. These sensors identified anomalies indicating potential failures, such as a dangerously degraded water pump motor. By spotting this issue early, Tenaris was able to conduct preemptive maintenance, thus preventing unexpected breakdowns and ensuring continuous, efficient operations.

IoT technology enables the integration of repair services with mobile applications. This integration allows customers to schedule repairs, track repair status, and communicate directly with service technicians from their smartphones. It enhances customer convenience and allows repair service providers to manage their workflows and dispatch resources effectively.

By analyzing real-time data from connected products, service providers can optimize the allocation of their technical resources. Predictive data models allow for anticipating repair demands, ensuring that technicians with the right skills are available and equipped with the necessary parts to handle specific types of repairs.

Connected products can also serve as training tools for repair technicians, providing real-time feedback and guidance during the repair process. This can be particularly valuable in complex repairs that require precise actions. Augmented reality (AR) and virtual reality (VR) technologies can overlay digital information, such as schematics and repair instructions, directly into the technician's field of view, improving repair accuracy and speed.

13.3.2 Enhancing Remanufacturing Models Through Connected Products

In this section, we treat refurbishment and remanufacturing under the same umbrella, collectively referring to them as remanufacturing. Connected products benefit remanufacturing processes by enabling precision, customization, and efficiency, addressing the challenges of restoring used products to meet like-new standards, and ensuring optimal performance and reliability. (See Sect. 11.4.2 for a process flow.)

Precision in Remanufacturing

Connected products offer sophisticated diagnostic tools that assess the health and viability of each component. This evaluation determines whether a component can be reused, reconditioned, or recycled. By accurately evaluating component conditions, remanufacturers can ensure only suitable parts reenter the production cycle, enhancing the reliability and quality of the final product.

IoT technology guides the disassembly process in remanufacturing by providing specific instructions based on each product's unique history and condition. This tailored guidance helps prevent damage to reusable components, maximize material retention, and reduce the need for new parts. The efficiency gained from optimized disassembly lowers labor costs and minimizes errors.

Customization in Remanufacturing

Detailed performance data for each component allows remanufacturers to identify underperforming parts or those likely to fail soon. This data-driven approach enables targeted upgrades, enhancing overall product performance and extending lifespan. By upgrading critical components without requiring complete overhauls, remanufacturers can improve product functionality and appeal.

Remanufacturers can utilize extensive usage data to customize products better to match the needs and preferences of future users. Suppose data shows certain features are rarely used, or there is heavy usage in specific areas. In that case, remanufacturers can modify the product to optimize its design for these patterns, adding value and increasing the marketability of remanufactured products.

Data from connected products enable remanufacturers to apply customized reconditioning processes tailored to the specific needs of each component. This bespoke approach ensures that all parts are restored to optimal functionality, maintaining the integrity and performance of complex machinery and equipment.

Efficiency in Remanufacturing

By precisely understanding the condition of each part of a product, remanufacturers can allocate resources more efficiently. This includes deciding which parts to replace, repair, and invest in for aesthetic enhancements. This precise allocation reduces costs and minimizes waste, supporting more sustainable remanufacturing practices.

Detailed insights from connected products allow remanufacturers to implement dynamic pricing models based on the actual condition and functionality of the product post-remanufacturing. Pricing can be adjusted based on new components added, the extent of remanufacturing, and the predicted reliability of the product, ensuring that pricing accurately reflects the value of the remanufactured item.

Quality Assurance in Remanufacturing

Connected products enable continuous monitoring during the testing phase of remanufacturing, ensuring all items meet specific performance criteria before release back into the market. During remanufacturing, connected devices continuously monitor the quality and performance of restored components. This real-time quality control maintains stringent standards, ensuring that each remanufactured product performs as well as, or better than, new products. This monitoring also helps to immediately identify and correct any issues, enhancing the overall efficiency of the remanufacturing process.

Connected products facilitate the automation of compliance checks and certification processes, ensuring all remanufactured products meet necessary industry standards and regulations. This automated documentation maintains customer transparency and trust, proving that remanufactured products are safe, reliable, and compliant with all relevant standards.

13.4 Recycling Phase

The recycling phase represents a transition where products are either reintroduced into the manufacturing cycle or responsibly discarded. While connected products enhance the decision-making and prediction stages of recycling, their direct involvement diminishes during collection, sorting, and the actual recycling processes.

Although sensors and IoT technologies enhance recycling operations within facilities, these intelligent products are outside the scope of our discussion on manufacturers' opportunities in the circular economy. The topic will only be touched briefly in the next section to enhance understanding of recycling. Still, we focus on the impact of connected products designed and integrated by manufacturers.

13.4.1 The Role of Sensors in the Recycling Phase

Sensors and IoT technologies enhance the efficiency and precision of the recycling process. These technologies are utilized across various stages, such as collection, sorting, and material processing.

In the collection phase, sensors in recycling bins and on collection vehicles provide real-time data on fill levels and locations, helping to optimize routes and pickup schedules. This not only improves the logistics of collection but also reduces the environmental impact of transportation.

During the sorting phase, advanced sorting systems equipped with sensors and AI capabilities quickly and accurately categorize materials based on their type, condition, and recyclability. This high level of precision ensures that materials are appropriately processed and directed toward suitable recycling pathways.

Advanced robots equipped with sensors are increasingly used to dismantle complex products. These robots utilize precision sensors to identify and separate different materials and components, enabling more efficient disassembly and better

Example 13.5 Apple's Daisy robot disassemble iPhones

Apple's[2] Daisy robot is designed to disassemble iPhones and recover valuable materials that can be reused in new products.

This advanced robotic arm is capable of breaking iPhones down into their parts—from screens to screws—at a rate of about 3.33 devices a minute. This means that Daisy can disassemble up to 200 iPhones per hour, or approximately 1.2 million devices annually. Daisy can identify and segregate different iPhone models, ensuring optimal material recovery.

Apple identified 14 priority materials—from metals, including gold and tungsten, to paper—that comprise 90 percent of the ingredients used in its devices and packaging. Many of these materials were being recovered in low quantities, in low quality, or not at all by existing recycling methods.

Daisy comprises 4 cells that break down an iPhone into 15 parts. Cell one opens up the phone; another uses −80 °C cold air to nullify the adhesive that attaches the battery to the housing; another punches out screws, while the final cell separates components from the housing. Armed with sophisticated AI, Daisy can now identify 23 different iPhone models and process 1 every 18 seconds, in whatever order they come.

[2] https://www.apple.com/

It can extract key components such as cobalt and lithium from batteries, gold and copper from cameras, and silver and platinum from logic boards.

One metric ton of recovered iPhone parts avoids mining 2000 metric tons of metal-rich rock.

By recovering high-value materials, Apple reduces its reliance on raw material suppliers, which mitigates price volatility and supply chain disruptions. This also translates to substantial cost savings.

With increasing global regulations on electronic waste, Daisy helps Apple comply with e-waste directives and avoid potential fines or sanctions. Proactively addressing these regulations positions Apple as a leader in corporate responsibility (Compton, 2023).

material recovery. This technology is beneficial in handling electronics and other products where manual disassembly would be time-consuming and potentially hazardous.

Finally, in the material processing stage, sensors continue to monitor the quality and condition of the materials being processed, ensuring that appropriate recycling methods are applied and that the final recycled materials meet the required standards. The integration of sensors throughout these stages underscores their indispensable role in modern recycling operations, improving the overall efficiency and effectiveness of the recycling process.

13.4.2 Decision and the Role of Digital Product Passport

Connected products primarily influence the recycling process during the initial decision-making stages. These products gather valuable lifecycle data that inform when and how a product should be recycled, enhancing decision-making with predictive insights into material degradation and end-of-life timing. This data ensures that recycling actions are timely and effective, maximizing resource recovery and aligning with sustainability objectives.

Digital Product Passports will play a role in product recycling. Typically accessible via QR codes or similar identifiers on the product, these passports provide detailed information about the product's material composition, usage history, and manufacturing details.

13.5 Manufacturer's IT Infrastructure for Connected Products

Establishing a robust connected product infrastructure is essential to leverage the benefit. This infrastructure must support a coherent architecture, ensure reliable connectivity, manage data efficiently, incorporate advanced analytics capabilities, and maintain stringent security measures.

13.5.1 Coherent Architecture for Connected Products

A coherent architecture provides a structured, unified framework that integrates various product lines within a manufacturer's portfolio. This architecture standardizes the approach to connectivity, data management, security, and user interactions across all connected devices, regardless of their specific applications or functions.

It brings standardization across protocols, interfaces, and data formats, reducing complexity and fostering efficiency across the manufacturing process. This standardization facilitates seamless interoperability between diverse devices, enhancing the overall functionality of the IoT ecosystem and ensuring that different products and systems can work together without friction. It simplifies maintenance and updates, allowing changes such as security patches or functionality enhancements to be rolled out uniformly, which ensures consistency and reliability across all connected products.

It results in cost savings and a faster time to market for innovations. The architecture also supports scalability, enabling manufacturers to add new product lines or expand into new markets without requiring extensive system redesign.

Despite these advantages, a unified architecture may introduce disadvantages, such as reduced flexibility in tailoring specific solutions to individual product lines or markets. This could limit innovation in niche areas where specialized solutions might be more effective. Additionally, implementing a comprehensive, coherent architecture requires upfront investment in time and resources, which might be a barrier for some manufacturers.

These disadvantages are generally outweighed by the long-term benefits of having a standardized, interoperable, and scalable infrastructure. The efficiencies gained from a unified approach typically result in lower total ownership costs and greater ease of management at scale. Therefore, it is often more beneficial for manufacturers to accept these trade-offs to leverage the broader advantages of a coherent architecture.

13.5.2 IoT Platform Connectivity

The IoT platform is the central nerve system of a manufacturer's connected product ecosystem. It provides the necessary infrastructure for connectivity and is an enabler of integrated operations, offering advanced functionalities beyond simple device management. It's a strategic asset that proactively manages product lifecycles, enhances service offerings, and creates new revenue streams through data-driven business models.

An IoT platform that supports robust connectivity options enables manufacturers to maintain an ongoing dialogue with their products throughout their lifecycle, even after they have been sold or redistributed. Continuous interaction is crucial for effective management, service, and end-of-life responsibilities.

The platform's unified interface simplifies the complex task of managing a diverse array of connected products. This centralized approach streamlines the administration of connectivity settings and enables manufacturers to efficiently monitor device statuses and manage data flows across their entire product portfolio. By consolidating control into a single interface, the platform ensures that manufacturers remotely can quickly identify and address issues, update settings, and deploy solutions across different devices and systems without needing separate management tools for each product line.

The platform seamlessly deploys firmware updates and security patches across all connected devices. By managing these updates through the unified interface, manufacturers can ensure that all devices are protected against the latest security threats and operating with the most up-to-date software, reducing vulnerabilities and enhancing functionality.

Example 13.6 Tesla's Over-the-Air updates

Tesla's Over-the-Air (OTA) updates allow the company to update the software of its electric vehicles remotely. These updates impact various aspects of vehicle operation, from improved battery management to enhanced driving dynamics or the introduction of new features such as Autopilot advancements through these updates.

Tesla's OTA extends the useful life of its vehicles by continually improving vehicle efficiency and performance without the need for physical modifications. This direct digital link to products in the field allows for continuous improvement after the point of sale (Tesla, 2024).

As manufacturers increasingly integrate IoT devices into their operations and product offerings, the complexity and scope of their digital ecosystems expand. This expansion necessitates a robust security infrastructure to safeguard against potential cyber threats. An infrastructure component is establishing an IoT Security Operations Center (SOC) dedicated to monitoring, detecting, and responding to security threats across owned and third-party devices in real time.

Example 13.7 Caterpillar is embedding security within its connected solutions

Caterpillar is taking a proactive approach to protecting data and embedding security within its connected solutions. The following principles form the basis of Caterpillar's connected solution security strategy, emphasizing due care in managing risk (Caterpillar, 2024).

Caterpillar has established a dedicated cybersecurity team focused on securing its connected solutions. This cross-functional team comprises professionals from product development, cybersecurity, legal, and compliance organizations. Their collective expertise ensures comprehensive security management for Caterpillar's connected solutions.

Caterpillar follows a risk-based approach to implement multiple layers of cybersecurity controls. They utilize standards-based processes and technologies to design, develop, and validate the security of their connected solutions, aiming to protect customer data from unauthorized access or disclosure.Caterpillar proactively identifies and addresses risks to their connected solutions. They continuously monitor and assess the cybersecurity posture of their connected solutions and environment, taking active steps to improve their security measures continuously.Caterpillar's cross-functional Computer Security Incident Response Team (CSIRT) is dedicated to threat intelligence, detection, and response to cyberattacks. This includes responding to incidents that may impact their connected solution environment.

13.5.3 Integration of IoT Platform with Internal and External Systems

Integrating the IoT platform with internal systems and third-party partners enhances operational efficiencies and enables collaborative and informed decision-making across the value chain.

The IoT platform is designed to connect effortlessly with a manufacturer's internal systems, such as enterprise resource planning (ERP), customer relationship management (CRM), and supply chain management (SCM). This connectivity enables automatic data flow between systems, reducing manual entry errors and increasing information processing speed. By integrating real-time data from IoT devices, manufacturers can directly influence supply chain decisions, trigger customer service actions, and adjust operational strategies swiftly.

APIs (Application Programming Interfaces) (Sect. 10.2) provide a robust framework for the IoT platform, defining the methods and data formats for system communication. This setup extends the platform's functionality, supporting various operations across various business areas. Alongside API-based integration, the IoT platform incorporates event-based integration (Sect. 10.3). This advanced feature enables internal and external systems to subscribe to specific events generated by IoT devices. For instance, if a sensor detects an abnormal temperature rise in equipment, the event-based system can trigger an alert that automatically initiates a maintenance protocol in the ERP system. This capability maintains continuous operational safety and efficiency, allowing immediate responses to potential issues without manual oversight.

Integrating the IoT platform through APIs and event-driven architecture facilitates enhanced collaboration between internal departments and external partners. It allows all parties to access and react to real-time information, enabling faster and more informed decision-making. This integration is particularly effective in automating workflows, where specific events detected by IoT devices can initiate predefined actions across connected systems, streamlining processes, reducing delays, and minimizing human error.

13.5.4 Advanced Analytics

Advanced analytics enables manufacturers to optimize product lifecycle management. These capabilities transform vast amounts of data collected from connected products into actionable insights, driving decisions that enhance sustainability, efficiency, and product value throughout their lifecycle.

Advanced analytics help manufacturers understand how their products are used in real-world conditions. By analyzing data on usage patterns, wear and tear, and operational efficiency, manufacturers can identify areas where product design can be improved to enhance durability and functionality. This extends the product's useful life and reduces waste and resource consumption.

By monitoring the real-time data from sensors embedded in products, analytics algorithms predict when a component will likely fail or when maintenance is needed. This proactive approach prevents breakdowns and prolongs product life. Furthermore, manufacturers can use these insights to offer tailored maintenance services to customers, enhancing product performance and customer satisfaction.

As products approach the end of their usable life, advanced analytics can help determine the best course of action. Whether refurbishing, recycling, or disposing of a product, analytics can help manufacturers make informed decisions based on its condition and residual value.

Beyond operational improvements, advanced analytics can enhance customer engagement by providing insights into how customers use and interact with products. This data can drive the development of new services and improvements in product design that more effectively meet customers' needs.

Analytics can help manufacturers ensure compliance with environmental regulations and standards by providing detailed reports on emissions, resource usage, and recycling rates.

13.5.5 Scalability and Flexibility

As the range and number of connected products expand, the IoT platform must scale accordingly, maintaining performance without compromise.

It should also remain flexible to adapt to evolving business models and market demands, especially as manufacturers continue to innovate in product stewardship and lifecycle management.

13.5.6 Edge Computing

Edge computing involves processing data near the network's edge, where it is generated by IoT devices, rather than relying solely on a centralized data center. This approach reduces latency, decreases bandwidth usage, and improves response times, enabling manufacturers to manage and analyze vast data streams from their products in real time.

Edge computing allows manufacturers to continuously monitor the condition and performance of their products at customer sites. For example, by processing data on-site, manufacturers can immediately detect anomalies or potential failures in industrial equipment and initiate corrective actions without delay.

By processing data locally, edge computing helps address data security and privacy concerns, an essential aspect of compliance in the circular economy. Sensitive data can be analyzed and acted upon locally, reducing the risks associated with data transmission over long distances.

13.5.7 The Importance of Data Privacy

Data privacy directly impacts user trust and the legal compliance of involved companies. Strong data privacy measures are essential as connected products may collect, transmit, and analyze vast amounts of user data, including sensitive information. This protects against unauthorized access, ensures data handling respects user preferences, and adheres to legal standards.

Companies must be transparent about what data is being collected, how it is being used, and with whom it is being shared. Clear communication with users about the data handling policies enhances trust and engagement.

Users must give explicit consent before data is collected and processed. Users should be able to opt in and, importantly, to opt out of data collection processes, giving them control over their information.

Collect only the necessary data to fulfill the intended service or purpose. This complies with privacy regulations and reduces the risk of data breaches, as less data is held.

Implement robust security measures to protect user data from breaches and unauthorized access. These measures include encryption, regular security audits, and secure data storage solutions.

Ensure that all data practices comply with relevant data protection laws, such as the GDPR in Europe, CCPA in California, or other regional data protection laws. This includes provisions for data protection by design and by default and the ability for users to request data deletion.

Educate users about the collected data and how it improves the service. An informed user is more likely to trust and engage with the service.

13.5.8 Multilayered Security in Connected Products

Connected products offer enhanced functionality, which exposes them to various security vulnerabilities. These vulnerabilities can lead to unauthorized access, data breaches, and even the control of the devices' physical functions. A multilayered security approach is required to mitigate these risks.

However, implementing multilayered security in connected products presents several challenges. One such challenge is the complexity of coordinating security measures across different layers. Additionally, there is a need for ongoing management and updates.

Adopting a holistic security framework, continuously monitoring security metrics, and educating users about security best practices are essential to overcome these challenges. This approach ensures that if one layer is compromised, additional layers of defense will protect the system. It includes access control, encryption, secure boot, secure firmware updates, and secure communications.

The following summarize some security measures manufacturers should implement to protect connected devices and their users. For a detailed discussion of securing connected products, please refer to NIST Cybersecurity for IoT Program (The National Institute of Standards and Technology (NIST), 2024) or similar sources.

- Use a Trusted Platform Module (TPM) or Hardware Security Module (HSM) to securely store cryptographic keys and ensure the safe execution of cryptographic operations.
- Implement the secure boot security standard to ensure that the device boots up using trusted software authorized by the Original Equipment Manufacturer (OEM) and prevents malicious software from loading during the startup process.
- Regularly update and patch firmware and software to protect against known vulnerabilities.
- Encrypt sensitive information at rest and in transit to protect it from unauthorized interception.
- Use firewalls and intrusion detection systems to monitor and control incoming and outgoing network traffic based on security rules.
- Utilize secure communication protocols like SSL/TLS for encrypted data transmission.
- Implement authentication and authorization methods, such as passwords, biometrics, or digital certificates, to ensure that only authorized users can access the device and its data.
- Apply role-based access control (RBAC) to limit access to information and computing resources based on individual user roles within an enterprise.
- Incorporate security considerations during the design and development phases of application creation, particularly for those applications that control or access connected devices.
- Regularly test applications for vulnerabilities to ensure the security of connected devices.

By implementing robust security measures at various layers—from the hardware level to the network and up to the application layer—manufacturers can ensure the integrity, confidentiality, and availability of their connected products, providing peace of mind for themselves and their customers.

Example 13.8 Caterpillar's Cat Connect optimizes the management and monitoring of equipment and machinery

Caterpillar's Cat Connect is designed to optimize the management and monitoring of equipment and machinery. The platform provides real-time data access and monitoring capabilities. Users can access web-based maps and view asset status, location, engine parameters, and performance data from anywhere, bridging the gap between on-site operations and remote management capabilities.

A feature of Cat Connect is its security framework, which protects sensitive operational data. The platform has multilayered security controls, including cryptographic measures to guard against unauthorized software changes, encrypted and authenticated remote connections, and a security architecture that prevents the device from engaging in or responding to general Internet traffic. Caterpillar's IT infrastructure uses widely recognized information security principles and practices, providing an additional layer of data integrity and privacy assurance (Caterpillar, 2024).

13.6 Digital Capability Map for Connected Products and Components in a Circular Economy

The capability map in Fig. 13.4 outlines the critical digital capabilities manufacturers need to develop and integrate to drive efficiency, sustainability, and profitability from connected products and components.

13.7 Checklist for Implementing Connected Products in a Circular Economy

This chapter has explored the potential of connected products and components within the circular economy. As manufacturers seek to integrate these technologies into their operations, a structured approach is required to ensure successful implementation. The following checklist guides manufacturers through the tasks, methodologies, expected outcomes, and risk mitigation strategies for effectively leveraging connected products. This checklist aims to help manufacturers optimize processes, enhance product lifecycle management, and contribute to a more sustainable and profitable circular economy.

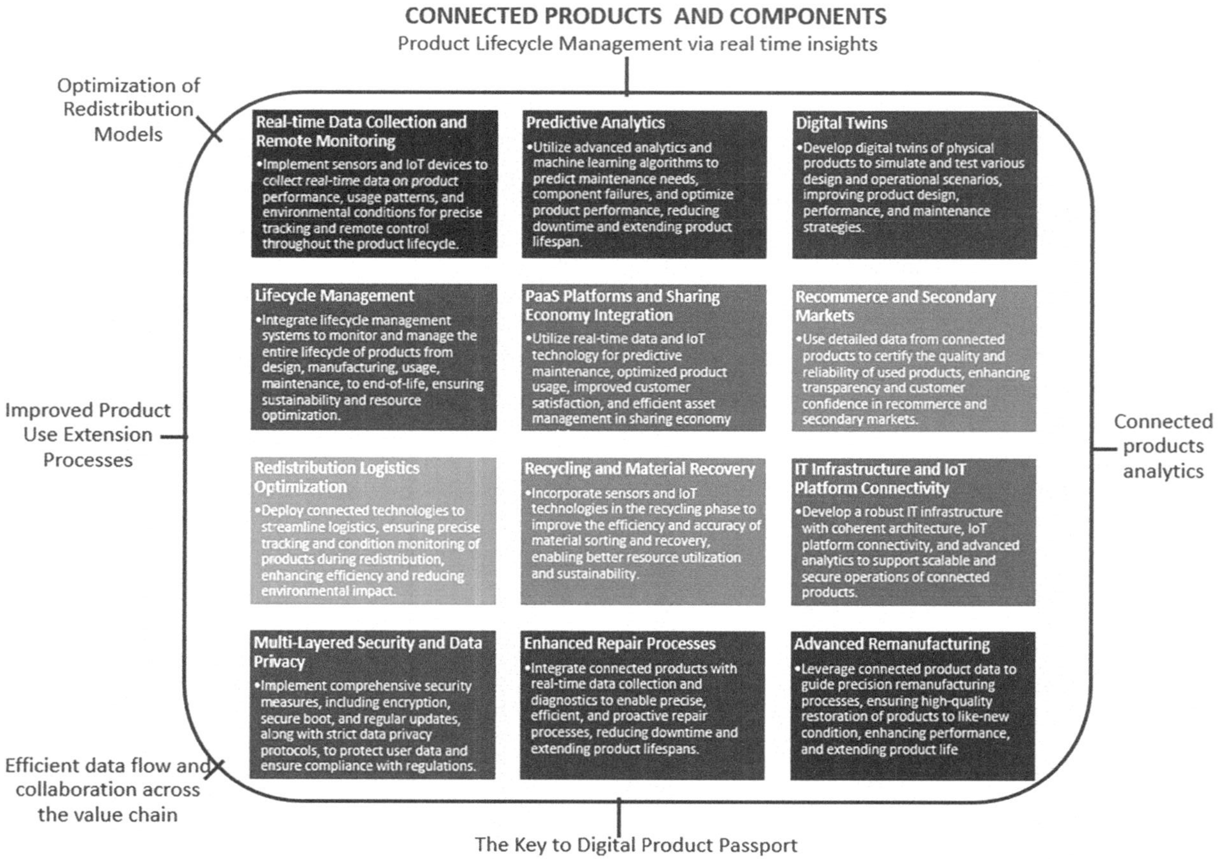

Fig. 13.4 Digital capability map for connected products and components in a circular economy

Task	Methodology	Expected outcome	Risk mitigation
Redesign for circularity	Utilize real-time data from connected products to inform design decisions	Enhanced product design, increased customer satisfaction, extended product lifespan	Mitigated risk of product failure through continuous feedback
Enable product-as-a-service (PaaS)	Integrate IoT technology for real-time monitoring and predictive maintenance	Improved service delivery, reduced downtime, enhanced customer engagement	Reduced risk of service interruptions with predictive maintenance
Enable sharing economy models	Deploy connected products with advanced tracking and security features	Efficient asset management, increased user trust, and transparency	Minimized risk of asset misuse and unauthorized access
Enhance recommerce and secondary markets	Use detailed product data to certify the quality and assess refurbishment needs	Increased customer trust in used products, optimized resale value	Addressed the risk of selling substandard used products
Optimize redistribution logistics	Implement connected technologies for precise tracking and condition monitoring	Efficient and timely redistribution of products	Lowered risk of logistical inefficiencies and delays
Extend product use	Apply continuous monitoring to detect early signs of wear and failure	Prolonged product lifespan, optimized maintenance schedules	Prevented unexpected product failures and maintenance costs
Develop robust IT infrastructure	Establish a coherent architecture with IoT platform connectivity and advanced analytics	Scalable and secure operations, improved data management	Mitigated risk of data breaches and operational inefficiencies
Ensure multilayered security in connected products	Implement comprehensive security measures, including encryption, secure boot, and regular updates	Protected user data, increased trust and compliance	Mitigated risk of unauthorized access, data breaches, and cyber threats
Ensure data privacy and security	Implement multilayered security measures and comply with data protection regulations	Protected user data, increased trust and compliance	Mitigated risk of data breaches and regulatory non-compliance

References

Caterpillar. (2024). *Connected solution security principles*. Retrieved from https://www.cat.com/en_ZA/support/technology/connected-solutions-principles/security.html

Compton, N. (2023, January). *What daisy did next: How Apple's evolving team of de-manufacturing machines battles e-waste*. Wallpaper. Retrieved from https://www.wallpaper.com/design-interiors/fmg-takes-technical-ceramics-out-of-this-world-in-a-new-campaign

Michelin. (2024, June). *Predictive tyre maintenance*. Retrieved from https://connectedfleet.michelin.com/solution/predictive-tyre-maintenance/

Rolls Royce. (2024, June). *Power by the hour*. Retrieved from https://www.rolls-royce.com/media/our-stories/discover/2017/totalcare.aspx

Tesla. (2024, June). *Software updates*. Retrieved from https://www.tesla.com/support/software-updates

The National Institute of Standards and Technology (NIST). (2024). *NIST cyber security for IoT program*. Retrieved from https://www.nist.gov/itl/applied-cybersecurity/nist-cybersecurity-iot-program

Digital Customer Touchpoint 14

Abstract

Digital customer engagement is pivotal in the circular economy, enhancing interaction throughout the product lifecycle. Manufacturers can foster circular consumption patterns by leveraging digital tools and strategies, creating seamless multichannel journeys, and building customer trust and loyalty. Augmented reality (AR) and virtual reality (VR) revolutionize customer experiences, making circular concepts accessible. Digital platforms facilitate recommerce, offering easy access to redistribution models and extending product lifecycles through repair and maintenance services. Apps streamline recycling by providing information and directing users to recycling centers. Comprehensive product lifecycle tracking fosters continuous customer dialogue and trust.

Ensuring digital readiness for third-party platforms enhances compatibility and customer satisfaction. Personalization, driven by customer analytics, encourages resource efficiency and waste reduction.

This chapter explores how manufacturers can enhance customer engagement in a circular economy, illustrated by the fictive example of SmartFlow Pumps Inc. and Alex, an operations manager, highlighting improved customer experiences and support for circular principles. The digital capability map and checklist provide manufacturers with a structured approach to implementing digital customer touchpoints, ensuring optimized processes, enhanced product lifecycle management, and a more sustainable and profitable circular economy.

H. H. Jensen, *Circular Economy Opportunities and Pathways for Manufacturers*, Future of Business and Finance, https://doi.org/10.1007/978-3-031-75279-7_14

Key Message

- *Digitization enhances customer interaction in the circular economy.* Manufacturers can foster circular consumption patterns by leveraging digital tools and strategies and maintaining engagement throughout the product lifecycle.
- *Creating a seamless multichannel customer journey.* A unified and consistent customer journey across all interaction channels builds trust and loyalty, ensuring personalized and consistent interactions.
- *AR and VR are revolutionizing customer engagement.* These technologies provide immersive experiences that help customers understand circularity concepts and make informed decisions about product use and sustainability.
- *Digital platforms facilitate easy access and interaction in redistribution models.* Online marketplaces and apps enable users to participate in recommerce and reuse, enhancing trust and convenience through digital contracts, payment systems, and user ratings.
- *Digital tools are vital for extending product lifecycles.* Platforms offering repair services, maintenance schedules, and DIY repair guidance ensure transparency and ease of service, making repair more appealing than replacement.
- *Streamlining recycling with digital engagement is key.* Apps and digital tools can inform users about recyclability, direct them to recycling centers, and provide detailed disassembly instructions.
- *Enabling product lifecycle tracking fosters deeper customer engagement.* Digital tools that provide comprehensive product histories, including repair and usage data, create a continuous loop of communication and trust between customers and manufacturers.
- *Manufacturers must ensure digital readiness for third-party-operated platforms.* Offering seamless access to digital warranties, repair manuals, and product passports through standardized data formats and APIs ensures compatibility and enhances customer trust.
- *Personalization drives circular behaviors.* Tailored product recommendations and services based on customer data encourage resource efficiency, product longevity, and waste reduction.
- *Customer analytics are vital for successful customer dialogues in the circular economy.* Analytics provide deep insights into customer behavior, enabling proactive maintenance, personalized sustainability recommendations, tracking the environmental impact of products, and supporting sustainable business practices.

The 1 + 5R model has revealed the growing significance of digital customer engagement in the circular economy. Value chain customers are no longer passive entities but active participants throughout the product lifecycle, enabling more insightful, dynamic, and responsive interaction.

Digital technologies are at the forefront of this transformation, allowing manufacturers to connect directly with end-users, often done through intermediaries in the linear economy. The focus on creating new digital services and customer interactions highlights the importance of a customer-centric approach in the circular economy. This approach aims to educate and engage customers in circular practices, providing them with tailored information to enable them to make and take informed choices that prolong the lifespan of products and explore end-of-life alternatives.

To illustrate how customers interact with a manufacturer and its products, let's consider a fictive example, where Alex is the operations manager of a large agricultural enterprise. By following Alex's journey with the fictive SmartFlow Pumps Inc., we can see how digital customer touchpoints improve engagement and support circular economy principles. This ensures a seamless and sustainable experience from purchase to end-of-life management.

Example 14.1 A fictive example of a customer's touchpoint

After installing the new SmartFlow pump, Alex downloads the SmartFlow mobile app. The app provides detailed usage instructions, and Alex can easily register the product for warranty. As Alex uses the pump, the app sends notifications for optimal usage and maintenance tips, ensuring the pump runs efficiently and effectively.

Some months later, the app notifies Alex that the pump is due for its first maintenance check. Using the app, Alex schedules a service appointment at a nearby SmartFlow service center. The service is booked quickly, and all service details are tracked within the app. This makes it easy for Alex to keep the pump in excellent condition without worrying about keeping physical records.

Alex uses the SmartFlow app to troubleshoot the issue when the pump shows signs of wear. The app provides step-by-step repair guidance, complete with AR overlays that make it easy to follow. For more complex issues, Alex can book a repair service directly through the app, ensuring minimal downtime for the irrigation system.

Over time, SmartFlow's analytics indicate that Alex's pump is becoming too small for the expanding irrigation needs of his company. The app sends a notification offering a recommerce opportunity: Alex can trade in the current pump and purchase a refurbished, larger model. This process is straightforward; Alex lists the current pump on SmartFlow's online marketplace through the app. After a quick AI-supported assessment, Alex can see offers from other users interested in buying the pump.

(continued)

After selling the old pump, Alex explores the refurbished pump options available on SmartFlow's marketplace. The app offers detailed information about each refurbished pump, including its service history and any replaced parts. Alex chooses a larger refurbished pump that fulfills the company's requirements and finalizes the purchase through the app.

The new, refurbished pump is seamlessly integrated into Alex's digital profile. The app informs Alex about future recycling options for parts. It directs him to the nearest recycling center when the components of the refurbished pump eventually reach the end of their life.

Alex participates in the SmartFlow community via social media and the SmartFlow customer engagement platform throughout the journey. Here, Alex can share experiences, offer feedback, and discuss new features and services.

SmartFlow's advanced digital tools and analytics ensure Alex receives relevant and timely information. Personalized product upgrades and maintenance recommendations are tailored to Alex's needs, ensuring the pump's longevity and efficiency.

14.1 Customer Interaction

The first aspect we will examine is customer interaction. Effective customer interaction fosters circular consumption patterns and maintains engagement throughout the product lifecycle. This section will explore how digital tools and strategies can enhance customer experiences, support circular practices, and drive long-term value for manufacturers and customers.

14.1.1 Seamless Multichannel Customer Journey

Manufacturers must ensure a seamless customer experience across all interaction channels. Whether directly interacting with the customer or through intermediaries such as resellers or circular service providers, a unified and consistent customer journey helps build trust and loyalty (Fig. 14.1).

Establishing a centralized system to manage customer data allows easy access to all customer interactions, preferences, and history across various touchpoints, such as in-store experiences, online platforms, repair services, and mobile apps. A unified view of customer data enables personalized and consistent interactions, regardless of the channel used.

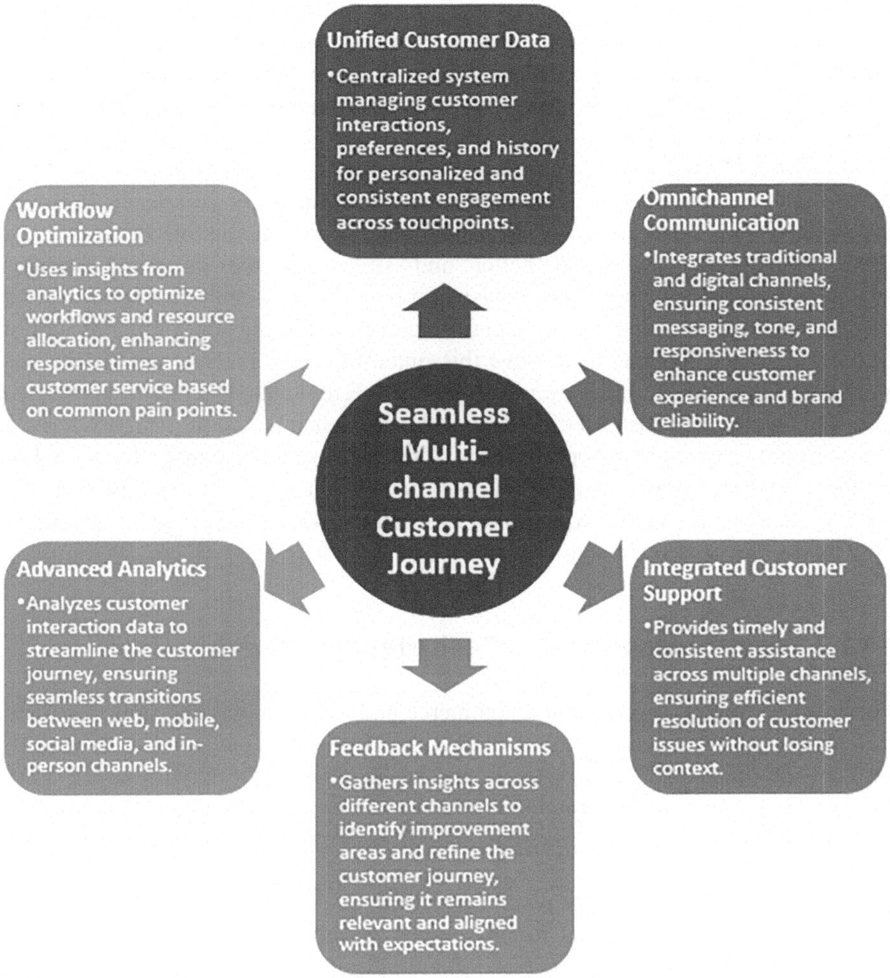

Fig. 14.1 Seamless multichannel customer journey

Leveraging omnichannel platforms helps to create a unified communication strategy that covers all aspects of customer service. This includes traditional in-person and telephone services and digital channels like social media, email, and chatbots. Consistency in messaging, tone, and responsiveness across all channels enhances the customer experience and reinforces brand reliability.

A well-integrated customer support system that works across multiple channels provides timely and consistent assistance and maintains customer satisfaction and loyalty. This system should be able to smoothly transition customer queries between channels without losing any context or information, ensuring an efficient and effective resolution of customer issues.

Businesses gather valuable insights into the customer experience by implementing feedback mechanisms across different channels. This helps them identify areas for improvement and make necessary changes. Regularly reviewing and refining the customer journey based on this feedback can help ensure that the experience remains relevant, seamless, and aligned with customer expectations.

Manufacturers use advanced analytics to improve the integration of various customer interaction channels, ensuring a seamless and consistent experience across all touchpoints. This capability involves analyzing customer interaction data from multiple channels to understand better and streamline the customer journey. Manufacturers make smooth and consistent transitions between web, mobile, social media, and in-person channels by identifying and addressing friction points within the multichannel journey. To achieve this, manufacturers analyze various metrics such as the time taken to resolve issues across different channels, the response rate of each channel, and customer satisfaction levels post-interaction. Insights derived from this data can guide the optimization of workflows and resource allocation. For example, manufacturers can adjust support protocols to quicken response times in slower channels or enhance training for customer service teams based on common pain points discovered through data analysis.

14.1.2 Digital Engagement in Redistribution Models

For business models centered on recommerce and reuse, digital platforms facilitate easy access and interaction. Online marketplaces and apps can connect users with available products for sharing, lease, or second-hand purchase, making participating in redistribution models as straightforward as shopping for new items. Features like digital contracts, payment systems, and user ratings enhance trust and convenience.

Manufacturers can generate revenue from products beyond their initial sale by creating a digital marketplace for pre-owned or refurbished items. This can be achieved through listing fees, transaction commissions, or offering certified refurbished products at a premium price. This approach helps to extend a product's revenue lifecycle and takes advantage of the growing demand for cost-effective, pre-owned goods.

Example 14.2 Harley-Davidson's digital marketplace for pre-owned motorcycles

Harley-Davidson has effectively extended its revenue streams beyond initial sales by establishing a digital marketplace for pre-owned motorcycles. In 2021, the company launched the H-D1™ Marketplace, an online platform that connects buyers and sellers of used Harley-Davidson motorcycles. This initiative allows the company to generate additional income through listing fees and transaction commissions.

Furthermore, Harley-Davidson introduced the H-D Certified™ program, offering certified pre-owned motorcycles that have undergone a comprehensive 110-point quality assurance inspection by certified technicians. These motorcycles come with a 12-month factory-backed limited warranty on the engine and transmission, providing customers with added confidence in their purchase.

Harley-Davidson capitalizes on the growing demand for cost-effective, reliable pre-owned goods by offering certified pre-owned motorcycles at a premium price. This strategy extends the revenue lifecycle of their products and reinforces customer loyalty by providing quality options within the Harley-Davidson ecosystem.

Manufacturers utilize a commission-based revenue model by creating digital platforms for peer-to-peer product sharing. Every platform transaction can generate a fee, whether renting out a tool for a weekend project or a bicycle for a city tour. This setup creates a continuous revenue stream without producing new goods.

The sharing economy's interactive platforms offer valuable insights into customer preferences and behavior. This data can be utilized to customize marketing strategies, create new products that cater to evolving needs, and identify opportunities for upselling and cross-selling, driving more sales and improving customer lifetime value.

14.1.3 Sharing Economy for Industrial Sectors[1]

The concept of a sharing economy is not just limited to consumer interactions; it also presents opportunities for manufacturers in the industrial sector (Sect. 5.3). Manufacturers can encourage industrial collaboration by creating digital support systems, which can lead to increased efficiency, innovation, and new revenue streams.

In the industrial sharing economy, businesses share resources, knowledge, and capabilities to achieve mutual benefits. Digital platforms can help companies share production facilities, logistics networks, or warehouses, leading to Business to Business (B2B) collaborations that enhance operational efficiency, reduce costs, and drive innovation. This business model aims to optimize the use of expensive assets and reduce the environmental impact caused by underutilized resources.

[1] https://www.harley-davidson.com/us/en/marketplace.html

14.1.4 Enhancing Product Use Extension Through Digital Tools

In models focused on repair, refurbishment, and remanufacturing, digital engagement extends product lifecycles. Manufacturers use digital platforms to offer repair services, schedule maintenance, or even guide customers through DIY repair processes via instructional videos or AR overlays. Digital booking systems, progress tracking, and direct communication channels ensure transparency and ease of service, making it more appealing for customers to choose repair over replacement.

Example 14.3 Apple's self service repair

In Sect. 6.4.6, we discussed Apple's Self Service Repair, which is supported by a digital platform. Customers can order genuine Apple parts and rent or buy the tools needed to repair their devices. They also get access to repair manuals and can return the replaced part for recycling. Additionally, customers may receive a credit for the return of certain parts (Apple, 2024).

Developing digital platforms that connect product owners with repair services or enable product swaps can introduce service fees or subscription models that contribute directly to the manufacturer's bottom line.

14.1.5 Streamlining Recycling with Digital Engagement

In recycling models, digital tools demystify the recycling process for end-users. Apps inform users about the recyclability of products or components and direct them to nearby recycling centers. Product QR codes can link to detailed information about properly disassembling and recycling each part. For more advanced circular sourcing models, digital platforms connect businesses with recycled material suppliers, facilitating the use of sustainable inputs in new products.

Digital customer engagement in these circular business models makes sustainable choices more accessible and attractive to consumers and creates operational efficiencies for manufacturers.

14.1.6 Enabling Product Lifecycle Tracking for Continuous Customer Dialogue

Manufacturers have an opportunity to foster deeper customer engagement by offering digital tools that enable product owners to track the entire lifecycle of their products. This capability extends beyond the point of sale, creating a continuous loop of communication and knowledge exchange that benefits both the customer and the manufacturer.

Customers access detailed records of all repairs performed, including dates, parts replaced, and service providers involved. This transparency builds trust and encourages customers to invest in maintenance and repairs rather than opting for replacements.

For remanufactured or redistributed products, tracking previous ownerships and uses provides a complete picture of the product's journey. This information can assure customers of the product's quality and sustainability.

IoT-enabled products continuously collect and report usage data, allowing owners to monitor performance, anticipate maintenance needs, and optimize usage patterns for longevity.

14.1.7 Enhancing Engagement with AR and VR

Augmented reality (AR) and virtual reality (VR) revolutionize how customers interact with products. They provide immersive experiences that enable customers to explore the entire lifecycle of products. AR allows customers to interact with digital overlays on physical products, providing insights into recyclability and sustainable design features. VR goes even further by, e.g., offering virtual tours of manufacturing processes and showcasing the use of sustainable materials and practices.

This hands-on approach helps customers grasp complex circularity concepts. It allows them to experiment with product features in real time, such as simulating upgrades or visualizing the environmental benefits of waste-efficient choices. This interactive exploration educates and empowers customers to make informed decisions about the products they use.

14.1.8 Ensuring Digital Readiness for Third-Party-Operated Platforms

When customers opt for a third-party digital platform, manufacturers must ensure they are an appealing digital partner ready for meaningful digital interaction. This includes offering seamless access to information and services that improve the customer experience through the third-party digital platform.

Manufacturers should provide digital warranties (Sect. 10.5) that can be easily accessed and managed through third-party platforms. This includes online registration, instant warranty validation, and automated reminders. Additionally, repair manuals should be readily available to empower customers and repair service providers to maintain and repair products.

Digital Product Passports enable transparency and traceability. They provide comprehensive information about a product's composition, origin, and lifecycle and should be easily accessible through third-party platforms.

Manufacturers should ensure interoperability and compatibility with various third-party platforms. This involves using standardized data formats, APIs, and event thinking to enable seamless integration. By ensuring compatibility, manufacturers can provide a consistent and reliable digital experience across different platforms, enhancing customer trust and engagement.

It is also important to build strong relationships with third-party platform operators. Manufacturers should collaborate with these partners to align digital strategies and ensure mutual benefits, including shared data analytics and co-developed digital tools that enhance the customer journey.

14.2 Personalization

In the circular economy context, personalization involves more than tailoring products and services to individual preferences. It also encourages behaviors that promote resource efficiency, product longevity, and waste reduction (Fig. 14.2).

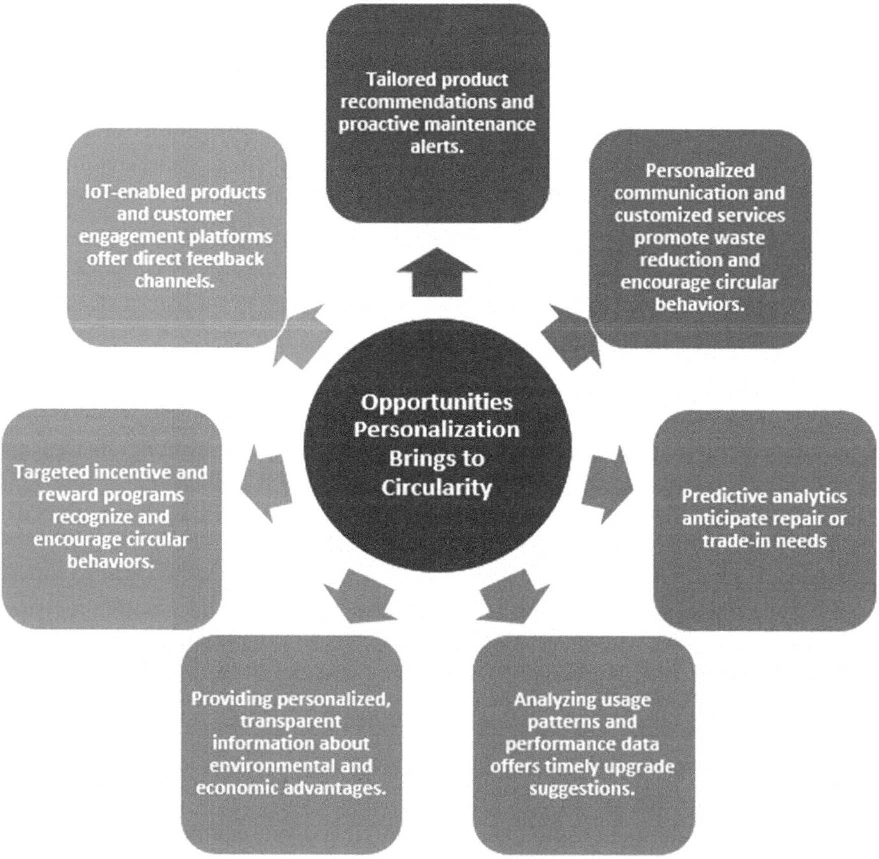

Fig. 14.2 Opportunities Personalization Brings to Circularity

Businesses can analyze customer data across different channels using advanced analytics and AI. This enables them to deliver personalized experiences that make the customer journey more engaging and relevant. Some of these personalized experiences include tailored product recommendations, customized services, and personalized communication based on the customer's previous interactions and preferences. For instance, tailored suggestions for product maintenance can extend the product's lifespan, options for refurbishing or upgrading existing products, and recommendations for recycling or participating in take-back schemes. Aligning these recommendations with individual customer habits and preferences increases the likelihood of adoption.

Predictive analytics can predict customers' needs and preferences in real time, allowing for proactive recommendations. For instance, even before a product reaches the end of its useful life, the customer can be given suggestions for repair services or trade-in options, thereby seamlessly integrating the principles of the circular economy into their overall customer experience. This anticipatory approach ensures that customers are presented with circular possibilities at the most relevant and impactful moments.

In Sect. 4.1.2, we discussed how building products with modules enables manufacturers to offer the product as a platform concept. By understanding each customer's platform configuration with its various modules, manufacturers can provide personalized recommendations for upgrading or modifying these modules. In addition to offering personalized upgrade suggestions, manufacturers can act as intermediaries for customers looking to upgrade their modules. Either via recommerce or if customers need extra capacity for a limited period, they can rent a module from another user rather than purchasing a new one. By analyzing usage patterns and performance data, manufacturers can identify when a customer might benefit from an upgrade or a new module. These insights help provide timely and relevant recommendations and enable manufacturers to anticipate future needs and trends.

Digital decision support systems play a role in encouraging customers to adopt more circular practices. These systems can provide personalized and transparent information regarding circular actions' environmental and economic advantages, such as selecting products designed for longevity or participating in a sharing economy platform.

Personalization can help create targeted incentive and reward programs that acknowledge and encourage circular behaviors. For example, customers who regularly engage in circular practices, such as returning products for recycling or choosing refurbished items, may receive personalized rewards or discounts.

By focusing on these personalized strategies, businesses can more effectively engage customers in the circular economy, encouraging practices that reduce waste, extend product life, and close material loops. Personalization thus becomes a powerful tool for enhancing customer experience and driving the systemic change needed for a more circular future.

Example 14.4 Burger King UK and Loop has implemented a digital incentive program

Burger King UK has implemented a digital incentive program to promote circular behaviors among its customers. In partnership with the global reuse platform Loop, the company introduced reusable packaging options for select menu items. Customers can opt for reusable cups or containers by paying a £1 deposit, which is refunded upon return[2].

The Loop app facilitates the process, where customers scan a unique QR code on the packaging to register the return. This digital interaction streamlines the return process and enables Burger King to track individual customer participation in the program. By analyzing this data, the company can potentially identify and reward customers who consistently engage in sustainable practices, such as returning reusable packaging.

14.2.1 Facilitating Direct Dialogue with End-Users

The digitization of customer interactions allows for direct communication with end-users and others in the value chain to promote circular practices and improve product lifecycle management.

Products embedded with IoT (Internet of Things) technologies offer a direct communication channel between manufacturers and their customers. These smart products gather and transmit real-time data on usage, performance metrics, and maintenance requirements, facilitating a continuous feedback loop. This connectivity enables manufacturers to provide personalized customer experiences, such as proactive maintenance alerts, tips for extending product life, and recommendations for recycling and refurbishment options.

Digital customer engagement platforms are online spaces that allow brands to interact directly with their customers in their value chain. These platforms can be integrated into a company's website or mobile app or exist as a standalone digital service. They offer various features such as live chat, forums, feedback submission forms, improvement suggestions, and interactive knowledge bases. Through this direct line of communication, manufacturers can gain valuable insights from their customers, which can drive product and service improvements. Additionally, these platforms offer the opportunity for customers to share ideas for new circular features or services.

[2] https://www.bitc.org.uk/case-study/burger-king-uk-minimising-waste-with-reusable-packaging/

Create platforms that can monitor and accurately communicate the sustainability metrics of products and services. These platforms should provide information about the product's origin, environmental impact throughout its lifecycle, and proper recycling or disposal guidelines. By doing so, value chain customers can gain insights into their purchases and use's environmental and social impacts.

14.3 Building Community Through Social Engagement and Collaboration

Social media platforms are vibrant forums for engaging with value chain customers, championing circular economy principles, and driving collaborative innovation. Their inherent two-way communication capacity allows businesses to connect with their audience, build communities, and foster a participatory culture in developing circular products and services.

Social media enables interactivity that traditional media cannot match, allowing for real-time conversations between businesses and customers. This two-way communication channel will enable customers to contribute ideas, express preferences, and provide feedback directly to manufacturers. For instance, businesses can involve their social media followers in prioritizing new product features or generating innovative ideas for circular design solutions, turning the product development process into a collaborative journey.

Manufacturers can use social collaboration to engage their audience in decision-making. These tools can gauge customer interest in potential circular features, such as product take-back programs, repair services, or sustainable material options. The insights gathered can guide businesses in aligning their offerings with the values and preferences of their community, ensuring that circular initiatives resonate with and meet the needs of their target audience.

Social media provides a fertile ground for crowdsourcing, where businesses can tap into their followers' collective wisdom and creativity to solve circular economy challenges. Whether finding new uses for by-products, improving product recyclability, or enhancing product longevity, the community can contribute valuable ideas and solutions. This collaborative approach accelerates innovation and fosters a sense of ownership and engagement among participants.

Social networks can be powerful platforms for disseminating information about circular practices, such as recycling, upcycling, product care, and repair tips. By sharing engaging content that educates and inspires, manufacturers can raise awareness about the importance and feasibility of circular behaviors. Highlighting success stories, sharing user-generated content related to circular practices, and offering practical advice can motivate followers to adopt more sustainable habits. Moreover, social media analytics can provide insights into customer attitudes toward circularity, helping businesses tailor their strategies to meet customer expectations better and drive change.

Creating dedicated online spaces or groups focusing on circular economy topics can help build a community of like-minded individuals. These forums can facilitate discussions, ideas exchange, and experience sharing, fostering participants' sense of belonging and collective action. Engaging with this community helps spread circular economy principles and understand customer needs and preferences, enabling more customer-centric circular innovations.

Social media marketing presents a powerful platform for advocating circular economy principles and engaging with audiences on sustainability. Through challenges and initiatives like "Zero-Waste Challenges," businesses can encourage participation in circular practices, fostering a sustainability-minded community. Partnering with influencers and collaborating with like-minded organizations amplifies this message, making circular principles accessible and actionable. Showcasing circular innovations and transparent design processes on social media educates customers and builds trust in the brand's commitment.

14.3.1 Gamification and Digital Loyalty Programs

Loyalty programs and gamification strategies are ways to encourage circular behaviors. Companies can increase customer engagement and promote circular practices by using digital platforms in conjunction with loyalty schemes. Digital loyalty programs allow customers to earn rewards for actions that contribute to circularity, like recycling, product refurbishment, and repair services. These rewards typically come in points, discounts, or access to exclusive services, providing customers with tangible benefits.

By incorporating gamification, businesses can make circular behaviors fun and competitive, motivating customers to participate more actively. Gamification involves applying game-design elements in non-game contexts to enhance user engagement and participation. This approach can transform routine activities into more dynamic and enjoyable experiences.

Gamification can be used to promote circular behaviors in various ways. For example, digital leaderboards can foster community and competition by displaying rankings based on users' recycling activities or choices for circular products. Challenges can be set up to encourage users to achieve specific goals, such as reducing waste or participating in recycling programs within a specific time frame. Completing these challenges may earn users achievement badges, visually representing their commitments and accomplishments.

14.4 Leveraging Customer Analytics

Customer analytics are essential for successful customer interactions in a circular economy. Manufacturers use data to improve their understanding of customer behavior, preferences, and needs. This understanding increases engagement and promotes circular practices throughout the product lifecycle.

Engaging with customers effectively goes beyond the initial transaction in a circular economy. It involves continuous interaction, feedback, and adaptation to ensure that products are used sustainably and resources are managed efficiently. Customer analytics provides the insights needed to support this ongoing dialogue, enabling manufacturers to offer personalized experiences, optimize resource use, and enhance overall customer satisfaction.

Previously, we've discussed how customer analytics is crucial in various opportunities. For instance, advanced analytics help create a smooth multichannel customer journey by integrating different customer interaction channels. This ensures a consistent and personalized experience across all touchpoints. By analyzing interaction data, manufacturers identify friction points and optimize workflows to enhance customer satisfaction.

In digital interaction within redistribution models, online marketplaces and digital platforms utilize analytics to comprehend customer preferences for renting, leasing, or purchasing pre-owned products. This data aids in tailoring offerings and enhancing the overall user experience.

By analyzing maintenance and usage data, manufacturers provide timely repair, upgrade, or refurbishment recommendations, extending product lifecycles and reducing waste. By streamlining recycling with digital engagement, customer analytics helps track product end-of-life decisions, informing manufacturers about recycling behaviors and preferences. This data is needed to design effective recycling programs and improve material recovery processes.

Analytics offers customers personalized recommendations, including energy-saving tips, optimal usage patterns, and advice on recycling or repurposing products. Manufacturers gain insights into customer perceptions and attitudes toward their products and sustainability efforts by analyzing customer feedback and sentiment from different channels such as social media, reviews, and surveys.

Analytics monitor the environmental impact of products from production to disposal. This data educates customers about the environmental consequences of their choices and emphasizes the impact of circular practices.

Please also see the discussion on data-driven circularity in Chap. 15.

14.5 Digital Customer Engagement in a Connected Circular Economy

In traditional linear economic models, the value chain customer and manufacturer relationship often concludes at the point of sale. A digitized circular economy breaks away from this one-time transaction framework, extending the relationship through the product's entire lifecycle, even into its end-of-life phase. Digitized circular engagement actively involves value chain customers at every step by deploying sophisticated digital tools like events, APIs, incentives, and versatile platforms.

Manufacturers improve their relationships with customers after they purchase a product by offering an easy-to-use digital dashboard or mobile application. This platform serves as a central hub for all interactions related to the product, such as usage instructions, maintenance tips, and options for utilizing circular services.

Integrating IoT technology and real-time analytics in the dashboard would provide personalized recommendations based on customer consumption patterns.

Automated notifications alert product owners about available circular pathways as the product approaches its end of use. These pathways include recycling, reselling, refurbishing, or remanufacturing. Each option has specific incentives like discounts on future purchases, loyalty points, or contributions to charitable causes. Gamification elements make circular consumption more attractive and straightforward, reducing hesitations or barriers customers might encounter.

Manufacturers engage with their customers beyond just transactional interactions. They ask for customer feedback about end-of-life decisions for their products, which is then used for analytics. This data is important as it allows manufacturers to improve their product designs, adjust their supply chain practices, and develop new circular business models. Such decisions are made based on direct customer insights.

Educational content and statistics on real-world impacts, such as waste diversion or carbon emission reductions, further enlighten and engage customers. This knowledge fosters a sense of community and shared responsibility.

By weaving advanced analytics into customer engagement practices, manufacturers are better positioned to anticipate needs, tailor interactions, and innovate to align with customers' need for circularity.

The journey to a circular economy is complex, but businesses can more effectively navigate this landscape by deepening customer connections through strategic digital customer engagement.

14.5.1 Essential Digital Capabilities for Enhancing the Customer Journey in a Circular Economy

Manufacturers must leverage a range of digital capabilities to support the digital customer journey in a circular economy successfully. Figure 14.3 shows the 12 key digital capabilities identified in the chapter.

14.5.2 Digital Customer Touchpoint Checklist

This chapter delved into how digitization can enhance customer interaction and engagement within the circular economy. The following checklist outlines the steps manufacturers should take to implement these strategies (Table 14.1).

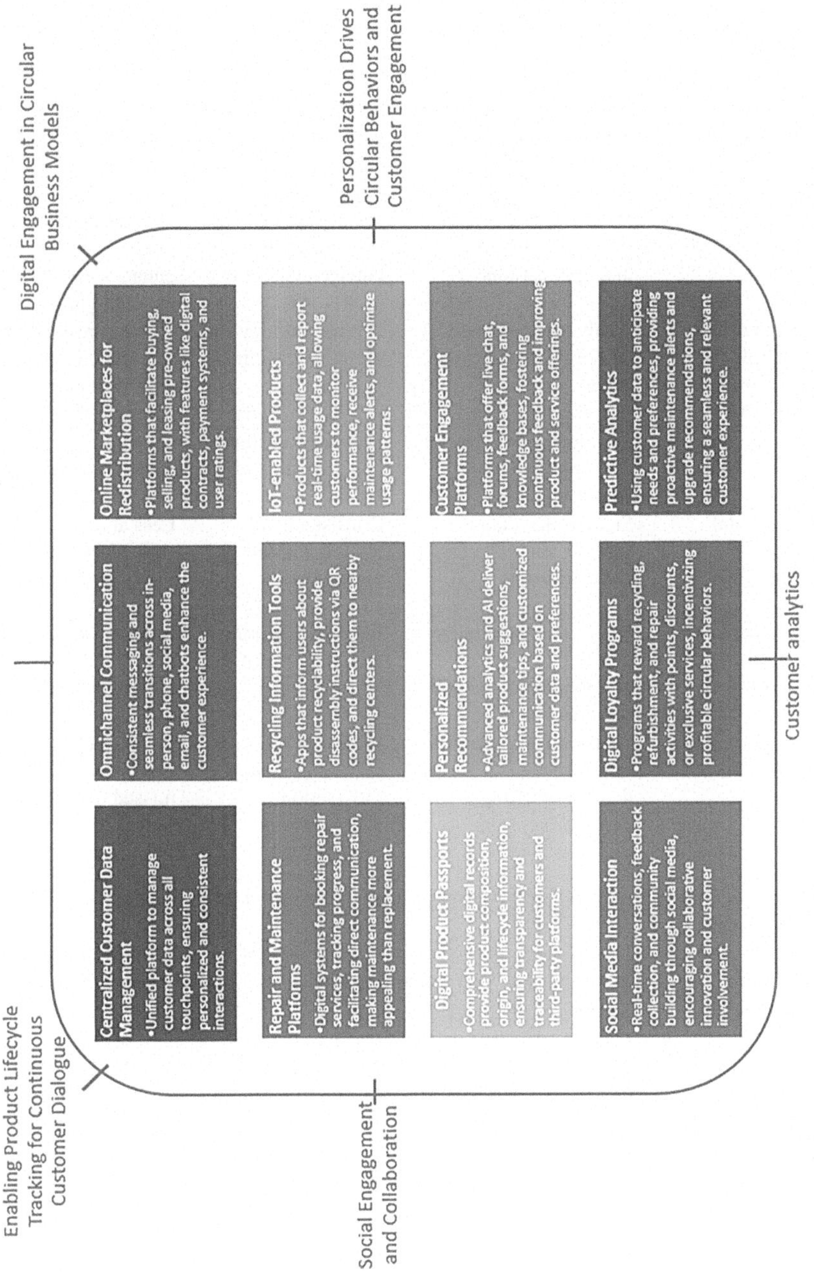

Fig. 14.3 Essential digital capabilities for enhancing the customer journey in a circular economy

Table 14.1 Digital customer touchpoint checklist

Task	Methodology	Expected outcome	Risk mitigated
Develop a multichannel support system	Implement an omnichannel platform	Consistent and personalized customer experience	Fragmented customer service across channels
Implement feedback mechanisms	Integrate feedback tools across all channels	Enhanced customer satisfaction and service improvement	Missing out on valuable customer insights
Familiarize yourself with AR/VR	Research and explore AR/VR technologies and applications	Awareness of immersive customer engagement tools	Lack of understanding of emerging engagement technologies
Investigate the desired role in digital customer interactions	Analyze market needs and evaluate potential roles	A clear strategy for digital engagement	A third party taking an important role in digital customer interactions
Enable product lifecycle tracking	Develop digital tools to track product history and usage data	Enhanced customer engagement and transparency	Customer disengagement due to lack of information
Ensure digital readiness for third-party platforms	Standardize data formats and APIs for compatibility	Consistent and reliable digital experience	Less attractiveness for customers using third-party platforms
Personalize customer interactions	Use analytics to tailor product recommendations and services	Increased customer satisfaction and loyalty	Generic interactions that fail to meet customer needs
Leverage customer analytics	Analyze customer data to inform decision-making	Improved resource use and customer satisfaction	Inefficient use of customer data leads to missed opportunities

Reference

Apple. (2024, 06). *Self service repair store for apple products*. From https://selfservicerepair.com/en-US/home

Data-Driven Circularity – The Brain of a Circular Economy

15

Abstract

Data-driven circularity is the central intelligence of the circular economy, integrating and leveraging data across customer interactions, business ecosystems, connected products, and internal IT systems to guide strategic decisions and enhance resource efficiency. Incorporating technologies such as big data, business intelligence (BI), artificial intelligence (AI), machine learning (ML), predictive analytics, and generative AI creates a robust framework that enhances operational efficiencies, drives sustainability, and fosters economic growth. Big data tracks material flows, optimizing resource use and minimizing waste. BI transforms raw data into actionable insights, improving operations and recycling programs. AI and ML optimize resource allocation, improve product design, and facilitate predictive maintenance and demand forecasting. Predictive analytics anticipates trends, improving product design for repairability and recyclability. Generative AI aids in innovative product designs and simulations. Digital Product Passports enhance transparency and lifecycle management. Data-driven circularity helps comply with regulations like right to repair and Extended Producer Responsibility (EPR), supports strategic decision-making in redistribution, and extends product lifecycles.

The chapter also outlines essential digital capabilities and provides a detailed capability map, emphasizing the integration of these technologies across various stages of the product lifecycle. Additionally, a comprehensive checklist guides manufacturers through implementing data-driven circular practices, ensuring structured adoption and effective outcomes. As part of the Sustainable Manufacturing Intelligence Framework (SMIF), data-driven circularity offers a comprehensive view of a manufacturer's circular business models, guiding strategic decisions and operational adjustments to drive profitability and resource efficiency.

H. H. Jensen, *Circular Economy Opportunities and Pathways for Manufacturers*, Future of Business and Finance, https://doi.org/10.1007/978-3-031-75279-7_15

Key Messages

- *Central Role of Data-Driven Circularity*: Data-driven circularity is the brain of the circular economy, integrating and leveraging data across customer interaction, business ecosystems, connected products, and internal IT systems to guide strategic decisions and enhance resource efficiency.
- *Technology Integration*: Incorporating technologies such as Big Data, Business Intelligence (BI), artificial intelligence (AI), machine learning (ML), predictive analytics, and Generative AI creates a robust framework that enhances operational efficiencies, drives sustainability, and fosters economic growth.
- *Big Data Utilization*: Big Data plays a crucial role in tracking the quantities and flows of materials, optimizing resource use, and minimizing waste, thereby supporting efficient and sustainable manufacturing practices.
- *Enhanced Business Intelligence*: BI transforms raw data into actionable insights, helping manufacturers understand their operations comprehensively and identify opportunities for improvement, particularly in recycling programs, resource utilization, and supply chain logistics.
- *AI and Machine Learning Synergy*: AI optimizes resource allocation, improves product design for sustainability, and enhances decision-making processes, while ML, as a subset of AI, enables systems to learn from data and make accurate predictions, facilitating predictive maintenance and demand forecasting.
- *Predictive Analytics*: Predictive analytics anticipates future trends and behaviors, allowing manufacturers to prepare for product end of life and improve designs for repairability and recyclability, thus enhancing product circularity.
- *Generative AI Innovation*: Generative AI aids in developing innovative product designs and simulations, optimizing for recyclability and durability, reducing the need for physical prototypes, and accelerating the innovation cycle.
- *Digital Product Passports*: Implementing Digital Product Passports (DPPs) enhances transparency and lifecycle management. They provide detailed information on product materials, origin, usage, and recyclability for informed decision-making and regulatory compliance.
- *Regulatory Compliance Through Data-Driven Circularity*: Data-driven circularity helps manufacturers comply with right to repair, packaging waste, and Extended Producer Responsibility (EPR) legislation by providing insights into component performance, failure rates, material usage, and waste generation. This supports product design for easier repairability, efficient recycling, and effective take-back programs, ensuring compliance with regulatory requirements.

(continued)

- *Strategic Decision-Making in Redistribution*: Data-driven insights optimize inventory, logistics, customer interactions, and maintenance in redistribution models, enhancing operational efficiency and customer satisfaction while promoting sustainable practices.
- *Product Use Extension*: Advanced analytics and predictive modeling support strategic decisions on repair, refurbishment, and remanufacturing, enabling businesses to extend product lifecycles efficiently and sustainably.
- *Operational Efficiency in Recycling*: Data analytics and ML optimize sourcing, lifecycle assessments, and quality management of recycled materials, ensuring compliance with regulations and maintaining product quality in manufacturing processes.

Data-driven circularity is pivotal in the Sustainable Manufacturing Intelligence Framework (SMIF), serving as the central intelligence or brain of a manufacturer's circular economy efforts. This capability integrates and leverages data from the other four capabilities of SMIF: customer interaction, business ecosystem, connected products, and internal IT systems. By merging and analyzing data across these dimensions, data-driven circularity offers a comprehensive view of a manufacturer's circular business models, guiding strategic decisions and operational adjustments that drive profitability and resource efficiency.

Data-driven circularity transition is critical for several reasons (Table 15.1).

The Sustainable Manufacturing Intelligence Framework (SMIF) is the foundation of data-driven circularity. It manages the movement of data that powers circular economy strategies. Each component of SMIF produces valuable data and employs the insights from the combined data to improve circular economy practices.

Internal IT systems generate a vast amount of data from internal processes. This data includes production data, resource usage, and efficiency metrics. Advanced analytics refine these processes, enhancing data security and improving decision-making. By increasing operational efficiency and supporting sustainable practices, the insights obtained from internal IT systems help streamline production, minimize waste, and ensure that business operations align with the principles of the circular economy.

The business ecosystem capability tracks the interactions and transactions within the supply chain and business partnerships, documenting the flow of resources and the lifecycle of materials across the ecosystem. Analyzing this data helps businesses to optimize their supply chain logistics, reduce dependencies, and increase the use of recycled materials. This fosters a more resilient and sustainable business model by improving supply chain sustainability and enabling a circular flow of materials.

Connected products and components continually transmit data related to their functioning, status, and efficiency. This real-time data is used to monitor product health and understand usage patterns. The insights from connected products are utilized for predictive maintenance, enhancing product longevity, and reducing

Table 15.1 Data-driven circularity focus area

Focus area	Key point	Role in circular economy models
Optimized resource use	Data-driven circularity enables manufacturers to make informed decisions that optimize resource allocation and minimize waste	This strategic insight leads to more efficient production processes, saving raw material costs and reducing waste management expenditures
Enhanced product design	Leveraging data across the product lifecycle allows manufacturers to enhance product design for durability and ease of recycling	This approach maximizes the value extracted from each product, reduces the replacement frequency, and supports sustainable consumption patterns
Customer insights	Data analytics provide deep insights into customer behaviors and preferences	This alignment enhances customer loyalty and strengthens the brand's market position
Regulatory adaptation	The agility of data-driven insights allows manufacturers to adapt to regulatory changes and market shifts	This proactive adaptation avoids potential fines and capitalizes on market opportunities promptly
Supply chain resilience	Data-driven strategies enhance visibility and coordination across the supply chain	Enabling manufacturers to anticipate disruptions, manage inventory more effectively, and maintain continuity in production This resilience is crucial in a global market where supply chain disruptions impact businesses
Service-based models	Comprehensive product usage and lifecycle data support the shift from traditional sales to service-based business models	Supports models such as Product-as-a-Service (PaaS) and repair services

waste. This results in better efficiency of repair, refurbishment, and remanufacturing processes, ensuring that products and resources are used optimally throughout their lifecycle.

The customer interaction capability aims to gather and examine comprehensive information about customer behavior, preferences, and product feedback. This data is crucial in understanding product performance and customer satisfaction in real-life situations. With the help of these insights, businesses can customize their product designs and offerings to better cater to customer needs, promote sustainable usage patterns, and engage in innovative practices that extend the product lifecycle. This includes improving repairability or optimizing recycling.

SmartFlow Pumps Inc. is a fictional company specializing in high-efficiency industrial pumps. The example is created to provide a coherent understanding of how a manufacturer can use data-driven decision-making in all aspects of its circular journey. The rest of the chapter will explore these opportunities further, illustrating how data-driven circularity enhances each stage of a product's lifecycle, from design to end-of-life management.

Example 15.1 Fictive example of Data-Driven Circularity

At the design and production stage, SmartFlow Pumps Inc. integrates advanced technologies to create products optimized for circularity. Generative AI aids in the innovative design of pumps by simulating various configurations and materials, ensuring that the final products are recyclable and durable. This approach reduces the need for physical prototypes and speeds up the innovation cycle. Big Data collects and analyzes extensive datasets from past designs, material usage, and customer feedback. This data-driven approach informs better design decisions, ensuring that the products meet customer needs and regulatory standards while minimizing waste and enhancing product longevity.

SmartFlow employs data-driven insights to optimize inventory management, logistics, and customer interactions in the sales and distribution phase. Collaboration and data sharing with suppliers and partners streamline supply chain logistics, reducing dependencies and enhancing operational efficiency. This approach improves customer satisfaction, promotes sustainable practices, and fosters a resilient business model, enabling a circular flow of materials throughout the supply chain.

During the usage and maintenance stage, SmartFlow Pumps are equipped with IoT devices that continuously transmit data on performance, usage patterns, and environmental conditions. Machine learning algorithms analyze this data to predict maintenance needs and optimize performance. This real-time monitoring ensures that the pumps operate at peak efficiency, reducing energy consumption and operational costs. Advanced analytics provide insights into customer behaviors and preferences, allowing SmartFlow to offer tailored maintenance schedules and proactive service reminders. Digital Product Passports (DPPs) also offer detailed information on product materials, origin, usage, and recyclability, enhancing customer understanding and engagement.

SmartFlow's approach to repairing involves leveraging predictive maintenance to minimize downtime and extend the operational life of the pumps. Machine learning algorithms analyze performance data to predict potential failures and maintenance needs, enabling timely repairs.

In terms of recommerce, data-driven insights help identify opportunities for reselling and reusing pumps that are still in good condition but no longer needed by the original customer. Business Intelligence tools manage inventory and logistics for the resale market, ensuring that recommerce operations are efficient and effective.

(continued)

In the refurbishment and remanufacturing phase, SmartFlow uses Big Data and AI to guide the process, analyzing which components need replacement or repair to restore the pump to like-new condition. Machine learning enhances decision-making by identifying which parts can be reused, refurbished, or replaced. Customer feedback from advanced analytics helps improve the refurbishment process and ensure high quality. This approach ensures that refurbished pumps meet high-quality and performance standards, providing a sustainable alternative to new products.

At the end-of-life management stage, SmartFlow employs predictive analytics to anticipate when pumps will reach the end of their useful life, allowing the company to plan for product take-back and recycling. Big Data and Business Intelligence tools analyze the flow of materials and identify opportunities for recycling and reuse. Data analytics ensure compliance with Extended Producer Responsibility (EPR) regulations and other environmental standards by tracking material usage and waste generation.

SmartFlow maintains an ongoing dialogue with customers throughout the lifecycle to build trust and loyalty. Digital Product Passports enhance transparency and lifecycle management by giving customers detailed information on their pump's journey and status. Continuous feedback loops, facilitated by advanced analytics and customer interaction platforms, ensure SmartFlow attests to customer needs and preferences. This robust engagement helps the company continuously evolve its products and services to meet market demands for sustainability and cost-effectiveness.

15.1 Technology Concepts Supporting Data-Driven Circularity

Manufacturers can support data-driven circularity by utilizing technology concepts such as Big Data, Business Intelligence (BI), artificial intelligence (AI), machine learning (ML), predictive analytics, and Generative AI. These technologies work together to create a robust framework for data-driven circularity, allowing manufacturers to leverage data to enhance operational efficiencies, drive sustainability, and foster economic growth. Each technology has its merits and works synergistically with others to provide a comprehensive approach to data-driven circularity.

Big Data involves collecting vast amounts of data from various sources throughout a product's lifecycle, including production, usage, disposal, and recycling. The primary purpose of Big Data is to provide extensive datasets that can be used for in-depth analysis and to train sophisticated models that can predict, analyze, and simulate. In a circular business model, Big Data plays a vital role in tracking the quantities and flows of materials, ensuring that resources are used efficiently and waste streams are kept to a minimum. Manufacturers can utilize Big Data to monitor resource consumption patterns, optimize material use, and reduce environmental impact while maximizing economic returns.

Business intelligence analyzes the raw data gathered by big data and turns it into actionable insights. This is achieved using various tools and processes that produce detailed reports, visualizations, and dashboards. These insights give businesses a comprehensive understanding of their operations, allowing them to identify areas of inefficiency and improve their performance.

In the context of circular business models, BI can be particularly useful in assessing the effectiveness of recycling programs, resource utilization, and supply chain logistics. By providing a clear picture of current operations, BI helps companies identify opportunities for improvement, such as areas where materials can be more effectively reused or recycled.

Artificial intelligence (AI) encompasses a broad range of technologies to create machines capable of performing tasks that typically require human intelligence. These tasks include problem-solving, decision-making, language understanding, and perception. In circular business models, AI can optimize resource allocation, improve product design for sustainability, and enhance decision-making processes. By integrating AI into their operations, manufacturers can achieve higher levels of efficiency and sustainability.

Machine learning, a subset of AI, enhances Business Intelligence capabilities by enabling systems to learn from data, detect patterns, and make accurate predictions without explicit programming. ML models improve their accuracy and relevance over time as they are fed more data. Predictive maintenance and demand forecasting in circular business models are some areas where ML can be advantageous. By anticipating when machines will require servicing or resources might become scarce, ML helps plan maintenance and resource procurement effectively, thus minimizing downtime and reducing excess inventory.

Example 15.2 Danfoss utilizes machine learning

Danfoss[1], a heating, ventilation, and air-conditioning (HVAC) system manufacturer, gathers a wide range of operational data from HVAC systems in commercial properties. This includes data on energy usage, operational efficiency, maintenance logs, and environmental conditions. The collected data is then analyzed using data processing tools to identify patterns and inefficiencies, such as frequent breakdowns or excessive energy consumption under certain conditions.

Danfoss utilizes machine learning (ML) to analyze historical performance data to predict potential failures or inefficiencies in HVAC system components. The system can detect operational issues like compressor failure or coil icing, providing practical guidance for resolution.

Predictive analytics is used to predict potential system failures and maintenance needs. The company can schedule maintenance or component replacements before actual system failures occur, minimizing downtime and extending the operational life of the HVAC systems.

[1] https://www.danfoss.com/en/

Danfoss focuses on deploying AI to decarbonize its systems. Since its launch in 2019, AI algorithms have saved 4 Mt CO_2 in the operation of multi-family houses globally. Early failure detection and continuous refrigeration system monitoring have helped save more than 100 tons of food loss on the retail side of the food industry.

Predictive analytics is a powerful tool that uses statistical algorithms and machine learning techniques to predict future scenarios based on historical data. This ML application is useful in anticipating future trends and behaviors, allowing manufacturers to act proactively rather than reactively. In circular business models, predictive analytics can help forecast products' end of life, enabling manufacturers to prepare for the return and recycling of products. Additionally, it can predict the failure rates of products and components, allowing manufacturers to design more easily repairable or recyclable products, thus enhancing their circularity.

Example 15.3 TK Elevator utilizes the Internet of Things (IoT), big data, and machine learning

TK Elevator, a global leader in elevator and escalator solutions, utilizes the Internet of Things (IoT), big data, and machine learning to improve the maintenance and performance of its elevators through a system called MAX.

TK Elevator's elevators are equipped with multiple sensors that constantly gather data on various aspects such as motor status, shaft alignment, and door functioning. This data is sent to the cloud and analyzed using advanced algorithms and machine learning based on data from over 175,000 connected devices worldwide.

MAX can predict maintenance needs before issues arise, reducing downtime by up to 50% and resulting in 30% fewer breakdowns. TK Elevator can dispatch technicians to repair equipment before a customer is even aware of a problem. This proactive maintenance approach ensures elevators operate at peak efficiency, offering a more reliable service for building occupants. This is crucial for high-rise buildings where elevator service is critical for people's day-to-day movement.

MAX integrates via APIs with existing building management systems to provide an overview of elevator status and health for building managers (TK Elevator, 2024a, b).

Generative AI, also known as GenAI, has a unique role in creating new data and simulations, although it is not traditionally involved in data analysis. GenAI can be used to innovate product designs in circular business models by simulating different configurations and materials. This can help identify those that optimize recyclability and durability.

GenAI can generate realistic data that can be used for training ML models when actual data is either insufficient or too costly to obtain. This capability is helpful for testing and improving product designs in a virtual environment. It reduces the need for physical prototypes and accelerates the innovation cycle.

15.2 Integrating Digital Product Passports in Data-Driven Circularity

Implementing Digital Product Passports (DPPs) in the European Union and potentially globally will transform the basis of data-driven practices within circular economies. DPPs will provide standardized, secure, and easily accessible data across product lifecycles, enhancing transparency and enabling effective lifecycle management of products.

DPPs will contain a comprehensive data record for every product, providing detailed information about its material composition, origin, usage instructions, and recyclability. This information will be vital for making informed decisions that promote sustainability and resource efficiency, as it ensures that all stakeholders, from manufacturers to consumers and recyclers, have access to accurate and reliable product information.

A household appliance manufacturer can use Digital Product Passports (DPPs) to improve product lifecycle management. For example, each appliance, such as a refrigerator or washing machine, will have a digital passport containing detailed information about the materials used, the manufacturing processes involved, and guidelines for repair and recycling. By integrating the DPP data into their Big Data systems, the manufacturer can use advanced analytics to monitor and analyze trends in material durability, common points of failure, and consumer usage patterns.

Manufacturers can use AI and analytics to drive the circular economy by ensuring that data from Digital Product Passports (DPPs) is fed into Big Data repositories. This helps with regulatory compliance and encourages market innovation, ultimately making businesses more competitive and sustainable. As DPPs are being implemented, manufacturers should prepare their data infrastructure to take advantage of this valuable source of information and incorporate it into their circular economy strategies.

15.3 How Data-Driven Circularity Supports the 1+5R Model

This section aims to inspire and illuminate how technologies such as Big Data, Business Intelligence (BI), machine learning (ML), predictive analytics, and Generative AI can be incorporated into the phases of the 1 + 5R model. The examples and applications discussed here are not exhaustive but indicative, intended to spark innovative thinking and encourage exploring further opportunities where these technologies can enhance manufacturers' circular capabilities.

15.3.1 Redesign

The redesign is the first step in the 1 + 5R model, which involves rethinking products and business models to ensure they are adaptable, repairable, and upgradable. Integrating advanced technologies can make the redesign process more efficient, data-driven, and aligned with circular principles.

Example 15.4 The Cyclometric project enhances the lifecycle-oriented development of automotive components

The Cyclometric project, led by the Fraunhofer Institute for Industrial Engineering IAO and other partners, aims to develop a decision-support tool to enhance the lifecycle-oriented development of automotive components. This tool ensures that all parts are recyclable from the development stage, thus promoting sustainability and circular economy principles in the automotive industry.

The project addresses the challenge of making recycling decisions during product development rather than at the end of a product's lifecycle. By integrating advanced systems engineering and lifecycle assessment methods, the Cyclometric tool analyzes data across all development phases and provides real-time feedback on the impact of design choices on producibility, recyclability, CO_2 emissions, and costs. This proactive approach helps developers make informed decisions that balance technological standards with environmental sustainability.

Insight Gathering and Customer Feedback

Big data and business intelligence (BI) can provide valuable insights into product usage, end-of-life outcomes, and customer preferences. Designers and engineers can create more durable and adaptable designs by analyzing large datasets about how products are used and identifying common failure points. BI tools can help visualize these patterns, enabling a better understanding of the specific aspects of a product that need redesigning to improve its lifecycle and reduce waste. Additionally, BI can facilitate lifecycle assessment (LCA) to evaluate the economic attractiveness of different circular business models, ensuring decisions are informed by both environmental impact and profitability.

User surveys and social media analysis are effective ways to gather user insights. Companies can extract valuable feedback from social media platforms and user-generated content by integrating AI-driven text and sentiment analysis tools. This information provides a direct path to understanding user preferences, pain points, and expectations, which can help inform the development of products that align better with user needs.

Predictive Modeling and Performance Forecasting

Machine learning allows designers to anticipate how modifications in design can influence a product's performance. ML can help recognize the most favorable design options that balance functionality, cost, and sustainability by creating models of various design alterations and their effects. For instance, ML algorithms can simulate the environmental and economic consequences of using various materials and components, guiding designers toward decisions that optimize profitability, recyclability, and minimal environmental impact.

Predictive analytics forecasts the future states of redesigned products under various economic, usage, and environmental conditions. Although it is closely related to machine learning, it is more specific in predicting the lifespan of new designs, anticipating maintenance needs, and estimating the timing of end of life. By doing so, predictive analytics ensures that products are designed to last longer and are easier to maintain and recycle.

Design Innovation and Prototyping

Generative AI can be used to develop new design prototypes. It optimizes the design based on specific criteria such as minimal resource usage or maximal ease of disassembly.

Generative AI can simulate how new designs perform under different conditions before being physically produced. This includes testing for durability under various usage scenarios and environmental impacts. By predicting how a design will behave over its lifecycle, manufacturers can make informed decisions about which designs will likely succeed in the market and meet sustainability targets.

Generative AI can deeply integrate with sustainable design principles by enabling the creation of complex and highly optimized designs that would be difficult to achieve manually. For instance, it can analyze many material properties and manufacturing processes to suggest designs that use the least material while maintaining structural integrity. This not only minimizes waste but also reduces the energy consumption and carbon footprint associated with the production of excess materials.

Regulatory Compliance and EPR Integration

Extended Producer Responsibility (EPR) (Sect. 2.3) is a policy approach that expands producers' responsibility for their products' environmental impacts throughout the product lifecycle. This includes take-back, recycling, and final disposal. When manufacturers are responsible for taking back their products, they are motivated to create products that are easier to disassemble and recycle. Data analytics can provide valuable insights into which product components are most frequently recovered and recycled, helping manufacturers improve their designs to meet EPR requirements.

Right to repair legislation requires manufacturers to provide consumers access to repair manuals, tools, and spare parts, ensuring products are designed for easy repairability. Data analytics tracks various components' performance and failure rates. This data can help manufacturers identify which parts are most prone to failure and should be designed for easier repair or replacement. Moreover, predictive analytics can forecast the need for spare parts, ensuring they are available when needed, thus supporting compliance with right to repair laws.

Packaging waste legislation mandates reducing, reusing, and recycling packaging materials. Data-driven circularity supports these goals by providing detailed insights into material usage and waste generation throughout the supply chain. By analyzing this data, manufacturers can identify opportunities to reduce packaging materials, design for recyclability, and improve recycling processes. For instance, data can highlight the effectiveness of different packaging designs in reducing waste and improving recycling rates, helping manufacturers to align with packaging waste regulations.

15.3.2 Leveraging Data-Driven Insights in Redistribution Strategies

The concept of redistribution involves extending the life and usefulness of products through models like recommerce, sharing economy, and Product-as-a-Service (PaaS). The effective use of data-driven insights is critical for the success of any redistribution strategy. These insights can help optimize inventory and logistics, enhance customer interactions, conduct economic analysis, and ensure proper product maintenance. Businesses can streamline operations by leveraging data, improving customer experiences, and promoting sustainable practices.

15.3.2.1 Customer Insight Management

Understanding customer behaviors and preferences is crucial for successful redistribution. Enhanced customer analytics provides insights into customer experiences, enabling manufacturers to customize their offerings to meet market demands and enhance user satisfaction. By utilizing data-driven insights for personalization, marketing and product offerings can be tailored to individual preferences, leading to better customer engagement and loyalty. Additionally, analyzing customer feedback across various platforms can provide actionable insights for product improvements and service enhancements, ensuring that products meet user expectations throughout their lifecycle.

15.3.2.2 Operational Efficiency

Effective inventory control balances supply and demand, particularly in models where products are returned for resale or reuse. Data analytics predicts product returns and demand fluctuations. This helps manufacturers prepare adequate inventory without overstocking, reducing holding costs and minimizing waste. Furthermore, monitoring products throughout their lifecycle provides valuable usage and longevity data. This information can be used to make informed inventory decisions for refurbished and reused items.

Optimizing logistics ensures that products are redistributed quickly and cost-effectively, thereby maintaining product value and customer satisfaction. By using data-driven models, delivery routes and pickup schedules can be optimized to reduce transportation costs and minimize environmental impact. Data-driven circularity enhances the efficiency of reverse logistics, especially for models involving returned or used products, to ensure that they are quickly reintegrated into the sales cycle or appropriately refurbished.

Advanced machine learning algorithms can analyze large volumes of data from different sources to accurately predict product demand and availability. This feature optimizes manufacturers' inventory levels and logistics operations, ensuring that products are available where they are most likely needed.

Predictive maintenance is essential for long-lasting goods, particularly those provided in PaaS or sharing models. It helps maintain the quality and functionality of the product, ensuring reliability and trust. Predictive analytics forecast maintenance requirements based on actual usage data, reducing downtime and extending the product's lifespan. Continuous monitoring of product conditions via sensors and IoT devices can proactively identify potential failures, allowing for prompt interventions.

Advanced machine learning algorithms and computer vision technologies can automate the inspection and categorization of returned products. By utilizing AI-powered visual inspection systems, recommerce sites can quickly and accurately assess the condition of returned items. This automation reduces the time and labor required for manual inspections, allowing faster processing and categorizing of products for resale, refurbishment, or recycling. The result is a more efficient recommerce process that maximizes the value of each returned item.

Example 15.5 Reezocar integrates advanced computer vision technologies into its recommerce processes

Reezocar[2], an online platform for buying and selling used cars in France, has improved operational efficiency by integrating advanced computer vision technologies into its recommerce processes. By implementing AI-powered visual inspection systems and a damage estimation model, the company can quickly and accurately assess the condition of returned vehicles.

Computer vision analyzes the car's images and identifies any damage, such as scratches, dents, or significant deterioration. After calculating the repair cost, Reezocar produces a post-repair estimate of the car's value. This estimate considers factors such as age, condition, and make to ensure maximum accuracy. With these tools, dealerships can offer more competitive pricing and determine whether a car should be refurbished or sent further down the circular path (Gleiser & Laurens, 2023).

15.3.2.3 Strategic Decision-Making

Economic analysis is a valuable tool for manufacturers to make strategic decisions, as it helps optimize their financial outcomes. Cost–benefit analysis can evaluate the economic impact of different redistribution strategies, allowing manufacturers to choose the most financially viable option. By analyzing pricing strategies and market trends, manufacturers can ensure their products are competitively priced and their revenue models are aligned with customer expectations and market dynamics.

[2] https://www.reezocar.com/

Manufacturers can better understand market dynamics that impact product supply and demand by integrating economic indicators, global supply chain data, and sector-specific trends. This broader data context helps anticipate market shifts and potential supply disruptions, allowing companies to make better-informed decisions and adjust their redistribution strategies to maintain efficiency and competitiveness.

Additional considerations include monitoring environmental impact through data analytics, which supports sustainability claims and compliance with regulatory requirements. This builds brand reputation and aligns with customer values. Data insights also play a pivotal role in identifying new markets or customer segments that could benefit from redistribution models, supporting business growth and diversification. These insights collectively enable businesses to adapt and thrive in a circular economy framework.

15.3.2.4 Data Sharing in the Redistribution Ecosystem

Data sharing and collaboration in the redistribution ecosystem can optimize the efficiency and efficacy of circular economy models. The entire ecosystem can benefit from enhanced insights and operational synergies by fostering a culture of open data exchange among key players, including manufacturers, retailers, and logistics providers. Data sharing can provide a comprehensive view of product lifecycles, customer demand patterns, and logistical efficiencies.

For effective collaboration, it is necessary to establish a shared understanding of which data benefits each participant in the ecosystem. This involves identifying relevant data points and developing standardized data collection, processing, and sharing methods that respect privacy and competitive boundaries. Efficient ways to share this data, such as through secure cloud-based platforms, can facilitate real-time data access and analysis, enabling dynamic adjustments in redistribution strategies.

Collaborative efforts can lead to more accurate demand forecasting, streamlined inventory management, and optimized logistics planning. By working together, ecosystem participants can leverage their collective data to reduce redundancies, minimize waste, and enhance the overall sustainability of their operations. This shared data approach ensures that redistribution models are more economically viable and responsive to the evolving market and environmental needs, establishing a genuinely data-driven circular economy.

The Digital Product Passport (DPP) simplifies the sharing of product-related information among various stakeholders involved in the redistribution process. It offers a comprehensive and accessible view of a product's origin, material composition, handling requirements, and previous usage history. This transparency enables informed decisions about the most appropriate redistribution strategies for different products, such as whether a product should be refurbished, resold, or recycled. It also helps ensure that all products meet the necessary quality and safety standards at each stage of their extended lifecycle.

15.3.3 Data-Driven Circularity to Support Product Use Extension

In this section, we will discuss how data-driven circularity can aid business models aiming to prolong the use of products. We will focus on the advantages beyond the data-driven insights addressed earlier in the redesign and redistribution phases. Therefore, we will not repeat the benefits such as customer insights, economic analysis, or redesign analysis. Instead, we will explore how data can facilitate decision-making processes related to repairing, refurbishing, and remanufacturing. Refurbishment and remanufacturing are mostly covered together under the term remanufacturing. Additionally, we will examine how capturing data can help enhance product maintenance and longevity by providing feedback to improve product redesign.

15.3.3.1 Strategic Decision-Making

Businesses can use big data and predictive analytics to decide whether to repair, refurbish, or remanufacture a product. It's about predicting when a product will fail and understanding the economic and environmental impacts of various end-of-life scenarios. These technologies allow companies to extend product lifecycles using actual usage data and detailed wear and tear forecasts.

Machine learning algorithms can analyze the outcomes of previous cycles of product extensions to improve the decision-making process for current products. For example, if historical data reveals that certain products or components frequently regain full functionality through refurbishment, similar future items can be directed down the same path. This can enhance efficiency and effectiveness in the production process.

Advanced analytics and machine learning can assist businesses in identifying the most appropriate repair or remanufacturing service providers based on market conditions. By analyzing the providers' availability, success rates, cost-effectiveness, and turnaround times, companies can choose partners that best meet their quality, affordability, and speed requirements, ensuring the most favorable product lifecycle extension.

15.3.3.2 Ecosystem Collaboration

Sharing data within the business ecosystem can improve the efficiency and intelligence of product use extension. Allowing data to flow between manufacturers, circular service providers, and recyclers enables each participant to predict demand better, adjust supply, and optimize operations while respecting privacy and competitive boundaries. This shared data environment encourages a more collaborative and transparent market space where all parties benefit from increased data access and insights.

For data sharing to be effective, the data being shared must be of high quality and standardized. Data can be trusted and used effectively for decision-making when consistent, accurate, and standardized. Standardized data formats among stakeholders make data integration and analysis easier from diverse sources, ultimately leading to better insights.

(continued)

For example, if a standard data protocol existed, all remanufacturing centers could consistently report their usage and failure data. This would make combining and analyzing data at a higher level easier, allowing for identifying trends and making strategic decisions. Implementing quality controls like regular audits and validations would help ensure the data remains accurate and timely, thus preserving the integrity of any business decisions based on this data.

Example 15.6 Catena-X enhances companies' decision-making on the most sustainable product-use extension pathways

Catena-X is a consortium of automotive networks that aims to create a digital ecosystem to promote traceability and sustainability across the entire value chain, from the production stage to the end-of-life processes. The network allows for the sharing of detailed information on the material composition and lifecycle of automotive components among various stakeholders, including manufacturers, suppliers, and service providers. This helps create a digital twin for each component, which aids in tracking and optimizing the reuse, refurbishment, and remanufacturing processes.

Catena-X uses a shared data environment to enhance companies' decision-making on the most sustainable product use extension pathways. For instance, the Catena-X Battery Pass allows for detailed tracking of battery components, ensuring they can be efficiently reused or repurposed instead of discarded. The system helps determine whether a battery should be repaired, refurbished, or remanufactured based on real-time data regarding its condition and life expectancy.

Furthermore, Catena-X promotes transparency and collaboration by allowing participants to access and share data while maintaining control over their proprietary information (Catena-X, 2024a, b).

15.3.3.3 Operational Optimization

Integrating predictive analytics can transform logistics in product use extension models by optimizing collection, repair, refurbishment, and redistribution routes. This leads to reduced transportation costs and lower carbon emissions. Smart logistics also ensure that products and components move through the repair, refurbishment, and remanufacturing processes more efficiently, minimizing downtime and speeding up the return to the market.

Machine learning algorithms have the potential to enhance inventory management by accurately predicting the timing and quantity of parts required for repair and refurbishment processes. This ability allows businesses to maintain an optimal inventory level, reducing holding costs and minimizing waste. Additionally, it ensures that parts are readily available when required, which is critical for maintaining the flow of operations and meeting customer demands on time.

Integrating IoT and AI into repair and remanufacturing processes improves efficiency and accuracy. With the help of IoT devices, it is possible to track the condition of products in real time and feed the data back to central systems for analysis. This data is used to predict future maintenance needs. AI also assists in diagnosing any issues and recommending the best repair methods.

15.3.3.4 Sustainability Assessment

Data analytics evaluate the environmental impacts of various options for extending the use of products. By utilizing comprehensive datasets, companies can assess the total environmental footprint of different pathways, such as repair, refurbishment, or remanufacturing. This analysis can include the energy consumption during the extension process, emissions produced, and the amount of raw materials saved. For instance, analytics can quantify the energy required to refurbish an appliance compared to manufacturing a new one. It can also calculate the reduction in carbon emissions achieved by repairing a product instead of replacing it. By comparing these metrics, companies can identify the most environmentally sustainable option, align their business practices with broader sustainability goals, reduce their environmental impact, and provide valuable data for reporting and compliance with environmental regulations.

15.3.4 Recycling

In the final section, we will discuss how manufacturers can utilize data-driven circularity to support business models based on recycling. It is important to note that this discussion will not cover how these technologies are used within the recycling industry. Instead, we will focus on how manufacturers can use these tools to improve their recycling strategies.

15.3.4.1 Strategic Forecasting and Planning

Manufacturers can use predictive analytics to collect and analyze market information, which can help them determine the most optimal times to initiate recycling for various products. This analysis involves understanding when products usually reach their end of life and forecasting market demand for recycled materials. The demand for recycling can vary by different regions and economic conditions. By incorporating demographic and geographical data, manufacturers can design targeted recycling campaigns that cater to specific regional regulations and customer behaviors. Predictive models can also forecast the potential recovery value of recycled materials, helping prioritize where recycling efforts can be most economically beneficial.

Manufacturers can benefit from using machine learning models to predict the demand for products made from recycled materials. By doing so, they can adjust their production schedules and raw material procurement to ensure that the supply of recycled materials aligns with market demand and reduces excess inventory. With the help of ML, manufacturers can perform scenario planning and risk assessment, evaluating how different variables could affect the demand for recycled materials. This includes assessing the impact of potential disruptions in the supply of recycled materials, changes in commodity prices, or shifts in customer sentiment toward sustainability. Manufacturers can devise strategies that maintain production continuity and market responsiveness by preparing for these scenarios.

15.3.4.2 Operational Efficiency and Compliance

Manufacturers use big data and business intelligence (BI) tools to analyze the market dynamically. This enables them to effectively balance sourcing recycled materials with virgin materials by assessing their availability, cost, and quality. Manufacturers can simulate various sourcing scenarios using AI algorithms and predict future market shifts. They can also integrate supplier performance data to ensure the reliability and quality of recycled materials. This approach helps maintain a resilient supply chain while adhering to sustainability standards.

Data analytics evaluate recycling options' environmental and economic impacts. Manufacturers can use lifecycle assessment (LCA) models to quantify the environmental effects, such as carbon footprint, water usage, and ecological implications of their recycling practices. Economically, analytics can model the return on investment (ROI) for various recycling activities. These models consider factors like operational costs, potential revenue from selling recycled materials, and savings from reduced waste disposal fees. This dual analysis helps manufacturers make informed decisions that optimize sustainability while enhancing financial performance.

Big data analytics enable manufacturers to comply with ever-increasing global recycling and waste management regulations. Extended Producer Responsibility (EPR) is an aspect that manufacturers must consider as part of these regulations. EPR policies put the responsibility of product disposal at the end of their lifecycle back on the producer, encouraging them to design products that are easy to recycle and to manage the recycling process.

Manufacturers use big data analytics to stay updated on EPR requirements and other regulatory obligations in different markets. This enables them to analyze vast amounts of compliance data efficiently, ensuring they meet legal standards without penalties. Furthermore, by utilizing this data strategically, manufacturers can optimize their product take-back, recycling systems, and material recovery processes, reducing waste and enhancing their environmental stewardship. Effective data management allows manufacturers to monitor and report on their compliance with these regulations, promoting transparency to regulators and building customer confidence.

15.3.4.3 Quality and Supply Chain Management

Recycled materials can have varying levels of quality due to factors like source, treatment, and age. To guarantee that these materials meet the required standards for manufacturing reuse, manufacturers can use machine learning algorithms to analyze and accurately predict material characteristics. ML models can be trained on a dataset that contains various attributes of recycled materials, such as purity, strength, and compatibility with new production processes. By analyzing patterns and outcomes from these datasets, ML algorithms can predict the suitability of recycled materials for specific manufacturing requirements. This ensures consistency and reliability in product quality.

Standardizing data throughout the recycling supply chain enables the seamless integration of recycled materials into manufacturing processes. Consistent data formats and quality standards enable manufacturers to evaluate the suitability of recycled materials from various sources. To achieve this standardization, all stakeholders must develop and implement common data protocols and interfaces, from collection points to processing facilities. This approach not only enhances the reliability of the data but also simplifies the process of integrating recycled materials into new product designs. Using standardized data, manufacturers can automate parts of their procurement and production processes, using algorithms to match material attributes with production requirements. Moreover, standardized data protocols encourage better communication and collaboration across the supply chain, enabling more efficient coordination and planning for using recycled materials.

Business Intelligence (BI) tools manage and analyze data from customer engagement programs that aim to encourage the return of end-of-life products for recycling. By analyzing customer interaction data, these tools can help manufacturers gain insights into how different customer segments respond to various recycling incentives. The patterns in data, such as participation rates, feedback, and redemption of recycling incentives, can be analyzed to refine these programs and make them more effective and appealing.

For example, BI tools can segment customers based on demographic data, past purchase behavior, and previous engagement with sustainability initiatives. This segmentation enables manufacturers to customize communications and recycling incentives for specific customer groups. For example, manufacturers may introduce app-based recycling reminders and rewards for younger demographics, who are more engaged with digital platforms. At the same time, more traditional communication methods or incentives may be effective for other groups.

15.4 Challenges for Data-Driven Circularity

Manufacturers face various challenges when adopting data-driven circularity, encompassing business practices' technical, operational, and strategic aspects.

Data-centric technologies can have high upfront and recurring expenses. These costs include investing in data infrastructure, analytics software, cybersecurity measures, and personnel training, all of which require financial resources. Balancing these expenditures with the anticipated return on investment from enhanced circular practices is a strategic challenge.

15.4.1 Access to Sufficient and Relevant Data

Access to high-quality, relevant data is essential for any data-driven initiative. Manufacturers frequently face challenges in gathering enough data about their products' lifecycles for effective analysis and decision-making. This involves collecting data on product usage, circular services, recycling processes, and customer feedback. Inadequate data can result in inaccurate predictions and suboptimal decisions.

To address challenges with insufficient data, manufacturers can utilize IoT technologies to gather real-time data from products in use. This allows them to gain valuable insights into how the products are being operated and when they may be at risk of failing. Additionally, improving customer feedback mechanisms through digital platforms helps to gather detailed user experiences and preferences.

Manufacturers can expand their access to a broader range of data by establishing data-sharing agreements with suppliers, recyclers, circular service providers, and other stakeholders. This allows for a more comprehensive view of the product lifecycle, enhancing the depth and quality of the data collected. As a result, manufacturers are better equipped to make informed decisions.

Advanced data aggregation platforms enable manufacturers to standardize and analyze data from diverse sources, ensuring consistency and accuracy.

15.4.2 Technical Challenges

Selecting and implementing the right analytics tools and platforms can be challenging for manufacturers. They require specialized tools that can handle the unique aspects of circular economy models, such as lifecycle assessment (LCA) tools or predictive analytics for product lifespan and recyclability. Integrating these tools into their existing IT infrastructures without disrupting current operations can add further complexity.

As companies increasingly rely on data to drive their operations, they often deal with a massive amount of data that can be difficult to manage. Manufacturers must be prepared for this challenge by investing in scalable data storage solutions and powerful processing capabilities that enable real-time data analysis. This will help them handle, store, and process large datasets efficiently and make the most of their data-driven initiatives.

Solutions must be practical and able to work on a larger scale across various parts of an organization. They should also be adaptable to different products and markets. However, scalability comes with challenges, such as managing larger data flows, maintaining consistent data quality across various units, and ensuring system performance without incurring significant costs.

As the importance of data privacy and protection grows, manufacturers need to ensure that their data practices align with international regulations such as EU's General Data Protection Regulation (GDPR). Cybersecurity is also a top concern since data breaches can reveal confidential company and customer information. Sharing data within the ecosystem requires balancing transparency and cooperation while protecting sensitive competitive information.

Manufacturers frequently use outdated legacy systems that may not be suitable for modern data-intensive operations. Integrating new data-driven solutions with these systems can be difficult due to compatibility issues or limitations in the older systems' capabilities. It is essential to find ways to connect new technologies with existing infrastructure without the need for extensive overhauls.

15.4.3 Cultural and Organizational Challenges

To adopt data-driven circularity, companies must undergo a cultural and operational shift. Employees at all levels need to understand the significance of using data to achieve sustainability goals. Training and developing a data-centric mindset is crucial to successfully implement these practices.

Manufacturers must ensure that suppliers and partners align with the data-sharing requirements of a circular economy model. This involves establishing clear protocols for data exchange, quality standards, and collaborative practices that support circularity without compromising proprietary information.

Manufacturers may have access to data and analytics tools, but interpreting this data correctly and making informed decisions requires data science and analytics expertise. Therefore, manufacturers should develop or acquire this expertise to accurately translate data insights into actionable, strategic decisions. This could involve hiring new talent or training existing employees, which also involves cultural and organizational changes.

To tackle these challenges, a comprehensive strategy that involves investments in technology, staff training, process reengineering, and often a shift in organizational culture is important. Successful implementation can result in enhanced sustainability, efficiency, and competitive advantage in the market.

15.5 Digital Capabilities That Manufacturers Must Develop to Support Data-Driven Circularity

Throughout the chapter, we explored the essential digital capabilities manufacturers must develop to support data-driven circularity. Each capability optimizes various aspects of the product lifecycle, from design and production to end-of-life management. By integrating these capabilities, manufacturers can harness the power of data to enhance operational efficiency, ensure regulatory compliance, and promote sustainability. The following capability map (Fig. 15.1) outlines the key technologies and systems for implementing a successful data-driven circular economy.

15.6 Checklist for Implementing Data-Driven Circularity

As explored in this chapter, implementing data-driven circularity can enhance a manufacturer's ability to optimize resources, reduce waste, and comply with regulatory requirements. The following checklist (Table 15.2) provides a structured approach to implementing key tasks associated with data-driven circularity. This checklist outlines each task's methodologies, expected outcomes, and risk mitigation strategies, ensuring a comprehensive and effective adoption of data-driven circular practices.

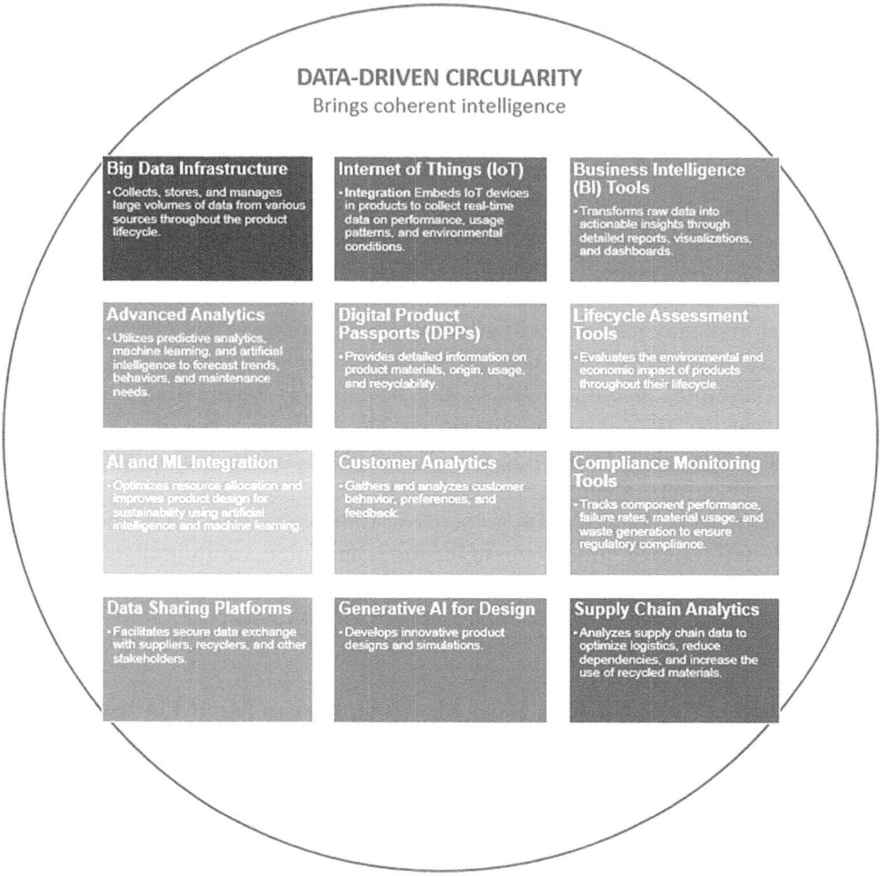

Fig. 15.1 Essential digital capabilities that manufacturers must develop to support data-driven circularity

Table 15.2 Checklist for implementing data-driven circularity

Task	Methodology	Expected outcome	Risk mitigation
Implement Big Data analytics	Collect and analyze data from various sources throughout the product lifecycle	Enhanced insights into material flows and resource usage	Inadequate visibility into the product lifecycle
Integrate Business Intelligence (BI)	Use BI tools to transform raw data into actionable insights	Improved operational efficiency and decision-making	Delayed decision-making due to slow data processing
Apply artificial intelligence (AI)	Utilize AI algorithms for resource allocation and product design optimization	Increased efficiency and sustainability in production processes	Manual evaluation of design options becomes cumbersome
Leverage machine learning (ML)	Develop ML models to predict maintenance needs and demand forecasting	Reduced downtime and optimized inventory management	Misunderstanding of model outputs
Utilize predictive analytics	Employ statistical algorithms to predict future scenarios based on historical data	Proactive decision-making and enhanced product lifecycle management	Inaccuracy in predictions
Incorporate Generative AI	Use Generative AI for innovative product design and simulation	Accelerated innovation cycle and optimized product designs	Falling behind competitors in innovation speed
Use DPPs for data-driven circularity	Develop and maintain DPPs for detailed product lifecycle information	Enhanced transparency and lifecycle management	Reduced supply chain visibility
Ensure regulatory compliance	Use data analytics to track component performance, material usage, and waste generation	Compliance with right to repair, packaging waste, and EPR legislation	High compliance costs
Optimize inventory and logistics	Apply data-driven insights to manage inventory and streamline logistics	Efficient redistribution and reduced operational costs	Excessive inventory and logistics costs
Enhance product use extension	Use advanced analytics for strategic decisions on repair, refurbishment, and remanufacturing	Extended product lifecycles and reduced waste	Lack of visibility into product status and performance
Improve recycling operations	Utilize ML and data analytics to optimize sourcing, lifecycle assessments, and quality management of recycled materials	High-quality recycled materials and compliance with recycling regulations	Decreased revenue from end-of-life product

References

Catena-X. (2024a, June). *Battery pass*. Retrieved from https://catena-x.net/en/benefits-pros/circular-economy

Catena-X. (2024b, June). *Data as basis for a successful circular economy*. Retrieved from https://catena-x.net/en/benefits-pros/circular-economy

Gleiser, I., & Laurens, F. (2023, August). *How computer vision is enabling a circular economy*. Retrieved from AWS HPC Blog: https://aws.amazon.com/blogs/hpc/how-computer-vision-is-enabling-a-circular-economy/

TK Elevator. (2024a, June). *MAX*. Retrieved from https://www.tkelevator.com/global-en/products-and-service/digital-solutions/max/

TK Elevator. (2024b, June). *Optimize every building's potential*. Retrieved from https://www.tkelevator.com/global-en/products-and-service/digital-solutions/max/

Digitizing Compliance 16

Abstract

Digitizing compliance transforms regulatory adherence into a strategic advantage for manufacturers by leveraging digital tools to streamline processes, enhance transparency, and optimize operations, thereby reducing costs and creating new business opportunities. Digital tools support Right to Repair initiatives by streamlining repair processes, enhancing service quality, and efficiently managing repair information. Implementing Digital Product Passports (DPPs) requires advanced data management systems, supply chain collaboration, IT interoperability, and customer engagement, enabling compliance, transparency, and sustainability. For Extended Producer Responsibility (EPR) compliance, manufacturers must utilize data management, IoT technologies, PLM software, and customer engagement platforms to ensure sustainability from design to disposal. Data analytics, digital design tools, real-time supply chain visibility, and consumer engagement platforms help manufacturers comply with packaging regulations, drive innovation, and optimize resource use for sustainable packaging solutions. A harmonized digital compliance system with advanced data analytics, predictive AI, and secure IT infrastructure allows manufacturers to navigate international sustainability regulations efficiently, enhancing operational efficiency and driving long-term growth.

The chapter also includes a capability map outlining the digital capabilities manufacturers must develop to support data-driven compliance. Additionally, a detailed checklist guides manufacturers through implementing these capabilities, ensuring structured adoption and effective outcomes in transforming compliance into a strategic business advantage.

H. H. Jensen, *Circular Economy Opportunities and Pathways for Manufacturers*, Future of Business and Finance, https://doi.org/10.1007/978-3-031-75279-7_16

Key Messages

- *Digitizing Compliance*: Digitization enables manufacturers to transform compliance into a strategic advantage by leveraging digital tools to streamline regulatory adherence, enhance transparency, and optimize operations, reducing costs and creating new business opportunities.
- *Digitization's Role in Supporting Right to Repair*: Digital tools streamline repair processes, enhance service quality, and manage repair information efficiently, aligning with legal requirements and boosting market competitiveness through customer-centric solutions and AI-driven predictive maintenance.
- *Digital Capabilities Needed to Prepare for and Benefit from a Digital Product Passport*: Advanced data management systems, supply chain collaboration, IT interoperability, and customer engagement are essential digital capabilities for implementing Digital Product Passports, enabling compliance, transparency, and sustainability.
- *Digital Capabilities for Extended Producer Responsibility Compliance*: Manufacturers must utilize data management, IoT technologies, PLM software, and customer engagement platforms to meet EPR obligations, ensure sustainability from design to disposal, and optimize supply chain processes.
- *Digital Requirements for Packaging and Packaging Waste*: Data analytics, digital design tools, real-time supply chain visibility, and consumer engagement platforms help manufacturers comply with packaging regulations, drive innovation, and optimize resource use for sustainable packaging solutions.
- *Unified Digital Support for Global Sustainability Compliance*: A harmonized digital compliance system with advanced data analytics, predictive AI, and secure IT infrastructure allows manufacturers to navigate international sustainability regulations efficiently, enhancing operational efficiency and driving long-term growth.

In Part I of this book, we introduced key legislations that underpin the circular economy, a theme we have touched upon throughout the chapters. This section aims to provide an overview of how digitization based on the SMIF framework can address these regulations' challenges and highlight the manufacturers' benefits.

By leveraging digital tools and technologies, manufacturers can transform compliance into a strategic advantage, enabling more efficient operations and fostering innovation. Digitization simplifies adherence to complex regulatory frameworks and enhances supply chain transparency, traceability, and accountability. This integration can help manufacturers meet regulatory demands while optimizing their processes, reducing costs, and creating new business opportunities.

16.1 Digitization's Role in Supporting Right to Repair

Digitization transforms Right to Repair into a strategic advantage for manufacturers. Companies can streamline repair processes, enhance service quality, and efficiently manage repair information and parts using digital tools (Fig. 16.1). This aligns with legal requirements and boosts market competitiveness by offering customer-centric solutions. Digital platforms offering repair guides, real-time AI assistance, and authenticated components enable compliance with legislation and build stronger, transparent relationships with customers. These digital touchpoints encourage consumer participation in product repair and maintenance, supporting responsible consumption and waste reduction.

Fig. 16.1 Digitization's role in supporting right to repair

AI and IoT technologies forecast spare parts demand and maintain optimal stock levels. AI analyzes historical repair data, seasonal trends, and product lifecycles to accurately predict parts demand, while IoT devices in products send early malfunction signals for preemptive restocking. This proactive approach minimizes inventory costs, ensures parts are available on time, and enhances overall repair efficiency.

Advanced digital interfaces facilitate easy repair requests, status tracking, and feedback. Features like chatbots and detailed timelines enable direct communication between customers and technicians, encouraging customer reviews and suggestions. Digital platforms also list spare parts, making it easy for customers to find and purchase parts that meet manufacturer specifications. This customer-centric shift enhances transparency and trust, requiring efficient internal IT systems to manage increased end-user interaction.

These systems store detailed repair manuals, instructional videos, and troubleshooting guides digitally, making repair information easily accessible to both professional technicians and DIY enthusiasts. Features like search functionality and interactive guides further streamline the repair process, making it more efficient and user-friendly. Additionally, AI-driven chatbots and augmented reality applications can guide users through real-time repair processes, simplifying self-repairs.

Embedded product sensors offer real-time diagnostics and predictive maintenance alerts, detecting early signs of wear or malfunction. Continuous monitoring allows preemptive repairs before major issues arise, reducing downtime, extending product lifespan, and offering a sophisticated, data-driven repair process.

Analyzing large sets of repair data to identify common issues informs product design improvements. AI algorithms detect patterns and trends, pinpointing recurring faults or weaknesses, leading to more robust and repairable designs in future product iterations. This AI-driven approach ensures that products become more durable and sustainable over time.

16.2 Digital Capabilities Needed to Prepare for and Benefit from a Digital Product Passport

As companies prepare to embrace the Digital Product Passport (DPP) paradigm, they must develop the necessary digital capabilities. These foundational capabilities enable businesses to implement, manage, and leverage the DPP's benefits (Fig. 16.2).

Companies need advanced data management systems to collect, store, and analyze extensive data for DPP compliance. This includes adapting existing systems to new data requirements and ensuring data security. The complexity and volume of data necessitate efficient and scalable systems. Integrating advanced technologies like cloud computing and AI can enhance data processing and management capabilities. Ensuring the integrity and accuracy of data throughout its lifecycle is paramount, as this data forms the backbone of the DPP's reliability.

Effective DPP implementation requires close collaboration across the supply chain. Manufacturers must engage with suppliers, manufacturers, and end-of-life operators to ensure data accuracy and completeness. This demands high-level

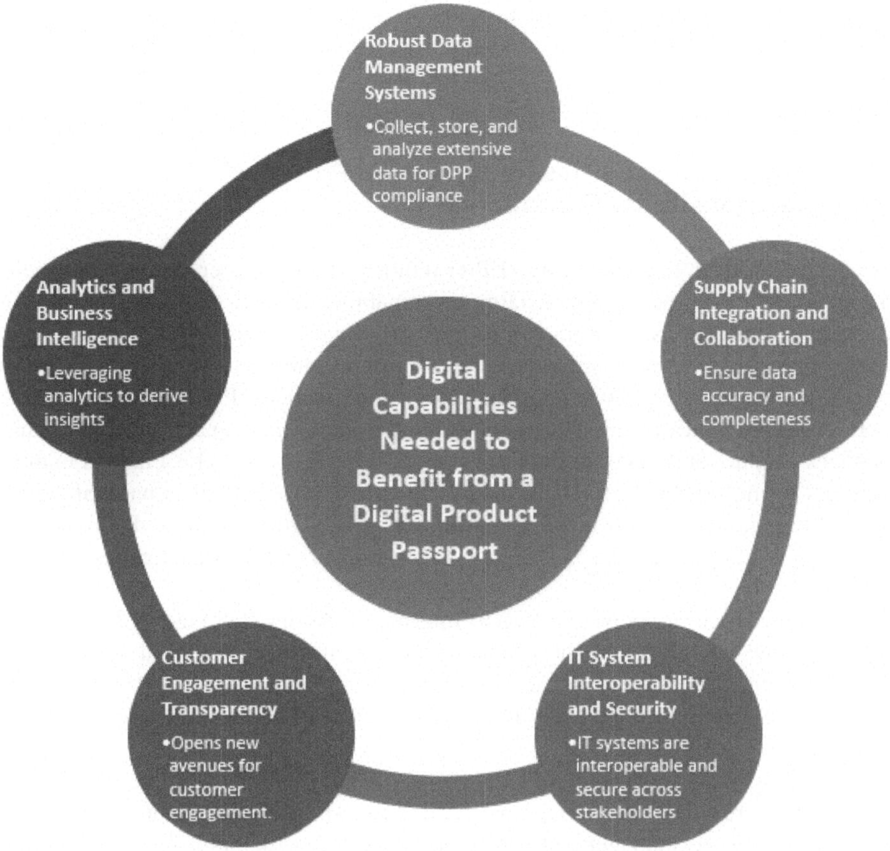

Fig. 16.2 Digital capabilities needed to benefit from a digital product passport

coordination and standardized protocols for data sharing and communication. By fostering a collaborative environment, companies can ensure the data in the DPP accurately represents the product's journey, enhancing credibility with customers and regulators.

Manufacturers must ensure that IT systems are interoperable across different stakeholders and secure against data breaches. Interoperability involves developing common standards and protocols that enable other systems to communicate and share data effectively. Robust security measures are required to protect sensitive data from unauthorized access and cyber threats, maintaining the trust of all stakeholders.

Implementing DPP opens new avenues for customer engagement. Companies can create continuous dialogue opportunities by providing detailed product information. Customers gain insights into the environmental impact, manufacturing processes, and sustainability features of products. This transparency allows manufacturers to distinguish their offerings in a competitive market.

Leveraging analytics to derive insights from DPP data can inform decision-making, optimize resource use, and identify opportunities for innovation and circular economy practices.

16.3 Digital Capabilities for Extended Producer Responsibility Compliance

Extended Producer Responsibility (EPR) requires manufacturers to manage their products' entire lifecycle, emphasizing sustainability from design to disposal. To meet these obligations, manufacturers must leverage various digital capabilities. These capabilities ensure compliance and offer opportunities to enhance efficiency, reduce costs, and engage consumers in sustainable practices (Fig. 16.3).

Implementing advanced data management systems and analytics tracks and manages product and material data throughout their lifecycle. This enables manufacturers to monitor and report on their product's environmental impact, aligning with EPR regulations. Advanced analytics optimize supply chain and production processes, leading to resource efficiency, cost savings, and the development of circular business models.

Digital Product Passports (DPP) and Internet of Things (IoT) technologies provide real-time visibility into the product lifecycle, from raw material sourcing to end-of-life disposal. This transparency ensures compliance with EPR regulations and fosters collaboration with suppliers and recyclers, enhancing the traceability of materials and components.

Integrating PLM software with EPR-focused features allows designers to design products that are easier to recycle, repair, and reuse. This proactive approach reduces material and waste management costs, meets customer demand for eco-friendly products, and opens new revenue streams from secondary markets or recycled materials.

These platforms streamline compliance processes by managing documentation, tracking real-time regulatory changes, and automating data compilation and report generation. This ensures timely and accurate compliance reporting, reducing non-compliance risk and saving time.

Digital platforms engage and educate customers about the environmental aspects of products, promoting recycling and reuse initiatives. They provide transparent product information, practical recycling guidance, and incentives for circular behavior, fostering a more conscious customer base.

AI and data analytics predict product end of life and enable proactive customer engagement for product returns. These technologies analyze large datasets to identify patterns and trends, informing product design and process efficiency improvements. AI-driven insights help manufacturers create more durable and sustainable products.

Fig. 16.3 Digital capabilities for extended producer responsibility compliance

16.4 Digital Requirements for Packaging and Packaging Waste

The EU's Proposal for Packaging and Packaging Waste Regulation necessitates a digitally integrated approach from manufacturers. By embracing various digital technologies, manufacturers can comply with regulatory demands, pioneer innovation, optimize supply chain processes, and engage customers (Fig. 16.4).

Implementing data analytics systems enables manufacturers to track packaging materials effectively, monitor compliance with recyclability and recycled content standards, and facilitate reporting on environmental impact metrics. These systems

Fig. 16.4 Digital requirements for packaging and packaging waste

also identify opportunities for improvement in packaging design and material usage, suggesting more sustainable alternatives and driving innovation in production processes.

Digital design tools develop packaging that meets PPWR's recyclability and reusability and minimizes size requirements. These tools allow for the simulation and testing of new materials and designs, integrating ecodesign principles to enhance sustainability efforts.

Digital tools like distributed databases and IoT provide real-time visibility into the supply chain, ensuring material traceability and facilitating collaboration between suppliers, manufacturers, and recyclers. This transparency optimizes resource use and minimizes waste, helping achieve reusability targets and manage recycled content effectively.

Systems for managing Declarations of Conformity and technical documentation securely store and retrieve documents, track compliance requirement changes, and ensure easy access to necessary information for regulatory purposes.

Digital solutions establish efficient collection systems for packaging waste and optimize reverse logistics. Technologies can create user-friendly return procedures, track returned packaging materials, and plan efficient transportation routes for recycling or repurposing.

Digital platforms engage customers in recycling and reuse initiatives. Manufacturers can use social media, mobile apps, and interactive websites to raise awareness, offer incentives, and communicate environmental benefits. Gamification and reward systems can encourage consumer participation, transforming interactions from passive receipt to active engagement and feedback.

Predictive analytics forecast future packaging needs and waste generation trends, helping manufacturers proactively plan resource procurement and waste management strategies, reducing overproduction and excess waste.

16.5 Checklist for Digitizing Compliance in Manufacturing

In this chapter, we have explored the role of digitization in transforming compliance processes within the manufacturing sector. We have examined how digital tools and technologies can streamline regulatory adherence, enhance transparency, and optimize operations, ultimately turning compliance into a strategic advantage.

This checklist (Table 16.1) provides a guide for manufacturers to digitize their compliance processes. By following these tasks and methodologies, manufacturers can ensure regulatory adherence, optimize operations, and mitigate risks effectively.

Table 16.1 Checklist for digitizing compliance in manufacturing

Task	Methodology	Expected outcome	Risk mitigation
Implement advanced data management systems	Deploy cloud-based data storage and management solutions, integrating AI for data analysis and processing	Enhanced data accuracy, efficient data handling, and compliance with regulatory standards	Mitigates risk of inaccurate data reporting by ensuring data integrity and security
Establish interoperable IT systems	Develop common standards and protocols for data sharing across stakeholders	Improved collaboration and seamless data exchange	Reduces risk of data silos and compliance gaps by standardizing data communication
Utilize IoT for real-time monitoring	Integrate IoT devices to monitor product lifecycle and environmental impact	Real-time data on product status, predictive maintenance, and enhanced traceability	Mitigates risk of non-compliance due to undetected issues by providing continuous monitoring and early detection

(continued)

Table 16.1 (continued)

Task	Methodology	Expected outcome	Risk mitigation
Implement AI-driven predictive analytics	Use AI to forecast demand, manage inventory, and predict maintenance needs	Optimized resource use, reduced downtime, and proactive maintenance	Reduces risk of regulatory non-compliance by ensuring timely maintenance and inventory management
Leverage Digital Product Passports (DPPs)	Create and manage digital records of product information throughout the lifecycle	Enhanced transparency, traceability, and consumer trust	Mitigates risk of non-compliance with EPR by ensuring accurate and comprehensive product data
Ensure supply chain collaboration	Use digital platforms to coordinate with suppliers, manufacturers, and recyclers	Enhanced data accuracy and process efficiency	Reduces risk of incomplete compliance data by ensuring all stakeholders are aligned and informed
Develop digital design tools for sustainable packaging	Use digital tools to design recyclable and reusable packaging	Improved compliance with packaging regulations and reduced environmental impact	Reduces risk of non-compliance with packaging waste regulations by ensuring designs meet standards
Implement data analytics for packaging compliance	Deploy data analytics systems to track packaging materials and recyclability	Effective monitoring of compliance with recyclability and recycled content standards	Mitigates risk of regulatory penalties by ensuring accurate reporting and compliance tracking
Establish secure systems for compliance documentation	Implement systems for managing and retrieving Declarations of Conformity and technical documentation	Efficient access to compliance documents and timely reporting	Mitigates risk of regulatory fines and operational disruptions by ensuring document accuracy and availability
Monitor and review compliance data regularly	Conduct regular audits and reviews of compliance data using digital tools	Continuous improvement and adherence to regulations	Reduces risk of falling out of compliance by ensuring ongoing monitoring and adjustments

17 Synthesizing Insights: The Role of Digitization in Circular Economy Transformation

Abstract

This chapter summarizes our journey with the Sustainable Manufacturing Intelligence Framework (SMIF), exploring the digital components essential for transitioning to circular business models.

Transitioning to a circular economy requires a comprehensive digital transformation that aligns internal improvements and external partnerships. SMIF provides a cohesive approach to navigating this transformation, ensuring seamless integration of digital initiatives. This framework is a practical toolkit for businesses ready to embrace digital transformation and advance circular economy principles, driving innovation, resource management, and economic success.

In our efforts to understand the shift to a circular economy, Part III focused on various digital touchstones that analyze the interconnected digital components necessary for the transition to circular business models. Chapter 10 introduced the Sustainable Manufacturing Intelligence Framework (SMIF), which integrates insights into an essential approach for manufacturers during this transformation.

Our journey started with a focus on Chap. 11. That emphasized the need for internal systems to adapt to new norms and regulations, ensuring product traceability and sustainable end-of-life strategies. Efficient API management, robust security measures, and scalable IT infrastructure are essential to support seamless integration within the digital ecosystem. These systems must be flexible to comply with new standards, enable product traceability, and implement end-of-life strategies effectively.

H. H. Jensen, *Circular Economy Opportunities and Pathways for Manufacturers*, Future of Business and Finance, https://doi.org/10.1007/978-3-031-75279-7_17

We explored and emphasized the significance of expanded partnerships in Chap. 12. This coordination of business ecosystems extends beyond supply chain alliances to include recyclers, repair services, and value chain customers, promoting a culture of shared responsibility and collaborative effort in achieving circularity. Digital platforms facilitate seamless interactions within the ecosystem, empowering participants to respond efficiently to new opportunities and challenges. For example, collaboration platforms support collective creativity, orchestration platforms streamline processes across multiple participants, and matching platforms connect supply with demand, optimizing resource utilization and operational efficiencies.

In Chap. 13, we then focused on connected products and components, acknowledging their importance in the circular economy. IoT technologies are crucial in real-time monitoring and data-driven decision-making, vital for extending product life and ensuring optimal resource utilization. Connected products and components continuously transmit data on their functioning status and efficiency, enabling predictive maintenance, improving product longevity, and reducing waste. The transparency and adaptability of IoT in product lifecycles inform sustainable designs and facilitate circular business models.

Our exploration led us to Chap. 14, where we recognized the growing importance of digital customer engagement in the circular economy. Customers in the value chain are no longer passive entities but active participants throughout the product lifecycle, enabling more insightful, dynamic, and responsive interaction. We emphasized engaging with customers beyond the point of sale, encouraging responsible consumption and stewardship of resources. Personalized experiences, facilitated by advanced analytics and AI, enable tailored product recommendations, proactive maintenance alerts, and incentives for circular behaviors, fostering deeper customer loyalty and sustainable usage patterns.

Chapter 15 emphasizes the importance of using data as the central intelligence of a manufacturer's circular economy efforts. This involves integrating and leveraging data from customer interactions, business ecosystems, connected products, and internal IT systems. By analyzing data across these dimensions, data-driven circularity offers a comprehensive view of a manufacturer's circular business models. This enables strategic decision-making and operational adjustments that improve profitability and resource efficiency. Big Data, Business Intelligence (BI), machine learning (ML), predictive analytics, and Generative AI collectively support these efforts, leading to enhanced decision-making, improved product lifecycle management, increased customer engagement, operational agility, and reduced supply chain vulnerabilities.

Transitioning to a circular economy is a complex challenge beyond changing mindsets or implementing isolated initiatives. It's not only about recycling or making minor improvements in waste management but rather a complete shift in how businesses view the lifecycle of their products, the value of their data, and their relationships with customers and other stakeholders. New digital capabilities are necessary to support this transition and require a comprehensive, strategically aligned digital transformation.

The Sustainable Manufacturing Intelligence Framework combines these elements in a cohesive approach to help manufacturers navigate the digital transformation required for a thriving circular economy. It serves as a guide through the uncharted territory of the circular economy, ensuring that every digital initiative—from IoT applications to predictive analytics—is not an isolated effort but a part of a larger, cohesive mechanism. This unified approach avoids fragmented digitization, which can lead to operational inefficiencies and hinder the seamless flow of a circular economy.

Without a cohesive guide, organizations can easily get lost in the complexity and nuances of the circular economy. Different departments might adopt different digital solutions with good intentions, leading to fragmentation and inefficiencies. Fragmented digital initiatives can result in operational silos, data incompatibilities, and disjointed customer experiences, all detrimental to the circular transition. In an ecosystem demanding unprecedented levels of real-time data sharing, collaboration, and transparency, a coherent digital landscape is not a luxury; it's a necessity. A standardized framework provides a unified vision and common language, aligning all stakeholders and ensuring the digital initiatives are cohesive and strategically aligned.

By implementing a comprehensive digital strategy that includes internal improvements and external partnerships, companies can promote transparent, responsible, and efficient relationships among all stakeholders, expediting the transition to a circular economy with significant environmental and economic advantages.

The time to take action is now. This framework is not just a theoretical concept; it's a practical toolkit for businesses prepared to adopt digital transformation and advance circular economy principles. As we envision the future, SMIF will serve as the compass that leads businesses toward a harmonious balance of innovation, resource management, and economic success in the circular economy landscape.

Part IV

Thriving Together: Business Growth Redefined for a Sustainable Future

Redefining growth through the circular economy empowers us to build resilient, profitable, and sustainable enterprises for the twenty-first century.

iStock Credit: M.photostock

Circular Economy as a Catalyst for Innovation and Growth

18

Abstract

This chapter summarizes our transformative journey, guided by the 1+5R model for transitioning to circular business models and underpinned by the Sustainable Manufacturing Intelligence Framework (SMIF) for digitizing these models. We explore how digitization can redefine business growth within the circular economy. We reflect on the Industrial Revolution's role in economic expansion and improved living standards while acknowledging its environmental costs. Today, our challenge is transitioning from linear consumption to circular systems that align with our planet's rhythms, ensuring continued economic development without compromising ecological integrity.

The circular economy offers innovative solutions to environmental challenges and new opportunities for economic growth. This model promises to increase global wealth, foster innovation, and minimize long-term environmental impacts. We can achieve inclusive, regenerative, and sustainable development by redefining growth and success.

This chapter presents the 10-Step Circular Advantage Guide to help manufacturers thrive in the circular economy. It emphasizes principles such as strategic deliberation, leveraging unique strengths, fostering collaboration, and innovating customer solutions. We also address challenges, including market acceptance, cultural shifts, regulatory compliance, and technological integration.

As we move toward 2030, embracing circular and digital transformation will enhance competitiveness, lower costs, and attract talent and investors. The path forward calls for immediate and strategic action, ensuring manufacturers build a sustainable, prosperous future for the economy and the planet. We conclude with actionable steps for manufacturers to take now, next, and later, providing a clear roadmap for integrating circular economy principles into their operations and ensuring long-term success.

H. H. Jensen, *Circular Economy Opportunities and Pathways for Manufacturers*, Future of Business and Finance, https://doi.org/10.1007/978-3-031-75279-7_18

Key Messages

- *Industrial Revolution's Impact*: The Industrial Revolution led to significant economic growth, improved living standards, and a burgeoning middle class, lifting billions out of poverty but at a profound environmental cost.
- *Environmental Consequences*: Unchecked industrial expansion consumed natural resources and disrupted ecosystems, establishing a "take-make-use-dispose" economy that externalized environmental costs.
- *Current Ecological Limits*: Our pursuit of prosperity has brought us close to ecological limits. Despite these challenges, there is a universal desire to secure a better future for the next generation.
- *Need for Economic Redefinition*: We must transition from linear consumption to systems that align with our planet's rhythms, promoting economic development that lifts people out of poverty without compromising the environment.
- *Balancing Prosperity and Ecology*: It is crucial to ensure that ecological damage does not negate human prosperity. Our economic progress must align with environmental sustainability and our children's well-being aspirations.
- *Circular Economy Solutions*: The circular economy offers solutions to environmental challenges while creating opportunities for innovation and growth, promoting inclusive, regenerative, and sustainable growth.
- *Collaborative Efforts*: Governments, businesses, and civil societies must collaborate to craft policies and solutions that prioritize long-term planetary health alongside immediate economic gains.
- *Embracing the Future*: We must embrace models where economic growth and environmental sustainability reinforce each other, leveraging the circular economy to usher in a new era of prosperity.
- *Architects of a New Economic Era*: As architects of a new economic era, we must embrace creativity, courage, and collaboration to forge a future where the planet and prosperity are partners in progress.
- *Winning in the Circular Economy*: The 10-Step Circular Advantage Guide provides a roadmap for manufacturers to succeed in the circular economy, driving innovation, sustainability, and profitability.

The Industrial Revolution catalyzed an explosion in productivity, leading to significant economic expansion, improved living standards, and the rise of a burgeoning middle class in industrialized nations. This period also played a crucial role in lifting billions out of poverty. The global spread of industrialization and its economic benefits widened access to education, improved health conditions, and unlocked new realms of human potential. However, this remarkable progress has come with a profound environmental cost.

Pursuing industrial dominance caused the environment to suffer due to unchecked expansion. Natural resources were consumed at an alarming rate, and industrial byproducts began disrupting ecosystems and taking a toll on the planet's health. The linear economy of "take-make-use-dispose" became the norm, externalizing the environmental costs of waste and pollution onto society rather than being accounted for by the businesses generating them or the consumers benefiting from their use.

Today, we face a precarious situation where our pursuit of prosperity has brought us close to ecological limits. Despite these challenges, parents worldwide universally desire to secure a better future for their children, prioritizing reduced poverty, better education, and improved health.

This highlights the urgent need to redefine our economic models. We must transition from linear consumption patterns that deplete natural resources to innovative systems that align with our planet's rhythms. This approach ensures that the pursuit of prosperity does not compromise the biosphere we depend on. It simultaneously promotes continued economic development that lifts more people out of poverty and guarantees a better future for their children.

We must ensure that irreversible ecological damage does not negate our gains in human prosperity. The challenge before us is not merely to sustain the momentum of growth but to elevate it to new dimensions, ensuring that our economic progress aligns with environmental sustainability and the fundamental aspirations of parents everywhere for their children's well-being.

The circular economy offers solutions to environmental challenges while creating new opportunities for economic innovation and growth. This economic model promises to increase global wealth, foster innovation, and minimize long-term environmental impact. It presents a strategic opportunity to redefine growth and success in the twenty-first century, closely connected to the environment's well-being. This isn't about sacrificing growth for the sake of sustainability; instead, it's about innovating our way toward an inclusive, regenerative, and sustainable form of growth.

This transformative journey requires a symphony of concerted efforts across all sectors and geographies. Governments, businesses, and civil societies must collaborate closely, crafting policies, innovating solutions, and cultivating a culture prioritizing long-term planetary health alongside immediate economic gains.

As we stand at this crossroads, the choice is clear. We can either cling to outdated models that pit economic growth against environmental sustainability or embrace a future where they thrive together, reinforcing each other. The promise of the circular economy is not just in its ability to mitigate ecological crises but in its potential to usher in a new era of prosperity.

We are called upon not just as stewards of the environment but as architects of a new economic era. Let us embrace this challenge with the creativity, courage, and collaboration it demands, forging a future where the planet and prosperity are partners in progress.

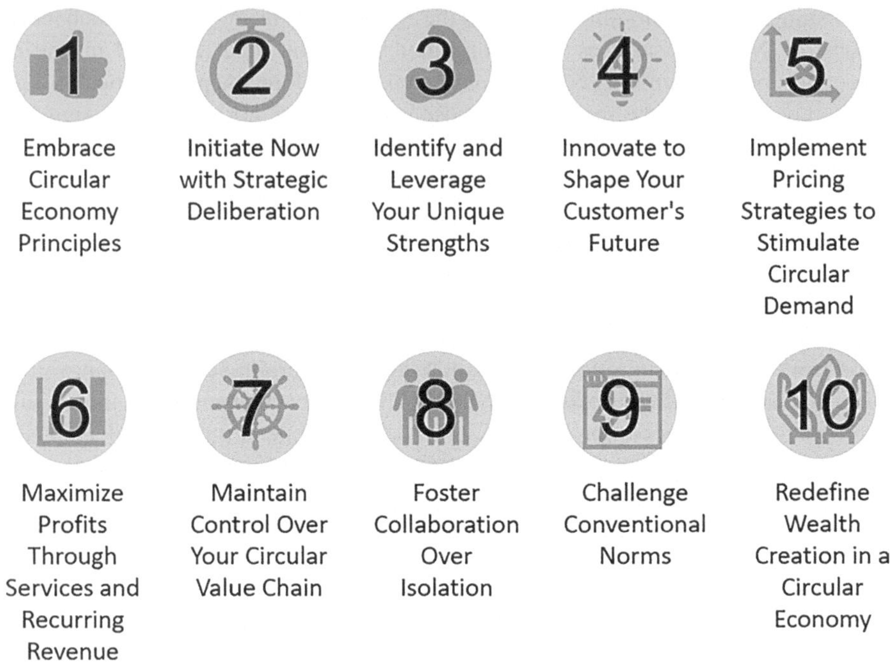

Fig. 18.1 The 10-step circular advantage guide

18.1 Winning in the Circular Economy: The 10-Step Circular Advantage Guide

This section presents the 10-Step Circular Advantage Guide for manufacturers to navigate and succeed in the circular economy (Fig. 18.1). Each step is an element in building a sustainable, resilient, and profitable business model that leverages circular economy principles. These steps draw on insights from digital disruption strategies, recent research, and strategic planning essentials and will help manufacturers thrive in the evolving economic landscape.

18.1.1 Embrace Circular Economy Principles

You must comprehend and incorporate circular principles into your business strategy to thrive in the circular economy. This involves creating products with longevity, reusability, and recyclability in mind and acknowledging that waste is an inefficiency that needs to be addressed. Prioritizing resource efficiency enables companies to harmonize sustainability with profitability, guaranteeing that environmental objectives are achieved while retaining a competitive edge.

18.1.2 Initiate Now with Strategic Deliberation

Starting your transition to a circular economy now while planning carefully allows you to take immediate action and adjust your strategies over time. Early adoption helps you stay ahead of competitors and regulatory changes, ensuring your business is well-positioned as the market evolves. Strategic planning should be adaptive, allowing flexibility and rapid response to market shifts, ensuring your initiatives remain relevant and practical.

18.1.3 Identify and Leverage Your Unique Strengths

Leverage your company's unique strengths and capabilities to excel in the circular economy. Identify what differentiates you from competitors and focus on areas where you have a competitive advantage. This ensures that your circular initiatives are not only sustainable but also profitable. Tailoring your strategy to your core strengths allows for more efficient use of resources and maximizes impact.

18.1.4 Innovate to Shape Your Customer's Future

Anticipate and shape the future needs of your customers by offering innovative circular solutions. Focusing on long-term customer relationships and delivering lifecycle value ensures your products and services meet evolving demands. Innovation should be customer-centric, integrating feedback and data to continuously improve and adapt offerings, fostering loyalty, and creating new revenue streams through circular practices like Product-as-a-Service models.

18.1.5 Implement Pricing Strategies to Stimulate Circular Demand

Use pricing strategies to encourage circular behaviors among your customers. Offer incentives for returning products for refurbishment or recycling, and develop pricing models that reflect the total lifecycle value of products. Strategic pricing can drive sustainable customer choices, making circular products and services more attractive and accessible and supporting the overall viability of circular business models.

18.1.6 Maximize Profits Through Services and Recurring Revenue

Generate revenue through services and recurring business models, such as maintenance, refurbishment, and leasing. These models extend product lifecycles and create continuous income streams, providing financial stability and enhancing customer relationships. Emphasizing services promotes resource efficiency and ensures ongoing engagement and value extraction from existing assets.

18.1.7 Maintain Control Over Your Circular Value Chain

Maintain control over your products and materials throughout their lifecycle by implementing robust tracking, management, and optimization systems. This ensures efficient reuse and recycling of materials, reduces waste, capitalizes on circular services, and meets regulatory requirements. Clear ownership and accountability across the value chain are essential for transparency and effective execution of circular strategies.

18.1.8 Foster Collaboration Over Isolation

Collaborate with stakeholders across the value chain, including suppliers, customers, and competitors. Building a collaborative network is essential for creating a thriving circular economy ecosystem. Collaboration fosters innovation, reduces costs, and ensures efficient resource use, building resilience against supply chain disruptions. Effective collaboration requires transparent communication and alignment of goals among all participants.

18.1.9 Challenge Conventional Norms

Question and rethink traditional business models and practices that do not align with circular economy principles. Being open to new ideas and willing to disrupt the status quo is crucial for innovation and progress. This mindset allows your company to find creative solutions to sustainability challenges and stay ahead in the market, continually evolving to meet changing demands and opportunities.

18.1.10 Redefine Wealth Creation in a Circular Economy

Shift the focus from traditional success metrics to those prioritizing sustainability, resource efficiency, and long-term value creation. Redefine what success looks like in a circular economy context, ensuring your business strategies align with global sustainability goals and contribute positively to society, the environment, and your bottom line. Companies can ensure long-term resilience and relevance by focusing on holistic value creation in a rapidly changing world.

By following these steps, manufacturers can navigate the complexities of the circular economy, driving innovation, sustainability, and profitability in equal measure. Each step builds on the insights from digital disruption and strategic planning, ensuring a robust and adaptable approach to the future.

18.2 Transformative Insights for a Circular Economy

As we conclude this transformative journey, we must reflect on the insights and strategies explored. The following statements from the previous chapters encapsulate the essence of the circular economy and its impact on manufacturing. These key takeaways represent our exploration's most pivotal and inspiring lessons, providing a blueprint for future success in a circular economy.

18.2.1 Embracing Circular Economy for Competitive Edge and Innovation

"The circular economy, supported by digital innovation, offers a path to sustainable and competitive manufacturing." Combining circular economy principles with digital technologies offers manufacturers a sustainable and competitive edge in the market. Embracing digital innovation allows companies to optimize their processes, reduce waste, and enhance overall efficiency (Sect. 1).

"The circular economy goes beyond sustainability efforts; it's a strong business strategy that enhances competitiveness by reducing reliance on finite resources, cutting costs, and creating new revenue streams." Adopting circular practices highlights the strategic benefits, secures a competitive advantage, reduces operational costs, and opens new revenue opportunities (Sect. 1).

"Companies must remain competitive in the existing linear market while adapting to circular practices." This balancing act is crucial—firms must innovate and invest within the circular model without losing their foothold in the traditional market. Managing this dual focus requires careful strategic planning and prioritization (Sect. 4.1.8).

"Countries increasingly focus on recycling and circular economy principles to enhance domestic resilience." Adopting circular economy principles strengthens resilience against global supply chain disruptions and environmental challenges, securing resources and reducing dependency on external sources (Sect. 7.8).

"Manufacturers' competitiveness depends on how effectively they integrate three key paradigms: cleaner production methods, digital technologies, and circular economy practices." Cleaner production methods minimize environmental and climate impacts by reducing carbon footprints. Digital technologies are essential to streamline operations, improve efficiency, and promote innovation. Circular economy practices are necessary to establish regenerative resource loops that extend product lifecycles and reduce waste (Sect. 1.3).

"Their focus remained on refining products for existing customers, leaving them vulnerable to new, groundbreaking business models." Innovating and adapting to new business models is vital for staying ahead of industry trends and ensuring long-term success. Technological shifts often blindsided established companies (Sect. 8.13).

"Industries must view this transformation not as a temporary change but as a fundamental shift that will shape the future of manufacturing." Integrating circular economy principles deeply into manufacturing firms' strategic and operational frameworks is essential for capturing the full benefits of circularity. This approach ensures that circular practices are embedded in every aspect of the business, from product design to end-of-life management (Sect. 1.4.5).

"The transition to a circular economy demands a cultural shift within organizations." Companies must move from a linear mindset of producing, selling, using, and disposing of products to a more holistic view that sees products and materials as valuable assets with extended lifecycles. This requires educating and training employees at all levels to understand and embrace circular economy principles (Sect. 9.4.2).

18.2.2 Revolutionizing Business Models with Circular Principles

"The emergence of 'born-circular' companies, founded with a circular business model at the core, promises to be as transformative as the impact of born-digital companies and disruptive firms leading the previous economic shifts." Born-circular companies integrate circular economy principles from the outset, driving significant industry shifts akin to the transformative impact of digital disruptors (Sect. 1).

"The circular economy changes how value is created, shifting it from the point of production to the continuous usage cycles of the entire product." This fundamental shift in value creation focuses on extending the product lifecycle rather than just the initial production phase, ensuring products remain valuable and functional for longer periods, maximizing their economic and environmental benefits (Sect. 1.2.6).

"Repair, refurbishment, and remanufacturing practices extend product life and create continuous revenue streams, shifting away from the traditional linear economy model." Focusing on extending product life through repair and refurbishment reduces waste and provides new opportunities for profit and customer engagement (Sect. 5.10).

"Recycling is the final stage in a product's lifecycle. This final stage determines whether it will be discarded as waste or given another life." Effective recycling processes reduce the need for virgin materials and lower environmental impacts by ensuring materials are continuously reused rather than discarded (Sect. 7.8).

"Modularity means that users have bought a platform they can constantly update." Designing products for easy updates and maintenance enhances their longevity and customer satisfaction, allowing continuous improvement without complete replacements (Sect. 4.1.2).

"The redesign imperative demands products crafted to fulfill an immediate need and endure multiple cycles of use and reuse." Designing products for durability and multiple life cycles reduces waste and increases value over time (Sect. 4).

18.2.3 Harnessing Digital Innovation for Circular Efficiency

"Internal IT systems facilitate manufacturers' transition to a circular economy." Efficient internal processes supported by advanced IT systems are crucial for tracking, managing, and optimizing resources throughout the product lifecycle. This technological backbone of circular business models promotes operational efficiency. It enhances the ability to innovate and adapt to changing market demands, making the transition to a circular economy feasible and sustainable (Sect. 11).

"Data-driven circularity is the brain of the circular economy." Leveraging data analytics enables manufacturers to understand and improve their operations, making them more sustainable and efficient (Sect. 14.6).

"This collective approach to data-driven decision-making enables all stakeholders to create decisions that benefit the ecosystem." When data flows freely and securely among ecosystem stakeholders, it forms the basis for collective intelligence that can tackle complex challenges beyond the capabilities of any individual company. Therefore, in a digitally interconnected ecosystem, data doesn't just inform—it transforms (Sect. 12.3.2).

"Connected products and components are the senses of the circular economy." IoT and intelligent technologies provide real-time data and insights critical for maintaining product longevity and efficiency, enabling continuous monitoring and feedback (Sect. 13).

"By implementing a comprehensive digital strategy, companies expedite the transition to a circular economy with significant environmental and economic advantages." A holistic digital strategy accelerates the shift towards circular practices, yielding both environmental benefits and economic gains (Sect. 17).

"Standardization and interoperability are frameworks that form the basis for scalable, adaptable, and efficient circular systems." Integrating digital technologies with circular economy principles enhances transparency, efficiency, and traceability across the supply chain, driving sustainable manufacturing practices (Sect. 12.3.5).

"Unlike traditional supply chains, where the focus is predominantly linear and confined within organizational boundaries, the supply chain in a circular digital ecosystem is an interconnected web of multiple stakeholders, each playing a unique role in a product's or material's lifecycle." Circular digital ecosystems feature supply chains as interconnected networks where multiple stakeholders collaboratively manage the lifecycle of products and materials (Sect. 12.3.4).

18.2.4 Rethinking Value and Resources in a Circular Context

"With circular business models, waste becomes an asset rather than a liability to discard." Viewing waste as a potential asset reduces the environmental footprint and creates new value from materials that would otherwise be discarded (Sect. 9.3.1).

"As history has demonstrated, those who fail to adapt to transformative changes are left behind." Embracing transformative changes like the circular economy is crucial for staying competitive. Innovating and evolving with industry trends is essential for long-term success and resilience in a rapidly changing market (Sect. 1).

" As we approach 2030, the perception of waste undergoes a profound transformation, propelled by a collective awakening among consumers and reinforced by decisive governmental action." Customers and citizens will increasingly view waste as unacceptable, demanding greater transparency and accountability from businesses regarding their environmental impact. Integrating circular practices prepares businesses for the future and positions them as industry leaders, ensuring long-term competitiveness and innovation. By 2030, there will be a significant shift in societal attitudes towards waste, driven by growing environmental awareness and stricter regulatory frameworks. Governments worldwide are expected to implement more stringent policies and regulations that mandate waste reduction, promote recycling, and encourage using sustainable materials (Sect. 1.4.6).

"In the circular economy, every material has a story to tell, and a transparent supply chain is the story's narrator." A transparent supply chain in the circular economy ensures that the journey of every material is traceable, fostering accountability and sustainability (Sect. 12.3.4).

"Ensuring parts and materials within their control never unintentionally exit their sphere of influence." Managing materials effectively throughout the product lifecycle ensures better resource utilization and minimizes waste (Sect. 4.2.2).

"It involves a shift in perspective from seeing products and components as disposable to recognizing them as valuable assets with extended lifecycles." Embracing a mindset that views products as long-term assets rather than disposable items is crucial for adopting circular economy principles (Sect. 5.5).

18.2.5 Addressing Environmental and Social Responsibilities

"These environmental burdens have fallen on society and natural ecosystems, creating a disconnect between the economic actions of manufacturers and their environmental and social impacts." Addressing traditional manufacturing practices' environmental and social consequences is essential for creating a more responsible and equitable economy (Sect. 5.10).

"Externalizing environmental costs have historically enabled business models focused on the unrepairability of products to be financially viable for manufacturers." Traditional business models that externalize environmental costs have thrived on product unrepairability, but this approach is increasingly unsustainable in a circular economy (Sect. 5.10).

18.3 Navigating the Challenges of the Circular Economy

Transitioning to a circular economy presents many opportunities, but it also comes with complex challenges that manufacturers must address to succeed. These challenges span various aspects of business operations, from technological integration to cultural shifts within organizations. In Sect. 9.4 we delved into the challenges identified, providing insights into how businesses can overcome them to embrace the circular economy fully. The key points are summarized in Table 18.1.

Table 18.1 Summary of challenges of the circular economy

Challenge Area	Key Points Summary
Market Acceptance and Customer Behavior	• Gaining market acceptance for circular products takes time and effort, especially in markets used to disposable goods. • Manufacturers need to educate customers on the benefits of circular products and build trust in their quality and longevity. • Marketing should highlight environmental and economic advantages. • Changing customer behavior through incentives and awareness campaigns is crucial.
Cultural and Organizational Shifts	• Transitioning to a circular economy requires a cultural shift within organizations. • Employees need education and training on circular economy principles. • Leadership must foster an environment encouraging innovation, collaboration, and sustainable practices. • Overcoming resistance to change and aligning all departments with the new vision is essential for success.
Regulatory Compliance and Standardization	• Manufacturers must navigate complex and evolving regulations related to sustainability. • Compliance with waste reduction, recycling, and sustainable materials laws is essential. • Standardization across the industry is crucial for integration within the circular economy, requiring stakeholder coordination.
Supply Chain and Resource Management	• Reconfiguring supply chains to support spare parts availability for repairs requires investment in warehousing and digital inventory tracking systems. • Establishing reverse logistics systems for end-of-life products is vital. • Companies must handle the complexities of collecting, sorting, and transporting used products. • Supply chain resilience is complicated by geopolitical and environmental challenges.
Redesign and Product Innovation	• Transitioning to circular product design focuses on easy disassembly, durability, and repairability. • This requires balancing performance and functionality with circularity. • Developing modular designs and standardizing components is necessary. • Engaging suppliers to produce components that support circularity adds complexity to the supply chain.

(continued)

Table 18.1 (continued)

Challenge Area	Key Points Summary
Collaboration Within the Business Ecosystem	• Aligning goals and practices across the business ecosystem, including manufacturers, suppliers, recyclers, and service providers, is essential for creating closed-loop systems. • Transparent communication, data sharing, and collaborative platforms are necessary. • Overcoming competitive barriers and fostering a culture of collaboration is crucial.
Financing the Transition	• Financing the transition to a circular economy while maintaining competitiveness in the linear economy is challenging. • Manufacturers must simultaneously invest in existing operations and circular initiatives. • Strategic financial planning and securing investment are crucial.
Technological Integration and Data Management	• Integrating advanced technologies and effective data management is challenging. • Investments in IT systems, IoT, AI, and analytics are needed to optimize resources. • High costs and the need for skilled personnel are significant barriers. • Ensuring data privacy and security is paramount.
Operational Challenges	• Shifting to circular practices requires capital expenditures for recycling, remanufacturing, and materials recovery processes. • Small- and medium-sized enterprises may struggle to secure funding. • Operational inefficiencies during the transition can disrupt production and increase costs. • Continuous operations updates are necessary to stay competitive.

18.4 The Opportunity for 2030: Embrace Clean, Circular, and Digital Transformation to Stay Competitive

In 2030, a forward-thinking manufacturer stands out in the competitive landscape by fully embracing clean, circular and digital transformation. This manufacturer has reduced costs through efficient resource use and waste minimization, resulting in streamlined operations and enhanced profitability. Their product lineup, characterized by sustainable and innovative designs, attracts a growing base of eco-conscious consumers, solidifying their market appeal and increase their revenue.

Harnessing the power of digitization, the manufacturer leverages data-driven insights to optimize every facet of their operations, from production to supply chain management, driving continuous innovation. By adhering to stringent environmental regulations, they avoid costly penalties and gain a distinct competitive edge, positioning themselves as leaders in compliance and sustainability.

This commitment to circular principles and cutting-edge technology makes the manufacturer a magnet for top talent, drawing in individuals passionate about sustainability and innovation. Their motivated and skilled workforce is crucial in sustaining their competitive advantage. Furthermore, the emphasis on ESG (Environmental, Social, and Governance) criteria makes the company attractive to investors seeking responsible and progressive investment opportunities.

The manufacturer's dedication to sustainable practices has enhanced its brand reputation, fostering customer trust and loyalty. It has built a resilient supply chain by implementing circular strategies, effectively mitigating risks associated with resource scarcity and geopolitical tensions and ensuring uninterrupted operations.

In this future landscape, the message is clear: being clean, circular, and digital has transformed this manufacturer into a necessity and a thriving example of how embracing these principles leads to unparalleled competitive advantage.

18.5 The Path Forward: A Call to Action for Manufacturers

As we conclude this book, it's essential to translate the insights and strategies discussed into actionable steps for manufacturers. The journey toward a sustainable, circular, and digital economy is necessary and urgent.

What Should a Manufacturer Do Now?

- *Assess and Integrate Circular Principles*: Evaluate your current operations and identify areas where circular economy principles can be integrated. This includes designing for durability, reusability, and recyclability.
- *Implement Immediate Changes*: Start with quick wins demonstrating economic benefits, such as reducing waste from production, improving energy efficiency, and using sustainable materials. Set clear, measurable goals for the profitability of your circularity initiatives.
- *Engage Stakeholders*: Communicate your commitment to circular economy principles to your stakeholders, including employees, suppliers, and customers. Build a coalition that supports your vision for sustainability.

What Should a Manufacturer Do Next?

- *Prepare Your IT for the Transition*: Ensure your IT infrastructure is ready to support circular economy initiatives. This includes modernizing systems, enhancing data analytics capabilities, and implementing digital tools for resource tracking, lifecycle management, customer interactions, and supply chain transparency.
- *Redesign Products and Processes*: Develop and launch new modular, repairable, and upgradeable products. Reengineer your processes to minimize environmental impact and maximize resource efficiency.
- *Pilot Circular Business Models*: Initiate pilot programs for circular business models such as take-back schemes, remanufacturing, and Product-as-a-Service. These pilots will help you understand circular practices' operational requirements and benefits before scaling them across your business.

What Should a Manufacturer Do Later?

- *Scale Circular Business Models*: Expand your circular initiatives to cover all aspects of your business.
- *Establish an Ecosystem of Circular Service Providers*: Build a network of partners, including repair shops, reverse logistics providers, and recycling facilities, to support your circular economy initiatives. Collaborating with these service providers ensures that products can be efficiently returned, repaired, refurbished, and recycled, creating a seamless circular value chain.
- *Digitize the Business Ecosystem*: Leverage digital technologies to create an interconnected, transparent, and efficient business ecosystem.

Embrace the transformation now to ensure your business survives and thrives. The time for action is now. We must build a sustainable, prosperous future that benefits our economy and planet.

Further Reading

Adidas. (2020). *Adidas aims to end plastic waste with innovation + partnerships as the solution*. From https://news.adidas.com/running/adidas-aims-to-end-plastic-waste-with-innovation%2D%2D-partnerships-as-the-solutions/s/be70ac18-1fc9-45c1-9413-d8abaac2e849

Amazon. (2024). *Grow your business by selling on Amazon renewed*. From https://sell.amazon.com/programs/renewed

Apple. (2021). *Product environmental report – iPhone 13*. From https://www.apple.com/environment/pdf/products/iphone/iPhone_13_PER_Sept2021.pdf

Apple. (2024a, 06). *Certified refurbished*. From https://www.apple.com/shop/refurbished

Apple. (2024b, 06). *Self service repair*. From https://support.apple.com/self-service-repair

Apple. (2024c, 06). *Self service repair store for Apple products*. From https://selfservicerepair.com/en-US/home

BCG. (2023, 08). *Building the supply chain of the future*. From BCG's Build for the Future series: https://www.bcg.com/publications/2023/building-the-supply-chain-of-the-future

Bland, R., & Shull, D. (2024, 03). *How HP is finding success in circularity*. From McKinsey Sustainability: https://www.mckinsey.com/capabilities/sustainability/our-insights/how-hp-is-finding-success-in-circularity

Bogdanich, I., Hardcastle, B., Donnelly, D., Axup, K., & Manderson, K. (2023). *Australia's critical minerals strategy 2023–2030*. Allens. From https://www.allens.com.au/insights-news/insights/2023/06/Australias-Critical-Minerals-Strategy-2023-2030/

Bolton, S., & Kao, G. (2015). *Valuing the net benefit of Dell's more sustainable plastic use at an industry scale*. Trucost. From https://i.dell.com/sites/doccontent/corporate/corp-comm/en/documents/circular-economy-net-benefits.pdf

Bosch. (2024, 06). *Online repair service*. From https://www.bosch-professional.com/gb/en/service/after-sales-service/online-repair-service/

Brown, A., Laubinger, F., & Börkey, P. (2023). *New Aspects of EPR: Extending producer responsibility to additional product groups and challenges throughout the product lifecycle* (OECD environment working papers). OECD – Organisation for Economic Co-operation and Development. From https://www.oecd-ilibrary.org/deliver/cfdc1bdc-en.pdf

Bruggers, J. (2022). *California passed a landmark law about plastic pollution. Why are some environmentalists still concerned?* Inside Climate News. From https://insideclimatenews.org/news/12102022/california-plastics-pollution-bill/

Cap Gemini Invent. (2021). *The sustainability impact of car sharing*. Cap Gemini Invent. From https://www.capgemini.com/se-en/wp-content/uploads/sites/20/2022/10/2022-09-21_The_Sustainability_Impact_of_Car_Sharing_A4_2021_v2_DIGITAL_KS.pdf

Catena-X. (2024a, 06). Catena-X. From https://catena-x.net/en/

Catena-X. (2024b, 06). *Data as basis for a successful circular economy*. From https://catena-x.net/en/benefits-pros/circular-economy

H. H. Jensen, *Circular Economy Opportunities and Pathways for Manufacturers*, Future of Business and Finance, https://doi.org/10.1007/978-3-031-75279-7

Caterpillar. (2024a). Cat® Reman. From https://www.cat.com/en_US/products/new/parts/reman.html

Caterpillar. (2024b). *Connected solution security principles*. From https://www.cat.com/en_ZA/support/technology/connected-solutions-principles/security.html

CATL. (2024, 04). *CATL and Volvo Cars join hands for sustainable development*. From https://www.catl.com/en/news/6234.html

Chandramouli, R. (2019, 08). *NIST SP 800-204 – Security strategies for microservices-based application systems*. From NIST – Computer Security Resource Center: https://csrc.nist.gov/pubs/sp/800/204/final

China Daily. (2012, 09). *Circular economy gets 5-year regulator boost*. From https://english.www.gov.cn/policies/policywatch/202107/08/content_WS60e639b0c6d0df57f98dc92b.html

Christensen, C. M. (1997). *The Innovator's dilemma: When new Technologies cause great firms to fail*. Harvard Business School Press.

Christensen, C. M., Raynor, M. E., & McDonald, R. (2015). *What is disruptive innovation?* Howard Business Review. From https://hbr.org/2015/12/what-is-disruptive-innovation

Circular Cars Initiative. (2022). *Driving ambitions: The business case for circular economy in the car industry*. World Econmic Forum. From https://www.weforum.org/projects/the-circular-cars-initiative/

Coherent Market Insights. (2024, 1). *Refurbished electronics marke analysis*. From https://www.coherentmarketinsights.com/market-insight/refurbished-electronics-market-6166

Compton, N. (2023, 01). *What daisy did next: How Apple's evolving team of de-manufacturing machines battles e-waste*. From Wallpaper: https://www.wallpaper.com/design-interiors/fmg-takes-technical-ceramics-out-of-this-world-in-a-new-campaign

Cummins. (2024). *Cummins Recon®*. From https://www.cummins.com/parts/recon

Cummins Inc. (2024, 02). *How Cummins Recon® products can help your sustainability goals*. From https://www.cummins.com/news/2024/02/01/how-cummins-reconr-products-can-help-your-sustainability-goals

Danfoss. (2022). *Annual report 2021 – The greenest energy is the energy we don't use*. Danfoss.

Dell. (2024a). *Closed-loop recycled content*. From Design for Environment: https://www.dell.com/learn/vg/en/vgcorp1/corp-comm/closed-loop-recycled-content

Dell. (2024b, 06). *Everything you need to know about refurbished computers*. From https://www.dell.com/en-us/dfh/lp/outlet-why-refurbished

Deloitte. (2023). *2023 gen Z and millennial survey*. Deloitte. From https://www.deloitte.com/global/en/issues/work/content/genzmillennialsurvey.html

Dentons. (2023, 07). *Extended producer responsibility: Mandatory implementation of a prevention and eco-design plan for each of the sectors to which you belong*. From https://www.dentons.com/en/insights/articles/2023/july/4/extended-producer-responsibility

Department for Environment, Food & Rural Affairs. (2018). *Resources and waste strategy for England*. From https://www.gov.uk/government/publications/resources-and-waste-strategy-for-england

Der Grüne Punkt. (2024, 06). *The German Pakcaging act – What's particular important for online retailers*. From https://www.gruener-punkt.de/en/packaging-licensing/packaging-act

DLA Piper. (2023). *European Union reduced vat rates for recycled products*. From https://www.dlapiper.com/en/insights/publications/vat-monthly-alert-series/2023/vat-monthly-alert-june-2023/european-union-reduced-vat-rates-for-recycled-products.

Elliott, R., Garcia, M. F., & Riglietti, G. (2023). *BCI supply chain resilience report 2023*. The Business Continuity. From https://www.thebci.org/news/bci-launches-supply-chain-resilience-report-2023.html

European Commission. (2020a). *A new circular economy action plan for a cleaner and more competitive Europe*. From https://environment.ec.europa.eu/strategy/circular-economy-action-plan_en

European Commission. (2020b, 01). *The European green deal*. From https://commission.europa.eu/strategy-and-policy/priorities-2019-2024/european-green-deal_en

European Commission. (2021). *Supporting climate action through the EU budget*. Directorate-General for Climate Action. From https://climate.ec.europa.eu/eu-action/eu-funding-climate-action/supporting-climate-action-through-eu-budget_en

European Commission. (2022a). *Ecodesign for sustainable products regulation*. From European Commission: https://commission.europa.eu/energy-climate-change-environment/standards-tools-and-labels/products-labelling-rules-and-requirements/sustainable-products/ecodesign-sustainable-products-regulation_en

European Commission. (2022b, 3 30). *Green Deal: New proposals to make sustainable products the norm and boost Europe's resource independence*. From https://ec.europa.eu/commission/presscorner/detail/en/ip_22_2013

European Commission. (2022c). *In focus: Solar energy—Harnessing the power of the sun*. Directorate-General for Communication. From https://commission.europa.eu/news/focus-solar-energy-harnessing-power-sun-2022-09-13_en#

European Commission. (2023a). *'Right to repair': Questions & answers*. From European Commission: https://ec.europa.eu/commission/presscorner/detail/es/qanda_23_1795

European Commission. (2023b, 08). *Circular economy: New law on more sustainable, circular and safe batteries enters into force*. From https://environment.ec.europa.eu/news/new-law-more-sustainable-circular-and-safe-batteries-enters-force-2023-08-17_en

European Commission. (2023c). *Critical raw materials act*. From https://single-market-economy.ec.europa.eu/sectors/raw-materials/areas-specific-interest/critical-raw-materials/critical-raw-materials-act_en

European Commission. (2024, 05). *Ecodesign for sustainable products regulation*. From https://commission.europa.eu/energy-climate-change-environment/standards-tools-and-labels/products-labelling-rules-and-requirements/sustainable-products/ecodesign-sustainable-products-regulation_en

European Commission. (n.d.). *Ecodesign for sustainable products regulation*. From European Commission: https://commission.europa.eu/energy-climate-change-environment/standards-tools-and-labels/products-labelling-rules-and-requirements/sustainable-products/ecodesign-sustainable-products-regulation_en

European Environment Agency. (2024). *The benefits to biodiversity of a strong circular economy*. From https://www.eea.europa.eu/publications/the-benefits-to-biodiversity

European Parliament. (2023, 10). *Packaging: New EU rules to reduce, reuse and recycle*. From https://www.europarl.europa.eu/news/en/press-room/20231023IPR08128/packaging-new-eu-rules-to-reduce-reuse-and-recycle

European Parliament. (2024). *The impact of textile production and waste on the environment*. From Topics European Parliament: https://www.europarl.europa.eu/topics/en/article/20201208STO93327/the-impact-of-textile-production-and-waste-on-the-environment-infographics

Excess Materials Exchange. (2019). *EME pilot report*. From https://excessmaterialsexchange-pilot-report.s3.eu-central-1.amazonaws.com/EME+Pilot+Report+compressed.pdf

FasterCapital. (2024). *Economic drivers of planned obsolescence: Profits over durability*. FasterCapital. From https://fastercapital.com/content/Economic-Drivers-of-Planned-Obsolescence%2D%2DProfits-over-Durability.html

First Insight. (2021). *The state of consumer spending. Gen Z influencing all generations to make sustainability-first pruchase decisions*. FIRST INSIGHT. From https://www.firstinsight.com/white-papers-posts/gen-z-influencing-all-generations-to-make-sustainability-first-purchasing-decisions

Fnac Darty. (2023, 09). *Darty max reaches 1 million subscribers*. From https://www.fnacdarty.com/en/1-million-dabonnes-a-darty-max/

Ford. (2021). *Leading a sustainale revolution: Ford and HP to collaborateto transform 3D waste into auto parts*. From https://media.ford.com/content/fordmedia/fna/us/en/news/2021/03/25/leading-a-sustainable-revolution.html

Fragkos, P. (2022). *Analysing the systemic implications of energy efficiency and circular economy strategies in the decarbonisation context*. AIMS Energy. From http://www.aimspress.com/journal/energy

Fraser, M. (2022). *Pioneers of the future: The countries leading the way with circular economy policy.* Circle Economy. From https://www.circle-economy.com/blogs/the-circular-economy-who-is-leading-the-way

Frey, S., Am, J. B., Doshi, V., Malik, A., & Noble, S. (2023). *Consumers care about sustainability—and back it up with their wallets.* McKinsey and NielsenIQ. From https://nielseniq.com/global/en/insights/report/2023/consumers-care-about-sustainability-and-back-it-up-with-their-wallets/

Gartner. (2019). *Gartner predicts circular economies will replace linear economies in 10 years.* Gartner. From https://www.gartner.com/en/newsroom/press-releases/2019-09-26-gartner-predicts-circular-economies-will-replace-line

GE Aerospace. (2024). *TrueChoice commercial services.* From https://www.geaerospace.com/commercial/services/true-choice

Giacovelli, C. (2018). *Single-use plastics: A roadmap for sustainability.* UN Environment Progamme. From https://www.unep.org/resources/report/single-use-plastics-roadmap-sustainability.

Girardi, B., Patrahau, I., Cisco, G., & Rademaker, M. (2023). *Strategic raw materials for defence mapping European industry needs.* 01. From https://hcss.nl/wp-content/uploads/2023/01/Strategic-Raw-Materials-for-Defence-HCSS-2023-2.pdf

Gleiser, I., & Laurens, F. (2023, 8). *How computer vision is enabling a circular economy.* From AWS HPC Blog: https://aws.amazon.com/blogs/hpc/how-computer-vision-is-enabling-a-circular-economy/

Government of Canada. (2021). *Get involved in the circular economy.* From https://www.canada.ca/en/services/environment/conservation/sustainability/circular-economy/get-involved.html.

Grundfos. (2023). *2023 sustanability report.* From https://www.grundfos.com/sustainability/sustainability-report-2023

H&M. (2024, 06). *Let's close the loop.* From https://www2.hm.com/en_gb/sustainability-at-hm/our-work/close-the-loop.html.

H&M Group. (2024, 06). How we work with materials. From https://hmgroup.com/sustainability/circularity-and-climate/materials/.

Henrich, J., Li, J., Mazuera, C., & Perez, F. (2022). *Future-proofing the supply chain.* McKinsey & Company.

HP. (2024a, 06). *HP all-in plan.* From https://www.hp.com/us-en/all-in-plan/printers.html

HP. (2024b, 05). *HP business outlet.* From https://www.hp.com/us-en/sbso/buspurchase_refurbished.html

Iberdrola. (2024). *Planned obsolescence and its environmental impact.* From Iberdrola: https://www.iberdrola.com/sustainability/planned-obsolescence

IKEA. (2024a, 06). *Designing for a circular future.* From https://www.ikea.com/global/en/our-business/people-planet/designing-for-a-circular-future/.

IKEA. (2024b). *Our circular agenda.* From https://www.ikea.com/global/en/our-business/people-planet/our-circular-agenda/

IMDS. (2024, 06). Welcome to the International Material Data System. From https://www.mdsystem.com/imdsnt/startpage/index.jsp

INEOS. (2024). *INEOS Infinia.* From https://www.ineos.com/businesses/ineos-aromatics/ineos-infinia/

Ingka Group. (2023). *Ingka group annual summary ingka group annual summary.* From https://www.ingka.com/static/ingka-group-annual-summary-and-sustainability-report-fy23.pdf

International Energy Agency (IEA). (2023). *World energy outlook 2023.* International Energy Agency (IEA).

IPCC, I. P. (2021). *Climate change widespread, rapid, and intensifying.* Intergovernmental Panel on Climate Change – IPCC. From https://www.ipcc.ch/2021/08/09/ar6-wg1-20210809-pr/

IRENA. (2023). *Renewables competitiveness accelerates, despite cost inflation.* The International Renewable Energy Agency (IRENA). From https://www.irena.org/News/pressreleases/2023/Aug/Renewables-Competitiveness-Accelerates-Despite-Cost-Inflation

IRENA – International Renewable Energy Agency. (2021). Renewable power generation costs in 2020. IRENA – International Renewable Energy Agency. From https://www.irena.org/publications/2021/Jun/Renewable-Power-Costs-in-2020

Jayawardane, H. (2020). *Eco-industrial parks.* From LinkedIn: https://www.linkedin.com/pulse/eco-industrial-parks-heshan-jayawardane/

Jensen, H. H. (2023a). *Digitizing compliance: Unpacking circular economy legislations and their digital demands.* From Circular Bytes: https://www.linkedin.com/pulse/digitizing-compliance-unpacking-circular-economy-digital-jensen-3x7ae/

Jensen, H. H. (2023b). *Digitizing sustainability: Navigating the new era of EU's packaging and packaging waste regulation.* From Circuar Bytes: https://www.linkedin.com/pulse/digitizing-sustainability-navigating-new-era-eus-packaging-jensen-dq2je/

Jensen, H. H. (2023c, 11). *Logistics reimagined: Pioneering the circular transformation.* From Circular Bytes: https://www.linkedin.com/pulse/logistics-reimagined-pioneering-circular-henrik-hvid-jensen-fcsye/

Jensen, H. H. (2024a). *Extended producer responsibility: Key points and the role of digitization in forging a sustainable circular economy.* From Circular bytes: https://www.linkedin.com/pulse/extended-producer-responsibility-key-points-role-forging-jensen-iqwhf/

Jensen, H. H. (2024b). *Global Ecodesign legislation: Navigating the digital transformation for a sustainable future.* From Circular Bytes: https://www.linkedin.com/pulse/global-ecodesign-legislation-navigating-digital-future-jensen-qzo1f/

Jensen, H. H. (2024c). *Navigating right to repair legislations through digital innovation.* From Circular Bytes: https://www.linkedin.com/pulse/navigating-right-repair-legislations-through-digital-jensen-qfjpf/

Jensen, H. H. (2024d). *Unlocking a new era of eco-conscious manufacturing with the digital product passport.* From Circular Bytes: https://www.linkedin.com/pulse/unlocking-new-era-eco-conscious-manufacturing-digital-jensen-vgltf/

Johannes, H. P., Kojima, M., Iwasaki, F., & Edita, E. P. (2021). Applying the extended producer responsibility towards plastic waste in Asian developing countries for reducing marine plastic debris. *Waste Management & Research, 39*(5), 69-702. From https://journals.sagepub.com/doi/pdf/10.1177/0734242X211013412

John Iniobong Beauty, S. A., & Aigbavboa, C. O. (2023). *Adoption of circular economy by construction industry SMEs: Organisational growth transition study.* MDPI. From https://www.mdpi.com/2071-1050/15/7/5929.

Kalundborg Symbiosi. (2024). *Kalundborg symbiosis surplus from circular production.* From https://www.dropbox.com/scl/fi/ryk0pmue9et4dja6awosn/Kalundborg_Symbiose_two-pager_17_partners_2024_english.pdf.

Kennerly, J. (2019). *Going solar in the America.* NC Clean Energy Technology Center – NC State University. From https://nccleantech.ncsu.edu/wp-content/uploads/2019/05/Going-Solar-in-America-Ranking-Solars-Value-to-Customers_FINAL.pdf

Kruse, T., Dechezleprêtre, A., Saffar, R., & Robert, L. (2022). *Measuring environmental policy stringency in OECD countries: An update of the OECD composite EPS indicator* (OECD Economics Department Working Papers). OECD. From https://doi.org/https://doi.org/10.1787/90ab82e8-en

Kumar, S. (2022). *Customer retention versus customer acquisition.* Forbes Business Council. From https://www.forbes.com/sites/forbesbusinesscouncil/2022/12/12/customer-retention-versus-customer-acquisition/

Lee, K., & Cha, J. (2020). Towards improved circular economy and resource security in South Korea. In *EARTH 2019-green technologies for resources and materials recycling.*

Lee, H., & Romero, J. (2023). *Climate change 2023: Synthesis report. Contribution of working groups I, II and III to the sixth assessment report of the intergovernmental panel on climate change.* IPCC.

Lindner, J. (2023). *Global water consumption statistics.* Gitnux Marketdata Report 2024. From https://gitnux.org/global-water-consumption-statistics/

Michelin. (2024a). *MICHELIN® Fleet solutions.* From https://business.michelinman.com/freight-transportation/freight-transportation-services/michelin-fleet-solutions

Michelin. (2024b, 06). *Predictive tyre maintenance.* From https://connectedfleet.michelin.com/solution/predictive-tyre-maintenance/

Mohindra, D. (2014). *Circular economy can generate US$ 1 trillion annually by 2025.* World Economic Forum. From https://www.weforum.org/press/2014/01/circular-economy-can-generate-us-1-trillion-annually-by-2025/

Morris, D. Z. (2016). *Today's cars are parked 95% of the time.* From Fotune: https://fortune.com/2016/03/13/cars-parked-95-percent-of-time/

Murywed, M. (n.d.). *Turbine transformation—A new lease of life for ageing wind turbines.* Peswind. From ABB: https://new.abb.com/docs/librariesprovider135/wind-power-solutions/turbine-transformation%2D%2D-a-new-lease-of-life-for-ageing-wind-turbines.pdf

n2s. (2024, 06). *Redefining the technology lifecycle.* From https://www.n2s.co.uk/

Negroponte, N. (1995). *Being digital.* Knopf Doubleday Publishing Group.

Nespresso. (2024, 06). *How to recycle your coffee pods.* From https://www.nespresso.com/uk/en/sustainability/recycling

Net Zero Tracker. (2023). *Net Zero Stocktake 2023.* NewClimate Institute, Oxford Net Zero, Energy & Climate Intelligence Unit and Data-Driven EnviroLab. From https://ca1-nzt.edcdn.com/Reports/Net_Zero_Stocktake_2023.pdf

Nielsen. (2023). *Global sustainability report.* From https://www.nielsen.com/about-us/responsibility-and-sustainability/esg-report/

Nike. (2024, 06). *Watch how nike refurbished works.* From https://about.nike.com/en/newsroom/releases/nike-refurbished-circularity-model

Nike Grind. (2024, 06). *Nike Grind.* From https://www.nikegrind.com/

NIST. (2024). *The CSF 1.1 five functions.* From https://www.nist.gov/cyberframework/getting-started/online-learning/five-functions

OECD. (2024). *Environmental country reviews.* OECD Environmental Performance Reviews (EPR) programme. From https://www.oecd.org/environment/country-reviews/

Openideo. (2024). *Designing circular solutions for the global plastic waste problem.* From https://www.openideo.com/case-studies/plastic-waste-solutions-in-circular-design-challenge

Pandora. (2024). *Recycled silver and gold.* From https://pandoragroup.com/sustainability/circular-innovation/recycled-silver-and-gold

Patagonia. (2024, 06). *Worn wear.* From https://eu.patagonia.com/gb/en/wornwear/

PDI Technologies. (2024, 04). From NACS: https://www.convenience.org/Media/Daily/2024/April/24/4-US-Consumers-Pay-Sustainable_Products_Research

Project CETEC. (n.d.). *New coalition of industry and academia to commercialise solution for full recyclability of wind turbine blades.* From https://www.project-cetec.dk/uk/about/

Refashion. (2021). *The platform that connects textile and footwear recycling professionals.* From https://recycle.refashion.fr/en/

REN21. (2023). *Renewables 2023 global status report.* Renewable Energy Policy Network for the 21st Century (REN21). From https://www.ren21.net/gsr-2023/

Renault Group. (2023, 12). *The Future Is NEUTRAL strengthens its coverage of the circular economy value chain.* From https://media.renaultgroup.com/the-future-is-neutral-strengthens-its-coverage-of-the-circular-economy-value-chain/

Robson, G. (2021, 12). *Pushing the boundaries of sustainable PC design: Concept Luna.* From Dell: https://www.dell.com/en-us/blog/pushing-the-boundaries-of-sustainable-pc-design-concept-luna/

Rollet, C. (2020). *Solar costs have fallen 82% since* 2010. pv magazine – Photovoltaics Markets and Technology. From https://www.pv-magazine.com/2020/06/03/solar-costs-have-fallen-82-since-2010/

Rolls Royce. (2024, 06). *Power by the hour.* From https://www.rolls-royce.com/media/our-stories/discover/2017/totalcare.aspx.

SAP. (2024). *Circular economy solutions.* From https://www.sap.com/products/sustainability/circular-economy.html

Schaeffler. (2022, 09). *From more efficient product design to data-based reconditioning service: Sustainability as a driver of innovation in rail transport.* From https://www.schaeffler.com/en/media/press-releases/press-releases-detail.jsp?id=87860997.

Shevchenko, T., & Cluzel, F. (2023). *A circular product design toolkit: Methodologial background, basic principles and building blocks* (p. 23). ICED.

Signify. (2024, 06). *Our purpose is to unlock the extraordinary potential of light for brighter lives and a better world.* From https://www.signify.com/global

SKF. (2024, 06). *SKF RecondOil.* From https://www.skf.com/dk/services/recondoil

Stellantis. (2022a, 03). *Dare forward* 2030. From Stellantis: https://www.stellantis.com/en/company/dare-forward-2030

Stellantis. (2022b). *Stellantis fosters circular economy ambitions with dedicated business unit to power new era of sustainable manufacturing and consumption.* From https://www.stellantis.com/en/news/press-releases/2022/october/stellantis-fosters-circular-economy-ambitions-with-dedicated-business-unit-to-power-new-era-of-sustainable-manufacturing-and-consumption

Stellantis. (2024). *Stellantis Circular Economy reported strong growth in 2023 and is on track to increase this trend in 2024.* From https://www.media.stellantis.com/em-en/corporate-communications/press/stellantis-circular-economy-reported-strong-growth-in-2023-and-is-on-track-to-increase-this-trend-in-2024

Stena Recycling. (2023, 12). *Collaborative project for recycling wind turbine blades boosts circularity in fossil-free wind power.* From https://www.stenarecycling.com/news-insights/newsroom/2023/wind-turbine-blade-recycling-boosts-circularity-in-fossil-free-wind-energy/

Tas, N., Tyrkko, K., Susan, C., Duru, S. D., Kechichian, E., Boll, M., & Felix, S. (2021). *An international framework for eco-industrial parks version 2.0.* The World Bank. From https://www.unido.org/sites/default/files/files/2021-04/An%20international%20framework%20for%20eco-industrial%20parks%20v2.0.pdf

Tesla. (2024, 06). *Software updates.* From https://www.tesla.com/support/software-updates.

Tetra Pak. (2024, 06). *Tetra Pak® upgrades.* From https://www.tetrapak.com/solutions/services/service-offerings/upgrades

Than, E. (2023). *Michelin: From the World's leading Tire manufacturers to a leader in mobility businesses driven by data and IoT.* sfiaCorporation. From https://medium.com/sfiacorporation/michelin-digital-transformation-canvas-4407ac584e5

The Australian Government. (2023). *Critical minerals strategy 2023–2030.* From https://www.industry.gov.au/sites/default/files/2023-06/critical-minerals-strategy-2023-2030.pdf

The Battery Pass consortium. (2023). *Battery passport content guidance- executive summary.* The Battery Pass consortium. From https://thebatterypass.eu/assets/images/content-guidance/pdf/2023_Battery_Passport_Content_Guidance_Executive_Summary.pdf

The California State Assembly. (2010). *California assembly bill 2398, chapter 681, statutes of 2010.* From Legiscan: https://legiscan.com/CA/text/AB2398/id/60892

The Ellen MacArthur Foundation. (2019). *The butterfly diagram: Visualising the circular economy.* From https://www.ellenmacarthurfoundation.org/circular-economy-diagram

The Global Sustainable Investment Alliance. (2023). *Global Sustainabilit investment review 2022.* HSBC Global Research. From https://www.gsi-alliance.org/wp-content/uploads/2023/12/GSIA-Report-2022.pdf

The International Energy Agency – IEA. (2022). *World Energy outlook 2022.* The International Energy Agency – IEA. From https://www.iea.org/reports/world-energy-outlook-2022

The National Institute of Standards and Technology (NIST). (2024). *NIST cyber security for IoT program.* From Information Technology Laboratory/Applied Cybersecurity Division: https://www.nist.gov/itl/applied-cybersecurity/nist-cybersecurity-iot-program

The Royal Mint. (2023, 01). *Recycled gold at The Royal Mint.* From https://www.royalmint.com/invest/discover/invest-in-gold/recycled-gold-at-the-royal-mint/

The White House. (2022, 08 09). *FACT SHEET: CHIPS and science act will lower costs, create jobs, strengthen supply chains, and counter China.* From The White House: https://www.whitehouse.gov/briefing-room/statements-releases/2022/08/09/fact-sheet-chips-and-science-act-will-lower-costs-create-jobs-strengthen-supply-chains-and-counter-china/

The World Economic Forum. (2023). *The global risks report 2023 18th edition.* The World Economic Forum. From https://www3.weforum.org/docs/WEF_Global_Risks_Report_2023.pdf

TK Elevator. (2024, 06). *Optimize every building's potential.* From https://www.tkelevator.com/global-en/products-and-service/digital-solutions/max/

Tohamy, N. (2023). *Hype cycle for supply chain strategy.* Gartner.

Trivium Communications. (2022). *Buying green report 2022.* From Trivium Packaging: https://www.triviumpackaging.com/news-media/reports/buying-green-report-2022/

Tukker, A., & Tischner, U. (2006). *Product-services as a research field: Past, present and future. Reflections from a decade of research.* Journal of Cleaner Production, *14*, 1552–1556. From https://www.sciencedirect.com/science/article/abs/pii/S0959652606000862

U.S. Government Publishing Office. (2022). *H.R.5376 – Inflation Reduction Act of 2022.* Congress.gov. From https://www.congress.gov/bill/117th-congress/house-bill/5376/text

US Energy Information Administration. (2023). *Annual energy outlook 2023.* From https://www.eia.gov/outlooks/aeo/narrative/

Vartavičiūtė, J., Milčiūnas, J., Titov, V., Honcharenko, A., & Jankauskaite, S. (2023). Importance of sustainability in business. In *International student and teacher scientific practical conference.*

Vela, R. A. (2024, 01 14). *Exploring remanufacturing and refurbishment processes.* From Planet SCM: https://www.linkedin.com/pulse/exploring-remanufacturing-refurbishment-processes-rafael-a-vela-yjzfe/

Vestas. (2024). *Vestas refurbished turbines.* From https://www.vestas.com/en/energy-solutions/refurbished-turbines

Volvo. (2024, 06). *It all revolves around the batteries.* From https://www.volvoenergy.com/en/how-we-do-it.html

Washington State Department of Ecology. (2021). *Recycled content minimums.* From https://ecology.wa.gov/waste-toxics/reducing-recycling-waste/plastics/2021-plastic-pollution-laws/recycled-content-minimums

Wood, J. (2019). *India is now producing the world's cheapest solar power.* The World Econmic Forum. From https://www.weforum.org/agenda/2019/06/india-is-now-producing-the-world-s-cheapest-solar-power/

Wood, J. (2022). *Gen Z cares about sustainability more than anyone else – And is starting to make others feel the same.* The World Econmic Forum. From https://www.weforum.org/agenda/2022/03/generation-z-sustainability-lifestyle-buying-decisions/

World Economic Forum. (2024). *Global risks report 2024.* Word Economic Forum.

The manufacturer's authorised representative in the EU is Springer
Nature Customer Service Centre GmbH, Europaplatz 3, 69115 Heidelberg,
Germany. If you have any concerns regarding our products, please
contact ProductSafety@springernature.com

Printed and bound by CPI Group (UK) Ltd, Croydon, CR0 4YY
01/10/2026
02225938-0006